Retirement Bible

Retirement Bible

Lynn O'Shaughnessy

Hungry Minds™

Hungry Minds, Inc.
An International Data Group Company

Indianapolis, IN ✦ Cleveland, OH ✦ New York, NY

Retirement Bible

Published by

Hungry Minds, Inc.
An International Data Group Company
909 Third Ave.
New York, NY 10022
www.hungryminds.com

Library of Congress Control Number: 00-109067

ISBN: 0-7645-5245-7

Printed in the United States of America

10 9 8 7 6 5 4 3 2 1

1O/QT/QV/QR/IN

Distributed in the United States by Hungry Minds, Inc.

Distributed by CDG Books Canada Inc. for Canada; by Transworld Publishers Limited in the United Kingdom; by IDG Norge Books for Norway; by IDG Sweden Books for Sweden; by IDG Books Australia Publishing Corporation Pty. Ltd. for Australia and New Zealand; by TransQuest Publishers Pte Ltd. for Singapore, Malaysia, Thailand, Indonesia, and Hong Kong; by Gotop Information Inc. for Taiwan; by ICG Muse, Inc. for Japan; by Intersoft for South Africa; by Eyrolles for France; by International Thomson Publishing for Germany, Austria, and Switzerland; by Distribuidora Cuspide for Argentina; by LR International for Brazil; by Galileo Libros for Chile; by Ediciones ZETA S.C.R. Ltda. for Peru; by WS Computer Publishing Corporation, Inc., for the Philippines; by Contemporanea de Ediciones for Venezuela; by Express Computer Distributors for the Caribbean and West Indies; by Micronesia Media Distributor, Inc. for Micronesia; by Chips Computadoras S.A. de C.V. for Mexico; by Editorial Norma de Panama S.A. for Panama; by American Bookshops for Finland.

For general information on Hungry Minds, Inc. books in the U.S., please call our Consumer Customer Service department at 800-762-2974. For reseller information, including discounts and premium sales, please call our Reseller Customer Service department at 800-434-3422.

For information on where to purchase Hungry Minds, Inc. books outside the U.S., please contact our International Sales department at 317-596-5530 or fax 317-572-4002.

For consumer information on foreign language translations, please contact our Customer Service department at 800-434-3422, fax 317-572-4002, or e-mail rights@hungryminds.com.

For information on licensing foreign or domestic rights, please contact our Sub-Rights Customer Care department at 212-884-5000.

For sales inquiries and special prices for bulk quantities, please contact our Order Services department at 800-434-3422 or write to the address above.

For information on using Hungry Minds, Inc. books in the classroom or for ordering examination copies, please contact our Educational Sales department at 800-434-2086 or fax 317-572-4005.

For press review copies, author interviews, or other publicity information, please contact our Public Relations department at 650-653-7000 or fax 650-653-7500.

For authorization to photocopy items for corporate, personal, or educational use, please contact Copyright Clearance Center, 222 Rosewood Drive, Danvers, MA 01923, or fax 978-750-4470.

Hungry Minds™ is a trademark of Hungry Minds, Inc.

About the Author

Lynn O'Shaughnessy, the author of *The Unofficial Guide to Investing*, has been writing about personal finance for nearly a decade. The former *Los Angeles Times* reporter has contributed countless articles to *Mutual Funds Magazine, Bloomberg Personal Finance Magazine, The Wall Street Journal, Forbes Magazine*'s Web site, and a variety of other magazines and online ventures. She is also a popular guest on Sage Online, a highly successful financial Internet site that has partnered with America Online for many years. Lynn, who graduated with honors from the University of Missouri's School of Journalism, worked as a reporter for the *Los Angeles Times* for nearly seven years. She is currently finishing up her third book, *Investing Bible*. She lives with her husband and two children in San Diego.

Credits

Acquisitions Editor
Jonathan Malysiak

Development Editor
Maureen Kelly

Production Editor
Stephanie Lucas

Technical Editors
Michael Molinski
Alan Simon
Robert Whitman

Copy Editors
Heather Stith
Krista Hansing

Project Coordinator
Maridee Ennis

Graphics and Production Specialists
Kendra Span
Brian Torwelle
Julie Tripetti

Quality Control Specialist
Laura Albert
Charles Spencer

Book Designer
Drew R. Moore

Proofreading and Indexing
York Production Services

Cover Image
Michelle Logan

To Bruce, Benjamin, and Caitlin.

And to the rest of my family in Denver, Pleasanton, and, of course, St. Louis.

Acknowledgments

When I was a reporter at *The Los Angeles Times*, a rival newspaper printed the kind of bizarre story that everybody reads. A small dog, belonging to a television actress, was killed one morning when the newspaper carrier hurled the incredibly heavy Sunday edition of the *L.A. Times* onto its lawn.

I was reminded of the story when I realized that my book was also fat enough to be a lethal weapon. Obviously, a book this thick can't be the work of just one person. Many people, including those I mention here, graciously helped me with this major undertaking.

First I want to thank Ed Slott, a CPA from Rockville Centre, New York, whom many personal financial journalists turn to when they need help reporting on Individual Retirement Accounts. While he was a tremendous help during my research, his biggest contribution was alerting me one weekend, shortly before the book was printed, about sweeping federal changes in IRA rules. With the help of Ed and Robert S. Keebler, a CPA in Green Bay, Wisconsin, I was able to rewrite the chapters in time to have the first book on the market that explains the new rules.

Perhaps even more complicated than IRA rules are the do's and dont's of estate planning. Navigating these chapters, however, was easier with the expert help of Bob Whitman, a law professor at the University of Connecticut, and Robert Wolf, a Pittsburgh attorney, who are both members of the American College of Trusts and Estates Counsel.

One of the most complicated issues facing retirees is how much money they can safely withdraw from their savings. I was able to turn to Christine Fahlund, a certified financial planner at T. Rowe Price, who has a knack for simplifying the complex. Steve Norwitz of T. Rowe Price was also, as usual, willing to assist in anyway he could. Equally helpful was Philip L. Cooley, a professor of finance at Trinity University and the lead author of a ground-breaking study on retirement withdrawal rates.

I also owe a large debt of thanks to the experts who assisted me with my chapters on trustees, trust services, and wealth management. They include Steven Kanaly, vice chairman of Kanaly Trust Company in Houston, Texas; Tom Prohaska, president of Idaho Trust Company in Coeur d'Alene, Idaho; and Douglas Regan, president of Northern Trust Bank in Palm Beach and Martin counties in Florida. Another indispensable source was Standish Smith, founder of HEIRs Inc., a nonprofit organization in Villanova, Pennsylvania. I'd also like to thank Bob Goss, former president of the Certified Financial Planner Board of Standards, as well Noel Maye, for fielding my questions on trends in the financial services industry.

The award for the most meticulous technical reviewer may go to Avram Sacks, a Social Security law analyst at CCH INCORPORATED, who aimed to verify every single word in my Social Security chapter. (I could tell by the No. 2 pencil tick marks he made on his copy.) Also graciously helping out were the staffers at the Social Security Administration's Richmond, California, office. I am also indebted to Karen Ferguson, director of the Pension Rights Center, and John Hotz, deputy director, who were a tremendous help with the pension chapter, as were experts at various pension rights offices, including Jeanne Medeiros, regional coordinator of the New England Pension Assistance Project.

Equally conscientious was James B. Potter, a highly respected planned giving consultant in Alexandria, Virginia, who guided me through the ins and outs of charitable giving. Anthony Steuer, a fee-only life insurance analyst in Larkspur, California, was an invaluable asset as I plodded through the insurance chapter, as were the experts at the United Seniors Health Cooperative. Joseph Rosanswank, editor and publisher of the *Comparative Annuity Reports* newsletter, was a lifesaver as I researched my chapters on 403(b)s and annuities. And I also appreciated the observations of Ted Benna, who created the nation's first 401(k).

Also deserving mention on this page is John Woerth, a principal at the Vanguard Group, who is always generous with his time. So too are the kind people at Morningstar, Lipper Inc., and Wiesenberger, who, at a moment's notice, will provide statistics as well as their own thoughts on investment trends. And a special thank you to Sue Stevens, a certified financial planner at Morningstar.

I also want to thank John Curran, managing editor of *Mutual Funds Magazine*, who gave me story assignments that tied in with book research. And I need to thank my littlest brother and favorite CPA, John O'Shaughnessy, who checked some of my financial figures, and, more importantly, gave me moral support. Also boosting my spirits were Susanna Starcevic, a true friend; Ken Vaillancourt (my biggest book fan outside my family); and, of course, my parents, Jacquelin and Vincent P. O'Shaughnessy.

These acknowledgments wouldn't be complete without mentioning the wonderful people at Hungry Minds, Inc., who helped on this project, including Jonathan Malysiak, Maureen Kelly, Kevin Thornton, Mark Butler, and most of all, Kathy Welton, who decided that I was the best person to write this book. I also owe a huge debt of gratitude to Joyce Lane Kennedy, who introduced me to the Hungry Minds editors. I also want to thank my agent, Daniel Greenberg of James Levine Communications.

Perhaps no one has devoted more hours to this book (besides me) than my two geriatric assistants. Berkeley and Riley, otherwise known as Golden Retrievers, spent long, long hours in my office sleeping under my desk.

I have reserved my warmest gratitude to the people dearest to my heart.

I am unbelievably lucky to be married to the same reporter who introduced himself to me 19 years ago in the *Kansas City Star/Times* newsroom. For all sorts of reasons, Bruce, you deserve a huge thanks. And finally, a big hug and a kiss go to Caitlin, our wonderfully creative 11-year-old writer, and Benjamin, our third-grade math brain, who asked me the other day, "Mom, why do people keep making you write books?" I didn't have an answer.

Lynn O'Shaughnessy
San Diego

Contents at a Glance

Contents

● ●

Part IV: Stocks and Mutual Funds for the Savvy Investor   217

Part VII: Being Generous for All the Right Reasons   471

Introduction

Does it ever seem like everybody, except perhaps you, will be rich by the time they retire? Stock options, which are getting passed around like Tic Tacs, are no longer just a standard perk for the tech heads of Silicon Valley. Even workers at places that make cough syrup, light bulbs, and refrigerators are counting their paper fortunes. At the same time, stock market performance in the [']90s, which was the longest bull market in American history, helped turn the 401(k) into the nation's healthiest addiction. Eight out of every 10 people who are eligible to participate in a 401(k) are socking something away. Not surprisingly, then, more and more retirees are calling it quits with six-figure 401(k)s. Today more Americans are covered by some kind of workplace retirement plan than at any other period in history.

The Bad News

Yet some of this seeming prosperity is only skin deep. When human resource directors get together, they spend hours fretting about what's going to happen to us all. They despair that most people treat their 401(k)s like Christmas Club accounts. About 68 percent of workers who leave their jobs cash out their 401(k)s. Half of all 401(k)s recently had balances of less than $12,000, which is hardly enough to subsidize a Carnival Cruise lifestyle.

401(k) delay

Making matters worse, corporations are sabotaging the retirement prospects of part-timers and new workers by denying them the opportunity to participate in a 401(k). They also make it difficult for the rest of us to hold onto a nice chunk of our own nest egg: Many workers will lose all or part of their employers' 401(k) matching contributions if they leave a job before becoming vested, even though they've been with the company several years.

Magical disappearing pensions

At the same time, pension benefits can no longer be taken for granted. Since the 1970s, tens of thousands of companies have abolished their pension plans. But even those lucky enough to still be covered by a plan can't afford to remain smug. Deep within the bowels of the nation's corporations, actuaries and consultants have been tinkering with Americans' traditional pension plans. The "new and improved" plans leave many middle-aged and older workers with pension benefits that are essentially frozen for years.

Fearsome feds

Corporate America isn't the only one that's booby-trapping our retirement plans. Federal regulations, which in many cases defy common sense and generate lots of billable hours for attorneys, are also culprits. One of the most troubling sets of regulations involves Individual Retirement Accounts. Following the correct procedures when inheriting or bequeathing an IRA to loved ones, for instance, can seem as tricky as dismantling a letter bomb, and the consequences of botching the job could be disastrous.

Federal rules about estate planning are just as infuriating. Although only about 2 percent of Americans pay estate taxes, it isn't just the people who make it onto *Forbes* magazine's annual billionaire list who end up writing those checks. People who consider themselves middle-class can inadvertently be tripped up by their own sentimentality. A husband and wife, for example, might leave all their possessions to each other in what estate attorneys derisively call "sweetheart wills." By doing this, however, the spouse who dies first forfeits the chance for his or her estate to claim a valuable estate tax exemption. As a result, the heirs will ultimately end up with much less money.

Perhaps it should be no surprise that deep down, American workers know they are in trouble. In a *USA Today* survey, the only things people confessed to worrying about more than retirement savings were cancer and car wrecks. Yet there is hope. No matter where you stand on the retirement timeline, your best protection is knowing the rules and your rights — and the most important of these are spelled out in this book.

The Good News

Choosing investments for your retirement accounts may seem difficult because of the enormous number of mutual funds and individual stocks and bonds on the market today. However, sifting through the glut of investment opportunities doesn't have to be time-consuming or difficult. In this book, you'll learn tricks to pinpoint the best investments for yourself, shelter your cash from Uncle Sam, and manage your nest egg so that it'll see you through one, two, or even three decades of retirement.

This is an exciting time for individual investors. The amount of high-quality information you can easily obtain on just about any type of investment has never been greater, and most of it is free. As you'll learn, the Internet has made investing much easier and more gratifying, as long as you stifle the urge to trade excessively. At the same time, promising new investment vehicles, such as exchange-traded funds, represents an excellent alternative to the multitude of mediocre mutual funds on the market. In another plus for the little guy, some financial institutions are now marketing tax-efficient ways to invest after decades of ignoring investors' tax pain.

The opportunity exists for each one of us to intelligently save for retirement. No matter what your age, *The Retirement Bible* can help you thoughtfully plan for a prosperous retirement. If you're already retired or nearing that milestone, this book can help you make the necessary adjustments to ensure that your money won't run out.

The Retirement Bible Quiz

If you're wondering if you really need this thick book to plan for your retirement, the quiz that follows might help you decide. If you discover that you don't know many answers, don't sweat it. The true purpose of this quiz is to give you a taste of what you'll discover in the next 30 chapters. Keep reading and you'll learn plenty.

1. Which of these statements about Social Security is true?

    A. You'll owe income taxes on Social Security benefits if you hold a job between the ages of 65 and 70.

    B. Most workers claim benefits at age 62.

    C. A company can never reduce pension benefits of any workers who are simultaneously receiving Social Security.

2. If you inherit an IRA from your mom or dad, you should

    A. Remove your parent's name from the account and transfer the money wherever you please.

    B. Cash out the account because the IRA's tax-deferred benefit dies with the owner.

    C. Keep your parent's name on the account and seek professional advice.

3. Brokerage customers can usually expect a higher level of service if their assets total at least

    A. $10,000.

    B. $100,000.

    C. $1 million.

4. Qubes, Spiders, and Diamonds are

    A. Saturday morning cartoon characters.

    B. Names of after-hours stock market exchanges.

    C. Nicknames of exchange-traded funds, an emerging investing phenomenon.

5. A will is the backbone of any estate plan. Which of these statements about wills is false?

    A. You can use a will to bequeath everything you own to loved ones.

    B. You can't direct who inherits your IRAs, 401(k) or 403(b) assets, life insurance, or annuities with a will.

    C. A will generally involves less paperwork than a living trust.

6. If your investment earns an average annual return of 10 percent, how many years will it take before your money doubles?

    A. 10 years

    B. 7 years

    C. 5 years

7. Which IRA is the best bet for most Americans?

    A. Deductible IRA

    B. Roth IRA

    C. Nondeductible IRA

8. If you can't fully fund both a 401(k) and a Roth IRA, if eligible, you should:

    A. Ignore the Roth and fund your 401(k).

    B. Put enough money in your 401(k) to capture the company match and then put any remaining money into a Roth.

    C. Invest $2,000 in a Roth. If any money's left, contribute to your 401(k).

9. When you leave a company, taking a lump sum is always better than opting for future pension checks.

    A. True

    B. False

10. If the contents of a safe-deposit box are stolen or damaged or destroyed by flood or fire, the bank is liable.

    A. True

    B. False

11. An ethical will

    A. Is not a legal document.

    B. Enables people to share their personal and spiritual values, life lessons, and forgiveness with heirs.

    C. All of the above.

12. When you begin tapping into your nest egg after retirement, it's generally better to

   A. Empty your taxable account first.

   B. Drain your IRA and other retirement accounts first.

   C. None of the above.

13. Which of the following statements about investing cash is false?

   A. The historical passbook savings account has been steadily declining for the past decade.

   B. Federal banking law prohibits someone from purchasing a certificate of deposit from a bank located in another state.

   C. Using the Internet, you may capture a CD rate that's 1 to 2 percent better than the average one.

14. Since the 1920s, the stock market has historically earned this average rate of return:

   A. 18 percent

   B. 11 percent

   C. 24 percent

15. Capital gains and income taxes can take a huge bite out of your investments. Which one of the following three investments is usually the least tax efficient?

   A. Index mutual funds

   B. Individual stocks

   C. Bond mutual funds

16. As an investment, utility stocks

   A. Are suitable only for ultraconservative investors.

   B. Have, in some cases, become a hot sector play.

   C. None of the above.

17. According to prominent researchers at Cornell University, the typical Baby Boomer will receive an inheritance of

   A. $25,000.

   B. $200,000.

   C. $90,000.

   D. $10,000.

18. Purchasing permanent life insurance

    A. Is an excellent way to discipline yourself to save.

    B. Is usually too expensive to make sense for most people.

    C. None of the above.

19. Stocks always provide a better return than bonds or money markets.

    A. True

    B. False

20. A full-service stockbroker

    A. Is a salesperson.

    B. Is a financial planner.

    C. Must have a college degree.

Answers

1.	B	11.	C
2.	C	12.	A
3.	B	13.	B
4.	C	14.	B
5.	A	15.	C
6.	B	16.	B
7.	B	17.	C
8.	B	18.	B
9.	B	19.	B
10.	B	20.	A

Planning Your Retirement: What You'll Need and What You'll Get

Part I helps you formulate a successful retirement savings strategy. Some of the tips may be new to you, such as the advice on using the Internet to help determine the amount you need to save. You'll also learn what you can expect from Social Security and company pensions, which together represent the bulk of many Americans' retirement income. You'll find advice on timing your Social Security benefit, as well as selecting the best payout plan for your pension benefit.

Get in the Game! Starting Your Savings

✦ ✦ ✦ ✦

In This Chapter

Figuring out how much you will need

Taking advantage of forced savings retirement plans

Estimating retirement costs with online resources

Asking yourself the right questions

Starting to save late in the game

✦ ✦ ✦ ✦

In this chapter, and throughout the book, you'll learn how to maximize your savings and identify the factors you need to consider when formulating a retirement strategy. In addition, this chapter includes quick tips on squeezing the most out of what you've saved so far. You'll also explore the explosion in online retirement planning, which is becoming popular among those who'd love a second opinion about their investing strategies. Finally, there's advice for those who are now struggling to play catch-up during that final stretch before retirement.

The Big Question

How much is enough? For many of us, that's the $1 million question. Or is it $2 million? Or maybe it's $899,999 or something far smaller? Just how much do you need to save for a happy, healthy, and, with any luck, long retirement? Pinpointing the right numbers can be as frustrating as herding cats. Some of the most learned people in financial academia contend that a definitive answer to this question doesn't exist.

However, a consensus does exist on this point: Gauging how much you need to stash away for retirement is one of the biggest financial challenges you will ever confront. If your calculations are wildly off base, retirement won't wait for you to catch up. Once the paychecks stop, your options begin evaporating.

For those who are already retired or nearing that milestone, the question is even more complicated: How much do they dare withdraw from their savings? Will the mishmash of stocks, bonds, and cash accumulated over a lifetime hold together like cement? Or will it unravel slowly like a loose yarn on a cardigan sweater?

Cross-Reference See Chapter 21 for details on withdrawal strategies that'll see you through.

No matter where you stand on the retirement timeline, inevitably you have to ask yourself this question: Am I investing wisely enough to get where I want to go? Smart investing, however, is only part of the equation. The age you begin saving seriously is also important. So too are the retirement benefits you may be entitled to at work. Even your family tree could influence your savings strategy. Did your parents or grandparents live long enough to celebrate the births of great-grandchildren? If so, you may be one of the increasing number of Americans who spend a third of their lives in retirement.

If you didn't start saving early (most people don't) and you're not a particularly astute investor, there's no need to be fatalistic. Here's a morale booster: The people who are living comfortably in retirement aren't always the ones who earned the biggest paychecks during their careers. Plenty of people pulling in six-figure salaries divert the bulk of their money into propping up opulent lifestyles. Other affluent Americans jeopardize their retirement years by favoring a macho investing style that's more like John Wayne than Warren Buffett.

Contrast this situation with the inspiring newspaper articles about ordinary middle-class folks who leave considerable sums behind to a charity, school, scholarship fund, or some other worthy cause. The media focuses on their generosity, yet their personal finance skills were no doubt equally inspiring. Anybody can follow the common-sense principles, such as buying and holding for the long haul, that these people followed when investing their money. And this chapter contains those very principles.

Tip Remember, how you invest your money—not necessarily how much you earn—ultimately will make the difference.

Setting Up Savings the Easy Way

If you're in your 20s or 30s, saving for retirement doesn't have to be a financially wrenching experience. Most people this age, who are socking away at least 10 percent of their income in a retirement account, should be fine.

 Tip Above and beyond the workplace plans, the Individual Retirement Account is an excellent repository for extra cash up to $2,000 a year. For those meeting the income qualifications, a Roth IRA is almost always the best choice.

Participating in a 401(k), a 403(b), or other workplace retirement plan can make saving incredibly easy because your employer automatically deducts from each paycheck the amount you specify for investing. If you aren't covered by a workplace retirement plan, you need to exert a bit more effort and set up your own savings plan. The easiest way is to establish an account with a brokerage firm or mutual fund company. Funding a yearly $2,000 IRA essentially means a weekly commitment of just over $38. Self-employed people can potentially sock away even more in a SEP-IRA.

Tip You can arrange with a mutual fund or a brokerage firm to automatically withdraw and invest a fixed amount out of your checking or saving account every month. This arrangement replicates one of the best features of a 401(k) plan: forced savings.

Take advantage of time

Folks in their 20s and 30s would be wise to take advantage of the longer length of time between themselves and retirement. Table 1-1 demonstrates how those regular deposits into a 401(k) or IRA can add up nicely with enough time and healthy returns.

Table 1-1 Monthly Investment Needed to Build a $500,000 Nest Egg by Age 65		
Investor Age	*Monthly Investment at 8% Return*	*Monthly Investment at 11% Return*
25	$142	$58
30	$217	$101
35	$333	$177
40	$522	$314
45	$843	$572
50	$1,435	$1,090
55	$2,715	$2,283

When time is not on your side

Table 1-1 also demonstrates how the savings curve climbs steeply as we age. Procrastinators who postpone setting aside money until their 40s or 50s need to save more aggressively. For these late bloomers, saving 15 to 20 percent of their income may be the best solution. For those who can stomach this kind of financial pain, choosing the right places to park this money is even more critical. Once a workplace retirement plan and an IRA are maxed out, the key is to exploit other tax-friendly investments. Index funds and a newer phenomenon called exchange-traded funds are both excellent low-cost alternatives (see Chapter 15). A tax-deferred annuity is another alternative, but the vast majority of these products are far too costly and will swallow too much of your earnings. Read Chapter 22 before choosing that route.

Tip   Those who start saving late should definitely seek outside advice. A financial planner may be able to spot areas where belt tightening can produce extra cash. Also, an expert is in a much better position to know whether someone's savings goals are on target and whether a retirement portfolio needs a tune-up or a major overhaul.

The Costs of Retirement

Financial planners often suggest that most retirees can live comfortably with 60 to 80 percent of their preretirement income. Once retired, many people's expenses decline. After all, they don't have to buy work clothes or pay Social Security and Medicare payroll taxes or wear down their car in a long commute. They also may have paid off the mortgage by then. Later in retirement, medical costs, particularly prescription drug bills, can strain a budget, but by then, other expenses, such as money devoted to entertainment, often decline.

Cross-Reference   See Chapters 4, 5, and 6 for details on working with a financial professional.

Of course, this range is just a general guideline. Someone living in a large home with considerable maintenance costs in a high-tax state such as New York or Minnesota would require a lot more money than a couple living in a modest two-bedroom condo in Nevada or Florida, which don't have a state income tax.

Note   Curiously, studies have suggested that wealthy retirees may need 100 percent or even more of their preretirement income. Why? They've gotten into the habit of spending with great gusto. No longer preoccupied with making money, they now have the time to enjoy and spend it.

You'll probably need to save more for retirement if

✦ You invest conservatively, primarily in bonds and cash.

✦ You want to retire early.

✦ You expect to spend 70 percent or more of your preretirement income after leaving the workforce.

✦ You face children's college costs.

✦ You don't start saving seriously until your 40s or 50s.

The Benefit of Just Asking the Question

Do you wonder how much you really need to save for retirement? Many people avoid asking this question because they are scared to learn the truth.

They simply assume they can't save enough for retirement. This negativity prevents many people from devising a savings roadmap. But a recent study shows that those who at least make an attempt to answer the retirement savings question are in better financial shape than those who don't, according to researchers at the nonprofit Employee Benefit Research Institute. According to its latest Retirement Confidence Survey, workers who try to calculate their future needs typically save considerably more money than those who remain clueless. Investors who did the math have socked away more than 4½ times as much as those who didn't bother. Why the difference? People escalated their savings, institute researchers suggest, because they were frightened by the results of their retirement research.

You can probably save less if

✦ You invest more aggressively.

✦ You plan to work part-time during retirement.

✦ You'll receive a pension.

✦ You can live on less than 70 percent of your preretirement income.

✦ You began saving at least 10 percent of your income in retirement accounts before hitting 40.

In the good old days, most retirement savers just winged it. They set aside what they could and crossed their fingers that it would be enough at the end. Today, the Internet is changing this with online calculators and Internet-based financial advisory services.

Online retirement calculators

Having quickly become as ubiquitous as sticky floors in theaters, retirement calculators are featured on countless financial Web sites. Any self-respecting financial Web site, from *Money* magazine's to the Motley Fool's to Investorama's, offers calculators to increase its foot traffic. It's easy to see why retirement calculators have become wildly popular. Many of them require answers to only a few questions: How many years until your retirement? What kind of rate of return do you expect? How much money have you stockpiled so far? How much do you plan to plow into your nest egg in the future? After you answer these questions, the online calculator spits out a verdict within seconds.

Caution These calculators can be a tremendous resource for people whose math skills are rusty, but beware: Some calculators produce meaningless numbers. The answers you receive from one software program may not even be remotely close to the answers another one flashes on the computer screen.

When *The Wall Street Journal* plugged the same figures into several free Web calculators, the results were astonishingly different. At one extreme, a mutual fund firm's software suggested that a hypothetical retirement saver would end up $1.1 million short. In contrast, the calculator of a popular stock-investing site concluded that the same investor would leave a $669,714 surplus to heirs.

Why the astounding discrepancies? Each Web calculator is calibrated with its own underlying assumptions and mathematical algorithms. In addition, the amount of information you must provide varies tremendously. Some forms can be completed in a few seconds; others may involve a half hour or more of your time.

Tip If you want to use the free retirement calculators, consider sticking with those requiring more grunt work on your part. In general, the more time you must spend filling in boxes, the more accurate and useful your results will be. And because results of these calculators do vary, don't limit yourself to just one.

The models assume that the data you're supplying is accurate and will remain so. But frankly, many people are just guessing during these exercises. For instance, these calculators often require you to plug in the rate of inflation for what may be many decades of retirement savings. Not even the Federal Reserve chairman would try to tackle that one.

You also are expected to type in how much you can stash away each year, as well as what rate of return all this dough can generate. Often you're allowed to supply only a fixed monthly or annual number. However, most people aren't going to contribute the same amount year after year. They often contribute a certain percentage of their paycheck through a 401(k). As someone's salary goes up, so do the contributions, but calculators don't typically reflect that. Savers also can't anticipate lean years when expensive medical bills or a legal nightmare might prevent any retirement contributions. What's more, the calculators can't provide advice about juggling investments to make up shortfalls.

Online investment advice

Although financial planning sites can generate much more than the sketchy information that online calculators provide, they are still largely in the Stone Age. When a leading technology research firm recently reviewed online retirement advisor services offered as an employee benefit, not a single one rated an "A" grade. Even today's most sophisticated models, including those offered by Morningstar and the much-vaunted Financial Engines, aren't bulletproof. But to its credit, the financial industry is working furiously to develop software that can provide even more sophisticated answers.

Note Not all these services are available to the general public. Some online retirement planning services, such as mPower and Standard & Poor's, are offered only as an employee benefit. However, those sponsored by Financial Engines, Morningstar, DirectAdvice, and Quicken gladly accept any paying customers.

To use one of these online planners, first rummage through your investment folders and pull out your recent statements. You'll typically be expected to provide information about your investing time horizon, your retirement savings goal, risk tolerance, your contribution levels, and your current investment choices inside and outside a workplace retirement plan.

Once all your data is logged in, you'll receive recommendations on ways to reshuffle your retirement portfolio to reach your goal. It might suggest that a younger worker scale back on a heavy reliance upon bond and money market funds and bulk up on stocks instead. An older worker might be urged to wean off a total dependence upon stocks. The advice is typically coupled with specific mutual fund recommendations. Although many services make recommendations only on 401(k) portfolios (the menu of choices is limited and thus, less complicated), some services, such as Financial Engines, are now offering counseling for other retirement accounts, such as IRAs.

So You Want to Be a Millionaire?

Contestants on television game shows can win $1 million in between commercials or by outlasting everyone at some desolate location. But most of us must work much harder to accumulate that kind of dough.

Some financial planners suggest that today's middle-aged savers can accumulate $1 million by the time they retire. But how much do you need to save now to reach that goal? Based upon what you've accumulated so far and the pace of your savings, FinanCenter.com (`www.financenter.com`) can give you a rough idea with its calculator. The operative word here is *rough*.

Let's see what the calculator concluded for a hypothetical 40-year-old who wants to be a millionaire by the time he's 65. So far, he's managed to save $100,000. If his money earned 11 percent a year, he'd need to save $610 a month to be a millionaire by his 65th birthday. If he contributed only $500 monthly, he'd have to wait until age 67 to reach a million.

You sure don't want to base your retirement plans on the verdict of this quick-and-dirty calculator, but it can give you something to think about or shoot for.

Some of the more comprehensive sites are providing personal service by combining computerized advice with live experts. Quicken 401k Advisor, at www.quicken.com, gives savers specific recommendations about which investments they should choose for their 401(k) and other retirement accounts. For a fee, you can have an in-depth consultation with a financial expert who will draw up a customized plan. The advice provided by all these online firms is far cheaper than an in-person meeting with a certified financial planner.

Tip   Some industry observers suggest that Internet advice resources, which charge modest fees, could be a lifesaver for middle-class investors, whose net worth isn't enough to pique a financial planner's interest.

Financial Engines' firepower

Financial Engines (www.financialengines.com) is clearly the online retirement advisor that has created the biggest buzz so far. The pedigree of its founder, Nobel laureate William F. Sharpe, helped give it instant credibility and panache, but the underpinnings of Financial Engines' calculator also have attracted a great deal of attention. Financial Engines uses Monte Carlo simulation software — a sophisticated approach to calculations based on real-world conditions — that has been developed and fine-tuned by math Ph.D.s as a substitute for more linear retirement saving projections.

Traditional software products predict that if you save for a certain number of years and earn a certain investment return over that time, you'll know whether you'll attain your goal. The creators of Financial Engines and other sophisticated retirement software scoff at such simplistic thinking. Instead, they tend to look at someone's retirement strategy as something of a game of chance. Rather than providing a yes-or-no answer as to whether you'll reach your goal, Financial Engines uses mathematical formulations that provide you with the probability of amassing a certain sum of money. Many experts suggest that being presented a range of probabilities is much more valuable to an individual than getting a black-and-white verdict. Institutional investors, such as pension fund administrators, have relied upon this type of sophisticated software for many years. Advances in technology, however, have allowed it to be offered to individuals only recently.

Getting real-world results

This new generation of software goes well beyond projecting what your portfolio would be worth based upon the historical performance of stocks, bonds, cash, and inflation. Mercifully, you don't have to guess what inflation is going to do or how well your own basket of investments will fare. Instead, the software analyzes an investor's specific retirement holdings and simulates how they might perform in thousands of economic scenarios. Plugged into the program is analytical information on thousands of mutual funds and individual stocks as well as the performance data on key asset classes, such as large-cap growth and value stocks, small-cap equities, and corporate and government bonds.

After all your data is plugged in, the software calculates your chances of reaching your financial retirement goal. The program might conclude that your portfolio of blue chip and technology stocks, along with a couple of index funds, provides you with a 65 percent chance of reaching your annual retirement income goal of $130,000. Along with the prognosis, you'll get a worst-case and a best-case scenario of what your portfolio could be worth on your retirement day. If the answer is scary, you can increase your savings, postpone your retirement age, or accept more risk by changing your investment mix. After you've fiddled with the figures online, the program crunches the numbers again.

 Chapter 20 can tell you even more about the use of Monte Carlo simulation software.

Frankly, the need for Monte Carlo simulations is more crucial for retirees or those on the verge of abandoning the rat race. Sure, the market is bound to gyrate during someone's career, but if the money remains invested for decades, the ups and downs should level out. Over time, a person's returns will probably come close to matching historical averages. A retiree, however, doesn't have the luxury of waiting out the bad times. See Chapter 20.

 If you want to learn more about Monte Carlo modeling, which was first used during World War II by American scientists developing the atomic bomb, visit the Web site of a pair of well-respected financial planners at www.montecarlo-simulation.com.

The online advice lineup

Here are major players in the online financial planning universe:

✦ Financial Engines at www.financialengines.com

✦ Mpower at www.mpower.com

✦ Morningstar's ClearFuture at www.morningstar.com

✦ Quicken 401k Advisor at www.quicken.com

✦ DirectAdvice at www.directadvice.com

The Internet isn't the only place you can find better-than-ballpark numbers. An increasing number of financial planners, for instance, are using sophisticated financial software. Do-it-yourselfers can also purchase stand-alone retirement savings software, including a modestly priced package from T. Rowe Price, the mutual fund firm.

 The T. Rowe Price Retirement Planning Analyzer software can be downloaded from the fund's Internet site or ordered by mail. The Web site is www.troweprice.com, and the phone number is (800) 541-8803.

Secrets to Success

Worried that your nest egg won't be big enough? Remember, you don't have to be rich to accumulate a fortune. Make the most of what you have by doing these simple things to get more mileage out of your savings. Each tip is addressed more in depth in later chapters.

✦ Reconsider leaving a job if you're close to vesting in workplace benefits, such as a pension, stock options, or an employer's 401(k) matching contributions. (See Chapters 3 and 8.)

✦ Don't assume every financial advisor knows his or her stuff; hire only the very best. (See Chapters 4, 5, and 6.)

✦ Invest regularly for retirement through dollar-cost averaging. (See Chapter 7.)

✦ Invest a major portion of your retirement savings into stocks. (See Chapter 12.)

✦ Favor mutual funds with below average expenses and above average historical returns. (See Chapter 14.)

✦ Invest in tax-efficient mutual funds. (See Chapter 16.)

✦ Consider putting your stock mutual funds in tax-deferred accounts such as IRAs and 401(k)s and stashing bonds in taxable accounts. Although counter to conventional wisdom, this strategy can pay off. (See Chapter 16.)

✦ If you are retired, avoid the extremely popular income-only portfolios. Invest for growth and the principal can often be touched without jeopardizing your lifestyle. (See Chapter 20.)

✦ When leaving a job or retiring, consider hiring an actuary to decide whether you'd be better off with future monthly pension checks or a lump sum. It's also wise to use an actuary, a CPA, or other financial expert to evaluate an early retirement buyout offer. (See Chapter 21.)

✦ When leaving a job, it's often best to transfer your workplace retirement plan into a rollover IRA. (See Chapter 21.)

✦ Don't use life insurance as a retirement investment. (See Chapter 30.)

✦ Insure your career with disability coverage. (See Chapter 30.)

Key Questions to Ask Yourself

Whiz-bang computer software is only as good as the information that you plug in. Before you can intelligently determine your needs, you must fill in some huge blanks. If you're in your 20s or 30s, nobody expects you to be able to answer most of these questions. Even if you do, chances are your situation will change significantly along the way. But the older you are, the more you should be paying attention to these retirement questions.

At what age do you want to retire?

Americans are abandoning work much earlier than in the past. The percentage of workers who are claiming Social Security benefits at age 62, which is the earliest age possible, is almost 58 percent. Nearly 76 percent of employees claim Social Security before celebrating their 65th birthday.

Before joining the herd, explore what benefits you could expect at different ages. Every month that you postpone receiving Social Security after reaching the age of 62, for instance, slightly increases the size of the checks you get later. In fact, the penalty for claiming Social Security before full retirement age is growing steeper. For instance, somebody born in 1960 or later who takes Social Security at age 62 will be able to claim only 70 percent of his or her full benefit. The incentives to postpone Social Security, however, evaporate completely at age 70. Pension benefits can also become more valuable if you delay retirement. That's because pensions are typically calculated upon the last few years of someone's career, which are usually the time of peak earnings.

Caution

Some retirees ultimately return to work because they've miscalculated how far their money will stretch. Most experts agree that if you want to retire quite early, say at 55 years of age, you'll need enough assets to last at least 30 years.

How much can you expect from Social Security and any pension?

The federal bureaucracy can help you with the first part of this question. Each year you should receive a Social Security statement, which forecasts your future benefits. The projection isn't perfect, though. It doesn't calculate inevitable salary increases you'll enjoy through your career. As you'll learn in Chapter 2, you may request that the Social Security office crunch more realistic numbers for you.

Deciphering pension statements you receive at work is more challenging. Pension law is so complicated that it can intimidate anyone who isn't an actuary. Aggravating the communication disconnect is this sad reality: An increasing number of corporations are rewriting their pension rules to whittle down future benefits for their workers.

How long do you expect to live?

Americans are living longer, but does that mean you will too? According to the federal government, the life expectancies for men and women are 73.8 years and 79.5 years respectively. Of course, these are just averages; you need to take into account your family's record of longevity and your own health.

If you'd like a rough idea of how long you might live, check out the Internet's life expectancy estimators. Typically, you have to answer just a handful of questions about your medical background; your parents' longevity; and your weight, height, and eating and exercise habits. The software estimates how many birthdays you have left. Remember, this estimate is just an actuarial guess. Try these two resources:

✦ MSN MoneyCentral at www.moneycentral.com

✦ Northwestern Mutual at www.nml.com/games/longevity

Without hopping on the Internet, retirees can refer to Table 1-2 for an estimate of how long they can expect to live.

Table 1-2
Probability of Surviving to Future Ages Starting at Age 65

Future Age	Female	Male
70	96%	92%
75	89%	81%
80	78%	65%
85	61%	45%
90	40%	26%
95	19%	11%
100	6%	3%

Can you survive financially if your spouse dies?

Many men who retire at their first opportunity don't realize that they may be condemning their widows to a life of poverty when they die. (See Chapter 2.) That's because the surviving spouse, who is most often the wife, must get by on a Social Security check that is one-third to one-half smaller. What's more, a pension is typically cut by half when the breadwinner dies. If a husband opts for a lump sum rather than monthly pension checks, this decision can also financially imperil a wife later on, as detailed in Chapter 3.

Caution   Many couples fail to develop a savings plan that protects whichever one lives the longest. When a husband or wife dies, often the survivor faces a severe reduction in income. Unfortunately, expenses usually don't decline by much when the first spouse dies.

How much money, if any, do you want to leave to heirs?

The financial gurus who are urging Americans to die broke have sold a ton of books. But not everybody wants to time their exit from this earth minutes after spending their last dollar. If you want to leave children or grandchildren money, you'll need to plug that information into your retirement calculations. But wishing to bequeath part of your nest egg requires more than just saving. Strategic planning is essential. There are right and wrong ways, for instance, to leave IRAs behind for loved ones, as covered in Chapter 11. Leaving a 401(k) at your old company when you quit is also unwise. Doing so can ultimately destroy the tax advantages of a 401(k) for your heirs. (See Chapter 8.)

What kind of investment return can you expect?

The transformation of the federal budget deficit into a surplus, low inflation, and increasing worker productivity helped contribute to the '90s' stupendous Wall Street performance. Here's just one amazing statistic from the recent past: From its low point in 1994 to its peak in January 2000, the Dow Jones Industrial Average soared 226 percent. The last time the Dow clocked those kinds of numbers was in the 1920s. As a result, many people in their 20s, 30s, and even 40s feel comfortable plowing all their retirement money into stocks. Younger investors who rely heavily on stocks shouldn't have to save as much as those who favor primarily bonds.

Caution   Although the 1990s provided phenomenal returns, don't get overconfident and assume that the party will go on forever with few or no hangovers. Financial experts warn that this type of stock market performance should not be expected to continue.

As we age, our ability to invest boldly vanishes. We need help from bonds to dampen our portfolio's potential risk. Despite their stodgy image, however, bonds can provide welcome stability without gutting stock returns. During the past 20 years, according to Wilson Associates International, an 80/20 portfolio of stocks and bonds returned 16.35 percent. An aggressive portfolio that was 95 percent stocks didn't do much better with its 17.63 percent return. At the same time, overdosing on bonds is dangerous because they typically have provided little to no growth. An all-bond portfolio has historically been riskier than a portfolio that keeps a small portion of its assets in stocks, as Table 1-3 indicates.

Table 1-3
Rewards of Asset Allocation

Portfolio	Stocks	Bonds	Cash	Average Annual Return	Best Year	Worst Year
Conservative	20%	45%	35%	10.36%	30.67%	−0.61%
Moderately Conservative	40%	40%	20%	12.44%	39.83%	−2.59%
Moderate	60%	30%	10%	14.39%	47.76%	−7.61%
Moderately Aggressive	80%	20%	0%	16.35%	55.69%	−12.62%
Aggressive	95%	5%	0%	17.63%	59.81%	−16.49%

Source: Wilson Associates International

Tip

As you can see in Table 1-3, stock lovers experience more volatility, but they also capture the biggest payoffs. The volatility isn't a big concern if the savings horizon is long enough to ride out financial tidal waves.

Some older investors, especially those who feel they haven't saved enough, believe that relying almost exclusively on stocks late in life will resolve their money woes. Becoming a stock kamikaze, however, can be extremely dangerous. That's not to say, however, that stocks should be chased out of a retirement portfolio. Not long ago seniors were traditionally advised to hunker down with bonds, CDs, and perhaps a conservative utility stock or two, but the need to keep the portfolio growing with equities is now recognized as crucial because Americans are living longer and retiring sooner. (See Chapter 20 for advice on what percentage of stocks is prudent for retirees.)

How much investment loss would you be willing to take?

It's perilous sitting on an aggressive retirement portfolio if you'd abandon it during a severe market correction. Could you stomach a 20, 30, or even 40 percent free fall? Of course, only you can make this kind of personal judgment call.

If you're not sure whether you have nerves of steel, consider visiting the Bear's Cave, a cozy Internet spot devoted to demonstrating the crushing power of a bear market. You'll find the Cave at the 401Kafe (www.401kafe.com), a Web site devoted to 401(k) participants. At the Cave, you'll discover how bloodied and bruised your portfolio would have been during one of the worst bear markets ever. During a period between January 1973 and September 1974, the Standard & Poor's 500 index, which is considered the stock market's most reliable barometer, plummeted by more than 50 percent. You can plug in your current asset allocation to see how your portfolio would have fared during this time. Table 1-4 provides a snapshot of the carnage inflicted upon a hypothetical $100,000 portfolio.

Table 1-4 Fate of $100,000 Portfolio During 1973–1974 Bear Market	
Asset Mix	*Value*
Long-term government bonds (100%)	$93,95
Long-term government bonds (50%) and large-cap stocks (50%)	$75,670
Long-term government bonds (30%), large-cap stocks (30%), small-cap stocks (20%), and international stocks (20%)	$69,710
Large-cap stocks (100%)	$57,380
Large-cap stocks (50%) and small-cap stocks (50%)	$57,080

Are you (and a spouse) protected by long-term care insurance?

One of Americans' biggest nightmares is spending the last years of their lives in a nursing home. Medicare won't pick up the tab for this expense. Consequently, many struggle to pay the bills for nursing home stays or at-home health costs. An increasing number of older Americans are buying long-term care insurance to protect themselves and their families from this financial ravaging. (See Chapter 30.)

Looking Past the Money

Many people's retirement daydreams end happily with a huge pile of cash at the finish line. Some people, bent on stockpiling lots of money, behave as if they have a savings scoreboard riveted to their forehead. In calculating what they have and what they'll need, eager-beaver savers postpone gratification until they retire, letting the money issue drive retirement decisions instead of being just a part of the preparation process.

Yet you can't fully enjoy the money you've diligently squirreled away if you don't focus on what you'd like to do when the alarm clock is no longer a necessity. Some affluent folks continue to work past retirement age not because they relish working, but because they don't know how else to fill the void. Many aren't sure what to do with their financial freedom beyond spending time with grandchildren and traveling. For those that remain puzzled, consider answering this question: What you would like to do if you had only five years to live?

Playing Catch-Up

What if you haven't started saving enough? What if you haven't saved at all? If you fit this description, you're not alone. According to one survey, the typical age when Americans who are 55 or older began saving for retirement was age 42. At this point, your biggest challenge may be convincing yourself that starting to save isn't futile. This section provides some drastic and some relatively painless catch-up techniques to show you that all hope is not lost.

Delay retirement.

Most Americans don't wait until age 65 to retire anymore. By postponing your retirement date, you'll receive proportionally more Social Security benefits. Delaying retirement can also lead to a fatter pension. Many pensions are calculated upon the final few years of a person's salary, which is presumably when your earnings are highest.

If there is a chance that you will abandon retirement later on, consider remaining in your current job. Folks who are forced back into the rat race typically make substantially less money than in the last job they held.

Max out your tax-deferred contributions.

Stuff the maximum allowed into your 401(k), 403(b), or other retirement plan. In addition, stick an extra $2,000 a year into a Roth IRA. (Those who make too much to qualify for a Roth should contribute to a nondeductible IRA instead.) A couple contributing a combined $4,000 for 10 years (at 11 percent return) to an IRA will ultimately pocket more than $57,000. If you've maxed out those options, start plowing money into tax-efficient investments. Two great low-cost candidates are index funds and exchange-traded funds, which are detailed in Chapter 15.

Tip   Don't overlook any opportunity to salt money away. Invest severance pay, salary raises, and bonuses into your retirement accounts.

Boost savings.

For those who fall short, aggressive savings is always an option. Suppose you're 40 and commit yourself to saving $100 a week in a stock mutual fund. The account earns 11 percent a year (the historic performance of stocks) for 20 years. By the time you celebrate your 65th birthday, your nest egg, before taxes, will have grown to $367,455. The longer you delay, however, the worse the sacrifice will be. A 50-year-old would have to bump up the savings to about $260 a week to make a comparable figure.

Carefully evaluate job moves.

Many Americans hop from one job to another without giving much thought to whether the move will jeopardize their retirement goals. Yet according to the U.S. Labor Department, workplace benefits represent nearly 30 percent of an employee's salary.

Quitting your current job can jeopardize your retirement plans if you aren't already vested in a pension or an employer's 401(k) match. You can also lose stock options if you leave a job prematurely. Carefully evaluate retirement benefits and other perks in a compensation package at a potential new workplace before making any decisions. Always ask yourself what you may be giving up by leaving. If the job proposal comes up short on retirement benefits, by all means submit a counter-offer. You may wish to ask for such things as a signing bonus, annual incentive bonuses, stock options, or stock up front.

Tip   Because it can be tricky evaluating different benefits plans, you may wish to consult a financial planner before making a decision.

Trade your house for a cheaper one.

If your house has appreciated in value, consider selling it and buying a cheaper one. Thanks to tax law changes, you won't owe any capital gains tax on the first $500,000 in profit. In the past, only people who were at least 55 could qualify for the free tax ride. This tax gift is powerful for those who start saving late. Take the money and invest it for retirement. Short of selling a house, find a cheaper mortgage. Refinancing can dramatically cut your monthly payments. Siphon the savings to your retirement account.

Seek outside advice.

A certified financial planner can construct a cash-flow analysis of your spending. A planner can spot ways to cut costs, such as replacing expensive insurance policies with cheaper ones and consolidating debt on a credit card offering the lowest interest rate.

Find a bridge job.

Many Americans don't just abruptly retire when they reach their 60s. Instead they transition out of the workplace with part-time or more flexible jobs. After leaving a full-time position, an electrical engineer might take up consulting on the side. A veteran newspaper reporter can freelance. A teacher can fill in as a substitute. Choosing this route can help ease a potential money crunch.

Summary

✦ When estimating what you'll need to save for retirement, take into account your health, family longevity, the content of your retirement portfolio, and your desired post-retirement lifestyle.

✦ Set up a system of forced savings through a workplace retirement plan or automatic bank draft.

✦ Consider taking advantage of online retirement advice, but keep in mind that the less information you put into a site's evaluation software, the less you'll get out of it.

✦ Boost your retirement investments with stock holdings.

✦ If you're coming in late to the savings game, carefully evaluate a job move if your retirement benefits are jeopardized. Consider delaying retirement and saving as much as you can. Take advantage of your home equity and think ahead to a transitional job for extra cash.

Gambling on Social Security

I n this chapter, you'll learn the Social Security basics and discover
Social Security's hidden perils. For instance, you may not know the
following facts:

- ◆ Many corporations decrease their pension payouts by the amount of Social Security benefits employees receive, which means that many workers who expect a pension may receive a shrunken one.

- ◆ Social Security benefits can be taxed. However, you can minimize the blow by using certain strategies.

- ◆ Women often must scrape by on a Social Security check that is decreased by as much as half after their husband's death.

- ◆ You may be entitled to an ex-spouse's Social Security benefits.

*If knowledge is power, then this chapter will make you powerful
indeed. Read on to get the lowdown on the ins and outs of applying
for benefits, contacting the Social Security administration, and working
around the sometimes-draconian taxes on your Social Security checks.*

The Media Debate:
All Hype, No Help

If you're saving for retirement, you can probably pinpoint,
with little difficulty, how much money you have stashed away
in a 401(k) or any Individual Retirement Accounts. You may
even know a fair amount about how to make all this money
grow. The media has certainly spent plenty of time and energy
coaching people on how to become extraordinary retirement
savers. What's missing from the constant media barrage is
practical advice on Social Security and pensions, yet these
two benefits represent the most valuable pieces in their retirement puzzle for millions of people. For the average American

The First Social Security Check

Five years after President Franklin D. Roosevelt signed the Social Security Act in 1935, the first check was mailed. The lucky retiree was Ida May Fuller of Ludlow, Vermont, who had paid just $24.75 into the system. Before dying, she received benefits totaling $22,889.

approaching retirement age, Social Security and pension coverage are worth as much as all other assets combined, including a house, IRA and 401(k), savings accounts, and life insurance policies.

Cross-Reference   See Chapter 3 for more details on pensions.

The press coverage on Social Security has been almost exclusively restricted to emotionally charged political argument about how to fix the Social Security system. Yet the vigorous debate on various Social Security reform proposals by Congress, policy wonks, and special-interest lobbyists does nothing to address the immediate concerns of a 61-year-old engineer who is struggling to decide whether it's smart to take a reduced Social Security benefit at age 62 or wait awhile. Nor will it help a divorced homemaker who wonders what claim, if any, she has to her ex-husband's Social Security benefit.

The Failing Health of Social Security

By a comfortable margin, most people believe that a pro wrestler stands a greater chance of getting elected president than they do of collecting all the Social Security money that's rightfully theirs. Another poll that drew lots of laughs insisted that more college kids believe in space aliens than they do the viability of the Social Security Administration. The truth is that most Americans consider the Social Security program about as sturdy as a house built from Tinker Toys.

Where Social Security Has Succeeded

Despite the spooky projections, Social Security has been one of the federal government's most crowning achievements. Forty years ago, 35 percent of elderly Americans were trapped in poverty. Social Security has helped to shrink the incidence of poverty among the elderly to about 1 in 10. Without Social Security, nearly 50 percent of today's elderly would be considered impoverished. Most Americans would find themselves in a very frightening place if Social Security checks stopped arriving. Right now $4 out of every $10 spent by retirees comes from Social Security. It's because the entitlement program has been so successful and sacrosanct that the debate enveloping Social Security has dragged on for many years.

The skepticism is understandable. Today, there's one Social Security recipient for every 3.4 workers paying payroll taxes. Yet the Social Security Trust Fund, which is now awash in cash, will be as empty as a kid's piggy bank in the year 2037. By that time, the prediction is that Social Security will be able to pay only 72 percent of the benefits owed. What's the reason? Beginning in 2015, recipients will pocket more money than workers pay into the system.

All of this gloom and doom isn't much of a revelation to anyone who has wondered how Generation X and the echo boom kids will brace themselves for the tremendous baby boom retirement bulge. By the time the trust fund is empty, just 2.1 workers will be supporting each Social Security recipient. Yet politicians, who may be more worried about their own election prospects than what's best for the Social Security program's future, have procrastinated in making the sort of decisions that are bound to infuriate one group or another.

Here are some of the most common suggestions for keeping the system solvent well into the 21st century:

- ✦ Shut out the richest elderly. Those who truly don't need the checks wouldn't receive them any longer.

- ✦ Continue raising the age when an individual can claim full Society Security benefits.

- ✦ Permit workers to shift part of their Social Security contributions into private investment accounts.

- ✦ Allow the government to partially invest in stocks rather than just ultra-safe Treasury bonds.

- ✦ Raise the income ceiling upon which Social Security taxes are calculated.

Of course, not even the shrewdest political observer can predict what will ultimately happen to Social Security. Although many strenuously insist Social Security won't be around by 2037, chances are good that the agency will still be cranking out checks. If the system imploded, the political firestorm would be too explosive. After all, for the average worker, a year's worth of Social Security checks now equals about 40 percent of his or her preretirement salary, which is hardly a chunk of change any of us could do without.

Many financial planners, who expect the worse, are counseling their richer clients to assume that Social Security won't be in the cards for them. Of course, ruling out Social Security is a luxury that only the young, who have decades to save, and the wealthy, who don't need the federal largess, can afford.

Tip   Your best strategy is to plan for less. If you aren't retiring in the next few years, play it safe and assume that your Social Security benefits won't be as generous.

There is some precedent for assuming that the younger you are, the less likely it is that you'll get what the government is promising today. The system is already on a diet. For anyone born after 1959, for instance, the age for full benefits has been pushed back to age 67. (See Table 2-1.) These younger Americans will still be able to claim partial payments at age 62, but the benefit will be reduced by 30 percent. In 2000, the checks for a 62-year-old taking early payments were cut by only 20 percent. Younger Americans will probably make even more Social Security sacrifices in the future.

Table 2-1
Age for Full Social Security Benefits

Year of Birth	Full Benefit Age
Prior to 1938	65
1938	65 and 2 months
1939	65 and 4 months
1940	65 and 6 months
1941	65 and 8 months
1942	65 and 10 months
1943 through 1954	66
1955	66 and 2 months
1956	66 and 4 months
1957	66 and 6 months
1958	66 and 8 months
1959	66 and 10 months
1960 and later	67

Source: Social Security Administration

Note   No matter what the current charts say you are entitled to receive, this reality won't change: If you want to live comfortably in retirement, you can't depend solely upon Social Security. Make it a priority to develop your own savings plan.

Here's a big splash of cold reality: Today's typical monthly retirement check from Social Security is just $845. Some people don't realize that the government, even in the 1930s, intended Social Security to be only a supplemental retirement program. As Social Security officials tour the country with their overhead projectors and slide shows, they talk repeatedly about the three-legged stool of retirement planning. Social Security is merely one leg; the other two are personal savings and workplace retirement plans.

Social Security FAQ

Here are answers to some common questions about Social Security:

What do I pay?

All of us who work are doing our part to keep the Social Security system solvent. Currently, 7.65 percent of our paychecks is siphoned into Social Security and Medicare. The Social Security portion of the tax is 6.2 percent; Medicare swallows the rest. Your employer picks up the other half of the tab, which brings the total tax to 15.3 percent.

Under this system, the self-employed get dinged twice. They must pay the 15.3 percent tax all by themselves. The self-employed, however, can claim half of this obligation as a tax deduction.

Social Security can't extract an unlimited amount of money from any one person or employer. There is a cap, which is adjusted annually, on how much Social Security can extract. In 2001, the maximum that a worker on somebody's payroll has to pay is 6.2 percent of $80,400. The Medicare portion of the tax, however, has no ceiling.

Are all workers covered by Social Security?

Most workers are covered by Social Security, but a few pockets of holdouts remain, thanks to past legislative action. Some federal, state, and local government employees still work outside the system, as do railroad employees and some church workers. Usually these people are covered by some other type of pension system.

Keep in mind that just because you're contributing to Social Security through payroll deductions doesn't automatically entitle you to future benefits. To qualify, you must earn 40 calendar quarters of coverage. As a practical matter, anybody who has contributed to Social Security for 10 years, which breaks down to 40 quarters, is covered. You don't have to work a decade to earn those 40 quarters, however. You can pocket four quarters quickly by meeting a minimum income requirement, although you can't earn more than four quarters in one year.

Example   In the year 2001, any worker who made $830 was credited with one quarter. Consequently, an individual making $3,320 (830 multiplied by 4) in a month or two would be guaranteed a year's worth of credits.

Most people will have an overabundance of quarters by retirement, but some people will be just shy of the requirement. A homemaker, for example, might have spent just a handful of years working within the Social Security system; a few more quarters of work could guarantee monthly Social Security checks. If you are nearing retirement age and aren't eligible yet for Social Security, find out how many quarters you'd need to guarantee that lifetime supply of Social Security checks. In some cases, it could make sense to postpone retirement until you've earned enough quarters.

Table 2-2 provides a breakdown of how much someone needed to earn during each of the past 10 years to qualify for one quarter of coverage and the yearly earnings needed for four quarters of coverage.

Table 2-2 Earnings Test Numbers 1990–2000		
Year	Amount of Earnings for One Quarter	Amount of Earnings for Four Quarters
2001	$830	$3,320
2000	$780	$3,120
1999	$740	$2,960
1998	$700	$2,800
1997	$670	$2,680
1996	$640	$2,560
1995	$630	$2,520
1994	$620	$2,480
1993	$590	$2,360
1992	$570	$2,280
1991	$540	$2,160
1990	$520	$2,080

Source: CCH INCORPORATED

Applying for Social Security

If you're nearing eligibility for Social Security, you should file an application three months before you want the benefits to begin. When you apply, you'll need these documents:

✦ Social Security number

✦ Birth certificate

✦ W-2 form or self-employment tax return for last year

✦ Military discharge papers, if applicable

✦ Proof of U.S. citizenship or lawful alien status if not born here

✦ Name of bank and account number for direct deposit

How are my benefits calculated?

In computing your benefits, the government averages for most workers the 35 highest-wage-earning years of an individual's salary history. (It is indexed to reflect the average increase in national wages during the same period.) Of course, not everybody has such a lengthy work record. Suppose you worked 25 years. The amount you earned during those 25 years will be averaged with 10 years' worth of zero income. Obviously, this method of calculation will shrink your benefit.

Caution This method of calculation can be a particular hardship for women who spent time at home raising their children. In later years, these same women often quit or scale back work to care for ailing parents or in-laws.

Social Security doesn't simply provide workers with a percentage of their average lifetime salaries. A person's age and date of retirement are also plugged into the calculations, and the earnings are indexed to national average earnings.

A progressive formula ensures that grocery checkers, daycare workers, secretaries, and other workers on the lower end of the salary range get to recoup a greater percentage of their preretirement salary than corporate executives, attorneys, doctors, and other highly paid people. Women also can expect proportionately higher checks because they historically have earned less than men. For the typical worker, Social Security replaces, on average, nearly 42 percent of his or her salary.

How much can I expect from Social Security?

To its credit, the Social Security Administration has made a stab at eliminating some of the guesswork concerning your future benefits. The federal government now mails yearly four-page statements that estimate what a worker's benefits will be upon retirement. Every worker who is 25 years of age or older should get one of these statements. You can expect the yearly mailing about three months before your birthday.

Tip Don't toss out your Social Security statements. Instead, double-check the figures. Yes, Social Security employees do make mistakes, which can cost you during retirement.

Your statement will list all your yearly earnings dating back to the start of your working career. If your earnings are understated, don't hesitate to complain. Remember, your earnings determine your benefit amount. Consequently, if the records are wrong, you might unfairly receive smaller checks.

One way to verify earnings is to review past tax returns or W-2 forms. You can contact Social Security through its toll-free number ((800) 772-1213) or Web site (www.ssa.gov). In addition, many local Social Security offices are scattered across the country. Make sure you take notes and get the name of anyone you talk with.

Hold, Please

Do you hate getting put on hold? If so, avoid calling Social Security's toll-free number early in the month, as well as early in the week. Representatives answer calls from 7 a.m. to 7 p.m. on business days. You can receive automated answers 24 hours a day.

Frequently, missing or incorrect earnings are the result of someone not reporting a name change from a marriage or divorce. Problems can also occur when an individual uses a nickname or incorrectly writes the wrong Social Security number on workplace paperwork. To ensure proper credit for your work experience, make sure the name and Social Security number listed on your W-2 precisely matches what's on your Social Security card.

When you receive your yearly statement, remember that it's just an estimate of future benefits. No guarantee comes with these benefit statements because neither bureaucrats nor anyone else know what kind of shape Social Security will be in. Plus, the assumptions built into the statement are based only on your current salary. Most people are going receive raises during their working careers, but Social Security ignores that possibility.

Tip   The Social Security Administration will send you a customized statement that includes your own future salary projections, but you must request it. These statements typically take about four weeks to receive.

Want a rough idea of what future benefits may be like? Tables 2-3 and 2-4 give projections of future benefits for average and highly paid workers. The figures were calculated by CCH INCORPORATED, a leading provider of tax law information and software, using data from the government's actuaries. For these charts, the benefits were calculated for average-paid workers, who were making about $31,000 in 2001 and who will be making about $43,000 by 2010. Workers were classified as highly paid if they bumped up against the Social Security earnings ceiling of $76,200 in 2000. (This ceiling is expected to increase to $105,000 by 2010.)

 Resource   You can obtain much quicker answers by using the agency's retirement calculators at www.ssa.gov. Two of the calculators can be used right on the site, but the most detailed software must be downloaded and installed on your computer.

Table 2-3
Annual Projected Social Security Benefits
for Those Retiring at Age 62

Year of Retirement	Average Paid Worker	Highly Paid Worker
2001	$10,446	$15,334
2002	$10,652	$15,760
2003	$10,890	$16,238
2004	$11,147	$16,749
2005	$11,424	$17,299
2006	$11,875	$18,102
2007	$12,345	$18,959
2008	$12,842	$19,845
2009	$13,374	$20,802
2010	$13,952	$21,795

Source: CCH INCORPORATED

Table 2-4
Annual Projected Social Security Benefits
for those Retiring at Age 65

Year of Retirement	Average Paid Worker	Highly Paid Worker
2001	$12,458	$18,242
2002	$13,313	$19,663
2003	$14,012	$20,869
2004	$14,520	$21,786
2005	$15,028	$22,728
2006	$15,630	$23,799
2007	$16,243	$24,894
2008	$16,834	$25,932
2009	$17,508	$27,146
2010	$18,206	$28,362

Source: CCH INCORPORATED

Does Social Security protect against inflation?

Social Security does offer one tremendous advantage over most private pension plans: It's designed to beat inflation. After 1974, cost-of-living adjustments (COLAs) have been automatic. Since that time, COLAs have ranged from 14.3 percent in 1980 to 1.3 percent in 1986 and 1998. In 2001, a 3.5 percent COLA bumped the average check up by $29. The government calculates the COLA every October, and the checks are adjusted in January. As you can see in Table 2-5, the average check is not a princely sum.

Table 2-5 Typical Monthly Checks Issued in 2001	
Type of Retiree	*Amount of Check*
All retired workers	$845
Elderly couple, both receiving benefits	$1,410
Widow or widower	$811

What many seniors discover, however, is that the inflation safety net is torn. The yearly increases are linked to the Consumer Price Index (CPI), which doesn't necessarily measure how seniors spend their money. Many items that the CPI dutifully tracks, such as price increases for cigarettes, new cars, and gasoline, aren't relevant to the spending pattern of seniors. Medical care, drugs, and housing gobble up more of their budgets.

Caution

The CPI also doesn't figure in the cost of Medicare premiums, which is a huge omission. The cost of medical care and prescriptions has been rising at a much higher rate than the CPI.

Land Mine No. 1: Timing Is Everything

In some ways, Social Security isn't as complicated as a 401(k) or an IRA. You don't have to worry about how to invest the money or what to do with a lump sum when you leave a job. All in all, Social Security is pretty cut-and-dry. But nonetheless, some devilish decisions could end up taunting you. Ideally, you'll want to avoid making decisions that could increase your taxes or jeopardize your family's future financial health.

Social Security Through Time

When President Franklin D. Roosevelt signed Social Security into law in 1935, the magic age to claim benefits was 65. Why 65? In searching for an appropriate age, Social Security's creators leaned heavily upon Germany's experience. Germany, which had been a pioneer in establishing a retirement system back in 1889, had been using 65 as its official retirement age since 1916. In the United States at the time, most fledgling retirement plans used either age 65 or 70.

Here are other Social Security milestones:

✦ 1939: Social Security's mandate was broadened to include workers' spouses and children.

✦ 1940: The first Social Security checks were mailed out.

✦ 1950: Social Security was expanded to provide benefits to disabled workers.

✦ 1961: President John F. Kennedy signed legislation allowing reduced retirement benefits at age 62.

✦ 1972: President Richard M. Nixon approved legislation creating automatic cost-of-living increases.

✦ 1983: President Ronald Reagan signed a bill permitting the taxation of Social Security benefits.

✦ 1996: Drug addicts and alcoholics were no longer eligible for Social Security disability checks.

✦ 2000: The Social Security earnings test for workers who reached full retirement age was killed.

When contemplating when to receive Social Security benefits, for example, you have many choices. The age of 62 is the first chance for retirees to cash Social Security checks. Although this age is by far the most popular age to retire (see Table 2-6), Social Security penalizes workplace dropouts for abandoning the 9-to-5 routine so soon by docking a portion of their checks. How large the cut will be depends upon their year of birth. In the past, retirees could expect the check to be 20 percent smaller than what they'd claim at the traditional retirement age of 65. That's no longer the case for people born after 1938. As you can see in Table 2-7, the penalty for taking early payments continues to grow. In contrast, the government rewards those who postpone retirement until age 70. These numbers simply reflect the reality that the traditional retirement age is inching up for everybody born since 1938.

Table 2-6
Ages When Americans Claim Social Security Benefits

Age	Percentage Who Claim
62	57.8%
63	7.8%
64	10.2%
65	16%
Between 66 and 69	4.8%
70 or older	3.5%

Table 2-7
Benefits of Delaying or Speeding Up Social Security Checks

Year of Birth	Age	Percentage of What You Could Expect at Normal Retirement Age
Before 1938	62	80%
Before 1938	63	87%
Before 1938	64	93%
Before 1938	65	100%
Before 1938	66	106.5%
Before 1938	67	113%
Before 1938	70	132.5%
1938	62	79%
1938	63	86%
1938	64	92%
1938	65	99%
1938	66	105%
1938	67	112%
1938	70	131%
1939	62	78%
1939	63	84%
1939	64	91%
1939	65	98%

Year of Birth	Age	Percentage of What You Could Expect at Normal Retirement Age
1939	66	105%
1939	67	112%
1939	70	133%
1940	62	77.5%
1940	63	83%
1940	64	90%
1940	65	97%
1940	66	103.5%
1940	67	110.5%
1940	70	131.5%
1941	62	77%
1941	63	82%
1941	64	89%
1941	65	96%
1941	66	102.5%
1941	67	110%
1941	70	132.5%
1942	62	76%
1942	63	81%
1942	64	88%
1942	65	94%
1942	66	101%
1942	67	109%
1942	70	131%
1943–1954	62	75%
1943–1954	63	80%
1943–1954	64	87%
1943–1954	65	93%
1943–1954	66	100%
1943–1954	67	108%

Continued

Table 2-7 *(continued)*		
Year of Birth	**Age**	**Percentage of What You Could Expect at Normal Retirement Age**
1943–1954	70	132%
1955	62	74%
1955	63	79%
1955	64	86%
1955	65	92%
1955	66	99%
1955	67	107%
1955	70	131%
1956	62	73%
1956	63	78%
1956	64	84%
1956	65	91%
1956	66	98%
1956	67	105%
1956	70	129%
1957	62	72.5%
1957	63	77.5%
1957	64	83%
1957	65	90%
1957	66	97%
1957	67	104%
1957	70	128%
1958	62	72%
1958	63	77%
1958	64	82%
1958	65	89%
1958	66	96%
1958	67	103%
1958	70	127%

Year of Birth	Age	Percentage of What You Could Expect at Normal Retirement Age
1959	62	71%
1959	63	76%
1959	64	81%
1959	65	88%
1959	66	94%
1959	67	101%
1959	70	125%
1960 and later	62	70%
1960 and later	63	75%
1960 and later	64	80%
1960 and later	65	87%
1960 and later	66	93%
1960 and later	67	100%
1960 and later	70	124%

Source: Social Security Administration, Office of the Chief Actuary

You can read the numbers yourself, but they won't necessarily provide you with the response to this critical question: When should I request my Social Security benefits? The government's actuaries made sure that there's no built-in advantage for whichever option you select. As a general rule, someone who claims Social Security at the earliest opportunity will get about the same amount of benefits over a lifetime as someone who waits until full retirement. If you apply early, for example, your checks will be lower, but chances are you'll cash more of them than somebody with bigger monthly payouts who waits until age 65.

Before deciding, consider these factors:

  ✦ How healthy are you?

  ✦ Is there a history of longevity in your family?

  ✦ Do you expect to continue working once Social Security kicks in?

  ✦ What kind of financial shape would your spouse be in if you died first?

  ✦ What other financial assets do you have?

No one-size-fits-all answer exists. Before making this incredibly important decision, you may wish to enlist the help of an actuary or accountant to crunch the numbers for you. For now, read on.

Claiming Social Security benefits at age 62: Issues to consider

Most people claim their benefits at this age, but before you join the crowd, consider these issues:

If your health is failing

Morbid as this fact is to contemplate, some people aren't going to live long after retiring. If you have a history of heart disease or you're fighting a cancer diagnosis, you may want to take the money now. Your family's health history may also play into your decision. Maybe your grandparents, parents, uncles, and aunts tended to die at relatively early ages. Smokers, alcoholics, the grossly overweight, or those who haven't been conscientious about taking care of themselves may also want to claim their Social Security stake as soon as possible.

If you need the money

If you're struggling financially, you may want to take the money and run, particularly if you are in poor health or have been laid off, with little chance of finding a new position in your field. If you have no desire to jump back into the work force or circumstances make that impossible, then Social Security could be your only way to stay afloat.

If you plan to invest the money

Some people who don't need the money may opt to postpone payments, but some financial planners urge their clients to take the cash and invest it instead. Sinking the money into the stock market could earn a greater windfall. Of course, investing in the stock market in your later years is also more perilous. If you plan to divert the cash into CDs, a savings account, or money market, you might be better off postponing Social Security.

If you continue to work

You could pay a heavy price if you begin taking Social Security benefits while you're still on the job. In 2001, federal law allows a Social Security recipient who is between 62 and full retirement age to make only $10,680 a year without being penalized. Once that limit is surpassed, workers forfeit $1 for every $2 they earn.

Note   Some people mistakenly believe that the earnings penalty was dismantled in 2000. The earnings penalty was abolished only for beneficiaries who have reached their full retirement age.

If your spouse would suffer financial hardship if you died first

Social Security is plagued by a gender gap. Because women live longer, they are the ones who usually face dramatic cutbacks in Social Security when a spouse dies. A widow (or widower) will receive a check that is just one-half or two-thirds of the couple's combined benefit.

Having Second Thoughts

Suppose you retire and your Social Security payments start. Then someone calls and offers you a job. Or maybe you're so bored watching old flicks on the A&E channel that you begin consulting on the side. Can you stop your Social Security checks? Luckily you can. For every month in which someone does not receive benefits, he or she is eligible for a benefit recomputation. The benefit can also be recalculated to take into account the increased earnings.

What hurts women is their historically lower salaries and their periodic absences from the workforce. Although Social Security retirement benefits are usually calculated upon the highest 35 years in a career, the typical woman works only 27 years. (The average man's career lasts 39 years.) All those missing years hurt when a woman's benefit is calculated.

Let's see what happens to a husband and wife who are both entitled to yearly $15,000 benefits based upon their own individual work histories. While they're both alive, they will annually pocket a combined $30,000. When the husband dies, the widow must live on a check that will be $15,000, or just slightly higher, based on such factors as her age, her husband's age at the time of death and the actual benefits he had received.

Now let's assume that the wife never worked outside the home. At the start, she'd claim half of her husband's $15,000 benefit, bringing the household income to $22,500. When her husband dies, the widow receives just $15,000 a year.

Finally, let's assume that the wife's benefit, based on her career, is somewhere between $7,500 and $15,000. She would receive that benefit until her husband died. Once that happened, she would essentially claim her husband's larger benefit.

Tip   Because benefits drop precipitously after the death of a spouse, the survivor, who is most often a woman, is better off if the original checks are as large as possible. Because men usually don't live as long, a husband might want to postpone his benefits if he is worried about his wife's financial future.

This largely feminine dilemma has been a huge concern for women's groups. When Congress examined whether workers who are drawing Social Security while still working should continue to face the 50 percent tax on their Social Security payouts, the National Women's Law Center and the National Council of Women's Organizations, which is a network of more than 100 women's groups, pleaded with Congress to keep the penalties in place for Social Security recipients who hadn't reached full retirement age. Eliminating that penalty would only encourage more men to take early benefits and thereby imperil the final years of more women. In fact, Social Security data suggested that up to 700,000 elderly women would have ultimately been pushed into poverty if the penalty had been eliminated.

Women and Social Security

The National Council of Women's Organizations, a nonpartisan network of women's groups, formed a Social Security task force in 1998 to address critical issues facing women. You can learn more by visiting the group's Women and Social Security Project Web site at www.women4socialsecurity.org.

If you're a woman

If you will receive benefits based upon your own work record, you may want to start those benefits early. (This advice assumes you are not continuing to work.) As previously noted, women enjoy an actuarial advantage over men because they live longer. Chances are a woman will remain alive long enough to overcome the built-in financial penalty for taking the money early because she'll draw many more checks over the years.

Claiming Social Security benefits at full retirement age or older: Issues to consider

Back when Social Security was launched, people often worked almost until their deaths because there was no national safety net. The retirement age that Congress originally envisioned for workers to claim their checks was 65, and it was assumed that many people would die before they reached this age. If you want full benefits and you were born prior to 1938, the age to claim full benefits is 65. For everyone else, the full retirement age keeps creeping up.

Note   If you decide to postpone Social Security when you reach 65, you should still sign up for Medicare. There is no financial incentive for delaying Medicare.

If you delay retirement until age 70, the amount of your ultimate monthly checks will increase anywhere from 4.5 percent to 8 percent a year. There is absolutely no point in waiting beyond age 70 because the benefits stop escalating (see Table 2-7). There's now even less need to wait until a 70th birthday because fewer retirees are being penalized for returning to work.

If you continue to work

Until the year 2000, the federal government didn't appreciate older beneficiaries working on the side. You've already read in this chapter about the penalties faced by the youngest recipients, but until recently the penalties didn't end there. Between the ages of 65 and 70, individuals were required to pay $1 for every $3 in wages after a salary ceiling was surpassed. In 2000, that ceiling was $17,000.

Social Security and Divorce

If you're trapped in a rocky marriage, you could understandably be anxious to start over. But if the marriage is near the 10-year milestone, you might want to postpone the breakup for a few months. If your marriage lasts that long, you can ultimately choose to collect Social Security checks that are based upon your spouse's earnings. (The federal government uses the official date of your divorce and not the beginning of a legal separation to determine the length of a marriage.) The benefit is about 50 percent of an ex-spouse's benefit if the person claiming the checks has reached full retirement age.

If you've been divorced twice, but you hung in there for at least 10 years both times, you have an option. You may claim a portion of the benefits of whichever former spouse managed to generate the biggest Social Security checks. The federal government can tell you which benefit would be greater, but you need to provide the agency with as much information as possible, including the spouse's Social Security number and birth date.

What did the earnings penalty mean in real-life terms? Suppose someone was entitled to the average $816 monthly Social Security check. If she earned $45,945, the amount of her Social Security check would have been a big fat zero. That's right, she would have been entitled to no benefits at all. Only when someone reached the age of 70 could he or she work the cash register at McDonald's for minimum wage or launch an Internet startup and make millions and the government wouldn't care. Either way, that person's Social Security checks wouldn't have been docked.

But for the first time in the history of Social Security, people who have reached full retirement age are no longer penalized if they continue to work. By unanimous votes in both the U.S. Senate and House in 2000, Congress repealed the rule that reduced benefit checks for Social Security beneficiaries ages 65 to 70 who continued to work.

With the penalty gone, many people who were working without Social Security benefits immediately applied for them.

If you have longevity on your side

Suppose you don't smoke or drink and you're a fitness nut. Your ancestors lived to ripe old ages. You may want to postpone the checks. If you reach your 80s, you will pocket more money than if you started payments earlier.

Here's how: In 2000, the maximum monthly payment was $1,433 or $17,196 a year. If you wait until age 70, the payments will jump 30 percent to $1,862 or $22,354. While waiting those five years, you'll pass on tens of thousands of dollars in missed benefits. But if you live into your mid 80s, you'll win the actuarial guessing game. At that time, your cumulative benefits will surpass benefits taken at 65.

If your tax bracket will decrease

As you'll learn later in the chapter, you can get heavily taxed on your Social Security benefits. Some affluent individuals who are in a high tax bracket, but expect it to decline somewhere between the ages of 65 and 70, might want to postpone their benefit until then.

Land Mine No. 2: Merging Pensions and Social Security

If you're vested in a pension, you're entitled to your full pension, right? The answer for millions of Americans could be no. This terrible surprise can be explained by a practice that experts call "integration."

Caution   An employer can significantly reduce a worker's pension benefits if he or she is receiving Social Security.

The more poorly paid workers, who can least absorb this body blow, are the ones who are hurt by this practice. On the other hand, the most highly paid employees at a company might enjoy even greater pension benefits than they originally anticipated.

While controversial, this practice is completely legal. In certain circumstances, a company can subtract a portion of your Social Security benefit from your pension. Many companies justify striping away pension benefits as a way to make things fairer for the best-paid employees.

The hazards of pension integration

Here's how this nightmare can happen: As mentioned earlier, employers are expected to kick in 6.2 percent of someone's pay up to a salary ceiling of $80,400 in 2001. Through payroll deduction, an employee contributes the identical amount. A company allocates the same percentage whether the employee is a corporate executive or a receptionist. But integration permits an employer to essentially take credit for the payroll tax representing a proportionately higher Social Security benefit for the lower paid workers. Remember, Social Security is a progressive system, which means the folks on the bottom of the wage scale will eventually recoup more of their salary from Social Security than somebody making tons of money.

Lower paid employees will retrieve more of their pay from Social Security, which many companies insist isn't fair to the well-paid employees. This argument, however, fails to take into consideration stock options, bonuses, and other executive compensation that can more than tip the scales the other way.

Companies try to even the playing field this way: By lowering pension benefits to the least fortunate, the total retirement package of pension plus Social Security now represents a more uniform percentage of final pay for all employees. Pension plans can use different approaches to slash benefits. One method offsets the Social Security dollars someone receives by reducing pension benefits by the same dollar amount.

Pension integration isn't some quirky fluke that will haunt only a few unfortunate souls. It's estimated that 32 percent of American workers who are participating in private pension plans could be affected. This potential time bomb isn't quite as big a threat for those who started working in 1988 or later. At that time, Congress required that employees be left with at least 50 percent of their pension. But that federal law only protects pension benefits earned after 1988. The old draconian formula can still be used for prior working years.

How to fight back

What can you do about pension integration? First, you need to find out what your company's policy is. Ask your human resources department and request a copy of your pension program's summary plan description. This document, which federal law requires to be easy to read, lays out how the plan works. It must precisely document how the integration is calculated.

 See Chapter 3 for a detailed treatment of pensions.

If your corporation uses integration, chances are most or all of your colleagues won't be aware of it. If enough people are angry by the arrangement, workplace sentiment might encourage the company to revisit the issue. You can also lobby Congress to outlaw integration altogether. U.S. Sen. Olympia Snowe (R-Maine) and Rep. Rob Andrews (D-N.J.) are both trying with their own legislation to banish integration from the workplace.

If you face the prospects of getting your pension reduced, find out how the calculations were made. If a company has used an estimate of your Social Security benefits in its calculations, you can ask for a recalculation. Consider consulting an actuary or an accountant to see how integration will affect you.

Land Mine No. 3: Triggering Taxes on Social Security Benefits

Social Security checks can be taxed. Some retirees are shocked when they discover this nasty surprise. Many people will never pay taxes on their Social Security checks, but plenty do. Whether you owe money will depend upon whether your income reaches a high enough level.

Social Security Handouts

The federal government offers a wide range of free publications concerning Social Security, including the following:

✦ *Social Security—Retirement Benefits* (Publication No. 05-10035)

✦ *Understanding the Benefits* (Publication No. 5-10024)

✦ *The Future of Social Security* (Publication No. 5-10055)

✦ *How Your Retirement Benefit Is Figured* (Publication No. 5-10070)

✦ *Government Pension Offset* (Publication No. 5-10007)

What you need to keep an eye on is something called your modified adjusted gross income (MAGI). Most of a person's income, whether it's taxable or not, is included in this formula. What's also thrown into the formula is 50 percent of the value of your Social Security benefits. If a single person's MAGI remains under $25,000, no taxes will be owed on the Social Security benefits. A married couple will also get a free ride if the adjusted income is below $32,000.

The tax pain is unavoidable, however, if this income formula exceeds $44,000 for a couple or $34,000 for an individual. For these folks, 85 percent of their Social Security benefits will be subject to tax. What about the people who fall in between these two groups? They will owe taxes, but not as much. In this case, the tax bill is based on the lesser of these two amounts: 50 percent of the Social Security benefits or 50 percent of the excess over the base amount ($25,000 for individuals and $32,000 for couples). Most states, by the way, don't tax Social Security benefits.

 Resource　To learn more about Social Security benefit taxation, you can order the IRS's Publication 554, *Tax Information for Older Americans.* Call the Internal Revenue Service at (800) 829-3676 or go to www.irs.gov.

Strategies to avoid taxation

Okay, that's the bad news. The good news is that some of this tax may be avoided.

Postpone Social Security benefits.

Affluent Americans can dodge or reduce the tax bite by postponing their Social Security benefits. As mentioned earlier, anyone under the age of 65 who is working and receiving benefits can get hit with a huge tax bill as well.

Time IRA distributions carefully.

Another way to lower your tax liability is to play it smart when timing any Individual Retirement Account distributions.

Many retirees are stunned to learn that their mandatory yearly withdrawals from traditional IRAs can trigger Social Security taxes. How does this happen? Large enough withdrawals can bump up someone's modified adjusted gross income and catapult that person into a higher federal tax bracket. In many cases, however, you can control how much of your Social Security will be taxed by thoughtfully controlling your IRA distributions.

Affluent Americans often withdraw just the bare minimum that's required by law from their IRAs. But that strategy can backfire when the IRA grows increasingly larger and the required yearly distributions become ever bigger as well. You should consult with an accountant or a financial planner on the optimal IRA withdrawal strategy.

Cross-Reference See Chapter 10 for details on IRAs and Chapter 20 for an overall spending game plan during your golden years.

Here's another way to avoid a potential tax on your Social Security checks. If you own a regular IRA, you'll be required to begin siphoning money out of it no later than April 1 of the year following the one in which you turn 70½. (Only Roth IRA owners can avoid this mandatory spending rule.) Retirees who would prefer not to touch their IRA loathe this deadline. Some instinctively postpone the inevitable until the very last minute, but that strategy could well trigger tax on your Social Security benefits.

If you turn 70½ in 2001, you could postpone your first withdrawal until April 1, 2002. But then you'll have to make two withdrawals in 2002 (your 2001 and 2002 distributions). If this is the case, it could be better to take the first distribution by December 31, 2001 to help lower your overall tax liabilities. However, if you expect an unusually large income in 2001 — perhaps from a final workplace bonus — and little income the next year, postponing both payments until 2002 could be preferable.

For some people, paying tax on their Social Security benefits is inevitable. If you fit into that category, you may want to have the federal tax automatically taken out of your Social Security checks. You can request taxes to be withheld when you apply for benefits. If you're already receiving benefits, contact the IRS and ask for form W-4V. You can also download the form from the IRS's Web site at www.irs.gov.

Summary

✦ If you're young, plan for skimpier Social Security benefits.

✦ Check your annual Social Security benefit statement for errors.

✦ Time your Social Security benefits carefully, taking into account the future needs of both yourself and your spouse.

✦ Understand the dangers of pension integration and find out before you retire what you can expect.

✦ Limit or avoid taxes on your Social Security checks by paying attention to the timing of IRA distributions and other income.

The Nation's Disappearing Pensions

Pensions have always been complicated, but the need to understand them has never been more critical. In this chapter, you learn what your rights are and what you need to understand about your pension. If your company is amending your pension plan or you think you're receiving the wrong amount, you'll find out where to turn for help. This chapter is also crucial for the spouses and ex-spouses of workers with pension plans. They'll learn what they need to do to protect themselves financially.

Pensions on the Defensive

If you still are covered by a pension plan, consider yourself lucky. Just under half of workers in the private sector still have pension programs available to them. But don't become complacent. The pensions that remain in place are complicated creatures, making them difficult for workers to understand and easy for employers to tinker with.

Corporate America has been quietly whittling away pension benefits for vast numbers of workers. Pension plan changes that are announced casually in a low-key company handout can in reality represent draconian cuts in workers' retirement benefits. A company can often eviscerate its future pension obligations without triggering a single complaint by smooth-talking its workers into thinking that the complex modifications are no big deal.

What can you do to protect yourself? Begin by reading this pension primer, which was written for workers of any age.

Cross-Reference In Chapter 21, folks set to retire soon can find out how to decide whether to take a lump sum pension payment or a monthly pension check.

The way we were

During his brief presidency, Gerald Ford was probably best remembered for two things: He pardoned Richard Nixon for Watergate, and he seemed to trip a lot when television cameras were rolling.

If you're saving for retirement, however, President Ford's most notable moment arguably happened in 1974 during a White House Rose Garden ceremony. Surrounded by politicians and bureaucrats, Ford signed into law a bill that sounded like a popular new name for a baby girl: ERISA. The Employee Retirement Income Security Act has helped to change forever the way Americans prepare for their retirement.

The brains behind ERISA were motivated by the sort of good intentions that only Robin Hood could match. Its supporters in Washington wanted to make sure that the pension plans for millions of Americans remained safe. After the landmark legislation was signed, a bureaucratic cottage industry sprung up to ensure that corporate pension promises to their employees were kept. No longer would a faithful factory worker lose his pension benefits because he was cut loose a few months shy of his 65th birthday. Nor would a retiree lose his pension because incompetent management drove a company into bankruptcy.

Note   ERISA has achieved pension security for millions. Yet it also may have inadvertently helped to cause thousands of American companies to get rid of their pension plans.

Many who track pension issues suggest that ERISA and its subsequent revisions made managing pension systems, which are also referred to as *defined benefit plans,* too expensive and cumbersome. When Ford signed the bill, 103,000 defined benefit plans existed. Today, the Employee Benefit Research Institute, a nonprofit organization, estimates that just 42,000 remain. Thousands of small employers, particularly those who had set up plans primarily as tax shelters to pay for their own retirements, balked at the new requirements and shuttered their plans. This practice was perfectly legal. A company must follow federal regulations in operating a pension plan, but there's no law preventing it from shutting one down and dispersing the assets to its employees. Pension plans are strictly voluntary, which is why so many have vanished.

Then in the early 1980s, the advent of the new 401(k) plans began stealing the limelight. Small companies began substituting these popular new savings plans for pensions and some larger employers added them as supplemental plans, while cutting back or freezing their pension plans.

Pensions in American History

America's first private pension plan was established in 1759 for the widows and children of Presbyterian ministers. It wasn't until 1875 that American Express created the first corporate pension plan for its employees.

The pension plan replaced: 401(k)s

With old-fashioned pensions, most workers were clueless about how their companies invested retirement dollars and how the benefits were calculated. Yet even someone who ignored all the company's pension handouts might have been okay. Within a few days of cutting the farewell sheet cake, those monthly checks would start appearing.

The checks arrived because, behind the scenes, armies of institutional money managers with backup from equity analysts, fixed-income and real estate experts, accountants, and asset allocation software made sure that corporate America's pension funds were safe, sound, and earning enough to meet all their obligations.

Today, however, your company may have replaced this sort of full-service financial firepower with something else: your 401(k) account, a do-it-yourself system where you are responsible for the financial choices once made by that army of corporate-sponsored money managers. Unlike the no-brainer pension system where workers could rightfully assume checks would just begin showing up, the 401(k) requires careful thought about how to make the money grow during the planning stage and how to make it last during the retirement years.

Cross-Reference See Chapter 8 for the lowdown on 401(k)s, the popular employer-sponsored retirement plan that has replaced so many pension plans.

Pension Patchwork Quilt

Surveys indicate that most American workers know little about their pension plans. Of course, it hasn't helped that pension issues, in comparison with Social Security, are trapped in a media black hole. You'll find very little news about pensions even though the stakes for both old and young employees are so high.

This media neglect is particularly unfortunate because what's sadly lacking in America's patchwork quilt of pension regulations and practices is a centralized place where everyone can seek help. The responsibility for pension administration is split among various federal agencies from the Departments of Labor and Treasury to the Internal Revenue Service. At least with Social Security, a taxpayer need call only one agency.

Pension Protection Strategies

Ultimately, it falls upon you to safeguard your own pension. The following sections explain what you should do.

Know your rights

Companies are free to tinker with their pension plans, but they aren't allowed to eliminate or reduce benefits you've already earned. If you have earned $100,000 in a pension plan that is now being radically altered, you'll still be entitled to that $100,000. However, if your company implements a stingier pension program, you may work for years without the value of your $100,000 pension budging one iota. ERISA can't Teflon-coat your benefits going forward. Your pension would essentially be frozen temporarily, but you probably wouldn't realize it.

Companies love to promote any proposed pension changes as good for employees and necessary to remain competitive. But remain wary. In recent years, most of the changes that employers have made to their pension changes hurt employees. Who is the winner? The corporations. Thanks to cutbacks, the surplus cash in corporate pension funds can soar—if pension payouts are decreased, the pension kitty grows fatter. A corporation can use this stockpile of money to make its earnings look better, which is the sort of move that shareholders adore.

Corporate America has put its pension plans on a variety of diets. Some of their favorite ways to cut pensions are the following:

✦ **Change the pay formula.** Many pension plans rely heavily upon the last three to five years of someone's pay to calculate the pension. This practice is favorable to you because you're presumably making the biggest bucks in those final years. However, some companies are now plugging into the equation a worker's salary going back as far as 10 years, which lowers a person's ultimate pension payout.

✦ **Another corporate strategy is to reduce a plan's pension *multiplier*.** A pension is typically calculated by multiplying three figures: years of service, pay, and a multiplier. The higher the multiplier, the better off you are. Suppose you worked at a company for 20 years with an average pay of $60,000 during the past three years. Multiply these figures with a pension multiplier of 1.4 percent and you'll arrive at a yearly pension payout of $16,800. If the company decreases the pension multiplier to 1 percent, the pension's annual value will plummet to $12,000.

✦ **Freeze the pension plan.** When a company freezes its pension plan, future raises and years on the job won't boost an individual's pension. When a pension is frozen, the company no longer makes contributions to the plan and whatever benefit a worker has earned begins to deteriorate at the rate of inflation.

✦ **Cap years of service.** Some companies institute a limit, say 25 years, on the years of service they use to calculate for pension benefits. Of course, a plan that uses the actual years of service is much better.

✦ **Convert to different type of pension plan.** Conversions to other types of pensions, such as a cash balance or pension-equity plan, can mean trouble for workers. You'll learn why later in this chapter.

Although companies enjoy tremendous latitude in shrinking pension benefits, you need to know how proposed changes will impact you. In some cases, workers, particularly older ones, have been grandfathered into a corporation's former and more generous pension plan. Meanwhile, some corporations have backed down or modified a proposed pension overhaul after employees complained loudly. If a company isn't dissuaded, you need to know enough to assess whether you should remain at the company, take early retirement (if possible), or pursue another job. You probably won't be able to determine that without help from an actuary or other expert. Later in the chapter, you'll learn how to find such an expert.

Keep all records

Most people become interested in their pensions only after they've retired. But unfortunately, once you're out the door, you have far less clout with your former employer than you did when you could waltz into the human resources department and buttonhole somebody. Just ask all those retirees with benefit questions who are now stuck trying to navigate automated voice systems.

Tip

If you are preparing to retire, make sure all of your pension documents are correct before you retire. Get all your questions answered before you leave.

Even if retirement is years away, you shouldn't be complacent. Establish a file folder and put all pension statements and documents you receive in it. This group of documents also includes any modifications made to your company's plan. Within this file, also keep a record of your yearly salaries and start and departure dates of all your career moves.

Keeping this backup material can be invaluable if you encounter problems later. Suppose you spend five years at a company, long enough to qualify for a pension, and then move on to other jobs in the intervening decades. If the firm later merges or goes out of business, your odds of still securing that pension will increase dramatically if you've kept the documents. If you haven't saved any paperwork, ask your employer to replicate as much of it as possible.

Here are the key pension documents you should have:

Your pension program's Summary Plan Description

Ask your employer for a copy of the Summary Plan Description, which outlines how your company's pension system works. This document explains what pension benefits are offered, eligibility requirements, and how pension calculations are made. Federal law, by the way, mandates that this document must be easy to read. No one would be able to determine whether your pension was correctly calculated without referring to this plan.

Individual pension benefit statement

Your statement tells you what pension benefits you have earned and how many years you've been enrolled in your employer's plan. The statement may include a projection of what your monthly checks will be when you retire as well as what a lump sum payment would be worth.

Tip   Look for errors on the paperwork, such as the wrong Social Security number or birth date and the wrong length of employment. If you spot mistakes, have your company's human resources office correct the error.

Your pension plan's annual report

If you or your colleagues are worried about the solvency of your pension plan or if you suspect the plan is greedily sitting on a mountain of cash, it's worth slogging through this document. The annual report includes information on the plan's financial condition, including its assets and liabilities plus income and expenses. (A worker should automatically receive a Summary Annual Report, which is a one-page overview of a private pension plan's finances.)

You should be able to obtain the annual document from your employer. It's also available from the U.S. Department of Labor's Pension and Welfare Benefits Administration through its public disclosure room in Washington D.C. or by mail: Pension and Welfare Benefits Administration, U.S. Department of Labor, 200 Constitution Ave., NW, Room N-5638, Washington, DC 20210. You can also contact the PWBA by phone (202) 219-8771 or on the Internet at www.dol.gov/dol/pwba.

Understand your pension payout choices

In the good old days, a retiree drew a monthly pension check. But today corporations are increasingly offering lump sum payments as an option. Not surprisingly, people favor cashing that one gigantic check. It sure seems like a better deal than those slow and steady monthly pension checks.

Although choosing the lump sum might seem like a no-brainer, it isn't. It won't always be the appropriate choice. In some cases, a person can unwittingly lose huge sums of money by taking the cash.

Caution

In the long run, the lump sum, even if you invest it all wisely, won't always match the stream of income that you're guaranteed with those monthly checks.

Many workers are incapable of evaluating which option is better because employers provide the raw figures with little or no analysis. Choosing between a lump sum and a monthly check is also tricky if you've been offered an early retirement subsidy. This subsidy has traditionally been offered to encourage older workers to leave. Here's what people don't realize: While the subsidy will be included in the calculation for monthly checks, a company can offer a departing worker a lump sum that doesn't take into consideration the value of the subsidy. By one estimate, some workers in their late 40s to late 50s who accept lump sums can effectively chop the value of their pensions in half. The U.S. Treasury Department is investigating whether employers are conducting themselves appropriately when they issue information on pension payouts.

It's critical that you consult an unbiased financial expert to help you decide how to proceed. Consider avoiding consulting a stockbroker on this important decision. Some energetic stockbrokers actually seek out workers on the verge of retiring at major companies in the area by using free retirement seminars as a hook. See Chapter 6 for information on this practice.

Caution

Stockbrokers will probably root for you to choose the lump sum. That way, they can help you invest the money and potentially generate commissions for themselves.

Ask the right questions

Knowing what can go wrong with pensions and what your rights are can only help you in the long run. Make sure you ask these crucial questions.

Do I have a pension?

Even if your company has a pension plan, don't assume you're covered. You need to specifically ask about yourself. The nation's pension laws permit employers to exclude people from their pension plans. Most commonly, the exclusions are by job category. For example, a plan might leave out all secretaries or even all hourly workers. But the exclusions can also be more arbitrary if certain rules are followed. For example, an employer could exclude anybody whose middle initial is "X," or just one person. The general rule is that companies can exclude up to 30 percent of their employees for any reason, and as many as 60 percent if complicated legal requirements are met.

Am I vested?

Your company might operate a generous pension plan, but you won't be entitled to any of it until you're vested. *Vesting* refers to the magical number of years you must toil at one place before you earn a pension stake. Once you are past the eligibility hurdle, you can receive monthly pension checks after reaching retirement age. In some cases, you'll be permitted to walk away with a lump sum when leaving a company even if you're young.

Tip   If you are contemplating a move to another job or early retirement, first double-check to make sure you are vested. If you are a year or a few months shy of eligibility, you could be far better off staying put for a short while.

Most people in companies and union pension plans are fully vested after five years of employment. Companies, however, are permitted to stretch out the vesting period as long as seven years. Plans covering state and local government employees, railroad workers and the military, aren't covered by ERISA provisions so the wait could be even longer — as much as 20 years in the case of military pensions. If you're lucky, your company provides instant vesting. In one survey, however, just 3 percent of companies were that magnanimous.

Vesting for union members

Until recently, many union members faced tougher rules for pension qualification than did other private sector workers. Those who worked in such fields as construction, mining, and trucking were covered by what's called a *multi-employer plan,* in which they could work for a number of different companies that had agreed to pay into the plan, but they had to work a total of 10 years to become vested. If they worked 9 years, they weren't entitled to a dime. Since 1999, 10-year vesting schedules are no longer allowed; however, the law change doesn't help those who retired prior to that year.

Tradespeople, because of the nature of their jobs, tend to be itinerant, and so need to make sure their pensions are portable when they move from one job to another. Multi-employer plans make such portability possible — the key is working only for employers who are obliged under the terms of a collective bargaining agreement to contribute to the same plan. Staying in the same union doesn't automatically ensure that you can take your pension from job to job. If you go to work for an employer who is contributing to a different pension fund from your last employer — even if you work for the same union — you need to find out whether a reciprocity agreement is in place between the plans. Without such an agreement, you could lose out on both pensions.

Will my spouse receive pension checks if I die first?

Too many widows are shocked to learn that when their husbands die, their claims to the pension die too. The pension checks stop after the funeral. How could this happen? Simple: The breadwinner decided on the eve of his retirement or when he

Pensions in the Good Old Days

If you have a workplace pension plan, you enjoy a better chance of being vested today than at any other time in American history. It wasn't that long ago, however, that vesting rules were outrageously stingy. In many cases, qualifying for a pension required Herculean devotion to a company. Even somebody who could boast of 40 years of service in one office could be routinely denied coverage. The reason? The person quit before reaching age 65. Thanks to federal law, pension-vesting rules can't be that draconian anymore.

left a company earlier in his career that he ultimately desired the biggest possible monthly pension check. (Women obviously have made the same choice, but for the current generation of retirees, the great majority of pensioners are men.) The only way to ensure the fattest check is to select payments as a single worker. You'll see this referred to as a *single-life annuity.*

For some of these workers, greed was the motivator. They wanted the maximum amount of income during their lifetimes. Their wives would just have to fend for themselves if they survived their husbands. In other cases, however, retirees were confused about their options and inadvertently imperiled their wives' final years.

To prevent this sort of travesty from happening, the federal government in the mid-1980s dictated that corporations should henceforth automatically assume that all future pensions would provide survivor benefits. This type of pension is classified as a *joint-and-survivor annuity.* Under this scenario, the payments continue being mailed to a spouse even after the worker dies. Then, after a death, the check amount is cut in half. Because one of these pensions covers two people instead of one, the monthly payouts are smaller to begin with. Often the checks are 15 to 20 percent lower, but sometimes the difference is greater. This is particularly so if the spouse is considerably younger than the pensioner.

Note Although the government did not outlaw the single-life payout option for married employees, today someone who doesn't want a joint-and-survivor annuity payout must first obtain the spouse's permission in writing.

Unfortunately, even this safeguard hasn't completely eliminated problems. A number of state, city, and county plans still let a worker make the decision as to whether to provide survivor protection. Some spouses still sign away their rights because they don't read or understand the paperwork they are signing. A federal study suggested that many of the legal consent forms being used by corporate America are difficult to read.

Fight back if you've lost benefits after a spouse's death

Paperwork that was signed prior to the mid-1980s can still end up booby-trapping new widows and widowers today. However, they may have a legal avenue to fight if the pension checks dry up. Transition rules implemented in the '80s required companies to notify workers of the pension changes. Your best chance to keep a pension alive is if those rules weren't meticulously followed.

Although the odds are stacked against you, occasionally a spouse can successfully reclaim the pension. Recently, the chances looked bleak for a Wisconsin widow whose husband died after just three months of retirement. His pension provided for no survivor benefits. She contacted the Pension Rights Project at the Minnesota Senior Federation, which agreed to intercede. (You'll find a list of similar organizations in the Resource Guide.) Unfortunately, the wife had signed the pension consent form, but the notary had not witnessed her signature. After the notary confessed to the transgression, the pension checks resumed.

A joint-and-survivor pension may be the best choice for most married couples. There are times, however, when it might be undesirable. Choosing a single-life pension might be more appropriate if the spouse is independently wealthy or terminally ill. (See Chapter 21.)

What happens to a pension in a divorce?

One of the most valuable assets up for grabs during a divorce is a pension. Typically, the husband enjoys the fatter pension. In fact, he may be the only one who has one. No matter whose pension it is, the other spouse may be awarded a portion of the pension checks once they start arriving.

Pension Seminar Shenanigans

If you are nearing retirement age, don't be surprised if you receive an invitation to a seminar that purports to share the secrets of a more financially rewarding retirement. Although you might not realize it as you sit on a folding chair listening to the pitch, the seminar speaker will probably be pushing pension maximization insurance. At these seminars, there may be no overt mention of life insurance, but that's what ends up being sold.

Here's how pension maximization, which is extremely controversial, works: If you are married, you elect to take your pension as a single-life annuity. This selection assures that you'll receive the highest possible monthly pension check. It's a treacherous move for married couples because the checks stop when the breadwinner dies.

An insurance agent, however, dismisses this high-stakes risk by suggesting that you buy life insurance with the extra pension money you'll pocket each month. If you die first, your husband or wife can rely upon the life insurance proceeds when the pension checks suddenly dry up.

Sounds plausible, right? Actually, it can be a dangerous move. These insurance policies aren't cheap, and the cost can negate any benefit of opting for the more generous pension payments. What's more, some retirees find they can't continue paying the insurance premiums and lose the policy coverage. Also, if insurance company investments don't do as well as expected, the insurance policy may not provide as much money as promised.

Caution Women frequently fail to claim a piece of their ex-husbands' pension benefits, which can cost an ex-wife dearly during her retirement years.

Mothers are often willing to surrender their rights to retirement benefits in exchange for the family home, but these women (and too many of their attorneys) don't comprehend the full ramifications of what they're relinquishing. The man can expect his pension and other workplace retirement plans to grow tax-deferred. Meanwhile, the woman will have to pay property taxes on the house, as well as make repairs and keep up on maintenance.

Anyone wishing a piece of a former spouse's pension won't be entitled to any of it without a court order, which for company and union plans is called a Qualified Domestic Relations Order (QDRO). (These court orders have other names under other retirement systems. A number of state and cities still do not provide for a division of retirement benefits for government employees at divorce.)

A QDRO instructs a pension plan administrator how and when to divide up the benefits after a marriage fails. If the QDRO isn't precise, the client could suffer big time years later. Even a QDRO that looks flawless can hide fatal mistakes. Imagine securing a QDRO that stipulates that a husband's pension must be shared with the ex-wife during retirement and the checks must continue even after the ex-husband dies. But if the attorney never specified that the ex-wife would also be entitled to the pension if her former husband died before he retired, she could be out of luck. She may be denied pension benefits simply because of an oversight.

It is also important for the court order to include future rights to early retirement subsidies or pension enhancements. An ex-spouse, for instance, may be entitled later on to a piece of a former husband or wife's early retirement subsidy.

Resource Women who need to learn more about this issue can obtain the book *Your Pension Rights at Divorce: What Women Need to Know* from the nonprofit Pension Rights Center. The cost is $23.95, which includes postage and handling. Write to the Pension Rights Center, 1140 19th St., NW, Suite 602, Washington, DC 20036; (202) 296-3776; www.pensionrights.org.

Because valuing pensions, 401(k) plans, stock options, and other workplace assets is so tricky, you should rely upon experts for advice on your particular situation. A solid resource is the Institute for Certified Divorce Planners. The Institute can provide the names of financial experts, including financial planners, attorneys, and certified public accountants, who have obtained the Certified Divorce Planner (CFP) designation.

Resource You can contact the Institute for Certified Divorce Planners at (800) 875-1760 or go to www.institutecdp.com.

Will my pension have built-in inflation protection?

Don't count on built-in inflation protection. Corporate America is far less benevolent than it used to be. In the past, many companies looked after their retirees by pumping up their monthly checks with periodic cost-of-living increases. Within some major corporations, the practice of passing along cost-of-living raises had been honored for many decades. As a result, many people who retire or accept early retirement packages assume that their monthly benefits will be able to withstand inflation threats.

But companies are not legally required to provide inflation protection. Consequently, when reviewing what assets you'll have during retirement, you should assume your payments will be frozen. Automatic cost-of-living increases are fairly rare except for government workers, and periodic increases are clearly declining. U.S. Census data shows that prior to 1975, 44 percent of pension recipients were getting cost-of-living raises. By the 1990s, the percentage had plummeted to 9 percent.

Unfortunately, inflation, even when it was quite modest during the 1990s, can have a corrosive effect on someone's purchasing power. Retirees who quit in 1980, for instance, have seen the spending power of their pension checks cut by more than 50 percent. If they lack other sources of retirement income, they must increasingly cut back on expenses — hardly an easy task.

What happens to my pension if my company goes out of business?

Your company going out of business isn't as scary a prospect as you might assume. One of ERISA's successes was the creation of the Pension Benefit Guaranty Corporation (PBGC), which guarantees the pensions of millions of workers and retirees. The program is funded by insurance premiums that private pension plans are required to pay into the system. The PBGC steps in when a company declares bankruptcy or for some catastrophic reason can't meet all of its pension obligations. The federal agency then meets the pension obligation. It's played the role of financial troubleshooter countless times.

However, the PBGC won't completely replace the most generous pension checks. A benefit ceiling exists, which means executives and other highly paid workers might not recoup their full benefits if disaster strikes. The benefit cap for a pension plan disbanded in 2001 was $3,392 a month for a 65-year-old retiree, $2,679 for a 62-year-old, and $1,526 for a 55-year-old. You can review all the maximum monthly guarantees by visiting the agency's Web site at www.pbgc.gov. The PBGC also won't reimburse a retiree for lost life insurance, health insurance, disability, or severance pay.

Not all employers are covered by the PBGC. Government employees, as well as those who work for churches and fraternal organizations, don't qualify. Neither do professional service employers, such as doctor and lawyer offices, which employ less than 25 workers.

Early Retirement Packages

Early retirement packages used to be as common as bad food on airplanes. Eager to downsize, corporations in the 1980s and early 1990s passed out retirement packages like bubble gum. But the practice, which has always been most prevalent among the corporate Goliaths, is no longer as popular. With years of steady growth in the economy, employers no longer are obsessed with cutting back their labor pools. Corporations also discovered that early retirement package weren't always a panacea. Sometimes the wrong people left or too many bolted for the door. Sometimes this situation forced companies that were paying pension benefits to retired workers to hire them back as consultants.

The typical age to qualify for an early retirement package is 55. According to one workplace study, the median early retirement benefit in corporate America was 56 percent of what someone could expect if he or she had remained until the age of 65. The earliest age that people could typically quit without jeopardizing a cut in their retirement benefits was 60.

Some corporations are now offering a new twist on early retirement plans by offering something called *phased-retirement programs.* Under these programs, an older worker can receive a pension in a lump sum while still working. In theory, the money allows an employee to drop to part-time work. The biggest winner, however, could be the company that's promoting the program. Employees who take a lump sum face the danger of spending it right away or investing it poorly. Meanwhile, their future pension benefits, which they are earning while still on the payroll, could accrue at a much smaller pace.

If you are offered an early retirement package, don't make a snap decision. Hire an expert to scrutinize the numbers.

Note In some cases, the PBGC can also help when someone is desperately trying to locate a long-lost pension benefit. As incredible as it may seem, a phenomenal number of Americans have yet to claim pension payments due to them. Like strays at an animal shelter, billions of lost pension dollars are waiting to be claimed.

Through the PBGC, you may be able to discover if you are owed a misplaced pension. On a voluntary basis, companies have listed with the PBGC, individuals, who are entitled to a pension, whom they can't find. These names are placed into a massive database. You can easily access the database by visiting the PBGC's Web site and clicking on the Pension Search link. Thousands of pensions have been found this way.

 Resource Before you start a search, order a free copy of the booklet, *Finding a Lost Pension,* from the PBGC by mail at Pension Benefit Guaranty Corporation, 1200 K St. NW, Washington, DC 20005-4026, on the Internet at www.pbgc.gov, or by phone at (800) 400-7242.

Often it is not the participants who have lost their pensions, but the plans that have lost their participants. Because there is no requirement to notify participants when a plan relocates, is bought, or is merged, former employees are left in the dark as to the location of their old company and its pension plan. How can you protect yourself? A former employee should always notify the sponsor of their pension plan whenever they relocate. Use certified mail and request a return receipt.

Am I getting the wrong pension?

Although many people dream about their retirement day, rarely does anybody stop to think about whether those future pension checks will be correct. But they should. Pension administrators can mess up. Pension miscalculations don't just hurt retirees: Anytime workers change jobs and take their pension benefit in a lump sum, they risk getting the wrong amount.

Note
Women can be especially vulnerable to pension miscalculations because they tend to move in and out of the workforce more frequently.

Mistakes aren't as rare as you might think. In one highly publicized survey in the 1990s, federal auditors estimated that about 8 percent of departing workers at 6,000 companies were receiving lump sum payouts that were far too skimpy. The focus of the survey was small businesses, where you might anticipate more problems, but even the big guns have been nailed. Corporations such as Chevron, Tyson Foods, Allstate Insurance, Continental Airlines, and International Paper have been caught mailing out inaccurate pension checks or calculating the wrong lump sum payments.

The mistakes don't represent some nefarious plot by employers to rip off departing workers; most mix-ups aren't intentional. One culprit is federal pension laws, which are incredibly difficult to understand even for experienced actuaries. Not only are the rules complex, they are also constantly changing. The other culprit is plain old human error.

Note
To give you some idea of how complex the maze of regulations can be, consider this: One particular federal pension rule that's just a sentence long requires 400 additional pages of explanatory text. No joke.

Top pension mistakes

According to the U.S. Department of Labor, companies often make these common errors when calculating a person's pension benefits:

✦ Your employer overlooked commissions, overtime, or bonuses when determining your pension.

✦ The company failed to include all your years of service. This error may occur if you have worked in different corporate divisions.

✦ The company used an incorrect benefits formula, such as the wrong interest rate.

✦ The firm relied upon the wrong Social Security number or birth date.

✦ Math mistakes were made in the calculation.

✦ Company mergers created confusion about the correct pension benefits.

✦ You failed to update the company personnel office with changes, such as marriage, divorce, or death of a spouse, that may affect your benefits.

When in doubt, seek help

Pensions are incredibly complicated, which is why you should seek qualified help when you have questions or concerns. You have several options at your disposal.

Actuaries

One option is consulting with an actuary who specializes in pension matters. Actuaries typically charge by the hour. Two groups can help you find actuaries in your area.

✦ **The American Academy of Actuaries,** a public policy and professional organization, can steer you to its members specializing in pensions. The academy maintains a free nationwide referral service, called the Pension Assistance List (PAL), which links people to actuaries willing to volunteer their services. You can contact the organization by mail at 1100 17th St. NW, 7th floor, Washington, DC 20036, by phone at (202) 223-8196, or on the Internet at www.actuary.org.

✦ **The American Society of Pension Actuaries** is a national organization devoted exclusively to the pension field. Its membership includes actuaries, attorneys, consultants, and others. You can contact the organization by mail at American Society of Pension Actuaries, 4245 N. Fairfax Dr., Suite 750, Arlington, VA 22203, by phone at (703) 516-9300, or on the Internet at www.aspa.org.

Caution

As you search for an actuary, keep this fact in mind: Most actuaries who specialize in pensions do a lot of work for corporations. Consequently, some actuaries may refuse to accept you as a client. Before hiring an actuary, find out what his or her background is and try to get a sense of any biases.

Federal Pension and Welfare Benefits Administration

The Pension and Welfare Benefits Administration, which is within the federal Department of Labor, can help people who are covered by private-sector pension plans. The PWBA receives more than 150,000 inquiries a year from participants and their beneficiaries. You can contact the PWBA at its headquarters in Washington,

D.C., or at one of its 10 regional offices. Here's the contact information: PWBA, U.S. Department of Labor, 200 Constitution Ave., NW, Washington, DC 20210; (202) 219-8776 (technical assistance); (800) 998-7542 (publications); www.dol.gov/dol/pwba.

The PWBA's publications include *How to File a Claim for Your Benefits, Protect Your Pension, What You Should Know About Your Pension Rights,* and *Cash Balance Plans: Questions and Answers.*

Nonprofit pension-counseling groups

Another little-known yet invaluable resource for workers is a network of pension-counseling projects that are partially funded by the federal Administration on Aging. These counseling outposts, which charge no fees, are scattered across the country in Alabama, Arizona, California, Illinois, Massachusetts, Michigan, Minnesota, Missouri, New York, and Virginia. Efforts are currently underway to expand the counseling project network to a national level, but until then it will remain a patchwork effort.

 See the Resource Guide for these nonprofit groups' contact information.

The counseling projects have collected millions of dollars for their clients. The Massachusetts office alone has put more than $5 million into retirees' pockets during its six-year history. Its director estimates that the center has been able to recover money for 20 to 25 percent of its clients.

The mandate of these centers goes beyond handling pension miscalculations. The projects also help track down lost pensions. The staffers can often be more thorough than the Pension Benefit Guaranty Corporation, and the service isn't impersonal. Some of the most heart-wrenching cases that counselors see are widows who were cut off from their husbands' pensions when they died. Restoring benefits for these women, who may have unwittingly signed paperwork waiving their rights to survivor benefits, is extremely difficult, but it can sometimes be done.

Certified financial planners

Another resource is a certified financial planner (CFP) who is comfortable with employee benefit issues. Some financial planners even specialize in the retirement benefits of specific companies or industries.

See Chapter 5 for details on locating CFPs and other financial experts.

Private retrieval companies

Another strategy that some people pursue is hiring a private company that specializes in retrieving lost or miscalculated pension benefits. Keep in mind that the price for this service is steep: These firms pocket a percentage of your recovered benefits until the pension checks stop coming. Using a nonprofit organization or an actuary is the best way to resolve your pension problems.

Do your homework

For your own protection, you should learn as much as you can about your pension rights. These resources are worth checking out:

✦ ***The Wall Street Journal,*** www.wsj.com: Very few journalists covered pension issues until *The Wall Street Journal* began critically examining corporate America's pension practices. To read the past coverage, visit the newspaper's archives at its Web site. You have to pay a fee for each article you download.

✦ **The Pension Rights Center,** 1140 19th St. NW, Suite 602, Washington, D.C. 20036; (202) 296-3776; www.pensionrights.org: This consumer organization advocates for pension changes that help workers and retirees. The nonprofit pension watchdog group offers helpful pension publications. Its Web site allows a visitor to locate his or her local pension assistance resources.

✦ **AARP,** 601 E. St., NW, Washington, DC 20049; (800) 424-3410; www.aarp.org: The senior advocacy group maintains a variety of information on pension issues on its Web site, including Congressional testimony by its officials.

Cash Balance Pension Brouhaha

Few workers thought much about their pensions until corporations began gutting their old pension plans and replacing them in the later 1990s with *cash balance pension plans* which, as you'll learn shortly, calculate benefits differently from the traditional pension plan. A growing lineup of corporate players, many with household names such as IBM, Avon, Boeing and AT&T, joined in. According to the federal General Accounting Office, nearly one in five corporation in the Fortune 1000 now sponsor a cash balance pension plan. The cash balance pension plan, more than any other type, has generated controversy in a field that used to excite only actuaries.

A cash balance plan is essentially a hybrid of defined benefit plans (such as the traditional pension, which is offered as a benefit by the employer) and defined contribution plans (such as a 401(k) or other account funded by employee contributions). In a typical cash balance plan, each year the employer distributes a "pay credit" (usually equal to a percentage of an employee's wages) and an "interest credit" (at either a fixed or variable rate) to an account in each employee's name. What's the key difference between traditional pensions and cash balance pensions? Traditional pensions define an employee's benefit as a series of monthly payments beginning upon retirement and continuing for life, but cash balance plans define the benefit in terms of each employee's account balance—and pay out no more than the total of those yearly contributions and interest payments.

At this point, you probably aren't going to be shocked to learn that cash balance plans save most corporations huge amounts of money. *The Wall Street Journal* wrote a story about tapes made at actuarial conferences that recorded these professionals talking candidly to their peers. Some speakers noted, for instance, that implementing a cash balance pension plan was a perfect strategy for a corporation that wants to slash pension benefits without being too obvious about it. The conversions can be so devilishly difficult for workers to understand, the speakers observed, that many don't even realize what's happening.

Cash balance plans began attracting the sort of attention usually reserved for Super Bowl Sunday. When AT&T unveiled the blueprints for its remodeled pension plan, thousands of employees stampeded the corporate Web site, which nearly shut it down. The merits of the cash balance approach are being fiercely debated and challenged in courtrooms, corporate cafeterias, Capitol Hill, and even Internet chat sessions.

Cash balance plan advantages

Some features of the cash balance pension plan work to the benefit of some employees.

Younger employees may fare better.

Younger employees and those who don't intend to be lifers at one job may fare better under a cash balance plan than they would under a traditional pension plan, but this is not a sure thing. Under traditional pension plans, benefits build at an excruciatingly slow pace until the last 5 or 10 years before retirement. At that point, someone's pension may balloon by 50 percent. The pension payout equals a percentage of a person's' final average earnings (often averaged from the last three to five years of employment) multiplied by the years of service. This traditional arrangement may not be ideal for somebody who has no intention of sticking around until those final years.

Note   Less than 10 percent of working Americans stay with one employer for 20 or more years.

A cash balance plan, however, lets workers accrue pension benefits more evenly from the start instead of waiting until 10 years before retirement for the company to start making decent-sized payments into their pensions. Workers no longer have to be pension slaves shackled to jobs they hate because they need a livable pension. Under a cash balance plan, companies usually contribute an amount equal to anywhere from 3 to 7 percent of a person's pay each year into the pension system. A worker's age or years of service sometimes affects this percentage.

Cash balance plans are as portable as a picnic cooler.

If you quit your job after you're vested in a cash balance pension plan, you can take your pension money with you. (The money will be subject to income taxes, and in some cases an early withdrawal penalty, unless it's transferred into an Individual Retirement Account.)

Most people covered by traditional pensions don't enjoy this luxury. Unless the pension amount is $5,000 or less, the majority of corporations do not permit departing employees to take their pensions as cash. Most people have to wait until they reach retirement age, which may be decades away, before they see that money in the form of monthly pension checks.

Cash balance plans are easier to decipher.

Just like a 401(k), participants in cash balance plans receive regular statements that show the buildup of cash within their pensions. (The accounts described in these statements are phantom accounts because the money is invested in a pool, but a formula is used to calculate an individual's share.) Cash balance updates are more understandable than traditional ones that forecast what a pension would be worth upon someone's retirement age. These traditional forecasts are just projections. Nobody knows for sure what kind of salary increases you'll receive throughout your career, whether you'll still be at the same desk on retirement day or whether future contribution rates to the plan will be reduced.

Cash balance plan disadvantages

These drawbacks are causing most of the controversy around cash balance plans.

Cash balance conversions hurt older employees.

Workers in their 40s, 50s, and 60s with lengthy service records have every right to be steamed by many cash balance conversions. Remember, the value of a traditional pension typically jumps significantly during the last few years of a career. Cash balance plans stop that acceleration. Even proponents of cash balance plans agree that cash balance plans can harm older workers who are financially squeezed during a transition from a regular to a cash balance pension. Some workers ultimately have their pension benefits shaved in half.

Because of concerns about how older workers fair under these plans, the Internal Revenue Service and the Equal Employment Opportunity Commission are investigating whether the plans are discriminatory.

A cash balance plan can freeze your benefits.

ERISA guarantees that you won't lose any pension benefits that you've accumulated before the pension conversion, but there's no guarantee that those benefits will keep growing. If your pension is worth $200,000, for instance, it will still be worth that amount on the day a cash balance plan begins. This might not be apparent when you examine your first cash balance account statement. The amount may be far smaller. In fact, it could take many years before your pension on paper once again reaches $200,000, much less exceeds it. This unpleasant phenomenon is euphemistically referred to as *wearaway*. If you retire, however, you are at least guaranteed the $200,000.

Wearaway occurs because your pension is rich in comparison to what you'd be getting under the new formula. In calculating opening balances, companies enjoy some latitude when plugging in assumptions about retirement age and interest rates, as well as mortality figures.

Cash balance plans hurt short-termers.

According to the U.S. Labor Department, the median job tenure for workers aged 25 to 34 is just 2.7 years. Cash balance plans are often worthless for workers who don't stay at a job for at least five years. Sure the money can start building faster with a cash balance, but you won't be entitled to it if you leave before you're vested.

Cash balance comparisons are difficult.

Comparing an old plan with a cash balance one isn't easy, and employers are typically not helpful. ERISA requires an employer to make a brief statement about a pension change only if the change will trigger a reduction in future benefits. That acknowledgement may be buried deep inside a corporate document.

Legislation has been floated in Washington to address corporate America's reluctance to candidly share in its company literature what a cash balance conversion would mean to each worker. The Congressional sponsors are dismayed at the lack of meaningful and individualized information that is distributed. One major bill would require companies with at least 1,000 employees to issue a statement that compares each worker's benefits under the new and old versions at various ages until retirement.

Cash balance plans make it easier to blow your pension payout.

Getting a lump sum upon leaving a company before retirement isn't in everyone's best interest. If the amount is low or a worker is fairly young, the temptation to blow it could be quite high. While receiving a lump sum upon departure is touted as a major positive feature of a cash balance plan, workers who are covered by these plans can always request to receive the traditional monthly payments instead.

Taking action

If your corporation is pushing through a cash balance plan, you can do more than simply consult an expert. Workers experiencing other pension changes can also use the tactics described in the following sections.

Cash Balance Beginnings

The first cash balance account was dreamed up for the Bank of America in the mid-1980s. In its 1987 annual report, the financial institution bragged that it had saved tens of millions of dollars by remodeling its existing defined benefit plan. But the financial institution's bold move pretty much remained an anomaly for years. During the tail end of the 1990s, however, the cash balance idea returned for a huge second act.

Ask if the change is all or nothing.

The critical issue when a company announces a pension shakeup is what protections, if any, it offers its senior people. At some companies, the oldest employees can remain in a traditional plan until retirement or for a limited time, such as 5 to 10 years, before getting transferred into a cash balance plan. In this case, an older worker's pension benefits should grow faster than they would otherwise. Other corporations may kick a higher percentage of an older worker's salary into the pension kitty so the money accumulates faster.

Often the pot is sweetened only for employees in their 50s and 60s. However, this limitation can trigger squeals of indignation from employees in their 40s who may also be financially penalized by the changes.

Organize.

If enough of your colleagues oppose a pension overhaul or want an employer to be more forthcoming, organize. Encouraged by a stream of negative press coverage, employees at corporations across the country are now trying to protect their pensions, and they've experienced some successes.

Example After enduring months of considerable employee agitation, IBM caved in and announced it would make concessions in its new cash balance plan.

One way that motivated employees have banded together is through the Internet. Retirees and current employees of such corporations as IBM, Duke Energy, SmithKline Beecham, and SBC Communications have formed their own Web sites or have staked out sites in Yahoo!'s club section.

 Resource To find these groups' meeting places, visit Yahoo! (www.yahoo.com), click on the "Clubs" hyperlink, and type in the keywords *pensions* or *cash balance.* Or visit the Web site of the Coalition for Retirement Security (www.pensions-r-us.org), a grassroots organization that fights pension inequities. Another employee-driven Web resource is cashpensions.org.

Contact your representative or senator.

The controversy being stirred up by the nation's pension changes has not escaped Capitol Hill's notice. Some people in Congress view the brouhaha as an opportunity to represent the little guy. Others are sponsoring legislation for corporations, which thirst for more freedom to dismantle pension programs.

Through your representative or senator, find out who the lead pro-consumer politicians on this issue are in Congress and then contact them. The U.S. Capitol switchboard's number is (202) 225-3121.

You can research Congressional action on pension issues by visiting a section of the Library of Congress' Web site that tracks all federal legislation and Congressional hearings: www.thomas.loc.gov. You can obtain the same information from the U.S. Senate and House of Representatives Web sites: www.senate.gov or www.house.gov.

Summary

✦ Never throw out pension documents.

✦ Always determine the impact pension changes will have on you at the time of the change; don't wait to be surprised at retirement time.

✦ Consult an actuary or other pension expert before making final decisions.

✦ Don't automatically choose a lump sum pension payment; explore your options.

✦ Check your paperwork for common pension mistakes.

✦   ✦   ✦

Getting Directions: A Guide to Financial Experts

PART

II

In Part II, you'll learn how to quickly eliminate from consideration the vast majority of financial experts who are clamoring for your business. You'll discover the best way to select a financial advisor, a brokerage firm, and wealth management services. This section also provides detailed advice for those seeking a highly qualified estate-planning attorney, an elder law lawyer, an insurance professional, or a certified public accountant.

The Best Advice That Money Can Buy: Wealth Management Services

Managing money isn't easy. Sometimes just picking a mutual fund from the thousands sitting on the shelves is enough to paralyze the most motivated investor. This chapter gives you the tools to discriminate between competing options and find the best help in the financial advice industry. For individuals who meet the new definition of wealth, this chapter also explores the phenomenal growth in wealth management services.

If all people had to do to manage their finances was choose a decent mutual fund, most of them could probably manage. But financial choices today can be far more complex, and the strategy you should be pursuing may, at times, seem as clear as an airline pilot's garbled announcements. As a result, more people than ever are paying for expert advice, although choosing the right experts is also becoming far more complicated than ever before. Knowing where to go is essential when you need solid advice on maximizing your retirement portfolio.

When Do You Need Professional Advice?

For many people, the financial picture grows more complex as time passes and retirement is no longer a distant dream. Something seems to happen when a person's portfolio jumps from five figures to six figures or higher. Many people who felt comfortable with a do-it-yourself approach get anxious about their future moves. This dilemma, admittedly a nice one, is occurring more and more frequently. Millions of Americans have ridden the coattails of history's longest bull market, stock options are being passed out like bubble gum, and the nation's greatest transfer of wealth from one generation to the next has already begun in earnest.

The sheer heft of a portfolio isn't the only reason why someone's finances become trickier. By the time the teenage ticket seller at the Cineplex assumes you're eligible for a senior citizen discount, economic decisions become more important, and the consequences of making the wrong calls become scarier. At this stage in life, somebody isn't just focused on getting richer. Wealth preservation becomes the goal, and that means estate planning, a prospect that terrifies many.

But you don't have to be eligible for AARP membership to require a professional's guidance. Most people at certain milestones in their lives need assistance in solving money dilemmas. The following questions highlight some of the issues that prompt people to seek help:

✦ Will I have enough money when I retire?

✦ Should I take early retirement?

✦ How slowly should I drain my retirement holdings?

✦ How can I keep an inherited IRA alive for decades?

✦ Do I need a living trust?

✦ How can I shelter my money from estate taxes?

✦ Does my 401(k) asset allocation make sense?

✦ What is the best way to limit taxes when cashing in stock options?

✦ Should I take my pension in a lump sum?

✦ Do I need an annuity?

✦ Which investments are most tax-efficient?

✦ How can I mix charitable giving with estate planning?

Your place in the financial revolution

Deciding where to seek help can be dizzying. Hundreds of thousands of people pass out business cards that identify them as financial experts, although considerably fewer are actually qualified to give financial advice.

At the same time, financial institutions are trespassing on each other's traditional territories. Banks are peddling insurance. Insurers are selling mutual funds and stocks. Mutual fund firms and discount brokers are offering trust department and financial advisory services, which would have been unheard of not long ago. Full-service brokers are selling their own federally insured bank investments. The Internet has brought newer contenders such as Intuit and Microsoft into the financial fray. Meanwhile, industrial behemoths such as General Electric, American Airlines, and General Motors are muscling their way through the crowd to market their own brands of mutual funds. All these changes contribute to providing more consumer choice now than at any time in history.

Not so long ago, your alternatives were far simpler. Most people stashed their money with a full-service broker, a mutual fund firm, or a bank. Wealthy Americans often turned to a bank trust department to oversee their fortunes and to supervise the handoff of all this money to their children and grandchildren. But the advent of the Individual Retirement Accounts and 401(k) plans and corporate America's decision to distance itself from traditional pension plans helped to dramatically change the dynamics of the financial services industry. The amounts of money that many of us are now personally responsible for are no longer considered chump change by the industry. And that's what has fueled the feeding frenzy.

The new definition of wealthy

Are you rich? Maybe not, but the financial industry might think you are. Its definition of wealth has changed. In the past, financial institutions that catered to the very wealthiest weren't impressed with anyone who couldn't claim kinship with other millionaires. But today, even some of the most blue-blooded financial preserves of America's wealthiest families are welcoming the merely affluent.

Note   You no longer have to be a millionaire to be treated like you have a million bucks. Even a $100,000 portfolio can create new opportunities for you.

The preferential treatment you can expect at brokerage firms, trust companies, elite investment banks, and money management firms becomes more deluxe as you inch up the financial food chain. A $1 million portfolio now opens doors at institutions that in the past may have remained tightly shut for anyone worth less than $5 million.

You may want to take advantage of these opportunities, but you don't want to get taken. You're likely to be most vulnerable when retirement is a short time away. When you're ready to retire, you may as well be walking around with a scarlet *R* for retiree on your forehead. To many stockbrokers, insurance agents, or financial planners, any graying worker with a 401(k) or pension payout is a tempting target. Some of these experts can provide invaluable services, but others will not. Read on so you'll know what's what when the phone calls and direct mail campaigns begin.

The Brokerage Industry's New Face

It used to be easy to tell the difference between discount brokers and their full-service competitors. But today's brokerage firms grow more alike in the following ways:

✦ Full-service brokers are behaving like discount brokers.

✦ Discounters are mimicking the full-service competition.

✦ Fee-based pricing is replacing commissions.

✦ Full-service brokers are touting themselves as financial advisors.

To understand how revolutionary these changes are and where you fit into the mix, you have to appreciate what led to the shattering of the status quo.

The old brokerage systems

In the old days, discount brokers merely filled trading orders. When you called, the person answering the telephone efficiently executed your order. You had no idea who the person was, and the next time you called somebody else wearing a headset in a cavernous room of phone representatives would handle your inquiry. Personal service was nonexistent. Usually there wasn't even a building to visit. This no-frills approach continued when customers began flocking to online trading. Do-it-yourselfers embraced the discounters because they were cheap. The commissions were a fraction of what the traditional brokerage houses were charging.

In contrast, someone choosing PaineWebber, Morgan Stanley Dean Witter, or one of the other national or regional full-service brokers expected hand-holding. If you had a substantial account, the person tracking your portfolio could be someone who had moved up the sales ranks to earn a title of vice president and a corner office with a mahogany desk. If you wanted to buy stock or ask about the tax advantages of municipal bonds, you called your own stockbroker. And that broker would check in periodically to see whether he could entice you into buying a variable annuity or 100 shares of IBM. He might even remember your birthday.

The full-service brokers made their money on steep commissions. But many people paid this price in return for the individual attention and access to the brokerage house's proprietary research. Even today each firm's think tank of stock analysts, economists, fixed-income experts, and others generate daily stock and bond tips along with economic predictions. For example, Merrill Lynch, the nation's biggest full-service broker, employs hundreds of analysts in more than two dozen countries to cover thousands of corporations worldwide.

At some point, however, the full-service customers grew antsy. They became jealous of the discounters' cheap trading costs. Meanwhile, the discount customers didn't think they had reached investing nirvana either. They began yearning for all the extras that the stripped-down discounters shunned. So what happened? Both types of brokerage firms decided to reinvent themselves.

Today, distinctions still exist among full-service firms and discounters, but these distinctions are far more subtle. This section covers what you can expect from both camps.

Discount brokers in the 21st century

Today's discount brokerage firms operate with split personalities. The deep discounters that advertise rock-bottom online trading prices continue to offer very little else. These firms attract frequent traders, who love paying just $7 or $8 for an online trade.

 The bare-bones cyber brokers usually aren't appropriate for beginning investors.

The biggest discount players, however, have distanced themselves from the rest of the pack. Prominent ones, such as Charles Schwab, Fidelity, TD Waterhouse, and E*Trade, have moved beyond being merely convenient and providing low-cost trading. Their commission prices typically aren't as cheap as the deep discounters, but they compensate with extra services.

Services galore

The bigger discount brokers now offer the following types of services:

Retirement planning	Credit and debit cards
Estate planning	Online bill payment
Mutual fund supermarkets	Access to initial public offerings (IPOs)
Institutional-class research	Mortgages
Real-time quotes	Term life insurance
Free checking	Wireless trading
Free ATM access	

Favoritism toward wealthier clients

The higher your net worth, the warmer your welcome is. With an investment of at least $100,000, you can expect better treatment. The perks become even more desirable when assets reach the $500,000 and $1 million levels.

As a larger client, you can expect cheaper commission rates, free in-depth stock research, priority access to IPOs, and possibly venture capital and hedge fund opportunities. Investors can also skip long waits for assistance on the telephone by using special toll-free numbers. Sink enough money into your account and you'll have access to financial specialists who can customize an individual bond portfolio for you, guide you through the process of investing in overseas securities, or help in many other ways. You may also be linked to outside financial planners who have been prescreened by the brokerage firms.

Meanwhile, to keep its wealthiest clients from leaving, the discounters have encroached upon the tony world of private banking and trust companies. Charles Schwab, for instance, gobbled up U.S. Trust, the nation's oldest trust company, which now allows it to offer more specialized services to its wealthier clients. In the past, discount brokerage customers with account balances that grew beyond $500,000 often bailed to other institutions.

Tip   Don't automatically assume that you won't qualify for red-carpet treatment. If you're a frequent stock trader, you can still enjoy some of these perks; be sure to ask.

Another way to ensure a higher range of services is to consolidate. Perhaps you have an IRA rollover at Fidelity, your spouse's IRA is at Prudential, and your children's custodial college savings accounts are kept at individual mutual fund firms. If you transfer your family's accounts to one discounter, you could meet the minimum investment requirement for special services. (The money wouldn't be mingled into one account, but all the accounts added together could satisfy the brokerage firm's minimum requirement.)

Broker Cheat Sheets

Brokerage firms are changing rapidly, but locating a superior one can be a fairly painless process. Many financial publications issue annual surveys that evaluate discount and full-service brokers on such criteria as the breadth of products, fees, customer service, and the quality of their Web sites.

The following magazines and organizations regularly rate brokerage firms:

✦ *Smart Money* at (800) 444-4204 or www.smartmoney.com

✦ *Business Week* at (800) 635-1200 or businessweek.com

✦ *Money Magazine* at (800) 633-9970 or www.money.com

✦ *Kiplinger's Personal Finance* at (800) 544-0155 or www.kiplinger.com

✦ American Association of Individual Investors at (312) 280-0170 or www.aaii.org

✦ Gomez Advisors at www.gomez.com

✦ CyberInvest at cyberinvest.com

✦ Forrester Research at www.forrester.com

Commission differences

Even in the discount world, commissions vary significantly. The fine print reveals whether someone is entitled to the cheapest prices. If the best rates are reserved for trades of at least 1,000 shares and you typically buy in smaller chunks, that great price is meaningless. In addition, some discounters reserve favorable pricing for heavy traders. You may also pay a higher price if you use limit orders to designate what price you are willing to pay for a stock.

 Caution Watch out for fees. Discounters can be sneaky, and they sometimes tack on charges for such things as wire asset transfers, custodial fees for IRA accounts, and mutual fund purchases.

Full-service brokers in the 21st century

The most striking difference in today's full-service brokerage firms is their fee schedules. The days of monster commissions will soon share the same fate as the Dodo bird. Full-service brokers are now heavily promoting other pricing schemes.

 Note You can still call your broker and invest in stocks, bonds, and other products the old-fashioned way, but you will pay for this traditional service with steep commissions.

Fee-based investing

With fee-based investing, you pay an annual percentage of the assets you keep at the brokerage firm or a yearly flat fee instead of commissions. One major full-service brokerage firm's minimum annual fee was recently $1,500.

This change could be good news for frequent traders. Heavy trading generates prohibitively high commission costs, but with a flat rate, costs can be contained.

In contrast, buy-and-hold investors may hate this approach. Suppose most of your money is tied up in municipal bonds and Treasuries. Do you really want to pay $1,500 a year or considerably more just so the firm can sit on your bonds? Small investors could also get gouged. Someone with a $30,000 stock portfolio, for example, would pay a disproportionately high price. Instead of shelling out, say, 1 percent in assets or $300, the investor would be stuck paying the minimum, which could be $1,500 or higher.

 Note The brokerage industry hopes that the new pricing will deflate the biggest gripe against full-service brokers, which is the built-in conflict of interest. Traditionally, a broker was paid only if a customer traded, which meant there was plenty of incentive to encourage clients to trade even when it was inappropriate.

Stock Trading on the Last Frontier

As recently as 1994, not even a single stock had been traded on the Internet. In the near future, however, the U.S. Securities and Exchange Commission predicts that the number of online brokerage accounts will roughly equal the combined populations of Seattle, San Francisco, Boston, Dallas, Denver, Miami, Atlanta, and Chicago.

Online investing

After stubbornly resisting for years, traditional brokerage houses began offering online investing. Merrill Lynch became the trailblazer by unveiling flat $29.95 online trades. By one estimate, this offer eviscerated the price of a typical trade at Merrill Lynch by 80 percent. On the surface, paying per trade might seem like the cheapest deal. But if you're a heavy trader, paying a flat fee for the whole year might save you money.

Meanwhile, if you choose the bare-bones online route, don't expect to qualify for all the perks that the other brokerage customers enjoy. You certainly won't have access to your own broker.

Enticing wealthy clients

Traditionally, the nation's wealthiest investors gravitated to private banking and trust services for their needs. But full-service brokerage firms are trying to entice many of them to stay by creating their own wealth management divisions. Under one roof, firms are offering money management, financial planning, lending, trust services, insurance, and tax planning. Just like the richest clients of discount brokers, top customers may also be invited to participate in hedge funds and venture capital deals.

Although customers with six- and seven-figure accounts can expect extra perks, everybody else might feel invisible. Small investors at full-service firms can no longer assume that they'll be assigned their own brokers. Instead, they may be directed to customer service hotlines. Small discount brokerage customers are beginning to feel equally unloved. Some discounters, for instance, are limiting the access that investors with modest accounts have to telephone representatives if they make too many calls.

Working with an Individual Broker

If you prefer the full-service route, knowing as much as possible about your personal broker is more important than ever. That's because brokers aren't just brokers anymore. Or at least that's what the industry wants you to believe. With the move toward fee-based pricing, your broker is now supposed to be your financial partner; brokers are even billing themselves as financial planners or consultants. You are supposed to rely on them for help in balancing your portfolio, developing a strategy for retirement savings, and handling other financial challenges.

This new definition of broker has created tremendous controversy in the financial world. Many experts question whether brokers are qualified to give advice. Historically, brokers have been just glorified salesmen. They never even had to register as investment advisors with regulatory agencies because what little counseling they provided was considered a tiny part of their job. Their chief job was to sell securities.

Caution   Realize that a broker's first loyalty is always to the firm. Brokers are expected to do what is best for the brokerage house. In practical terms, that means that they may sometimes recommend investments that aren't the best for their customers.

Unlike financial planners, brokers don't have a fiduciary responsibility to their customers. That means that they aren't required to put the interests of their clients above all else. Here's where the controversy comes in: Because financial planners have a fiduciary responsibility to their clients, shouldn't brokers who now call themselves financial planners have to abide by the same rule of fiduciary responsibility? Federal regulators have yet to answer this basic question.

The broker accountability issue isn't a burning one for discount customers yet. However, as discounters start offering tailored advice to their clients, checking out the qualifications of the employees providing this advice becomes necessary. The following sections explain some of the pointed questions you should ask.

How long have you been a broker?

With fat commissions disappearing, many veteran brokers are fleeing the business. At the same time, fewer young business majors aspire to spend their early professional years cold-calling clients. Recent college grads can't replenish the ranks alone. You'll also see carpet salesmen, cooks, assembly workers, teachers, and store managers signing up for second careers as brokers.

Caution   Never allow a rookie to handle your account. Try to stick with someone with several years' experience.

What are your qualifications?

Your best bet is to find a broker whose training goes beyond selling securities. Look for a broker who has earned such certifications or designations as Certified Financial Planner (CFP), chartered financial analyst (CFA), or chartered financial consultant (ChFC). These designations are hard to get and are handed out by independent accrediting bodies. Brokerage firms typically reserve the best-trained brokers for their biggest clients.

See Chapter 5 for tips on selecting and working with a CFP, and for contact information on CFP accrediting bodies.

What's on your Central Registration Depository report?

You should definitely read a broker's Central Registration Depository (CRD) report. Thousands of these reports are stored in a massive computer database in Maryland that's jointly operated by the National Association of Securities Dealers (NASD), which regulates the brokerage industry, and the North American Securities Administrators Association (NASAA), which represents the 50 states' financial watchdog agencies.

If a broker does claim some type of accreditation, make sure you understand what it is and how difficult it was to obtain. Then double-check with the accrediting body.

If a broker is trying to hide anything, chances are it'll show up on this report. This report contains the following types of information:

✦ Broker's past employment

✦ Any disciplinary actions taken by state or federal securities agencies

✦ Civil judgment involving securities

✦ Arbitration with clients

✦ Criminal convictions or indictments

Contact one of the following associations to obtain this free report:

✦ National Association of Securities Dealers, P.O. Box 9401, Gaithersburg, MD 20898-9401; (800) 289-9999; www.nasdr.com.

✦ North American Securities Administrators Association, 10 G St. NE, Suite 710, Washington, DC 20002; (202) 737-0900; www.nasaa.org. The NASAA doesn't provide a copy of the report itself, but it can give you the phone number of your state's securities department, which can send the report to you.

Where do you get your investment ideas?

Traditionally, brokerage houses funnel stock ideas generated by their in-house analysts to their sales crew. Of course, some brokerage firms are better at stock picking than others. *The Wall Street Journal* publishes a quarterly ranking of the major firms' long- and short-term stock selection prowess. Ask for the performance track record of the firm's recommended stock list. Even better, ask for a copy of *The Wall Street Journal*'s latest brokerage house roundup.

What happens if your financial advisor leaves the firm?

Every Friday as another session of the New York Stock Exchange gavels to a close, brokers across the country clean out their desks and abruptly quit. In the brokerage business, the courtesy of a two-week notice is laughable. Two minutes is even too much.

Once the bombshell drops, the branch manager, with the precision of a well-rehearsed fire drill, summons the remaining brokers and carves up the traitor's client list. Throughout the weekend, the troops try to discourage hundreds of customers from deserting the firm as well. While all this is happening, the departing broker is following his own finely honed game plan. The most popular time for these surprise farewells, 4 p.m. Eastern time Friday, is calculated to foil old colleagues. This time gives a broker who is forbidden from soliciting his or her clients before an official resignation all weekend to contact them by phone.

You might dismiss this kind of behavior as an example of broker high jinks, but the job shuffle isn't confined to full-service brokers. As the financial industry experiences tumultuous change, planners, investment advisors, certified public accountants, and other professionals are being swept up by mergers, career repositioning, and the age-old desire to make more dough.

Note Partly because of all this jockeying between firms, Americans recently switched 3.2 million investment accounts from one brokerage firm to another in one year, but this switch was less than seamless. Bungled transfer accounts rank as the Security and Exchange Commission's top consumer complaint.

Should you accept your advisor's wanderlust and tag along? There is no easy answer. But the departure provides an excellent chance to reassess the professional relationship. If you've been unimpressed with your advisor's performance, but you lacked the chutzpah to escape, here's an excellent excuse to bail. If you ultimately decide to remain loyal, you may be able to finagle some concessions.

As you mull over your options, ask the following key questions.

Did you get paid to leave?

If your broker sounds incredibly perky in his new surroundings, it's no wonder. He probably sold out for big bucks. Hot producers are receiving the kind of bonuses from rival brokerage houses that only a Heisman trophy contender would take for granted. A successful broker can typically pocket a bonus equaling 50 to 100 percent of his or her trailing 12-month revenues just for moving to an office across town. Someone who generated $1 million in commissions during the last year could walk off with a check cut for the same amount.

SEC Chairman Arthur Levitt has been grumbling unsuccessfully about broker bounties for years. What's the harm? Although brokers bitterly deny it, consumer advocates complain that the practice encourages financial hired guns to generate super-sized fees for their new firms while ignoring what's best for their customers. A hefty sign-on bonus for the broker should definitely raise a red flag for you the client.

Why are you leaving?

Here's what you'll probably hear: "I'm pursing a new opportunity which will allow me to serve you and my other clients better." Nevertheless, you should eliminate the possibility that your trusted advisor was pushed out for improprieties. If your broker has anything to hide, it should show up on his or her CRD report.

If you've been relying upon a registered investment advisor (most financial planners fit into that category), examine his or her ADV Form (Part I and II). You can obtain the exhaustive report from the Securities & Exchange Commission by calling (202) 942-8090 or, in some cases, by contacting your state securities department.

What's going to happen to my fees?

If your departing broker is begging you to remain loyal, your chances of getting a break on fees have never been better. If asked, a broker will typically offer reduced prices for a temporary period of time, such as six months. You may even want to trigger a bidding war. The spurned brokerage firm is often eager to make fee concessions as well.

If a financial planner is making the move, price breaks aren't automatic, but it can't hurt to inquire. You also need to find out if the size of your portfolio could pose a problem. Some firms charge minimum investment fees each year, which could be expensive for someone with a modest portfolio.

Will your role change?

Although many advisors are emptying their desks for bigger firms, others are bucking the trend and striking out on their own. Either way, finding out what your advisor's new responsibilities will be is crucial.

If your advisor goes solo, you'll want to know who'll be taking care of the back office services. You don't want your financial touchstone to be spending a lot of time stuffing envelopes. If your advisor is now positioning himself as a jack-of-all trades, find out if he was previously fulfilling that role. For instance, to what extent, if any, was your account handled by other partners? If someone else made investment decisions while your advisor did the financial planning, you'll want to know. To get a more candid answer, make an anonymous call to find out about the various staff's responsibilities.

Transfer Snafus

Most of the time, investors' accounts are transferred from one brokerage firm to another within two to three weeks. But glitches can gum up the works. Sometimes customers mistakenly substitute IRA paperwork for a taxable account form or fill out the transfer form incorrectly. Even something as innocent as failing to include your middle name on a transfer form when you used it on your old account can create hassles.

Keep in mind that some securities just can't be moved. Trying to do so just causes a delay. Limited partnerships, a brokerage firm's proprietary mutual funds, and annuities may have to stay put. If you want completely out of a certain firm, you may have to sell these assets.

If problems occur, contact your new or previous brokerage firm. You may want to speak with the offending firm's compliance officer. If that doesn't work, call the New York Stock Exchange (212) 656-2772 or the National Association of Securities Dealers (212) 858-4400 to explain your problem. Which one you call depends upon where your brokerage firm is a member.

If your advisor is a little fish swimming to a bigger tank, other issues must be hashed out. Will your advisor continue to handle all your needs, or will the tasks be parceled out to others? What are the qualifications of the other involved people? Meanwhile, how accessible will your advisor continue to be?

Can I get caught in crossfire?

Dealing with account transfer forms can be a pain, but nobody expects to get trapped by bitter litigation after signing one. But it happens all too often. Some brokerage firms are known for suing escaping brokers for allegedly violating contractual agreements. If you've signed transfer paperwork, your account could end up in limbo until the dueling parties drop their swords.

Caution You can be pulled into a tug-of-war between a brokerage firm and a departing broker for your loyalty. The firm may try to hold on to as many of your assets as possible and make it as difficult as possible to let you follow the departing broker.

Once you're caught in the crosshairs, a truce may not be declared for weeks or even months. Typically, a firm receives a temporary restraining order to block accounts from being transferred. The next step is arbitration, but often a broker's new firm settles to make the legal attack dogs go away. Typically, the payoff ranges from 5 to 25 percent of the broker's most recent one-year revenues.

Tip If you're trapped in a legal brawl, you can always avoid the fray by transferring your account to a third financial institution.

Wealth Management Services: Can You Qualify?

Wealth management is hot. Clever marketers have started investors buzzing about services that they thought were available only from traditional millionaire haunts such as Northern Trust and J.P. Morgan. Today many more financial contenders are chasing after investors with newer money. And you don't have to be a blue-haired dowager to cash in on the phenomenon.

Brokerage firms, banks, trust companies, and other financial institutions now boast that they can simplify your life by coordinating your financial needs with seamless service. Whether you want to boost your portfolio's performance, buy a house, borrow money for a business deal, or fund a trust, you can do it in one place. At least that's what the advertisements claim. It's up to you to decide whether they're bluffing.

With more institutions bragging about their wealth management capabilities, the term is in danger of losing its cache. Many institutions categorize wealth management as everything outside the realm of traditional checking and savings accounts. Private banking, as it's often called, offers both mundane services as well as the gee-whiz variety. Here's some of what you can expect:

✦ A private bank officer

✦ Personal lines of credit

✦ Mortgages

✦ Business loans

✦ Personalized portfolio management

✦ Trust services

What this sterile list can't capture are the extra flourishes that can make life easier for pampered customers. Some private bankers gladly scout for the best deal on a luxury car, investigate assisted-living facilities for an ailing client, and tutor a widow or a client's college-age children on the basics of money and investing. A private banker may also offer suggestions on developing a prime piece of real estate or liquidating a closely held business. Meanwhile, money managers within these institutions are used to tailoring portfolios to their clients' needs. An investment manager, for example, will honor a widower's wishes to keep any tobacco stocks out of his holdings because his wife died from lung cancer.

Private banking is typically available only to those who can claim at least $250,000 in investable assets. If you want to park your money at the nation's finest institutions and qualify for all the goodies, you'll need at least $1 million.

If you have that much cash and are shopping for private banking services, here's what the candidates should offer.

Personal attention

On a first visit to a private banking institution, are you introduced to your own banker? Do you get the opportunity to shake hands with any others who may be part of your team? You will often have at least three people assigned to your account: a private banker, an administrator, and a portfolio manager. A nearby row of phones could signal trouble. If you're asked to dial a toll-free number to establish an account, that's a tip off that personalized service is going to be a joke.

Portfolio building

One of private banking's biggest perks is gaining access to your own investment manager. An in-house investment manager oversees your portfolio of stocks, bonds, and cash. The institution should be completely familiar with your investment goals before any money changes hands. Is your top priority preserving principal with reasonable growth? What kind of income stream, if any, do you need? Investment professionals should ask these basic questions at the start.

What you don't want to see is your money dumped in a bank's own brand of mutual funds. This strategy makes money for the bank, but it's usually bad news for the poor shareholders.

Caution

Bank mutual funds have historically fared poorly compared to the rest of the fund universe. If you have at least a $500,000 portfolio, you'll probably have enough leverage to avoid these proprietary funds.

Pay close attention to the institution's investment track record, as well as its ability to limit risk. Make sure that the investment managers are compliant with the standards set by the Association for Investment Management and Research. You can contact the association at 560 Ray C. Hunt Dr., Charlottesville, VA 22903; (800) 247-8132; www.aimr.org.

Background material

Request meaningful background material instead of just accepting the puffy sales literature. Ask for the biographies of the people you'd be working with. How long have they been in the field? What are their qualifications? Ask about employee turnover. With bank mergers, staff continuity is hard to maintain.

Make sure you obtain the fee schedule. With a $1 million portfolio, the annual fee should be about 1 percent. Be leery if the firm or bank primarily makes money from its clients through transactions. That method may encourage frequent trading, which could endanger the more prudent buy-and-hold strategy.

Tip

For your own protection, stick with a fee-based arrangement in which you pay a percentage of the assets you invest instead of paying commissions.

Family Offices and Snob Appeal

The *family office* is a bland name to describe a tony enterprise. Back in the 1920s and 1930s, some of America's wealthiest families decided they no longer wanted to parcel out the job of managing their millions to outsiders. On payrolls that already included butlers, maids, horse groomers, and gardeners, they began adding their own attorneys, accountants, and investment pros. The hired help managed the financial affairs of the original families and continued on the job as the families grew and multiplied long after the patriarch and matriarch had died. Eventually, the families concluded that they could cut their costs by opening their doors and charging others for the financial services.

Families such as the Phipps (Carnegie Steel heirs), the Pews (Sun oil money), and the Pitcairns (PPG Industries heirs) now share their services with minor millionaires.

You can obtain more information by contacting the Family Office Exchange, an organization that includes 900 families and family office executives who are scattered from New York to Hong Kong. The Exchange is located at 137 N. Oak Park Ave., Suite 310, Oak Park, IL 60301; (708) 848-2030; www.familyoffice.com.

References

Solicit the opinion of customers, as well as professional references. Keep in mind that an estate attorney, a CPA, or some other professional could be hiding his or her own interests. If someone in the finance industry refers to a particular bank, ask your source what his or her relationship is with the institution he or she is praising. Sometimes attorneys send business to a bank or trust company, and in return the institution funnels clients back.

Trust services

Evaluating the aid of a trust department, whether it's an arm of a brokerage firm, bank, or another financial institution, is tricky, but it can be extremely important not only for you, but your heirs as well.

You can find tips on how to evaluate trust services in Chapter 26.

Your Own Private Money Manager

In the past, only multimillionaires could realistically hire their own personal money managers. An exclusive money management firm that maintained a roster of institutional clients would have snubbed someone's overtures if he or she wasn't worth $5 to $10 million or more. Today, institutional money management has become far more practical for those who aren't lucky enough to be filthy rich. Technological advances have made it economically feasible for these elite institutions to compete for the assets of the Volvo crowd.

Note Many firms, which oversee portfolios for pension funds, endowments, and multi-millionaires, will now manage an individual's portfolio if it's worth at least $100,000 to $250,000.

Of course, professional money managers run mutual funds, and the minimum investment for them is usually just a few thousand dollars. So why, you might wonder, does someone need a personal financial whiz? Here are the top reasons:

✦ Potential to better control taxes

✦ Ability to own individual stocks

✦ Possibility of better performance

✦ Customized account

Because keeping tax liabilities low is a major incentive, most people use private money managers to oversee their taxable accounts. They may invest their IRAs and IRA rollovers elsewhere. Personal portfolio managers are usually sensitive to their affluent clients' tax liabilities and try to keep the tax pain to a minimum. Such managers can also customize a portfolio to meet a client's unique needs. Suppose someone owned a huge position in Cisco Systems thanks to stock options. That person's money manager can steer clear of Cisco and other computer networking stocks to maintain a diversified portfolio.

How do you find a money manager?

There are two ways to hire a money manager: Hire someone directly or use a finder's service. To hire someone directly, realistically you must have several million dollars to invest.

As you may have guessed, most investors rely upon an intermediary to find and evaluate money managers. This service can be worth the extra money because locating someone by yourself can be tricky. Performance records, for instance, aren't uniform. Unlike mutual funds, you can't look up the statistics of an individual money manager in the daily newspaper. These investment managers typically specialize in one field, such as large-cap value or small-cap growth, so you'll need to know what type of investing prowess is appropriate for you.

Here's where you can find the intermediaries to help:

Major full-service brokerage houses

If you're a brokerage client, your broker can link you with outside money management firms that have survived a screening process. These programs are commonly referred to as *wrap accounts*.

Charles Schwab's Managed Account Connection

Charles Schwab has a stable of hundreds of outside money managers affiliated with its program. However, you can't ask for a list and start dialing. The program requires that you seek assistance from one of the thousands of fee-only financial planners who are in Schwab's referral network.

Investment advisory firms

Independent firms also evaluate money management firms. Once again, these firms only work directly with a financial advisor. You can't just pay the firm to provide the names. Two prominent players in this field are the following firms:

✦ Lockwood Financial Services: 10 Valley Stream Parkway, Malvern, PA 19355; (800) 309-2360; www.lockwoodfinancial.com.

✦ Portfolio Management Consultants: 555 17th St., 14th floor, Denver, CO 80202; (800) 852-1177; www.pmcdenver.com.

Who should not work with a private money manager?

Although hiring a money manager to oversee an investment account is now a possibility for more Americans, who are flush with bull market winnings, it isn't feasible for somebody who can only scrape together the minimum investment. The reason for this caution is that when you hire a manager, you're buying into one particular investment style, whether that's large-cap growth, small-cap value, or some other discipline. You'd need a lot more than a $100,000 account to diversify. One way around this dilemma is to supplement part of your portfolio with mutual funds while you leave the rest in the money manager's hands.

You should know upfront, too, that you won't have the same kind of interaction with your money manager as you'd enjoy with a broker or financial planner. You're paying the money manager to make decisions largely without your input. Money managers typically prefer not to hear from you. Any communication is usually done through your financial advisor. If this loss of control bothers you, don't sign up for it.

On the other hand, if this type of investing appeals to you, realize that although the money manager's performance is important, keeping costs down is crucial as well. If you're not careful, fees could eat up your potential tax savings. The good news is that fees have been going down, and there's room to negotiate. Brokerage firm literature suggests that wrap accounts annually cost 2.5 to 3 percent. This amount is excessive. One industry survey, however, concluded that the typical fee is much closer to 2 percent. In other words, remember to dicker. The total cost of going through Schwab or one of the independent firms should be at the low end of the scale. Even services on the lower end of the fee scale won't necessarily be a bargain. A private money manager has to have nurtured an outstanding record to overcome the built-in expenses.

Summary

✦ The brokerage industry revolution means you can get more service with less money.

✦ Use the surveys from financial publications and other financial organizations to help you evaluate brokerage firms.

✦ Play detective with your broker: Evaluate credentials and check the CRD report.

✦ Make sure an institution's wealth management services are worth the money.

✦ Private money manager may provide tax-efficient, customized accounts for people with at least several hundred thousand dollars to invest.

✦   ✦   ✦

Finding a Financial Planner

✦   ✦   ✦   ✦

In This Chapter

Understanding what financial planners do

Knowing where to turn to find a top planner in your area

Evaluating credentials

Grilling prospective planners

✦   ✦   ✦   ✦

This chapter presents information on selecting an Ivy League-caliber financial planner, including the organizations and Web sites that provide referrals, a rundown of planner pricing, and leads on free (albeit rudimentary) advice you can get over the Internet.

Never have more Americans been in need of sophisticated financial help, especially those who suddenly realize that retirement is no longer a tiny speck on the horizon and that they have no pension plan to fall back on. For those who require guidance and advice, the best solution is often to find a qualified financial planner.

Finding a financial planner, however, can be daunting. Thousands of advisors are jostling for your business. One reason for the abundance of advisors? Financial planning is an easy field to crack. No uniform standards exist to weed out the less capable or the crooked. You don't need a college degree or even a high school diploma to get started. Some people who are searching for a second career gravitate to the profession because financial software has made it easy to develop boilerplate financial plans for customers. Use this chapter to help you weed out the mediocre and select an eminently qualified planner.

Financial Planners for Good Financial Health

Locating an excellent financial planner is worth the hassle. A first-rate one functions in much the same way as a trusted family doctor: Before a planner makes comprehensive recommendations, you'll typically undergo a top-to-bottom financial checkup. Your retirement goals, insurance needs, cash flow requirements, estate-planning preparation, and much more will be closely examined. You might be dying to know if you should buy shares in Pfizer or Intel, but a reputable financial planner won't even touch investment questions until he or she has a good grasp of your overall financial health.

Note Some planners specialize in advising particular groups, such as millionaires, widows, divorcees, teachers, or parents with disabled children. Other planners may do a lot of insurance work, estate planning, small business advising, or stock-option counseling.

When looking for a planner, you should seek out someone whose client roster contains a lot of people who share your same needs or goals. Your situation dictates the type of plan you'll need. The following are the most common types of financial plans:

✦ The comprehensive plan is comparable to a complete physical. Nothing should be overlooked. One of these plans covers retirement and investment strategies, employee benefits, tax and estate planning, and insurance coverage. The final document will not only analyze your family's financial health, but it will also set goals.

✦ A specialty plan focuses on a specific financial goal, such as saving for retirement, starting a business, or funding a college education.

✦ Hourly consultation. Maybe you already have a financial plan, or you feel capable of going it alone. In an hourly consultation, a planner can answer your questions on a single issue, such as exercising employee stock options, buying versus leasing a car, and handling a 401(k) distribution.

Paying a Planner

Whom should you pick? That question alone keeps many people from ever seeking help from a financial planner. The best way to eliminate most financial planners from consideration is to decide how you want to pay for the services. The three methods of payment for financial planners are commissions, fee-only, and fee-based.

Commissions

Stockbrokers aren't the only ones who pocket commissions; many financial planners earn commissions as well. Investors who feel that they can't afford expensive financial advice gravitate to these planners with the mistaken belief that their advice is free. But what these investors don't understand is that the costs are merely hidden.

Commissioned planners favor investments that generate sales charges. If you ask a commissioned planner to select mutual funds for a retirement portfolio, for instance, you'll probably end up with load mutual funds. Load funds come with sales charges that can typically be 4 or 5 percent or higher. (See Chapter 14 for information on mutual funds' sales loads.) If you invest $10,000 in a fund with an upfront 5 percent load, $500 will be skimmed off the top. The planner pockets some of this money, and your initial investment drops to $9,500. Consequently, you're paying for the fund recommendation, although you may not realize it. Some funds, recommended by commissioned planners, don't appear to charge any load, but the yearly fund expenses are significantly higher. And these extra annual charges can last as long as you own the fund.

Caution Some commission-based planners may steer you to buy investment products that generate even juicier commissions such as whole life insurance, variable annuities, and limited partnerships.

In some respects, using a commissioned planner will limit your options since the planner, who depends upon commissions for a livelihood, would starve if he or she steered you to worthwhile investments that don't generate them. You may be better off with a couple of high-performing yet inexpensive index funds from the Vanguard Group, for instance, but you might never get the chance because Vanguard, the highly regarded mutual fund company, doesn't pay commissions.

In their defense, commissioned planners can provide an easier way to obtain financial advise for some middle-class people who can't afford an upfront fee for a comprehensive plan, which sometimes reaches into the thousands of dollars. The existence of commissioned planners ensures that individuals of modest means won't be shut out by fee-only advisors, who tend to prefer affluent clients.

Fee-only

A fee-only planner typically provides services by the hour, for a flat fee or a percentage of the assets being managed. For a quick financial consultation, you typically pay by the hour. A flat fee is usually charged for more ambitious financial plans. In addition, if a financial planner manages your assets, the annual investment fee can often range from 1 to 2 percent of your total investment.

Tip The fee-only approach is usually the best way to pay for financial advice.

A fee-only advisor is theoretically free to make the best investments decisions rather than steer you toward mutual funds or annuities that trigger commissions. The financial press clearly favors fee-only advising, which is why more advisors are trying to break free of commissioned work. But it's extremely hard for planners to wean themselves off of those dependable kickbacks. The vast majority of planners depend at least partially on commissions.

Don't Let the Initials Fool You

Not all acronyms should impress you. Plenty of them are just about meaningless. For instance, those folks who call themselves *registered investment advisors* (RIA) have a very low hurdle to jump. To become an RIA, the federal Securities & Exchange Commission requires a person to simply pay a small fee and fill out an ADV Form (a document covered later in this chapter). In 2000, almost all states began requiring new RIAs to pass a three-hour competency exam that tests a person's knowledge of investments, which is still a fairly low hurdle. Meanwhile, another fancy title you might run across is *registered representative* — which is just another name for stockbroker.

Paying a reasonable fee is one thing; getting gouged is another. One way to economize when you seek the help of a fee-only planner is to manage your own portfolio. If the planner does oversee your assets, find out what discounts he or she provides for larger portfolios. Typically, the investment fee decreases as your assets grow. For instance, a planner might charge 1 percent of assets for managing a portfolio, but for a client with a $1 million portfolio, the fee slips to .8 percent.

Fee-only planners, who depend upon asset management fees, aren't entirely free of potential conflicts. These planners will earn more when their clients' portfolios grow. Let's say, for instance, that a client, leaving a job, is debating whether to roll a 401(k) into an Individual Retirement Account or keep it at his old employer. Obviously, the planner will benefit if the money gets moved into an account that he or she oversees.

Since fee-only planners are in the minority, it can be harder to find them. In a moment, you'll learn how to contact an association that represents them. Not all of these advisors will want your business. Some prefer to work with clients who have at least $500,000 or $1 million in assets or more. The search for one of these planners, however, can be well worth the hunt.

Fee-based

A fee-based financial planner plays it both ways. These planners charge fees and collect commissions. An increasing number of financial planners, who used to depend exclusively on commissions, are adopting this method of compensation. Some of these planners will charge a fee and offset this cost when they recommend an investment product that offers a commission. You should ask these planners, as well as those who exclusively live on commissions, how much they will pocket on every investment they recommend.

Caution   With the fee-based approach, you could end up paying for a plan that recommends load products, which you could have gotten free from a commissioned planner.

Regardless of how a planner is paid, no one type enjoys a monopoly on integrity and wisdom. It will be up to you to evaluate whether a planner, regardless of the method of payment, will suit your needs.

Checking Credentials

Once you decide how you'd like to pay for financial planning, focus next on credentials. Look for what has come to be regarded as the badge of honor for financial planners: the Certified Financial Planner (CFP) certification. To earn this certification from the Certified Financial Planner Board of Standards, planners must pass a rigorous 10-hour exam, have three to five years experience in the field, adhere to a strict code of ethics, and attend continuing education courses. More than 36,000 planners are now authorized to use the CFP mark, which is a trademarked designation. The leading organizations for Certified Financial Planners are the National Association of Personal Financial Advisors (NAPFA) and the Financial Planning Association (FPA). These organizations can provide you with the names of CFPs in your area.

National Association of Personal Financial Advisors

The National Association of Personal Financial Advisors (NAPFA) represents the elite of the financial planning universe. By industry standards, NAPFA's size is minuscule. Fewer than 700 financial planners belong, but they are visible far beyond their numbers. Its members are often quoted in *The Wall Street Journal, The New York Times,* and many personal finance magazines.

Qualifying for this group is tough, which goes a long way towards explaining its modest membership. Any NAPFA wannabe can't accept any commissions because all NAPFA members have proclaimed themselves fee-only planners.

Beyond the fee issue, applicants must let NAPFA snoop into their background. An outside expert scrutinizes the information that's contained in the forms that financial planners must file with the SEC or the state. An applicant must also submit for

A CFP Litmus Test

Do you want independent confirmation that finding a Certified Financial Planner is worthwhile? Each September, *Worth* magazine publishes a list that contains who it considers to be the nation's top 300 financial advisors. This list is hardly a scientific survey, but the editorial staff puts a great deal of effort into it, including conducting background checks and reviewing work samples. The candidates are recommended by financial experts, professional associations, and *Worth* readers. In a recent issue, 85 percent of those who made the list were Certified Financial Planners.

peer review a financial plan previously prepared for a real client. If the plan is mediocre, membership is denied. Once accepted, a new member can't coast. The continuing education requirements are stiff.

You can contact NAPFA by mail at 355 W. Dundee Rd., Suite 200, Buffalo Grove, IL 60089; by phone at (888) FEE-ONLY; or on the Internet at www.napfa.org.

Financial Planning Association

In the planning world, the Financial Planning Association (FPA) is the 800-pound gorilla. It encompasses a hodgepodge of financial expertise. Its members include Certified Financial Planners, stockbrokers, attorneys, accountants, and other financial professionals. If you don't recognize the name of this organization, it's not surprising. The FPA is a fairly new organization, with roughly 29,000 members, that combines two professional groups with very different memberships. After an off-and-on again courtship, the Institute of Certified Financial Planners in Denver and the International Association for Financial Planning in Atlanta officially merged in 2000.

Despite its eclectic membership, if you call FPA for a financial planner, you will receive only the names of Certified Financial Planners. Unlike NAPFA members, many CFPs in this organization accept commissions. You can contact the FPA by calling (800) 282-PLAN or visiting its Web site (www.fpanet.org).

Cyberspace leads

Some folks are turning to their computer to find financial planners. Microsoft, the software giant, sponsors a matchmaking program at its Web site, MSN MoneyCentral, that links Internet users with financial planners around the nation. In so doing, Microsoft is directly challenging Charles Schwab, the long-time online planner matching service.

After you fill out a questionnaire at the Microsoft site (www.moneycentral.com), the software matches your answers with a database of several thousand financial planners. Within seconds, you obtain the names of planners who are supposed to match your criteria, including planner profiles and information about fees and location. However, don't assume that names in the database represent the best in the business; Microsoft's screens aren't too tough. Planners must have a blemish-free regulatory record for the past five years. They also have to be full-time planners with a significant number of clients and at least a five-year track record.

Schwab's AdvisorSource program (www.schwab.com) screens more rigorously. For example, it requires that planners oversee client assets worth at least $25 million. But the most important distinction between the two programs is that Schwab requires that its planners shun all commissions. Remember, a planner who charges fees rather than pocketing commissions is less likely to get tripped up by a conflict of interest.

Note   Whether you find an advisor online or through more traditional means, you still need to rigorously check them out the same way.

Whittling Down Your Choices

Once you've gathered the names of financial planner prospects, here's what you need to do to narrow the list.

Sit down for an initial interview.

The first visit with a financial planner is usually free. During the meeting, determine whether you could comfortably work with this person. Remember, you're going to be sharing highly personal information with the planner you pick. A planner could be brilliant, but if he or she has the personality of a calculator, you may wish to look elsewhere. You also don't want to choose somebody who can't explain financial strategies without being condescending.

Tip   Resist the urge to sign up with the first person you meet. Try to interview at least two or three planners.

Request a resume in advance.

If you can read the planner's resume ahead of time, you'll be less rushed at the initial meeting. Reading the resume should either answer key questions or raise questions you can ask at the initial meeting.

Bring a list of questions to the first meeting.

Make sure you ask these key questions when you interview a financial planner.

- ✦ How are you compensated?
- ✦ What is your experience?
- ✦ Do you specialize in certain types of financial planning?
- ✦ What professional affiliations do you have?
- ✦ How do you keep current?
- ✦ Do you personally research products you recommend?
- ✦ How often would we meet?
- ✦ Do you have references that I could check?

    ✦ Can I see a sample financial plan?

    ✦ Is your investment style aggressive or conservative? (You'll want an investment approach that fits your comfort level.)

    ✦ Will you provide a written analysis of my financial situation, along with recommendations? (This feature should be a standard part of the analysis package.)

Tip

Getting a sample financial plan from each potential planner helps you to quickly compare the candidates — and what they can and will do for you.

Get a copy of the ADV Form.

Before you sign on with a financial planner, do a little more digging. You'll want to pore over a candidate's ADV Form. Any planners you are considering should have submitted this form to the Securities and Exchange Commission (SEC) or their state securities department. A planner files the paperwork with the SEC unless he or she manages less than $25 million in client assets. Those managing smaller amounts of money are expected to file their ADV Form with their respective state securities departments. You can contact the SEC by mail at 450 Fifth St., Washington, DC 20549; by phone (800) 732-0330; or on the Internet at www.sec.gov. You can find the appropriate phone number for a state agency by contacting the North American Securities Administrators Association at the mailing address 10 G St. NE, Suite 710, Washington, DC 20002; the phone number (202) 737-0900; or the Web site www.nasaa.org.

Caution

If a financial planner hasn't filled out the ADV Form or doesn't want to provide you with a copy, cross him or her off your list.

Although the ADV Form isn't the easiest document to read, it can be a treasure trove of information about an individual financial planner. Here are some of the things you can find out about a planner's background:

    ✦ Education

    ✦ Professional history

    ✦ Disciplinary record

    ✦ Lawsuits and arbitration proceedings

    ✦ Method of payment

    ✦ Types of investments the planner recommends

    ✦ Potential conflicts of interest

A planner is legally obligated to give you only Part II of the ADV Form. But you'll want to obtain Part I as well.

Double-check on a CFP.

If the planner you're considering is a Certified Financial Planner, make one more call to ensure that your prospect is entitled to claim the CFP certification. You should also inquire about any disciplinary actions. You can do this easily by calling the Certified Financial Planner Board of Standards at (888) CFP-MARK. You can also reach the board by mail at 1700 Broadway, Suite 2101, Denver, CO 80290-2101; or on the Internet at www.CFP-Board.org. If you ever feel that a CFP has acted unethically or dishonestly, you can lodge a complaint with the regulatory board as well.

Summary

✦ When searching for a qualified financial planner, determine which method of payment is best for you.

✦ Stick with planners who have the Certified Financial Planner designation.

✦ Prepare for a first visit with a planner by getting his or her resume and compiling a list of questions.

✦ Check with the pertinent regulators before choosing a planner.

✦   ✦   ✦

Working with Specialists

In this chapter, you discover how to find the best financial experts available in the nation. At the same time, you learn which credentials matter, particularly in specialized fields that you usually don't hear much about. Also provided is a primer on retirement seminars, which are a favorite way of bona fide experts, as well as charlatans, to drum up business.

This chapter is crucial for so many folks out there. Why? Americans often wind up getting financial advice by accident. A dear friend's daughter has decided to be an insurance agent. Guess where she's paying one of her first courtesy calls? Or maybe the new neighbor is an accountant who's trawling for clients, and you get snagged while trimming the rose bushes. Or you decide to attend one of those free retirement seminars because it comes with a free dinner. Nobody needs to tell you that finding help this way is full of peril, particularly when so many of us must take full responsibility for funding our retirement in this age of dwindling Social Security and disappearing pensions.

A major reason why so many people fall victim to cold calling and the pressure tactics of financial salespeople is because their financial and legal affairs desperately need attention.

Plenty of people should draw up an estate plan, for example, but the prospects of finding the right attorney is daunting. Most of us will require help from one or more professionals at some point in their lives, but the person cold calling us at dinnertime may not be the best choice. Read on for the lowdown on those folks seeking your business.

 Cross-Reference This chapter covers niche advisors; Chapter 5 addresses financial planners who deal out more general advice about your overall financial picture, particularly your investments.

Retirement Seminars: Hold onto Your Wallet

If you're nearing retirement age and you haven't been invited to a retirement seminar, just wait — you'll be invited soon. Brokers, financial planners, and perhaps your own employer want to present their take on what awaits you after you've cleared out your desk. The competition for your ear is fierce. Retirement communities are pelted with invitations for free seminars. Brokerage firms buy mailing lists from personal finance magazines to ferret out prospective seminar attendees ages 50 and up. If you open the business section of your local paper, you'll probably find ads for free retirement presentations.

Meanwhile, corporate America, as well as public pension systems, are stepping in to provide parting financial advice. Increasingly, corporations have concluded that bestowing a retiring employee with a package of benefits and a farewell sheet cake just isn't cutting it. A person who is retiring is now likely to have a chance to attend a retirement seminar before the last payroll check is processed.

Before you RSVP to one of these seminars, you need to understand a few things. A seminar is like an hors d'oeuvre: it can wet your appetite, but it won't fill you up. At their best, seminars prod you into thinking about all the issues you need to face. Yet not every talking head clutching a microphone at a seminar is worth listening to.

Caution The credentials of some seminar presenters may be thinner than a computer chip. Some speakers are strictly hunting for new clients to sell specific products to rather than looking to provide solutions customized to an individual's needs.

At a free seminar, most people anticipate a sales pitch, but you might not be prepared for a sales delivery that is so slick you won't realize what's happening. What's billed as a retirement seminar, for example, may really be a pitch for life insurance, annuities, or living trusts. If you attend a retirement presentation, a personal finance fair, or some investment extravaganza, remain leery. Look for ideas and different opinions, but don't expect easy answers. To protect yourself, follow these steps:

Request credentials.

Find out who'll be talking. At some seminars, speakers simply bill themselves as retirement planners, which is a broad, meaningless term. Call and ask the sponsor of the seminar to send the biography of the speaker and the firm. The material should include the person's experience in the financial industry, his or her area of expertise, and a list of credentials and education.

 Cross-Reference Contact the National Association of Securities Dealers (NASD), the securities industry regulator, to learn whether the speaker or the firm has ever been in trouble. See the Resource Guide for contact information.

Inquire about fees.

Ask how the speaker presenter is paid. Plenty of people who attend free seminars and complimentary follow-up consultations think the freebies last indefinitely. They don't. You end up paying one way or another. Some brokers and advisors never fully explain the commission schedules.

Watch for red flags.

Brokers and financial planners aren't free to blurt out whatever they'd like when they invite the public to a seminar. If a speaker is regulated by the NASD (as salespeople selling securities-based products are), his or her script may need to obtain the regulator's seal of approval. Before the script ever gets that far, a financial institution's in-house compliance department is supposed to screen scripts for unacceptable claims, though some investment representatives ignore this requirement.

Caution Words such as "guaranteed," "sure thing," and "risk-free," promises of specific returns, and charts or graphs that indicate what will happen to an investment in the future are unethical. No one can accurately predict what return an investment will generate, and NASD specifically restricts agents from making such promises.

Beware of the sales pitch.

When you attend retirement seminars, be prepared for the sales pitch. Sometimes discerning what product a speaker is pushing is tough. For example, a speaker may be gushing enthusiastically about how audience members can boost their future pension income. You may sit through the entire event without ever realizing that the host is talking about a controversial strategy called pension maximization, which requires the purchase of life insurance. At the seminar, there may be no overt mention of life insurance, but that's what is being sold.

Tip During a presentation, ask yourself whether the topic is appropriate for the audience. For instance, if a speaker is praising variable annuity investments to an elderly gathering, you should be suspicious. Variable annuities are meant as long-term investments and are hardly appropriate for this age group.

Don't feel obligated.

Seminar sponsors often serve breakfasts, desserts, or lasagna dinners to encourage people to come. But don't feel obligated because the free food. Never become a client of the seminar presenter because you think it's the polite thing to do. Just because someone spends time with you and provides a few pastries doesn't mean that person deserves to handle your money.

Avoid information overload.

One potential drawback with any seminar is that sometimes there's too much information to absorb. Don't assume that you can learn everything you need to know by eating your way through free seminars. Use these seminars as a starting point for further research.

Tip   If you learn just one valuable concept (and get a square meal), a seminar may be worth your time.

Be wary of workplace-sponsored retirement seminars.

If your employer sponsors a retirement seminar, you should remain just as guarded about the presentation. Some companies try to wing it with their human resources staffers, but the caliber of in-house speakers can be erratic. HR staffers may be efficient at running a 401(k) enrollment meeting, but they are often out of their league discussing complex retirement issues.

Many companies instead bring in outside brokerage firms, financial planners, or insurance agents. Employers are relieved when a brokerage firm or insurance agency offers to hold workshops. Usually these speakers don't charge a cent. They may even bring in cartons of complimentary three-ring binders filled with glossy financial material for the audience.

Caution   If an outside expert has been invited in, don't assume that your company has granted the speaker its seal of approval. The presenter might have just caught an HR exec's administrative assistant on a good day.

These sessions can be thinly disguised sales pitches. Organizers of these events lament that when speakers promise to avoid self promotion, it happens anyway. Guests can be subjected to an even harder sell later. Attendees are typically invited to attend free private consultations at a speaker's office.

Note   Some companies combat this glaring conflict of interest by hiring independent consulting firms such as Hewitt Associates and Buck Consultants to hold workplace seminars. These employee benefits firms charge for their educational services; they aren't peddling anything.

When you attend workplace retirement seminars, consider the presenter's built-in biases. A full-service stockbroker, for instance, isn't going to discuss the virtues of a discount brokerage account or disclose that brokers aren't technically qualified to provide investment advice.

Estate-Planning Attorneys: Finding the Best

Although a million attorneys practice law in this country, only a fraction of them can confidently navigate the Byzantine world of estate planning. Roughly 25,000 lawyers devote their practices to this specialty.

Note Many types of attorneys are capable of drawing up a will, but their knowledge of estates and trusts is often superficial. Unless your assets are quite modest, choose an attorney who specializes in this complex and evolving field of law.

Finding the sharpest practitioners isn't all that easy. Estate-planning attorneys are not, by nature, a flamboyant fraternity. You won't see them working a jury in front of television cameras or making headlines in a local newspaper. Estate-planning attorneys prefer to keep their most creative efforts quiet. If they devise an ingenious estate-planning strategy that saves their clients thousands or millions of dollars, publicity might draw an IRS audit or even congressional legislation to plug a loophole.

Sources for estate-planning attorneys

Where can you find these smart attorneys? The following sources are the best places to look.

The American College of Trust & Estate Counsel

Do you want a lawyer who's admired by his or her competition? Contact the American College of Trust & Estate Counsel. Membership in this exclusive organization is by invitation only. To qualify as a fellow of the counsel, an attorney must be nominated by other members in his or her geographic area. Candidates are then elected by the membership at large. To be considered, an attorney must have made "substantial contributions" to the field of estate planning through lecturing, writing, teaching, and bar activities. In addition, an attorney must have practiced estate-planning law for at least 10 years.

The nonprofit group's 2,700 members are scattered across the country. To locate members who practice in your area, send a letter to the American College of Trust & Estate Counsel, 3415 S. Sepulveda Blvd., Suite 330, Los Angeles, CA 90034. Alternatively, you can call (310) 398-1888 or visit the Web site at www.actec.org.

State bars

Contact your state bar to see whether it issues special estate-planning certification for highly skilled estate and trust attorneys. In California, Texas, North Carolina, and some other states, estate-planning attorneys can earn this extra designation. To qualify, attorneys typically must be a veteran in the field, pass periodic exams, and complete continuing education courses annually.

In those states that don't issue the special certification, your state and local bars can still provide names of estate-planning attorneys, but don't consider them recommendations — the bars can't play favorites. Attorneys may have even paid to have their names included on the referral list.

 Resource   If you're not sure how to contact your state bar, these two Web sites can provide the appropriate link: Findlaw.com at www.findlaw.com and the California State Bar at www.calbar.org.

Other attorneys

Look for an attorney who is sought out by his or her peers. It's a good sign, for instance, if an attorney is a popular estate-planning speaker at professional conferences; your state or local bar association should be able to provide the names of conference presenters. In addition, a lawyer who is a member of one of the estate-planning and taxation committees that are maintained by the American Bar Association (www.abanet.org) and state and local bars is more likely to be aware of cutting-edge developments in the field.

Local bank trust officers

Trust officers are like baseball scouts. They know the good attorneys and the ones that strike out a lot because they regularly deal with them all.

Evaluating and selecting an estate-planning attorney

An estate-planning attorney may have a phenomenal pedigree, but if you don't feel comfortable on a personal level with a true expert, it will be a miserable match. You can judge that for yourself at an introductory meeting.

Tip   Typically, the first visit with an estate-planning attorney is free, which permits you to interview more than one attorney.

During the initial meeting, the attorney should share his or her credentials and ask general questions about your needs. Ask for the attorney's resume in advance so that you can examine it ahead of time. The following questions are good ones to ask at this first meeting:

✦ How long have you been in practice?

✦ How much time do you devote to the practice of estate-planning law?

✦ How long have you specialized in estate planning?

✦ What professional organizations do you belong to?

✦ Have you lectured or written on the subject?

✦ Do you have special estate-planning credentials from your state bar?

AARP's Legal Services Network

Are you looking for an attorney with lots of experience and reasonable rates? The AARP Legal Services Network links prescreened attorneys with potential clients.

To join the legal network, lawyers must have at least four years of experience in the area of law he or she handles for AARP members. Each lawyer is in good standing with bar groups and has current malpractice coverage. In addition, all the participating attorneys have agreed to provide significant fee discounts for AARP members. The attorney also must provide a free half-hour consultation by phone or in person and give clients a written fee agreement. To find participating attorneys, visit the AARP's Web site at www.aarp.org/lsn. You can also contact the organization at AARP, LSN Fulfillment, P.O. Box 100084, Pittsburgh, PA 15290; (800) 424-3410.

✦ Do you actively participate in local or state bar activities dealing with trusts and estates?

✦ How are fees computed?

✦ How much will my estate-planning documents cost? When you retain a lawyer, you should receive a written fee agreement so there should be no surprises.

✦ What information do you need me to provide?

✦ What institution do you typically recommend to serve as trustee for clients' trusts? What is the nature of your relationship with that institution?

Note Fees vary by lawyer and region; call around to get an idea of reasonable rates for your area.

Finding an Elder Law Attorney

Elder law attorneys specialize in the legal needs of the aged. They may handle general estate-planning issues, but their scope goes beyond inheritance matters. Elder law attorneys are also tied into networks of social workers, psychologists, and other gerontology experts who may be able to help with problems beyond the traditional legal ones.

Resource An easy way to find potential elder law attorneys is by visiting the Web site of the National Academy of Elder Law Attorneys at www.naela.com. You can also reach the organization at (520) 881-4005 or 1604 N. Country Club Rd., Tucson, AZ 85716.

The specialties of elder law attorneys include the following:

✦ Preservation or transfer of assets when a spouse enters a nursing home

✦ Medicare claims and appeals

✦ Social Security and disability claims and appeals

✦ Conservatorships and guardianships

✦ Long-term care placements in nursing homes and life care communities

✦ Nursing home patient rights

✦ Elder abuse and fraud recovery cases

✦ Workplace age discrimination

✦ Mental health law

✦ Housing issues, including discrimination

Tip   The majority of elder law attorneys don't specialize in all these areas. Consequently, you should make sure that the elder law attorney that you're consulting spends a sizable amount of time dealing with the particular issue that you or a relative is facing.

The following groups may be able to help you locate elder law attorneys:

✦ Alzheimer's Association at www.alz.org or 1-800-272-3900

✦ National Citizen's Coalition of Nursing Home Reform at www.nccnhr.org or 202-332-2275

✦ Older Women's League at www.owl-national.org or 1-800-TAKE-OWL

✦ AARP at www.aarp.org or 1-800-424-3410

✦ Support groups for specific diseases

✦ A local area agency or council on aging

✦ State or local bar associations

✦ Children of aging parents

Just like their estate-planning colleagues, elder law attorneys can earn extra credentialing. This extra credential can represent one more piece of evidence than an attorney is an expert in this field. Some state bars, including Florida's with its large senior citizen population, offer elder law certification. The National Elder Law Foundation also offers an elder law certification designation (CELA) for lawyers across the country. It is the only national elder law designation that is recognized by the American Bar Association.

Tip   You can contact the National Academy of Elder Law Attorneys to find out which of its members have earned the CELA mark.

Eldercare Internet Resources

Check out these information-filled sites concerning eldercare issues:

✦ **AARP at** www.aarp.org

✦ **American Bar Association Section on Legal Problems of the Elderly at** www.abanet.org/elderly

✦ **American Bar Association – Real Property, Probate & Trust Law at** www.abanet.org/rppt/home.html

✦ **ElderWeb at** www.elderweb.com

✦ **CaregiverZone at** www.caregiverzone.com

✦ **Careguide at** www.careguide.com

✦ **CareScout at** www.carescout.com

✦ **Medicare at** www.medicare.gov

✦ **Medicare Rights Center at** www.medicarerights.org

✦ **National Alliance for Caregiving at** www.caregiving.org

✦ **National Family Caregivers Association at** www.nfcacares.org

✦ **National Senior Citizens Law Center at** www.nsclc.org

✦ **Social Security Administration at** www.ssa.gov

✦ **United Seniors Health Cooperative at** www.unitedseniorhealth.org

When you have a list of candidates, evaluate elder law attorneys the same way you would an estate-planning attorney (see listing of key questions in the previous section).

Getting an Insurance Agent – If You Still Need One

Insurance agents haven't become obsolete, but fewer people need them anymore. Auto, home, and umbrella liability policies can be bought directly from many major insurers who don't employ agents. This self-service phenomenon hasn't gone unnoticed by insurance agents, who are attempting to recreate themselves. The most visible sign of change was the decision of a prominent insurance agent organization to dump its name. In late 1990s, the American Society of Chartered Life Underwriters & Chartered Financial Consultants renamed itself the Society of Financial Service Professionals.

With the advent of insurance quote services via telephone and the Internet, people can purchase term life insurance without ever talking to an agent. See Chapter 30 for more information on quote services.

Insurance agents are increasingly portraying themselves as one-stop financial advisors. They will be happy to advise you on estate-planning issues, investment strategies, retirement savings, and much more. Life insurance is no longer the only product in their repertoire. Many now sell variable annuities, mutual funds, and other investments. However, just because an agent wants to be your financial guru doesn't mean it's a good idea.

Evaluate an agent the same way you would a traditional financial planner by asking how he or she is compensated for advice and what training and experience he or she has beyond selling insurance policies.

Uses for life insurance in an estate

Despite the changing times, insurance advice will always be needed. People who require cash-value life insurance when a term policy isn't appropriate especially need such advice. Retirees sometimes desire this type of life insurance for estate planning purposes. For example, a couple who wants to pass along a private business to the next generation may use life insurance to compensate children who'd rather have cash than a stake in the family enterprise. Aging parents with a disabled child may require cash-value life insurance to fund the child's care after their deaths. A life insurance policy can also be the glue that holds together sophisticated charitable giving plans.

Chapters 23 and 24 cover the fundamentals of estate planning.

All these scenarios are complicated and take a great deal more thought than shopping for cheap term life insurance. Yet finding a source of unbiased advice can be exasperating. If you contact a life insurance agent, chances are he or she is going to heartily endorse your need for a particular kind of policy. Suppose a couple is wondering whether they should buy life insurance to pay their eventual estate taxes so their grown kids can enjoy a bigger inheritance. Even if an agent knows there's a cheaper alternative to life insurance, it may be too tempting to turn away the business and lose a fat commission. Perhaps all the couple needs is a bypass shelter trust, which can be drawn up by any competent estate attorney (as is detailed in Chapter 25).

Chapter 5 tells you all about finding and evaluating financial planners.

An insurance agent's motivation

Certainly many insurance agents don't intentionally mislead their clients, but the system is rigged against consumers. As with the brokerage industry, insurance agents feel great pressure to push policies. An agent isn't rewarded for dispensing sage advice. She or he gets paid only after sealing a deal. Consequently, it's only natural for you to wonder about the veracity of an agent who has spread glossy insurance illustrations across your dining room table.

However, not all insurance experts are saddled with this built-in conflict. Fee-for-service life insurance advisors don't take commissions. As the name suggests, you pay a flat fee for any guidance. These advisors, who are sometimes former agents, don't work for insurance companies and can recommend policies they believe are superior for your situation.

Tip Fee-for-service advisors also enjoy access to life insurance plans' wholesale prices. Advisors avoid traditional policies with huge commissions and choose "low-load" policies instead, which are stripped of commissions.

Unfortunately, the number of fee-for-service insurance advisors could probably fit inside a hotel ballroom. In the state of California, for instance, fewer than four dozen exist. Locating these insurance pros is tricky, but it's not impossible. Try calling these three resources for names:

✦ Life Insurance Advisers Association at (800) 521-4578

✦ Financial Advisors Insurance Resources, Inc at (877) 411-FAIR (or go to www.lowloadinsurance.com)

Questions to ask a prospective agent

Before committing yourself to an insurance agent, pose these questions.

Can I see a copy of your insurance license?

Don't assume that an agent has a current state license unless you see it. You can obtain a copy from your state insurance department. The state agency should also be able to tell you whether the license has expired or been revoked. You obviously want an agent with a clean regulatory record. Some states can also provide you

Letting Someone Else Pick

Even if you need sizable life insurance protection, you may never have to deal directly with an insurance agent. If you're working with a Certified Financial Planner or a CPA, for instance, he or she may consult insurance agents. Because insurance is such a complicated industry, even financial planners must often rely upon outside experts.

with the names of an agent's insurance affiliations, as well as any continuing education classes he or she has taken. Finally, check with your local Better Business Bureau to see whether the agent has been the target of complaints.

Do you have any professional designations?

Look for agents who have earned either one or both of these designations: Charter Life Underwriter (CLU) and Chartered Financial Consultant (ChFC). To claim either of these titles, an agent must take a series of courses in such areas as life insurance, estate planning, and business and employee benefit planning. The correspondence courses are overseen by the American College in Bryn Mawr, Pennsylvania.

Tip   For a consumer, the ChFC designation is the more impressive one. The course work for a CLU is primarily focused on insurance; the ChFC course work involves a more holistic financial planning approach.

Do you have a particular area of expertise?

Some agents have specialized knowledge on particular insurance needs. For example, an agent may know a great deal about life insurance products for wealthy individuals who want to combine philanthropy with their estate planning. If an agent is working in this field, ask whether he or she belongs to a local planned giving council or some related group. In addition, ask whether the agent has taken education courses in his or her field of expertise. For example, an agent who sells insurance to small businesses should be familiar with key person insurance, buy-sell agreements, and group benefits.

Resource   You can find agents with CLU and ChFC designations by contacting the Society of Financial Service Professionals by mail at 270 S. Bryn Mawr Ave., Bryn Mawr, PA 19010-2195; by phone at (888) 243-2258; or on the Internet at www. financialpro.org.

What qualifications do you have beyond selling insurance?

If an insurance agent is billing himself or herself as a financial advisor, ask the agent to elaborate on his or her financial planning experience. Some insurance agents have indeed become Certified Financial Planners, but they are vastly outnumbered. Of the 32,000 active members of the Society of Financial Service Professionals, only 735 recently listed themselves as CFPs.

How are you paid?

If customers discovered how much they're paying in commissions, some might balk at signing the paperwork. It's common for 50 to 100 percent of a first-year's life insurance premium to be swallowed by the agent's commission. Find out what the agent would earn on any policy proposed to you. If the amount is more than you are comfortable paying for the policy, your best alternative is a low-load policy, issued by insurance companies that do not use agents. (See Chapter 30 for more information on finding such companies.)

Finding Your State's Insurance Regulator

If you don't know how to contact your state's insurance department, visit the Web site of the nonprofit National Association of Insurance Commissioners at www.naic.org. You can also contact the organization by mail at 2301 McGee, Suite 800, Kansas City, MO 64108 or by phone at (816) 842-3600.

The association, which represents insurance regulators in all 50 states, provides links, addresses, and phone numbers for each state's insurance division. The NAIC also publishes brochures to help consumers select life insurance and Medicare gap insurance.

How many insurance companies do you represent?

"Captive" agents represent only a single insurer; independent agents sell policies from many insurance companies. The more choices you have, the better off you'll be.

Can I see a copy of your ethics code?

If the agent doesn't have a copy of the ethics code or isn't sure whether his or her company has one, you may want to find another agent. An agent with the CLU or ChFC designation operates under the ethics code established by the Society of Financial Service Professionals.

Can you provide me with referrals?

An agent isn't going to release the names of disgruntled customers, but there are ways to finesse information from an agent's past clients. Ask former customers if they would recommend the agent to their mother or a close friend. Also ask whether the agent was helpful after the insurance policy sale.

Tip Also ask for professional references from CPAs, lawyers, or Certified Financial Planners.

Will you provide service after the sale?

After the deal is sealed, will your agent disappear? What kind of help can you expect later on? You won't find this information spelled out in the insurance contract. Ask whether the agent makes a practice of periodically checking back with clients to find out whether their coverage needs have changed. Such life events as the birth of a child, marriage, divorce, or a first home purchase often require updates to insurance coverage — but that's hardly a task most people place high on their lists of things to do. An agent who remains committed to his or her clients can really pick up the ball here.

The Changing Role of CPAs

Most people start thinking about certified public accountants in February or March during the thick of tax season. But increasingly, CPAs want you to consider them during the other 11 months. No longer willing to fit into a typecast role of dull but dependable tax preparers, CPAs are aggressively branching out into the financial planning arena as well.

One reason for the migration is strictly financial. For many CPAs, the bulk of their business is clustered around the annual tax season. To spread out the revenues more evenly throughout the year, they are looking for extra business. CPAs also are competing against cheap software, such as Turbo Tax and Quicken, that has allowed many taxpayers to complete their own tax returns.

Broadening their businesses

More than a quarter of the CPAs who belong to the American Institute of Certified Public Accountants are now providing financial advice, and that number is expected to rise even more dramatically in the next 10 years. Along with dispensing tax and accounting advice, today's CPA is also likely to sell an array of financial products, including stocks, insurance, and annuities. Some CPAs are also beginning to provide eldercare services that might include everything from finding adult daycare services to making sure that an elderly client's lawn is regularly mowed. The number of CPA firms that offer only traditional tax advice is shrinking dramatically.

If you trust your CPA and would prefer to receive all your financial services from one place, you might applaud this new trend. But consumers also face some potential dangers. As a profession, CPAs enjoy a sterling reputation for honesty. Yet some observers question whether CPAs can retain their well-respected impartiality when they're now peddling products — especially those that carry commissions. In recent years, the vast majority of states have removed regulatory barriers that once prohibited CPAs from accepting commissions or referral fees.

Tip   The best way to avoid any ethical stickiness is to seek out a CPA who avoids commissions. Favor accountants who use the traditional methods of charging by the hour or basing the bill on the amount of assets under discussion.

A CPA who is a whiz at taxes, however, isn't necessarily going to be adept at devising a worthwhile financial game plan for your retirement. A CPA who has spent his or her professional career focused on the federal tax code has a learning curve regarding financial planning. Ask yourself if you want to be a CPA's guinea pig when plenty of other qualified financial planners are available.

One way to gauge whether a CPA is committed to financial planning is to ask whether he or she has extra certification. A CPA who specializes in financial planning can earn a designation of personal finance specialist (PFS) through the

American Institute of Certified Public Accountants. To become credentialed as a PFS, a CPA must have devoted at least 250 hours to financial planning work in each of the past three years. A candidate must also submit six references to substantiate the work experience and pass a rigorous exam. Several thousand CPAs have earned this designation. Some CPAs have gone so far as to obtain the Certified Financial Planner (CFP) certification. (See Chapter 5 for details on CFPs.)

 Resource To locate a CPA with personal finance training, contact the American Institute of Certified Public Accountants, Personal Financial Planning Division, 1211 Avenue of the Americas, New York, NY 10036; (888) 999-9256; www.aicpa.org.

Using a CPA for your taxes

Even if you're content to let your CPA or another tax professional simply handle your tax returns, finding the right one is worth the effort. Choosing the best professional may save you money and reduce your own tax anxieties.

The first step is deciding whether you need any help at all. If you file a simple return with a year-end W-2 wage and tax statement and claim no deductions, you can probably do it yourself. If you need a little hand-holding, consider calling the IRS's free tax assistance line at (800) 829-1040. Another alternative is driving to your nearest H&R Block.

Locating a CPA or an enrolled agent

For more complicated returns, good options exist. You may want to hire a CPA or an enrolled agent.

 Caution In business schools, future CPAs devote a great deal of time to learning how to audit corporate America's books. Someone who is most comfortable in the arcane world of corporate financial reports and taxation probably isn't going to be too helpful if you're just wondering whether you qualify for a home office deduction.

Some CPAs specialize in individuals' tax needs. You can find these CPAs at Big Five and regional accounting firms; others practice alone. An advantage to using a bigger accounting firm is that it will have more resources to keep track of tax code changes, and that's a massive job. Since 1986, the federal tax code has been changed more than 8,000 times. Someone practicing accounting solo would have a much harder time staying current.

Another option is to hire an enrolled agent, who is licensed by the federal government. Only enrolled agents and CPAs are authorized to appear in place of a taxpayer during an IRS audit. Many of the nation's 34,000 enrolled agents are former IRS agents who worked at least five years for the agency. Others qualify if they pass a grueling two-day tax exam administered by the IRS. The majority of the test takers flunk the exam, which covers taxation issues for individuals, partnerships, estates and trusts, and corporations. In addition, before earning the enrolled agent (EA) designation, applicants must survive a federal background check. Enrolled agents are also required to take a certain number of continuing education classes throughout their careers.

Tip   Don't begin your search for a tax advisor during tax season. Think ahead.

You can find enrolled agents in your community by contacting the National Association of Enrolled Agents, 200 Orchard Ridge Dr., Suite 302, Gaithersburg, MD 20878; (800) 424-4339; www.naea.org.

Members of the National Association of Enrolled Agents must meet stiff continuing education requirements, as well as obey a code of ethics.

Grilling your prospective tax preparer

When searching for a tax preparer, you should pose these questions (and go with the preparer whose answers make you feel most comfortable):

✦ What are your qualifications?

✦ How do you keep current with the tax laws?

✦ Do you have a tax specialty?

✦ Can you provide me with references?

✦ Are you available to answer questions year round?

✦ Are you familiar with the laws of states in which I am subject to taxes?

✦ How aggressively do you pursue deductions?

✦ What percentage of your prepared returns are similar to mine? (You'll want to hire someone who handles a lot of returns just like yours, whether you're a physician, a small business owner, a writer, or a member of some other profession.)

✦ Will you represent me if I'm audited?

✦ Have you ever been audited?

✦ How many of your clients have undergone an audit?

A Civil War Beginning

Enrolled agents trace their roots to Chester Arthur's presidency. Disgusted with fishy Civil War claims, Congress created the enrolled agent to represent aggrieved citizens who had filed petitions with the U.S. Treasury Department. The enrolled agent's focus shifted when the federal income tax was created in 1913.

✦ Can I talk to one of your audited clients?

✦ How much do you charge?

✦ Will you provide me with an organizer to help sort my financial records?

You should also assess whether a tax preparer is a daredevil. A survey from Indiana University suggests that taxpayers are in no mood to make big gambles on their returns. Those questioned said they would be willing to try for a deduction in a gray area if their preparers were 70 percent sure of their interpretation of the tax law. But the IRS permits tax preparers far more leeway than is allowed to individuals preparing their own returns. The tax preparer won't get in hot water as long as the deduction could realistically be upheld in an audit. What's realistic? The agency considers a position realistic if a tax expert could conclude that a controversial deduction had at least a 33 percent chance of being right. Of course, if your tax preparer is wrong, you're the one who pays any penalties and back taxes.

The study also uncovered a communications gap between the tax preparer and the client. Indiana University researchers asked tax preparers this question: Do your clients want you to be more aggressive? The tax preparers resoundingly answered yes. But when asked the same question, clients, particularly those using CPA firms, complained that their tax preparers were too aggressive.

Tip   To avoid problems, ask your tax preparer how certain he or she must be about a potential deduction before recommending it. Press your preparer to give a percentage figure.

Polishing your rotten apple radar

The tax preparation industry still resembles the Wild West. Only a handful of states regulate tax preparers. In many places, anybody can rent an office and declare himself a tax preparer. It's up to you to check out your tax preparer as thoroughly as possible. Unfortunately, playing Dick Tracy is much easier when you're checking out a broker or a certified financial planner because of the organizations that regulate such professions. If a tax preparer is dirty, it can be difficult to uncover. The following sections describe some potential sources of help.

Think Ahead

Avoid relying upon a seasonal tax preparer. Tax planning is a year-round activity, especially if you file an itemized return. Many important tax strategies that can reduce the pain on April 15 must be taken before December 31. If you can't talk to your preparer before the winter holidays end, you could pay an inflated tax bill.

Look for the Lightning Bolt

If you want to avoid becoming audit bait, consider sticking with a tax preparer who has permission from the IRS to file tax returns over the Internet. Such permission means that the IRS has closely scrutinized the tax preparer's qualifications. It makes sure that such tax preparers have filed their own taxes, and it checks with the regional IRS offices to eliminate problem tax preparers. In addition, some tax preparers must undergo fingerprinting, which is reviewed by the Federal Bureau of Investigation. Those tax preparers who pass the screen are allowed to use a yellow lightning bolt on their business cards, stationery, and advertisements.

Caution Rogue tax preparers are one of the prime reasons why unwitting taxpayers are audited. The local IRS directors know who the bad tax preparers are and are gunning for them.

IRS's Office of the Director of Practice

The IRS's Office of the Director of Practice can tell you if an enrolled agent, a CPA, or an attorney is eligible to represent taxpayers with the agency. It will also share whether the IRS has disciplined any of these practitioners. Keep in mind that although the IRS investigates consumer complaints about unethical tax preparers, the tiny investigative team is swamped with cases. Contact the office at (202) 694-1891 or through the general Web site at www.irs.gov.

American Institute of Certified Public Accountants

The American Institute of Certified Public Accountants (AICPA), which represents more than 330,000 CPAs, tries to police its own profession. Every year, disciplinary committees review hundreds of cases. The AICPA will tell you over the phone whether a CPA is a member (about 80 percent of CPAs belong) if you call (888) 777-7077. To obtain information about disciplinary actions, however, you must write the organization at this address: AICPA, Harborside Financial Center, Attn: Member Satisfaction, 201 Plaza 3, Jersey City, NJ 07311-3881.

State Accounting Boards

Each state is responsible for licensing and regulating accountants. Make sure an accountant is licensed by the appropriate state accounting board. Also, check with the state group to see whether any complaints have been filed against the accountant you're considering. How forthcoming the boards are varies from state to state. To obtain the phone number for your state board, visit the Web site of the National Association of State Boards of Accountancy at www.nasba.org.

Better Business Bureau

Check with your local Better Business Bureau, a state consumer affairs office, or other appropriate regulatory office to see whether it can provide any information on a particular tax preparer.

Summary

✦ Remain wary of sales pitches at retirement seminars, and don't feel obligated to sign on with the presenters just because the seminar is free of charge.

✦ Look for an estate-planning attorney who's admired by peers.

✦ Hire an elder law attorney who has earned extra credentials.

✦ Take the extra steps to find a well-qualified insurance expert.

✦ Decide whether you want your CPA to handle your investments.

✦ Consider using an enrolled agent for your tax needs.

✦   ✦   ✦

Instant Advice: Four Simple Shortcuts to Financial Success

Not every aspect of retirement planning is complicated enough to require a consultation with a professional. Begin getting your house in order with this chapter's four simple and sure-fire steps to improve your fiscal outlook. Taking these steps diminishes the time you need to spend brooding about your finances and can make you wealthier as well.

Shortcut No. 1: Take Cash Seriously

As people age, they instinctively look for the safest harbors to shield larger portions of their portfolios from risk. Younger investors need to squeeze the most out of their cash as well. Yet Americans' favorite place to park cash remains the traditional bank savings account, which pays next to nothing in interest. In fact, the interest rates for these accounts have been steadily deteriorating for more than a decade, from 5.17 percent in 1989 to 1.65 percent in 2000.

Clearly banks don't feel pressured to offer competitive rates, and customers pay dearly for their own complacency. If you are setting aside money for a rainy day, a house down payment, or another good cause, the worst thing you can do is take your cash for granted, especially when you can easily fatten the interest your cash is generating. As Table 7-1 illustrates, finding an investment that surpasses a passbook account yield by 2 or 3 percent can generate huge profits over time.

Table 7-1 Value of a $25,000 Investment		
Years to Invest	**Interest Rates**	**Value of Investment**
5	2%	$27,602
5	4%	$30,416
5	6%	$33,456
5	7%	$35,064
10	2%	$30,475
10	4%	$37,006
10	6%	$44,771
10	7%	$49,179
15	2%	$33,647
15	4%	$45,024
15	6%	$59,914
15	7%	$68,976
20	2%	$37,149
20	4%	$54,778
20	6%	$80,178
20	7%	$96,742

If you'd like to treat your cash more seriously and get higher returns, consider these three alternatives to a passbook savings account:

✦ Certificates of deposit

✦ Money markets

✦ U.S. Treasuries

Certificates of deposit

A CD promises a fixed rate of interest, and in return the investor agrees to keep the money locked inside one for 90 days, 1 year, 5 years, or some other fixed period.

Because the money is off limits for a while, you're compensated with a higher return than you'd expect with a regular bank savings account. But you sacrifice flexibility. The longer the cash is tied up, the higher the interest rate is. Investors who fear even an iota of risk love CDs because, unlike money markets, CDs are insured up to $100,000 per account by the Federal Deposit Insurance Corp. (FDIC).

Caution Prematurely withdrawing money from a CD triggers a stiff penalty. Many institutions deduct three to six months' worth of interest. Always make sure you are comfortable with the withdrawal penalty terms before investing in a CD.

Although buying a CD at your local bank is convenient, you may find a much better deal two or three time zones away. Luckily, when purchasing a CD, distance doesn't matter. A CD from St. Louis is the same as one from Memphis or San Diego.

Long-distance CDs

Shopping long distance might seem like a hassle, but the payoff can be worth it. You could capture a rate that is 1 or 2 percent higher than the average local CD. Tracking down the best rates is easy. In many Sunday newspapers, you'll find a list of the top-yielding CDs offered nationwide, along with each bank's toll-free number. On the Internet, you can find similar lists by visiting these sites:

- ✦ Bank Rate Monitor at `www.bankrate.com`
- ✦ iMoneyNet.com at `imoneynet.com`
- ✦ BanxQuote at `www.banxquote.com`

The newest wrinkle in long-distance CD shopping is CD auctions, which are expected to proliferate in the future. An Internet site operated by MaxRate.com (`www.maxrate.com`) acts as an intermediary between potential customers and dozens of banks. At the site, you type in the CD rate you'd desire and how much you plan to invest. In just seconds, you'll know if any participating banks are willing to bite.

Tip Unlike banks, MaxRate.com is open 24 hours a day and doesn't charge investors a fee for choosing a CD.

Don't ignore local institutions altogether. Smaller banks, even if they're offering fat yields, aren't always included in the national surveys. You also may want to try negotiating a higher yield with your neighborhood bank.

Brokered CDs

Another way to hunt for a generous CD is through a stockbroker. Brokerage firms search the country for the most tantalizing CD opportunities. These CDs often offer a slightly better interest rate than conventional ones.

Laddering CDs

No matter what type of CD you buy, you face the risk that interest rates will climb later on. You'll feel miserable if you're holding an old CD paying 5.5 percent while new customers are snatching up CDs offering 7 percent. You can address this problem by *laddering* your CDs. You do this by purchasing CDs with differing maturities. If interest rates are rising, you take the money out of a CD that has just matured, which means it's reached its full term, and put it into a CD that reflects the higher interest rate. You can use the same strategy when buying U.S. Treasuries.

A brokered CD also provides versatility that the others don't. If you want to bail, a broker can sell your CD without triggering an early withdrawal penalty. How is this possible? If you buy a CD from a broker, say Merrill Lynch, the broker holds the CD in its own name though the money belongs to you. If Merrill Lynch sells the CD to someone else, then you won't be liable for the early withdrawal penalty because technically the money was never in your name.

Because these CDs can be traded, they act more like bonds. The value of the CD, in other words, can change. If interest rates are falling when you sell a CD, you may make a profit. You could lose money if you let the CD go during escalating interest rates. The fluctuations of a brokered CD won't matter if you plan to hold on to it until its maturity.

Tip   A broker shouldn't charge you a commission for purchasing a CD on your behalf. Rather, the firm makes money through the difference between what you pay for the CD and what the bank sells it for.

Money markets: the cash magnet

The biggest threat to the sleepy savings account is the money market. Since the first one was unveiled in 1972, the money market has become the darling of Americans who are disenchanted with savings account returns. Money markets have grown so popular that the cash flowing into them sometimes eclipses the dollars gushing into stock mutual funds.

Money market accounts, which can be opened at any brokerage house and most mutual fund firms, enjoy several advantages over traditional CDs:

✦ They often generate a higher yield.

✦ They offer tax-free and taxable versions.

✦ They're more convenient.

✦ Withdrawals don't trigger penalties.

✦ You can write checks with a money market account.

Note Some banks offer money market accounts, but tend to offer lower rates than do brokerages and mutual fund firms.

Despite the name, a money market is a mutual fund that invests in ultra short-term securities. A money market differs from other mutual funds in a significant way: The value of a single money market share is always $1. You make money on the dividends that these shares spin off. This amount is referred to as the *yield.* In contrast, shares in other mutual funds can vary dramatically depending upon what's happening in the stock and bond markets.

Some folks remain leery of money markets because they aren't federally insured. That $1 share price could theoretically dip to 99 cents or much lower. There have been a few harrowing close calls in recent years that forced fund sponsors to financially prop up their money markets. So far, however, not a single individual shareholder has ever lost a dollar.

Shopping for a money market

With hundreds of money markets in existence, how do you find the best one? Here's a hint: The funds bragging about the highest yields typically charge little or no expenses. This is one of those rare times when the old adage of "You get what you pay for" doesn't apply. How does this happen? Chalk it up to marketing gimmicks. To lure customers to its array of other mutual funds, a fund sponsor will roll out a money market that temporarily charges a laughably low fee or none at all. To achieve this lower rate, the fund *subsidizes* its cash accounts by eating the expenses during the promotional period to keep the costs artificially low.

Calming the Jitters

Some people shun money markets because they lack FDIC insurance. If you're one of them, a little-known development in the industry may reassure you. Some mutual fund companies, including Fidelity, Federated, Massachusetts Financial Services, Putnam, and Vanguard, have bought private insurance to protect their money market assets.

Fund companies, which worry that investors might confuse this insurance with FDIC coverage, don't advertise this added layer of protection, and chances are you won't see it mentioned in a fund's literature. However, industry observers predict that the coverage will become standard for money markets in the next few years.

In the meantime, anyone concerned about risk can select a money market that invests exclusively in ultra-safe U.S. Treasuries. As an added bonus, you receive a state tax break on the income. Meanwhile, risk-averse investors may want to avoid smaller money markets and stick with the big-name players. Chances are if money markets begin hemorrhaging during a catastrophic market meltdown, the nation's largest fund families, as well as the major brokerage houses, wouldn't dare jeopardize their reputations by passing losses on to shareholders.

What's the Difference?

Some might argue that comparing money market funds is like choosing between two cartons of vanilla ice cream. Admittedly, you won't see huge differences in yields.

The reason for this lack of difference is that the Securities and Exchange Commission, wishing to preserve money markets as safe havens, keeps a tight rein on what can go into one. For example, a fund can contain only investments with maturities of less than 13 months. What's more, the average maturity of a fund's holdings cannot exceed 90 days.

Although a free lunch is still unusual in money market circles, a free dessert is not. According to one industry survey, almost 6 out of every 10 money markets waive a portion of their fees. You should snub money markets that charge as a standard rate more than the average .83 percent in annual expenses, which breaks down to a yearly charge of $8.30 for every $1,000 you invest.

Tip　To pinpoint the highest-yielding money market funds, visit iMoneyNet.com's Web site (www.imoneynet.com). You can also check money market performance by looking in many local newspapers, as well as *The Wall Street Journal* and *Barron's.*

Few people have the stamina to locate the best bargain-basement money market and then abandon it when the promotional period is over and the standard, higher fees kick in. An excellent alternative is to simply stick your cash in a Vanguard money market and forget about it. Vanguard never subsidizes its cash accounts, yet they consistently rank among the cheapest and best-performing money markets.

Features to ask about

When shopping for a money market, you don't necessarily want to focus exclusively on yield. Active investors might want to sacrifice a bit of yield for convenience. You may, for example, want to write unlimited checks with your money market account, and you don't want to be shackled by minimum check requirements. Some money markets require that checks be written for at least $500.

You might also prefer a money market linked to your mutual funds or brokerage account so that dividends or the sale of an investment can be swept into it. A money market linked in this way enables you to move in and out of stocks, bonds, or cash with a quick phone call or a click of a mouse.

Money markets are increasingly positioning themselves to behave more like checking accounts. Charles Schwab, Fidelity Investments, T. Rowe Price, and the full-service brokerage houses, such as Merrill Lynch, offer cash management accounts that include unlimited check writing, daily sweeps of earnings into the account, and the use of a debit card. Some investors no longer use a bank at all. They directly deposit their paychecks into these cash management accounts.

Caution   You pay a price for bells and whistles. A money market's yield will suffer if the money market is loaded with fancy features.

If you're a refugee from the bank deposit ranks and desire only a more profitable place to park your cash, then searching for a no-frills money market makes the most sense. Keep in mind that capturing the plumpest yield is going to be more lucrative if you have at least $20,000 to $50,000 to invest. With any less than that, a slight edge on yield won't necessarily amount to much.

Money market math: taxable or not?

You must decide whether to invest in a taxable or a tax-free money market. Some investors instinctively choose the tax-free version just because they hate taxes. But that decision can be shortsighted. The best decision hinges upon your tax bracket.

Tip   If you're in the 28 percent bracket or higher, it'll pay to explore whether the taxable or tax-free money market provides the best deal.

Tax-free funds offer skimpier yields, but the income is exempt from federal and sometimes state taxes. The higher your tax bracket, the more significant the tax advantage can be. Tax-free money markets invest in short-term obligations of municipal and state authorities. Individuals in certain states can avoid state taxes as well by investing in money markets that limit the investments within taxpayers' own state borders. These funds are available to investors in such states as California, New York, Michigan, New Jersey, Pennsylvania, Ohio, and Virginia.

To determine which variety of money market is better for you, you need to plug numbers into this math formula:

   Taxable equivalent yield = tax-free yield / (1 – federal income tax rate)

Suppose you're in the 36 percent tax bracket and are trying to decide which is a better deal: a tax-free money market yielding 3 percent or a taxable one offering 5 percent. Use the formula to compare the two money markets:

1. Subtract .36 (the tax bracket rate) from 1 to reach the figure .64.

2. Divide the tax-free yield of .03 by .64 to reach the figure .0468, or 4.68 percent, which is the taxable equivalent yield.

3. Compare the taxable equivalent yield (4.68 percent in this example) with the yield on the taxable money market. In this example, the taxable money market is the better choice at a full 5 percent yield.

Short-Term Bond Funds

"Forget money markets. Stick with a short-term bond fund. You'll be happy you did." That's a line you'll hear from stockbrokers, who may try to steer your cash into a short-term bond fund. The brokers have a point, but they may tell you only half the story.

Short-term bond funds can outperform money markets, but that ability sometimes comes at a steep price. The bond funds that full-service brokers recommend typically carry a sales charge or load. Because the historic returns for short-term bond funds are modest, being hit with a load could wipe out most or all of your gains.

Suppose that you deposit $50,000 into a short-term bond fund that charges a 3 percent load. At the start, your investment shrinks to $48,500 due to the load. To avoid this kind of financial pain, stick with no-load funds. Also snub any fund that charges above-average expenses. According to Lipper Inc., the average expense ratio for short-term bond funds was recently .94 percent. That means yearly expenses on a $10,000 investment would be $94. Expense ratios currently range from a low of .2 percent to an outrageous 3.5 percent. Stick with an inexpensive fund.

Short-term bond funds also are riskier than money markets. The prices of the individual bonds within a fund fluctuate depending upon interest rate movements. You could lose principal if interest rates spiked.

U.S. Treasuries

U.S. Treasuries are arguably the safest investments on the planet. Backed by the federal government, the nation's capitol would have to crumble under an enemy invasion before it failed to honor its Treasury obligations.

Treasuries are bonds that come with varying lengths of maturity (see Chapter 17 for details):

✦ Treasury bill (T-bill): 13 or 26 weeks

✦ Treasury note: 2 to 10 years

✦ Treasury bond: 10 to 30 years

As with any fixed-income investment, the longer the maturity, the greater chance for volatility. Treasury bonds usually offer the fattest yields; you are rewarded for assuming more risk. The value of your Treasuries can zig and zag, but this fluctuation doesn't matter if you're a buy-and-hold investor.

T-bills and Treasury notes are the only appropriate Treasuries for money you might need in five years or less. Ultra-conservative investors may feel most comfortable investing in T-bills. A T-bill's life span can be as short as 13 weeks.

Treasury notes and bills typically provide a better yield than CDs, and they offer greater liquidity. If you need to sell your Treasuries before maturity, there will be plenty of buyers. Another benefit: You can buy any Treasury for as little as $1,000. All Treasury purchases must be in increments of $1,000.

Tip   Treasuries especially reward those investors who live in a high-tax state such as California or New York with a tax break. You'll pay federal taxes on the interest a Treasury generates, but no state taxes.

One of the nicest features about Treasuries is that you can purchase them directly. There's no financial incentive to use a bank or a broker who will tack on a sales charge. The government handles transactions for free. The U.S. Treasury has tried to make the process as seamless as possible. To obtain the initial paperwork for the Treasury Direct program, call your nearest Federal Reserve Bank branch. You can also download an application from the Treasury Department's Web site at www.publicdebt.treas.gov.

Shortcut No. 2: Consolidate Your Holdings

Few people enjoy the administrative end of investing, but it can be hard to avoid. If you have a brokerage account or two, some mutual fund accounts, plus 401(k) statements and stock options to watch, and perhaps some CDs marching toward maturity, the flurry of paperwork can commandeer a filing cabinet.

This influx of paperwork represents more than a housekeeping headache. With assets scattered among various financial institutions, pinpointing your net worth can be impossible without a time-consuming scavenger hunt. Developing a rational financial strategy under such circumstances is also difficult.

Supermarket brokerages

Many brokerage firms and mutual fund firms can minimize the hassles of multiple accounts through their mutual fund supermarkets. This approach enables investors to find just about any fund they could possibly covet in one place. If you want to buy shares in Janus Enterprise Fund in Denver, American Century Ultra in Kansas City, Strong Growth & Income Fund in Menomonee Falls, Wisconsin, or thousands of other funds, you can do so with just one phone call to a brokerage firm. Once purchased, all these funds are tucked into a single brokerage account, where all transactions and tax information are listed in a single convenient statement.

Fund-shopping networks make selling shares just as easy. With one phone call or a visit to a brokerage firm's Web site, an investor can abandon one fund and jump into the next effortlessly.

Note   Within a supermarket account, fund swapping can be completed within a day or two, and there's no paperwork to fill out.

Here's how the old, plodding system of fund swapping used to work and still does for millions of Americans: You contact your fund family and instruct it to sell all or some of your shares. If you want your money fast, you'll pay a fee to have the cash wired into your bank account. For everybody else, the process moves to the turtle track. Eventually, your redemption check arrives in the mail. After you receive the cash, you have to write a check to the new fund company and wait for confirmation by mail that the money arrived at its destination. The process also drags on if you shift money out of an Individual Retirement Account and into another one. Suppose you'd prefer to have your IRA money transferred directly from one fund family to another. (This happens to be the safest approach because you won't inadvertently trigger taxes.) You request a transfer form from your new fund company, fill it out, and mail it back. Once that's done, the transaction could take weeks.

In addition to speedier and easier transactions, supermarket accounts offer a convenient way to corral your other investments. After all, to take advantage of a brokerage firm's fund choices, you must sign up for a brokerage account. One of these accounts is the most logical place to also park your individual stock and bond holdings.

Note

A fund supermarket might not sound revolutionary in the year 2001, but it truly was in 1992 when Charles Schwab unveiled the first fund supermarket. Before then, Americans had to open up separate accounts with individual fund families. If someone owned shares in 10 funds, they may have had 10 accounts to track.

Most discount brokerage firms, including Charles Schwab, E*Trade, TD Waterhouse, CSFBdirect, and National Discount Brokers, operate their own supermarket programs. So do major no-load fund families, such as Fidelity, Vanguard, American Century, and T. Rowe Price. Once you've opened a brokerage account with one of these firms, you can typically choose from among thousands of mutual funds.

If your funds are currently scattered among various fund families, you can apply for a brokerage account and ask the firm for transfer forms. Once these forms are filled out, your new brokerage firm will make sure that the funds you hold elsewhere are moved to your new account.

The Hazards of Overindulging

The danger to using a financial supermarket is that investing may get too easy. With one call or 60 seconds at the computer, you can shift money from one fund to another or into individual stocks. The ability to trade so quickly without getting slowed down by licking a stamp can be hazardous for impetuous investors.

What's more, all this merging has a limit. Even if you'd love to keep all your money in one account, for most people that's an impossible dream. Why? Because you can't mix certain assets. Money you have stashed in an Individual Retirement Account, for instance, can't be mixed with money in a nonretirement account. And of course, money invested in a 401(k) plan at work can't be transferred to a brokerage account until you retire or quit.

Questions to ask before you pick a brokerage

If you want to take advantage of a fund supermarket, ask the brokerage firm the following questions before you sign up.

How many funds does the brokerage offer?

The numbers on this question are all over the board. Some brokerage firms offer a few hundred, but many institutions boast of several thousand or more choices. Recently, brokerage customers at National Discount Brokers and Ameritrade chose from more than 9,000 funds. If you're interested in particular funds, find out in advance whether the supermarket stocks them.

How many funds come without a transaction fee?

You don't want to pay extra for convenience, but you'll face a transaction fee when trading many funds at many of the supermarkets. A typical transaction fee is $25, but the charges do vary.

If you're wondering why you're hit with a fee for some funds and not others, the answer boils down to economics. Every brokerage firm expects to be compensated for peddling competitors' funds. When a fund family declines to pay, however, the money must come from you instead. You can't blame a fund company for not coughing up the cash. Vanguard, for instance, permits its funds to be sold through brokerage firms, but it won't pay for the privilege. If it did so, Vanguard would have to hike the yearly expenses that it passes on to every shareholder. Typically, a fund that doesn't carry a transaction fee has decided to make all its investors pay slightly higher yearly expenses to subsidize its availability in the supermarkets.

Tip

If you're interested in a fund that carries a transaction fee, it's best to make one big purchase. Otherwise, you'll be dinged with the extra cost every time you purchase shares, even in modest amounts.

Does the financial institution provide a helping hand?

Knowing that your brokerage firm offers thousands of fund choices can be intimidating. Excessive options make for difficult decisions just when you're striving to simplify your life by having fewer accounts. What you need is a helping hand. Some brokerage firms offer their shareholders regular publications listing performance statistics, yearly expenses, minimum purchase requirements, and other information for the funds on their menus. You may also find this type of information on their Web sites. Firms may recommend funds they particularly favor in such categories as large-cap growth stocks, small-cap value stocks, and foreign funds. Before establishing a brokerage account, find out if the firm offers similar guidance.

What's the minimum investment to open an account?

Each brokerage firm imposes its own requirements. You can open some accounts for as little as $500 or $1,000; others insist on a commitment of $2,000 to $5,000. Typically the minimum hurdles established for IRA accounts are lower than those set for taxable accounts. Many brokerage firms permit an IRA account to be opened for as little as $1,000 or $2,000.

Internet linking sites

Sure, it's nice to be able to lump all your investment holdings together in a brokerage account. But imagine pushing a button and having your bank and brokerage accounts, credit card balances, car loan status, your frequent flyer mile tally, and more all on one screen. This isn't a pie-in-the-sky wish: It's now possible to know precisely what your up-to-the-minute net worth is simply by using a personalized financial Web site. These sites lump all your assets and liabilities together onto one screen.

If you haven't heard about this phenomenon, you will soon. Although the pioneers of this idea were little-known Internet companies, financial heavyweights such as Citigroup, Merrill Lynch, and Chase Manhattan have recently launched their own services for financial couch potatoes or are on the verge of doing so.

All this consolidation can be incredibly convenient, but consumer advocates are petrified that all this personal information could end up in the wrong hands. The scary part of using these personalized sites is that you have to divulge the password to all your computerized accounts. With these passwords, the so-called screen scrapers can pull information from your far-flung accounts and dump all the numbers onto your computer screen. Although these Internet companies say they won't share the information, they're too new to have a proven track record of responsibility. You also need to worry about the behavior of the well-known banks and brokerage firms that are joining the competition. What you don't want is a brokerage firm, for instance, sharing your information with its own sales forces.

Caution

Even if you're not dismayed by the privacy issues, protect yourself as best you can. First, read the paperwork you're asked to approve. Know what a company can and can't do with your data. Also stick with a prominent financial institution rather than trust a fledgling Internet entrepreneur with your privacy.

Shortcut No. 3: Use Dollar-Cost Averaging

The principle of dollar-cost averaging is quite simple: You make a commitment to stash away a certain amount of money on a regular basis. The easiest way to accomplish this is by signing up for an automatic savings plan with a mutual fund, credit union, or some other financial institution. You decide how much money is taken out of a checking or savings account on a regular interval and deposited in a mutual fund or other investment.

Millions of people take advantage of dollar-cost averaging at their workplace. Every week, employees bring home paychecks with their 401(k) contributions already deducted. One reason why 401(k)s are so successful is because this way of investing is relatively painless. Because the money is sucked out before a worker can cash it, there's no temptation to spend the money on a pizza or a new pair of shoes.

The advantages of dollar-cost averaging

Dollar-cost averaging provides many additional investing advantages. Here are the main ones:

It buys time.

Suppose you're suddenly faced with the task of investing a large amount of money when you receive an inheritance or bonus, win the lottery (don't count on it), or retire with a hefty lump sum from your pension or other workplace retirement plan. Investing what may be the largest sum of money you've ever received at one time can pose a monumental challenge.

Someone who is skittish about the market's direction or unsure how to proceed can gradually invest this money into the financial markets over a period of months, years, or more.

It helps you buy stocks on sale.

Many investors are understandably squeamish about the stock and bond markets' volatility. Dollar-cost averaging can bolster your courage to hang tight when markets are getting pushed around like toy boats in a bathtub. If the markets are taking a nosedive, you'll hate your temporary paper losses, but you'll have a great consolation prize.

With your automatic investments, you'll be buying stocks or bonds when the prices are cheaper. Consequently, your money will stretch further.

It discourages market timing.

Many people wait on the sidelines for a calamitous market crash so they can jump in and invest. That sounds like a good strategy, but nobody owns a crystal ball that accurately predicts when the market will hit bottom. Consequently, many glum people sit on the sidelines for years as they wait for their big chance. With slow, steady investing, you don't have to time your purchases exactly.

The Case Against Dollar-Cost Averaging

Academics tend to scoff at dollar-cost averaging. Many studies have suggested that this strategy won't produce the highest returns if the alternative is one lump-sum investment. If you have the courage or the know-how to invest all at once, fine. If you're unsure where to direct the money or if you're tempted to place a bet on a hot stock or two, it's better to proceed slowly. When economists poke holes in dollar-cost averaging, they don't plug human nature into their equations.

It doesn't require discipline.

Sure you want to tuck away money for retirement, a child's college education, or maybe a vacation home in the mountains. Although your intentions are great, your resolve could be paper-thin. If you decide to stash away money when you have extra cash, you may never pocket the keys to that mountain chalet. Realistically, there are too many daily demands for that money. If the cash is automatically withdrawn from your checking account, however, meeting your savings goal is much more realistic.

It can get you into more exclusive mutual funds.

Dollar-cost averaging can solve a potentially big problem for some investing neophytes: saving up enough to get into a mutual fund. Many funds require a minimum investment of $2,000, $3,000, or more. But if you sign up for a fund's automatic investment plan, the minimum is sometimes waived. The monthly investment in a fund can be as little as $50.

Dollar-cost averaging and stocks

Dollar-cost averaging is an ideal way to invest in mutual funds, and it's gotten even easier. Not too long ago, you didn't have many options if you wanted to automatically deposit your money into a mutual fund at regular intervals. Many fund companies didn't allow you to pick what day you wanted the money moved. What's more, you were tied into investing on a monthly basis. Now you can often decide whether you want to invest biweekly, quarterly, or even yearly. You also pick the date to invest.

Investing in individual stocks with dollar-cost averaging is not as practical. If you purchase a tiny number of shares regularly, the commissions can gnaw at your returns. However, this cost is less of a concern now than it was when brokerage fees were prohibitively expensive. Today, some no-frills discounters charge just a few dollars to perform a trade.

For fans of dollar-cost averaging who want to avoid the constant drain of commissions, two potential solutions exist: dividend reinvestment plans (DRIPs) and direct stock plans (DSPs). A DRIP generally allows investors to buy stock shares directly from a sponsoring corporation, and to purchase shares through reinvested dividends. To participate, a person must buy the first share of stock through a broker. A DSP also allows investors to purchase shares directly from a corporation, but there is no need to obtain that initial share from a broker. Both DRIPs and DSPs allow the investor to either reinvest the dividends or pocket them.

Making the most of DRIPs and DSPs

Here's how a DSP works: If you want to invest regularly in Pfizer, for example, you can do so by sending the pharmaceutical giant an initial check of at least $500. After that, you can send Pfizer checks for as little as $50. At Home Depot, $250 will get you started, and checks later on can be for as little as $25. You can invest directly with hundreds of corporations by simply contacting the ones you like and filling out the paperwork. In some cases, you can enroll on the Internet.

Establishing a DRIP is just a little bit more trouble, since you'll need that first share of stock to get started. You can obtain a single share for certain companies either from a broker or through the National Association of Investors Corp., the nation-wide investment club organization (see Chapter 13). You have to join the nonprofit group to be eligible. For more information, contact the National Association of Investors Corp., P.O. Box 220, Royal Oak, Michigan 48068. You can also call NAIC at (248) 583-NAIC or visit its Web site at www.better-investing.org.

The vast majority of companies that participate in these plans are well established and widely known in their regions or nationally (see Table 7-2 for some of the bigger names). Unfortunately, you won't be able to invest in a wide range of technology or small-cap stocks using this method.

Table 7-2
Sample of Corporations Offering Direct Stock Plans

Aetna	IBM	American Express
Pfizer	Home Depot	Lehman Brothers
Enron	Wal-Mart	Mellon Bank
General Electric	SBC Communications	Intimate Brands
Lucent Technologies	Compaq Computer	Tandy
BellSouth	Motorola	Sears, Roebuck
Nokia	McGraw-Hill	Walgreen

Source: NetStock Direct (www.netstockdirect.com)

Note   Before you sign up, find out what expenses, if any, a corporation will pass along. Some corporations charge several dollars for each stock transaction. In this case, if you are buying small amounts, this method won't make economic sense.

Resources for Buying Direct

Want to learn more about stock investing without a broker? Log onto DRIP Central (www.dripcentral.com), a clearinghouse of DRIP information. Another source is NetStock Direct (www.netstockdirect.com), which operates a search engine for corporate investment plans. You can hunt for stock plans by industry and examine the details of an individual corporation's stock purchase plans.

For those not plugged into the Internet, entire books have been devoted to the subject. Two prominent ones are authored by Charles Carlson: *Buying Stocks Without a Broker* (McGraw-Hill, 1995) and *No-Load Stocks: How to Buy Your First Share and Every Share Directly From the Company With No Broker's Fee* (McGraw-Hill, 1996).

Shortcut No. 4: Keep Your Paperwork Safe

If something ever happened to you, would your family know where to track down your investment holdings? What about your estate-planning documents and other critically important papers? Having one place for all your important papers is only one of the solid reasons why it makes sense to rent a safety-deposit box.

Safety-deposit boxes have been around since the Egyptian pharaohs, and it's easy to appreciate why. A safety-deposit box is a cheap way to store a family's most important papers and possessions for just pennies a day.

Box rental rates vary from bank to bank, as well as region to region. The size of the box is also a factor in the cost. The smallest boxes are five inches by two inches and two feet deep. The larger boxes can be four feet square. The average yearly charge for the popular three-inch by five-inch box is $30.

Tip   You may be able to negotiate an even better deal on a safety-deposit box if you're a bank's valued customer. According to the American Bankers Association, most banks offer a discount to valued customers, and some waive rental fees entirely.

Safety-deposit box contents

Among the items that people should keep in these boxes are papers documenting the important legal and financial events in a family's lifetime, as well as special treasures that have been acquired. Items in a safety-deposit box could include the following:

✦ Stock and bond certificates

✦ Inventory of all financial holdings

✦ Estate-planning documents

✦ Birth and marriage certificates

✦ Adoption papers

✦ Military service records

✦ Citizenship papers

✦ Business agreements

✦ Titles to home and cars

✦ Divorce decrees

✦ Pension documents

✦ Death certificates

✦ Appraisals and video for art, jewelry, antiques, and other valuables

✦ Jewelry

✦ Coin and stamp collections

Antique Stock Certificates

You never know what you may find in a person's safety-deposit box. Plenty of heirs discover old stock certificates inside. In some cases, the company issuing the certificates went broke or was swallowed up by a competitor.

Determining whether these yellowed stock certificates are valuable, however, doesn't have to turn into a huge hassle. You can pay $75 to $100 to a search company such as R.M. Smythe & Co. in New York (call (212) 943-1880) to do the hunting. R.M. Smythe, which has been playing stock detective since 1880, can also determine whether the certificates have any value to collectors.

If you'd prefer to play sleuth, find a library that contains these two securities reference guides: *Financial Stock Guide Service,* which is published by Financial Information, Inc. in New Jersey, and *Robert D. Fisher Manual of Valuable and Worthless Securities.* The latter book was last published in 1926. Another resource is the secretary of state's office in the state where the company was incorporated.

Don't keep the only copy of your will and other estate documents in your safety-deposit box. A few states still seal the contents of the box upon a renter's death. If only one person rented the box, an heir will need a court order to examine the contents. If two persons rented the box, the survivor will, in most cases, have complete access to it after a death.

Caution

Think twice before placing cash inside a box. Many rental contracts forbid you to store currency in a safety-deposit box. If money were missing, it would be tough to argue that the bank was liable.

Safety-deposit box security

Don't assume that your rental fee buys you invincibility. The metal safety-deposit boxes aren't fireproof or waterproof. In the lingo of the banking industry, the containers are merely "resistant" to water and flames. Fires have destroyed or damaged valuables kept in boxes. During the massive Midwestern flooding in the mid-1990s, water seeped into many boxes and damaged contents. After that experience, banks started advising customers to place objects that could be ruined by water into resealable plastic bags.

Thieves are another potential threat to your safety-deposit box. To reduce the chances of problems, don't rent a box at a financial institution with careless safety procedures. Find out if the bank always checks customers' signature cards before escorting them to their boxes. Although this procedure is standard, some institutions are lax. Security lapses like these can result in a thief rifling through a box.

Properly insuring the contents

A lot of people assume that a bank is liable if a fire, flood, or clever crook penetrates its security system. It isn't. Banks don't insure the items sitting in a safety-deposit box, and FDIC insurance doesn't extend to valuables kept in these boxes.

Unfortunately, your homeowner's insurance policy might not be too helpful either. Typically these policies reimburse you for only up to $1,000 in loss or damage. To skirt this problem, you can obtain safety-deposit insurance as a rider on your homeowner policy. Insuring valuables this way can cost one-fourth to one-third the price you'd pay with regular homeowner coverage.

Caution   If you take valuables out of the bank for any period of time, you could endanger your safety-deposit rider.

What if you want to wear your grandmother's diamond necklace to your daughter's wedding? Some insurance companies allow people to switch between regular homeowner's and safety-deposit coverage. Tell your insurance agent when you intend to take jewelry or other valuables out of the bank. For that period of time, you'll be charged the higher insurance rate.

Some banks are experimenting with purchasing private insurance up to $10,000 of coverage per box for their safety-deposit customers. The cost to the customers for this protection is about $25 per year. Ask your bank if it's available.

Replacing a lost key

Ask your bank what would happen if you lose one of your two keys. Some banks simply cut a new one. This no-hassle policy sounds appealing, but the American Safe Deposit Association warns against it. Instead, choose a bank that will assign you a new box to provide extra protection. After all, if someone found your lost key and forged your signature, the crook could clean out your box.

Meanwhile, never let a bank employee hold your key for any length of time. In some cases, unscrupulous bank workers have secretly made an imprint of a customer's key by pressing it into paraffin wax that's concealed in their palms. And don't store your safety-deposit keys in an envelope with the box number, your name, and the name of the financial institution on it. That's just asking for trouble.

Summary

✦ Squeeze as much return as you can out of your cash by looking beyond passbook savings to CDs, money markets, and Treasuries.

✦ Know what you own: Consolidate your investments into a brokerage account.

✦ Try dollar-cost averaging for automatic-pilot investing.

✦ Don't overlook a safety-deposit box as an inexpensive way to keep all your crucial documents in one place.

✦   ✦   ✦

Vehicles to Get You There Safely

In Part III, you'll learn to squeeze the most mileage out of America's two vastly popular retirement plans—the 401(k) and the Individual Retirement Account. Not to be left out is a chapter devoted to the retirement plans of teachers, civil servants, and those who work in the nonprofit field. This section also reveals the secrets of keeping an IRA alive long after its first owner has died.

Managing Your 401(k) Like a Pro

In this chapter, you'll learn ways to squeeze the most out of your 401(k). Maximizing your 401(k) is more than a goal; it's a necessity. Getting the most out of your 401(k) is more important than ever before. In the old days, employers provided for workers' retirement years through pension plans. But fewer corporations now offer pension programs; they have substituted 401(k) plans instead. It's harder for workers to stash away as much in their 401(k) accounts as pensions would have provided them.

Do you ever wonder if your 401(k) is on the right track? Unfortunately, 401(k) strategies aren't scored like Olympic events; there's no panel of judges holding up placards that rate financial prowess. Most people are on their own. Some enjoy tremendous success balancing their 401(k) choices, and others somehow muddle through with mediocre results.

Cross-Reference Equally important to investing well is withdrawing wisely. See Chapter 21 for withdrawal strategies upon retirement.

Your decisions about investing and using your 401(k) money can make all the difference to your retirement years, but you need to play it smart. The best way to proceed is to know how the 401(k) works, what risks are involved, and what your options are. Then you can take control.

Heads Up: What Your 401(k) Can't Do

No matter how delighted Americans are with their 401(k) plans, replacing a pension with a 401(k) isn't always an even trade. Many workers would have been better off with a regular pension. The fact is that what a pension pays is typically superior to what you can accumulate within a 401(k). With a pension, you receive a lifetime guarantee of monthly checks. With a 401(k), you get a pile of money at retirement that you must then invest so it becomes as valuable as a pension, and pulling this off will be tricky for many workers. (See Chapter 20 for your best investing strategies.)

The cruelest difference between pensions and 401(k) plans is this: Pension systems covered most workers. It didn't matter if you were the chief financial officer or the guy who refilled the paper towels in the restroom, most people on the payroll received some sort of pension. That's not so with 401(k)s.

Caution   Poorly paid employees don't participate as much in 401(k)s, yet these workers are the ones who most desperately need a retirement cushion. If an employee doesn't contribute to a 401(k), the boss won't kick in a dime.

Other reasons exist why workers need to be more diligent. Some of the most influential people in the retirement field, including the consultant credited with creating the 401(k), are predicting that the 401(k) is on the verge of revolutionary change. In this new era, employers, who chafe at selecting investment choices for their workers, would no longer serve as 401(k) gatekeepers. Employees would be able to invest in just about anything they want to. Instead of a menu of eight or nine investment options that were picked by their companies, everyone would face thousands upon thousands of choices. While this freedom would be a welcome boon to many, it will overwhelm others.

Regardless of what the guy in the next cubicle does, you can make a difference, but you need to play it smart. The best way to proceed is to know what your 401(k) options are. Then take control.

401(k)s and Your Financial Health

By now, most of us understand that investing in a 401(k) is as healthy for us as eating broccoli. During the past decade, the value of the money we've stashed into 401(k) accounts skyrocketed roughly 500 percent. At the start of the new millennium, at least 31 million of us own one.

Yet some workers are still immune to the 401(k)'s charms, declining to even sign up for the 401(k); others have put their 401(k)s on starvation diets, contributing a mere pittance. Many 401(k) participants don't make the maximum contributions. If you are one of those workers who are still not sold on the power and glory of a 401(k), there are at least five reasons why you should be.

It's easy.

You simply instruct your employer to extract a certain percentage of your salary out of each paycheck. Saving this way is often less of a struggle because you never touch the money.

It's a fabulous tax shelter.

The 401(k) provides a wonderful way to stockpile a fortune while keeping the Internal Revenue Service at a safe distance. All the money deposited into a 401(k) avoids taxes up front because the money is automatically withdrawn before federal and state income taxes can be assessed.

Your 401(k)'s instant return is phenomenal.

Thanks to that immediate tax savings, your return is far superior to what the overall stock market can muster even during a spectacular year. Unconvinced? See for yourself how it can pencil out. Suppose you're in the 28 percent tax bracket. Every dollar you deposit into your 401(k) essentially costs you just 72 cents. That's because each dollar escapes a federal tax of 28 cents. (When you figure in any state taxes, your cost is even cheaper.) If you contribute $5,000 in your 401(k) one year, your investment is really just $3,600.

You pocket free money.

To encourage participation in 401(k) plans, about 97 percent of companies, by one estimate, provide a match for their employees' contributions. Suppose your employer kicks in 50 cents for every dollar you deposit. Your initial investment of just 72 cents in the previous example, blossoms to $1.50. That's an instant return of more than 100 percent.

The 401(k) tax break keeps on ticking.

Your 401(k) may mushroom to five or six figures or more over the years, but the IRS still can't touch it. Only when you withdraw the money do you pay taxes.

401(k) Contribution Strategies

Obviously, the more you sock away in a 401(k), the better off you'll be in retirement. Although the maximum annual contribution set by the feds in 2001 was $10,500, the ceiling can change yearly. However, most people can't set aside that much even if they could afford it because companies set their own limits on the maximum percentage that an employee can contribute annually. For example, an engineer making $65,000 with a company-imposed 10 percent cap on contributions could kick in a maximum of $6,500 a year.

In an ideal world, anyone with a 401(k) should stuff as much money as is legally permitted into it. Unfortunately, that's not always possible in a world that's also cluttered with SUV payments, broken dishwashers, and leaky roofs. If you can't fully fund your 401(k), you'll need to put your money where it gets the best mileage. Ultimately, you'll have to decide whether to sink all your retirement money into your 401(k) or divert some of it into an IRA.

Tip   Your best bet is to feed your 401(k) enough to at least guarantee a full company match.

When you are deciding how much to contribute to your 401(k), keep in mind that one of the main benefits of a 401(k) is the company matching funds. However, you must contribute a certain amount to the 401(k) in order to qualify for the maximum matching amount. The most common arrangement is a 50 percent match on the first 6 percent you kick in. For that engineer earning $65,000 a year, a 6 percent contribution would equal $3,900. In this scenario, the company contribution would be $1,950. That's free money, so you don't want to walk from it.

Ideally, you can also contribute an annual $2,000 into a Roth IRA after securing your 401(k) match. If you can kick in more money after funding a Roth, put the remaining money into your 401(k).

Cross-Reference   See Chapter 10 for more information on Roth IRAs.

With a Roth IRA, you won't be entitled to claim a tax deduction for your contribution, but the Roth compensates for that niggling drawback by bestowing a lifetime of tax-free investing. All the money percolating in your Roth won't get hit with taxes when you start draining the proceeds during retirement. In comparison, when you eventually tap into your 401(k), you'll have to pay taxes based on your tax rate.

Not everyone is eligible for a Roth. You are shut out from making even a partial contribution if your adjusted gross annual income exceeds $160,000 if you're filing a joint return or $110,000 as a single taxpayer. Someone who is ineligible for a Roth can contribute $2,000 a year instead to a nondeductible IRA, which even welcomes billionaires. This IRA doesn't provide a tax deduction either, but like a Roth investment, the money grows tax-free as long as it's kept in the account. Unlike a Roth, you will owe taxes when you withdraw the money from the nondeductible IRA.

Note   You shouldn't consider funding a nondeductible IRA until you max out your 401(k) contributions.

If you're a savings dynamo, you may still be raring to save after funding your 401(k) and an IRA. What's next? Unfortunately, most people have to stash other retirement savings into taxable accounts. Consequently, you want to carefully choose investments that don't inflict excruciating tax pain. Individual stocks, index funds, and the newer exchange-traded funds are three good candidates. (See Chapters 13 and 15 for details on individual stocks and these funds.)

The Six Worst 401(k) Mistakes

Everybody knows what they should do to live longer: Skip greasy double cheese-burgers, stop smoking, and take the stairs instead of the elevator. If you're just as conscientious with your retirement money, your 401(k) can outlast you. But to pull that off, you have to sidestep mistakes. Even if you're contributing to a 403(b), a 457 plan, or a small-business retirement plan (all of which are covered in Chapter 9), some of the same errors can trip you up. This section explains the biggest no-no's concerning 401(k)s.

Mistake no. 1: Failing to diversify

With the 24-hour access available to many 401(k)s, it's now incredibly easy to push money around as if were in a shopping cart. When blue chips are hot, investors stampede into these stalwarts. When technology is smoking, everyone wants to own a fund that contains Cisco Systems, Oracle, and JDS Uniphase. Avoid the temptation. Trying to outsmart the market is futile. *Forbes* magazine's annual list of America's wealthiest people never includes market timers.

Chasing the latest hot stock distracts you from the more mundane task of determining whether your 401(k) asset allocation is appropriate for your age and tolerance for risk. Even the best-intentioned investors often fail to choose the best combination of assets for their situation. Why? People tend to evenly spread their money among the available 401(k) funds. If a workplace offers three bond funds and two stock funds, the ratio of bond and stock assets in the typical employee's portfolio is three to two. This is the wrong way to divvy up your money. The younger you are, the more likely you should be invested heavily in stocks. And older investors will want bonds to play a bigger role in their 401(k) portfolio.

Mistake no. 2: Loading up on company stock

People love to grumble about their jobs, but as investors, they are amazingly loyal to their companies. In fact, they're too loyal. Employees up and down the corporate food chain invest too much cash in their own companies' stock.

Although loyalty is admirable, pinning your career and your retirement dreams on one stock is not wise. Suppose you work for a company that becomes obsolete thanks to a competitor that sells more innovative products faster and cheaper. The fortunes of your company disintegrates, the stock tanks, and you get a layoff notice through interoffice mail. Obviously, linking your career with your financial future carries its own hazards.

Many people who toil at America's best-known companies apparently believe they are immune to this sort of calamity. According to a survey conducted by *Pension & Investments,* a prominent trade publication, workplace retirement accounts at many blue chips are bursting with in-house stock. Employees at Procter & Gamble, the maker of Ivory soap, Crest toothpaste, and Pampers, have sunk nearly 96 percent of their defined contribution money into company stock. The employees who dreamed up Viagra for Pfizer have 88 percent in company stock, and the workers at General Electric, which makes everything from light bulbs to locomotives, have earmarked 73 percent of their 401(k) assets to GE stock.

Caution

A 401(k) crammed with in-house stock can't possibly be diversified, which makes it vulnerable to wild swings.

The potential danger of this strategy is evident when you consider this fact: On a single day in the spring of 2000, for instance, Procter & Gamble's stock plummeted 31 percent. If you work for a brand-name company that's been in business a long time, you might dismiss the P&G fiasco as a fluke. Don't. Plenty of well-known companies become trapped in extended periods of dreadful stock performance. Employees of Kmart, Toys R Us, Dole Foods, J.C. Penney, and Hilton Hotels understand this. While investors were celebrating larger-than-life stock gains during the 1990s, these stocks stunk. For the entire decade, the annual return for Toys R Us' stock was a negative 5 percent. The others in this sorry fraternity did only slightly better.

Corporations often remain mum about their workers' misplaced loyalty. After all, when employees own a large amount of stock, a hostile corporate takeover is less likely. Executives also assume that workers are more motivated when their fortunes are intertwined with the company's stock price.

Note

What's ironic is that a corporation would never paralyze its own retirement investments with a heavy dose of in-house stock. Such an act would be so foolhardy that the federal government forbids it. A corporate pension plan can only invest 10 percent of its assets in its own company stock.

Although avoiding or severely limiting company stock in your 401(k) and other investment portfolios is the best strategy, it's often not easy to do. Almost half of the nation's corporations offer in-house stock as a 401(k) option, and most of them match their employees' contributions with, you guessed it, company shares.

Some corporations do allow workers to sell their stock and shift the money to other 401(k) options. If you don't enjoy this flexibility, you should at least avoid putting any of your own dollars into company stock.

Tip

Another way to reduce your dependence on your employer's stock is to avoid investing in mutual funds that own a chunk of your company or other stocks in your industry.

Mistake no. 3: Failing to double-check

How often have you counted the dollar bills a store clerk hands you before slipping them into your wallet? No doubt, you've done it a lot. But how frequently have you checked the accuracy of your 401(k)?

Many never bother because they assume their employers are honest. But honesty usually isn't an issue. Most often the errors spotted in retirement accounts can be traced back to unintentional mistakes. Paycheck contributions are inadvertently deposited into the wrong workers' accounts, and 401(k) investment choices are sometimes switched without anybody ever authorizing it. Consider this scenario: You think your contributions are being deposited into a stock fund within your 401(k), but when you examine your latest statement, the cash is loitering in a money market. This situation sometimes happens when a company changes its 401(k) investment menu or when a worker fails to fill out key paperwork. You can also make mistakes when you are tinkering with your investment mix by computer or with a telephone keypad.

> **Tip** Your best defense against 401(k) errors is good records. Don't toss your 401(k) documents.

After you receive a 401(k) statement, add up your pay stubs for the period to see how much you contributed to your account. See if that amount matches the statement.

While you're at it, double-check that you're getting the correct company match. Finally, review your investment options to make sure your money is making it into the correct pigeonholes.

Mistake no. 4: Borrowing from your 401(k)

Many people strenuously argue that tapping into a 401(k) is hardly a crime. It's certainly not in the same league, they insist, as getting a cash advance from a credit card that's charging 21 percent interest. With a 401(k) loan, after all, you're borrowing from your own account. Instead of a credit card company collecting the interest, your 401(k) account does.

> **Caution** Although less expensive than a credit card advance, most 401(k) loans are still usually a bad idea. Treating your retirement plan like a credit card can ultimately jeopardize your retirement.

About 92 percent of workplaces, according to one major survey, offer 401(k) loans. When obtaining a 401(k) loan, you typically borrow at 1 percent or so above prime rate, which is the rate banks charge their favored business clients. This rate might seem like a good deal, but what many 401(k) participants fail to consider is their lost opportunities. You may be paying 8 percent interest, for example, but at the same time, the stock fund that you emptied in your 401(k) could be faring much better. During the past 20 years, large-cap stocks have rewarded their owners with a return of close to 18 percent. A 401(k) loan can never flash numbers like that.

> **Note** When people are struggling to repay 401(k) loans, they often stop making contributions to their 401(k)s. Most loans need to be repaid within five years, which is a long time to ignore contributing to the retirement kitty.

Finally, a 401(k) loan can chain you to your cubicle. If you leave a company, whether you're laid off, fired, or depart for a better opportunity, the 401(k) loan must be paid in full. Usually, you're given just 30 to 90 days to come up with the cash. If you don't promptly settle the debt, the federal government will consider the outstanding amount a premature withdrawal. Then you'll owe federal and state taxes, and if you're under 59½, you could owe a 10 percent penalty as well. When you add up this liability, you could easily owe 40 percent or more in taxes and penalties on your loan balance.

Mistake no. 5: Fumbling the handoff

What happens to all the money you sacrificed so hard to save when you leave your job? Your employer will cut you a check, but what should you do with it? When the 401(k) phenomenon was still in its infancy, the financial stakes weren't high. The typical account balance was minuscule. But today, the average worker in his or her 60s now sits on a balance of $135,000.

The people who can least afford it are the most likely to cash in their windfalls. Yet even sophisticated investors who wouldn't dream of blowing their 401(k) loot make inadvertent mistakes. A person might assume, for instance, that he or she should roll over the entire 401(k) into an IRA. Although this strategy is usually the best, it might make more financial sense to sell the portion that is in company stock, pay the taxes, and put those proceeds into a taxable account.

 Cross-Reference Check out Chapter 20 for the best investment strategies to follow when you're ready to retire.

To navigate all the land mines, most people should seek professional help. But many don't, fearing sales pressure. This fear is understandable. It doesn't take much imagination to picture yourself in an office with a persuasive broker who is brimming with investment ideas, which may result in hefty commissions.

Tip When deciding how to best invest your 401(k) proceeds at retirement, you may fare better if you choose a fee-only certified financial planner for advice rather than a broker.

Mistake No. 6: Ignoring estate-planning options

If you want your children to inherit some or all of your 401(k) money, how you handle your windfall is critical. What's appealing about a 401(k) is its ability to grow without being encumbered by taxes. What parents wouldn't want to pass that great feature along to their kids? But if you cash out your 401(k) and pay the taxes on the money, that great gift of tax-deferred investing is lost forever. Heirs other than a spouse would also lose the tax protection if you fail to move your 401(k) assets when leaving your job.

What should you do? Consider rolling your 401(k) over into an IRA. If you do this, your children will inherit a tax-deferred IRA account that they can often keep alive for decades. What most people don't understand is that this great tax-dodging gift may vanish if they die with their money still sitting in their old 401(k). There's an exception for widows and widowers, who may roll the money over into an IRA. But for everybody else, the tax protection evaporates once your old employer disperses the money to the beneficiaries.

Note Also keep in mind that the 401(k) beneficiary for a married person must legally be the spouse. Even if you've designated children from a first marriage on your beneficiary form, these other beneficiaries will be valid only if the spouse signs a waiver relinquishing his or her rights to the account.

Challenging Conventional Investment Wisdom

Maybe you're already an A+ retirement saver. You max out your 401(k) contribution each year, feed your IRA regularly, and resist any temptation to raid your retirement nest egg. What else can you possibly do? Look closely at where you're stashing your money.

The traditional approach to tax shelters

Conventional wisdom suggests that you reserve the most tax-efficient investments, that is individual stocks and stock funds, for your taxable accounts. At the same time, you're supposed to corral the true tax hogs in your portfolio — individual taxable bonds and bond funds — into tax-deferred retirement accounts like a 401(k). Their sin is that they generate interest income, which is taxed at whatever your tax bracket is. If your tax bracket is 39.6 percent, the IRS will skim off 39.6 percent of your bond interest. In contrast, the tax hit for stock investors isn't as brutal. The maximum capital gains tax ceiling for stocks held more than a year is 20 percent. For persons in the lowest tax bracket, the capital gains rate is only 10 percent.

A new take on sheltering your returns

But financial experts at T. Rowe Price, the mutual fund family, and elsewhere suggest that long-term retirement investors should reexamine their strategy. The research shows that many mutual fund investors would be better off segregating stock funds in retirement accounts and bond funds in taxable accounts.

Using historical data from the 1970s through to the late 1990s, the study examined what would happen if $10,000 was invested in both a bond and a growth stock fund using this counterintuitive strategy. During a 20-year period, an investor in the 28 percent tax bracket would have netted $197,700 after taxes versus $184,500 using the traditional approach.

The investor fared better because the stock fund's appreciation dramatically overshadowed the income generated by the bond fund. Even though a stock fund enjoys a lower rate of taxation, its appreciation can be so much greater than a bond fund that the ultimate tax bite will in fact be bigger. Consequently, sheltering stock funds, with their potential for blockbuster returns, in tax-deferred accounts such as 401(k)s and IRAs can be the smarter strategy. In contrast, the bond funds, with more modest income distributions, could be best sequestered in taxable accounts.

Is the new approach for you?

In general, the higher your tax bracket in retirement and the shorter your investing time horizon, the more it makes sense to follow the conventional wisdom. In contrast, the lower your tax bracket and the longer your time horizon, the more it makes sense to try the nonconventional approach.

You may be wondering why people in the highest tax brackets (36 percent and 39.6 percent) might not want to follow this approach. The reason is that money eventually extracted from an IRA, a 401(k), or other retirement account is taxed at that stiffer individual tax rate rather than at the more favorable long-term capital gains rate of 20 percent or even 10 percent.

Example

When cashing out, a wealthy retiree in the 39.6 percent tax bracket who maintained a $500,000 stock fund in a retirement account would face a tax bite of $198,000. If someone in the same tax bracket kept that $500,000 stock fund in a taxable account, the capital gains tax bill of 20 percent would come to only $100,000.

This unconventional strategy of putting stock funds into tax-deferred accounts makes even more sense if you plan to put your stock fund in a Roth IRA. Unlike 401(k)s and other types of IRAs, the money that's pulled out of a Roth during retirement is not taxed. Consequently, it's best to put your most aggressive stock funds, the ones with the best potential to soar in value, in a Roth.

 Resource

If you're wondering if this approach makes sense for you personally, you can read a detailed analysis of the research on T. Rowe Price's Web site at www. troweprice.com. Click on the site's Tax Center.

The Gold Standard for 401(k)s

The concept of a 401(k) is wonderful, but that doesn't mean that dreadful plans don't exist. If you're wondering where your 401(k) fits in the spectrum, consider the following list a set of standards your 401(k) should ideally live up to. If your company flunks the test, remember that you don't necessarily have to tolerate a lousy plan. As 401(k) balances swell and employees begin to realize the importance of the plans to their futures, they've become increasingly vocal. They expect more from their 401(k) providers, and they are starting to get it (this topic is detailed in the next section).

High-quality fund selection

Employers vary widely in the quality of funds that they offer. At some companies, the 401(k) menu is a meager four or five selections. In contrast, other companies offer dozens of choices. You want a plan that at least provides all the building blocks necessary for a well-diversified portfolio.

At a minimum, you should find the following types of funds represented on the menu:

✦ Large-cap stock fund

✦ Small-cap stock fund

✦ International stock fund

✦ Bond fund

✦ Money market

Beyond these basics, a 401(k) provider should offer stock funds that feature value and growth strategies or a blend of the two. For instance, a plan may offer a large-cap mutual fund like Janus Olympus, which invests in large corporations. Two choices for small-cap or mid-cap funds would also be ideal, to provide exposure to smaller to medium-sized companies. In addition, the mix should include an index fund that tracks large-cap stocks or, even better, the entire stock market. A superior plan would also offer more than one fixed-income option; for example, it may provide a general-purpose bond that invests in corporate and government bonds, as well as a fund that specializes in high-yield corporate bonds.

Cross-Reference See Chapter 12 for a description of value and growth strategies, and definitions of small-, mid-, and large-cap stocks.

Some trailblazing companies may soon be offering employees the opportunity to invest in a nearly limitless selection of investments, while still maintaining a lineup of solid, pre-screened funds for those employees who are unnerved by the freedom to choose from so many options.

Generous employer match

Most companies provide a match. As mentioned earlier, the match is typically 50 cents for each dollar you invest up to 6 percent of your salary. The best plans provide a more generous match, and the matching funds are in hard currency. That is, the employer gives you a cash match rather than one in company stock. This way, you decide how this money is invested among your 401(k) options.

The best plans also permit you to immediately claim a company's match. Many workers, however, must wait three to seven years to qualify for a full match. Because of unfairly rigged rules, only a small fraction of workers at some companies are ever fully vested, meaning they can pocket their employer's entire match upon leaving the company. Individuals who are partially vested lose a percentage of their match when they quit. What's more, some companies kick in lower matches for those who are younger, have less seniority, or earn smaller paychecks.

Easy entry

Excellent plans permit 401(k) enrollment on a person's first day on the job. There's no logical reason why companies forbid new arrivals from participating until they've been on the payroll for six months or a year. By federal law, the maximum waiting period can be no more than 12 months. To remain competitive, some workplaces are now shrinking the wait to 90 days or less. A huge loophole though permits corporations to exclude part-timers from ever participating.

Tip If you're completely shut out of your company's 401(k) program or are waiting for eligibility, your best alternative is to contribute to a Roth IRA. Once that's maxed out, consider investing in a tax-efficient mutual fund, such as a stock index fund.

Low expenses

Maybe you're lucky enough to own a gold-plated 401(k) with investment choices galore, a 24-hour hotline at your disposal, and instant account updates — all that's missing is valet parking. But guess what? Somebody is paying for all these features, and chances are that somebody is you. High 401(k) fees are the financial industry's dirty little secret. Millions of 401(k) participants are being gouged each year. In contrast, the best 401(k) plans pass along minimal expenses.

Most of the people in your office probably assume that every dollar they sink into a 401(k) is invested in their fund choices. That's often untrue. A percentage of your 401(k) dollars is eaten up by administrative and investment management fees. Because 401(k) participants may foot the entire bill for these fees, human resources departments don't necessarily feel pressure to sign up the most cost-efficient 401(k) administrator.

Tip To quickly discover whether your 401(k) is gouging you, check the yearly or quarterly returns on the mutual funds in your 401(k) and compare those to the performance of the same funds listed in the newspaper. If funds in the paper enjoy a 1 percent or higher return than yours, then high fees are eroding your 401(k)'s performance.

What fee amount is reasonable? If fees are gobbling up more than 1.5 percent of your 401(k) assets, you're paying too much. Annual expenses that are 1 percent or 2 percent higher than that might not seem like a big deal. But over time, the difference can be devastating. As you can see in Table 8-1, a 401(k) with a 1 percent annual fee can handily beat a pricier one over time.

Table 8-1 Value of Annual $3,000 Contributions into Two 401(k)s		
401(k) Account	**Annual Expenses**	**Value 20 Years Later***
A	3%	$304,993
B	1%	$457,768

* Assumes 10% annual return

The two main fees to watch for are administrative fees and investment fees:

✦ Administrative fees pay for record-keeping, toll-free service lines, and account statements. In the best plans, employers pick up this tab. Nevertheless, the number of companies that make employees foot this bill has increased.

✦ Investment fees swallow the biggest chunk of money. This money compensates the managers who run the funds within your 401(k) and the plan administrator who selects and oversees the investment choices. These fees warrant close attention because employees usually foot this bill.

Resource

Learn more about 401(k) expenses by obtaining a free copy of *A Look at 401(k) Plan Fees for Employees,* which can be downloaded from the Pension and Welfare Benefits Administration Web site at www.dol.gov/dol/pwba or ordered by phone by calling (800) 998-7542.

Use of low-cost mutual funds substitutes

We all appreciate brand names whether its Jif peanut butter or Gillette razor blades It's no different with mutual funds. We naturally feel safer if we recognize well-known funds in our 401(k) from firms such as Fidelity, Janus, Putnam, Franklin, and AIM. But retail funds come with retail (that is, expensive) price tags. Smart employers now realize this fact. Even though it might seem hard to believe, shaving just a fraction of a percent off expenses can give your 401(k) portfolio a tremendous boost over time. Consider this: slicing a mere one-tenth of 1 percent off the $1.5 trillion invested in 401(k)s would annually save workers $150 million.

To reduce costs (as illustrated in Table 8-2), more workplaces are plowing 401(k) assets into these three alternatives:

✦ Institutional mutual funds

✦ Separately managed accounts

✦ Commingled trust funds

Institutional mutual funds

Institutional mutual funds are nearly clones of retail mutual funds. The difference is that the institutional funds are cheaper. Institutional funds are so named because they are reserved for huge customers, such as pension funds and endowments. Because these funds don't cater to individuals, they save considerably on marketing and other costs. Those savings translate into lower expenses.

Note   In 2001, $13 out of every $100 flowing into 401(k)s were expected to be heading into institutional funds.

Separately managed accounts

With separately managed accounts, major corporations essentially hire their own portfolio managers to invest the money. These private-label 401(k)s are an option only for America's biggest employers because the minimum investment required to obtain this personalized attention can be hundreds of millions of dollars.

This approach is not without risks for the employer or employees: Corporations can botch the job of picking private investment firms. They have to hire investment managers with excellent pedigrees, but this task isn't as easy as it may sound. Investment managers may hype the performance of certain portfolios while hiding the performance of wretched ones.

Commingled trust funds

Commingled trust funds, which are governed by bank trust laws, are cheaper than institutional funds. They are an alternative for a corporation that doesn't have hundreds of millions to invest, but would still like personalized money management. The manager of a commingled fund may oversee the 401(k) assets from three or four dozen companies.

Table 8-2 401(k) Expense Comparison			
Type of 401(k)	*Large-Cap Stock Funds*	*Small-Cap Stock Funds*	*Bond Funds*
Retail mutual funds	1.22%	1.49%	.88%
Institutional mutual funds	.83%	1.09%	.59%
Commingled trust funds	.63%	.87%	.46%
Separately managed account	.49%	.78%	.29%

Source: Cerulli Associates

Commingled funds and separately managed accounts present other challenges. Unlike retail mutual funds, you can't look up their performance statistics in a newspaper. But employers are addressing that drawback by making daily returns available by phone or through intranet sites.

Getting the 401(k) That You Deserve

If your 401(k) flunks the gold-standard test, you can do more than brood. Try persuading your company to change its ways. Impossible? Hardly. Corporate 401(k)s evolve more than you might realize. A survey by the Investment Company Institute, the mutual fund industry trade group, revealed that 1 out of 10 companies expected to hire a different investment manager within the next year. One out of every five companies surveyed said it would be adding new investment choices.

Much of the time, companies tinker with their plans in a vacuum. They don't hear from employees, who mistakenly assume the folks in the human resources department know how to assemble a crackerjack 401(k) plan. Yet the human resources department may choose an investment provider simply because the arrangement seemed cheap or the decision makers were hooked by an impressive sales presentation.

If you're willing to lobby for a better 401(k), this section tells you how to forge ahead.

Solicit moral support.

You'll enjoy more credibility by enlisting other disillusioned souls in the office. Explore what irks your colleagues about the current plan and discuss how they'd like to see it improved. As always, strength is in numbers

Find the right place to lodge your complaints.

Contact your company's benefits director and arrange a meeting to discuss concerns. Before the meeting, send the director a letter that outlines why you feel the 401(k) plan is inadequate and what steps you'd like taken.

Be constructive.

Don't just complain that the company's fund choices stink. Instead, use performance benchmarks such as the Standard & Poor's 500, the Russell 2000, and other appropriate indexes to illustrate how the company's funds have perennially lagged behind the market.

Don't give up.

If your reasoned approach falls flat, consider soliciting the aid of employee or union groups and volunteer for a seat on your company's benefits committee. Another option is to buttonhole a top executive. Remember that the company's top officers probably have more sunk into their 401(k)s than you do. They might be too preoccupied to realize how lousy their plan is. Finally, be patient. Don't get discouraged if change doesn't happen immediately.

Finding Unbiased 401(k) Investing Advice

For the first time in 401(k) history, you can easily get unbiased guidance about whether your investment choices will deliver you to the finish line. With very little effort, you can learn if your savings are on target and whether your mix of investments spells disaster or salvation.

For the most part, employers pick up the tab for these financial checkups, which are primarily delivered over the Internet. If your company isn't willing to pay, you can subscribe to some of these services for very little money. In some cases, the caliber of information you receive was previously available only to institutional investors and the very wealthiest people.

Why the sudden interest in 401(k) hand-holding? Corporations are starting to realize that employees need help with loads of difficult questions concerning nitty-gritty dilemmas like these:

✦ A 42-year-old has $60,000 in her 401(k) and $85,000 in a rollover IRA. The money is evenly divided between funds devoted to long-term bonds and large-cap stocks. If she continues to save 10 percent of her salary annually, what are the chances that she'll be able to withdraw $80,000 a year during retirement without seriously depleting her portfolio?

✦ A 56-year-old conservative investor wants to limit his exposure to the stock market. He knows, however, that he can't depend exclusively on bonds to get him to the finish line. Based on his 401(k) menu, what mix of stock, bond, and money market funds will keep his risks low but still provide some octane for his portfolio?

Answers to questions like these have always been impossible for employers to answer. Typically the extent of advice begins and ends with a 401(k) enrollment meeting in the company cafeteria. A company representative explains how to fill out forms, and everybody leaves with brochures generally devoid of anything too meaningful. If you were stumped by your 401(k) choices and struggling over whether to pick T. Rowe Price Science & Technology Fund or AXP New Dimensions Fund, that was your tough luck.

Note Companies have been historically skittish about fielding questions concerning specific investment decisions for legal reasons. Corporate attorneys still worry that some guy in the mailroom, complaining of lost money due to poor advice, will sue.

Companies today fret that keeping silent while their workers struggle with monumental 401(k) investing decisions will spawn lawsuits. The number of corporations cautiously tiptoeing into the advice business is increasing dramatically. But a company that manufactures radial tires or candy bars doesn't have the experience to serve as a financial coach. That's why there has been an explosion of online retirement advice services geared toward 401(k) participants.

Online advice

Some of these online advisory services are available only if your employer has signed up. But others, such as Financial Engines and Morningstar's Clear Future, provide advice directly to individuals. None of the online 401(k) advisors costs much. Typically, a company can annually provide the service for $20 to $60 per worker. If your company doesn't offer such a service, urge it to do so.

Here are some of the major online retirement advisory services:

✦ Financial Engines at `www.financialengines.com`

✦ 401(k) Forum at `www.401kforum.com`

✦ Standard & Poor's at `www.sp401k.com`

✦ DirectAdvice.com at `www.directadvice.com`

✦ Morningstar at `www.morningstar.com`

✦ Fidelity Investments at `www.fidelity.com`

✦ Vanguard Group at `www.vanguard.com`

These players have developed sophisticated Web-based software that's designed to be brutally frank about your investment choices. They may not only provide specific recommendations based upon your 401(k) portfolio, but also predict how your choices might perform in the years or decades ahead. Fancier software analyzes your specific retirement holdings and simulates how they'll perform in thousands of economic scenarios in the future.

The Internet front runner: Financial Engines

Arguably, the firm that has created the most buzz is Financial Engines. The I.Q. behind Financial Engines belongs to William F. Sharpe, the Nobel Prize laureate in economics and professor emeritus at Stanford University. Financial Engines essentially combines Sharpe's life work with advances in financial analytics and software technology. The result of all this high-tech firepower is an easy-to-use tool for an investor who may be wondering whether he has too much money riding on the Janus Twenty mutual fund and not enough on Harbor Bond Fund.

Within seconds, Financial Engines' software can estimate (with a percentage) your chances of having enough income to retire. For instance, the program might conclude that your portfolio of company stock, bonds, and large-cap stocks gives you a 79 percent chance of reaching your annual retirement income goal of $120,000. It also provides a worst- and best-case scenario of what your portfolio could be worth the day you cut your retirement cake. If the odds aren't so hot, the software won't strand you. You can tinker with several factors under your control, such as your projected retirement age, your yearly retirement contributions, and your risk tolerance.

The paper-and-pencil method

Even if you live in a computer-free zone, you can make some sense of what you have set aside for retirement in just one evening. First, jot down your long-term retirement holdings and how much each is worth on a legal pad. Don't include money that's set aside for a house payment, a car, or any other nonretirement use. Place these investments in categories: stocks, bonds, and cash. Then subdivide the stock and bond assets into subcategories, such as large-caps, small-caps, and foreign holdings. Once that's done, you need to figure out whether your equity investments fit into the value, growth, or blend niche.

Tip   If you aren't sure how to place your various assets in the right column, fund literature should clear up any confusion. You can also turn to Morningstar's mutual fund reports, which you can often find in your local library's reference department.

Now look for overlaps. Do you have five funds devoted to Goliath companies such as Microsoft and Coca-Cola, but none to small companies? Maybe you have three long-term bond funds, which does nothing for your diversification but adds to your expenses.

Tip   Married couples need to coordinate their 401(k)s just as they do with vacations and kid's schedules.

Between two plans, couples have the opportunity to design a far better workplace retirement portfolio than most singles could hope for. If you and your spouse can afford it, both of you should contribute as much money as your 401(k)s allow. But if that's an impossible financial burden, scrutinizing both plans can pay off. You may want to put the most money into whichever plan offers the more generous company match. Couples should also coordinate their investment options. When determining where to allocate the money, you both need to pay attention to the quality of the mutual fund choices.

Example   Say a husband's workplace offers an excellent large-cap index fund, but mediocre bond funds. The wife, on the other hand, has access to a superior small-cap stock fund and an intermediate bond fund. Play to each plan's strengths.

Mom's 401(k)

Women plunder their 401(k) accounts more than men. One reason is that families are more likely to treat the mother or wife's 401(k) or IRA as a rainy day fund. A study by the Employee Benefits Research Institute, a nonprofit workplace think tank, indicates that about one out of every four women who receive a lump-sum amount from their retirement plan spend it all.

Treating a mom's 401(k) as if it's a financial kitty is dangerous. In saving for retirement, women are already at a disadvantage. Women typically have less squirreled away in their 401(k)s than men. This fact isn't surprising because women earn lower salaries and hop in and out of the workforce more because of childcare responsibilities.

What's scary about this situation is that the average woman is going to need her retirement nest egg to last much longer. Today, the average life expectancy for a man is 72; the typical woman lives until 82. Roughly half the number of women who are over 65 years old are widows. Not surprisingly, about 80 percent of women will be the sole financial decision makers at some point in their lives.

Summary

✦ Sacrificing some of your paycheck to a 401(k) now may seem like a hardship, but you will benefit greatly in the long run.

✦ Don't make the common 401(k) mistakes: consider your strategy, options, and paperwork carefully.

✦ Check out all the options when deciding your 401(k) exit strategy.

✦ Assess your 401(k) plan to see if it measures up. If your plan is mediocre, negotiate for a better one.

✦ Use online advisory services to evaluate your 401(k) strategy.

✦   ✦   ✦

The Forgotten Retirement Plans: 403(b)s, 457s, and Small Business Plans

Although 401(k) plans continue to hog the nation's attention, the smaller retirement plans are left out in the cold, both media-wise and in terms of employee participation. This chapter fills in some of the blanks for the non-401(k) crowd and gives a rundown on the Retirement Plans That the Media Forgot:

◆ 403(b)s

◆ 457s

◆ SEP-IRAs

◆ SIMPLE-IRAs

◆ Keoghs

◆ Small business 401(k)s

In addition, this chapter explores two little-discussed options for those who work at major corporations: profit sharing and deferred compensation plans.

> **Tip**
> Even if you don't have access to a 401(k), make sure you know about the retirement plan your employer does offer and take advantage of it to the fullest extent.

Do some of these plans sound unfamiliar? It's no wonder: By one estimate, only about half of all those eligible to participate in 403(b) retirement plans are contributing. Some workers don't bother with their employer-sponsored retirement plan because of the plan's inherent *flaws. For example, certain people enrolled in Section 457 retirement plans aren't even guaranteed that the money they sock away in these plans will be there at retirement. If a nonprofit organization declares bankruptcy, its workers could stand in line with all the other creditors. Meanwhile, most people who work for small businesses have no workplace retirement coverage at all. Although this one chapter can't replace the media barrage (and the accompanying flood of advice and ratings) that surrounds 401(k) plans, it provides solid information to help you make the best retirement plan choices for your employment situation.*

The 403(b): A Strange Bird

"The 403(b) market is a very weird market. It's bizarre."

—Patrick Reinkemeyer, a Morningstar editor

A 403(b) investor may already appreciate what the expert from Morningstar is talking about. The 403(b) world is not only weird, but it's misunderstood as well. Although the 403(b) resembles the 401(k) in many ways, the several differences between the two tend to confuse people.

Note   Unlike investors in the media's darling, the 401(k), 403(b) investors often receive questionable advice or none at all, which is shameful because they face far more complex challenges.

Although weird and potentially confusing, 403(b) plans can be worth the headaches. Once you understand the convoluted rules, your 403(b) can provide far more flexibility than a 401(k) ever could. For instance, if you don't like the investment choices at your workplace, you may be free to shop for a better provider. In some cases, you can also make up for years when you contributed little or nothing to the plan.

The advantage of a 403(b)

If you're participating in a 403(b), chances are you're a teacher, school administrator, or a professor. Doctors, nurses, and others working in nonprofit hospitals are also enrolled in these plans, as are those on the payrolls of charities and churches. The six million people with 403(b) accounts have been enticed by the same golden promise: They can save retirement dollars without getting hammered by taxes.

Just like in 401(k)s, the money contributed to a 403(b) is not taxed up front, and earnings grow tax-deferred. It's only when the money is withdrawn that the 403(b) participant must pay taxes based upon his or her tax bracket. Some employers provide matching contributions to sweeten the deal. Even without employer contributions, such an opportunity beats post-tax investing hands-down. Yet a 403(b) has some disadvantages as well.

Playing Catch-Up: The 403(b) Advantage

The 403(b) enjoys a fantastic advantage that's denied to all 401(k)s fans: You can play catch-up. Perhaps you made meager contributions to your 403(b) when you were younger, or maybe you quit your job when your children were babies. Now, however, you want to turbo-charge your 403(b) by investing more than the maximum yearly contribution, which in 2000 was $10,500. Consult your employer and a certified financial planner to learn whether you qualify and how much you can kick in.

The drawbacks of a 403(b)

Before you can choose wisely, you need to know what the chief challenges are when participating in a 403(b) plan. The following sections describe the big ones.

Nobody screens the choices — or the salespeople.

Within a 401(k) plan, workers choose from a limited menu of investment options that their employers hand-pick. Some workplaces that offer 403(b)s do the same thing by presenting employees with a fixed lineup. But many school districts, hospitals, and charities don't narrow down the 403(b) selections. Instead, employers welcome just about anybody who wants to sell a teacher or a hospital lab worker legitimate investment products.

This open-door policy encourages 403(b) salesmen, who are often insurance agents, to deluge participants with investment literature and sales pitches. Even after someone has signed up, the sales pressure doesn't necessarily disappear. Eager agents will continue to try to wheedle second-grade teachers into transferring all their 403(b) money to the agent's insurance company.

Employers don't like to get involved.

While teachers fend off insurance salesmen, their school district's responsibility often begins and ends with payroll duties. School districts make sure that an employee's 403(b) deduction is withdrawn from each paycheck and sent to the right investment company, but often that's the limit of the district's involvement. If a teacher has questions about the district's 403(b) program, staff may be unable (or unwilling) to answer them. With employers not eager to get involved, many workers aren't even aware that they can contribute to a 403(b). And it's no wonder that the districts don't wish to get involved with their employees' concerns and decisions — many districts, out of concern about fairness, maintain an open door policy which may encourage dozens of providers to prospect for clients. With so many 403(b) providers vying for clients in one district, it can be impossible for either employer or employee to keep track of options and make decisions.

Many 403(b) investment plans are invested poorly.

One recent study suggested that 85 percent of all 403(b) money is invested in annuities, which are insurance products. Annuities are often an unfortunate choice because they **can** charge outlandishly high fees, include punitive surrender charges, and provide insurance coverage and other features that are unnecessary for long-term savers.

Annuities: The dominant investment in 403(b) plans

History explains why annuities dominate the 403(b) market. When the federal government first sanctioned 403(b)s in the late 1930s, annuities were the only legal option. In 1974, Congress wisely decided to expand the 403(b) universe to include mutual funds. Now major mutual fund groups, such as Fidelity Investments, Vanguard, T. Rowe Price, and Strong, offer their funds through 403(b) plans. Yet a quarter of a century later, the insurance industry still hasn't loosened its hammerlock on the market. Many 403(b) participants even call their plans *TSAs* or tax-sheltered annuities. Annuities are a creation of the insurance industry, which is why armies of insurance agents are the ones extolling the virtues of 403(b)s.

Cross-Reference   An *annuity* is a financial hybrid, which offers an investment product that's protected with an insurance policy. (See Chapter 22.)

Annuities come in two flavors: fixed and variable.

Fixed annuities

A fixed annuity is the ultra-conservative option. It promises to pay a certain rate of interest on your investment. Typically, the interest rate is guaranteed for a certain period of time, which is often one year. After that, the rate can be adjusted. When inflation is falling, you can expect the rate to drop. Fixed-rate annuities, however, guarantee that rates won't fall below a certain level.

Caution   Too many teachers invest the bulk of their 403(b)s into fixed annuities. Anyone stuck in a fixed annuity during the 1990s would have missed out on the stock market's historic climb. For a teacher with a long way to go before retirement, remaining loyal to fixed annuities, which may barely keep pace with inflation, is a poor idea.

Variable annuities

Variable annuities allow investors to participate in the stock market. Within a variable annuity, an investor divides his or her money among a limited selection of mutual funds, which are called subaccounts. In better 403(b) annuities, the subaccount choices are diverse enough to appeal to both conservative and more aggressive savers. The menu might include well-known funds from firms such as Janus, Alliance, AIM, Fidelity, and American. As an investor, you can mix and match these funds to construct a diversified portfolio. This kind of annuity is called "variable" because the return depends upon the performance of the underlying funds. The return is not guaranteed.

A variable annuity's dubious death benefit

Although the variable annuity is riskier, it comes wrapped with a so-called death benefit. This dollop of insurance protects the value of your investment if you die during a stubborn bear market. The insurance can't help you, but it could make your heirs happier.

Insurance agents love to boast about the 403(b)'s variable annuity death benefit. The classic annuity guarantee promises that the value of your initial investment will not drop below the contributions you made. Suppose that you contributed $60,000 into your 403(b) annuity during your working lifetime. If you die and the balance is, say, $55,000, your estate will receive $60,000 instead. In recent years, fancier variations of this asset protection have been unveiled.

Tip

A variable annuity's insurance might sound appealing, but the chances of needing it are slim.

Even insurance executives acknowledge that the 403(b) death benefit is rarely used. Remember, retirement savings usually occur over someone's entire career. Consequently, the odds of a portfolio remaining submerged in the red for very long periods are remote.

TIAA-CREF: One Annuity That's Worthwhile

One notable exception to the high-fee annuity pox is the nation's premier 403(b) annuity provider: Teachers Insurance and Annuity Association—College Retirement Equities Fund, or *TIAA-CREF* for short. The financial institution traces its roots to 1918 when philanthropist Andrew Carnegie, who worried about the fate of aging university professors, donated money to start a retirement fund for them. Since that start, TIAA-CREF has become the operator of the world's largest private pension system with a reputation for top-notch money management and excellent customer service. It has a huge presence in the higher education 403(b) field.

TIAA-CREF, which is based in New York City, is fanatical about keeping costs low for its customers. Unlike other insurers, it doesn't believe in using surrender charges, and it doesn't offer mortality coverage because it thinks it's waste of money. It also doesn't maintain a sales force, so you won't find commissions built into its prices. The company's fees are lower than most mutual funds. TIAA-CREF is often compared to the Vanguard Group, the mutual fund firm, which is best known for its index funds and rock-bottom expenses.

In comparing expenses, TIAA-CREF handily beats its average competitor by at least 1.5 percent. This amount might not seem like a lot, but it adds up to a lot of money. Invest in TIAA-CREF's largest stock fund, and you'll be charged 31 cents for every $100 invested. In contrast, the typical large-cap variable annuity fund charges nearly $2 for every $100 investment. Let's assume two people invested $10,000 in both funds, which provided 8 percent returns for 30 years. At the finish line, the race wouldn't be close. The TIAA-CREF fund would be worth $92,313. The expensive one would be worth just $58,089.

Annuities' big fees

The death benefit is as useful as a car hood ornament, but what's the harm? The harm is that you'll pay dearly for the insurance coverage. Variable annuities are historically loaded with stiff fees, which can sabotage your investment return.

 Caution   Annuities can stick to your portfolio like Velcro. Getting rid of one could cost you big bucks thanks to so-called surrender fees. If you sign up for an annuity and decide to bail a year later, the insurance company can assess a stiff penalty.

All these annuity fees buy you something else you don't need: double tax protection. An annuity by its very nature is a tax-deferred product because you don't pay the IRS until the money's taken out. Sounds just like a 403(b)'s tax advantage, right? Yes. And that's the point. Putting money into an annuity within a 403(b) is overkill. The 403(b) already automatically provides the tax protection, so what do you need an expensive variable annuity for?

Who might want an annuity?

Although the gripe against most annuities' steep fees is legitimate, an annuity can be godsend for retirees, who are petrified of investing money on their own. What an annuity does best is provide a stream of monthly income for the rest of a person's life.

A retired female teacher with an annuity, for instance, can opt to receive the money that's accumulated in her account in monthly checks, with the guarantee that she will receive a check each month for the rest of her life. The insurer makes all the investing decisions and assumes the risk that the teacher will live longer than anyone expected. If the teacher sprints past the actuarial predictions, she can end up pocketing far more money than she ever contributed during her career. On the other hand, the retired female teacher could decide not to annuitize but instead empty her 403(b) and invest the money herself. If she makes terrible financial decisions, her nest egg may vanish before she dies.

Tip   You don't need to invest in an expensive 403(b) annuity throughout your career to receive those dependable monthly checks later on. You can wait until retirement to buy what's called an *immediate annuity*—a product that kicks out monthly checks. The cash can come from a 403(b), private savings, or anywhere else.

Mutual Funds: The forgotten 403(b) option

If annuities don't sound appealing, you can invest your 403(b) money in no-load mutual funds. High-quality fund companies that participate in the 403(b) market include Fidelity Investments, Strong, T. Rowe Price, and the Vanguard Group.

Tip   By choosing a no-load fund company, you can avoid the sticker shock associated with annuities and loaded funds; *no-load* means no sales commission.

Mutual funds don't dominate the 403(b) world as they do the 401(k) universe, because no one is extolling their virtues. An insurance agent selling annuities won't mind making the rounds to chat with nurses in a hospital cafeteria or sit with teachers in a school lounge. In contrast, mutual fund firms don't have the staff or the desire to make house calls to potential 403(b) clients. Many people who could choose the mutual fund option don't even know that it is available.

See Chapter 14 for more information on selecting a mutual fund.

Questions to ask about your 403(b)

Whether you're enrolling in a 403(b) or contemplating a switch to another provider, you need to ask these key questions:

Will I be penalized for transferring my 403(b) elsewhere?

Insurers tend to penalize investors who bail. During the first few years of an annuity, you may have to pay a surrender charge when transferring to another insurer or mutual fund. Often this fee starts at 7 or 8 percent and declines by a percentage point every year.

The most stubborn surrender fees, however, never vanish. Sometimes they even increase over the years. You'll typically discover this nasty surprise with "two-tiered" fixed annuities. Two-tiered annuities work this way: The insurer promises customers a higher interest rate on their assets if they ultimately agree to "annuitize" their investment upon retirement. That is, customers forego the opportunity to withdraw their money in a lump sum and instead allow the insurer to send them monthly checks.

Realize that you'll suffer a significant financial blow if you decide later that you'd rather take the money from a two-tiered annuity in a lump sum — that option gives you a punier, lower-tiered rate.

The great disparity between the two interest tiers has turned a lot of unhappy customers into hostages. Many times, people aren't aware of the trap until many years after signing their contract. Those who move their money anyway sometimes face a 20 percent penalty on their first-year contributions. In other words, they could lose $20 out of every $100 originally invested in their account.

If you want to get out of a two-tiered annuity, do it soon: the surrender fees can be a lower dollar amount in the early years.

Unless you're approaching retirement age, you'll probably want to escape from one of these annuities, but before you do, consult a financial planner who is familiar with 403(b) plans. If you invest in no-load mutual funds within your 403(b) plan, surrender fees won't be an issue.

What investment fees will I pay?

Whether you choose to invest in an annuity or through regular mutual funds, be sure to pin down costs and any sales charges. Focus on each investment's *expense ratio,* which is the percentage of an investment that is eaten up by fees each year. The average variable annuity expense ratio is 2.14 percent. The average mutual fund expense ratio is 1.37 percent. Therefore, a $10,000 investment in the typical variable annuity would generate $214 in annual fees, versus $137 for the average mutual fund.

You can find the expense ratio listed in the prospectus of any mutual fund or variable annuity. Another way to check expense ratios is to look in *The Wall Street Journal* and *Barron's,* which regularly list annuity costs near the stock and bond tables.

How is your insurance company rated?

If you invest in a fixed annuity, you need to know how sound the insurance carrier is. You might assume that your money is protected within a fixed annuity, but there's no guarantee. That's because the money in a fixed annuity is not segregated from the rest of the company's funds. Your money, therefore, can be at risk if the insurer declares bankruptcy. In contrast, variable annuities are kept separate from the rest of an insurance company's assets.

Review the ratings of the insurance carrier you're considering from at least two insurance rating services. Many times, the information you obtain by phone is free. The major rating firms are as follows:

A.M. Best	(800) 424-BEST
Duff & Phelps	(312) 368-3198
Standard & Poor's	(212) 208-1527
Weiss	(800) 289-9222

What are my investment choices?

Whether you invest through a variable annuity or traditional mutual funds, you'll want top-notch performers. Check the track records of any mutual funds before investing. If you prefer a variable annuity, you'll want to know which mutual funds underlie the annuity's performance. Investigate the performance figures of these mutual funds as well. Ideally, a menu of funds should cover all the major investing categories: large- and small-cap funds, bonds, foreign exposure, and a money market.

Tip

Morningstar evaluates variable annuity subaccounts, but you won't find these rankings in the library. Because Morningstar's variable annuity publications are very expensive, it's best to ask an insurance agent for copies of the pertinent pages.

Changing 403(b) providers

You may want to switch to a different 403(b) provider for any one of the following reasons:

✦ Variable annuity expenses are too high.

✦ Returns are mediocre or worse.

✦ Investment choices are few.

✦ You want to consolidate multiple 403(b) accounts.

✦ Assets are confined within a fixed annuity.

✦ You desire a 403(b) provider who offers better features.

If you aren't pleased with your 403(b) choices, take heart. You have options; just take the steps outlined in the following sections.

Contact your employee benefits department.

Request a list of the outside investment providers now available through your 403(b). You may discover investment alternatives that you didn't know existed.

Request better choices.

If you want to invest with a mutual fund firm that's not on the list, ask your employer to add it to the official list. Some school districts and universities rubberstamp approval for just about any investment firm; other employers rebuff requests for more selections.

Enlist moral support.

If your employer balks at adding more investment choices, bring in reinforcements. If fellow workers are clamoring for better investment options, your chances of success should increase.

Rescue your 403(b).

If, despite your best efforts, your employer refuses to add the mutual fund company you want to the approved list of investment choices, you can periodically pull money that's accumulated in your lackluster 403(b) plan and direct it to your outside 403(b) account. To do this, you need to make arrangements directly with whatever fund company or insurer you want to invest with. This firm will then send you the paperwork.

Tip

Unless your employer specifically prohibits it, you can transfer your assets to any mutual fund company or insurer that maintains a 403(b) program.

The 457 Blues

Most of the two million people or so participating in a Section 457 deferred compensation plan work for state and local governments, nonprofit hospitals, charities, or certain nonprofit organizations, such as chambers of commerce, blood banks, symphonies, and sports associations, that can't qualify for a better arrangement under the current crazy-quilt tax code.

Just like in a 401(k) or 403(b) plan, someone in a 457 plan can shelter pretax money from Uncle Sam's sticky fingers. The investment grows within a 457 without ever triggering a tax bill.

Caution   Annuities dominate this market. Consequently, you should read the admonitions earlier in this chapter about 403(b) annuity investing.

The downside of 457s

A 457 isn't as desirable as other retirement plans because it's technically not classified as one. The federal government considers it a type of deferred compensation, which (as you'll learn later in this chapter) is a retirement savings option that's primarily used by wealthy executives. They stuff big bucks into their deferred compensation plans after maxing out their 401(k)s. Deferred compensation, whether it's for a receptionist at a blood bank or a chief executive officer, doesn't provide the security of a 401(k).

Caution   Unless you are in a 457 plan offered by a governmental body, nobody can completely guarantee that the money you put in a 457 plan will be waiting for you at retirement. Your investment won't automatically belong to you if your employer declares bankruptcy.

It used to be that if an employer declared bankruptcy, a 457 participant's claim wasn't automatically protected. The clerks, building inspectors, and others working for Orange County, California, discovered this problem back in the 1990s when the county government declared bankruptcy. At one point, workers were told they might be entitled to just 90 cents for every dollar in their 457s. In addressing this injustice, Congress changed the laws, but not everybody is protected. Today, government workers' 457 money is safe if their employer plunges into bankruptcy. But unfortunately, employees who work for non-profit organizations don't enjoy the same protection.

Unfortunately, the 457 plan, which takes its name from a section in the federal tax code, is funded entirely by the worker. The employer rarely kicks in matching funds. In 2000, the maximum contribution was $8,000 or 33 percent of someone's salary, whichever was lower. The contribution ceiling is far lower than a 401(k)'s. What's more, the 457 isn't portable. When someone leaves a job, the 457 stays behind unless the next job also offers one. Workers are also prohibited from tucking their nest egg into an IRA rollover plan.

Hope for the 457

Don't abandon hope for a less prickly 457. Back in Washington, legislators, most notably U.S. Rep. Earl Pomeroy (D-North Dakota), have been attempting to remodel this pseudo-retirement plan. One promising bill would allow a departing worker to move a 457 into an IRA rollover, a 401(k), a 403(b), or any other similar plan.

In addition, a growing number of government employers are scrapping their Scrooge-like plans for something more attractive: the 401(a) plan. Although 401(a)s have been around for awhile, state governments, in particular, have begun switching to them only in the last couple of years. The 401(a) closely resembles a 401(k). These plans allow for employer matches, and they are as portable as a Sony Walkman. When someone leaves a public sector job, he or she can roll the 401(a) into an IRA or a new employer's 401(k) plan.

The upside of 457s

The small consolation prize for the inflexibility of the 457 is that the IRS won't hit workers with a 10 percent penalty if they start spending their 457 money before the age of 59$\frac{1}{2}$.

The 457 hasn't attracted a lot of fans. Yet even though roughly 75 percent of workers snub their 457 plans, the 457 is still a valuable tool. Despite the flaws, a 457 permits participants to shelter retirement money from taxes for many years, possibly decades.

Note   The 457 offers a great feature that 401(k)s lack: a catch-up provision. Some plans permit employees to kick in considerably more into their plan during any of the last three years before normal retirement age, which is a real boon to procrastinators.

Retirement Options at Large Companies

If you're lucky, you work at a place that offers a 401(k) plan and a pension. But large corporations, in particular, will sometimes go one step farther and provide even more.

Profit-sharing plans

Profit-sharing plans have been eclipsed by 401(k) plans, but even so they still cover millions of workers. Under a profit-sharing plan, a company distributes a portion of its profits among its employees. In some cases, the cash or stock is doled out directly to workers, but most often the money is invested within tax-deferred accounts.

Caution   Cash profit-sharing plans aren't as valuable a tool for retirement savings because many people treat the windfall as a bonus. Unfortunately, the money is more likely to be spent than tucked away.

The maximum employer contribution in a profit-sharing plan is usually limited to no more than 15 percent of total outlay for payroll. Companies typically make contributions to workers even if the workers don't contribute to the plan, unlike with a 401(k). If you don't participate in a 401(k), the employer sets aside nothing for you. Consequently, a profit-sharing plan can be especially valuable for young employees and lower paid workers, who typically don't enroll in 401(k) plans or who are prevented from doing so.

How much profit do corporations share? It depends. Some companies leave it up to their board of directors, so there's no predictability. A business often determines the amount by using a pre-set formula that's tied to its overall profitability. For example, the pot might equal 15 percent of a company's pretax profit. If there's no profit one year, there's nothing to divide. Companies are not required to kick money into the profit-sharing kitty every year. However, contributions can be made even in years when the company doesn't make a profit.

Usually new employees have to wait 90 days to a year before they are eligible to participate in profit-sharing plans. Less than 1 company in 10 immediately welcomes new employees to participate in sharing profits.

How Profit-Sharing Began

Profit-sharing plans predate 401(k) plans by almost two centuries. The Treasury Secretary during President Thomas Jefferson's administration dreamed up the first one for workers at his glass factory in 1797.

In the 20th century, Procter & Gamble revived the idea during a period when labor unrest was spreading through the nation's factories. William Cooper Procter, the founder's grandson, believed that sharing profits would empower workers and give P&G a competitive edge. Within a few years, Eastman Kodak, Sears, Roebuck & Co., and other companies were offering their own plans. However, 7 out of every 10 profit-sharing plans were disbanded during the Great Depression.

During World War II, the notion caught on again. By 1955, when ex-GIs were moving their families into the suburbs, 8,500 plans were in place across the country. Twenty years later, the number was pushing 200,000.

The passage of the Employee Retirement Income Security Act (ERISA) in 1974, however, pretty much killed their proliferation. Too much confusion existed about what the landmark legislation meant for profit-sharing plans. Ironically, legislation passed in 1978 to reinvigorate profit-sharing did the opposite—when Congress enacted Section 401(k) to the tax code, it paved the way for the 401(k), and the rest, as we say, is history.

Deferred compensation plans

For millions of Americans, building a substantial 401(k) account isn't enough. Those who are high on the corporate food chain expect more. Executives demand generous deferred compensation plans that dodge the retirement savings rules that other workers must follow.

Tip Deferred compensation plans can be ideal for anybody making a six-figure salary who feels hemmed in by the IRS's limits on what workers can sock away.

For someone making a six-figure salary, the annual 401(k) cap on contributions amounts to peanuts. Deferred compensation plans permit higher paid employees to thumb their noses at 401(k) caps. Just like a 401(k), any money funneled into a deferred compensation plan avoids up-front income taxes, and the cash remains in a tax-free zone until it is withdrawn. Presumably by the time a retiree taps into this money, he or she is at a lower income tax bracket. The government doesn't even care how much money is stashed away. Each corporation decides limits for itself. Corporations also determine what rate of return the money earns. The return is often linked to an index, such as the Standard & Poor's 500, U. S. Treasuries, or the prime rate.

The tax advantages make these plans so alluring. Suppose that an executive funnels $50,000 into one of these plans for 12 years. Earning 10 percent a year, the assets would grow to $1.2 million. The numbers wouldn't pencil out as nice if that yearly $50,000 contribution was ravaged by taxes. If a person faced a combined state and federal tax rate of 40 percent, the nest egg's value, if earnings grew at the same 10 percent, would reach just $944,000.

More people qualify for this perk than you might guess. The federal guidelines are vague, but the person's salary must exceed $80,000. These plans are as common a fixture as drinking fountains among the nation's largest corporations. Some smaller companies also offer them as a way to attract and retain key executives.

Threats to deferred compensation plan assets

All of the benefits of deferred compensation plans undoubtedly sound great, but these plans aren't foolproof. The biggest mistake you could make is assuming that you're tucking money into a 401(k) clone. If deferred compensation plans offered the same legal protections as a 401(k), the feds would banish them from the workplace. Consequently, don't expect an iron-clad guarantee that your money will be there when you retire. If your company declares bankruptcy, you may lose all or part of your investment. The money could also be endangered if another corporation gobbles yours up. The corporate newcomer might reinterpret the agreement, for instance, which could ultimately result in less money for you. Remember, you don't have access to this money until withdrawal time. If the worst happens, it could be just you and your $200-an-hour lawyer fighting this injustice. The federal government can't protect you.

Protecting deferred assets

Safeguards against losing your deferred compensation plan investments, though imperfect, do exist. Your investment should be safer if the corporation tucks your contributions into a trust. The rabbi trust is the most common. Named after a Baltimore rabbi who wanted some kind of assurance that a future congregation couldn't dip into his retirement cache, a *rabbi trust* prevents an employer from diverting the money for its own operations, but it can't protect the assets from bankruptcy. Other less-popular trusts exist as does the possibility of insurance coverage. This insurance, however, can be costly, and few carriers write such policies. Although an individual is supposed to pay the insurance cost, corporations sometimes find ways to pick up the tab.

To protect your future retirement fund, be hard-nosed during negotiations. Before signing an agreement, ask about escape hatches. Ask your corporation to stipulate that you can retrieve your money if you're fired or leave voluntarily. You also want the freedom to bail if your company is acquired. Executives are typically savvy enough to demand that the new corporate owner assume the deferred compensation obligation. As long as executives work within a company among management that they know and trust, they should feel safe letting the money ride.

Small Business Retirement Plans

If you work for a company with fewer than 100 employees, you probably aren't covered by an employer retirement plan. By one estimate, only 13 percent of these tiny workplaces offer a 401(k) plan. At companies with fewer than 500 employees, just one in three workers enjoys the benefits of a 401(k). In contrast, 97 percent of corporate giants (those with work forces of at least 5,000 people) have 401(k)s in their employee benefit lineup.

Small businesses often haven't had the resources or the savvy to create retirement benefit programs. Owners conclude that, without the economies of scale enjoyed by large corporations, the benefits to employees don't justify owner expense. But there's no reason why a small business can't offer retirement coverage. The federal government has made it easier than ever for small businesses and their employees to prepare for retirement. But what really might spark more small business involvement is the financial industry. With the 401(k) market having reached the saturation point among America's large companies, financial providers are focused on the underserved small fry. The following sections provide a rundown of what's available.

Simplified employee pension plans (SEP-IRA)

The SEP-IRA is the ultimate no-hassle retirement plan for small businesses. Employees who are eligible for SEP-IRAs can establish their individual accounts at whatever brokerage firm, bank, insurance company, or mutual fund they please.

They enjoy the freedom to direct their investments within their SEP-IRAs anyway they want. They can play it safe with government bonds or gamble with initial public offerings. It's up to them.

Unlike 401(k)s, however, employees can't make their own pre-tax contributions to their SEP-IRA. Only employers can contribute to the employees' account. An employer can contribute up to 15 percent of a worker's compensation into a SEP-IRA or $24,000, whichever is smaller. The maximum contribution is adjusted annually for inflation.

Note A business can prohibit some people from participating in a SEP-IRA. Legally it can exclude persons under age 21, people who have not worked for the employer in at least three of the past five years, and those who are covered by a collective bargaining agreement.

In one respect, the SEP-IRA is a great equalizer. If the boss contributes 10 percent of his or her salary into a SEP, all eligible employees can expect the same 10 percent of their pay deposited into their accounts. They can't, however, count on this windfall every year. A company isn't obligated to set aside the same amount annually, and a business doesn't have to contribute anything at all some years.

Benefits to employees and employers

SEP-IRAs require very little record keeping. Employees aren't even required to report contributions on their tax returns. And just like other retirement plans, the SEP-IRA provides a tax break. Just like a 401(k) or a regular IRA, the money inside a SEP-IRA grows without being taxed until it's withdrawn. Once that happens, the cash is taxed at a person's ordinary income tax rate. Companies also claim a tax deduction for the money they contribute to their workers' SEP-IRAs.

Look Before You Leap

Thinking of job hopping? Don't let a big salary increase blind you. A big bump in take-home pay may not be in your best interest if your retirement package stinks. Ask a prospective employer about retirement program eligibility, vesting requirements, an employer match, and investment choices. You'll also want to know whether the company offers a pension plan. Many companies have scrapped or drastically altered pensions.

If you're contemplating a move to a small company with little or no retirement benefits, consider this move carefully. The danger is that there are few avenues to save for retirement outside a workplace. You can put money into an IRA, but that's limited to $2,000 a year.

Suppose you contribute $10,000 a year, which includes the employer match, into a 401(k) plan at your current job. If the money earned an annual 10 percent return for 30 years, you'd pocket $1.6 million. In contrast, a small company offers you an extra $25,000 in salary a year and more autonomy. Trouble is, the retirement plan kicks in only a yearly $2,000 into a SEP-IRA. If that money earned the same 10 percent a year, your nest egg would grow to only $328,988.

SEPs for the self-employed

SEP-IRAs are also attractive for self-employed people, who obviously must make their own tax-deductible contributions. SEP-IRAs are especially popular with independent consultants, contractors, and freelancers.

Example

Suppose an independent contractor contributed $10,000 to his SEP-IRA and happened to be in the 31 percent tax bracket. His tax deduction would be worth $3,100.

Savings incentive match plan for employees (SIMPLE-IRA)

The SIMPLE-IRA is tailored for companies with 100 or fewer employees. Among the businesses that typically benefit from these plans are restaurants, retailers, law and accounting firms, and small manufacturers. These plans, which have been available only since 1997, seem to be most popular with businesses that employ 10 or fewer people.

Cross-Reference

Both SIMPLE- and SEP-IRAs follow the many of the same guidelines as regular IRAs; see Chapter 10 for a detailed treatment of IRAs.

The SIMPLE-IRA advantage

With the SIMPLE-IRA, both the boss and the worker can stash money into the tax-deferred account. Like the other options, an employee can establish his or her account at any financial institution. The employer may contribute one of two ways:

✦ Provide a dollar-for-dollar match up to 3 percent of each participating employee's salary. Employers are free to decrease that percentage in any two years out of five.

✦ Contribute 2 percent of salary on behalf of all eligible employees regardless of whether they're kicking in money to their SIMPLE-IRA.

SIMPLE-IRA disadvantages

A big drawback of the SIMPLE-IRA is the plan's contribution ceiling. The maximum amount that a person can contribute is $6,000 annually. For a higher-paid employee, this amount breaks down to far less than the ceiling caps on a 401(k) or a SEP-IRA. But at least participants in SIMPLE-IRAs are vested immediately. Employees who quit their jobs can take an employer's match with them.

IRAs: The More the Better

Participating in a SEP-IRA or a SIMPLE-IRA doesn't disqualify you from investing in a regular IRA. Even if you max out your SEP-IRA or SIMPLE-IRA, you're still eligible to contribute up to the maximum $2,000 a year into a traditional or Roth IRA.

Caution   Beware of a deadly time bomb if you're tempted to cash in your SIMPLE-IRA account. If you withdraw money from your SIMPLE-IRA within the first two years of your initial participation, you could be subject to a 25 percent penalty.

Small business owners have not warmly embraced SIMPLE-IRA plans, but they are even less enthusiastic about SIMPLE-401(k)s. Unlike the SIMPLE-IRA, the SIMPLE-401(k) doesn't allow companies to reduce their matching contributions below 3 percent. SIMPLE-401(k)s also generate a lot more paperwork. Many big mutual fund companies don't even offer them.

Keoghs

The Keogh, which was named after a New York legislator who championed the concept four decades ago, is tailored for self-employed entrepreneurs and small-business owners. Although the Keogh enjoys the same tax perks as a SEP-IRA, many don't consider it as desirable because it demands considerably more paperwork. The consolation prize for the red tape is that you can stuff more money into a Keogh than into IRAs. In some circumstances, an individual may contribute up to 25 percent of his or her compensation each year or $30,000, whichever is less. Some Keogh plans may have vesting schedules. As a general rule, Keogh plan participants face the same restrictions on distribution as IRAs.

Confused? Here's Help

Confused about your retirement options? Many mutual funds and brokerage firms provide literature on different small-business retirement choices. To receive the free materials, just call a firm's toll-free number. Mutual fund and brokerage firms' Web sites can also provide a wealth of information. Fidelity's Internet site, for instance, provides calculators that help individuals determine how much they can legally contribute to a Keogh or SEP-IRA.

For a drier, but exhaustive, treatment of small workplace retirement choices, call the IRS at (800) 829-1040 and ask for Publication 560, *Retirement Plans for Small Businesses.*

Because of the higher contribution ceiling, Keoghs are often attractive to physicians, dentists, veterinarians, engineers, attorneys, and accountants; there are different types of Keoghs for various situations. However, the Keogh is a complicated animal, so consult an experienced accountant or financial planner to determine whether a Keogh is best for your situation.

Note

A new Keogh must be opened before the end of a calendar year to qualify for the tax deduction. You can, however, delay any contributions until April 15 and still snag the tax break for the previous year. In contrast, you can establish a SEP-IRA or any other IRA as late as April 15 and still claim the tax deduction for the previous year.

Small-business 401(k)s

Many small businesses have shied away from 401(k)s because of the administrative costs. But now that the 401(k) market is approaching the saturation point with larger companies, financial marketers are focusing more attention on companies with less than 100 employees. Insurance companies have dominated this niche, which isn't a happy development for workers. Annuities, as you've already learned in this chapter, are notorious for their high fees. Mutual fund firms and brokerage firms, however, are now experiencing success in capturing some of the business by using the Internet to decrease program costs.

In 1999, for instance, Fidelity unveiled the first Internet-based 401(k), geared exclusively toward small businesses. Because all transactions are conducted on the Internet, the costs are cheaper. While online, employees can enroll, obtain educational materials, check their portfolios, and change their investment choices. American Century, another major mutual fund family, has also set its sights on the mini-401(k) market, and others are following. Participants in these new programs can access their accounts by an automated phone system or through the Internet.

Tip

Today even a company with two dozen employees can participate in a 401(k) plan with very modest costs. If your company insists that 401(k) programs are too expensive, explain that times have changed.

Table 9-1 provides a quick comparison of the four major plans for small businesses and the self-employed.

Table 9-1 Small-Business Retirement Plan Comparisons				
	SEP-IRA	**SIMPLE-IRA**	**Keogh**	**401(k)**
Eligibility	Self-employed, business owners, anyone with self-employed income.	Businesses with 100 or fewer eligible employees.	Self-employed, business owners, anyone with self-employed	Typically companies with 25 or more employees. income.
Key Advantage	Easy to establish and maintain.	Both employer and employee can contribute.	Highest contributions permitted.	Popular retirement plan with high employee participation.
Annual Contributions	Up to 15% of compensation, maximum of $24,000.	Maximum for employees is $6,000; different formulas exist for employers.	Up to 25% of compensation, maximum $30,000.	Maximum employee contribution is $10,500. Most companies provide some sort of match.
Vesting of Contributions	Immediate.	Immediate.	May have vesting schedule.	Vesting for employer contributions varies; it's usually not immediate.
Access to Assets	Withdrawals anytime, subject to income tax and possible 10% early withdrawal penalty.	Withdrawals at anytime, but may be subject to 25% penalty if taken out within the first two years. After the second year, a 10% penalty is a possibility.	Withdrawal allowed at retirement, leaving company, and job dismissal. A 10% early withdrawal penalty may apply.	Withdrawals allowed at retirement, leaving company, and job dismissal. A 10% early withdrawal penalty may apply.

Summary

- ✦ When investing in a 403(b), avoid expensive annuities; investigate all the investment options available in your plan.

- ✦ Escape from a lousy 403(b) by lobbying for changes or quietly moving out your money.

- ✦ Don't spurn a 457 plan; take advantage of it when it's offered.

- ✦ Protect your deferred compensation investment with upfront agreements about how it is to be handled.

- ✦ Think twice before accepting a job without retirement benefits: the increased salary may not make up for the loss of tax-sheltered retirement cash.

- ✦ Employees at small businesses and the self-employed can still set up tax-sheltered retirement accounts in the form of SEP-IRAs, SIMPLE-IRAs, and Keoghs.

- ✦ Small businesses are now participating in less expensive 401(k) programs.

✦   ✦   ✦

The ABCs of IRAs (Individual Retirement Accounts)

This chapter is a crash course on IRA investing. You'll discover how to comparison shop among the different types of IRAs and decide whether to convert any traditional IRAs you currently own into a Roth IRA. You'll also become familiar with how to start an IRA account and learn the truth behind common IRA myths.

Why Is the IRA So Popular?

Back in 1974, most Americans knew who Archie Bunker was, but few probably could explain what the initials IRA meant. Now, 27 years after its birth, the IRA has become as popular as *All in the Family* ever was. With the future of Social Security uncertain and company pension plans disappearing, millions of Americans regard their IRAs as their ace in the hole. The size of a person's IRA can ultimately determine whether someone spends retirement driving a golf cart or riding the bus.

Whether someone uses an IRA rollover to shield a small fortune or faithfully deposits up to $2,000 a year into a regular IRA, the attraction is the same. The IRA can make you richer. Although the different kinds of IRAs operate under different rules, they all share the same fantastic feature: As long as the money stays safely tucked inside one, you won't owe any taxes. It doesn't matter if the IRA contains $1,000 or $10 million. The feds can't claim a piece of it unless you withdraw the money. With the Roth IRA, the latest IRA choice, you may *never* owe any income taxes, not even when you withdraw your money. As you can see in Tables 10-1 and 10-2, the fact that this money can grow for many years or decades without taxation helps trigger explosive growth.

Rollover-a-Rama

Traditionally, if you asked your neighbor or a golfing buddy what their biggest asset was, chances were the response was automatic: the house. But for many workers today, their IRAs are their biggest asset. All that wealth, however, can't be traced back to those modest $2,000 checks we're allowed to deposit into our IRAs each year. The $2,000 annual limit, which stubbornly defies inflationary reality, hasn't been bumped up since 1981. The nation's IRAs are groaning with cash for one huge reason: the IRA rollover. The IRA has become a favored way station for millions of workers leaving or retiring from their jobs with fat 401(k)s and pension payouts.

For departing workers, who don't want old employers overseeing their money, the IRA rollover is the only way to shield all this loot from taxes. A twenty-something who quits a job at Starbucks when making lattes gets old might have just a tiny amount from his or her 401(k) to stash into an IRA rollover. A retiring executive from a Fortune 500 may stuff a seven-figure sum into his or her rollover. Unlike a regular IRA, any amount of money transferred from a qualified workplace retirement plan can be deposited all at once inside a rollover IRA. The IRS doesn't care whether you roll over $5,000 or $2 million or any other amount.

Table 10-1
$100,000 Investment Placed in an IRA Rollover Versus a Taxable Account*

Years to Invest	Taxable Account	IRA Rollover
10 years	$184,218	$259,374
15 years	$250,034	$417,725
20 years	$339,364	$672,750

*This table assumes a 10% return for investor in 31% federal tax bracket who pays 6% in state taxes.

Table 10-2
Annual $2,000 Contributions in IRA Versus a Taxable Account*

Number of Years Contributing	Taxable Account	IRA
10 years	$26,736	$31,875
15 years	$47,630	$63,545
20 years	$75,988	$114,550

Number of Years Contributing	Taxable Account	IRA
25 years	$114,479	$196,694
30 years	$166,721	$328,988

*This table assumes a 10% return for an investor in the 31% federal tax bracket, who pays 6% in state taxes.

IRAs have also grown in popularity thanks to Congress's decision to make these retirement accounts look more like all-purpose savings accounts. You can now use IRAs to buy a home, pay your kid's college dorm fees, or subsidize a face-lift and tummy tuck during a mid-life crisis. One of the newer ones, the Education IRA, doesn't have anything to do with retirement at all. Keep in mind, however, that robbing your IRAs to pay for other expenses, no matter how noble, can quickly develop into a dangerous habit. If the money is gone, it won't be there at retirement, when there will be no more pay raises, much less paychecks, to help you play catch-up.

The downside of IRAs: tricky regulation

IRA investing isn't too tough to master, as you'll see in this chapter. However, withdrawing that wisely invested money used to be incredibly complicated. Only the most diligent tax authorities, who consulted dog-eared copies of the U.S. Tax Code, could keep track of the rules governing inherited IRAs and IRA withdrawals during retirement. But the good news is that in 2001 the IRS completely revamped and simplified the IRA rules in these two areas. The transition from the old to the new regulations, however, is creating confusion, so it's best to consult an expert if you are now making mandatory withdrawals from an IRA or have inherited an IRA.

Cross-Reference

To learn more about the sweeping changes made to the IRA regulations, see Chapters 11 and 21.

Creating an IRA

Some novice investors believe that an IRA is a specific type of investment. It's not. The IRA account itself is just a shell: You select one or more investments to fill it. You can open up any kind of investment account—for example, a mutual fund, a particular stock or stock portfolio, a bond, a passbook savings account, a certificate of deposit, or a money market account—and do the paperwork to declare it an IRA, giving that account all the attributes of an IRA, such as freedom from taxation and the $2,000 yearly contribution limitation. Just about any brokerage firm, mutual fund company, bank, savings and loan, or insurance company would welcome your account. When you contact your institution of choice, specify that you want the application form for an IRA account.

The brokerage firm advantage

Where your IRA money ends up depends upon what you want to do with it and how large your account is. If you have a sizable IRA, you'll probably want to keep it at a brokerage firm. With a brokerage account, you enjoy ultimate flexibility whether you personally oversee your investments or rely upon a financial planner or broker. Through a brokerage firm, you can trade individual stocks and bonds and invest in mutual funds as well as certificates of deposit within your IRA.

Note   If you're just starting out, a brokerage account probably won't be practical. Many brokerage firms won't let you open an account with just $2,000, which is the maximum yearly IRA contribution.

Great vehicles for beginners

If you're establishing your first IRA account, a mutual fund company may be your best bet. You can start with nothing, invest only $50 or $100 per month, and have access to some excellent investment vehicles. What kinds of funds should you consider?

✦ A large-cap growth fund, which contains America's most recognizable and biggest corporations, is a solid place to put your money.

✦ Consider also an index mutual fund that tracks Standard & Poor's 500, which is a collection of the nation's largest corporations.

✦ Perhaps a better alternative is an index fund that tracks an even broader stock benchmark, such as the Wilshire 5000, which includes most of the nation's publicly traded companies, both big and small.

✦ An all-purpose bond fund, such as the Vanguard Total Bond Market Index Fund, is ideal for fixed-income folks.

Annuities are an option as well; major mutual fund families, as well as brokerage firms and insurance companies, offer annuities. If you'd prefer to safeguard your money in certificates of deposit, look to a bank, a savings and loan, a credit union, or a brokerage firm.

Cross-Reference   If you're ready to retire and desire a steady income, transferring a portion of your IRA assets into an immediate annuity could be the answer. See Chapter 22 for details on annuities.

When selecting an IRA custodian, be pragmatic. Are you easily distracted from your retirement savings goals? If so, choose a place that allows you to make automatic deposits into your IRA. This method is perhaps the closest you can come to pain-free investing. Many mutual fund companies offer this option. Instead of writing one or more checks each year, you can instruct the mutual fund firm to deduct an agreed upon amount each month or quarter from your checking or savings account. Most funds allow you to contribute as little as $50 a month this way. To meet the yearly $2,000 maximum contribution, your automatic monthly withdrawal would be slightly more than $166.

IRA Investment No-No's

The IRS is picky about what you can invest in an IRA. Even if you're sure that hoarding rare Beanie Babies or Pokémon cards in a vault will someday make you rich, the cuddly critters and Japanese pocket monsters aren't eligible to be part of IRAs. The following are also forbidden:

✦ Artwork

✦ Rugs

✦ Antiques

✦ Stamps

✦ Gems

✦ Rare wine (or any other kind of alcoholic beverage)

Most coins are also taboo, but exceptions exist, such as certain U.S.-minted gold and silver coins. Gold, silver, and platinum bullion is also generally acceptable. In addition, some brokerage firms frown upon what they consider to be inappropriate retirement investments. They may forbid IRA customers from trading in options, for example.

Choosing the Right IRA for You

Unlike the selections you face at Baskin Robbins, your IRA choices are far more limited. When you retire or quit your job, a rollover IRA is the only place you can move the funds from your 401(k), another qualified retirement plan, or a pension lump sum to retain their tax-free status. Once established, a rollover IRA behaves just like a traditional IRA. The money grows without being subject to taxes until it is withdrawn. Like a traditional IRA, an owner must begin pulling money out of the account not long after reaching the age of 70½. And that money is subject to income taxes. There are no eligibility rules regarding who can transfer workplace retirement money into an IRA rollover. If you leave a company and wish to take your 401(k) loot with you, you can establish an IRA rollover account at just about any financial institution.

If you want to create a brand new IRA — as opposed to transferring a workplace account — you have these three choices:

✦ Traditional deductible IRA

✦ Traditional nondeductible IRA

✦ Roth IRA

Until the Roth IRA hit the scene in 1998, the traditional deductible IRA was the best of the bunch. But the deductible IRA now has a tough time competing against the Roth, and not everyone is eligible for it. The ugly duckling in this trio is the nondeductible IRA, but it's still a fine choice for wealthy Americans, who can't qualify for any other kind.

Deductible IRA

Although every type of IRA provides some tax protection, only the deductible IRA guarantees instant tax gratification. Up front, you're guaranteed a tax deduction on your contribution. If you deposit $2,000 during the year, for instance, you'll lock in the opportunity to shave a modest amount off your annual tax bill. Just how big the slice will be depends upon your tax bracket.

Example   If you're in the 28 percent tax bracket, you can write off 28 percent of your $2,000 contribution, which is $560. Someone in the 15 percent bracket who contributes $2,000 could claim a $300 tax break. Note that a smaller contribution results in a smaller deduction.

Because you enjoy this tax perk up front, you will owe income taxes on the money you withdraw from the IRA during your retirement years. Let's say you're retired and want to withdraw $10,000 from your $75,000 IRA. If you're in the 28 percent tax bracket, your federal tax hit would be $2,800, and any applicable state tax would take its share too. If you dip into your IRA account before reaching 59½, you will probably be hit with a 10 percent penalty. For those in the highest tax brackets, this double whammy of taxes and penalty can erode more than 50 percent of their cash. A $50,000 withdrawal can shrink to less than $25,000 after someone finishes paying off the IRS and any state taxing authority.

In some limited exceptions, the 10 percent penalty is waived, but the taxes aren't. You can dodge the penalty in the following circumstances:

✦ You become permanently disabled.

✦ The money is used to pay medical bills exceeding 7.5 percent of your adjusted gross income. (It's not necessary to itemize your tax return to avoid the penalty.)

✦ The money is earmarked for college expenses.

✦ You withdraw up to $10,000 to buy a first home for yourself or family member.

✦ You die.

By the way, the federal government relies upon its own peculiar definition of "first-time home buyer." You may have had mortgages on several homes in the past, but if you haven't owned a house in the past two years, you meet the criteria.

See IRS Publication 590, *Individual Retirement Arrangements,* for details on all aspects of the IRA. You can download IRS publications and forms at www.irs.gov. Because of the major changes in the IRS regulations for mandatory IRA withdrawals and inheritances, make sure the copy you receive is an updated one.

Qualifying for deductible IRAs

Those smitten by deductible IRAs won't necessarily be eligible for one. If neither you nor your spouse is covered by a workplace retirement program, such as a pension plan, 401(k), 403(b), or something comparable, you're automatically eligible to contribute to a deductible IRA even if you're a millionaire.

If you have a workplace retirement plan, however, you can take the full tax deduction only if your adjusted gross income (AGI) doesn't exceed certain limits. For a married couple filing a joint tax return, that limit is $53,000 for 2001 and $54,000 in 2002. For a single person, the ceiling is $33,000 for 2001, and it bumps up by an additional $1,000 in 2002. The caps continue inching up until 2007 when the limits for couples and single taxpayers are $80,000 and $50,000 respectively.

As you can see in Table 10-3, you may be able to claim a partial tax deduction for a deductible IRA if your income falls within certain ranges. These ceilings continue climbing until 2007.

What's an Adjusted Gross Income?

Whether you will qualify for certain IRAs often depends upon your adjusted gross income (AGI). Your *AGI* is listed on your latest federal 1040 tax return and is determined by adding up all your income, including wages, tips, investment income, capital gains and losses, and alimony, and subtracting the deductions listed on the bottom of Page 1 of the 1040 form. Unfortunately, itemized deductions and deductions for children can't lower your AGI.

The hodgepodge of deductions that reduce your AGI include the following:

✦ Contributions to 401(k)s, 403(b)s, Keoghs, SEP-IRAs, and SIMPLE-IRAs

✦ Alimony

✦ Moving expenses

✦ Student loan interest

✦ Stock losses

✦ Rental real estate losses

✦ Self-employed health insurance

✦ One-half of self-employment tax

Table 10-3 Eligibility for a Partial Deductible IRA		
Year	Married-Joint Returns	Single
2001	$53,000–$63,000	$33,000–$43,000
2002	$54,000–$64,000	$34,000–$44,000
2003	$60,000–$70,000	$40,000–$50,000
2004	$65,000–$75,000	$45,000–$55,000
2005	$70,000–$80,000	$50,000–$60,000
2006	$75,000–$85,000	$50,000–$60,000
2007	$80,000–$100,000	$50,000–$60,000

Nondeductible IRA

The nondeductible IRA doesn't generate much enthusiasm. It used to be the only alternative for Americans who made too much money to qualify for the traditional deductible IRA. However, that situation changed with the passage of the Taxpayer Relief Act of 1997 when the Roth IRA was born. Thanks to this landmark legislation, most Americans now can invest in the more attractive Roth.

Just like the Roth, someone contributing to a nondeductible IRA, as its name suggests, can't claim an upfront tax deduction.

Caution Unlike the Roth, the nondeductible IRA doesn't offer a tax break on the back end. Taxes are due on a portion of the money withdrawn during retirement. And if the money is taken out before the age of 59½, that pesky 10 percent penalty typically is assessed.

The nondeductible IRA enjoys one distinct advantage: It doesn't have an income limitation for investors. Consequently, wealthy Americans who are prohibited from contributing to a Roth or a deductible IRA can choose this one. Even Microsoft's Bill Gates qualifies.

Roth IRA

For many years, banks, mutual funds, and brokerage houses valiantly touted the wonders of IRAs, but few people listened. This disinterest can be traced back to Congress, which in 1986 sabotaged the IRA. Before that year, anybody who contributed to an IRA could claim a tax deduction. But Capitol Hill took that perk away from all but those making modest salaries. The result was dramatic. The next year, IRA contributions plummeted by two-thirds.

The Roth IRA, which is the namesake of former Sen. William V. Roth Jr.(R), a septua-genarian from Delaware, was designed to get people excited about IRAs again. If anything will spur Americans to open IRAs, the Roth IRA is it. Just like the two kinds of traditional IRAs, you can sink up to $2,000 a year into one.

Freedom from taxation

The Roth's main virtue is that investors don't pay taxes on any of the earnings and contributions that grow inside the account, no matter how flush the account gets. Imagine contributing $2,000 a year into a Roth for three decades. If this cash grew at 11 percent, the stock market's historical rate, your brokerage statement would ulti-mately reach $400,000. When you retire, you could withdraw all the funds at once, nibble on the account as needed, or pass the whole amount to your heirs — and nei-ther you nor your heirs pay Uncle Sam income tax on that money. This is the chief advantage over the traditional IRAs, which require owners to pay taxes when they withdraw cash during retirement. If someone with a traditional IRA amassed the same $400,000 over their working lifetime, when they pulled out the money, they'd owe taxes at their income tax bracket. In this case, a person in the 31 percent bracket, would pay $124,000 in federal taxes! And a state taxing agency could expect its own cut too.

In exchange for its great tax ride, the Roth does have one drawback, but it's decid-edly a minor one. The Roth doesn't provide an upfront tax break like the deductible IRA. When you plunk money into a Roth, you can't deduct the contribution off your annual income tax return.

Example

Imagine contributing $2,000 a year into a Roth for three decades. If this cash grew at 11 percent (the historical rate of earnings of the stock market), your brokerage statement would ultimately reach $398,042. That's a lot of tax-free earnings.

The joy of accessibility

Lots of people have avoided IRAs because they've been too petrified to tie their money up for decades. What if they encounter a medical emergency? Or what if they're slapped with a costly lawsuit? If they pulled the money out prematurely, they'd be hit with taxes and possibly that 10 percent penalty. With a Roth IRA, you don't have to worry about locking up your money for what might seem like an eter-nity. (Though that is the preferable option.)

The Roth provides a trap door for those wishing to access their money without incurring financial penalties. For starters, the Roth allows someone of any age to withdraw yearly contributions at any time without financial repercussions. Suppose that you contributed $2,000 to a Roth IRA, and your car was totaled six months later. You could pull that $2,000 out of the Roth IRA to pay for the car repair without facing any taxes or penalties from the IRS.

You can also withdraw earnings from a Roth before your retirement, but in many cases income taxes and a penalty will be assessed. First off, you will owe income taxes and a 10 percent penalty if you touch the earnings before five years have passed since your first Roth contribution. Even if they wait the required five years, however, most people will be hit with taxes and the penalty if they haven't reached the age of 59½.

The Roth IRA, however, offers limited ways around the tax landmine. As long as you have had the Roth IRA for five years, you can take out money for a first-time home purchase without triggering income taxes or the penalty. (The Roth has the same wacky definition of a first-time buyer as the deductible IRA does.) The lifetime maximum amount on this type of withdrawal is $10,000.

Tip

> You can also use Roth IRA proceeds to pay for college expenses for you or relatives. In this case, you don't pay a penalty, but you will owe income taxes on the money when you withdraw it from the account.

Additional advantages of the all-star Roth

The Roth IRA is superior for other reasons as well. These reasons are explained in the following sections.

A Roth can be left alone.

An affluent retiree can leave a Roth undisturbed for a lifetime. Distributions are not mandatory. In contrast, an investor with a traditional IRA must crack it open after reaching age 70½ and begin making yearly withdrawals of a certain amount based upon an IRS formula.

A Roth allows heirs to skip income taxes.

The Roth tax break lives on even after you're gone. Your heirs won't have to pay income taxes on the money they pull out of your Roth IRA. And as long as they keep the money in the Roth, the assets grow tax-free. Although some heirs may have to pay estate taxes on a Roth or any other assets, most Americans can avoid this bill because the amount that's allowed to be sheltered from estate taxes continues to rise.

Qualifying for a Roth IRA

A Roth IRA is great, but not everyone qualifies for one. You can't take full advantage of the Roth IRA if your adjusted gross income exceeds $150,000 (married taxpayers) or $95,000 (single taxpayers). As with the deductible IRAs, you are eligible for a partial contribution if your income is slightly higher than these limits. A married couple filing jointly can make a smaller Roth contribution if their income doesn't exceed $160,000. A single person can make a partial contribution if his or her income is no more than $110,000.

Deductible IRA versus the Roth

Deciding whether to invest in a deductible IRA or a Roth IRA doesn't require King Solomon's wisdom. The case for the Roth is overwhelming. It's a rare scenario indeed when the deductible IRA fares better. Let's look at how the numbers pencil out. Let's say Roslyn faithfully stashes $2,000 into a Roth for the next 25 years. During the same period, Caitlin prefers putting her $2,000 checks into a deductible IRA. Each account grows at an annual 11 percent clip. When both women are ready to retire, their nest eggs are each worth $228,827. Yet Roslyn has more to celebrate. She owes zero income taxes as she taps into her account. Better still, her heirs owe no income taxes on this money if she leaves any of it behind. Poor Caitlin, however, faces a painful tax bill. If she's in the 28 percent tax bracket, her taxes will total $64,071, which shrinks her nest egg to $164,756. Table 10-4 lays out the numbers.

Table 10-4 Totals for Investing $2,000 in an IRA for 25 Years*		
	Roth IRA	**Traditional IRA**
Account Value After 25 Years	$228,827	$228,827
Taxes Owed Upon Withdrawal	$0	$64,071
Total Value	$228,827	$164,756

* This table assumes 11% annual growth and an investor in the 28% federal tax bracket.

Is this an unfair comparison? Deductible IRA fans might insist that it is because the example ignores those yearly tax breaks Caitlin enjoyed for a quarter century. Nice try, but the Roth is still a slam-dunk. Assuming that Caitlin had been in the 28 percent tax bracket all those years, her yearly tax break would amount to $560 for a grand total of $14,000. Even when you add that into the equation, Roslyn is still $50,071 ahead.

Getting realistic with the Roth

Although the Roth IRA is an infinitely better deal, you wouldn't necessarily make that conclusion if you examined the informational materials on IRAs that are mass-produced by brokerage firms, mutual funds, and other financial juggernauts. The literature can hem and haw so much that you might think that choosing between the two IRAs is comparable to deciding which of your children you love the most. Yet if you closely examine how these financial institutions compare the two IRAs, you'll see that they make conclusions about Americans' spending and investing habits that are arguably farfetched.

Here's the scenario that's typically presented in the literature of financial institutions: Someone invests $2,000 a year in either a Roth IRA or a deductible IRA. Okay, so far. But then those financial brochures make this huge assumption: The person contributing to the deductible IRA puts the tax savings in a taxable account for the next 20 or 30 years. How many people are realistically going to do that? Isn't the whole point of getting a tax break to lower tax liability or possibly receive a big tax refund check in May or June? If someone receives a refund, isn't he or she more likely to use this bonanza to pay off a credit card, buy radial tires, underwrite a weekend trip, or reduce the cost of a kid's summer camp adventures?

But even if you do assume that somebody was disciplined enough to segregate their deductible tax savings in a separate account, the Roth is usually still superior. Let's say Caitlin did invest her $560 tax savings every year, and it also earns 11 percent. Ultimately, her separate taxable account would grow to $40,464, but she still isn't as rich as Roslyn. Roslyn's account would be ahead by $23,607.

Converting to a Roth IRA

Converting a traditional IRA or an IRA rollover into a Roth can make a great deal of sense for people who can survive the initial sticker shock. It won't, however, be appropriate for everybody. If you proceed, you will pay taxes. These taxes scare off lots of otherwise motivated investors. The magnitude of the tax bite depends upon how much money you have squirreled away in your traditional IRA.

Here's where the tax pain comes in: If you convert your IRA, you will owe income taxes on the amount that you convert the next time you file your annual federal tax return. If you transfer $50,000 from a rollover IRA into a Roth, for example, that's the amount that will be taxed. Your bill will depend upon your tax bracket. Someone in the 28 percent bracket would owe $14,000. Why does the federal government make you pay tax even though you are just switching the money from one IRA to another? The IRS wants the money now because it could be its last chance. Remember, money inside a Roth IRA can grow for a lifetime without ever being subject to income taxes again.

The most affluent Americans are spared agonizing over this decision because they don't qualify for a Roth conversion. The adjusted gross income (AGI) of a couple who files tax returns jointly cannot exceed $100,000 during the year of an intended conversion to a Roth IRA. The same ceiling applies to single taxpayers. If you are married, but you file taxes separately from your spouse, you can't convert to a Roth IRA at all.

Reasons to convert

Whether converting to a Roth is an intelligent move depends upon a lot of factors. If you match the descriptions in the following sections, a conversion to a Roth is probably a good idea for you.

Your tax bracket will be the same or higher when you retire.

Most people don't leapfrog to a higher tax bracket in retirement, but if that's going to happen, a conversion to a Roth looks mighty attractive. It's also desirable even if your tax bracket doesn't budge.

Suppose you have a $50,000 deductible IRA, you're in the 28 percent tax bracket, and you decide not to convert. You don't touch the IRA, which generates an 8 percent annual return for 20 years. Your investment would grow to $129,033. When you withdraw the money, assuming for the sake of this illustration that you withdraw it all at once, you'll sacrifice $36,129 to taxes and be left with $92,904.

Thou Shalt Not Convert

The IRS has mailed out warnings to tens of thousands of taxpayers who unwittingly defy the eligibility rules for converting to a Roth IRA. This is not the sort of letter to ignore. The penalties for an illegal conversion are brutal: The taxpayer is liable for income taxes on the entire taxable portion of the amount converted, and the IRS will assess an annual 6 percent penalty. If you find yourself in this situation, you can undo the damage if you don't procrastinate. Swiftly move the money in the new Roth back into a traditional IRA or retitle the Roth account as a traditional IRA. You must accomplish this task by April 15, unless you receive a filing extension.

If you think you might bump up against the eligibility ceiling, consider delaying your conversion until later in the year when you'll know better how much income you'll make.

If you'd like to convert your IRA into a Roth, but you know you earn too much to qualify, you can use these tricks to temporarily shrink your taxable income:

✦ Contribute more to your 401(k), 403(b), or other tax-deferred workplace retirement plan.

✦ Delay a year-end bonus until January.

✦ If you're eligible, add to a Keogh, SEP-IRA, or a SIMPLE-IRA (see Chapter 9 for more information).

✦ Declare stock losses for the year.

✦ Pay January's alimony check a month early.

✦ If you're self-employed, delay mailing invoices and accelerate expenses.

Had you converted the deductible IRA to a Roth, you would have owed $14,000 in taxes (28 percent of $50,000) at the time of the conversion. Assuming that you paid the tax bill with funds *not* from the IRA and received the same 8 percent annual rate of return for two decades, you could have kept that $36,129 at retirement time. The longer the investment period and the higher the rate of return, the better the conversion will look.

You're middle-aged or younger.

If you're young, you have little reason not to convert. Chances are you don't have much in your IRA yet, so the tax pain won't be great. And the younger you are, the more time you'll have to recuperate from the tax hit.

You don't need to use your IRA to pay for the conversion.

You can cripple the ultimate tax savings of a conversion if you dip into your IRA to pay the IRS. Recalling the earlier example, if you had withdrawn $14,000 out of the $50,000 account to pay the conversion tab, the account would be valued at $92,904 instead of $129,033 at retirement time. In other words, the conversion would have been a wash. In addition, you'd owe income taxes on the $14,000 you took from the

IRA. For somebody in the 28 percent tax bracket, that amount would be another $3,920 in taxes. Throw in the 10 percent withdrawal penalty if you're younger than 59½ for an additional tax hit of $1,400.

Caution   You worsen your tax bite if you rob an IRA to pay for the conversion to a Roth IRA.

You plan to leave your IRA to your heirs.

By converting a regular IRA to a Roth IRA, you shrink your taxable estate. That is, all that tax money that you spent converting to a Roth will no longer be in the estate. Since its gone, it can't be subject to estate taxes. For wealthy Americans, who are fortunate to be sitting on large estates, the savings to the heirs can be considerable.

Reasons not to convert

Although a conversion to a Roth has its advantages, it might not make sense for you if you match the characteristics described in the following sections.

You expect your income tax bracket to drop after retirement.

Let's say you're in the 31 percent federal tax bracket, and you expect to be in the 15 percent bracket when you quit your last job. It could require decades for the conversion to make financial sense.

Table 10-5 illustrates how many years it would take for the benefits of conversion to out pace the initial conversion tax pain. As you'll see, the higher your expected rate of return, the shorter the period of time it will take for the conversion to a Roth to make sense. Right now, Roth conversions are permitted only for those in the 31 percent tax bracket or lower, but Congress has debated the possibility of giving wealthier Americans this option. Because of this possibility, Table 10-5 also indicates the feasibility of conversion for persons in all but the highest tax brackets.

Table 10-5 Roth IRA Conversion Chart			
Tax Rate Now	**Retirement Tax Rate**	**Rate of Return**	**Years Until Benefit***
36%	15%	4%	>70
36%	15%	6%	64
36%	15%	8%	49
36%	15%	10%	40
36%	15%	12%	34
36%	15%	14%	29

Tax Rate Now	Retirement Tax Rate	Rate of Return	Years Until Benefit*
36%	28%	4%	17
36%	28%	6%	12
36%	28%	8%	9
36%	28%	10%	8
36%	28%	12%	7
36%	28%	14%	6
36%	31%	4%	10
36%	31%	6%	7
36%	31%	8%	5
36%	31%	10%	<5
36%	31%	12%	<5
36%	31%	14%	<5
31%	15%	4%	>70
31%	15%	6%	52
31%	15%	8%	40
31%	15%	10%	33
31%	15%	12%	28
31%	15%	14%	24
31%	28%	4%	7
31%	28%	6%	5
31%	28%	8%	<5
31%	28%	10%	<5
31%	28%	12%	<5
31%	28%	14%	<5
28%	15%	4%	65
28%	15%	6%	44
28%	15%	8%	34
28%	15%	10%	28
28%	15%	12%	24
28%	15%	14%	21

* This column shows the number of years it will take before the benefits of a Roth conversion exceed the upfront tax bill. This number is based on the assumption of a state income tax rate of 5%.

Source: "Roth IRAs After 1998 Tax Law Changes," CCH INCORPORATED, and Brian L. Anderson, JD, LLM, CPA of DeWitt, Ross & Stevens in Madison, WI.

Web Sites to the Rescue

A financial planner or a Certified Public Accountant can help you decide whether a Roth conversion makes sense. If you just want general IRA suggestions, however, quite a few financial Web sites offer free analyzers that can weigh in on whether a Roth conversion is worthwhile, as well as which IRA is best for you. These sites offer this kind of assistance:

- ✦ Quicken at www.quicken.com
- ✦ Charles Schwab at www.schwab.com
- ✦ Vanguard at www.vanguard.com
- ✦ Fidelity at www.fidelity.com
- ✦ T. Rowe Price at www.troweprice.com
- ✦ Strong at www.estrong.com

You don't have spare cash.

As mentioned earlier, don't convert your IRA if you must rob your IRA to pay the taxes. If paying the conversion taxes would wreak havoc on your finances, forget the idea or convert only a portion of an IRA.

You greatly fear changes in tax laws.

Some people have balked at converting to Roth IRAs because they suspect that the federal government will someday change the tax rules again. They can't see the advantage of paying voluntary taxes now when the Roth could conceivably be gutted or replaced with an even better IRA. Although Congress does love to tinker with tax laws, it's unlikely that the Roth's advantages would ever be plucked from those who have one. Precedent strongly suggests that the advantages enjoyed by Roth investors would be grandfathered in if tax laws were changed.

The Roth conversion tax whammy

The tax liability for converting to a Roth IRA is most brutal for those investors in the higher tax brackets. For example, somebody in the 31 percent tax bracket would owe $31 for every $100 within the IRA. You won't necessarily pay taxes on all the cash within your IRA though.

Example

Say you faithfully deposited $2,000 annually for 12 years into a traditional IRA, which grew into $50,000. Because your income level was too high to allow you to take tax deductions on the $24,000 you originally contributed, you won't owe taxes on the contributions. You are liable only for taxes on the $26,000 in earnings.

The tax bill can be much higher for somebody who wants to convert into a Roth an IRA rollover that was funded with 401(k), 403(b), or some other qualified retirement

plan. Because taxes were never paid on any of this cash when an employer originally whisked it out of someone's paycheck, the conversion to a Roth triggers a tax
bill on *all* of it.

Uncle Sam is watching you.

Some people think they've figured out a clever way to outsmart the IRS. They pro-
pose pulling out only money that wouldn't get slammed by taxes. They might want
to leave their old 401(k) rollover money alone and just convert all those nondeductible $2,000 contributions. Don't bother trying this stunt. The IRS won't permit
it. Even if all your contributions to an IRA are nondeductible, you'll still owe taxes
on the earnings.

If you have an account with deductible and nondeductible contributions in it, you
might still think you can limit the liability by withdrawing just the nondeductible
portion. Sorry, you can't dodge taxes this way either. If you convert only a portion
of your IRA, the conversion will reflect the ratio of nondeductible money to the
total IRA balance.

Something else to keep in mind is that the lump sum you convert isn't counted
against you when you calculate your adjusted gross income for Roth IRA conversion eligibility. As mentioned earlier, if your AGI is too high, it disqualifies you to
convert a Roth. Suppose your AGI is $90,000, and you convert a $50,000 IRA. The
$50,00 won't be considered income—for conversion purposes so you are free to
move the money into a Roth. Nonetheless, an IRS land mine is lurking in the regulations. By converting your IRA, you may inadvertently bump yourself up into a
higher income tax bracket. That's because the amount of money that you transfer
into a Roth is considered income by the IRS. For instance, normally you might be in
the 15 percent bracket, but the conversion might temporarily bump you up into the
28 percent tax bracket. It's important to ask an accountant or other tax professional
if a contemplated conversion could push you into a higher tax bracket for one year.
Converting could also temporarily disqualify you for other tax perks, such as child
credits and education tax breaks.

Here are some of the tax breaks you might lose with the higher tax bracket that
could result from a conversion:

✦ **Child credits.** A $500 credit per child under the age of 17 begins to phase out
for parents earning $110,000 and for individuals making $75,000.

✦ **Miscellaneous itemized deductions.** It feels good to be able to deduct things
such as union dues, tax preparer fees, and unreimbursed business expenses
on your income tax return. But you aren't entitled to do this unless these
oddball deductions exceed 2 percent of your adjusted gross income. If your
income has been artificially inflated by a one-time conversion, you might not
meet the criteria.

✦ **Medical deductions.** Here you could face the same dilemma about qualifying
as you did with the miscellaneous itemized deductions. The threshold to
write off medical expenses is 7.5 percent of your gross adjusted income.

If you are worried about the financial implications of a Roth conversion, talk with a tax professional. He or she may suggest that you complete the conversion in phases to preserve tax write-offs and thereby avoid inching up to a more punitive tax bracket.

Conversion cold feet

If you convert your IRA, can you change your mind? Yes. It's possible to withdraw money from a Roth and return it to a traditional IRA. However, most people who make the conversion aren't overwhelmed by regret. Rather they are shrewd investors who are glad to shrink their tax bills.

> **Tip**   Bailing out of a traditional IRA during a market plunge might be wise: If you convert when the financial markets are depressed, your tax bill will be smaller.

Jumping in and out of a Roth conversion can potentially save you thousands of dollars. Suppose somebody converted a $75,000 IRA from a traditional to a Roth. Within a few months, the market tanks, and the IRA, which contained a lot of volatile stocks, loses $15,000 in value. If the investor holds onto the Roth, he or she owes taxes on a $75,000 IRA even though the portfolio is now worth only $60,000. To avoid paying a higher tax, the investor can fill out paperwork at whatever financial institution is safeguarding his or her IRA to convert the Roth back into a traditional IRA. After this is done, the traditional IRA can once again be converted to a Roth to capture the lower portfolio valuation. In this example, the taxpayer would owe income tax on a $60,000 conversion instead of a $75,000 one. This maneuver can be executed only if the tax on the conversion has yet to be paid. The tax is owed the year the conversion takes place. For instance, if you converted an IRA in 2002, the tax would be due when you filed your 2002 tax return (by April 15, 2003).

When the Roth first arrived on the scene, investors could dance back and forth between a traditional and Roth IRA as many times as they pleased. The IRS, however, was not amused. Today, you can only flip-flop once a year. If you dismantle your Roth IRA in 2001, for instance, you must wait until 2002 to reconvert that money into a new Roth. If you try this in December, you must wait 30 days before reconverting.

IRA Myths

Many misperceptions exist about IRA investing. Your can make the most of your investments if you know the truth behind some common IRA myths.

I can't contribute to an IRA after I retire.

A traditional IRA forbids anyone from making contributions after age 70½, but that's not the case with the Roth IRA. You can also funnel money into your spouse's IRA. The total contributions for both of you, however, can't exceed what you're earning on the side.

Tip

As long as you continue drawing some income, whether it's from consulting, selling crafts, or other ventures, you can contribute to a Roth IRA throughout your retirement.

Because my wife is a stay-at-home mom, she can't open an IRA.

Luckily, a husband or wife who doesn't work outside the home is no longer discriminated against. A few years ago, the rules were changed, and now a spouse who doesn't earn a paycheck can contribute the full $2,000 a year into his or her own IRA.

I can roll a 401(k) or the proceeds of another workplace retirement plan directly into a Roth IRA.

Not so fast. This money could ultimately end up in a Roth, but you must first transfer the money into a traditional IRA. Once the money is inside a regular IRA, you have to pay the conversion taxes before moving that money into a Roth. This same two-step process must be followed for some other retirement plans, such as a 403(b) and a Keogh. A regular IRA, as well as a SEP-IRA and SIMPLE-IRA, can be converted directly into a Roth IRA.

Kids can't own IRAs.

IRAs for kids are a great idea. Even if a child puts a pittance into a Roth IRA when he or she is young, the money can grow a lot before he or she retires. The numbers look even more awesome if a teenager feeds an IRA every year. Suppose an 18-year-old starts tucking $2,000 annually into an IRA until the age of 65. Assuming an 11 percent return, the payoff for such diligence will be a whopping $2.7 million.

Example

Suppose a 15-year-old opens an IRA with $1,000 she made designing Web pages and then ignores the account until she's 65. With an 11 percent return, that $1,000 will mushroom to $184,565. The advantage of a head start is tremendous. If that 15-year-old waited until age 21 to do the same thing, the IRA would be worth just $98,676 when she's 65.

Of course, convincing a child or grandchild to sock money away for decades is a tough sell. As an incentive, you might promise to match whatever money the child deposits into an IRA. Or you could contribute the entire amount yourself.

Take care, however, that the total contribution doesn't exceed the amount of money your child or grandchild earned during the year. If your daughter made $1,100 babysitting one year, that's all she's legally allowed to put into an IRA. For that reason, younger children, unless they're child movie stars, aren't financially eligible for IRAs—they have to have some sort of earned income in order to contribute.

When converting a traditional IRA into a Roth, you can spread the tax pain over four years.

That used to be true, but the privilege is now extended only to those who made the move by December 31, 1998. The tax bill for conversions after that date is due the year the conversions are made.

> **Tip**   If you'd like to make the switch to a Roth, but don't want to foot a sizable tax bill in just one year, convert just a portion of your traditional IRA annually.

Contributions to a Roth IRA shouldn't be mingled with a Roth conversion account.

This idea was popular when Roths were first introduced, but mixing Roth accounts is no longer considered taboo. If you have a regular Roth and a converted Roth account, you can combine them; just call your IRA custodian to arrange it. By merging Roth accounts, you'll avoid paying more than one annual custodial fee, and you'll reduce the paperwork.

If I don't contribute to an IRA by New Year's Eve, I'm out of luck.

You have more time than that. The federal government always gives you 15½ months to stash money into an IRA. For the 2002 tax year, for example, your window of opportunity extends from January 1, 2002 until April 15, 2003. Don't assume you have to write one check. You can mail in smaller amounts throughout the year. To maximize your investment, contribute as early in the year as possible.

Before I retire, I must consolidate all my retirement assets within one IRA for distribution purposes.

No matter what your age, you can have as many IRAs as you please. You might have an IRA residing in a bank while another IRA hibernates in a brokerage account or a mutual fund.

Of course, the more IRAs you have, the more difficult it is to keep track of them—and the more paperwork and custodial fees you generate.

I can transfer my IRA among different IRA providers as often as I please without triggering taxes.

Generally that's true, but there's a big exception. If you instruct your IRA custodian to mail the money directly to you—not a good idea, by the way—you have 60 days to put it into another IRA account. But you can do this only once a year. If a second check is mailed to you within 12 months, the IRS will consider it a payout. You will owe taxes on the face value of the check and possibly a 10 percent penalty. To avoid this catastrophe, instruct your IRA custodian to send your money directly to another IRA account at the other financial institution. This kind of institutional transfer never triggers taxes, no matter how many times your money bounces around.

Summary

✦ You can establish an IRA at any financial institution with very little paper-work.

✦ IRAs provide a great way to shelter your money from taxes.

✦ If you're opening up your first IRA, consider establishing an account with a mutual fund company.

✦ Among the three IRA choices, the Roth IRA is almost always superior.

✦ Although the process involves significant tax costs, converting a traditional IRA into a Roth can be a smart move.

✦ Understand all the tax consequences of converting an IRA into a Roth before you proceed.

Inherited IRAs: What You Should Know

Chances are good that some of the money in your Individual Retirement Account is going to outlive you. This chapter familiarizes you with IRA distribution and inheritance rules so that you can keep that IRA living long after you're gone. Whether you expect to inherit an IRA or give one away, you need to familiarize yourself with the IRS's new rules to keep the tax shelter standing.

Nobody wants to spend a lifetime building a sizable IRA for the IRS, but it has happened plenty of times. Some IRAs have been devastated as much as 75 percent by inadvertent mistakes that thousands of Americans and their financial advisors make every day. The ill-advised moves of countless parents and grandparents have diminished the value of IRAs that their loved ones inherit by thousands or even millions of dollars.

The biggest culprit of this vast cash hemorrhage has been the federal government. Regulations issued in 1987 that governed how older Americans could tap into their IRA nest eggs and ultimately pass along what was left to their loved ones were booby-trapped with complicated instructions. Even banks, brokerage firms, and other financial institutions that oversaw these retirement accounts got confused. But now those dark days are behind us, for the most part.

The New Deal

In a sudden and surprising move, the IRS issued new IRA regulations in 2001 that dramatically simplify the rules for millions of Americans and give a second chance to elderly people who made mistakes when calculating what is officially referred to as their *required minimum distributions*. These required minimum distributions kick in after someone reaches the age of

70^1/$_2$. (You'll learn more about required IRA withdrawals in Chapter 21.) At that point, a person is required to take at least a minimum amount of money out of his or her IRA each year. In the past, inadvertent errors made at this crucial age were most often irrevocable.

The new regulations have created something else to cheer about. In some cases, family and friends who have already inherited flawed IRAs may be able to undo the damage.

The revamped regulations don't affect just IRA accounts. The new rules also apply to different types of qualified retirement plans, including 401(k)s and 403(b)s. Much of the time, money from a workplace retirement plan is transferred into an IRA when someone leaves a company or retires. But some people prefer to leave the money in their 401(k) accounts during retirement. These rules affect the mandatory withdrawals from these accounts as well. In fact, the new rules make leaving money behind in a 401(k) or other workplace accounts even less desirable an option than it was previously.

Cross-Reference   You'll get details on required withdrawals from your retirement nest egg in Chapter 21.

With the sweeping changes, it's now even more critical that you take the time to learn the rules. For example, you should understand up front that IRA withdrawals in retirement still follow a *distribution timeline*. When the original owner decides to begin tapping into an IRA, he or she uses a simple formula based on the IRS life expectancy tables to determine the minimum that must be withdrawn each year. That quick calculation does factor into the length of time an heir gets to enjoy the IRA's tax-protected status, as you'll learn in this chapter.

Making the most of the new regulations is crucial both for retirees who are contemplating passing along assets to family, friends, or charities and for folks who expect to inherit an IRA or other retirement plan proceeds.

What Hasn't Changed

The sweeping federal changes don't affect all IRA rules. Savers who are still contributing to IRAs rather than taking the money out in retirement won't notice any differences. For instance, the annual ceiling on IRA contributions remains $2,000. The income requirements to qualify for certain IRAs also haven't budged. (See Chapter 10 for the basic IRA saving rules.) Nor have the penalties changed for prematurely withdrawing money out of an IRA.

If You're the IRA Owner

To get the outcome you want, protect yourself by playing the IRA game by the rules. Keep the following tips in mind when you plan to give an IRA away.

Don't rely upon free advice.

Many people have gotten into trouble because they turn to a bank officer, a representative answering the phones at a mutual fund company, or their broker for advice about IRA issues involving distributions and inheritance. Such ad-hoc advisors mean well. The people manning the phones at a mutual fund company are trained to answer investment questions, though; they aren't equipped to handle estate and taxation matters. Even the literature from a mutual fund or a brokerage firm can sometimes be inadvertently misleading—or completely outdated.

Get the most up-to-date information.

With the dramatic overhaul of the rules issued in January 2001, there will no doubt be a lead time before all the financial institutions are familiar with the new IRA regulations, which filled 108 single-spaced pages.

Caution Any brochures or literature on IRA distributions and inheritance that were published before January 2001 will be wrong.

Before using an IRA publication, ask the source, such as a mutual fund company or brokerage firm, whether it contains the new IRA distribution rules. Meanwhile, don't assume that the information on financial Web sites is current just because the material can be updated easily. Despite the immediacy of the Web, articles posted in cyberspace can be quite old.

Unfortunately, misinformation is far too prevalent. When the new regulations came out, for instance, even some of the nation's leading newspapers got some of its coverage wrong.

Of course, you can obtain the straight scoop from the IRS. The IRS is rewriting or replacing its Publication No. 590, which contained all the rules involving IRA distributions. The free publication lists the life expectancy tables that have always been used to calculate IRA distributions for IRA participants and heirs. You can contact the IRS by calling (800) 829-1040 or visiting its Web site, at www.irs.gov.

Tip You'll know that a publication on IRA distributions and inheritance is horribly outdated if it includes such phrases as *term certain* and *recalculation methods.* These calculations have been abolished.

Stick with the experts.

If you are already taking mandatory withdrawals from an IRA or other retirement plan, you may need advice to make sense of the new rules. Paying an expert is worth the price. This advice is especially sound now as millions of Americans transition from the old retirement distribution rules to the new ones. You may need more than one person, though, because the knowledge of professional advisors is fragmented. An attorney, for instance, might be well versed in trusts and estates, but a certified public accountant might be familiar with the latest IRA regulation wrinkles.

Just because somebody has an advanced degree won't guarantee expertise in this arcane area, either. In one case that made headlines in *The Wall Street Journal* before the regulations were changed, a New York resident who happened to be a volunteer tax instructor contacted the IRS, three banks, three brokerage firms, and the staff of the U.S. Senate Finance Committee — and was still unsure how to proceed with an inherited IRA.

So how do you find someone who understands the tax code inside and out? Look for experts who are sought out by their peers. Often these experts, such as CPAs and estate attorneys, are popular speakers on estate-planning matters at professional conferences.

Tip   Members of the estate-planning and taxation committees maintained by well-regarded organizations such as the American Bar Association, state bars, and the state CPA societies are usually on the cutting edge of IRA and estate-planning rules.

One way to find bona fide experts who fit these criteria is to call the American Bar Association, the state CPA societies, and the American College of Trust & Estate Counsel. This last group is a prestigious organization that includes only attorneys who have made substantial contributions in the field. (See the Resource Guide at the end of this book for addresses and phone numbers.)

When you locate a hot prospect, you needn't commit until you've met face-to-face. Often this first meeting is free; it helps you determine whether you can comfortably work with this person. During the meeting, play detective. Ask the attorney or CPA where he or she keeps his or her copy of the federal tax code. You don't want to hear that it's sitting in the law library down the hall. The ones who can recite tax code citations easier than the grades in their child's last report card keep the ponderous book on a shelf within reach or on the desk.

Tip   If the advisor's copy of the federal tax code is highlighted with markers and stuffed with adhesive notes, that's a good sign; this advisor very likely knows the code backward and forward.

IRA Cyber Answers

A relatively cheap and easy way to tap into some of this high-caliber IRA advice is to subscribe to Ed Slott's *IRA Advisor,* a newsletter. Slott, a CPA in Rockville Centre, New York, is one of the first experts personal finance journalists turn to when they are researching IRA issues. He was among the first professionals in the nation to obtain and interpret the new IRA regulations. This newsletter also contains articles penned by some of the nation's other leading IRA experts. To order the newsletter, call (800) 663-1340. Slott and other experts also answers visitors' IRA questions, including those on the new regulations, on his Web site at www.irahelp.com. Hundreds of the responses are archived on the site. Slott also has posted the complete text of the revised IRS regulations.

Know who your beneficiaries are.

Do you remember when you first filled out paperwork for an IRA? If you're married, is your husband or wife listed as the beneficiary of the accounts? Are all the children named as secondary or contingent beneficiaries? Just as important, are you named on your spouse's accounts? Double-checking is critical. Taking a few minutes to make phones calls or to look up old documents can prevent a great deal of heartache and save a phenomenal amount of money later.

What can happen if you don't do it? For starters, the wrong person can some day wind up with all this money. Someone may be happily married to a man for years before he dies suddenly of a heart attack. Only then does the wife discover that he forgot to take his ex-wife off his IRA. What happens in a case like that may seem outrageous, but it's perfectly legal. The ex-wife can walk away with the IRA — that's right, all of it.

This nightmare doesn't just apply to second marriages. The same thing could happen, for instance, if your future spouse established an IRA years before you met Maybe parents or a sibling were listed as the beneficiaries, and it was never changed. Meanwhile, if parents fill out beneficiary paperwork but never add a child born later, that child is out of luck.

What's scary about these snafus is that the damage can't be undone even if a will exists. The will might stipulate that the surviving spouse gets everything from the sterling silver tea set to the portfolio of blue chip stocks, but that won't matter. If an ex-wife or ex-husband is still listed as the beneficiary of an IRA, he or she gets it.

Feel free to revisit beneficiary decisions.

Here's one of the huge pluses of the new IRA regulations: You can erase some beneficiary mistakes even if you are past the age of $70^1/_2$. Under the old rules, once the beneficiaries were chosen, the owner couldn't later undo the effects of the decision after the date passed for the first mandatory IRA distribution. This *required beginning date,* as it's officially called, is still April 1 following the year in which someone turns 70^1/$_2$.

Here's one illustration of why this inflexibility often caused great hardship. Suppose a retiree originally selected his own estate as beneficiary of his IRA, a phenomenon that unfortunately happens all the time. Only later did he realize that making this innocent designation condemned his IRA to an early death for his heirs, a situation detailed later in this section. (After his death, the IRA would have to be disbanded. When this occurred, taxes would be owed on the full amount, and the money could no longer grow tax-deferred.) Having learned belatedly about this rule, this retiree might have tried to rectify the mistake by naming his son as the beneficiary. Although switching the identity of the beneficiary was no problem, the switch could not change the ultimate disposition of the IRA. The IRA's fate was sealed by his previous beneficiary selection, which he did not change before his 70^1/$_2$ birthday. Consequently, the son would have inherited the money in the IRA, but he would have been prevented from sheltering that cash throughout his lifetime.

Today, the timing on selecting beneficiaries is no longer a make-or-break decision. An IRA owner's decision at or before 70^1/$_2$ won't lock in the retirement account's fate. In fact, now an IRA owner can change beneficiaries at any time, at any age. So, if the retiree in the previous example switched his beneficiary designation from his estate to his son when he was 80 or 90 or even 100 years old, the son would not be forced to crack open the entire IRA immediately after death.

Tip   Review your beneficiary designations to determine whether you need to make any changes. If you haven't named a beneficiary for your IRA or a workplace retirement plan, do so as soon as possible.

Name a person, not your estate, as beneficiary.

Failing to name someone as the recipient of your IRA on the account paperwork filed with a financial institution can be the quickest way to kill an IRA after you die. If you fail to name a beneficiary before you die, your estate may automatically be the recipient. Sometimes well-meaning people intentionally designate their estate as the beneficiary. They believe that their loved ones, having been named as beneficiaries in a will, shall receive the IRA when the estate is settled. And they will. But by that time, the IRA's value to the survivors will be greatly diminished.

If an estate is named as the IRA beneficiary, the IRA will often end up on life support. How long the IRA can be kept alive typically depends upon the deceased's age. If the IRA holder dies before making mandatory IRA withdrawals, the entire IRA must be distributed no later than five years after the year of the death. If the IRA owner had already begun mandatory withdrawals, the IRA beneficiary actually gets a better deal. The heir can preserve the IRA based on the distribution timeline that was already in place when the owner died.

Naming the estate as the IRA beneficiary won't always lead to a premature disbanding of the IRA. Loopholes exist. For instance, suppose a husband left the IRA to his estate but named his wife as his IRA beneficiary in his will. In a case like this, the wife can shelter the inherited IRA throughout her lifetime if she can meet one condition: She has to be the executor of her husband's estate.

Caution   It can also be a risky move to name a revocable living trust or some other trusts as the IRA beneficiary. Frankly, many attorneys don't know how to structure a trust to make it foolproof.

Not all trusts will trigger an IRA meltdown, however. In certain circumstances, a trust might be needed. You might want one if your beneficiary is a child or an adult who handles money recklessly. This arrangement could also be a useful tool in second or third marriages. Perhaps a man want his IRA to initially go to his latest wife, but he worries that she'll ultimately pass any remaining money on to her own children. However, he wants his kids to pocket the cash. A trust could ensure that this happens.

You certainly don't want to name a trust as an IRA beneficiary without fully appreciating the future tax consequences, though. Definitely consult an estate attorney or other expert before making any arrangements.

Decide whether your spouse needs the IRA.

What could be a better show of your love than bequeathing all your earthly possessions (including your IRA) to your faithful soul mate? It's hard to argue with sentimentality. Nonetheless, you should avoid automatically assuming that your partner should inherit your IRA. If your husband or wife will ultimately need that IRA to pay the electric bill, car insurance, and the Blockbuster video charges, then by all means pass along the entire IRA to him or her.

This decision gets trickier for everybody else. In general, the larger the estate and the older the spouse, the less sense it makes to name the husband or wife as the exclusive IRA beneficiary. For instance, if a wife has access to mutual funds, stocks, and bonds in sizable taxable accounts, and if she's eligible for a pension, her heirs might ultimately save a bundle in taxes if the IRA skips over her.

If you're uneasy about shutting out your spouse, you can compromise. With a $600,000, IRA, for instance, you could leave $300,000 to your spouse and the rest to one or more children. You can split an IRA any way you want.

The new IRA regulations can help couples grappling with how much of an IRA should be directly passed to the widow or widower, and how much, if any, should be bequeathed to children, grandchildren, or other loved ones. The surviving spouse now enjoys the luxury of making that determination after the death, but the IRA must be structured properly ahead of time. It can work only if an IRA owner designates both a primary beneficiary for the IRA and one or more contingent beneficiaries. Usually a contingent beneficiary inherits the IRA only if the primary beneficiary is dead. However, the designation can also provide a loophole for heirs. Say that a wife dies after naming her husband as the beneficiary and naming her son as the contingent beneficiary. If the husband decides he doesn't need the IRA, he can "disclaim" or waive the right to his inheritance so that the contingent beneficiary, his son, gets the cash.

Tip   If you have an existing IRA, make sure the original paperwork that you filed with your IRA custodian names backup beneficiaries. Many people name only a primary, which can backfire later.

Consider rolling your workplace retirement plan into an IRA.

Upon leaving a company, many people automatically transfer the assets from their employer-sponsored retirement plan into an IRA. But plenty of individuals keep the money where it is, apparently out of loyalty to their old company or perhaps just lack of initiative.

However, the revamped regulations make moving the cash worth the effort. Here's why: If your money is stashed inside an IRA, what's left when you die can largely be sheltered throughout your heir's lifetime. Beyond mandated yearly withdrawals, for instance, a son or a daughter could keep the money shielded from taxes for decades.

This happy outcome is unlikely, however, if loved ones inherit your retirement nest egg through a 401(k) or other qualified workplace retirement plan. Corporations aren't required to accommodate heirs who want to stretch out Mom or Dad's 401(k) over their lifetimes. Cold as it may sound, when a former worker dies, the corporation wants to close the books on that retirement account as soon as legally possible. What happens instead is this: A company is permitted to limit payouts to beneficiaries for five years.

When the five years are up, the retirement account loses its tax protection. The money is removed, and heirs owe income taxes on what's left.

Divide your IRA intelligently.

When naming children and grandchildren as beneficiaries, it's best not to list them all on one IRA. Instead, divide up an IRA beforehand so that each beneficiary will ultimately have his or her own. If you have a $100,000 IRA and you want to ultimately pass it along to your two sons, split the IRA in two, and name each son as the beneficiary of one of the two accounts.

Children and IRAs

If your heir is a minor, don't name the child as your IRA beneficiary. Instead, designate a custodial account or a trust to receive the money on the child's behalf. Why the extra step? A child can't directly inherit money. By leaving the money to a trust or a custodial account, you can name the person who will oversee the money until the child is of age. (Note that some states define minors as anyone under the age of 18; some states use age 21.) If you don't set up the gift this way, a judge might select an outside guardian to handle the money, someone who would not be of your choosing.

Of course, lumping all your heirs together in one IRA is the easiest route to take. But by doing this, you potentially rob the younger ones of a richer inheritance.

If your children inherited the same IRA, all of them would be forced to make mandatory withdrawals based on the oldest sibling's life expectancy, a real disadvantage for younger children interested in preserving the IRA for as long as possible. Say that a mother left her IRA to her two daughters, ages 52 and 42, and to her 18-year-old grandson. According to IRS life expectancy tables, a 52-year-old's life expectancy is 31.3 years, but a 42-year-old's life expectancy is 40.6 years. An 18-year-old's life expectancy is 63.9 years.

If the children each inherited their own IRA, they would be entitled to the use their own life expectancy. So, the 18-year-old would be allowed to stretch out his IRA payments for more than 63 years instead of 31.3 years, giving him an extra 32 years to capitalize on the earnings.

As you'll learn later in the chapter, a solution may now exist to undo the potential harm if an IRA owner bequeathed a single IRA to a group of individuals; see the "Understand your options" section.

Keep an eye on the paperwork.

In many cases, IRA beneficiary paperwork hasn't changed much over the years. Many forms were developed when the IRA was still in its infancy. When the paperwork was designed, no one envisioned that IRAs would one day swell to six and seven figures. Nor was there much, if any, thought given to whether these forms would be adequate when IRA customers started dying. For example, suppose that you've inherited an IRA, and you want to name your own beneficiary in case you die before the IRA is emptied. Not all IRA forms accommodate this desire. In some cases, you might need to have your attorney draw up a specialized form for your inherited assets.

Inadequate forms aren't the only problem. Missing ones can create even more havoc. Merger mania among banks and other financial institutions has increased the chances that your IRA forms have been lost or misplaced in a basement or warehouse. The consequences of this carelessness can be disastrous for heirs. Employees at several New York banks, for instance, searched in vain for beneficiary forms for some of their deceased customers. Because no official records of the IRA beneficiaries could be found, the IRAs had to be disbanded. The loved ones didn't sue because they didn't possess the original beneficiary forms that would have proven their case. They pocketed the money from the disbanded IRAs, but they missed out on many years of invaluable tax-deferred growth.

To protect your family's inheritance, ask your IRA custodian for a copy of the original beneficiary form that you filled out. Keep copies of this document with your attorney, in your safe deposit box, and in your personal files.

Tip When you mail in a beneficiary form, request that your financial institution stamp "received" on a copy, date it, and send back a copy.

Think about a Roth IRA conversion.

Most older people assume Roth IRAs are only for the young. Most would never consider converting a traditional IRA into a Roth IRA because the conversion results in a large tax bill. Less than 1 percent of conversions at one major discount brokerage firm were initiated by those older than 70. But a Roth conversion could be an excellent idea for seniors if they won't need the money in the IRA during their lifetimes. Even a death-bed conversion could be worthwhile.

 Cross-Reference See Chapter 10 for details on Roth conversions.

An inherited Roth is far more valuable than a regular one because heirs won't have to pay any income tax on a Roth windfall as it's withdrawn. If an heir withdraws the money over his or her lifetime, the tax-free compounding and the free ride on withdrawals can be a tremendous boon. (Heirs must pay taxes on withdrawals of all other IRAs.)

Consider life insurance.

Ideally, you want your children to enjoy the fruits of your IRA for many decades. But your hopes could be dashed if the IRA must be cannibalized to pay estate taxes as well as income taxes. In some cases, substantial accounts could be subject to income and estate taxes that reach 75 percent. If you own a huge IRA and most of your assets are wrapped up in it, you might want to obtain life insurance to pay the estate taxes.

IRA Inheritance Checklist

IRA inheritance rules can be confusing. This quick list highlights what you need to do, whether you are the IRA owner or an heir.

Advice for an IRA owner:

- ✦ See how the new IRA rules might affect your IRA beneficiary decisions.

- ✦ Avoid naming your estate as the IRA beneficiary.

- ✦ Insist that your financial institution acknowledge in writing that it received your IRA beneficiary paperwork.

- ✦ Consider using customized IRA forms if no standard forms cover your situation.

- ✦ Double-check whom you've listed as IRA beneficiaries, and name contingency beneficiaries.

- ✦ Seek out professional advice on IRA inheritance issues.

- ✦ If you're currently making mandatory withdrawals from your IRA, calculate your new minimum required distribution. It may be considerably less than what you are now forced to take out.

- ✦ You can begin taking out the lower mandatory withdrawals beginning in 2001.

Advice for an IRA beneficiary:

- ✦ Keep your inherited IRA alive as long as possible.

- ✦ Discuss with your parents their intentions for passing along their IRAs.

- ✦ If a relative dies, don't move or touch the loved one's IRA without receiving tax advice.

- ✦ Explore how IRA mistakes may be rectified after the IRA owner has died.

- ✦ Don't erase the benefactor's name from an inherited account.

- ✦ If you inherited an IRA in 2000, you should be able to use the more favorable IRA payout schedule.

- ✦ Make provisions to pass on an inherited IRA to your own kids.

Don't pay life insurance premiums to cover estate taxes if you have reason to expect that the federal estate tax will be eliminated. One of the big campaign promises of President George W. Bush was to eliminate the estate tax. Some politicians on Capitol Hill, however, suggest that a scale-back of the tax is a more likely outcome.

Second-to-die insurance, which is typically cheaper than a regular life insurance policy, can be an ideal solution for a married couple. When the remaining spouse dies, the insurance pays out. This money is used to cover any estate tax liabilities. If life insurance is structured correctly, it doesn't generate estate or income taxes of its own. In this case, the insurance beneficiary, such as an adult son or daughter, must own the policy.

Withdraw the right amount of your IRA or retirement plan.

Despite the streamlined, user-friendly rules, people who are now making mandatory withdrawals from a retirement cache need to be vigilant. Harsh tax penalties exist for those who don't follow the new regulations. Someone who underestimates the mandatory withdrawal faces paying a 50 percent penalty on the amount that he or she failed to extract. In the past, this punishment was rarely imposed, but now thanks to new reporting requirements for financial institutions, it will be easy for the IRS to know who isn't following the rules.

You should also review the amount of money you are currently taking from your IRA. Under the revamped rules, most people will be permitted to withdraw far less money each year. (There's no ceiling on the maximum amount you can pull out — anything goes.) That's because the shift in the life-expectancy table is substantial. For instance, in the past, a 70-year-old was expected to make IRA withdrawals within a 16-year period. Under the new regulations, it can be spread out over 26.2 years or more.

This is exciting news for anybody who loathes taking money out of his or her IRA. More affluent retirees who don't need the money might prefer not to touch their retirement accounts because they want to shelter their money from taxes as long as possible. See more on this issue in Chapter 21.

If You're the Inheritor

Mishandling an inherited IRA can cost you plenty in money, time, and exasperation. Here you'll find some ways to avoid costly mistakes.

Talk to your parents.

Perhaps your mom and dad have no intention of spending their entire IRAs. They may be among the lucky ones who can live quite comfortably off other sources of income. If they intend to pass along all or some of their IRA assets to their kids, they need to know how to structure the handoff.

The only way you'll get a sense of whether your parents understand the issues involved in passing along an IRA is to ask. This conversation will be difficult for some people and maybe impossible for others. Of course, even if parents confide in their children, the family might not know whether the IRAs are structured properly. With their parents' acquiescence, some baby boomers are hiring attorneys and CPAs to double-check their parents' arrangements. Obviously, Mom and Dad can do this themselves, but they may resent the added expense.

Understand your options.

In the past, heirs could do little if their benefactors had inadvertently botched the IRA handoff from one generation to the next. But beneficiaries now enjoy greater freedoms to correct mistakes that Mom and Dad or other dearly departed benefactors might have made.

Posthumous estate planning, for example, could now rectify a potential mistake mentioned earlier in the chapter: leaving one IRA to more than one beneficiary. IRA regulations may now permit a division of the IRA after the owner dies that allow each heir to use his or her own life expectancy. In some cases, this could lengthen the life of an IRA for a considerably longer period for some heirs. To be able to successfully pull this off, however, it must be clear how the benefactor intended the IRA proceeds to be distributed. For instance, a mother might have indicated in her will that her three children were to each receive a third of the account.

Note It's important to consult an estate attorney or other expert who is familiar with IRS regulations if you want to rectify planning mistakes when you inherit an IRA.

The new regulations allow families at least a year — and most often even more time — to correct, in a limited way, a deceased's estate plan mistakes. That's because beneficiaries aren't officially recognized by the IRS until December 31 of the year after the IRA owner's death.

This posthumous planning provides other opportunities as well. It can resolve the problem that occurs when someone leaves an IRA jointly to a person and a charity. Remember that an IRA must be disbanded much quicker if the beneficiary is an estate? Well, similar rules apply to a charity. In the eyes of the IRS, the charity has a zero life expectancy, so any IRA that is bequeathed to a charity must be dissolved after the death of the owner. This is true even if the IRA is to be shared with a person. It's now possible to divert this disaster, however, by cashing out a charity. That is, the amount intended for the charity is withdrawn from the IRA while preserving the IRA and its tax benefits to the real-life beneficiaries. The arrangement must be worked out between the charity and the other beneficiary.

Consider disclaiming an IRA.

If you inherit an IRA but don't need the money, consider disclaiming it. In other words, you waive the rights to the IRA in favor of somebody else. (Admittedly this won't apply — or appeal — to most people.)

Don't Stop with the First Opinion

After you inherit an IRA, behave as you would if your physician had just recommended a heart bypass. Get a second and preferably third opinion on how to proceed. IRA inheritance rules can be confusing, so it's best to hear more than one slant on what you should do with your windfall. You'll want to consult the sort of experts that were discussed earlier in the chapter.

Why would somebody prefer not to inherit an IRA? An affluent widow, for instance, might prefer that the IRA be inherited by her child, who could enjoy the tax benefits of the IRA for a much longer period of time.

The disclaimer, which was conceived back in the 1970s, can be a creative tool to rescue a variety of botched estate plans. Although married couples enjoy a more liberal use of disclaimers, others can rely upon the strategy as well. Disclaimers can be very tricky, though; anyone contemplating such a move needs to be advised by an experienced estate-planning attorney.

Decide whether you need to spend or save.

When you inherit an IRA, you might be anxious to cash it out all at once rather than taking it in yearly distributions as you are entitled to by law. If you cash out an inherited IRA, you pay income taxes on the entire amount. But if you don't need the money immediately, you might be able to keep the IRA alive for many decades.

In general, an inherited IRA can mushroom dramatically over the years if someone pulls out just the minimum amount of money required by tax laws. Under the new rules, these minimum distributions will be calculated upon a beneficiary's life expectancy, which is calculated using his or her age in the year after the benefactor's death.

When you do withdraw money from an inherited IRA, whether it's the minimum required or more, you will pay income taxes on the cash. The Roth IRA provides the only exception. Someone lucky enough to inherit a Roth won't have to pay taxes on the withdrawals.

Caution Loved ones who inherit an IRA often don't know what to do with it. A study conducted by Oppenheimer Funds indicates that people who inherit at least $50,000 spend just one week thinking about their action plan. No one should be in that big of a hurry.

Don't wipe Mom or Dad's name off the account.

When you're dealing with inherited IRAs, using common sense can get you into deep trouble. When you inherit an IRA, you might assume that the account, whether it's at Fidelity, Merrill Lynch, a bank trust department, or someplace else, is yours. That's true, but you'd better leave your benefactor's name on the account. Only a spouse can put an inherited IRA in his or her name. If you substitute your own name on an IRA that you inherited from anyone other than your spouse, the IRS will consider this innocent act as a complete cashing out of the IRA. Oops, you'll owe taxes on the full amount.

You not only have to watch your own actions, but you have to watch the financial institution's as well. In one sad case, a bank, acting upon an estate attorney's advice, attempted to swiftly distribute a dead father's $400,000 IRA to his four children. The dad's name was removed, and four new accounts were opened. As a result, the IRS demanded immediate tax payment, and the IRA was disbanded. Instead of the $400,000 being allowed to grow into millions over many years, the tax-deferral advantage evaporated, much to the anger of the heirs. Although this very error has happened countless times, by the time it's noticed, the damage can't be undone.

Tip   To protect yourself, keep the inherited IRA in the original account owner's name, but make sure the IRA custodian adds your name and Social Security number to the account and notes on the paperwork the date of your benefactor's death.

Sharing an IRA with someone who has died can create other frustrations, too. You might encounter problems moving that IRA. Suppose that someone's dad, for instance, parked his IRA in a certificate of deposit at his lifelong bank. A son or daughter might be itching to transfer this money into a brokerage account where it won't be restricted to ultraconservative investments. Because the dad obviously can't okay the move, the bank's custodian must approve the transfer plan. The place where the child wants the money sent must sign off on the transaction, too. Some financial institutions balk at approving such transactions because of general phobia about inherited IRA snafus. If you encounter problems, remain persistent. The financial institutions must legally permit you to move the money.

Anticipate your own mortality.

With any luck, you'll still be enjoying that inherited IRA when you start contemplating your own mortality. If you want to name your kids as beneficiaries of their grandmother's original IRA, however, your own IRA custodian may try to stop you. In the past, mutual funds and brokerage firms have balked at permitting customers to extend the lives of their IRAs for another generation. If a custodian refuses, you might want to have your attorney, CPA, or a financial planner get involved. Sometimes just the hint of a lawsuit works wonders.

Luckily, this institutional reluctance is slowly beginning to evaporate. Some financial institutions are now developing special paperwork that allows IRA inheritors to designate their own beneficiaries. However, some IRA custodians accept the special paperwork but then decline to pass on the IRA as directed when the customer dies. Instead, the financial institution might direct the money to the deceased's estate, which in effect kills the IRA. Before the custodian does anything with the IRA after the owner's death, contact the custodian to ensure that the written agreement will be honored.

Tip Don't despair if your bank or brokerage firm doesn't have its own beneficiary forms. An attorney can create a customized form.

When you mail in a customized form, make sure you get a mailed acknowledgement from the institution that it received and approved your form. Sometimes firms accept special forms only if the customer has invested a significant amount of assets (at least six figures) at the institution.

Summary

✦ Review your IRA holdings in light of the sweeping changes in IRS regulations regarding IRA distributions.

✦ Don't touch an inherited IRA without seeking professional advice.

✦ It may be possible to correct IRA inheritance mistakes even after the IRA owner has died.

✦ Beneficiaries should resist plundering their IRA windfall because the tax protection is invaluable.

✦ Make sure all your IRA and workplace retirement plan paperwork is in order and that you have copies of the documents.

✦ Keep Mom or Dad's name on your inherited IRA so that it isn't broken apart.

Stocks and Mutual Funds for the Savvy Investor

P A R T

IV

◆ ◆ ◆ ◆

In This Part

Chapter 12
Stocks: Who, What, When, Where, and How

Chapter 13
Stock Picking 101

Chapter 14
Selecting the Right Mutual Funds

Chapter 15
Index Funds and Exchange-Traded Funds

Chapter 16
Protecting Stocks and Mutual Funds from Taxes

◆ ◆ ◆ ◆

Part IV explores how Americans can turbo charge their retirement savings by investing in stocks. You will learn how to intelligently analyze mutual funds and individual stocks before including them in your portfolio. This part also examines a relatively new type of equity investing called exchange-traded funds and compares it to another fine alternative, index mutual funds. Finally, the many tips included in this section teach you how to invest in the stock market without getting gouged by taxes.

Stocks: Who, What, When, Where, and How

Understanding, selecting, and purchasing stocks is a big topic. This chapter nibbles away at it by explaining what kinds of stocks are available, how they work, and how different type of stocks have performed over time. Whether you are planning for or are already in retirement, stocks should play a pivotal role in most portfolios.

Here are some basics for newcomers to the equities scene: When you buy shares in a stock, you're purchasing a miniature piece of a corporation. Your tiny stake in the company is your equity, which is why stocks are often referred to as equities. Once you buy shares, you're entitled to any dividends — a cut of the company's earnings — that the company issues. Companies that are growing at a rapid clip often don't generate dividends. Instead, you hope to enjoy a great ride with the price of each of your shares increasing. This price acceleration is referred to as capital appreciation. Investors buy the vast majority of stocks through the New York Stock Exchange, the Nasdaq and the American Stock Exchange. The New York Stock Exchange, which is sometimes referred to as the Big Board, is the oldest and largest exchange. Many of the biggest blue chip names are listed here. A significant number of the companies traded on the Nasdaq, which is the youngest exchange, are smaller companies with a heavy tech influence. In the shadows is the American Stock Exchange which has been gaining more attention by listing the bulk of exchange-traded funds, a new type of mutual fund traded like a stock (and one that is detailed in Chapter 15).

The Advantages of Stocks

Why invest in stocks? Back in the 1990s, this question wasn't one that many people pondered. The answer appeared self-evident. Techno-geek millionaires bought Lamborghinis on their lunch hour. Secretaries with stock options retired before the first gray hairs ever appeared in their combs. And the 401(k), that unlyrical subsection of the U.S. Tax Code, infiltrated the public's consciousness to become a household name. When the 20th century ended, the longest bull market in American history stampeded across the fallen confetti and charged right into the new millennium — at least for a little while.

Note

When the stock prices overall are increasing for a prolonged period, it's called a bull market. When stock values decline overall for an extended time, it's called a bear market.

Years from now, historians will probably look back on this era as a phenomenon. It was a time when stock returns and investors' ambitious expectations were clearly out of whack with the historical averages of the stock market. Investing milestones seemed to be set every few days during the longest and most volatile bull market in history. During the 90s, America Online soared in value by more than 70,000 percent, and it had an amazing amount of company. At the same time, however, it wasn't unusual for some high-flying stocks to plummet 20 or 30 percent in just one day.

Note

Wild stock market rides are nothing new: In 1907, for instance, the Dow Jones Industrial Average plummeted a negative 37.7 percent; the next year it bounced back 48.2 percent.

Top performers over time

The reason why stocks are the bedrock of retirement investing, however, remains the same whether Wall Street is marveling at the Dow Jones Industrial Average's new high or struggling as it did in the 1930s when the Dow's return for the entire decade was a negative 39 percent. Throughout modern history, stocks have clearly outperformed bonds and cash by an impressive margin. Since the eve of the Great Crash in 1929, the stock market has been up more than twice as many years as it has been down.

Stocks clearly belong in most individuals' portfolios, including retirees and those about to retire. Some financial experts suggest that retirees should devote 60 or 70 percent or more of their portfolio to stocks. The reason behind this advice is the fact that people are living longer. In just the past couple of decades, the average American's life expectancy has jumped more than three years to 77 years of age, and the pharmaceutical giants are hell-bent on stretching that much further. Of course, millions of Americans live well beyond that average.

Cross-Reference

See Chapter 20 for details on building and maintaining a portfolio during your years of retirement.

Ease of investing

Investing in stocks has become much easier since the first investors traded stocks under a buttonwood tree along an unremarkable New York City road called Wall Street more than 200 years ago. The explosion of discount brokerage services has reduced the average transaction fee that investors pay for buying a block of stock to less than the price of a tank of gas. Valuable research that used to be the exclusive domain of institutional investors is now free. Index funds, which were once ridiculed by financial pundits, are enabling amateur investors to soundly beat the pros with better investment returns. Wall Street has even created a new way to invest in equities for those who are torn between individual stocks and mutual funds: the exchange-traded funds. Such funds provide a great option for reluctant investors who love the idea of owning individual stocks, but lack the desire or the knowledge to go the distance with individual stock trading.

Cross-Reference   For the first time in history, top-notch money managers, who used to pick stocks exclusively for pension funds, endowments, and multimillionaires, are now helping the merely affluent. See Chapter 4 for more information.

You don't need a lot of money to begin investing in individual stocks or stock mutual funds. You can now open a trading account at a discount broker for as little as $500, and some mutual fund companies will get you started for $50 provided that you commit to investing a small amount of cash each month. What's more, hundreds of companies are now offering direct-purchase stock plans in which you can bypass a broker altogether and buy as little as $50 worth of shares in a company for a low fee or none at all. (See Chapter 7's section on DSPs and DRIPs.)

Whether the market is up or down, some things have not changed. You still need to know what stocks to put in your portfolio, whether that's a 401(k), an Individual Retirement Account, a taxable brokerage account, or some other kind of account. You'll also need to know what is a prudent amount of stocks for your own comfort level. Exposing your portfolio to unacceptable risk can lead to financial disaster.

Stock Classification

A space alien listening to breathless Wall Street dispatches from the media might have recently assumed that only two types of stocks existed on this planet: blue chip, which refers to the stock of widely recognized corporation that possesses a long record of growth (and named for the color of the most valuable poker chips) and explosive technology stocks. Yet an entire world of worthwhile stocks falls in between.

The most common way to characterize stocks is through their *market capitalization.* To determine a stock's market capitalization, you multiply the price of a single share by the number of stock shares held by individuals. The market capitalization of Microsoft, the biggest company in the Dow Jones Industrial Average, was recently $262 billion, making it most definitely a "large-cap" stock.

The typical size classifications of stocks break down this way:

✦ **Large-cap:** $10 billion plus

✦ **Mid-cap:** $2 billion to $10 billion

✦ **Small-cap:** $1 billion to $2 billion

✦ **Micro-cap:** Usually well under $1 billion

Winners attract the most cash—it's human nature. For most of the 1990s, the winners were large-cap stocks. In the early 1990s, however, small-caps were hot. In the mid-1980s, foreign stocks were the market darlings. And in 2000, mid-cap stocks were the stars. The trouble with positioning yourself at ground zero of a scorching market is that you don't know when the fire will shift. Markets can change with breathtaking speed, and trying to predict the market's direction is futile. In fact, while technology stocks were hot for much of the 1990s, investors who piled in late for the ride were truly whipsawed. In 2000, the tech heavy Nasdaq plummeted 39 percent, which was the worst year in its history

Tip

Because the stock and bond market is a moving target, keeping a broad mix of assets in any long-range portfolio is essential. Some industry research has long suggested that over time your mix of stocks, bonds, and cash will affect your returns more dramatically than the individual brand names in your portfolio.

Large-cap stocks

For quite awhile now, investors have preferred to stuff their portfolios with corporations such as AT&T, IBM, Hewlett Packard, and the rest of the nation's industrial Goliaths. By one estimate, 93 percent of all the money invested in stock mutual funds was recently sitting in large-cap stocks.

This loyalty to large-caps is understandable. During the past five years, the Standard & Poor's 500 Index, which tracks large-cap stocks, has averaged returns of more than 18 percent. The Nasdaq 100, which is stuffed with many of the most successful and biggest technology companies in the galaxy, claims even more spectacular performance figures. During the same period, it has averaged annual returns of more than 32 percent. (See the section on indexes later in this chapter for more details on market performance.)

Beyond the latest numbers, Americans gravitate to the big boys for this reason: Large-caps, having survived the brutal weeding-out process, are generally more dependable and less volatile when the stock market is getting pounded. Many large-cap stocks, such as Hershey's, Johnson & Johnson, and Ford Motor Company, have been around for decades reliably making products that Americans keep in their kitchens, medicine cabinets, bedrooms, or driveways. It's doubtful that anybody is going to chase them out of the marketplace. Designating large-cap stocks as the core holdings in a long-term retirement portfolio makes a great deal of sense.

Tip The easiest way to give your retirement portfolio a solid core of large-caps is to purchase shares in a mutual fund.

If you prefer to construct your own stock portfolio instead of buying mutual fund shares, consider putting the bulk of your investments in the highest quality stocks. After all, would you rather place a bet on the seventh best player in an industry and hope it can rise to fourth place, or start out with the pick of the litter? If you invest in individual stocks, diversification across several different industries, such as technology, health, retail, financials, utilities, and consumer staples is also critical.

Mid-cap stocks

If you're looking for something spicier than a large-cap but can't stomach the volatility of small-cap stocks, look to mid-caps as an option that won't give you much indigestion. They add spice to a portfolio, but the inherent risks aren't as high as with small-caps.

In the mutual fund world, your mid-cap options are just a fraction of the choices you'll find with large-cap and small-cap funds. One reason is that mid-cap stocks are a moving target. A portfolio of mid-cap stocks won't stay in that category. A high-flying mid-cap will evolve into a large-cap while a losing mid-cap will slip into the small-cap category.

Note Some analysts suggest you don't even need mid-cap stocks in your portfolio, asserting that a mix of large- and small-caps will evenly balance your portfolio.

Well-known mid-cap stocks include the following:

Abercrombie & Fitch	Harley-Davidson
Alaska Air	Tiffany & Co.
Callaway Golf	Office Depot
Sotheby's	Smucker's
Best Buy	Scholastic

Small-cap stocks

Many people dismiss small-cap stocks as too risky. Although plenty of flashy high-tech startups are lurking in the small-cap universe, many littler companies aren't nearly so exotic. You might be surprised at how many players you could recognize. Here are a few:

Swiss Army Brands	Lillian Vernon
Ethan Allen Interiors	Pier 1 Imports
La-Z-Boy	Sports Authority

Chiquita Brands International	Nautica Enterprises
Oshkosh B'Gosh	Toro
Jack in the Box	Gymboree

Admittedly, small-caps are inherently more volatile and therefore riskier than large-caps. One of these tiny tots may offer only one or two product lines, and they can be hit harder during a recession or when one or two key managers leave. These stocks also aren't traded as heavily as the bigger ones, which can cause wider price swings. Yet despite these characteristics, small-caps can reduce a portfolio's risk.

Tip Studies indicate that adding a 10 percent small-cap exposure to a large-cap portfolio will boost returns over time without increasing risks. The mix of big and small companies dampens the volatility of the investments.

Recent years indicate that large- and small-cap stocks don't move in tandem. With each captive to its own mysterious cycles, both types of stocks can move in dramatically different directions. When large-caps stumble, small-caps may excel. A portfolio that is loaded with just one type of investment, whether it's blue chips, bonds, real estate, or certificates of deposit, is much more susceptible to financial hazards such as inflation or a bear market.

What's quirky about small-caps is that their periods of excellent performance can be unpredictably sudden and relatively short-lived. However, their bad years can be truly dreadful. Small-caps are like the little girl in the nursery rhyme. When she's good, she's very, very good. When she's bad, she's horrid.

Note Since the 1920s, small-caps have outperformed large-caps by 3 or 4 percent.

Micro-cap stocks

The tiniest companies huddle together in their own category. Because they are so little by Wall Street standards, you can expect these munchkins to be even more volatile than small-caps. Even within the mercurial micro-cap world, however, you'll find long-time companies that most people would consider quite tame. Among the ranks of micro-caps, for example, you'll find quite a few community banks.

Most financial experts suggest that an aggressive investor dedicate no more than 5 percent of his or her portfolio to micro-caps. Because researching these stocks individually is so difficult, the best way to invest in micro-caps is through a mutual fund. The selection of this type of fund, however, is small.

 Resource Intrepid investors who'd like to do their own picking should consider first reading *Mastering Microcaps: Strategies, Trends, and Stock Selection* by Daniel P. Coker, published by Bloomberg Press.

Stay Away from Penny Stocks

If you're intrigued by small-cap investing, don't get suckered into purchasing penny stocks. Penny stocks are the cheapest of the cheap. Usually you can buy a share for under $5, and sometimes the price is less than what you'd pay for a candy bar.

There's often a good reason why these shares are selling for a pittance. The risks are extremely high. Investing in many penny stock companies, which may not have real businesses behind them, is so speculative that you may as well be feeding a slot machine.

Often penny stocks are promoted by obscure brokerage firms that rely heavily upon telephone cold-calling to find gullible customers. Don't buy anything from an unknown broker who contacts you by phone. Also stick with stocks that are traded on the New York Stock Exchange, the Nasdaq, and the American Stock Exchange. The financial requirements these exchanges impose on their listing companies effectively shut out the penny stocks.

The Great Balancing Act: Value and Growth Stocks

Size matters when balancing your portfolio, but it shouldn't be your only consideration. Before you can be truly diversified, you need to determine how to divide your equity holdings between value and growth stocks.

Value stocks are essentially garage-sale buys. Often these stocks, which can be of any size from micro- to large-cap, are beaten down because their industries, such as natural resources, heavy manufacturing, or banks, have been temporarily shunned. There may be nothing inherently wrong with these companies, which is what attracts bargain hunters. Often these companies' shares are attractively priced and offer above average *dividend yields* (the average dividend hardly reached 3 percent in the 1990s). These characteristics mean that these companies are considered less risky than their go-go growth competition.

Note
The *dividend yield* is the ratio of the dividend to the share price. For example, if a company's share price is $10, and the company pays out $1 a year in dividends, its dividend yield is 10 percent.

Growth stocks are sexier and often far more expensive than value stocks. Investors are willing to pay more for these companies, which often offer strong earnings and revenue growth, because they that believe their torrid expansion pace will continue. Well-known growth companies include the likes of Charles Schwab, Home Depot, JDS Uniphase, Amgen, Applied Materials, and Oracle. Growth companies rarely generate dividends to their stockholders.

The case for value stocks

In recent years, value stocks have been about as popular as political commercials. The flow of money into generally safer value stock funds has evaporated. The reason why value degenerated into a dirty word on Wall Street in the 1990s is easy to see: growth stocks averaged returns of 20.6 percent while value stocks lagged behind at 15.4 percent. However, value funds don't deserve the rude treatment they've received over the last decade. Over the very long haul, value stocks have fared a bit better. Until the tail end of the 1990s, value stocks edged out growth rivals during a period stretching back to 1975. While value and growth stocks have produced similar returns, they each have enjoyed periods where they've been top dog.

Note Value does capture the performance title if you look at a longer period. The majority of history's most celebrated investors, including Nebraska billionaire Warren Buffett and his mentor, Benjamin Graham, have remained faithful value stock disciples.

Balancing your portfolio with value stocks

Trying to guess whether growth stocks will stumble or value stocks will regain their momentum is futile. Yet you don't need to make such predictions if you hedge your bet and sink money into both types of funds. However, diversification isn't the only reason to embrace value stocks. With growth stocks performing stupendously in recent years, many investors' portfolios remain heavily weighted in these riskier stocks. Adding value stocks may bring balance to lopsided portfolios.

Note With growth stocks performing stupendously for so many years, your portfolio may be overweighted in high-octane stocks and therefore exposed to more risk than you'd like. A lopsided portfolio can pose a threat to retirees' finances.

The easiest way to get your value fix is through mutual funds. When you shop for value stocks, however, beware of what you're buying. Although most value funds have floundered in recent years, some have shined with superb numbers. Gravitating to the winners, however, might not be prudent for conservative investors. That's because many of the most successful value funds hold stakes in companies that would make traditional value disciples cringe.

Legg Mason Value Trust, which is probably the most successful value fund in recent memory, was recently stuffed with such traditional high flyers as Dell Computer, Gateway, and other technology stocks. Fund manager William H. Miller III, who believes that investing predominantly in the traditional smokestack industries is questionable, sees value in new economy companies such as Nextel and Worldcom. So does Wally Weitz, another acclaimed value manager, who has been committed to volatile cable stocks. Meanwhile, Kevin Landis, the manager of Firsthand Technology Value Fund (one of the best-performing mutual funds in recent years), stuffs his portfolio with technology stocks that he considers undervalued. Industry observers are still shaking their heads that a fund smoking with these firecrackers could ever be considered a value fund.

Buy and Hold and Hold and Hold

If you are investing over a period of many years, your best strategy is to stay put no matter what the market is doing. Don't panic. Research has shown that dodging in and out of the market even for just a few days can be disastrous. Take a study that focused on what would have happened to $1,000 invested in fund based on the S&P 500 index during one recent 10-year period. The portfolio would ultimately have grown to $4,014. But if the investor had missed the 10 best days on Wall Street during that time, the portfolio would be worth only $2,653. By sitting out just the 20 best days, the profits would have been cut nearly in half to $2,034.

Research also indicates that rapid-fire trading can be just as dangerous. A well-publicized study conducted by a couple of professors at the University of California revealed that frequent traders earned an annual return of 11.4 percent, but those who tended to hold on to their stocks realized annual gains of 18.5 percent. These numbers were generated after scrutinizing 60,000 discount brokerage accounts during a six-year period ending in 1997. A follow-up study done by the same researchers has since revealed a similar trend.

Nonetheless, plenty of people are tuning out these admonitions. Today many investors are holding stocks for just months or even minutes, instead of years. Even fund fans have caught the speculative bug. By one estimate, the average investor now ditches a fund in less than four years; just a decade ago, a fund typically stayed inside a portfolio for 11 years. The last time investors were so trigger-happy was in the years leading up to the 1929 stock market crash.

You must decide whether you want to follow the lead of the new breed of value funds or stick with a traditional one. Both types are represented in the following list of funds that you may want to consider:

- ✦ Legg Mason Value Trust; (800) 822-5544
- ✦ Ameristock; (800) 394-5064
- ✦ Vanguard Windsor II; (800) 635-1511
- ✦ Davis New York Venture; (800) 279-0279
- ✦ Weitz Partners Value; (800) 232-4161
- ✦ Vanguard Value Index; (800) 635-1511
- ✦ Firsthand Technology Value; (888) 884-2675

Stock Indexes: A Handy Reference

Indexes are an excellent tool to help investors evaluate how well or poorly their portfolios are faring. Indexes are essentially listings designed to reflect the performance of a certain segments of the market. They were originally created for huge institutional investors, such as pension funds and insurance companies, which wanted benchmarks to evaluate the performance of their own money managers. Today thousands of indexes exist. However, you need to be aware of only a handful that can be found in most newspapers. One of the nation's best known indexes, for instance, is the Standard & Poor's 500. It contains most of the nation's most prominent corporations. Knowing how the S&P 500 has fared can easily help you evaluate your own holdings. For example, if you own a large-cap mutual fund that inched up a total of 11 percent during a three-year period, but the Standard & Poor's 500 index soared 40 percent, you'll want to evaluate whether you should remain loyal to that mutual fund because it lagged so far behind the benchmark.

There are other practical ways to use indexes. When you're shopping for mutual funds, you need to find out what indexes prospective funds use as their benchmarks so you won't end up with multiple funds sharing the same mission. For instance, you don't need three large-cap growth funds that each measure their performance against the S&P 500. Meanwhile, if you're an index fund aficionado, you should have some sense of which companies are in an index before you select a fund because index funds limit their investments to the companies listed on that particular index.

Note   An index fund is not the same as an index. You can't directly invest in an index. But index mutual funds were created to allow you to invest in all or many of the corporations that are represented in an index—a topic detailed in Chapter 15.

Wilshire 5000

The Wilshire 5000 is America's biggest stock index and the only one that covers the performance of the entire U.S. stock market. Despite its misleading name, the index encompasses more than 7,000 companies. Although the index has received far less attention than the Standard & Poor's 500, both track records are nearly identical. Since it was created in 1971, the Wilshire 5000 has enjoyed an annualized return of 13.7 percent compared with the S&P 500's 13.8 percent.

Tip   The Wilshire 5000 should perform slightly better than the Standard & Poor's 500 during periods when small-caps shine.

Standard & Poor's 500

If you own shares in an index fund, it's probably linked to the Standard & Poor's 500, which, true to its name, contains 500 hand-picked Goliaths that trade primarily on the New York Stock Exchange. This elite group of corporate titans represents about 80 percent of the market value of all U.S. stocks.

Recently, the 10 largest corporation in the index were the following:

Microsoft	Intel
General Electric	Lucent Technologies
Cisco Systems	IBM
Wal-Mart	Citigroup
Exxon Mobil	America Online

As this lineup suggests, the index is currently heavily weighted in high-priced technology stocks; technology stocks now make up about 30 percent of the index. This development is stunning when you realize that technology represented only 13 percent of the index just a few years ago. At the start of the 1990s, IBM was the only technology stock in the top 10 list.

The S&P 500 has experienced a backlash lately from professional money managers, who insist that the Wilshire 5000 is a superior proxy for the U.S. stock market because it includes small- and mid-cap stocks as well. The Wilshire 5000 might be a slightly safer bet for conservative investors or retirees who worry about technology-driven volatility or for any investor whose goal is to mimic the returns of the entire stock market rather than just large-cap stocks. Nonetheless, even the Wilshire 5000 is heavily weighted with America's biggest corporations.

Dow Jones Industrial Average

When you hear a television network anchor or your neighbor commenting on how the stock market did today, they are referring to the Dow Jones Industrial Average. Ironically, the Dow, which was created by newspaper editor Charles H. Dow in 1896, isn't as broad an indicator as many assume. Just 30 huge companies are included. The editors of *The Wall Street Journal* occasionally tinker with the lineup to make it a better market bellwether. Not long ago, the editors booted such old-line companies as Goodyear Tire & Rubber and Sears, Roebuck & Co. to make way for Microsoft, Intel, and other new economy stocks.

You can find all 30 Dow stocks listed together each day in *The Wall Street Journal.*

Nasdaq Composite

This benchmark, launched in 1971, contains all the corporations, both domestic and foreign, that are listed on the Nasdaq stock market. The composite includes more than 5,000 companies. Nasdaq has become synonymous with technology for good reason. About 70 percent of the composite's valuation can be traced to technology stocks.

Nasdaq 100

Created in 1985, the Nasdaq 100 index includes the largest and most actively traded corporations in the Nasdaq stock market. At this writing, the Nasdaq 100 is devoted almost entirely to technology stocks to the exclusion of other industries. (The financial industry is kept out of the mix intentionally, because the Nasdaq created a separate index for financials in 1985 — the Nasdaq Financial 100 Index.) The Nasdaq 100 has outperformed all major domestic and foreign indexes during the past decade.

Members of this elite index include the following companies:

Microsoft	Amazon.com
Apple Computer	Worldcom
Cisco Systems	Bed, Bath & Beyond
Qualcomm	Staples
Starbucks	Sun Microsystems
Yahoo!	Northwest Airlines

Russell 2000

The Russell 2000, the oldest small-cap index, was created two decades ago by the Frank Russell Co., a prestigious money management firm in Tacoma, Washington. Its original purpose was to make it easier for institutional investors to track the small-cap universe. Each summer, the company pinpoints the nation's 3,000 biggest companies and lops off the bottom two-thirds to form the Russell 2000. The market value of all 2,000 companies still wouldn't surpass the market value of a handful of blue chip stocks.

Standard & Poor's SmallCap 600

As the name suggests, the S&P SmallCap 600 doesn't cast as wide a net. The companies that make the cut are slightly bigger companies than what you'd find in the Russell 2000.

Note   As you'll see in Table 12-1, the S&P SmallCap 600 has performed significantly better during the past five years than the Russell 2000.

Standard & Poor's MidCap 400

You might assume that the S&P MidCap 400 index was carved out of the S&P 500, but it's not. The S&P 500 comprises 70 percent of the total stock market, but this mid-cap index represents the next 10 percent of the market.

Indexes on the Web

Next time you're surfing the Web, check out the following stock indexes:

✦ Dow Jones Industrial Average at `www.averages.dowjones.com`

✦ Standard & Poor's 500 at `www.spglobal.com`

✦ Nasdaq 100 and Nasdaq Composite at `www.nasdaq.com`

✦ Wilshire 5000 at `www.wilshire.com`

✦ Russell 2000 at `www.russell.com`

Morgan Stanley Capital International Europe, Australasia, and Far East Index (EAFE)

The EAFE index, which is pronounced *Ee-feh,* tracks the fortunes of foreign companies that are located in such developed nations as Germany, Great Britain, France, Ireland, and Singapore. This index is the most popular foreign index, and it's the one used most often to compare an individual's own foreign mutual fund performance.

How do these indexes perform?

Table 12-1 lays out the performance of major indexes over the last 5 years.

Table 12-1 Performance of Leading Indexes			
Index	*1 year*	*3 years*	*5 years*
Wilshire 5000	−10.73%	10.83%	16.72%
S&P 500	−9.11%	12.26%	18.33%
Dow Jones Industrial Average	−4.85%	12.63%	18.13%
Nasdaq Composite	−39.29%	16.53%	19.00%
Nasdaq 100	−36.84%	33.2%	32.37%
Russell 2000	−12.7%	1.04%	8.02%
S&P SmallCap 600	11.8%	7.44%	13.57%
S&P MidCap 400	17.51%	17.1%	20.41%
MSCI EAFE	−13.96%	9.64%	7.43%

Data through Dec. 31, 2000

Source: Wiesenberger

Summary

✦ Diversify your portfolio with different size stocks.

✦ Balance your portfolio: Don't snub value stocks.

✦ Avoid flitting in and out of stocks; buying and holding is your best strategy.

✦ Know which indexes matter to your investment goals and compare your investments' performance to the indexes.

✦   ✦   ✦

Stock Picking 101

In this chapter, you learn the basic rules of stock picking as well as sources of unbiased information and some key strategies to increase your chances of picking winners.

Why buy individual stocks at all when mutual funds represent the very best way to invest for most folks? The truth is that mutual funds can also be a bit dull. Sure, most funds make money over time, but they aren't capable of making the awesome leaps in value that a solitary stock can. An increasing number of restless investors have begun adding a few stocks to their portfolios.

Finding Stock Candidates

Owning individual stocks can be both lucrative and treacherous. Do you think you can distinguish the stinkers from the winners? Lots of people would love to give you advice, from the guys who post anonymous messages on Internet bulletin boards to your dry cleaner. But ultimately it's your money that's at stake. To begin your search for winners, you'll want to start out with some ideas to explore. In addition to relying upon your personal expertise, try the following strategies to flush out some candidates.

Cross-Reference If you aren't yet familiar with stock lingo and basic stock concepts, check out Chapter 12 to make for smoother reading ahead.

Plug into the media.

Stock investing has become such an obsession that almost any issue of a personal finance magazine or a newspaper contains a few ideas. Arguably the most thoughtful and sophisticated magazine devoted to individual stock pickers is

Bloomberg Personal Finance magazine. Television watchers can also gather tips by watching the two financial news cable channels: CNBC and CNNfn. If you prefer to use the Internet, visit their Web sites at www.cnbc.com and www.cnnfn.com.

Stay alert to trends.

Listening to the news can spawn ideas. When Coca-Cola is hit hard because a contaminated batch in Europe made some people ill, you might decide it's a buying opportunity. Or maybe you hear that Wal-Mart is forming an alliance with another company, and you suspect that stock will soar.

Use stock screens.

Free stock screens, which are widely available on financial Internet sites, sift out the big losers and suggest some solid prospects. The mother of all stock-screening services is Market Guide (www.marketguide.com). Most of the other financial Internet sites that offer stock screening buy their data from this service.

Caution   Don't embrace the first idea you run across. Screening is only the first step. If you have neither the time nor the desire to research your picks, you're better off with mutual funds.

Get creative when looking for small- to mid-caps.

Finding promising smaller stocks is more challenging because the giants get most of the attention. With a company like Disney having dozens of stock analysts covering every hiccup in its business cycle, there aren't going to be many corporate surprises from that end. With such thorough coverage, the stock may pretty much be priced "efficiently" — that is, the price is where it should be. But a small-cap stock may have just one analyst or none at all covering it. There are, after all, more than 10,000 small-cap stocks! Financial experts refer to the small-cap market as an "inefficient" market. Consequently, you may be able to find hidden jewels among the legions of small-cap companies publicly traded nationwide.

So where do you find these stock jewels? Stock screens are always an option. If you don't have a computer, however, don't despair. You may want to buy a copy of *Standard & Poor's SmallCap 600 Guide* or *Standard & Poor's MidCap 400 Guide.* These thick books, which are updated annually, contain valuable information on all the companies listed in these S&P indexes. S&P stock researchers provide a business profile of each company, a list of recent notable developments for each company, and a chart of each company's historic stock performance and key financial figures. The books can be ordered through any bookstore.

Also consider visiting the cyber headquarters of *The Red Chip Review,* a highly regarded small-cap newsletter (www.redchip.com). Some of the content is free, but signing up for a free trial membership provides access to more of the goodies. Red Chip's screens have narrowed the small-cap universe to 300 promising companies.

Mixing and Matching

Investing in stocks doesn't have to be an all-or-nothing proposition. If you're a novice, placing your biggest bets on mutual funds is the safest strategy. But beyond that, the combinations are endless. You might decide to own an index fund for large-caps and pick individual small-caps if you're eager to discover your own hidden gems. Or you may prefer to own individual stocks, but you don't have the patience or the intellectual stamina to stay abreast of technological advances. If you fit into that category, you share something in common with billionaire Warren Buffett, who balks at holding high-tech stocks because he doesn't understand them. In this case, you could get your technology fix by investing in a technology sector fund. Chapter 14 tells you all about picking mutual funds.

You may also want to steal ideas from the pros. Call the toll-free number of a mutual fund family that offers a top-notch small-cap or mid-cap fund and ask for a copy of its annual report.

Tip　A mutual fund's annual report lists the fund's stock holdings and may include a manager's reasons for favoring certain stocks, which is information you can use.

The Dividend Dilemma

A dividend is a company's distribution of earnings to investors who own stock or mutual fund shares. Once upon a time, dividends provided decent and steady payouts. Today, however, anybody who is retired is probably keenly aware that today's stock dividends are pathetic. Lately, the average blue chip dividend yield barely surpassed 1 percent. Obviously, a retiree on a fixed income can't count on this sort of payout to pay grocery bills.

In recent years, doomsayers have touted puny dividend yields as proof that the stock market is wildly overvalued. In the past, dividend yields served as a good barometer of the health of the market. From the 1870s until 1990, the stock market usually stumbled whenever dividend yields dipped below 3 percent. But dividend yields have been stuck below that mark since the autumn of 1992.

Note　Many experts now all but state that an Elvis Presley reincarnation is more likely than a return to high dividends. In 1978, 66 percent of all publicly traded American companies rewarded shareholders with dividends. Today, less than 21 percent do.

For dividend stock fans, the pickings are slim. Tobacco stocks are an option, but many would-be investors are spooked by endless courtroom dramas pitting frail lung cancer patients against cigarette makers. Even utilities are no longer a dependable dividend oasis. With deregulation arriving on the scene, once sleepy utilities are hustling to remain competitive, and they are sacrificing some of their dividend booty to do so. If you look hard enough, however, you should be able to find stocks in these two sectors, as well as in real estate, financials, and consumer staples, that can pay as much as four times the going dividend rate.

Before beginning your search, ask yourself this question: Should I invest in stocks offering the highest yield or the ones offering the highest rate of dividend growth? Often the companies sporting today's juiciest yields tend to have the worse prospects for future dividend growth.

Tip   During your stock research, be sure to check a stock's average yield and dividend growth rate during the past five years as well as its current yield.

For regular payout streams, bonds, real estate investment trusts (REITs), and convertible securities are always options. Meanwhile, stock investors may want to gravitate to an equity-income or growth and income mutual fund for a dividend fix. These managers are more likely to invest in corporations that spin out dividends.

 Resource   An easy way to compare dividend yields and growth rates for individual stocks is to visit Market Guide (www.marketguide.com). Or go to your local library and ask the librarian for a copy of *Value Line Investment Survey,* the stock guide.

Required Reading

Most of the elementary information that you need to evaluate a stock can be obtained free through the Internet or by calling a corporation's toll-free number. When contacting a company directly, you need to ask for an annual report, a 10K, and a 10Q.

Annual report

In this glossy document, a corporation tries to put a positive spin on the past year's activities. The exhaustive financial statements are in the back. The report's balance sheet and income statement are critical in evaluating a company's financial health. The annual report can also answer what the company does, which might be more extensive than you think.

10K

This yearly report, devoid of the fluff, is meatier than the annual report. It contains the same financial numbers as well as a candid discussion of what went right or wrong during the past 12 months. You'll find this information under the heading "Management's Discussion and Analysis of Financial Condition." In one of its 10Ks, Nike, for instance, discussed how Americans snapped up shoes endorsed by basketball star Michael Jordan, but ignored a lot of other Nike sports gear lingering on shelves, including inline skating and roller hockey gear.

10Q

These quarterly reports are released about six weeks after a quarter ends. The reports contain financial figures that are broken down into quarters. The 10Qs are designed to update current stockholders, who are already aware of a company's financial fundamentals.

Analyzing income statements, balance sheets, statement of cash flows, and other financial information isn't easy. To do a proper job requires education. Many Web sites assume you already know how to scrutinize a company's balance sheet or understand what a P/E is or what other financial ratios mean. In contrast, Web sites such as Motley Fool (www.fool.com) and Market Guide (www.marketguide.com) don't take this knowledge for granted; they shepherd novices through the process.

Entire books are devoted to understanding 10Qs. To find a few, visit your local bookstore or library, or log onto Amazon.com and type "financial statements" into the search box.

Many people, however, resist the heavy lifting and instead rely upon others to do all the analysis. This method may be adequate as long as those outside resources are reliable. One tried-and-true source of information is Value Line (800-634-3583), which has been ranking stocks in terms of timeliness and safety for decades. As mentioned earlier in this chapter, you can find Value Line's regular updated coverage of stocks in many libraries.

Morningstar also rates stocks, though not as exhaustively. Subscribers to the monthly *Morningstar Stock Investor* (800-735-0770) receive a compendium of 300 stocks in a variety of industries that survive the Chicago firm's own rigorous screening. Morningstar's Web site (www.morningstar.com) also provides stock commentary and analysis.

Cyber Research

Thanks to cyberspace, you can now share in the same comprehensive and timely stock information that the wizards of Wall Street have historically paid exorbitant amounts of money to obtain. With tons of free data all just a click away, the trick is not wasting your time or getting buried. One way is to limit yourself to the must-see financial sites.

If you're shaky on the stock market basics, an excellent way to begin is by visiting the Web sites of the nation's personal finance publications and financial television networks. You can immerse yourself in stock basics, evaluate companies, pick up portfolio diversification tips, and much more. Consider visiting these worthwhile and free sites:

✦ Money Magazine at www.money.com

✦ CNBC at www.cnbc.com

✦ CNNfn at `www.cnnfn.com`

✦ Bloomberg Personal Finance Magazine at `www.bloomberg.com`

✦ Smart Money Magazine at `www.smartmoney.com`

✦ Worth Magazine at `www.worth.com`

✦ USA Today's money section at `www.usatoday.com/money`

All-Star Investment Sites

Don't feel like hopping from one site to another when you're researching investment opportunities? In that case, you'll definitely want to become acquainted with the mega investing sites, which you may see referred to as financial Internet portals. These sites aim to provide it all from investing primers to financial data on specific stocks. Here are some notable ones:

MoneyCentral

MSN MoneyCentral (`www.moneycentral.com`) is undoubtedly the Internet's best investing way station. The site's Research Wizard is a godsend for both novice and sophisticated investors. In easy to understand steps, Research Wizard produces a comprehensive, financial blueprint for countless stocks by gathering an exhaustive amount of data, including figures on sales, earnings, debt, and profit margin, as well as stock price prospects, analysts' opinions, and potential business catalysts. MoneyCentral also manages to present all this data in an understandable way. The software is a time saver because the analysis isn't presented in a vacuum. It provides comparisons of other companies in the same industry.

MoneyCentral also provides stock screens, including cheapest large-cap growth stocks and the S&P 500's highest yielding stocks. You can find Wall Street commentary and feature articles on such topics as technology investing, 401(k)s, retirement, estate planning, and Social Security here as well.

Yahoo!

Yahoo! (`www.yahoo.com`), the incredibly popular search engine, maintains a vast financial section. You can track a stock's daily price swings, punch up its historical price charts, and read the latest news affecting any specific company. Yahoo! also provides profiles of thousands of companies as well as data on a corporation's underlying financial fundamentals, its corporate growth prospects, and analysts' opinions. You can also find handy comparisons if you want to determine how a particular company ranks with others in the same industry.

CBS MarketWatch (www.csbmarketwatch.com)

CBS MarketWatch provides the same stockpile of research you can get from the previous two sites and similar investing tools. The site finds a variety of ways to dice financial data, including compiling charts of how dozens of different industries have performed over the years. The site also maintains libraries on such topics as retirement, taxes, investing, small business, and real estate. It also keeps tabs on IPO developments, market trends, and daily financial news.

Edgar and its user-friendly clones

Edgar isn't a financial portal, but for serious stock pickers, Edgar (www.sec.gov) is the ultimate place to head for raw stock data. Maintained by the Securities and Exchange Commission (SEC), Edgar is the vast depository for all the documents that publicly traded companies are required to file with the government. If you want copies of all Edgar's available material on, say, General Electric, your printer could be tied up for a very long time. You can get the same information by calling a corporation, but with Edgar you won't have to wait for the mail.

Unfortunately, SEC bureaucrats are not Web-savvy. Edgar's Web site can be difficult to navigate, and it's as homely as its name. Consequently, you may want to get the same raw data from this more user-friendly source, FreeEDGAR (www.freeedgar.com).

To Buy or Not to Buy

Once you've gathered the treasure trove of data, you're faced with the dilemma of what to do with it. Here then are key concepts you need to use when deciding whether to buy a particular stock:

Price-to-earnings ratio

Stock A sells for $20 a share. Stock B sells for $30. Which is cheaper? Novice investors might assume that the first one is the cheapest, but the price itself is meaningless. What's far more relevant is a stock's *price-to-earnings (P/E) ratio.* The P/E ratio gives an investor a quick way to see the relationship between a company's recent earnings and its stock price and is often a clue as to whether a stock is worth acquiring. It's calculated by dividing the price of a single share of stock by the stock's annual earnings per share. You don't have to do the math because stock P/E ratios are listed daily in newspapers. A P/E ratio based on the past year's earnings is called a *trailing P/E;* a *forward P/E ratio* is formulated on what analysts suggest earnings will be in the year ahead.

Note   A stock is considered fairly priced if its P/E ratio equals its earnings growth rate. A company that is growing at a 20 percent clip with a 20 P/E ratio would fit into this category.

Value-oriented investors love to uncover companies with growth rates that outstrip their P/E ratios. A corporation expanding annually at a rate of 25 percent with a P/E ratio of 15 would fit that criteria. Unfortunately, a company that sports a laughably low P/E ratio isn't always a bargain. Many times, P/E ratios only appear low. Wall Street has often punished companies that happen to be priced cheaply for incompetence, bad luck, or a dearth of new products or ideas. Sometimes all the stocks in one sector, such as financials, semiconductors, retail, or housing stocks, are in the dumps. At these times, value-oriented investors start salivating.

Tip   Even when an entire industry is depressed, however, it pays to discriminate. The best approach is usually to choose the strongest stock in the litter.

In contrast, aggressive investors remain unfazed by high P/E ratios. Cisco Systems, which makes computer networking equipment, is the kind of stock they love. One point in 2000, Cisco earnings were expected to grow 28 percent in 2001, but at the same time its P/E ratio was a stratospheric 159. Nonetheless, analysts were insisting that Cisco was a great buy. Growth investors were willing to pay a premium for a corporation such as Cisco because it's been one of Wall Street's superior performers. High P/E stocks, however, not even the most highly regarded ones are infallible. In late 2001 and early 2001, for instance, Cisco's stock price was hammered.

Revenue and earnings growth

Choosy investors expect to see decent yearly growth in a corporation's earnings and sales. You'll have to set your own parameters on what kind of growth is acceptable, but many professional money managers prefer companies with sales and earnings growth of at least 15 percent to 20 percent. The average growth rates for industries vary widely so it's important to compare within the stock's own industry; for example, don't compare a drug or financial stock with stock in the semiconductor industry.

Caution   Don't put too much faith into one year's growth rate. If a company had a rotten 12 months followed by a respectable year, management will appear to doing spectacularly. Conversely, if a corporation experienced a fabulous year followed by an average one, the latest figures will stink. Look at a company's performance over several years and it's projected prospects several years into the future.

Ideally, you want a company that has earnings growing faster than its revenues, because such growth indicates that the company is squeezing more profits from the sale of its products or services. Typically, this situation means that costs are being effectively controlled. But cost savings inevitably taper off at some point, and real revenue growth has to take up any slack. Healthy earnings growth can also be generated if a company's products enjoy a large and growing market share.

Note   A small, emerging company can post phenomenal growth rates much more easily than a larger company because the small company is starting from zero.

A pint-sized company with sales jumping from $1 million to $2 million in one year experiences a 100 percent growth rate. A corporate giant like Wal-Mart, with recent sales of $138 billion, would have to record sales of $276 billion the next year to match the feat. This kind of growth isn't likely.

You may not want to be as demanding with the small-caps. The little guys aren't as resilient as the blue chips, which is why you shouldn't necessarily shun a small-cap that produces lackluster earnings over a couple of quarters or even a year. This company could be experiencing normal growing pains. Instead, determine what the small-cap's average earnings growth has been over three years. High growth rates in the early corporate stages typically can't be sustained over long periods of time. That's okay, as long as the current growth rate is acceptable to you.

Economic factors

To outsiders, Wall Street's preoccupation with interest rate movements may seem as unfathomable as a Poke[as]mon or scooter obsession. Surely some of the attention paid to the Federal Reserve Board chairman's luncheon speeches and congressional appearances can be explained away as inside baseball. But economic conditions, tedious as they might be to contemplate, can affect the value of your portfolio, which is a big concern for retirees who are living off their portfolio's earnings. Younger folks with a decade or so to go before retirement need not concern themselves as much with such swings because they have time to ride out the storm.

What everyone should appreciate is that stock valuations (that is, P/E ratios) are typically higher when interest rates and inflation remain low. That's because anemic interest rates and inflation make things rosier for stocks. If interest rates are hovering at 5 percent or 6 percent, people aren't too likely to invest in certificates of deposit (CDs) or Treasuries. At those rates, the payoff is too skimpy. Consequently, the logical place to be in this kind of economic climate is the stock market. At least in the stock market, the chances of besting the return of a five-year CD are much greater. Under these circumstances, investors usually pay premiums for stocks. Low interest rates are also important for stocks because they make it easier for consumers to spend money, which helps corporate earnings, and cheap borrowing rates make it less costly for companies to invest in their own growth.

Stock prices tend to float higher during periods of low inflation because investors are willing to assume higher risks for fatter returns. They pay two or three times what a blue chip stock such as IBM or Coca-Cola is worth. However, stock prices may plummet when inflation kicks in and interest rates soar. A CD or a Treasury offering 8 percent or 9 percent then becomes appealing. Some people question why they should remain loyal to a wobbly, overpriced stock when they can invest in a sure thing?

Analysts' opinions

Wall Street is driven by what stock analysts say, but they can be as objective as a proud mother bragging about her kids. These industry experts can't always be candid because doing so could cost their own companies millions in lost investment banking business. Companies turn peevish when analysts criticize their operations. Sometimes corporate officers even stop talking to the offending analysts.

This situation largely explains why you'll rarely see analysts issuing "sell" recommendations. Even "neutral" ratings are unusual. All that's left are various shades of "buy" recommendations. Although you wouldn't want to scoop up a stock based solely on what cheerful analysts are saying, you should know what their consensus is. A recent academic study that examined 360,000 analyst recommendations concluded that the stocks that garnered the highest analyst praise earned the highest returns. Those stocks that the analysts panned fared the worst.

The easiest place to learn what analysts are saying is the Internet. Visit these sites to find the latest opinions:

✦ First Call at `www.thomsoninvest.net`

✦ Zacks Investment Research at `www.zacks.com`

✦ Multex at `www.multex.com`

Investment Clubs

If you're intrigued but anxious about investing in individual stocks, consider joining an investment club. In a club, you can mingle with more experienced investors and see how they choose their stock picks. Typically members in a club meet once a month and share stock research and updates on the club's stock portfolio. Stock trades are authorized by a vote of the majority of a club's members. Some clubs allow members to invest as little as $25 or so a month into the kitty.

Historically, older investors, who typically have more time and money to invest, have gravitated to investment clubs. The median age of club members is about 50, and the majority of members are women. But the demographics are changing as younger people express interest in joining and technology reinvigorates the club movement. Not all clubs meet in living rooms: virtual clubs allow members to live anywhere in the world as long as they have a modem. Meetings take place online. Even clubs that prefer to meet in person can use the Internet to their advantage. The Motley Fool, which is an excellent financial Web site (`www.fool.com`), establishes a free message board for any club that desires one. This message board allows members to kick around stock ideas and discuss the portfolio's performance when they aren't sitting around a table. Another great resource for clubs' is Bivio (www.bivio.com), which provides clubs excellent (and free) accounting software and features columnists, who regularly answer visitors' club questions.

 Resource   For a free package of investment club information, write the National Association of Investors Corp at P.O. Box 220, Royal Oak, Michigan 48068. You can also call NAIC at (248) 583-NAIC or visit its Web site at www.better-investing.org.

Start your search for a club by contacting the nonprofit National Association of Investors Corp., which oversees more than 36,500 clubs and 650,000 members. Even if you prefer investing solo, you can still join the National Association of Investors Corp. (NAIC) and take advantage of the organization's stock analysis software and publications. The NAIC doesn't urge its members to make a fast buck on the stock market. It favors buying and holding growth stocks at reasonable prices. If you follow NAIC's investing guidelines and/or use its stock analysis software, for instance, you'd dare not touch a wireless startup with absolutely no earnings.

Club criteria

When evaluating a stock prospect, club members ask these questions:

Can I double my money in five years?

Investment clubs favor stocks they believe can double in five years. This amount breaks down to compounded annual returns of 14.9 percent. Although this percentage hasn't seemed flashy in more recent years, it's considerably better than the stock market's historic return.

Is this a growth stock?

Clubs love well-managed companies in rapidly growing industries. They get especially excited about corporations with the highest profit margins and earnings on invested capital. Keep in mind that hunting for prospects in the hottest industries isn't for the faint-hearted. At a minimum, the NAIC recommends that a company must be increasing its earnings by at least 10 percent.

What's a reasonable price for a stock?

Falling in love with a stock is one thing; tying the knot is another. Club members don't want to pay a ridiculous price for a stock. The NAIC guidelines favor companies where earnings are keeping pace or outdistancing revenues. They look skeptically at a company with robust sales and stagnating earnings.

Club member focus, in part, on the P/E ratio as a measure of a stock's fair value. They also look at a company's historic P/E ratios, including high, low, and median, to help gauge whether the stock is fairly priced.

Favorite investment club stocks

The most popular stocks held by NAIC investment clubs in the year 2000 were the following:

1. Intel	**11.** Diebold
2. Lucent Technologies	**12.** Clayton Homes
3. Home Depot	**13.** Wal-Mart
4. Cisco Systems	**14.** Motorola
5. Merck & Co.	**15.** General Motors
6. Pepsico	**16.** Coca-Cola
7. Pfizer	**17.** AT&T
8. AFLAC	**18.** Oracle
9. Pfizer	**19.** Disney
10. McDonald's	**20.** Worldcom

Watch Out for Cyber Crooks

Psst, wanna make a bundle on an Internet shopping mall stock that could earn 600 percent in the next 12 months? Or perhaps you'd be willing to look overseas for stupendous returns. You can buy a stake in a Costa Rican coconut chip factory or an ethanol plant in the Dominican Republic.

If these deals all sound fishy, you're right. Watchdogs at the federal Securities and Exchange Commission and at the state level have issued warnings on these and many other dubious investments. Unfortunately, when the stock market was booming, scam artists flourished. It's easy to see why: Wild claims of astronomical returns on phony get-rich schemes don't seem outlandish when the stock market was behaving as if it was on steroids.

Although pinpointing just how successful the scam artists have been at duping innocent people is impossible, the projections are alarming. The North American Securities Administrators Association (NASAA), which represents state securities regulators, at one point estimated that investment fraud was costing Americans about $1 million an hour.

Even if you consider yourself a prudent investor who would never fall for an investment scam, you might be vulnerable in ways you never anticipated. Internet scam artists have worked especially hard to make their cons difficult to detect. Deception without detection has been easier to achieve because their anonymity is assured on the Internet. No one, after all, really knows who is posting stock tips on message boards or even who is sponsoring many financial Web sites.

One of the more ingenious types of stock scams is referred to as a pump-and-dump. In this scam, tiny companies, eager for publicity, pay investment Web sites, financial radio show hosts, or newsletters to promote their stocks. An unethical Web site might send free e-mail alerts to subscribers about stocks poised for triple-digit returns. Falling for the media hype, investors unwittingly sink money into these stocks. All the new money generated by the enthusiastic coverage may artificially pump up a company's stock price. When the price spikes up, company insiders dump their shares at a fabulous profit. Unfortunately for those who hold onto their shares, the price often plummets.

These scams work because the stock promoters, whether they operate on the Internet or elsewhere, know that people are basically trusting. Investors assume that what they are reading or hearing is unbiased, top-notch stock research. But what they are really getting is paid advertisements.

To protect yourself, ignore any advice that doesn't come from a reputable brokerage house or a financial publication such as the *Wall Street Journal.* Stay away from Internet financial sites that aren't sponsored by well-regarded and nationally known organizations. Stick with credible sources you are familiar with. Don't risk your money on the advice of an anonymous stranger on the Internet.

Want to learn more about stock scams? An excellent place to explore is the FinancialWeb's Stock Detective section (www.financialweb.com). It regularly reports on stock rip-offs it unearths, as well as SEC actions. The SEC also posts many examples of investment fraud on its Web site; its "CyberForce" of regulators surf the Net for violators. The SEC's online complaint center receives hundreds of complaints a day. If you believe you're a victim of securities fraud, contact the Security and Exchange Commission, Division of Enforcement Complaint Center at 450 Fifth St. NW, Washington, DC 20549-0710. Its Web site is www.sec.gov, or you can e-mail the SEC at enforcement@sec.gov.

Summary

✦ Know where to look for solid stock ideas, including using stock screens and financial publications.

✦ You will need to be patient if you're hunting for stocks that provide decent stock dividends.

✦ Pour through a company's financial statements before investing in it and compare what you discover with other corporations in the same industry.

✦ Consider using one of the major one-stop investing sites on the Internet as you research stocks.

[lb]   If you're timid about buying individual stocks and need a helping hand, consider forming or joining an investment club.

✦   ✦   ✦

Selecting the Right Mutual Funds

Mutual funds are America's investment darling. This chapter explains the workings of mutual funds and how you can use funds as building blocks for your investment strategy.

What Makes Mutual Funds So Popular?

Investing with mutual funds is a lot like relying upon a department store's personal shopper. With your money, a professional shopper selects a wardrobe that makes you look stunning. Using your cash, the manager of a mutual fund devises a dream portfolio that (with any luck) makes you look like an investing genius.

In either case, you don't have to do much work. The professionals make the tough calls. Americans, who wouldn't dream of watching television without a remote control, overwhelmingly favor this effortless way to invest in the financial markets. Mutual funds have never been so popular: More than 82 million Americans are mutual fund investors, with nearly one out of every two households owning at least a few shares.

But the land of mutual funds is not all wine and roses. Critics accuse funds of producing mediocre returns, chasing investing fads, and being too darned expensive. Fund families have deflected this grousing for years, but today they're sweating. The biggest competition these days comes from discount brokers, whose low transaction fees permit small investors to build their own portfolios of stocks inexpensively.

However, no one is predicting that mutual funds will wither away. They will always have a place in investing. Consequently, everyone with spare dollars to invest needs to understand how to deftly include mutual funds in their portfolios.

Mutual Fund Basics

A mutual fund operates by pooling the money of thousands of investors. For example, you might mail in a $1,000 check to a fund family while others might write checks for $50 or $10,000 or more. Popular funds may have millions of dollars pouring into them every day.

What happens with all this money? A manager in charge of the fund decides where to invest it. He or she might invest it in stocks or bonds or leave a chunk of it in cash. The manager isn't free to stuff his portfolio with whatever he or she pleases. Each fund must be run according to the terms outlined in a document called the *prospectus*. A bond fund, for instance, might be limited in the percentage of junk bonds it can invest in. A domestic stock fund may be prohibited from investing more than 25 percent in foreign companies.

The beauty of diversification

No matter what ends up in a fund's portfolio, you own a tiny piece of it, and that's what makes a fund so great. Most investors couldn't possibly duplicate the diversification they can receive instantly through a mutual fund. For an investment of just $1,000 or $2,000, you can buy into an impressive lineup of stocks, bonds, or both.

Example

In 2000, the Janus Mercury fund's top 10 holdings included Amazon.com, AT&T, Cisco Systems, Enron Corp., Time Warner, and JDS Uniphase. In addition, about $1 out of every $4 in the fund was invested in Europe, the Pacific Rim, or Latin America.

For example, one recently popular fund, the Janus Mercury fund, provides shareholders with large holdings in a variety of companies as well as overseas exposure. Can you imagine how much time it would take you to construct a similar portfolio? Most of us don't have the time to research individual stocks or bonds or the know-how and willpower to make the investments.

Making money with mutual funds

You make money with mutual funds through capital gains and income. Racking up capital gains is the sexy way to make money. When stocks or bonds inside a fund jump in value, your stake in the fund jumps, too. Because the prices of a fund's holdings change daily, the fund's share price hops around, too. To find the latest price of your fund, check the business section of your newspaper, your fund's Web site, or a financial Internet portal, such as CBS.MarketWatch.com or Morningstar.com.

What's often overlooked when evaluating a fund's price performance is its income. A shareholder can also earn money if a fund spins off income from its investments. This income can be generated from interest from bonds or cash or through stock dividends. Depending on the fund, income may be paid out monthly, quarterly, or less frequently. Retirees may want to receive this income in cash; investors who are far from retirement may prefer to have this money reinvested in more fund shares. Funds that spin off income are generally more conservative.

Choosing Mutual Funds

With roughly 16,500 choices, the number of mutual funds eclipses the number of stocks traded on the New York Stock Exchange. The mutual fund industry churns out a new fund on just about a daily basis. However, the task of selecting a fund doesn't have to be a grind. Before fine-tuning a fund portfolio or starting from scratch, you need to know what types of funds are available and how certain fund types fit in with your retirement goals.

Here then is a breakdown of the types of funds based on the major investment objectives. In this listing, the fund choices grow progressively riskier.

Objective: Risk-free income

Risk-free income is the objective for people who fear losing even a few dollars of their investment — particularly retirees with smaller nest eggs or those folks preparing to retire in the next year or two. The best fund for people with this objective is a money market.

Although money markets aren't technically risk-free, no individual investor has ever lost any money in one. In addition to being an excellent place for retirees to stash their cash, a money market is also ideal for anyone saving for a big expense (such as a house, car, or boat) who will need the money within two or three years.

Two types of money markets exist: taxable and tax-free. Which one is best for you depends upon your tax bracket. The higher your tax bracket is, the more likely that a tax-free version will be the superior one for you.

 Cross-Reference   See Chapter 7 for more information on choosing a money market.

Objective: Income

Income-oriented investors are interested in a conservative investment that spins off income while leaving the principal untouched, which is the arrangement some retirees find ideal. These investors should consider bond funds. Like money markets, bond funds come in two types: taxable and tax-free.

Taxable bond funds

This broad category of funds includes just about all bonds except municipals. The prime attraction to most of these funds is the income they spin off. When choosing a bond fund, the yield isn't the only factor. Bond funds vary in overall credit risk and average maturity. For someone looking for an all-purpose bond investment, a general bond fund, which is often referred to as an intermediate-term bond fund, is a sensible choice. These funds usually invest in a mix of corporate and government bonds. Two strong funds in this category are Harbor Bond and Dodge & Cox Income.

Tip   Because bond funds don't offer a lot of price appreciation, be sure to select a fund that charges very low expenses. Otherwise, the fees will swallow a healthy percentage of your income.

Tax-free bond funds

Tax-free bonds, such as municipal bonds, appeal to wealthier Americans. Municipal bonds (*munis*) are highly valued for their tax break; investors aren't saddled with federal income taxes on the interest. Because of this tax break, munis typically offer a lower yield. Although munis pose some risk of default, more of these bonds are hitting the marketplace with insurance. Before choosing between tax-free and taxable bonds, do the math to see which is the better deal for you.

Cross-Reference   See Chapter 17 for more information on bonds of all kinds.

Objective: Income and capital growth

These investors hope their investment grows in value, but they may want to siphon off income. They have several types of funds to choose from to meet their objective.

Balanced funds

Balanced funds invest in stocks and bonds. Stocks usually represent anywhere from 40 to 60 percent of a balanced fund's portfolio. Some investors use a balanced fund as a one-stop way to diversify with equities and bonds. Others want the appreciation that stocks can provide, but they also want the stability of bonds.

Many balanced fund managers love value-oriented stocks, such as utilities, tobacco stocks, and real estate investment trusts (REITs). The bonds and dividend yielding cyclical and commodity stocks produce the fund's income. Yet some balanced fund managers are bypassing old favorites and loading up on more growth plays instead. For example, the Janus Balanced Fund has shown a penchant for technology and cable stocks.

Tip   Find out what type of fund you're diving into before making the plunge by checking out the list of companies a fund is invested in before sending in your checks.

Equity-income and growth-and-income funds

Equity-income and growth-and-income fund managers like to load up on large-cap growth stocks that offer dividends. To increase the yield, some managers invest in bonds. These funds are more conservative and consequently should produce smaller returns than pure growth funds. On the flip side, they shouldn't do as poorly during bear markets.

Just like balanced funds, some funds in this pool are riskier than others. To learn what kind of risk you're taking on, find out what type of companies a fund invests in. One way to uncover this information is to read a fund's annual or semi-annual report. You'll learn other ways to investigate a fund later in the chapter.

Objective: Growth

Growth investors are unexcited about dividends and are not looking for an income stream; they just want their fund to appreciate in price over the long run. These folks have years (maybe decades) to go before retirement.

Growth funds

Managers of growth funds love to invest in companies that are growing at a faster pace than the economy as a whole. These funds tend to invest in the kind of huge companies that are in the Standard & Poor's 500. Like other types of funds, the volatility of growth funds can vary dramatically. Some fund managers stick with tried-and-true blue chips such as General Electric and Johnson & Johnson; others try to push the envelope by taking on more risk with smaller, less well-known hot shots.

Tip
A large-cap growth fund can function as the largest core holding in a long-term portfolio.

International growth funds

Most experts agree that long-term investors should also maintain an international fund as a core holding. If you keep all your money at home, you'll miss out on tremendous growth opportunities on the rest of the planet. These funds vary in risk. A fund that places heavy bets on emerging market nations is far more volatile than one that contains a lot of blue chip European stocks. If you're going to hold just one international growth fund, make it an all-purpose, large-cap international fund that invests in established corporations in the developed world.

Investing internationally is wise, but think twice before choosing a global fund rather than a pure international fund. (Global funds invest in both U.S. companies and overseas.) Americans discovered global funds back in the 1990s when Janus Worldwide came out of nowhere to become one of the most successful funds around. So much money poured into Janus Worldwide that the firm eventually closed the fund to new investors. What's wrong with investing in these funds? If you're invested in a domestic fund, you face the danger of duplicating what you own. Most investors should stick with a pure international fund.

Value Fund Alternative

While growth funds have hogged the spotlight in recent years, value funds rightfully deserve a place in just about anyone's fund portfolio. Traditionally, value funds, whether they invest in large or small-cap companies, aren't as volatile as their growth cousins. Value fund managers typically look for beaten-down stocks or companies that happen to be in sectors that are out of favor. Usually stocks paying decent dividends are considered value plays. Some mutual fund managers are die-hard growth players, while others are just as committed to value investing. If you can't decide, choose a blended fund that dabbles in both styles. (See Chapter 12 for a more detailed description of value versus growth investing.)

Objective: Aggressive growth

Funds in the aggressive growth category are firecrackers. The returns can be explosive, but the dips can be nauseating. In recent years, these funds have bet heavily on technology companies. Only a dedicated risk-taker with several years to ride out the ups and down should invest in these sorts of funds.

Aggressive growth funds

Aggressive growth funds are permitted to be chameleons. A manager in pursuit of the hottest stock prospects enjoys the flexibility to invest in any size company. A prospect may be a multinational corporation or a fledgling startup that had trouble paying its light bill last year. Depending upon what's happening in the economy, fund managers can easily switch investments among large, middle-sized, or small companies to capture the best returns. Alger Capital Appreciation and Fidelity New Millennium have been among the most successful funds in pursuing this strategy.

Small-cap stocks

Small-cap growth stock funds are considered riskier than ones that invest in blue chip stocks because the smaller companies aren't as well established. No one need worry that a Goliath such as Pepsico is going to declare bankruptcy, but it's a real possibility for the little guys holding the slingshots. A fledgling company may offer just a couple of products that become obsolete or are improved upon by a bigger competitor. Although small-cap funds were overshadowed by large-caps for most of the 1990s, historically they have provided a higher return than large-caps. This higher return is supposed to compensate investors for assuming more risk.

Tip

Because of the volatility of small-cap stocks, you shouldn't even consider handling these hot potatoes if you aren't willing to hold them for at least five years. Yet they do play an important role in a long-term, retirement portfolio. Because they are riskier than large-cap stocks, they probably shouldn't represent more than 25 percent of most people's holdings.

Life-Cycle Funds: A Simple Solution

Do you crave simplicity? Consider a type of fund that promises to eliminate investment guesswork, both when you start with the fund and as you grow older and your investment needs change. These funds go by different names, such as life cycle, lifestyle, or target retirement funds, but they essentially work the same way. Instead of struggling to build your own successful portfolio of domestic and foreign stock funds, bonds, and cash, you can purchase just one of these funds to get instant diversification: The fund uses pre-determined formulas to automatically pick the right mix of stocks, bonds, and cash according to the investor's age and risk tolerance.

These funds, which are often found on 401(k) menus, provide one-stop shopping. You do, however, have to make some decisions. You must determine, for instance, whether you want a fund that invests aggressively, conservatively, or somewhere in between. Mutual fund families often offer more than one choice. The mix of stocks, bonds, and cash in any given life cycle fund can vary dramatically. What Charles Schwab calls a conservative life cycle fund isn't necessarily the same working definition that Vanguard or Dreyfus uses.

Some life cycle funds automatically grow more conservative as you age. These funds, which invest heavily in stocks when you're in your 30s or 40s, increasingly rely upon bonds as you head closer to retirement and no longer can tolerate the volatility of a portfolio dominated by stocks. These evolving life cycle funds, which are offered by Vanguard, Fidelity, and others, are tied to future retirement dates.

Life cycle funds, however, have not caught on because they're misunderstood. Many people mistakenly compare the performance of these diversified funds with growth funds invested exclusively in stocks. A life cycle fund's returns during bull markets won't be as good as a pure stock funds, but the cash and bonds within its portfolio should provide protection against future market volatility. Over the long haul, you'll give up some return with a life cycle fund, but it should be safer than a stock fund.

Sector funds

Sector funds focus on a particular industry, such as aerospace, banking, healthcare, and technology. Although the returns are often quite volatile, the payoffs can be phenomenal. Quite often the best-performing funds in any given year are sector funds. However, the worst performing funds in any given year are also sector funds.

Many investors have concluded that the risks are too monumental to invest in such a narrow niche. Only the boldest investors should consider sector funds. For those interested, these three mutual fund families offer the largest selections:

✦ Fidelity Investments at (800) 544-8888 or www.fidelity.com

✦ Invesco at (800) 525-8085 or www.invesco.com

✦ Rydex at (800) 820-0888 or www.rydexfunds.com

Sector funds tend to attract *market timers,* those investors who jump in and out of stocks, attempting to anticipate the market's directions. But sector investing can also interest buy-and-hold investors, who stick with the most promising long-term sectors, such as health care, financial services, and technology. Even for the most aggressive investor, a 5 percent or 10 percent sector stake within a portfolio is often plenty. Use sector funds for seasoning in a portfolio, not the main course.

Tip If you expect to flit in and out of sectors, you'll save yourself money by keeping this trading confined to a tax-deferred retirement account. If you hold a sector fund in a taxable account for a year or less, you'll be hit with short-term capital gains taxes.

Assembling a World-Class Portfolio

Constructing a mutual fund portfolio that's the envy of your neighborhood watch group doesn't have to be difficult. Just follow these suggestions:

Caution Never buy a fund—no matter how tantalizing it is—without first considering how it would affect your overall portfolio.

Stick with your strategy.

Once you familiarize yourself with the types of funds, resist the urge to pick the hottest fund on the market. If you pick funds from the current year's best-performing lists that are trumpeted by financial magazines, you will commit one of the most common mutual fund mistakes. The Roman candles that explode to the top each year typically make highly aggressive stock bets and often concentrate on only one industry, such as technology or financial stocks. During a market meltdown, these funds can tank quickly. For instance, American Heritage, the nation's best-performing fund in 1997 with a return of 75 percent, became the absolute worst fund the next year by plummeting 61 percent.

The best way to pick funds is to first review your risk tolerance, financial goals, and the amount of time you have before you need the money. Next, decide what percentage of your assets you'd like in large- and small-cap domestic stocks, bonds, international funds, and a money market. Then stick with that game plan.

 Cross-Reference Chapters 1 and 20 have details on developing a spending and saving plan for retirement.

Pay attention to track records.

Don't be hypnotized by a portfolio manager's flash of brilliance. Select a fund that has nurtured an above-average track record spanning at least three years and preferably five. Make sure to compare a fund against its appropriate benchmark.

You wouldn't want to use the S&P 500 index, for instance, to evaluate the performance of a small-cap fund. Instead, you would look at the Russell 2000 or the S&P SmallCap 600 index. Avoid simply looking at a fund's raw performance numbers. The fact that a fund slumped 15 percent in one year is meaningless unless you know what funds in the same category did in that same time period. An excellent resource for comparing a fund to its appropriate benchmark is Morningstar (www.morningstar.com). Each of its fund profiles graphically compares the fund's performance to its peer group and benchmark index.

Once you've made your choices, resist abandoning your funds during rough times. You certainly shouldn't bail after one poor year. Even the best funds experience hard times. On the other hand, consider selling if your fund has eked out mediocre returns for a couple of years while similar funds have enjoyed appreciably better results.

 Resource For more insights on the art of fund selling, check out a Web site called FundAlarm at www.fundalarm.com.

Think small.

With the popularity of mutual funds at an all-time high, the most popular funds are far too crowded. Super-sizing might work for McDonald's, but it bombs in the fund world. When too much money is sloshing around in a fund, a manager often can't deliver top returns because he or she runs out of fabulous stock ideas. All of us can think of five friends, but can you name 500 or more? That's the kind of challenge facing fund managers who have billions of dollars sitting in their portfolios.

How big is too big? Some experts suggest that investors should avoid large-cap funds with more than $10 billion in assets and small-cap funds with assets exceeding $1 billion. But others contend that's too simplistic of a rule. While some popular funds do fine when money gushes in, others struggle to stay afloat.

As a general rule, a small-cap fund's size is more critical than a large-cap's size. When the portfolio becomes bloated with cash, a small-cap fund manager can be forced to invest in larger corporations when he or she can't find enough solid small-cap ideas. A fast-growing asset base, however, can be perilous for growth funds, no matter what their size. That's because these funds tend to place bets on the most popular stocks and with huge amounts of money to invest, large trades can boost stock prices or alternatively depress them when a portfolio manager tries to dump a lot of stock. Value funds seem to be better protected from the dangers of monster cash flows. The easiest way to discover a fund's asset size is to call its toll-free number and ask the telephone representative.

The Beta Barometer

Even if you're retired, chances are you'll need some stocks to sustain you till the end. How do you minimize the extra risk? One way is to focus on a fund's beta.

Beta is a nifty measurement that indicates how volatile a fund or an individual stock is — relative to the market — during both good and bad times. A high-beta fund is the most volatile. When stocks soar, one of these funds should perform better than the market. When the market tanks, stocks and funds with high betas should crash harder. In contrast, a low-beta investment won't have as much to celebrate when Wall Street is rejoicing, but it should be able to break its fall when the market experiences a lull.

The average beta is designated as 1.0. A fund with a beta as high as 1.1 or 1.2 has a history of being more volatile than the market. If the market slumped 20 percent, a fund with a 1.25 beta could be expected to dive 25 percent. On the other hand, a fund with a beta of .85 should drop just 17 percent.

If you prefer more tranquil funds, stick with funds that have a beta no greater than 1.0. Index funds usually have a 1.0 beta because they are engineered to match the market as closely as possible — the typical index fund passively invests in all the corporations in a given benchmark, such as the S&P 500. Therefore, these funds should be no more volatile than the market.

However, don't expect a fund to behave exactly as its beta predicts. Betas aren't foolproof. The betas of gold and international funds, for instance, aren't much help at all. Gold funds have low betas, but they aren't low-risk plays. Despite this shortcoming, a beta can provide a good estimate of a fund or stock's built-in risk.

Any mutual fund firm should be able to tell you what a fund's beta is. Morningstar's fund publications also list betas, as well as other risk measurements. Many financial Web sites can provide a stock's beta as well.

An even quicker approach is using the Portfolio Forecaster at *Mutual Funds Magazine's* Web site (`www.mutual-funds.com/mfmag`). The software can evaluate how risky your stock and fund holdings are compared to the average investor's.

Whenever possible, avoid load funds.

If you buy funds through a broker or a financial planner who works on commission, you almost certainly will invest in a *load fund,* which means that you will pay sales charges. Everyone else, however, should stick with no-load funds; *no-load funds* are funds that don't carry built-in sales charges.

Clever marketers would like you to believe that the fund world is doing you a favor by offering a kaleidoscope of load choices. What these choices mostly do is confuse investors, who often pick the wrong one.

You have three main choices:

Front-end load (A shares)

You pay the commission upfront on A shares. If you purchase $15,000 worth of a fund carrying a 5 percent load, you'd face a $750 sales charge. This charge decreases your initial investment to $14,250. Unfortunately, the majority of investors mistakenly shun front-end loads. Over the long run, these funds are much cheaper than other load funds because of their lower yearly expenses.

Tip   If you must buy into a load fund, in most cases go with A shares.

Back-end loads (B shares)

The back-end load enables you to skip the sales charge until you sell shares. If you hold a fund long enough, you might not face any back-end costs. It sounds tempting, but beware. Such funds can gouge you with high 12b-1 fees, which are earmarked for a fund's marketing efforts.

Level loads (C shares)

These shares typically charge an extra 1 percent ongoing fee to compensate the broker for as long as you hold the fund. So if you keep your shares for 10 years, your broker will continue to be compensated for that long-ago recommendation. Once again, you'll find this added cost in the fund's 12b-1 fee. In addition, level loads typically charge a redemption fee if you bail within the first 12 to 18 months.

Among load funds, C shares have become phenomenally popular because investors assume they are dodging a commission. In fact, C shares can be the worst deal possible for a long-term investment.

Anyone relying upon a broker's advice should always ask why he or she recommends a particular load fund and request a cost comparison of various loads for different time periods. Another option is to use load calculators at these two Web sites:

✦ Quicken at www.quicken.com

✦ FinanCenter.com at www.calcbuilder.com

Snub expensive funds.

When you shop for a new car, the first thing you look at is the price pasted on the window. Unfortunately, mutual fund investors rarely ask about price. Many people blow off the whole notion of expenses. After all, if a fund has been returning 20 percent or better a year, does it matter that the investment is a tad too pricey? The answer is yes.

Mutual fund companies make their money by charging you fees to invest in their funds. These fees, which cover everything from the salaries of the fund managers to the sales and distribution costs of the funds, are embedded into the price of the fund. Some of these fees are high; some are not. You can compare the costs of each fund by looking at their *expense ratios*, which fund firms are required by law to disclose on the prospectuses they mail to you at least twice a year. The expense ratio is the percentage of the share price of a fund that is made up of the fund's total expenses.

The only costs not included in the expense ratio are load fees, which are one-time fees that fund firms impose as a way to reimburse the broker or financial advisor who sold you the fund.

Over the long run, shopping for the best deal can save you a ton of money. Believe it or not, the cost of your mutual funds, as well as their tax efficiency, are the factors that have the most impact your yearly returns.

 Cross-Reference   You'll find tax strategies for individual stocks and funds in Chapter 16.

Suppose you're debating whether to invest in a stock fund that maintains a 1 percent annual expense ratio or one with a 1.5 percent annual expense ratio. The difference hardly seems worth quibbling about. But if you choose the cheaper fund, you could ultimately save yourself thousands of dollars. If you invested $10,000 in the cheaper fund and both funds generated 8 percent returns over the next 20 years, your fund would earn an extra $3,000.

Skeptics may suggest that shaving costs can backfire. After all, if motorists valued price over performance, we'd all be driving Hyundais. Obviously, a fund that couples cheap expenses with lousy performance is not a marvelous deal. But curiously enough, top performance is often linked to low expenses.

Note   Often the cheap expenses, not the fund manager's genius, are what catapults a fund to the top.

This phenomenon was illustrated recently when Morningstar undertook a study of fund expenses for *The Wall Street Journal*. Morningstar looked at five-year fund performances in 10 categories, including small-, mid-, and large-cap stocks; foreign stocks; municipal bonds; and short-term and intermediate government bonds. In all but one category (small-cap stocks), the funds that made it into the top quartile during those five years offered the lowest fees. The funds that placed in the next highest quartile offered the second cheapest fees. The pathetic funds sitting in the basement charged the highest fees.

If you aren't sure what your funds are costing you, don't chide yourself. Cost is often a mystery because you don't write yearly checks to your fund companies. Without fanfare, the fees are automatically deducted from your accounts. You can, however, find out what these fees are by ordering a fund's prospectus. The U.S. Securities and Exchange Commission requires each fund to disclose its assortment of fees in a table near the front of this document.

Even with a prospectus, however, you won't be able to pinpoint precisely what you're paying in expenses. That's because the expense charts are standardized with a generic investment sum. For instance, the literature might assume that all investors originally sink $10,000 into a fund. To circumvent this problem, an increasing number of Web sites, including the following, are making it much easier to get a handle on your actual costs:

✦ Personal Fund at www.personalfund.com

✦ Morningstar at www.morningstar.com

✦ Quicken at www.quicken.com

 The SEC introduced its own fund cost calculator in 1999 (www.sec.gov/mfcc/mfcc-int.htm). One of the calculator's creators was a government economist, who had encountered his own troubles figuring out how much his funds were costing him.

If all this sounds like too much work, relax. Try this shortcut: Just stay away from funds that charge above-average fees. Decide what's reasonable after looking at Table 14-1.

Table 14-1
Average Mutual Fund Expense Ratios

Domestic Stock Funds

Type of Fund	Expense Ratio
Large-cap growth stock funds	1.4%
Large-cap value stock funds	1.3%
Small-cap growth stock funds	1.6%
Small-cap value stock funds	1.5%
S&P 500 index funds	.6%
Equity income funds	1.4%
Balanced funds	1.3%
Technology and science funds	1.7%
Real-estate funds	1.5%
Utility funds	1.5%
Gold funds	1.9%

Continued

Table 14-1   *(continued)*

Foreign Stock Funds

Type of Fund	Expense Ratio
International stock funds	1.7%
Global funds	1.8%
Emerging markets funds	1.7%
European funds	1.7%

Fixed-Income Funds

Type of Fund	Expense Ratio
Municipal bond funds	1.1%
General bond funds	1.1%
Corporate bond funds	1%
Junk bond funds	1%
Treasury bond funds	.8%
GNMA funds	1.1%

Source: Lipper Inc.

Don't skip the research.

Mutual fund analysis isn't as complicated as programming your VCR. Thumbing through a fund's prospectus, which is a more readable document than it used to be should provide you with answers to the basic questions. If you're like most Americans, who refuse to read the thing, at least look at what *Morningstar Mutual Funds* or *The Value Line Mutual Fund Survey* has to say. Each publication provides a one-page report for many funds that includes a discussion of a fund's investing style and its manager. It also squeezes in statistics on tax efficiency, volatility, performance, expenses, and portfolio holdings.

Resource

To obtain their fund analysis publications, contact Morningstar at (800) 735-0700 or www.morningstar.com; you can reach Value Line at (800) 634-3583 or www.valueline.com.

The Advantages of Institutional Funds

If you want to buy into a good fund for peanuts, you may be interested in institutional mutual funds. What distinguishes institutional funds from regular mutual funds are the customers. Historically, institutional funds were reserved for endowments, corporate pension funds, and the filthy rich. These funds were interested only in investors who could write a check for at least $1 million. However, the financial snobbery is disappearing. Officially, institutional funds still maintain extremely high investment minimums, but now you can purchase shares through discount brokerage firms such as Fidelity Investments, Charles Schwab, Muriel Siebert, and TD Waterhouse. In many cases, you can invest for $2,500 or less. Well-respected money management firms that now allow the average investor to buy shares in their institutional mutual funds include PIMCO Advisors, Loomis Sayles, and Miller Anderson & Sherrerd (MAS).

Why should you care about this institutional change of heart? In a word, performance. Studies suggest that institutional funds enjoy an edge over their retail competitors. In one Morningstar study that spanned 5½ years, the average institutional fund beat its retail competitor by 8 percent. An investor who stashed $10,000 in an institutional fund during that period would have been $800 richer.

The institutional funds' secret weapon is low expense. Unlike other funds, institutional players aren't saddled with the high costs of customer service operations and advertising. Further, institutional funds aren't known for attracting trigger-happy clients, which can be a plus during volatile markets. During troubled times on Wall Street, institutional managers need not worry about massive redemptions.

Institutional players don't advertise their track records, but one way to chase down solid prospects is by checking Morningstar. Don't get discouraged if one discount broker doesn't carry a certain fund because the discounters offer different ones. It pays to shop around. Not all institutional funds, however, are worth owning. Don't buy shares just to own a stake in an institutional fund. Make sure it fits your needs.

Meanwhile, the Internet has made screening for solid funds far easier. Morningstar's Web site, for instance, is packed with fund ideas, as well as analysis and commentaries on countless funds. You can also screen thousands of mutual funds at the major financial portals and online brokerage firms:

✦ Fidelity at `www.fidelity.com`

✦ Microsoft's MoneyCentral at `www.moneycentral.com`

✦ CBS MarketWatch at `www.cbs.marketwatch.com`

✦ Charles Schwab at `www.schwab.com`

✦ Yahoo! at `www.yahoo.com`

Mutual Funds Versus Individual Stocks

If you aren't sure whether to go with the instant diversification of a mutual fund or the more spectacular returns of individual stocks, this section provides some compelling reasons for both to help you steer your course.

Reasons to own individual stocks

In recent years, investors have become increasingly interested in owning individual stocks. Here are the most common reasons:

You like the performance potential.

If you invest in individual stocks, you enjoy the potential of hitting a home run. In contrast, mutual fund investing is steadier, and the chances for dramatic returns aren't as great. Of course, while you're swinging for the fences, you can also strike out. Only you can judge whether you have the moxie and the knowledge to be a stock picker.

You're committed to holding a well-rounded portfolio of stocks.

Unlike a mutual fund portfolio, stocks can be tailored to your individual needs. Although individual stock picking can be a riskier pursuit than fund investing, it doesn't need to be if you have enough money to spread around. You can be comfortably diversified in blue chip growth stocks, for instance, if your portfolio contains 15 to 20 companies in unrelated industries.

You're tired of tax-sloppy mutual funds.

By holding individual stocks, you control your own tax bill. For instance, during the past decade, Cisco Systems stock skyrocketed 65,500 percent. If you were lucky enough to own that stock during that period, you would have paid no capital gains taxes. That's right: Absolutely nothing. As long as you don't sell Cisco or any other stock for that matter, no capital gains taxes are generated no matter how long your stock defies gravity.

You can't get this same guarantee with mutual funds because portfolio managers buy and sell stocks throughout the year. Managers traded Cisco countless times during the past 10 years, and those sales triggered capital gains taxes for all fund shareholders.

You want to capitalize on your own expertise.

Perhaps you work in the Silicon Valley and can sift the technological wheat from the chaff. If you're in the financial industry, you might have insight into what banks won't get hammered by bad loans or are good candidates for mergers. Meanwhile, an avid newspaper reader may enjoy keeping tabs on the top companies in his or her area. A Cincinnati resident gets a heavy dose of Proctor & Gamble news coverage, a St. Louisian reads a great deal about Anheuser Busch and Emerson Electric, and Miami investors get their fill of news about Royal Caribbean Cruises and Carnival Corp. These investors may obtain enough knowledge of their local companies to intelligently pick solid regional stocks.

You have time to babysit.

At the very least, you need to check on your stocks four times a year when quarterly earnings are released. The amount of time you must devote to your stock portfolio will be less if you do your research on the Internet.

Reasons to own mutual funds

Not everybody should become a stock jockey. Here are the main reasons to stick with mutual funds:

Investments bore you.

If keeping up-to-date on individual stocks' performance and researching new picks make you slackjawed, you should let fund managers, who obsess about stocks all day, make the decisions. As you gain more confidence and experience, you may want to acquire a few individual stocks that complement your portfolio. For most people, however, mutual funds remain their biggest holdings.

You don't have enough cash to diversify into individual stocks.

Money stretches farther with mutual funds. The initial investment for many funds is $2,000 or $3,000. Often even these modest minimums are lowered if you establish an Individual Retirement Account. With just a small investment, you can own a tiny piece of dozens, if not hundreds, of stocks through one or two mutual funds. The same $2,000 doesn't go far if you hanker to invest in individual stocks.

You intend to invest regularly in modest amounts.

A mutual fund firm will gladly arrange for you to invest a specific amount each month or quarter. The money is withdrawn from your checking or savings account on prearranged dates. This slow, steady method of investing isn't as practical with stocks because every purchase generates a commission.

Individual Bonds Versus Bond Funds

You can purchase bonds through a mutual fund or buy them individually. Experts have spent a lot of psychic energy debating which is the best approach, but there is no one-size-fits-all answer. The pros and cons for each strategy are highlighted in the following sections.

Reasons to own individual bonds

More sophisticated investors and those who have a hefty amount of money to sink into bonds may want to own individual ones. Here are the major reasons why:

Cross-Reference   For detailed information on individual bonds, see Chapters 17 and 18.

You can't lose principal.

If you're a buy-and-hold bond investor, wild fluctuations in interest rates aren't going to spook you. Your coupon payments will continue as they always have. If you hold $10,000 worth of Treasury bonds that offer a 6.5 percent coupon rate, you will receive a total of $650 a year in interest payments regardless of what happens in the market. When the bonds mature, you'll get your $10,000 back. Only if you bail out prematurely and sell your bonds could you lose money. (The rare chance exists, however, that the company or government institution issuing the bond will default on the debt payments—particularly in the realm of high-risk bonds such as emerging markets or corporate junk bonds.)

You can't get this same assurance with a bond fund. Fund managers don't sit on their bond portfolios. Managers trade bonds, which means a $10,000 investment in a fund could drop in value or appreciate. In contrast, buy-and-hold bond investors who don't reinvest income will never see their holdings grow.

Your income stream is predictable.

When holding individual bonds, you know exactly how much your income checks will be. With a bond fund, no set coupon rate exists. The payouts vary depending upon the current bonds in the fund's portfolio.

Individual bonds may be cheaper.

Once you purchase a bond, you're finished with your out-of-pocket expenses. The tricky part about buying individual bonds is not getting gouged by the brokerage houses. Buying bonds yourself should be cheaper, but it's not a given.

A study conducted by Charles Schwab, the discount broker, suggests that purchasing individual bonds costs about as much as investing in inexpensive bond funds. But this is true only if an investor has at least $50,000 to sink into individual bonds. That's because bond-trading costs should decrease with more sizable bond purchases. If an investor has less than $50,000 to devote to bonds, a low-cost bond fund should be a more attractive alternative.

You have enough cash to diversify.

Many experts suggest that you need at least $50,000 to $100,000 to seriously consider picking your own bonds. You require that much to safely diversify among a variety of bonds of different maturities and durations.

Reasons to own bond funds

For most people, assembling an individual bond portfolio will never make it onto their must-do lists. Here are the reasons to stick with bond funds:

You get instant diversification.

Buy shares in a fund and you instantly own a wide swath of the bond market. The holdings of Harbor Bond Fund, which is one of the most successful general bond funds around, illustrate this point. In the summer of 2000, Harbor owned a hodge-podge of bonds issued by Worldcom, Bank One, Citicorp, Nabors Industries (an oil driller), the U.S. Treasury, and Ginnie Mae. Getting that kind of breadth on your own would require tremendous amounts of cash and a great deal of effort. Another benefit of diversification: In the rare event that a company should default on its debt payments, the default is barely noticeable to a fund that holds the bonds of a hundred companies.

You don't need lots of money.

You can sign up for a bond fund for as little as $1,000. Once you're in a fund, you can divert additional money into the fund in amounts as little as $50 or $100. This sort of modest, steady investments in individual bonds isn't practical.

Funds are low maintenance.

Somebody who has spent enough hours in the front of the TV to memorize his or her favorite commercials might have enough free time to pick bonds, but most people don't have that kind of free time. The sheer number of bonds available is enough to paralyze most investors. With a fund, the bond professionals are paid to decide, for instance, whether to buy a California water treatment utility bond or a Missouri public housing issue.

Funds can be a better way to go if your taste in bonds goes beyond the plain vanilla Treasuries and insured municipal bonds. Some bonds, such as mortgage-backed debt, can require you to learn an entire new language. If you don't know what collateorized mortgage obligations (CMOs), callable pass-throughs, and tranches are, you should let a fund do the picking. Corporate bond selection can also be treacherous.

The income stream is more frequent.

Most bond funds distribute interest income every month. This regular payment can be a big plus for retirees. Individual bonds usually mail their checks only twice a year.

Summary

✦ Understand what types of funds are available before constructing a mutual fund portfolio.

✦ Don't buy into additional funds without considering whether they will truly improve your portfolio.

✦ Sticking with funds with low expenses increases your chances of outperforming the market.

✦ If you are going to pick your own funds, avoid investing in those that carry sales charges.

✦ Unless you are truly committed to selecting individual bonds and stocks, stick with mutual funds.

Index Funds and Exchange-Traded Funds

As much as we love our mutual funds, sometimes they flounder for a variety of reasons. This chapter explores two investment tools for fund lovers (index funds and exchange-traded funds) that could, over time, improve your overall investment performance. You learn the basics of both these investment options in this chapter. You also learn how to compare index funds and exchange-traded funds and how they can help you construct a well-rounded portfolio for your retirement years.

The Honeymoon's Over for Mutual Funds

The nation's increasing preoccupation with saving for retirement has led to skyrocketing growth in mutual funds. Currently, $7 trillion is sunk into mutual funds — compared with a mere $4.6 billion just two decades ago — and the majority of that money is sitting in retirement accounts. But like most love affairs, the infatuation with mutual funds has faded a bit. Investors, particularly the more sophisticated ones, understand that mutual funds aren't a panacea.

Drawbacks of a traditional mutual fund

Funds can be expensive, fund performance can be erratic, and fund managers, who are only human, can't always resist chasing the hottest stocks rather than sticking to their true investing principles. Even if you do latch onto a fabulous fund that's feted on the front cover of Money magazine, your success is not guaranteed to last.

◆   ◆   ◆   ◆

In This Chapter

Appreciating the downside of mutual funds

Understanding the pros and cons of index funds

Avoiding index overdose

Assessing the exchange-traded fund phenomenon

Considering the pros and cons of exchange-traded funds

◆   ◆   ◆   ◆

Success can wreck the most popular funds. A fund with spectacular returns inevitably generates media attention, which inevitably attracts hordes of new fans. Unfortunately, all that new money sloshing around in a fund can jeopardize returns because too much cash is chasing too few stock ideas. When that happens, today's brilliant fund manager can be tomorrow's toad.

Note
Despite the warts, mutual funds will always be around. For an overwhelming number of investors, mutual funds are the most practical way to buy exposure in the stock and bond markets.

Alternatives to traditional funds

If you've become disenchanted with traditional mutual funds, you may want to consider these two options: index funds and exchange-traded funds. Fans of both of these funds snatch up shares for identical reasons:

✦ Low cost

✦ Tax efficiency

✦ Instant diversification

✦ Less guesswork involved than buying individual stocks

Index funds, which try to match the performance of a given stock index, are familiar to most investors, but exchange-traded funds, which are a hybrid of mutual funds and stocks, remain a mystery to most people. Although professional investors are already using this promising investing technique, word has only begun trickling out to the public. What's exciting about exchange-traded funds is the opportunity they present for people who are too scared to invest in individual stocks, but are discouraged by mutual funds' inherent disadvantages.

Executives in the mutual fund industry are petrified that this new way to invest will steal business away from them, and they are right to be anxious. The popularity of this new investment option has been explosive. Industry insiders are no longer shocked when the most popular of these exchange-traded funds end the day as the most actively traded issues on the American Stock Exchange, where most of them are currently listed.

Are index funds and exchange-traded funds right for you? Perhaps. But you need to understand how they work and what your choices are before making that decision. Read on to find out the basics behind these two fund varieties and how to enhance your portfolio with them.

Index Funds

Index funds are designed to replicate the performance of a given index, such as Standard and Poor's 500. The Vanguard 500 Index Fund, the index movement's flagship, is the nation's most popular mutual fund. Despite the hoopla that Vanguard's index funds have generated, index funds still represent a tiny fraction of the money invested in the mutual fund universe.

Cross-Reference   See Chapter 12 for a listing of the biggest indexes.

The advantages of index funds

Here are the reasons why you might want to consider index funds:

Indexing provides instant diversification.

The beauty of investing in an index fund is that you can own a stake in a huge chunk of the U.S. stock market for as little as $2,000 or $3,000. That modest investment buys exposure in the mightiest of blue chips all the way down the food chain to aggressive Internet startups. Buy shares in a bond index fund and your reach into the fixed-income universe will extend far beyond the clutch of municipal bonds or Treasuries you might currently possess.

You can purchase shares in monster index funds that not only guarantee broad exposure to both stock and bond markets, but to overseas markets as well. What's more, you can buy index funds that are linked to the fortunes of technology, real estate, and emerging markets. Mutual fund firms, which never dreamed they'd be swept up in the indexing business, are now scrambling to offer their own indexing creations.

Index funds provide superior returns.

When the first index fund, sponsored by the Vanguard Group, rumbled off the conveyer belt back in 1976, the financial world laughed at the concept. Critics believed that indexing was sheer lunacy because it condemned an investor to a lifetime of average returns. On the surface, the gripe seems legitimate. By its very nature, an index fund isn't supposed to do any better or worse than the benchmark it tracks. An index fund that shadows the Standard & Poor's 500, for instance, isn't designed to outperform the popular benchmark. Its sole mission is to match the benchmark as closely as possible.

This single-minded drive to provide investors with returns that mimic the financial market's overall performance drives detractors nuts. Would you, they argue, send your child to an average pediatrician or pay an average car mechanic to overhaul your engine? Would you enjoy sitting through an average performance of *The Nutcracker Suite?*

Cyber Cafe for Index Junkies

Are you an index fund junkie? On the Internet, your best source for news on index and exchange-traded funds is IndexFunds.com (www.indexfunds.com). This Web site provides commentary for sophisticated and beginning index investors, fund profiles, links to index benchmarks, and more. Meanwhile, Morningstar (www.morningstar.com), in addition to its long-time coverage of index funds, has devoted a section of its Web site to exchange-traded funds.

The problem with all these analogies is that average returns in the stock market end up being better than what most investors typically get. An increasing number of Americans now appreciate this fact. A big reason index funds can perform better, as you'll learn a little later, is that the expenses are quite low. Index funds don't try to outguess the market by jumping in and out of stocks, as do some investors.

Index funds don't require stock-picking prowess.

Index funds are largely immune from human stock-picking frailties. An index fund manager doesn't have to agonize about which stocks to hold or sell in the portfolio. If the fund is an S&P 500 index fund, the manager automatically holds shares in all 500 corporations from General Electric, which was recently the biggest, down to the littlest, which lately was Alberto-Culver Co., a health and beauty supplier. If the fund is linked to a small-cap index, it will contain most or all of the stocks in the Russell 2000 or the Standard & Poor's SmallCap 600.

Index funds that try to keep pace with the entire stock market have a trickier task. A fund like Vanguard Total Stock Market Index is linked to the Wilshire 5000, which encompasses most of the nation's publicly traded stocks. Owning stock in all the companies that are part of this index is impractical for a fund. Instead, it contains a representative sampling of a few thousand companies.

The mandate of all these index funds is to cruise on autopilot. In contrast, managers of actively managed funds — that includes all but the indexing variety — don't have that luxury. They make their trading decisions in the hopes of beating the market average. They might stockpile cash in their funds because they're nervous that the market's going to plummet. Or they may place big bets on pharmaceutical or bank stocks or conclude that a heavy dose of telecommunication stock is the shrewdest strategy. Yet no matter how prescient or intelligent these guys are, outsmarting the market has been extremely difficult, especially for large-cap managers. Most actively managed funds that invest in large companies have failed to beat that market's average.

Indexing is cheap.

A cineplex can charge more for a movie ticket than you'll pay all year for a money manager to babysit your index fund shares. The average stock index fund's yearly expense ratio is a mere .60 percent. That means for every $1,000 invested in a fund, you pay $6 a year for its maintenance. The Vanguard Group even undercuts that price by much more than half. (Some exchange-traded funds, as you'll learn later in this chapter, can even undercut Vanguard's prices!) In contrast, the average stock fund charges about 1.5 percent. That might not seem like much, but it is. If your stock fund returns 11 percent and expenses are 1.5 percent, 13.6 percent of your gain is eaten up by taxes.

Index funds are cheap because overhead is low. You don't need the services of a stellar stock picker, who commands a hefty salary, or backup from a phalanx of stock analysts. Trading is minimal, which also keeps costs down. The traditional mutual fund can easily cost three to five times as much as an index fund. This price advantage helps catapult index funds past many of their competitors.

Note Although traditional fund expenses might not seem so outrageous when Wall Street is scorching, the indexing cost edge is quite noticeable during normal years.

Index funds track more than the S&P 500.

The most popular index funds are linked to the Standard & Poor's 500, which is packed with many of the nation's instantly recognizable companies from Disney to Johnson & Johnson. But many experts warn that ignoring the broader stock market in favor of these 500 brutes can be a mistake.

Note S&P 500 loyalists were rewarded with phenomenal returns in the 1990s, but the returns, just like a helium balloon, couldn't float high indefinitely.

Investing in a total stock market index fund, which is linked to an index such as the Wilshire 5000, is arguably a slightly better strategy. With one of these funds, your financial future isn't riding exclusively on the fate of 500 stocks, but on thousands. These funds aren't quite so risky because they don't place such a concentrated bet on one corner of the market. Although blue chips dominate the Wilshire 5000 just as they do in the S&P 500, the funds that track the Wilshire 5000 do invest in small- and mid-cap stocks.

Note Large-caps predominate the Wilshire 5000 and the S&P 500 because the indexes are *market weighted* — the fortunes of just a few of the nation's biggest corporate titans influence index movement far more than do thousands of the smaller stocks.

Although total stock market funds aren't nearly as common as the S&P 500 variety, the leading no-load mutual fund firms (such as Vanguard, Fidelity, and T. Rowe Price) do offer them. In addition, Wilshire Associates, which maintains the Wilshire 5000 index, markets its own index funds, as do Charles Schwab and E*Trade.

Indexing offers maximum convenience.

Certain index funds can bundle stock and bond index choices together into a mega index fund. This kind of fund can represent the ultimate in indexing convenience. Fidelity, T. Rowe Price, and Vanguard package a handful of index funds into one fund. Fidelity's "Four-in-One" index fund, for example, contains four of its proprietary stock and bond index funds. Buy shares in this fund of funds and you'll attain instant diversification in blue chips, small-caps, and overseas stocks, as well as the broad bond market. Investing in a bundled index fund can be an ideal way to achieve effortless diversification for beginners or those who don't want to bother with selecting funds.

Bond Index Funds: Your Best Bet

The lowly bond index fund shares something in common with the ugliest mutt at the animal pound: Most investors don't even slow down to take a look. Recently only $2 out of every $100 being plowed into bond funds were tied to an index. This lack of attention is unfortunate because bond index funds provide good returns.

You can buy individual bonds yourself, but you typically need an investment of at least $50,000 to $100,000 to be safely diversified. With an index fund, you attain sweeping coverage instantly. The most common index funds offer the broadest exposure by tracking the Lehman Brothers Aggregate Bond Index, which is divided among Treasuries, government and corporate bonds, and mortgage-backed securities. Index funds can also specialize in short-, intermediate-, or long-term bonds.

How good are bond index funds? During a recent three-year period, the Vanguard Total Bond Index, which is the country's largest bond index fund, outperformed 89 percent of actively managed bond funds. Other bond index funds (less than three dozen exist) have also typically trounced most peers. Charles Schwab, the brokerage firm, became so enamored with the merits of bond indexing that it transformed two of its government bond funds into indexed products.

Low expenses also give bond index funds a decisive advantage over other bond mutual funds. The average bond index fund charges just 45 cents for every $100 invested, and some excellent funds charge less than half that. This pricing edge is even more critical in the fixed-income world because bonds are more modest performers.

Suppose you invested $10,000 in one of Vanguard's bond index funds, which carries a tiny 0.2 percent expense ratio. The fund is yielding 5 percent, so after expenses the actual yield drops to 4.8 percent. Compounded over 5 years, the account would be worth $12,642. But if that $10,000 is placed in a bond fund offering the same yield, but charging 1 percent for expenses (about the national bond fund average), you'd pocket $12,167 or $475 less.

The price advantage helps explain why bond index funds nudged out their actively managed competition for the top performance title during the past decade. Maybe the bond index funds' built-in cost advantage wouldn't matter if the bond world was full of portfolio managers who could produce extra returns out of sheer brilliance. But that hasn't happened. What you see over and over again is that the difference between good and bad bond funds can be traced back to their expenses.

Indexing can be particularly appealing for shorter-term bond holdings. With the short maturities, managers have even less of an opportunity to pull ahead of the pack because the prices are so similar. In other words, even a great deal on these bonds won't be appreciably better than a mediocre transaction.

If you're interested in bond index funds, consider the following:

✦ **Schwab Short-Term Bond Market Index Fund.** Call (800) 266-5623 or go to the Web site www.schwab.com for more information.

✦ **Schwab Total Bond Market Index Fund.** Call (800) 266-5623 or go to the Web site at www.schwab.com for more information.

✦ **Vanguard Short-Term Bond Index Fund.** Call (800) 635-1511 or go to the Web site at www.vanguard.com for more information.

✦ **Vanguard Intermediate-Term Bond Index Fund.** Call (800) 635-1511 or go to the Web site at www.vanguard.com for more information.

✦ **Vanguard Total Bond Market Index Fund.** Call (800) 635-1511 or go to the Web site at www.vanguard.com for more information.

✦ **Vanguard Long-Term Bond Index Fund.** Call (800) 635-1511 or go to the Web site at www.vanguard.com for more information.

Index funds are tax efficient.

Too many mutual fund managers don't give a hoot about taxes. They trade stocks frequently without considering how this activity generates painful capital gains taxes for you and me. Index funds, however, generally don't create these taxing problems. They are tax efficient because of their buy-and-hold mantra.

Total stock market index funds win the award for tax efficiency. After all, there's not much call to trade when a fund's mission is to track the entire stock market. Large-cap index funds are also extremely tax efficient. Because of their tax efficiency, index funds are excellent candidates for taxable investment accounts. (Of course, the superior performance of index funds makes them good candidates for tax-sheltered retirement accounts as well.)

Note

Small-cap index funds don't repel taxes as well as large-cap index funds do because frequent changes in the small-cap index can require managers to buy or sell hundreds of stocks. Even so, small-cap index funds are generally far more tax efficient than actively managed small-cap funds.

Index fund disadvantages

Consider these aspects of an index fund before making a final decision to buy.

Indexing all markets is difficult.

The argument for overseas and small-cap index funds isn't nearly as compelling as the argument for domestic large-cap index funds. In the global marketplace, smart stock-pickers can beat the indexers fairly easily. During the past decade, the majority of managers have beaten the Morgan Stanley Capital International Europe, Australasia, and Far East Index (MSCI EAFE), the most popular overseas benchmark.

Why have foreign index funds generally performed poorly? Active managers might enjoy an edge because the world stock markets are broad enough to allow for surprises. An industrious manager may find a hidden jewel in Switzerland or Vietnam that the rest of the financial world hasn't yet discovered. This kind of surprise just doesn't happen with the Standard & Poor's 500 crowd. On our own shores, small-cap managers can uncover obscure companies that the rest of the pack has overlooked, which explains why small-cap managers have fared better than small-cap index funds.

Another important aspect to foreign index funds is the Japanese factor. Most foreign index funds are tied to the MSCI EAFE, which Japanese stocks dominate. For many years, however, the Japanese market was a financial basket case. While indexers had no choice but to maintain a large Japanese exposure in their portfolio, active managers treated Japanese stocks like road kill and stayed away. The MSCI EAFE's Japanese exposure, however, has been shrinking.

Note

Investors shouldn't necessarily shun foreign and small-cap index funds. Later in this chapter, you'll see suggestions for the ideal mix of actively managed and index funds in these categories.

Not all index funds are cheap.

Most index funds lure investors with Wal-Mart prices, but dozens of index funds are now being peddled with sales charges that can exceed 5 percent. What's more, some of these funds are gouging unsuspecting customers with annual expenses that are seven or eight times as expensive as the low-cost indexing leaders. The biggest culprits are typically proprietary bank index funds and those sold through full-service brokers.

Tip

You won't get suckered if you choose a fund that charges less than the average fund's yearly expense ratio. See the prospectus, which a fund company mails free to potential investors, to find out fund expenses. Compare those expenses with the list of typical expense ratios in Chapter 14.

Leveraged index funds can be dangerous.

Remember how index funds are supposed to match their respective benchmarks or come darn close? The newer *leveraged* or *enhanced* index funds have smashed that assumption. A handful of mutual fund firms (including Rydex, ProFunds, and Potomac) oversee index funds that are intentionally designed to fare much better or worse than the markets they track. During jubilant times, these funds sprint to the pinnacle of those yearly lists of the nation's best-performing funds.

Caution In bear markets, leveraged index funds could easily lose 20, 30, or even 40 percent or more of their value.

How risky can these funds be? The dead giveaway is a fund's *beta*, which is a measure of volatility. If the S&P 500 jumps 10 percent, then a traditional index fund with a beta of 1.0, such as the Vanguard 500 Index, should return nearly 10 percent. It's a one-to-one correlation. But look what happens with ProFund UltraOTC, which is enhanced with an earth-shattering 2.0 beta. When the Nasdaq 100, which is crammed with technology stocks, scoots up 10 percent, the fund, which tracks this benchmark, should advance about 20 percent. If the Nasdaq 100 drops 25 percent during a bear market, the value of ProFund UltraOTC should plummet about 50 percent. Not all the leveraged funds, however, are quite so volatile. For instance, Potomac OTC Plus, which is linked to the Nasdaq 100, has a 1.25 beta.

These leveraged funds exaggerate index movements by using exotic investment techniques. The funds initially appealed to financial professionals who dart in and out of the market. Rydex, ProFunds, and Potomac have become halfway houses for market timers, who are loathed by other fund groups who prefer buy-and-hold customers. But as news spread of the spectacular returns during the 1990s, traditional investors began snapping up shares.

Caution These turbo-charged funds aren't appropriate for retirees or anyone else who can't afford investment implosion. A better fit is the portfolio of an aggressive, long-term investor who has the guts to hang on during scary periods.

To keep away the unsophisticated, the fund families set high initial minimum investments ranging from $10,000 to $25,000, though shares can be purchased for much smaller amounts through discount brokerage firms. The following fund families carry leveraged funds:

◆ Rydex Funds at (800) 820-0888 or www.rydexfunds.com

◆ ProFunds at (888) 776-3637 or www.profunds.com

◆ Potomac Funds at (800) 851-0511 or www.potomacfunds.com

Indexing Possibilities

Are you in the market for a stock index fund? Consider these candidates:

Standard & Poor's 500 Index Fund	Phone Number
Bridgeway Ultra-Large 35 Index	(800) 661-3550
Fidelity Spartan Market Index	(800) 544-8888
Vanguard 500 Index	(800) 635-1511

Total Stock Market Index Fund	Phone Number
Fidelity Spartan Extended Market Index	(800) 544-8888
Schwab 1000	(800) 266-5623
Vanguard Total Stock Market Index	(800) 635-1511
Wilshire Target Large-Cap Growth	(888) 200-6796
Wilshire Target Large-Cap Value	(888) 200-6796

Small-Cap Index Fund	Phone Number
Bridgeway Ultra-Small Index	(800) 661-3550
E*Trade Extended Market Index	(800) 786-2575
Schwab Small-Cap Index	(800) 266-5623
Vanguard Small-Cap Index	(800) 635-1511
Vanguard Extended Market Index	(800) 635-1511

Morgan Stanley EAFE	Phone Number
Fidelity Spartan International Index	(800) 544-8888
Schwab International Index	(800) 266-5623
Vanguard Developed Markets Index	(800) 635-1511

Index funds don't always make money.

Index funds are not invincible. History strongly suggests that the superlative returns in the 20 percent and 30 percent range that were common in the 1990s were unusual. During most of the twentieth century, stocks have averaged gains of 11 percent a year. But even that kind of return is no sure thing. Because of the potential volatility, you shouldn't consider investing in any index fund if you can't hold your investment for at least several years.

Indexing Your Portfolio: When Enough Is Enough

You can fill your entire portfolio with index funds and be done with it. A total stock market index or exchange-traded fund (a product detailed later in this chapter) along with a bond index fund provides immediate diversification. Or you could choose one index fund that combines both stocks and bonds. Add a foreign index fund into the mix and you'd be covered globally as well.

More sophisticated investors might want to use indexing as their portfolio's corner-stone. They can then choose individual stocks or mutual funds for small-cap and foreign investing or for concentrated bets on the market. Index funds could not meet all the needs of someone interested in exposure to such industries as real estate, natural resources, and utilities. Exchange-traded funds can provide a better way to gain exposure in the market's smaller niches.

Tip

If you don't have enough money to diversify properly, investing in an all-purpose index fund can provide a nice solution. As your assets grow, some of this money can be funneled into other types of investments as well.

But for millions of Americans who have enough money to spread around, the key question is: Is it possible to overdose on index funds? Vanguard, the indisputable indexing giant, suggests it's possible. Vanguard has historically recommended that 50 percent to 60 percent of a typical investor's total portfolio should be devoted to index funds. The fund family, however, provides little guidance on how the pie should be sliced beyond that. Vanguard firmly believes that there's no magic for-mula for indexing versus active investing.

Not long ago, Charles Schwab's researchers tackled this issue by examining the his-toric performance of more than 2,700 hypothetical mutual fund portfolios in the 1990s. The mutual funds selected for the study were historically high-performing funds. The number crunchers examined whether investors would be better off with an all-index approach, a portfolio of all actively managed funds, or some combina-tion of the two. The asset allocation breakdown of each portfolio was large-caps (40 percent), small-caps (25 percent), international (30 percent), and cash in money market accounts (5 percent).

Here are the research highlights:

- ✦ A combination of index and actively managed funds enjoyed a better chance of outperforming the market than a pure indexed portfolio. Two-thirds of these combo portfolios beat the all-index approach's total return of 19.3 percent.

- ✦ A mix of index and actively managed funds was 57 percent less volatile than portfolios containing no index funds.

- ✦ Using actively managed small-cap and international funds with a large-cap index fund increases an investor's chances of beating the market.

Institutions Love Index Funds

While Schwab and Vanguard have been quibbling about how much indexing is appropriate, the nation's mightiest investors have been employing a mixed approach for many years. Institutional investors are the heaviest users of indexed investing. Boeing, AT&T, Ford Motor, IBM, and the massive public pension systems in California, New York, and Florida are just a few of the huge index investors. It's no longer unusual for a corporation's financial decision makers to devote up to 75 percent of their stock holdings to index investments. The remaining money is often used to try to hit home runs with active money managers.

Institutional heavyweights have increasingly turned to indexing because they can't find dynamo managers who routinely beat the market. If finding such strong managers is difficult for professionals, imagine how much more difficult it is for individual investors.

In screening for the best investment combinations, the Schwab researchers arrived at what they considered to be the optimum mix of index and actively managed funds. In the performance race, the researchers concluded that it was tough improving upon a large-cap index fund. In contrast, international and small-cap index funds, not surprisingly, didn't perform nearly as well as their actively managed peers.

The following recommended proportions, according to Schwab's research, represent the best opportunity to beat the market or, during rocky times, at least underperfom it by the smallest percentage:

✦ **Large-cap stock holdings:** 80 percent index and 20 percent actively managed

✦ **Small-cap stock holdings:** 40 percent index and 60 percent actively managed

✦ **International stock holdings:** 30 percent index and 70 percent actively managed

The one wrinkle in this research is that Schwab study, which is believed to be the first one of its kind, didn't use any mediocre funds. The funds selected to simulate portfolio returns were (like the kids in Lake Woebegone) all above average. The funds used in the study came from Schwab's Mutual Fund Select List, which is composed of traditionally high-performing funds available through the discount broker. The funds included in the research came from such fund families as Janus, Strong, T. Rowe Price, Fidelity, and American Century. A computer generated the portfolio combinations. Although using highly rated funds might seem to unfairly stack the deck against indexing, Schwab researchers defended the move. Investors, they noted, tend to gravitate to the highest-performing funds, whether they generate ideas through the popular Schwab list, Morningstar, fund screening software or the media.

Note   The Schwab study results were meant to serve as a guideline. Some investors may want to index their whole portfolio. Others, who seek to outperform the market and have strong convictions about individual mutual funds or market trends, may lean more toward actively managed funds.

Exchange-Traded Funds

More and more index fans are sinking money into exchange-traded funds, which behave remarkably like index funds, but are traded like stocks.

Just like index funds, exchange-traded funds hold stocks in companies that make up a given benchmark, such as the S&P 500 or the Nasdaq 100. If you hold an exchange-traded fund that mimics the S&P 500 or the Russell 2000 (a popular benchmark for small-cap stocks), your return should very closely match the corresponding index.

Spiders, Diamonds, and Qubes, oh my!

If you've never heard of exchange-traded funds, you may recognize some of the off-beat nicknames of three of the most well-known exchange-traded funds so far:

✦ **Qubes (stock symbol QQQ):** Named for the QQQ ticker symbol, this fund tracks the tech-heavy Nasdaq 100. Official name is the Nasdaq-100 Index Tracking Stock.

✦ **Diamonds (stock symbol DIA):** This fund shadows the 30 corporations in the Dow Jones Industrial Average.

✦ **Spiders (stock symbol SPY):** Short for Standard & Poor's Depository Receipts, this fund contains all the stocks in the S&P 500 index.

Exchange-traded funds were introduced way back in 1993, but they were initially treated as a curiosity. Then, in 1999, Qubes burst onto the scene. With technology stocks on fire at that time, investors rushed to buy Qubes as an effortless way to ride the technology wave. The tech-heavy Nasdaq 100 includes such stocks as Cisco Systems, Apple Computer, Sun Microsystems, Worldcom, and Qualcomm. (It's not all tech stocks, however. Also included are corporations likes Starbucks and Bed, Bath & Beyond.)

Resource   To find out more about exchange-traded funds, visit Nasdaq's Web site at www. nasdaq.com.

The Nasdaq tracking stock remains so popular that it's typically the most heavily traded stock on the American Stock Exchange. Its popularity didn't go unnoticed in the financial world. Barclays Global Investors made a splash in 2000 by introducing more than 50 new exchange-traded funds that also trade on the American Stock Exchange. Many other companies are also scrambling to get into the act. Time Warner announced plans to launch an exchange-traded fund that tracks *Fortune* magazine's Internet index. Another fund holds 40 stocks that make up *Wired* magazine's New Economy Index. Meanwhile, the New York Stock Exchange is exploring offering its own line of funds.

Not to be left out, Vanguard announced that it would soon offer its own brand of exchange-traded funds, nicknamed VIPERs. It's expected to offer exchange-traded funds for a few of its existing funds, including Vanguard Growth Index, Vanguard Value Index, Vanguard Total Stock Market Index, and Vanguard Small-Cap Index.

Exchange-traded fund advantages

Wonder if exchange-traded funds are right for you? Here's how these funds can shine:

Exchange-traded funds are cheap.

Exchange-traded funds can be quite inexpensive. For example, the annual cost of owning a Spider, excluding transaction fees, is vastly cheaper than the cost of a run-of-the-mill mutual fund. It is also more economical than the average index fund, as you can see in Table 15-1.

Table 15-1	
Average Yearly Cost of a $10,000 Investment	
Type of Investment	*Average Annual Cost*
Spider	$18
S&P 500 Index Fund	$61
Average stock fund	$154

Exchange-traded funds provide an in for someone who doesn't have enough money for an index fund's minimum initial investment. For instance, you'll typically need $3,000 to invest in one of Vanguard's index funds. With an exchange-traded fund, you could get started with a much smaller amount of money.

These funds, which are sometimes referred to as index shares or tracking stocks, are generally cheap because the sponsors don't have the overhead of a mutual fund company. For instance, branch offices and telephone centers are unnecessary because there is no direct dealing with the public; all trading goes through brokers.

With the field becoming more crowded, the competition is lowering the prices even further. A $10,000 investment in an exchange-traded S&P 500 clone from Barclays Global Investors generates yearly expenses of just $9.45.

It would be a mistake, however, to think that ETFs are always cheaper than index funds. The most inexpensive index funds, such as the ones offered by Vanguard, offer the same rock-bottom expenses.

Caution Don't forget to factor in the cost of trading ETFs. Just like stocks, you must purchase exchange-traded funds through a broker. An ETF's savings over an index fund could vanish after the brokerage firm is paid.

The funds are tax-friendly.

Although mutual funds can be terribly tax inefficient, index shares often aren't haunted by the same tax gremlins. As long as you hold onto index funds, capital gains taxes will often be a rarer occurrence. Many exchange-traded funds are even more tax efficient than their index fund counterparts.

Cross-Reference Even a regular mutual fund that ends the year in the red can sometimes generate a nightmarish tax bill for its hapless shareholders. See Chapter 16 for more details.

Experts also predict that exchange-traded funds could be a godsend during nasty market downturns, if panicking shareholders pull massive amounts of money out of traditional mutual funds. If this happens, funds could be forced to sell truckloads of stock to pay off their fleeing customers. These sales would create a terrible capital gains tax liability for those remaining behind. A similar flight from exchange-traded funds wouldn't necessarily trigger taxes due to the way the funds are structured.

Keep in mind, however, that ETFs are not entirely insulated from taxes. An ETF, for instance, has to sell stock if a company in its respective benchmark is removed from the index for a variety of reasons, such as a corporate merger. Selling shares can trigger capital gains taxes.

Another ETF Option

Merill Lynch HOLDRs, which stands for Holding Company Depositary Receipts, are lumped into the exchange-traded category, but they have unique features. Like other ETFs, an investor in a HOLDR will own a basket of stocks. However, a HOLDR doesn't automatically own a piece of all the companies in a given index. Each HOLDR typically contains just 20 stocks in a fixed, unmanaged portfolio. Another unique feature: HOLDRs can only be bought in increments of 100 shares, which is known as a round lot. Consequently, the price will be a deterrent to some.

Exchange-traded funds can be solid core holdings.

Some investors are using exchange-traded funds as their core large-cap stock holding. Investors could buy shares in a Spider for their large-cap exposure, but plenty of other choices are also available, including those offered by Barclays Global Investors, which have nicknamed their funds iShares. Among the iShares' offerings are broad funds that track the Russell 3000 Index, the Russell 1000 Growth Index, the Dow Jones U.S. Total Stock Market Index, and the S&P 500.

Meanwhile, if you want to bet aggressively on technology, you could gravitate to Qubes or another tech-oriented fund, such as iShares Dow Jones U.S. Technology Sector Index Fund. Another popular source is Merrill Lynch's HOLDRs. What's especially appealing about these tech offerings is that there aren't many traditional index funds for tech heads, and some of the existing ones pass along extremely high expenses.

A sophisticated investor who feels bullish about the prospects of a foreign country's stocks might want to supplement an overseas mutual fund with funds that specialize in foreign countries. Through Barclays' iShares, someone can invest in well over a dozen different countries, including Japan, Canada, Australia, Italy, Germany, Hong Kong, Mexico, Singapore, and the United Kingdom.

Exchange-traded funds can also be ideal if you are interested in buying individual stocks, but aren't ready to make your move. They can also provide a solution if you aren't sure which stocks to buy in a particular sector.

Example

If you want to buy individual utility stocks, but aren't sure which ones, you can tuck the money inside iShare's Dow Jones U.S. Utilities or Dow Jones U.S. Tele-communication funds.

Exchange-Traded Fund Contacts

Here's how you can reach the major sources of exchange-traded funds:

✦ American Stock Exchange at (800) THE-AMEX ext. 1 or www.amex.com

✦ Barclays Global Investors at (800) 474-2737 or www.ishares.com

✦ Merrill Lynch Holdrs at www.holdrs.com or contact your local Merrill Lynch branch.

Before investing in an exchange-traded fund, be sure to read the prospectus that details the expenses and potential risks.

For a great deal of commentary on the exchange-traded phenomenon visit these two online sites:

✦ TheStreet.com at www.thestreet.com

✦ Morningstar at www.morningstar.com

These funds are flexible.

You can buy and sell Spiders, Diamonds, and the other baskets of stocks through-out the trading day. The prices, like any other stock, fluctuate during market hours. In contrast, traditional mutual funds are priced only once a day after the market's close.

This flexibility is proving irresistible to both aggressive traders and long-term investors. Active traders are attracted to the opportunity to be choosy about their price. They can buy shares through a market order, which ensures they pay the best price available at the time the order is processed. Or they can set their own target price with a limit order. You can't buy regular mutual funds with a limit order. Aggressive players can also buy shares on margin or sell shares short.

Disadvantages of exchange-traded funds

Here are the drawbacks to exchange-traded funds:

Exchange-traded funds encourage market timers.

When exchange-traded funds were first unveiled, it was primarily the market timers who took notice. These guys, who like to flit in and out of investments frequently, have traditionally been scorned by regular mutual fund companies. Their frequent trading jacks up the expenses for other fund shareholders and can generate unwanted taxes. Mutual funds were designed for buy-and-hold investors and not for market timers.

The ability to buy and sell exchange-traded funds throughout the day encourages frenetic trading. But the overwhelming consensus drawn from years of academic research suggests that you can't outsmart Wall Street with frequent trading.

These funds aren't for the faint of heart.

Exchange-traded funds that specialize in one niche of the total stock market can be extremely volatile. Investing in Qubes, for instance, can be hair raising. Stocks such as eBay, Yahoo!, and CMGI, which can all be found within a Qube, are capable of losing 10 or 20 percent or much more in just one day. In fact, with the Nasdaq in a free fall in 2000, the value of a Qube dropped nearly 37 percent that year. Conservative investors and those who can't afford to sit on their investment for at least several years should stay away.

The other sector bets can also be scary. The three main sources for sector exposure are Select Spiders, which were created after unbundling the S&P 500 into broad industries, Barclays' iShares and Merrill Lynch's HOLDRs. This partial list from all three sources gives you an idea of what's available:

Select Spiders:
+ Basic industries (stock symbol XLB)
+ Consumer services (stock symbol XLV)
+ Consumer staples (stock symbol XLP)
+ Energy (stock symbol XLE)
+ Financial (stock symbol XLF)
+ Industrial (stock symbol XLI)
+ Technology (stock symbol XLK)
+ Utilities (stock symbol XLU)

iShares sector funds:
+ Dow Jones U.S. Chemicals (stock symbol IYD)
+ Dow Jones U.S. Consumer Cyclical (stock symbol IYC)
+ Dow Jones U.S. Industrial (stock symbol IYJ)
+ Dow Jones U.S. Energy (stock symbol IYE)
+ Dow Jones U.S. Internet (stock symbol IYV)
+ Dow Jones U.S. Healthcare (stock symbol IYH)

Merrill Lynch HOLDRs:
+ Biotech (stock symbol BBH)
+ Broadband (stock symbol BDH)
+ B2B Internet (stock symbol BHH)
+ Internet (stock symbol HHH)
+ Pharmaceutical (stock symbol PPH)
+ Regional bank (stock symbol RKH)
+ Semiconductor (stock symbol SMH)
+ Telecom (stock symbol TTH)
+ Utilities (stock symbol UTH)

What you have to worry about with these sector funds is getting too much exposure to two or three corporations. With some of these funds, the top three holdings may represent a third or even more of the fund's assets.

The choices are getting confusing.

With more exchange-traded funds being introduced all the time, the options could become bewildering very quickly.

ETFs can be impractical for dollar-cost averaging.

If you're a fan of dollar-cost averaging, exchange-traded fund aren't practical. Remember, every time you invest in an exchange-traded fund, you must pay a stock commission to the brokerage firm. Imagine contributing $50 or $100 a month into one of these funds. The commissions would kill you. Mutual funds are the best way to invest in this slow and steady way.

Summary

✦ Stick with cheap index funds.

✦ Handle leveraged index funds carefully.

✦ Invest in both traditional funds as well as index funds to make the most of your money.

✦ Don't overlook bond index funds.

✦ Exchange-traded funds can be a solid indexing substitute.

✦   ✦   ✦

Protecting Stocks and Mutual Funds from Taxes

♦ ♦ ♦ ♦

In This Chapter

Knowing why capital gains tax rates matter

Reducing taxes when selling stocks at a profit

Understanding the effects of taxes on mutual fund returns

Learning tax strategies for mutual funds

♦ ♦ ♦ ♦

This chapter presents tactics to keep your investing tax bills to a minimum. You'll learn about tax-efficient trading strategies, which investments are most tax friendly, and knowing what investments may be best kept in your retirement versus your taxable accounts.

Of course, the easiest way to keep most of your profits from Uncle Sam is to stuff as much money as you can in retirement accounts for as long as possible. This way, the money can grow for years or even decades beyond the reach of the IRS's sticky fingers. Within a retirement account, you can switch in and out of mutual funds, stocks, or bonds without triggering capital gains taxes. Income generated within your retirement portfolios isn't taxed either. It's only when you begin draining the money out of these sheltered accounts that you'll encounter a tax bill.

If you're a super retirement saver, you already appreciate the fact that hiding all your money from the Internal Revenue Service is difficult. Sure, you can stash a decent chunk in your 401(k) or other workplace retirement plan. If you're still working, you're also eligible to deposit up to $2,000 each year into an Individual Retirement Account. But what if you still have money left over? Chances are you have that cash invested in taxable accounts where it can get slammed by taxes. Read on for solutions to your tax dilemmas.

How Taxes Affect Individual Stocks

Counting paper profits is certainly more fun than worrying about how much of that money will be chewed up by taxes, but the tax consequences of stock trading can sap your net worth. Luckily, you can do something to stop the bleeding.

Tip   You're most in control of your tax destiny if you invest in individual stocks.

Investing in stocks can be incredibly tax-friendly because you essentially decide when you're going to pay the IRS. If you own individual stocks that don't spin off dividends, you can watch your stocks escalate in value for years or decades without paying a single cent in taxes. You never owe any taxes on stocks until you sell. That's a guarantee that investors who were lucky enough to invest in some of the best-performing stocks of the 20th century can be especially grateful for.

Example   During the 1990s, Dell Computer rewarded its shareholders with annual returns of 97.3 percent. The value of a $10,000 investment in Dell exploded to $8.9 million. Yet shareholders who have held tight to their shares have still not paid any capital gains taxes on that miraculous windfall.

When stock investors sell shares, however, they owe taxes on their gains. Stock investors can face three types of taxes:

✦ Short-term capital gains tax

✦ Long-term capital gains tax

✦ Tax on dividend and interest income

Short-term capital gains tax

Trigger-happy investors face the harshest tax pain. If you hold a stock for a year or less, the profits are subject to the short-term capital gains tax. These quick profits are taxed at the same rate as ordinary income, just like your paycheck.

The tax you pay depends upon your income tax bracket, which ranges from 15 percent to 39.6 percent. Suppose someone in the 39.6 percent tax bracket made $10,000 on a quick sale of Yahoo! stock. The government's cut of the profits would be nearly $4,000. If the Yahoo! fan had kept the stock for at least 366 days (a year, plus one day), the tax bill would have shriveled to $2,000 because the profit would have been classified as a long-term capital gain instead.

Tip   Whenever possible, you want to avoid the pain of the short-term capital gains tax. If you hold off selling even one day beyond the 365-day period following your purchase of the stock, you pay less tax.

Long-term capital gains tax

If taxes on your stock trades are inevitable, paying the long-term capital gains tax is preferable to paying the short-term tax because the rate is lower. Like the short-term variety, you'll trigger this capital gains tax only when you unload a stock for a profit. You also must be patient enough to hold the stock for at least a year and a day to qualify for the lower long-term rate.

Example   Say you bought stock in the Gap at $30 a share, and you bailed two years later when shares were priced at $50. You would have to pay long-term capital gains taxes on the $20 per share profit.

The ceiling for long-term capital gains taxes is 20 percent. For those in the 15 percent tax bracket, the tax drops to 10 percent. In addition, these rates are slated to decline. Stocks which were bought in the year 2001 or later and held for at least five years will be subject to a maximum long-term capital gains rate of 18 percent. For those in the 15 percent tax bracket, the rate slips to 8 percent.

Tax on dividend and interest income

There's no clever way to dodge taxes on stock dividends. A *dividend* is a fraction of a company's earnings that the company decides to distribute to its shareholders. Slower growing companies typically use dividends, which are usually paid quarterly, as a carrot to whet investors' appetites. Many corporations don't offer dividends anymore or have become less generous in the ones they distribute.

Caution   Unfortunately, you can't use the buy-and-hold strategy to avoid paying taxes on dividends, and you have to pay taxes regardless of whether you pocket the cash or reinvest it to buy more stock shares. Even if you don't sell a stock, you still pay annual taxes on any dividends.

Dividends are always taxed as ordinary income. That means your tax rate equals your tax bracket. Interest income generated by bonds, certificates of deposit, savings accounts, and any other income generators are taxed the same way.

Taxes on dividends can swallow a huge chunk of your profits. Philip Morris stock, for example, recently sported a dividend yield of 7.66 percent or $1.92 a share. However, that princely dividend doesn't look so handsome after the taxes are paid. The yearly dividend payout to someone holding 1,000 shares of the cigarette maker would be $1,920. If this shareholder is in the 31 percent tax bracket, the dividend would effectively shrink to $1,324 after paying taxes. This tax on dividends might not seem fair, but that's how the tax laws work.

Tax Strategies for Stocks

In addition to holding onto stocks for more than a year, you can keep your tax liabilities low in other ways.

Sell the stinkers.

Some stock picks are real dogs. But you can take advantage of your unlucky selections by using them to offset the capital gains taxes you might owe from mutual funds or the sale of winning stocks or bonds.

Suppose you sell a stock, and the sale generates $22,000 in capital gains tax. To soften that tax blow, you decide to get rid of a stock that has dropped $10,000 in value since its purchase. You can turn around and use that $10,000 loss to reduce your capital gains tax obligation. By doing this, you effectively are no longer liable for a tax on a $22,000 capital gain, but a $12,000 one instead.

What if you like the stock that's been struggling and hesitate to dump it? No problem. Sell the stock, take the loss, and then buy back the stock no sooner than 31 days later. If you jump back in the stock before the 31 days have passed, you can't deduct your loss off your tax return. Of course, investors who do this, face the possibility of the stock soaring while they are sitting on the sidelines. One possible solution is to buy a similar stock in the same industry with the proceeds from the sale; check with your tax advisor before doing this. Another possible solution would be to double up on the shares you own with the stock price depressed and then wait 31 days to sell your original block of stock for a loss.

Tip   What if you don't have any capital gains to offset? You can still capitalize on the sale of a losing stock by deducting the loss from your ordinary income when you file your income tax.

One hitch to this strategy is that you can't shave more than $3,000 off your total income, which includes such things as your salary, using this approach in any given year. If your loss exceeds the $3,000 ceiling, though, it's not an insurmountable problem. You can carry the leftover loss over to future years. Before you use this strategy, consult your accountant or other tax expert. Such people should be privy to the latest tax rules on stock sales.

Got Tax Questions?

The IRS is ready to help. You can call the IRS at (800) TAX-1040 to ask specific tax questions. Meanwhile, you can order a variety of free IRS publications and forms by calling (800) TAX-FORM. These materials are also available on the agency's Web site (www.irs.gov).

Know Your Cost Basis

When you sell a stock or fund for a profit, you aren't necessarily liable for the entire profit. Your tax liability is based upon what's called the *cost basis*. Let's suppose you bought $10,000 worth of fund shares and sold it years later for $18,000. On the surface, your cost basis appears to be $10,000 (the original price of the investment) so you'd have a tax liability for an $8,000 profit. But also included in the cost basis are any sales charges or transaction fees you paid during your trading. Suppose you paid your discount broker a total of $70 to buy and later sell your fund shares. That adds $70 to your cost basis, which brings it up to $10,070, which obviously reduces your taxable profit. Any reinvested capital gains distributions and dividends you received over the years are also included in the cost basis. In some cases, these additions can boost an investment's cost basis considerably and ultimately save you a lot in capital gains taxes.

Tip When seeking advice on this strategy, keep in mind that you may be more likely to receive unbiased advice from a CPA than from a stockbroker or a commission-based financial planner who could profit from a potential stock sale.

Unload the most expensive shares.

When selling stock or mutual funds, consider getting rid of the priciest shares first. Suppose you bought American Express at $82 and then increased your stake when the stock hit $130. Now the stock is sitting at $160. Your tax burden will be lighter if you specifically sell the shares you bought for $130 each instead of the ones you bought at $82 because the capital gains tax would be calculated on a gain of $30 per share rather than $78. If you proceed with this approach, you'll have to specify which shares you want to unload to your brokerage firm. You do this by noting the day that these shares were originally purchased. (This is one excellent reason why investors should keep good records.) When you receive the sales confirmation later from your broker, double-check to make sure your instructions were followed.

Caution You might not want to use this approach if the designated shares were bought within the past year and are therefore subject to the brutal short-term capital gains rate. This method also won't work if you identify the stock shares to be sold after the sale.

For mutual fund investors, another strategy allows you to calculate your gains based upon the average price paid for all shares held. This strategy can be helpful if you periodically bought shares over a long period of time and reinvested dividends and capital gains to purchase even more.

Note that the Internal Revenue Service assumes that you use the "first in, first out" (FIFO) method when selling stock or mutual funds. In this scenario, shares are sold in the order they are bought. This method is often costly for investors and a boon for the IRS because the first shares are typically the most valuable because they've

Stiffing the IRS: Conventional Wisdom Versus New Research

If you want to shrink your tax bill, pay attention to where you're investing your stocks and bonds. The traditional advice is to keep tax hogs (investments that generate dividends, interest income, and short-term capital gains) in your retirement accounts. Remember, you don't have to pay taxes on the interest or dividends generated by any investment that's wrapped inside an IRA, a 401(k), or other retirement plan. For that reason, bonds are a favorite investment to tuck into retirement accounts because bonds generate cash regularly. In contrast, people have traditionally been advised to reserve stocks for taxable accounts because they are inherently tax efficient. Remember, capital gains on a stock, even in a taxable account, aren't taxed until the shares are sold.

The conventional wisdom, however, has been challenged by studies done by T. Rowe Price and others that explore which type of investments work best in retirement and taxable accounts. If the investment horizon is a long one, bonds might be better kept in a taxable account, and stocks may do better in a retirement account. (See Chapter 8 for more on the findings.) To read the study, visit T. Rowe Price's Web site at www.troweprice.com and check out its tax center.

had time to appreciate. Oddly enough, the IRS won't know which shares you sold unless it conducts an audit, at which point the taxpayer is asked for proof. So if you follow this strategy and use the resulting calculation for your taxes, keep all the paperwork should you need to provide proof later.

Pass stocks along to heirs or charities.

The way to avoid ever paying capital gains taxes on stocks is to never sell the stocks. Instead, you leave your stock portfolio to heirs or a charity. When heirs inherit stock, they receive a true tax gift from the government. Suppose your father sat on a favorite stock for decades. His original investment grew from $5,000 to $100,000. If he had sold that stock, he'd have owed taxes on a whopping profit. Instead, he stipulated in his will that you inherit the stock. Once you get the stock, the government essentially pretends that the huge gain never existed. Your cost basis, which is largely based upon the investment's original price, is recalibrated to $100,000. The tax savings on this posthumous transfer of ownership is invaluable.

You can also benefit by donating stock that has soared in value to a favorite charity. Suppose you bought $10,000 worth of IBM shares years ago, and it's now worth $80,000. If you give the stock to a charity, you can claim a tax deduction based on its current rather than original value. Also, you owe no capital gains tax when you give the stock to charity.

Cross-Reference   See Chapter 28 for information on leaving stocks and other assets to charity.

Limit stock trading to your retirement accounts.

Remember that trades inside tax-deferred retirement accounts don't trigger any taxes at all. Consequently, you'll save money if you confine most of your trades to these tax-deferred accounts rather than taxable ones.

How Taxes Affect Mutual Funds

If you're a mutual fund investor, dodging an onerous tax bill each year can be a crapshoot. While some fund managers are very good about keeping the tax bill for shareholders quite low, others, who could be preoccupied with snagging the highest possible yearly return, may disregard the tax consequences of their actions. In order to claim a magical five-star rating from Morningstar or to win a year-end bonus, a manager might ignore the capital gains tax implications of frequent stock trading.

Even a fund manager who loathes taxes as much as you do can get ambushed during shaky markets. If equities plunge and terrified investors flee, a manager may be forced to sell winning stocks to pay off massive redemptions. And guess what? The faithful shareholders who are left behind will stagger from an even bigger tax whammy when the capital gains are distributed. Too many fund managers don't consider it their job to keep tax liabilities low for you and the rest of their shareholders.

And the Winner Is . . .

Certain categories of funds are more tax efficient than others. This rundown lists the most tax-efficient funds from the top down:

✦ Stock index funds

✦ Small company and aggressive growth funds

✦ Growth funds

✦ Foreign funds

✦ Growth and income and equity income funds

Generalities, however, can only go so far. There is a vast difference in the tax sensitivity of the nation's mutual funds. Incredibly, some funds lose several percentage points from their returns each year to taxes. In contrast, the after-tax returns of the most tax-efficient fund may lose a tiny fraction of one percentage point to taxes.

The Securities and Exchange Commission, which had been concerned about this tax erosion for some time, did something about it in 2001. The SEC now requires fund companies to provide shareholders with more realistic performance data by including *after-tax* returns in their fund prospectuses and annual reports. In addition, Morningstar's mutual fund materials, which can be found in most libraries and on its Internet site (www.morningstar. com), provide information on the historic tax efficiency of individual funds.

Caution   KPMG Peat Marwick concluded that the average mutual fund loses 2.6 percentage points of its yearly gains to taxes. Considering that stocks have historically returned 11 percent, a 2.6 percent tax bite represents 28 percent of the return.

Although an individual stock investor can avoid all capital gain taxes by not selling, a fund investor can't. Every year mutual funds are required by law to pass along any realized capital gains to their shareholders. That makes all fund investors sitting ducks. They typically don't know until near the end of the year whether funds will distribute any capital gains.

Caution   You can even be hit with taxes on capital gains you never got to enjoy. If you joined a fund late in the year, you will still owe capital gains on any high-flying stocks sold for hefty profits during the spring or summer.

Not all investors appreciate why capital gains distributions are something to dread. So what if you have to pay taxes when your account is now flush with extra money from a distribution? But when a fund distributes yearly capital gains to shareholders, it simultaneously reduces the underlying net asset value of each share accordingly, so the capital gains are a wash. Because you reinvest this money, you'll own more shares, but each share will be worth less. And of course, you'll be stuck paying those taxes.

Note   If your mutual fund investments are tied up in tax-deferred retirement accounts, however, distributions won't matter. The tax consequences are zero.

Because fund companies typically pass out capital gains distributions late in the year, you should call a fund company's toll-free number to find out when that date is. If you want to invest in a fund for a taxable account in November or December and the distribution date is a few days away, by all means wait until after the distribution. If you had been contemplating selling a fund, you will probably want to do so before the distribution.

Tax Strategies for Mutual Funds

The good news is that taxes, which represent the single largest cost of mutual fund investments, can be controlled. First, you can employ some of the same tax strategies that were outlined earlier in this chapter for stock investors. Beyond that, try to find funds that take tax concerns seriously. The search will be much easier now that the SEC is making funds publish their after-tax figures.

In addition, some investors seek to shrink their tax exposure by signing on with one of these three notably tax-efficient vehicles:

✦ Index and exchange-traded funds

✦ Tax-managed funds

✦ Privately managed accounts

Index and exchange-traded funds

Index funds provide an excellent way to keep your tax liabilities low. Because index funds generally hold onto their stocks with a vise grip, very little trading occurs within these funds. Consequently, capital gains taxes are held to a minimum. Exchange-traded funds, which are hybrids between mutual funds and individual stocks, can be just as tax-friendly.

Cross-Reference

See Chapter 15 for more info on the advantages of index and exchange-traded funds.

Tax-managed funds

Figuring out whether a mutual fund is tax efficient is very difficult. But if the fund is labeled a tax-managed fund, tax efficiency is not such a guessing game. Just like an ordinary mutual fund, the tax-managed variety strives for the highest yearly return. But unlike ordinary mutual funds, tax-managed funds focus on a performance figure not mentioned in the fund world's glossy brochures: the after-tax return. What really counts for these funds is what shareholders keep in their pocket.

In order to succeed without triggering an obscene tax bill, tax-managed fund managers have many methods, none of which is terribly complicated. They strive to avoid any capital gains distributions, especially those punitive short-term ones. Managers are also careful about which stocks they sell; they prefer to unload those with the highest cost basis and thus the least tax liability. In addition, a tax-managed fund also looks for opportunities to balance the sale of a phenomenally profitable stock by tossing the lemons.

Tax-managed funds are still in the toddler stage. Morningstar tracks about five dozen, but more fund families are planning to offer them. The Vanguard Group pioneered the tax-managed movement when it launched the first three funds, and it has since added more to its lineup. The impressive performance of Vanguard Tax-Managed Growth & Income, in particular, has swayed some skeptics, who argue that tax considerations can distract a manager from achieving the very best performance. Since its creation in the mid 1990s, the fund has slightly outperformed the firm's flagship offering, the Vanguard 500 Index Fund, which is the nation's most popular fund.

Consider these tax-managed funds:

Fidelity Tax-Managed Stock	(800) 544-6666
Eaton Vance Tax-Managed Growth	(800) 225-6265
T. Rowe Price Tax-Efficient Growth	(800) 638-5660
Schwab 1000 Fund	(800) 266-5623
Vanguard Tax-Managed Growth & Income	(800) 635-1511
Vanguard Tax-Managed Capital Appreciation	(800) 635-1511
Vanguard Tax-Managed Balanced	(800) 635-1511
Vanguard Tax-Managed Small Cap	(800) 635-1511

Privately managed accounts and taxes

Once upon a time, mutual funds could do no wrong, and Americans couldn't get enough of them. But that's changing. An increasing number of sophisticated investors who are disenchanted with tax-inefficient funds and subpar returns think they've discovered something better. They are stashing money into stocks within privately managed accounts. In contrast to mutual funds that commingle everybody's cash, the only money in a privately managed account is your own. The person handling your stock portfolio could also be managing money for a Fortune 500 company.

Those investors who choose this route primarily want to avoid getting clobbered by the Internal Revenue Service. Most of the money being squirreled away in these accounts is taxable assets and not retirement money. The financial pros who run customized portfolios are usually already sensitive to tax issues and work to keep tax liabilities as low as possible.

Cross-Reference   For more on this tax strategy, see Chapter 4.

Summary

✦ Avoid short-term capital gains taxes by holding stocks at least a year and a day.

✦ Watch what you put in retirement accounts because gains on investments sheltered in retirement accounts are not taxed until you begin making withdrawals in retirement.

✦ Selectively sell stock shares: trade the most expensive first.

✦ Limit active trading to retirement accounts.

✦ Consider using the most tax-efficient mutual funds.

✦   ✦   ✦

All About Bonds

Part V demystifies bonds. You will learn the types of bonds on the market and whether they might be appropriate for your portfolio. You will also discover the risks that bond investing poses. Finally, you'll find a primer on other alternatives for income-producing investments, such as convertible securities, real estate investment trusts (REITs), and utility stocks.

A Bond Primer

This chapter covers the basics about that favorite fixed-income investment, the bond, in its many manifestations: Treasuries, zero coupon bonds, inflation-indexed bonds, municipal bonds, investment-grade bonds, junk corporate bonds, and savings bonds. You'll learn how they work and how they can be invaluable whether you are saving for retirement or have already done so.

Bond Basics

A bond is an IOU. When you buy a bond, you're essentially lending cash to a debtor, such as the U.S. Treasury, an airport authority, a wireless startup, or some other organization or company. How well you'll profit from your loan partially depends upon how desperate the borrower is to generate cash. If the borrower isn't terribly trustworthy, you should be rewarded upfront with a better deal.

Most bonds are priced at $1,000. Even when a pension fund or some other huge institutional player buys a multimillion-dollar block of bonds, they are doled out in $1,000 increments. The amount of money you lend is called the *principal;* the bond's face value is referred to as *par.*

Of course, when you lend money, you want something in return. A bond provides that through its coupon. A *coupon* is the amount of money or interest that the issuer agrees to pay each year over the life of the bond. Coupons make bonds ideal for those investors who desire a predictable income stream from their investments.

Example

A $1,000 junk bond with a 9 percent coupon from Apple Computer would pay $90 annually. Most bonds distribute interest biannually. So in this case, the Apple lender would receive a $45 payment twice a year.

Neither you nor the debtor wants your money tied up forever, so every bond eventually expires. In fixed-income jargon, the time when the bond expires is called the bond's *maturity.* You can choose from a wide assortment of maturities. Treasuries, for instance, peddle their debt with maturities as short as

In This Chapter

Understanding a bond's behavior

Recognizing the many advantages of bonds

Considering bond disadvantages

Laying out your best bond strategies

Avoiding the biggest bond mistakes

3 months and as long as 30 years. In extremely rare cases, some corporations, such as Disney, have issued 100-year bonds. These bonds are typically bought by pension funds and other institutional investors. When a bond reaches maturity, the investor gets back the original $1,000 investment.

Bonds are classified by their maturities:

✦ Short-term bonds last 1 to 3 years.

✦ Intermediate-term bonds last 3 to 10 years.

✦ Long-term bonds last more than 10 years.

Bonds and Yields

When bond shopping, you need to understand the concept of *yield,* but there's more than one yield to worry about. Keep these yields in mind:

✦ **Simple yield:** The simple yield equals the coupon rate. For example, if you buy a $1,000 bond with a 7 percent coupon, the simple yield would be 7 percent.

✦ **Current yield:** Once you buy a bond, its value fluctuates, and this fluctuation determines the current yield. To obtain the current yield, you divide the bond's annual interest by its current trading price. If the trading price of your bond with a simple yield of 7 percent slipped to $850, for instance, the current yield would rise to 8.2 percent ($70 divided by $850). (For details on how bond prices can fall, see the "Bond Risks" section in this chapter.)

✦ **Yield to maturity:** This yield is a more realistic measure of what you can expect if you hold onto your bond until it matures. This yield is calculated by figuring such things as the interest payments you'll pocket and the money you can make by reinvesting those biannual interest checks.

✦ **Yield to call:** This yield is a crucial one to know before choosing a bond. Unfortunately for investors, most bond issuers enjoy the freedom to pay off their loans prematurely, which is referred to as *calling back* the bond. (Investors in U.S. Treasuries don't have to worry about this.) This privilege may seem unfair, unless you consider it from a debtor's point of view. Suppose your state highway department sold bonds for bridge construction when the going interest rate for a municipal bond was 7 percent, and now they could float the same bonds for 5 percent. You can imagine that the politicians and taxpayers would love the fact that the department could pay back the 7 percent loans and take out new 5 percent loans instead.

Always find out how quickly a lender can renege on the deal. A *callable bond* stipulates the dates when the bond can be redeemed. The yield to call is based on the first call date. If the yield to call is considerably smaller than the bond's yield to maturity, search for a more attractive bond.

Usually, investors who are willing to lend money for the longest periods (which is often not a wise move) can expect more compensation. Consequently, someone investing in a 30-year Treasury bond expects a higher coupon than somebody lending the Treasury money for 5 or 10 years. There are occasionally periods, such as 2000, when the coupons for the shorter Treasuries were greater than the longest ones.

You expect extra compensation because you are assuming more risk with a long-term bond. If you tie up your money in a 30-year bond with a 6.5 percent coupon, you may find that five years later interest rates climb, and now everybody else is grabbing bonds yielding 10 percent or 12 percent. If you want to bail and latch on to a more tantalizing bond, you can. Plenty of people will happily buy your sorry bond, but they will do so only at a fire sale price. Consequently, the price of your bond will plummet, which means the yield skyrockets for the next owner (see sidebar on yields). You will lose some of your original principal, but that's the only way to unload the bond.

Tip   Because investors can't accurately predict interest rate movements, many financial experts suggest that long-term fixed-income fans, who desire the highest interest rates with the least amount of risk, stick with bonds that mature in the 7 to 10 year range.

Advantages of Bonds

Because stocks have hogged the media spotlight for so long, few folks appreciate how vast the bond market is. A regular reader of a local newspaper's business section might assume that the number of bond deals being struck each day is minuscule. While several pages of type are devoted to stock prices and mutual funds, a tiny listing of bond prices is often shoved in a corner. But this lack of media attention is misleading. It would take about 90 pages in a newspaper to list all the outstanding municipal bond deals. Meanwhile, corporate bond issues that are traded on the New York Stock Exchange vastly outnumber the companies listed on the exchange.

In many respects, bonds work the same way as they did when the federal government was issuing them during George Washington's days. What can make them a compelling investment? What follows are the top reasons why bonds matter.

Predictable income stream

With today's stocks paying little or no dividends, bonds are a refuge for retirees and others who depend upon a steady stream of income.

Safety

Bonds are considered safer than stocks. A bond isn't going to lose half of its value within a matter of hours. Not even the bluest of the blue chips can beat a Treasury bond for downright security. No one who has held onto a Treasury until maturity has ever lost a dime with the investment and almost certainly never will. Not all bonds can boast of that impeccable safety record, but for those who want to stick with the most reliable bonds, a well-established credit ratings system that categorizes bond safety exists (this rating system is covered later in this chapter).

Tax savings

Because bonds can be a tough sell, some are equipped with tax advantages to entice the reluctant. A bond offering a puny yield might not look attractive, but it may provide insulation from federal or state taxes. (See Chapter 18 for more information on tax-free municipal bonds.)

Partners in diversification

Since the 1920s, large-cap stocks have generated 11 percent annual returns while bonds have trailed behind with yearly returns of about 5 percent. But that fact doesn't tell the entire story. Stocks are cursed with higher volatility, which makes pairing them with steadier bonds an ideal strategy to reduce an investor's fear factor.

Tip   You can diversify your own bond portfolio instantly by buying shares in a *bond fund,* which is a mutual fund whose holdings consist entirely of bonds.

Bond Risks

Bonds do present some solid advantages, but every investment has its downside. What follows are the risks inherent in bond investments.

Interest rate threats

Although retirees embrace bonds for their steady income, bonds aren't as solid as some assume. The fixed-income world's biggest boogeyman is interest rate hikes, which can make the bond's face value fall lower than the $1,000 you paid for it.

Interest rates are likely to creep up during inflationary times. That occurs when the economy is steaming ahead, the stock market is going up, and unemployment is way down. During these times, people feel like spending more because they're confident about holding onto their jobs and have possibly made a killing on Wall Street. They blow money on new Volvos, remodel their kitchens, and fly to Club Med. If enough people indulge in spending sprees, the folks selling them all this stuff will screw up the courage to hike prices. When enough prices are hiked, inflation sets in.

The 1990s were remarkable because despite a robust economy, a killer stock market, and historically high employment, inflation never materialized. One major reason: American workers, with some help from technology, became more and more productive. Also, the Federal Reserve, headed by Chairman Alan Greenspan, kept down inflation by gradually increasing short-term interest rates.

Caution   Why should high interest rates matter to bond holders? Because bonds lose value with interest rate creep up.

Remember, the best feature of bonds is their typically modest yields. Unlike stocks, most bonds don't provide much in the way of capital appreciation. A Treasury bond jumping in price by just one point in one day is a really big deal.

So if interest rates climb, guess what happens? Other ultra-safe investments look very appealing. Banks start advertising yields on certificates of deposit that could make your bond coupons look laughable. People dump bonds and gravitate to CDs, which are federally insured, or money markets. The value of the abandoned bonds plummets.

Happily, this disaster has a flip side. When interest rates drop, bonds grow more valuable. Suppose you have a bond with a 7 percent coupon, and interest rates fall to 5 percent. Buyers would pay a premium to purchase your bond to snag that higher coupon. Consequently, when interest rates shrivel, the bond market celebrates.

Inflation threats

During inflationary times, a bond portfolio also loses purchasing power. This loss can happen even when inflation is low. If inflation ran a modest 3 percent for five years, the value of a $100 semi-annual interest check would drop to just $86 in actual purchasing power. Younger retirees often lose sight of the effect of inflation when they construct portfolios that are heavily weighted in bonds.

Credit risks

Are there people in your life that you'd never lend money to? Maybe you have an unreliable brother-in-law or a neighbor who blows too much on lottery tickets. In the bond world, debtors with the shakiest reputation for repaying must entice would-be lenders with better interest rates.

The world of institutional debtors has a clear pecking order. Starting at the top, here's the list of the most reliable down to the truly iffy debtors:

✦ U.S. Treasuries

✦ Federal government agency bonds

✦ Municipal bonds

✦ High-grade corporate bonds

✦ High-yield (junk) corporate bonds

✦ Emerging markets (Third World) bonds

Of course, a wide credit disparity can exist even among bond issuers in the same category. That's why bond investors pay attention to the opinions of a handful of credit rating agencies; Moody's and Standard & Poor's are the two most popular ones. Table 17-1 explains the system they use to rank bond issuers.

Table 17-1
Credit Quality Ratings for Bonds

Moody's	Standard & Poor's	Description
Aaa	AAA	These top ratings are enjoyed by Treasuries and federal agency bonds, which are considered to offer the highest quality with the lowest risk.
Aa	AA	Bonds with this rating are also of excellent quality; they're just a step below the very best.
A	A	This rating is bestowed on high medium-grade bonds.
Baa	BBB	This rating is the lowest for investment-grade bonds. A bond with this rating is characterized as a medium-grade bond; such a bond is creditworthy, but it has a moderate risk.
Ba	BB	A bond with this rating has a moderate chance of remaining safe. Bonds that receive this grade and those ranked lower are considered speculative; that's why they're called junk or high-yield bonds.
B	B	The chances of your principal and interest payments continuing uninterrupted could be small if you purchase bonds with this rating.
Caa	CCC	The bond issuer for bonds of this poor quality might need favorable business and economic conditions to meet its obligations.
C	CC	These bonds at this rock-bottom grade could be in default or teetering toward it.

Source: Moody's Investor Services and Standard & Poor's

Tip

Before buying a bond, always check its credit rating. (Don't worry about the credit rating of Treasuries; they automatically carry the highest rating.)

You won't be overwhelmed with choices if you limit yourself to the most credit-worthy creditors. Recently Standard & Poor's had bestowed its highest AAA rating upon just nine American corporations:

✦ Bell South

✦ Abbot Laboratories

✦ Exxon Mobil

✦ Johnson & Johnson

✦ General Electric

✦ Pfizer

✦ Merck

✦ UPS

✦ Bristol Meyers Squibb

The second highest S&P rating category, AA, is also exclusive. About 60 companies qualify, with a heavy concentration of oil, telephone, and drug companies. They include Microsoft, American Airlines, and Hewlett Packard. Meanwhile, more than half of American corporations are classified in the junk category. Among the companies snagging S&P's junk designation are Alaska Airlines, Apple Computer, and Budget Group (car rentals).

Note Rating services are not infallible. Bond analysts have missed some tremendous financial crises, including the Orange County, California bankruptcy and the Asian economic meltdown, both in the 1990s.

Your Best Bond Strategies

Use these strategies to get the most out of your bond holdings.

Pay attention to the yield curve.

Did you buy your bonds at a good price? You won't necessarily know if you haven't checked the Treasury *yield curve,* which charts the yields of Treasury bonds at different maturities. The yield curve, which changes every day, is easy to plot. To draw one, you just need to know what Treasuries are yielding, from the short three-month bills all the way out to the 30-year bonds. Once all the dots are connected, you have a yield curve. The yield curve is published daily in *The Wall Street Journal.*

The yield curve often looks like a sloping hill. When this happens, the more aggressive investors, who buy longer term Treasuries, pocket the best yield. But sometimes the yield curve morphs into something different. Recently, for instance, the yield curve looked like a camel's back because the intermediate Treasury bonds provided the highest yields.

Tip

By looking at the yield curve, you can instantly pinpoint which Treasury maturities are providing the best yields.

Even odder is an inverted yield curve. That's when the shorter-term Treasuries offer the best deal. This phenomenon usually happens when economists expect inflation to hit and short-term interest rates to rise. Investors not wanting to miss profiting from this increase pull their money out of long-term bonds and funnel it into the short-term bonds.

If you're interested in corporate bonds, municipal bonds, or some other kinds, you still need to know how Treasuries are faring because they have historically served as the bond benchmark. Other bonds are priced with the Treasury rates in mind. Because other bonds aren't as safe as Treasuries, they are expected to give investors a better spread. The *spread* is the difference between the coupon for Treasuries and other types of bonds.

Tip

Check *The Wall Street Journal* to find out bond yields. Near the yield curve graphic are yield comparisons of corporate, junk, municipal, federal agency, and mortgage-backed bonds.

This method of evaluating bond yields sounds simple, but there's a potential problem. The Treasury benchmark may be in danger because the federal government, which has been enjoying budget surpluses, wishes to ease out of the debt business. The U.S. government has slowed the pace of its 30-year Treasury issues and has been buying back a small fraction of them. It hopes to pay off its Treasury debt by 2013. Of course, no one knows whether this will happen. A lot will depend upon politics and the state of the economy.

The buy back isn't totally unprecedented. The first one occurred during George Washington's administration, and it's happened at least two or three times since. However, the prospect of life without Treasuries has left bond experts scrambling to find a benchmark replacement. Widespread worry that 30-year Treasuries may someday disappear boosted their price recently. Consequently, the 30-year Treasury is no longer considered the standard benchmark. The 10-year Treasury has taken its place. If Treasuries become even rarer, some bond experts are anticipating the day when another type of bond will have to fill in. Many are suggesting that the substitute benchmark be so-called agency bonds. These bonds are issued by quasi-government entities, including the Federal National Mortgage Association (Fannie Mae) and the Federal Home Loan Mortgage Corp. (Freddie Mac).

Tip

Regardless of what benchmark forms the basis of the yield curve, you should take note of that benchmark before shopping for bonds.

Are Bonds Necessary?

Unlike stocks, not everybody needs bonds. If you're in your 20s or 30s, there may be no compelling reason to buy bonds. Even mildly aggressive investors in their 40s might not find them necessary, given that a 40-year-old's life span could easily stretch another four decades or more.

Decide how much is enough.

How many bonds do you need? That may be the trickiest question of all, with different answers coming from different experts. Some suggest, for instance, that the percentage of bonds in your portfolio should equal your age. A 60-year-old, for instance, should devote 60 percent of his or her holdings to bonds. Others say to multiply your age by 80 percent for the right proportion of bonds. Beware of such simplistic formulas. How much you need depends upon your time horizon, your investment goals, and your tolerance for risk. That said, here are some very rough guidelines that you might want to consider in Table 17-2.

Table 17-2
Investor Guidelines

Type of Investor	Stocks	Bonds	Cash	Characteristics
Aggressive	100%	0%	0%	Is interested only in growth and is not worried about volatility.
Moderately aggressive	80%	15%	5%	Is focused on growth and doesn't need current income.
Moderate	60%	30%	10%	Doesn't need current income, but is not willing to make oversized stock bets.
Moderately conservative	40%	45%	15%	Desires some portfolio growth, but needs current income.
Conservative	20%	55%	25%	Needs stability and current income.

Ladder your bonds.

Smart bond investors know when to make their moves. When interest rates are poised to drop, they scoop up longer-term bonds that guarantee high yields. If rates are about to rise, they go with short-term bonds. In this way, they can keep capturing higher rates as short-term holdings mature during inflationary times. The only problem with using this strategy is that predicting interest rate movements is as impossible as correctly guessing the direction of the stock market.

So what's the next best thing? Consider bond *laddering*. With this strategy, you hedge your bets by investing equal amounts of money in individual bonds with maturities of varying lengths. Each rung of the ladder contains one or more bonds that mature at roughly the same time. Laddering should produce a higher return than keeping a stockpile of short-term bonds. At the same time, your risk won't be as great as it is for someone who holds only long-term bonds. Suppose you laddered a portfolio with bonds maturing in 2, 4, 6, 8, and 10 years. When a bond matured, you could use the proceeds to buy a replacement with a 10-year life expectancy. Conservative investors may want to construct a ladder with maturities that range from one year to five or six.

Another option is using a *barbell* strategy in which you distribute your bonds on either end of the yield curve. You might hold, for instance, 1-year and 20-year bonds.

Tip   Laddering with Treasuries is easiest because there is no need to fret about diversifying. Every Treasury is extremely creditworthy; the only risk is a movement in interest rates.

Laddering is trickier with corporate and municipal (*muni*) bonds because of differing credit risks and those darn call features. Most of these bonds are callable, which means an issuer can retrieve their bonds and return your principal if they wish. Consequently, laddering with these bonds isn't a sure thing.

Typical Bond Mistakes

Shopping for bonds? Don't make these common mistakes.

Judging bond funds by yield alone

Retirees, in particular, tend to focus exclusively on bond yields. But chasing hot yields is dangerous. By fixating on yield, investors miss an even more crucial figure: the total return. The *total return* equals the yield plus a fund's capital appreciation or losses. With retirees living longer, their portfolios need to do more than generate reliable income. Their bonds need to appreciate in value. You can tell how well a bond or bond fund has done by checking its total return. Suppose you bought a $1,000 bond with an $80 coupon, and you sold it for $1,060 a year later. Your total return is $140 ($80 in interest and $60 capital gain) or 14 percent. If a retiree is buying bonds and intends to hold them until maturity, total return is irrelevant. In contrast, total return is a crucial factor for anybody hunting for a bond mutual fund.

These investors will want income plus capital appreciation. You can easily find out a fund's total return by checking with Morningstar's mutual fund publication, which many libraries carry or by visiting its Web site (www.morningstar.com).

Caution A bond fund with a tantalizingly high yield can be hiding an ugly surprise: risk. Before committing to a bond fund, examine a portfolio's contents.

If a general bond fund's yield is far superior to its peers, you have to wonder why. The fund could be juicing its yield with high-risk junk bonds from such borrowers as casino riverboats ventures and human genome startups and the portfolio could contain speculative foreign bonds. Even Treasury bond funds have been known to contain exotic bonds.

Tip Bond issuers can experience difficulties and receive credit quality downgrades. Find out whether your brokerage firm keeps tabs on your corporate or governmental borrowers.

Bonds and the Internet

Financial Web sites will soon outnumber the grains of sand on a beach, or at least it seems that way. Curiously, although countless Web sites are devoted to stocks, few are devoted to bonds. Here are three notable ones:

✦ The Bond Market Association (www.investinginbonds.com) is a solid bond source for those who want to learn bond basics. You can obtain guides on investing in municipal, corporate, zero coupon, and other types of bonds. You'll also find a calculator that compares a municipal bond's tax-free yield with an equivalent taxable one. The Bond Market Association, which is an industry trade association, also posts daily prices of various types of bonds and provides many links to bond dealers.

✦ The U.S. Bureau of Public Debt (www.publicdebt.treas.gov) Web site enables you to bone up on Treasuries and savings bonds. You will find answers to investors' frequently asked questions as well as a glossary and a savings bond calculator. You can also learn about Treasury bond scams (plenty are out there) as well as determine what the current Treasury and savings bonds investment rates are. You also may buy Treasuries and savings bonds direct from this site.

✦ Bonds Online (www.bondsonline.com), which is sponsored by a fixed-income financial services company, offers free economic and bond commentary, news, and research. You can obtain quotes on thousands of bonds as well as take advantage of screening software that allows you to plug in the type of bond you want as well as the desired maturity, yield, and credit rating. The site also sells access to fixed-income newsletters.

You should also visit TheStreet.com (www.thestreet.com) and Morningstar.com (www.morningstar.com). Although both Web sites devote most of their energies to the stock market, they have stockpiled an impressive number of bond articles for novices as well as more sophisticated investors.

How do you know what's in a bond fund's portfolio? Your best bet is to check the annual or semiannual report, which lists a fund's holdings. Because that list can become outdated fairly quickly, make sure you visit the fund company's Web site as well. Some managers update their list of holdings more frequently. And you can always check Morningstar's analysis of a fund. Meanwhile, a fund's prospectus can give you a sense of whether a manager enjoys the freedom to become a fixed-income swashbuckler or whether he or she must steer a conservative course.

Another way to measure a bond fund's volatility is to look at the fund's *standard deviation,* which measures how far a stock or bond fund's more recent performance has strayed from its long-term average. The higher the standard deviation is, the greater the chances for volatility. Morningstar provides this statistic in its fund evaluations. Also look at a fund's *style box,* which Morningstar uses to rate its credit quality and interest rate sensitivity.

Cross-
Reference
For more details on bond funds, see Chapter 14.

Making the wrong comparisons

When shopping for bonds, make sure you are comparing apples to apples. Comparing the yield of a short-term bond with one offering a much longer maturity is dangerous; instead compare bonds with similar features.

If you're looking at bond funds, you can level the playing field by using as a point of reference the fund's *average weighted maturity,* a figure that tells you when, on average, the bonds in the portfolio are scheduled to come due. The average is weighted because larger bonds count for more than bonds representing a smaller portion of the portfolio. Equally important is comparing the average credit quality ratings of bond funds that you are considering.

Forgetting about expenses

You're not going to get rich investing in bonds. Bonds can't approach the total returns possible with stocks. Consequently, keeping expenses extremely low when investing in bonds or bond funds is crucial.

When you purchase a bond fund, absolutely avoid those carrying a load. A *load fund* charges a commission that could range from 2 percent to 5 percent or higher. What you want instead is a *no-load fund,* which means it generates no commission. That sounds like a no-brainer, but if you work through a full-service broker or a commissioned financial advisor, that person will steer you to load funds because he or she depends upon commissions.

Key Terms for Bond Comparisons

Knowing these terms ahead of time will aid your research.

✦ **Yield to worst call:** Refers to the bond issuer's right to repay the loan at a pre-arranged yield set sometime in the future that would be the least advantageous to you, the lender.

✦ **Bid and ask prices:** The bid refers to the price that an investor is willing to pay for a bond, while the ask is the price that someone is willing to sell it.

✦ **Spread:** The difference between the bid and ask prices. This figure includes the broker's commission. The goal is to buy a bond with the narrowest spread possible. Don't be afraid to haggle with the broker over the spread.

✦ **Liquidity:** Indicates the marketability of a bond on the secondary market. The narrower the spread between asking and bid price, the greater the bond's liquidity. Liquid bonds have no trouble attracting buyers; illiquid bonds are more difficult to sell.

✦ **Credit watch:** A bond rating agency will put a bond on a credit watch if it's investigating whether to improve or downgrade a bond's credit quality rating.

Some brokers insist that the load isn't an issue. They may even convince you that a load fund doesn't have a load at all by peddling a fund with a back-end load, which is designed to disappear if you hold onto the shares for enough years. What they don't explain is that these back-end load shares pass along higher annual expenses. Consequently, you are almost always better off choosing a front-end load if you're limited to load choices.

Cross-Reference See Chapter 14 for more information on mutual fund expenses.

Loads aren't the only peril for frugal investors. A fund's annual expense ratio can also swallow a big bite out of modest bond returns. Avoid any bond fund that charges more than 1 percent in annual expenses a year. You can find expense information in a bond fund's prospectus.

Failing to do your homework

Most investors purchase individual, nongovernment bonds through a broker or financial advisor. Make sure you ask these questions before committing yourself:

✦ What kind of bond is it?

✦ Why is this bond a good fit for my portfolio?

✦ What is the maturity of this bond?

✦ How is this bond affected by interest rate fluctuations?

✦ What can you tell me about this bond's creditworthiness?

✦ Is this bond callable?

✦ If the bond is callable, what is its yield to worst call?

✦ How liquid is this bond?

✦ Has this bond been sitting in your inventory?

✦ How closely does your brokerage firm follow the government agency or corporation issuing the bond?

✦ Is the bond on credit watch?

✦ What is the bid and ask price on the bond?

Forgetting about the tax consequences

Know which bonds need to be sheltered from taxes. Putting tax-immune municipal bonds inside a tax-sheltered retirement account is like using an umbrella inside a house. On the other hand, it's important to place corporate bonds inside a retirement account so that you can defer taxes on all the interest income that the bonds generate. With bond payouts historically modest, you don't want to lose gains to taxes.

If you keep corporate or federal agency bonds outside a retirement account, the taxes on the interest income can be stiff because they are based on your tax bracket. Consequently, if you're in the 33 percent tax bracket, you would lose 33 cents for every $1 in interest.

Failing to diversify

Accumulating bonds with different maturities isn't the only way to protect yourself against fixed income predators. You should hold different types of bonds issued by governments and by private industry. If you gravitate toward junk bonds, your overall risk won't be as great if you also invest in blue chip corporate bonds and government issues.

Buying pricey bonds

Financial pundits are always warning people to stay away from brand new stock issues, which are better known as *initial public offerings*. On the first day that a stock is publicly traded, the price can fluctuate wildly. This rule, however, doesn't apply to bonds. Investing in a new bond can be better than buying older bonds that somebody else wants to unload.

The Bad Old Days and Better Times Ahead

The bond market has always been a murky, impenetrable place, which has made it easy for middlemen to fleece investors. However, the emerging phenomenon of online bond trading is making price gouging harder to pull off.

Although investors take access to real-time stock quotes for granted, the fossilized bond business has long appeared frozen in a time warp that was impenetrable to technological advances. It hasn't helped that the American bond market, which is the world's biggest financial market, has always operated in a fragmented fashion. No central exchanges exist, and there is no mandatory reporting for bid and ask prices. In the bond world, it was laughable if you wanted to know the current price for a bond, much less trade bonds in a forum that wasn't rigged. Historically, bond traders have operated in a clubby environment where favored customers, who are most often the institutional ones, were offered the best bond prices.

Plus, being a do-it-yourself bond picker was hard. Although stock fans could pick and choose their own stocks, bond customers were pretty much stuck relying upon a broker. In the common scenario, the broker would depend upon an in-house bond trader to find an appropriate pick for an individual investor within the firm's catalog. No one at the brokerage house had any great incentive to comb through the vast fixed-income universe when there were some bonds gathering dust on the shelf. In some cases, an outside bond dealer was called in to assist in the scavenger hunt.

The deck isn't quite so stacked against the individual today. Some brokerage firms, such as E*Trade, Morgan Stanley Dean Witter, and Charles Schwab, are offering online bond trading. Meanwhile, Internet sites such as BondAgent.com (www.bondagent.com) are providing a self-service source for individual bond investors. The Bond Market Association, which was mentioned earlier, provides daily pricing information for some corporate and municipal bonds. Meanwhile, the U.S. Securities and Exchange Commission is pushing the bond industry to make a much better effort at lifting the secrecy veil.

Tip

Pricing is more likely to be favorable with a new bond issue. That's because small bond investors enjoy the same price as the big institutional players.

When you buy an older bond on the secondary market, it's going to include a (often excessive) bond dealer's markup. The *markup* is the price between what the broker pays and what he or she charges you. Brokers aren't obligated to fill you in on these commissions and are often rewarded for peddling stale bonds sitting in a brokerage firm's inventory rather than searching for the best bond on the open market.

Caution

Grill your broker if he or she is pushing a particular bond. Ask if the firm is offering the broker any incentives to hype particular bonds.

Summary

✦ Understand how interest rate fluctuations affect your bond holdings.

✦ Bone up on bonds on the Internet.

✦ Don't judge a bond fund by yield alone.

✦ Know how to interpret a yield curve.

✦ Don't let a broker unload stale bonds in your account.

✦   ✦   ✦

Building a Bond Portfolio

The previous chapter covered bond basics: what makes them tick,
how they can enhance your retirement portfolio, and how to buy
them. This chapter details the many types of bonds on the market:
Treasuries, federal agency/mortgage-backed securities, inflation-
indexed bonds, zero coupon bonds, municipal bonds, high-quality
corporate bonds, and junk bonds.

Bonds: Back in the Game

While the longest bull market in America's history stampeded
through the 1990s, it was hard to make a compelling case for
bonds. But a curious thing happened when the stock market
faltered, at least temporarily, in the new century. No longer
did everyone sneer at bonds. Brokerage houses began reporting that investors in their 20s, 30s, and 40s were snatching
them up. Having watched well-respected stocks such as
Worldcom, Microsoft, Home Depot, the Gap, and Proctor &
Gamble drop 20 or 30 percent or more in just a matter or days
or weeks, bond newcomers concluded that placing some bets
on fixed-income tortoises wasn't such a bad idea.

Our increasing longevity has influenced the fixed-income portion of our portfolios, too. Millions of Americans will live at
least a couple of decades in retirement. Financial planners,
charged with devising portfolios that will last as long as their
retiring clients, are now plugging in life expectancies that
reach 100. With advances in medical research, some experts
are now suggesting that Americans may someday routinely
live to be 120 or older. These longer life spans are playing
havoc with traditional bond strategies. It used to be that
retirees rested easily with an assortment of bonds and perhaps some utility stocks. But now experts are warning that a
retiree's excessive reliance upon bonds is a sure-fire way to
run out of money.

Cross-Reference   See Chapter 20 for information on supplementing bonds with stocks for a winning retirement portfolio.

Further, the historically hidebound bond industry is struggling to adapt to the new economy. Technology, which has already revolutionized the way investors buy and research stocks, is beginning to do the same thing for bond buyers. Consequently, bond pricing, which for all individual investors knew may have been determined with tea leaves, is finally being exposed to the sunlight. Meanwhile, a new type of Treasury is trying to address one of the bond's world's most dreaded enemies: inflation.

Dwarfing other developments is a move by the U.S. Treasury Department that stunned the bond world. The federal government, which is the nation's largest debtor, announced that it no longer wants to behave like a college kid with a wallet full of credit cards. With money flowing into the Treasury after years of unprecedented economic growth, the feds don't feel compelled to keep borrowing at such a frenetic pace and may even attempt to eliminate Treasury bonds. You'll find out in this chapter why that development matters to bondholders.

Treasuries

Treasuries are arguably the safest bonds in the universe. Why? They are backed by the full faith and credit of the federal government. Not surprisingly then, Treasuries are the nation's highest-rated bonds and the most popular. Individual and institutional investors hold more than $3 trillion in Treasury debt. However, you shouldn't confuse Treasuries' rock-solid reliability with their investment value. Just like any other bonds, Treasuries can experience tremendous fluctuations in value. A Treasury's volatility depends to a great extent on its maturity.

Treasuries come in three flavors based on the length of their maturities:

✦ Treasury bills (T-bills) have maturities of 13 weeks, 26 weeks, or 1 year.

✦ Treasury notes have maturities ranging from 2 years to 10 years.

✦ Treasury bonds have maturities ranging from 10 years to 30 years.

Advantages of Treasuries

Here are the major reasons why Treasuries are so popular with Americans:

Treasuries are the ultimate security blanket.

Economic crises are inevitable, and Treasuries always provide a port in a storm. Whether it's an Asian economic implosion or a fiscal crisis in Russia or economic problems in our own backyard, nervous Nellies flee to Treasuries during times of financial trouble.

Treasuries aren't callable.

Most bonds exhibit an irritating personality defect: they can be *called.* That is, a bond issuer can repay its loan early. This repayment typically happens when the debtor feels it can issue bonds at a lower interest rate. When bonds are called, bondholders usually feel ripped off. Interest rates are typically dropping, which makes it tough for investors to find a decent fixed-income replacement for the returned money. But you don't have to worry about the federal government calling back your Treasuries.

You get a break on state taxes.

The income from Treasuries is not taxable by either state or local governments. (You will owe federal tax, though.) This tax break can be attractive to investors living in states with high state income taxes. Curiously enough, a lot of Treasury fans live in New York City, where residents are buffeted by the double whammy of onerous state and local taxes.

Treasuries have a low minimum investment.

The admission ticket to buy Treasury bills used to be as high as $10,000. But now the minimum investment for all Treasuries is just $1,000. Because Treasuries are super safe, you don't have to worry about diversifying as you would with some other types of bonds.

Tip Because of the low entry price, you can easily construct your own Treasury ladder. This investing strategy allows you to invest the principal of maturing bonds into higher yielding investments if inflation is rising. See Chapter 17 for details on laddering.

Treasuries provide a safe place to stash cash.

Like certificates of deposit, Treasuries are a safe cash haven. Unlike CDs, however, Treasuries enjoy that built-in tax break for state or local taxes. Consequently, some people prefer keeping their emergency fund or money that they're saving for a house or car in short-term Treasuries.

Treasuries are easy to buy.

Buying Treasuries on your own used to be as irritating as standing in a post office line during the holiday rush. You had to obtain a certified check from a bank and then mail in the investment. To sell your bonds, you sometimes had to wait weeks before your Treasuries could be transferred to a bank or brokerage firm, which would then unload the bonds. But thanks to the government's Treasury Direct program, you can now buy Treasuries directly from the federal government by having money transferred from your bank account.

Caution You can also purchase Treasuries through a broker, but often a broker charges $50 to $75 to conduct the simple transaction. You'll pay nothing if you buy direct from the government.

To get started, you need to fill out a form that can be downloaded from the Treasury Department's Web site (`www.publicdebt.treas.gov`) or ordered by calling (800) 722-2678.

Once you've established an account, you can purchase Treasuries on the Internet or by phone. The government will also sell Treasuries for you by soliciting three bids and then selling to the highest bidder. This service has a small fee.

Caution

You can invest in Treasuries through mutual funds, but you'll waste money on yearly fund expenses by doing do. Further, in addition to federal agency bonds, a Treasury bond fund may contain bonds with no connection to the federal government, which means less security and more volatility.

Disadvantages of Treasuries

Along with the silver lining come the clouds: Treasuries have a couple of drawbacks.

Treasuries might not be around forever.

The federal government hopes to one day eliminate Treasuries. In 2000, the government began to very slowly buy back some of the longest-term Treasuries that were held by institutional investors. If the economy remains robust and if Washington remains determined to get out of debt, Treasuries may someday become extinct. But those are two big ifs.

Yields aren't the highest.

Because Treasuries are ultra-safe, it doesn't take courage to invest in one. Consequently, the market isn't going to reward income investors with fat yields. You have to look elsewhere for a bigger payoff. Federal agency debt, which is just a bit riskier, typically offers a slightly better yield.

Federal Agency/Mortgage-Backed Securities

The best-known mortgage-backed securities go by such funny names as Fannie Mae (Federal National Mortgage Association), Freddie Mac (Federal Home Loan Mortgage Corp), and Ginnie Mae (Government National Mortgage Association). The federal government created these entities in the hopes of keeping home-loan interest rates reasonable for American families. Since Ginnie Mae, which is a federal agency, issued the first mortgage security in 1970, the threesome have ensured that vastly more money is available for lending.

Ginnie Mae takes huge numbers of mortgages that are guaranteed by the federal government, such as mortgages through the Veterans Administration and Federal Housing Administration, and packages them for sale to primarily institutional investors. Fannie Mae and Freddie Mac, which are federally chartered but publicly traded companies, also bundle up vast numbers of mortgages and offer them for sale to investors.

Advantages of mortgage-backed securities

Mortgage-backed securities have a couple of favorable attributes.

They are creditworthy.

No bond can beat Treasuries for reliability, but federal agency bonds come close. Although the federal government has never pledged it would bail out these bonds, there's an implied guarantee that it would do so. Ginnie Mae bonds are considered safer than Fannie Mae and Freddie Mac bonds because the issuing body is a branch of the federal government. Fannie Mae and Freddie Mac have never defaulted on any of their interest payments.

They provide a better yield.

Although the credit risk is just about nil for all these bonds, the yield is typically better than a Treasury's. Bondholders are rewarded for inching a bit further out on the credit spectrum.

Disadvantages of mortgage-backed securities

Mortgage-backed securities also have their disadvantages.

Income isn't a sure thing.

Mortgage-backed securities don't distribute income the way regular bonds do. Instead of twice yearly payouts, the checks arrive every month, which could be a plus. However, you're never certain what the check amount will be until you open the envelope. There's no steady coupon payment. Your payout depends upon the repayment pace of mortgages in those huge pools.

Mortgage-Backed Securities on the Internet

If you'd like to learn more about the sources of mortgage-backed securities, check the issuers' Web sites:

✦ Ginnie Mae at www.ginniemae.gov

✦ Freddie Mac at www.freddiemac.com

✦ Fannie Mae at www.fanniemae.com

Note What many investors don't understand is that those monthly checks also include a portion of the principal. By the time the bond matures, all the principal will have been returned to you. (The monthly statement provides the income and principal breakdown.) So don't spend the principal if you want to transfer it into another bond.

There's no tax break.

Unlike Treasuries, mortgage-backed securities don't enjoy a state tax break. Like Treasuries, they're also subject to federal taxes.

Tip Mortgage-backed funds typically do best when the economy is percolating along with fairly stable interest rates.

Mortgage-backed securities are sensitive to interest rate fluctuations.

Investors in mortgage-backed securities dread declining interest rates because lower interest rates cause homeowners to refinance their mortgages, which means that more of their principal is returned in their monthly checks. They will then be forced to reinvest their principal at a time when interest rates are lower. Rising interest rates can be a threat as well because increasing rates can slow the pace of mortgage repayments. If the pace slows, the rate at which you can reinvest your principal will slow too.

 Caution The worst thing that an individual investor can do is to buy mortgage-backed securities during a high inflation period that then melts away.

They are harder to buy.

Because mortgage-backed securities are becoming more popular, Fannie Mae and the other issuers are trying to make the bonds more accessible. Currently, however, you can't buy the bonds directly; you must go through a broker.

Tip An easy way to purchase these bonds is to buy mutual funds composed primarily of mortgage-backed securities. These bond funds can also respond to interest rate moves.

Mortgage-backed mutual funds

If you're interested in a mortgage-backed mutual fund, you can choose a fund that primarily invests in Ginnie Maes; such funds often contain the abbreviation GNMA in the name. General mortgage funds are also available.

Consider these top GNMA candidates:

✦ Vanguard GNMA at (800) 635-1511 or www.vanguard.com

✦ American Century GNMA at (800) 345-2021 or www.americancentury.com

✦ Fidelity Ginnie Mae at (800) 544-6666 or www.fidelity.com

Inflation-Indexed Bonds

Inflation has always posed a threat to bonds. But a new breed of bonds, which has been woefully unappreciated, can help tame that financial monster. Inflation-indexed Treasury bonds are unique because they offer an inflation hedge. They do this by guaranteeing a rate of return above inflation.

Note This inflation protection is revolutionary for bonds. When runaway interest rates are clobbering regular bonds, TIPs should do just fine. TIPs also enjoy the same rock-solid credit assurance as other Treasuries.

If you haven't heard about *TIP*s, which stands for Treasury Inflation-Protection Securities, it's no surprise. The federal government's timing on the introduction of these bonds couldn't have been worse. After the launch in 1997, inflation wasn't a worry, which condemned TIPs to lackluster performance. Investor interest never materialized. But when inflation fears threaten, TIPs suddenly look appealing. So far, institutional players are the primary investors in these bonds.

Like regular Treasuries, a TIP pays out a set interest rate for the life of the bond. What's different is that the bond's principal value is adjusted twice a year to reflect any inflation indicated by the Consumer Price Index. Suppose the Treasury was paying a base interest rate of 3 percent and inflation was 1 percent. If inflation jumped 1 percent, the principal of a $1,000 TIP would bump up to $1,010. The semi-annual coupon payment would be then be based on $1,010; as the issuer, the feds have to pony up the additional cash for the payouts.

Note, however, that during the years you hold the bond, you pocket only payments based on the original interest rate. You don't receive the inflation-adjusted amounts until your TIP matures.

Caution Be aware that TIPs can provide a nasty tax surprise: Investors are obliged to pay income tax on those phantom yearly adjustments. So keep TIPs in a tax-deferred or tax-free retirement account.

You can buy individual TIPs from the Treasury Direct program for no cost, or you can spend more money by using a broker. You can also choose to invest through mutual funds, a route that offers convenience. Portfolio managers may be able to tweak a fund's total return by trading among different TIP maturities. So far, a paltry number of funds are devoted to these bonds. Here are three to research:

✦ Vanguard Inflation-Protected Securities Fund: (800) 635-1511

✦ American Century Inflation Adjusted Treasuries Fund: (800) 3435-2021

✦ 59 Wall Street Inflation-Indexed Securities Fund: (800) 625-5759

Zero Coupon Bonds

The zero coupon bond (or zero) has a funny name and an even quirkier personality. The zero got its name because the bond's coupon, or interest, is removed before the bond is sold. In the days when bonds were still printed on paper, the coupon was literally snipped off. Zeroes are also called *strips* for the same reason.

Suppose you're retiring in 2011, so you invest in zero coupon bonds that mature in 10 years. A $1,000 zero with a 10-year maturity would cost about $590 in early 2001. (A longer-term zero would have been even cheaper.) In 2011, you'd pocket the $1,000 when the zero matures. In comparison, if you purchased a $1,000 Treasury or other type of bond, you'd pay the $1,000 face value upfront. But those bonds would kick out regular interest payments every six months or so. Consequently, you would be profiting from your bond throughout its lifetime.

With a zero, you have to wait until the bond matures before you pocket any of the interest. This delay won't matter if you don't need the steady income, but if you depend upon bond income, zeroes aren't appropriate for you. Because you don't enjoy regular income with a zero, the bond's initial discount is your compensation.

Note   What makes zeroes so unusual is their split personality. They appeal to two vastly different groups of investors: the most conservative and the most aggressive.

The Treasury Department issues most of the nation's zero coupon bonds. Municipal zeroes are also an option. Although not as safe, these municipal zeroes are attractive to more affluent investors because they enable these investors to avoid federal and sometimes state taxes on the interest. In addition, corporations issue billions of dollars' worth of zeroes every year.

Advantages of zero-coupon bonds

Here's what's attractive about zero-coupon bonds.

Little upfront money is needed.

When you buy a regular bond, you pay full price and then pocket a steady stream of income over the bond's lifetime. But a zero is priced at a discount; you never pay its face value. Instead, you buy it at a discount to get the interest in a lump sum at maturity.

Zeroes are safe for the patient investor.

Zeroes can be as safe as a certificate of deposit. An ultraconservative investor will know to the exact penny what the bond will be worth when it matures. If you purchase a Treasury zero that will pay $1,000 on August 31, 2025, that's precisely the amount you'll collect on that date. Zeroes can be a practical solution for someone needing rock-solid assurance that a specific amount of money will be available at a future date. Some parents use zero coupons as a way to save for college.

Tip   Zeroes can be particularly useful when a child is in or entering high school. That's when parents often want to move college money out of stocks and stock funds and into safer investments.

There's no reinvestment risk.

With other bonds, you have to reinvest your regular income checks somewhere else. That money might end up in a savings account, money market, or another bond offering a puny yield. Continual reinvestment isn't an issue with zeroes because you receive your interest payment in one lump sum.

Treasury zeroes aren't callable.

Treasury zeroes can be attractive to investors who hate losing their bonds prematurely because zeroes aren't callable. Municipal and corporate zeroes, however, don't provide this protection.

Disadvantages of zero-coupon bonds

Here's the bad news about zeroes.

The tax bite can hurt.

Some people avoid zeroes for tax reasons. Although long-term zero holders may face 10, 20, or 30 years before pocketing their earnings, the IRS won't be that patient. The IRS expects you to pay taxes each year on all the interest zeroes generate on paper annually.

Tip   Because of the tax time bomb, keep your zeroes in a tax-protected retirement account.

Inflation and Savings Bonds

Historically geared toward smaller, conservative investors, savings bonds are issued by the U.S. Treasury. Unlike Treasuries, savings bonds are not traded on the market, so their holders cannot lose money on these bonds no matter what happens on Wall Street. They are not immune to inflation, however: Inflation has traditionally hurt savings bond investors as much as any other bondholder. But individuals who appreciate the safety of a good old savings bond can now protect their investment against inflation.

The interest rate for inflation-protected savings bonds, which have been nicknamed *I Bonds,* is set in two ways. Every six months, the federal government establishes a base rate on its newest crop of I Bonds. An investor is guaranteed to receive at least this rate for the bond's lifetime. But even better, the bonds are adjusted for inflation twice a year; a benefit bondholders can truly appreciate when the bond is cashed in. That extra interest is added to the bond's value monthly and paid when the bond is cashed in (rather than being included in the bondholder's yearly interest checks).

Just like a TIP, the interest from the Series I bond is subject to federal tax, but not state and local taxes. But there's a key difference. You don't have to pay income taxes on the interest until the bond is cashed in.

I Bonds, which are issued in maturities up to 30 years, can be bought at face value in various amounts from $50 to $10,000. They may be ordered at just about any financial institution.

While financial experts have been touting the advantages of I bonds, most savings bond investors still don't know about them. The vast majority of customers gravitate to the traditional EE savings bonds. In most cases, the I bond is the wiser choice.

Savings Bond Resources

Want to brush up on your savings bond IQ? Here's where to turn for help:

✦ **Bureau of the Public Debt:** The Bureau's Savings Bond Calculator can help you determine such things as the value of your bonds now and in the near future, as well as when bonds will stop earning interest. Or you can make the calculation offline, by downloading the Savings Bond Wizard. The phone number is (304) 480-6112, or try the automated line at (800) 4US-BOND. The Web address is www.savingsbonds.gov.

✦ **Savings Bond Customer Service Unit:** You can reach representatives at Federal Reserve Bank at (800) 333-2919; their hours are 8:00 a.m. to 6:00 p.m. Central Time, Monday through Friday.

✦ **Morningstar:** Would you love to hear people argue about the merits of I Bonds versus TIPS? You'll be surprised at how many knowledgeable investors pontificate on subjects like these in Morningstar's forums. Most of the conversations about savings bonds and TIPS take place in the Bond Squad and Vanguard Diehards forums. Go to www.morningstar.com.

✦ **Savings Bond Informer:** You receive regular statements for your checking, brokerage, and mutual fund accounts, but the federal government doesn't provide them for its savings bond customers. Sign up with the Savings Bond Informer and you'll receive a customized analysis of your savings bonds inventory that can help you track and evaluate your holdings. Through this private bond service, you can also obtain Daniel J. Pedersen's book, *Savings Bonds: When to Hold, When to Fold and Everything In-Between* (Sage Creek). Call (800) 927-1901 or go to www.bondinformer.com.

Zeroes can be terrifying for the faint-hearted.

A zero is boringly predictable if you hang on till the bitter end. But watch out if you need to sell the zero before its maturity date. If the price volatility of a zero coupon were traced on paper, the graph could look like a jagged piece of broken glass. The reason for the wild gyrations is simple: Zeroes don't provide the regular income that other bonds spin off, which would dampen some of the swings.

A Zero Source

Investors who don't relish shopping for Treasury zeroes have an alternative: zero coupon mutual funds. Only a handful of these funds exist. The granddaddy of zero funds is American Century. The fund family offers six fund choices in the American Century Target series that currently contain portfolios of Treasury zeroes that mature every five years from 2005 to 2025. You select a fund based on the bond maturity you want. Contact American Century at www.americancentury.com or (800) 345-2021.

Unlike other mutual funds, the American Century funds are designed to shut down when their portfolio of zeroes matures. A future target redemption amount is established each time one of these funds is created. The funds with the most distant maturities are the most volatile. When interest rates are dropping, speculators stampede into these funds. It's no wonder. When rates crumble, the American Century zero coupon funds can be the year's best bond performers. In 1995, when interest rates plunged, for instance, American Century Target 2020 soared 61.34 percent. A trio of American Century zero coupon funds claimed the titles as the No. 1, 2, and 3 best performing bond funds for the year 2000.

On the flip side, the zero coupon funds with the longest maturity can fall apart when interest rates climb. When this happened in 1999, for instance, American Century 2025 returned a negative 20.8 percent.

Changes in interest rates trigger the wild rides. Zero speculators love to see interest rates drop, but they cringe when rates inch up. The longer a zero's maturity is, the more harrowing or exhilarating the ride. For instance, if you own a 30-year zero coupon bond and interest rates drop 1 percent, the value of the zero (the amount you would get for it if you sold it today) soars 30 percent. If interest rates increase 1 percent, your zero's value plummets 30 percent. A 1 percent move in interest rates in either direction with a 10-year zero triggers a 10 percent change either up or down.

When interest rates seem poised to shrink, speculative investors load up on long-term zeroes in hopes of generating a phenomenal profit. Gambling on interest rates, however, is best left to the most fearless investors because a wrong bet could be disastrous.

Zeroes are subject to sales gouging.

Unfortunately, you can't buy federal zeroes directly from the Treasury, which means you'll need a broker. Shop around because prices can vary dramatically. Stockbrokers love to sell zeroes because commissions are fairly high; zero commissions are based on the bond's face value rather than the amount invested.

Municipal Bonds

Wonder where the technology millionaires headed when Internet stocks tanked in 2000? Some of that cash is sitting in municipal bonds (called *munis*). Because of the muni's tax-friendly nature, it's a favorite diversification move for wealthy Americans whether they are near retirement or decades from it. It's estimated that more than five million households own either individual munis or muni mutual funds.

A bewildering number of munis are available. More than 50,000 state and local government entities float bonds to pay for everything from college dormitories to sewage plants. But not all of these bonds are equally appealing, so you need to do your homework.

Advantages of municipal bonds

Why do some investors love munis? Here's why.

Munis provide tax breaks.

The muni's best selling point is its tax break. If you buy a muni, the income it generates is not subject to federal income tax. The tax break can get even better: If you invest in individual bonds or a bond fund that concentrates exclusively on debt in your state, you can skip state taxes as well. Some investors even finagle a triple play by buying bonds that are issued by their particular municipality, a move that can eliminate any local tax on the income.

On the surface, muni yields may not look competitive. Because of the tax break, however, you can't compare a muni's yield with the yield of a taxable bond. To make a fair comparison, you must use this formula:

Taxable equivalent yield = tax-exempt yield / (1 – federal income tax rate)

Suppose the municipal bond was yielding 6.5 percent and the investor was in the 36 percent tax bracket; here's how the equation would work in this situation:

1. Subtract .36 (the federal income tax rate) from 1 to reach the figure .64.

2. Divide the tax-exempt yield of .065 by .64 to reach the figure .101 (10.1 percent), which is the taxable equivalent yield.

3. Compare the taxable equivalent yield for the muni with the yield of a taxable bond. A taxable bond would have to offer a yield of more than 10.1 percent to make it a better deal than the muni.

If you hate math, don't worry. Plenty of Web sites offer yield conversion calculators. Here are some places to look:

✦ Financenter.com at www.financenter.com

✦ Bond Market Association at www.investinginbonds.com

✦ BondAgent.com at www.bondagent.com

Insured munis can increase your portfolio's safety.

Municipal bonds are riskier than federal government bonds, but the gap isn't as wide as you might assume. That's because more than half of muni issuers now insure their bonds. What does that mean to the investor? If an issuer defaults on payments to its lenders, whether institutional or individuals, the insurer guarantees that the interest payments continue to be mailed out. The insurance company also will make sure that you ultimately receive your principal back. Insurance doesn't protect bondholders from fluctuations in bond prices though.

Tip   Before you invest, check the issuer's credit history.

To check the credit history of a bond issuer, you can wade through the *official statements* or *offering circulars,* the documents in which issuers disclose details of their financial conditions. Or you can find out what the bond rating agencies think. If you're investing in a muni bond fund, check its prospectus and annual report.

Your Muni Bond: What's It Worth?

A shareholder in Cisco Systems or Boeing can check the newspaper everyday to find out what a share is worth. A bondholder has a more difficult time finding out what his or her investment is worth. For a modest fee, you can call the Standard & Poor's/The Bond Market Association Municipal Bond Service (800) BOND-INFO to get recent bond price transactions for muni bonds you hold. Your broker might also be able to help, especially if he or she has access to Bloomberg, a computerized investment information service that most wealthy investors use to analyze bonds.

Certain types of bonds are inherently riskier than others. The safest are general obligation bonds, which are approved by voters and secured by the full faith and credit of the issuer. Revenue bonds are a notch below in safety. They are dependent upon money generated by public projects, such as airports, bridges, low-income housing, and water and sewage treatment facilities.

Disadvantages of municipal bonds

Consider the downside of munis when making investment choices.

Munis aren't always tax-free.

Some investors are stunned to discover that they owe taxes on a supposedly tax-free investment. Munis are only tax-free if you hold onto them until maturity, and they aren't immune from capital gains. For instance, if you buy $20,000 worth of municipal bonds and you later unload them for $23,000, you will owe income taxes on the $3,000 gain.

This nasty surprise isn't just limited to bondholders who sell. Bond mutual fund shareholders can get these capital gains distributions passed on to them if their portfolio manager sells bonds at a profit. You might think that getting distributions would increase the value of your investment, but it doesn't. The value of each share in your muni bond fund drops in correlation with any capital gains distribution, so it's a wash. You, however, will be stuck on April 15 paying capital gains taxes on a distribution that did you no good at all.

Meanwhile, you definitely should avoid being snared by a bond (or holdings in a bond fund) that is subject to the dreaded *alternative minimum tax* (AMT). The AMT is supposed to prevent wealthier people from claiming too many deductions on their tax returns. The AMT can apply to interest generated from *private activity* bonds, such as those issued for airports, industrial development, and stadiums. Aiming to tweak their yields, many municipal bond funds hold this type of bond.

The tax break isn't attractive for everybody.

There's a reason why America's most affluent investors load up on municipal bonds. The higher a person's tax bracket is, the better the deal. But if your tax bracket is 15 percent, buying munis is usually pointless because munis won't provide you with enough of a tax break to compensate for their lower yields. Munis are sometimes worthwhile for those in the 28 percent tax bracket; they're more of a sure thing for people in the highest brackets.

Maximizing the tax break can increase your risks.

People like to snatch up bonds issued in their own state for the biggest tax savings. Diversification isn't on their agenda. This strategy can be riskier because a city, county, or state can be affected simultaneously by the same economic disasters. Imagine owning a ton of California muni bonds when the earthquake of the century hits.

Investment-Grade and High-Yield (Junk) Corporate Bonds

Governments aren't the only ones peddling debt. Private industry also issues bonds. A distinct dividing line exists between corporations considered a shoo-in to pay off their lenders and those who may stumble. The riskier debt is characterized as *high yield* or *junk;* the debt of the most responsible debtors is classified as *investment grade.*

Because junk bonds are riskier, their issuers must entice would-be lenders with better yields. Just because these bonds are called junk, however, doesn't mean that all the borrowers are irresponsible or seat-of-the-pants technology startups. The companies in the junk category include Burlington Industries, Avis, Boise Cascade, and Air Canada.

> **Tip**
> Unless you relish the task of evaluating individual corporate bonds, you're better off investing in a top-notch bond mutual fund that has a heavy concentration in corporate bonds.

You will often see bond funds with big holdings in corporate bonds referred to simply as *intermediate-term bond funds.* These funds, which can be an excellent choice to serve as a core fixed-income holding in a portfolio, invest in both corporate and different types of government bonds.

Advantages of corporate bonds

Here's why you may be interested in corporate bonds.

The Odds of Defaulting

Certain industries, according to a Standard & Poor's survey, are more inclined to default than others. The following table from Standard & Poor's shows the default rate by industry for the period between 1981 and 2000.

Industry	Period 1981–2000			2000	
	Number of Obligors	Number of Defaults	Default Rate (%)	Number of Defaults	Default Rate (%)
Aerospace/automotive/ capital goods/metal	1,030	108	10.49	19	1.84
High tech/computers/ office equipment	415	33	7.95	6	1.45
Consumer/service sector	1,326	185	13.95	32	2.41
Leisure time/media	755	109	14.44	17	2.25
Healthcare/chemicals	503	45	8.95	10	1.99
Forest/building products/ home builders	368	47	12.77	9	2.45
Energy/natural resources	496	65	13.10	4	0.81
Utilities	803	16	1.99	3	0.37
Telecommunications	394	18	4.57	7	1.78
Transportation	396	44	11.11	7	1.77
Financial institutions	1,771	47	2.65	2	0.11
Insurance/real estate	912	29	3.18	1	0.11
Total	9,169	746	8.14	117	1.28

Source: Standard & Poor's CreditWeek, January 31, 2001. Note: This table is not a recommendation to buy, hold, or sell any securities.

Corporate bonds can provide a better yield.

Although more affluent Americans often prefer munis because of the tax break, corporate bonds can be an attractive alternative if the bonds are tucked inside a retirement plan. If bonds are in a tax-protected retirement account, there's no incentive to choose munis. Corporate bonds can also make sense for investors in low tax brackets who aren't a good match for munis. Corporate bonds typically pay more interest than Treasuries.

Junk Bond Hall of Shame

Not all companies that default on their bonds are obscure ones. You may recognize these offenders:

- ✦ Fruit of the Loom
- ✦ Planet Hollywood International
- ✦ Loehmann's Inc.
- ✦ AMF Bowling Inc.
- ✦ Just for Feet
- ✦ Claridge Hotel & Casino Corp.
- ✦ Family Golf Centers

Corporate bonds' value can increase along with stock.

Corporate bonds can cling to the coattails of a soaring stock. If a company is flourishing and its stock is skyrocketing, its debt might be more highly valued. Junk bonds, in particular, react more quickly to a company's overall value. At the same time, corporate debt is a safer investment than a company's stock. A stock can plummet to zero, but bondholders enjoy a better chance of recouping some of their initial investment.

Disadvantages of corporate bonds

Corporate bonds aren't for everyone; here's why:

Corporate bonds can get clobbered during financially shaky times.

When an economic catastrophe occurs in another part of the world, investors back home tend to panic. During such times, fixed-income junkies flee to "quality." They feel safer scooping up Treasuries and blue chip stocks. Corporate bonds, especially junk bonds, can get clobbered as their prices shrivel. (Note: Investors who hold onto their corporate bonds during turbulent periods receive the same interest checks.) During hard times, a corporation could see its credit rating slashed, which would puncture its market value. In addition, a struggling corporation may go belly-up. In that worst case scenario, failed corporations must follow a particular order in paying back debtors when any assets are divided up, and bondholders stand fairly close to the head of the line.

Evaluating corporate debt is tough.

The danger with buying individual corporate bonds is evaluating their reliability. Will the hot telecommunications newcomer that just issued $500 million worth of debt honor its obligations? It's hard to know that without being comfortable analyzing a corporation's financial figures.

Tip   Frankly, most of us don't have enough time to pour through a company's financial information. Couch potatoes should invest in corporate bonds through a mutual fund.

Corporate bonds aren't shielded from taxes.

Unlike munis, Treasuries, and government agency bonds, corporate bonds have absolutely no tax protection. They are subject to federal, state, and, where applicable, local income taxes.

Corporate bonds aren't easy to buy.

One of the knocks against corporate bond trading for individuals is that it isn't as easy to buy corporate bonds as it is to buy other types of bonds. Getting exploited by bond brokers is just one hazard you have to try to avoid. Some blue chips, including Ford Motor and General Electric, have attempted to make corporate bonds more liquid by regularly issuing debt in large amounts.

Summary

✦ If safety is your top concern, try Treasuries.

✦ When you invest in mortgage-backed securities, stick with mutual funds.

✦ As a hedge against inflation, look into inflation-indexed bonds.

✦ Understand the risks of a zero coupon bond's split personality.

✦ Check your tax bracket before investing in municipal bonds.

✦ Keep corporate bonds inside a retirement account.

✦   ✦   ✦

Beyond Bonds: Other Income Alternatives

✦   ✦   ✦   ✦

In This Chapter

Powering up with utility investments

Playing the stock market with convertible securities

Remembering preferred stock: the forgotten income option

Investing in real estate with REITs

✦   ✦   ✦   ✦

Need a fixed-income fix beyond bonds? This chapter gives you the scoop on such income alternatives as utility stocks, convertible securities, preferred stock, and real estate investment trusts (REITs). These other income options have been undergoing tremendous changes and can be impressive income generators. In some cases, they can offer what bonds traditionally can't provide: octane for your income portfolio. Investors can still pocket that regular stream of income, but they may be pleasantly surprised to see the value of their holdings grow at the same time.

Even the most intrepid bond fans can stretch a bit with this miscellaneous category of investment vehicles, particularly considering the updated versions. You may not recognize today's new breed of utility stocks that invest in wireless companies and other hot telecommunications plays. Jittery investors who wouldn't dare dabble in technology stocks are instead turning to convertible securities for less risky exposure. Meanwhile, REITs have been making a comeback in the new century after some rough patches in the 1990s.

Utilities in the New Economy

Throughout most of stock market history, utilities were predictable because they operated as monopolies. An electric utility didn't have to worry about customers shopping for cheaper electricity; there was no other place to go.

In this environment, utility stocks were an ideal setup for retirees or other investors who desired a dependable income stream. With captive customers, a utility company's earnings were usually steady. The dividends (those company distributions of earnings to investors who own stock) were fat and reliable because utilities had nothing better to do with their cash. Unlike such corporate conquistadors, such as Home Depot or the Gap, a local utility wasn't going to embark on cross-continental empire building.

Sweeping deregulation has obliterated the old rules. The telecommunications (telecom) industry has experienced the most dramatic changes. It's been many years since Americans had only one option for just about all their telephone service: that corporate monolith known lovingly as Ma Bell. The feds then broke Ma Bell into smaller independent companies called the Baby Bells. Yet the telephone monopoly breakup was only the prelude for revolutionary changes brought about by the subsequent cannibalization of the Baby Bells and by high-flying wireless technology. Meanwhile, deregulation among gas utilities has rewarded ambitious companies that are furiously expanding pipeline and distribution networks. Even in the electric utilities industry, where deregulatory changes have created turmoil in California, some energy providers are behaving more like aggressors than stodgy slowpokes.

 Example During a recent 12-month period, the stock value of Calpine Corporation, a relentless acquirer and operator of power plants, surged more than 75 percent. This isn't the kind of slow-paced, conservative utility stock that grandma likes.

For anyone hooked on a regular dividend fix from utilities, the dynamic changes are not necessarily good news. No longer protected by cozy monopoly arrangements, utilities aren't as anxious to plow their capital into dividends. Instead, some are using profits to invest in new projects, expand their territory, and protect themselves against interlopers. Consequently, dividend opportunities, although still plentiful, are shrinking.

Utility mutual funds, however, provide a slightly better yield than you can expect from the general stock market. The average utility fund, according to Morningstar, was recently yielding a dividend of 1.74 percent. The yield of the typical corporate dividend in the Standard & Poor's 500 was 1.1 percent. Yet the dividend erosion in the utility universe has been dramatic. As recently as 1997, for instance, the average utility was paying a 3 percent dividend.

The good and bad sides of utilities

Utilities remain a fine investment, but for many people the rationale for including them in their portfolios has changed. Depending on your investment goals, utilities can be either advantageous or disastrous. This section provides the reasons for and against investing in utility stocks.

Utilities provide a hedge against volatility.

Like bonds, real estate investment trusts (REITs), and precious metal stocks, utilities usually are not affected by the stock market's performance. Little historical correlation exists between utilities and the broader market. At the same time, utilities have historically been less volatile than REITs and precious metals; during the 90s, the average utility fund outperformed the typical REIT or metals fund.

Judging a Fund's Relationship to the Market

If you want to know how closely a fund tracks the larger market, look at a measurement called *r-squared*. Statisticians assign a fund a rating from 1 to 100, called the r-squared, based on how closely it matches the performance of the S&P 500. A rating of 100 signifies that the fund matches the index perfectly. Funds with low r-squared numbers are often considered good diversification hedges against the stock market. Recently, the average utility fund's r-squared rating was 44. The average r-squared rating for REIT mutual funds was much lower. Morningstar reports these numbers in its fund evaluations.

Utilities' value increases when interest rates decline.

Like bonds, utility stocks and funds are allergic to interest rate hikes because utility companies are often highly leveraged. When interest rates decline, these stocks typically get a boost, which is a fine thing during the planning stages of retirement when you are shooting for the most dramatic increases in your portfolio.

Caution   When rates go up, the utilities' costs of doing business increase as well. These increased costs further decrease the dividend income stream retirees rely on.

A utility pick can be a play on a hot sector.

Utilities are welcoming a different breed of investor, one not interested in income. This new breed craves exposure to the telecom industry, which has become a premiere economic growth area. One of the most explosive areas is in wireless phones and other products. Rapid technological advances have made wireless services cheap, convenient, and incredibly popular. With an insatiable demand, the industry has plenty of room to grow. Note, however, that many of the most popular companies are generating huge annual losses as they plow all their cash into expansion efforts. This helps explain why the performance of the high-flying telecom industry hit a speed bump in the year 2000.

Caution   Evaluating many of these telecom players is extremely difficult because they defy traditional measurements. To play it safe, most people should invest in telecom companies through mutual funds.

Picking the right utility mutual fund

If utility mutual funds intrigue you, you have three categories to consider: traditional, growth-oriented, and global.

Cross-Reference   Chapter 13 provides general guidelines for evaluating any type of stock; you can learn about bond issuer credit ratings in Chapter 18.

Utility Stock Picking

If you prefer buying individual utility stocks, make sure you ask these questions:

✦ What is the company's prospect for growth?

✦ How does the company's price-to-earnings ratio compare with its growth rate?

✦ How is the utility dealing with deregulation?

✦ What is the company's dividend yield?

✦ What is the company's return on equity?

✦ What reputation does the management have?

✦ What is the company's bond rating?

Finally, you should also ask what effect is deregulation having upon a utility. For instance, two huge public electric utilities in California announced in 2001 they might be forced to declare bankruptcy because of deregulatory changes that have occurred in that state. At the same time, a few electric utilities in some other states, which are scheduled to undergo deregulation, were experiencing hits to their stock prices. These examples are extreme cases, but you need to be aware of any potential booby traps.

Traditional utility funds

These funds continue to invest primarily in the traditional dividend-paying utility stocks, which represent the safest category of utility funds. When the stock market is smoking, these funds can't keep up, but during turbulent markets, they typically lose less of their value.

Investors primarily concerned with income and capital preservation should consider these two fund candidates:

✦ Vanguard Utilities Income at (800) 635-1511 or www.vanguard.com

✦ AXP Utilities Income at (800) 328-8300 or www.americanexpress.com/advisors

Growth-oriented utility funds

Aggressive utility funds invest a large bulk of their money into telecom stocks. A smaller portion of the portfolios is devoted to electric utilities. The yield offered by these funds is typically mediocre. The returns can be impressive, but they can also be much more volatile than your old-fashioned utility fund. These funds are appropriate for more aggressive investors, who want to bet on this sector.

Tip

These hard-charging funds allow more timid investors, frightened by the volatility of technology stocks, to dabble in the technology sector. A utility fund with a high telecom exposure is actually a quasi-technology fund.

Although these funds don't benefit when the market is celebrating one new high after another, they won't do as poorly when a market hangover sets in. These funds are capable of providing returns that exceed the Standard & Poor's 500 return, the large-cap benchmark. If these funds interest you, start your research with the following two options:

✦ Fidelity Utilities Fund at (800) 544-8888 or `www.fidelity.com`

✦ MFS Utilities Fund at (800) 225-2606 or `www.mfs.com`

Meanwhile, investors who prefer to chuck the electric utilities and stick strictly with telecommunications firms can choose risky sector funds that do just that. Here are two candidates:

✦ Fidelity Select Telecommunications at (800) 544-8888 or `www.fidelity.com`

✦ Turner Wireless & Communications at (800) 224-6312 or `www.turner-invest.com`

Note With funds that invest only in telecommunications companies, you can usually forget about a dividend.

Global utility funds

Foreign utilities funds can be ideal for those investors who believe that overseas companies offer better growth prospects and for those who want to diversify a domestic portfolio. These funds typically invest in both American and foreign utilities. These funds are generally considered a safer alternative to a diversified foreign fund. The funds, however, do carry additional risks because of currency exposure and the potential for political instability in emerging markets. Just like their domestic counterparts, global funds vary dramatically in their risk profiles. Some funds load up on telecoms; others prefer electric utilities.

Beware of High Yields

As dividends shrivel, it's only natural for fixed-income fans to hunt for utilities that continue to provide a robust payout. But buyer beware. The utilities offering the biggest dividends are often not the best. The yield may be high because the stock price has been pummeled by Wall Street, which doesn't like the utility's prospects. When a stock's price plummets, the *yield,* which is the dividend as a percentage of the stock's price, rises.

You need to be equally leery of utility funds boasting of unusually high yields. Although the yield looks phenomenal, the total return could be dreadful. That can happen when a manager loads up on stocks with high yields, but terrible growth prospects. Some funds also fatten their yields by using risky investment strategies.

How to Identify Funds

Maybe you want a traditional utility fund or perhaps you're leaning toward a growth-oriented one. A fund's name won't tip you off to its built-in bias. How do you tell? Call the fund company and request a copy of the firm's prospectus. It describes what the fund can invest in. Often, the fund's annual or semi-annual report discusses the manager's investing style. If you're still not certain, contact the firm and ask.

These two historically high-performing global funds are worth considering:

✦ AIM Global Utilities at (800) 959-4246 or www.aimfunds.com

✦ Warburg Pincus Global Telecommunications at (800) 927-2874 or www.warburg.com

Convertible Securities

Do you crave the potential returns of stocks, but feel safer with bonds? If so, consider shopping for convertible securities. Convertibles have a split personality: They offer the regular income of a bond, but they also hold out promise of potential gains like a stock.

Cross-Reference   For more details on how bonds and stocks work, see Chapters 12 and 17.

Just like a bond, a convertible is sold in increments of $1,000 and is callable. When a convertible matures, the bondholder receives the original investment back. The yield won't be as generous as either junk or blue chip corporate bonds, but a convertible compensates by providing an equity kicker: Investors have the right to redeem their convertibles into the issuer's common stock at any time. When you buy a convertible, you know up front what the conversion ratio is. The *conversion ratio* is how many shares of stock each bond can convert to.

Example   When Amazon.com issued the biggest convertible offering of its kind in 1999, investors received a 4.5 percent coupon for each $1,000 investment. They also obtained the right to convert each of those bonds into 6.4 shares of Amazon.com. The conversion rate at the time was valued at about $156.

Advantages of convertible securities

Here are reasons why you might want to consider convertibles:

Convertibles aren't as risky as common stock.

Convertibles essentially permit you to ride the Wall Street roller coaster with a seat-belt. If the stock crashes, a convertible holder typically experiences only a portion of the fall. On the other hand, a convertible holder can't enjoy a stock's entire mete-oric rise. If the worst happens and a company declares bankruptcy, a convertible holder's claim will take priority over common stockholders.

Note   Convertible bonds of established blue chips can be attractive to conservative investors.

Convertibles provide safer bets for daring investors.

Convertibles are attracting more aggressive investors, who use them to place more cautioned bets on young, innovative companies in the technology, wireless, and biotech fields. Among the companies that have issued convertibles are Qualcomm, Global Crossing, Costco, and Veritas Software. A Merrill Lynch study suggested that more than 50 percent of convertible issuers today are technology firms. Speculative companies love convertibles because they can avoid paying bondholders as much interest as they would have to if they issued junk bonds.

Convertibles generate income.

The yield of the typical convertible, with its steady income stream, is much higher than what a regular stock can muster.

Disadvantages of convertible securities

Although convertibles can be handy sources of income, would-be investors need to consider the downsides as well.

Picking a convertible takes energy.

Evaluating convertible candidates is horribly difficult. Convertibles are influenced by earnings, just as any stock is, as well as interest rates, just as bonds are. Conse-quently, you not only have to evaluate a company as a potential stock holder, but you must also scrutinize the bond offering.

Convertibles can fuel unrealistic expectations.

If you're excited about convertibles, make sure your expectations are realistic. Some financial advisors complain that clients grow dissatisfied with convertibles even when they behave just as they should. The investors crave greater upside potential when a company skyrockets. They want more than a percentage of the gain. What these folks tend to forget is they are also capturing income.

> **Tip**   If you think you'd be too exasperated with convertibles, you may instead want to invest in a combination of growth stocks and bonds. Or stick with a balanced mutual fund that typically invests 60 percent in stocks and 40 percent in fixed income.

Convertibles aren't liquid.

Trading shares of a company's convertible isn't as easy as trading its stock. There aren't nearly as many interested convertible buyers. Some days, there isn't any activity at all. Consequently, if you want out quickly, you might be disappointed. What's more, most convertibles are sold in huge blocks to institutional players, which creates a pricing vacuum for individual investors, making them easy prey for broker's commissions.

Convertible mutual fund choices

Until high-flying tech companies, who were desperate for cash came along, convertibles were not money magnets. Consequently, the number of mutual funds devoted to convertible securities remains small. A flurry of new funds has appeared in recent times, but the grand total still doesn't exceed about six dozen.

You might be tempted to choose a fund with the highest return, but stifle that impulse. Funds with super-sized returns are probably invested in the most speculative companies. They may be holding a lot of converted common stock, which is obviously more volatile. Make sure you look at a fund's holdings before investing. Also compare how different funds have fared during rough times in the market, such as in 2000.

You may want to consider these funds, which have long-term track records:

✦ Fidelity Convertible Securities Fund at (800) 544-8888 or www.fidelity.com

✦ Value Line Convertible Fund at (800) 233-0818 or www.valueline.com

✦ Vanguard Convertible Securities Fund at (800) 635-1511 or www.vanguard.com

Web Site for Convertible Fans

To immerse yourself in convertibles, visit ConvertBond.com at www.convertbond.com. Visitors will find a convertible tutorial, but beyond that the site is geared toward already knowledgeable investors.

Preferred Stocks

Holding preferred stocks is another way to increase income for retirees. Despite the name, preferred stocks behave more like bonds than common stock because they pay out income quarterly. Unlike convertibles, whose performance is linked to a company's welfare, a preferred stock reacts more strongly to interest rate movements.

Caution

If you want to hit a home run with smart stock picking, preferred stocks aren't for you. Unless you buy convertible preferred stocks, there's no potential for growth.

What a preferred stock does offer is a way for conservative investors to bolster their income without the same level of volatility that bonds face. The yield can be attractive. For bondholders to capture an equivalent yield, they must typically invest in riskier junk bonds. If disaster strikes, preferred stock does provide a level of safety. If a company liquidates, preferred shareholders get any crumbs remaining before common stock shareholders do. But preferred investors must wait behind all bondholders.

Example

An IBM preferred stock recently offered a yield of 7.35 percent, but traded in a range of just 25 to 26¼ during the previous 12 months. During the same period, IBM's common stock trading range was 80¹⁄₁₆ to 134¹⁵⁄₁₆ and it's dividend yield was well under 1 percent.

Preferred stocks also exhibit the same vexing characteristic that bonds do: They can be called. If interest rates slump, a company may redeem preferred shares because it can now borrow money more cheaply. New preferred stocks often carry a five-year moratorium on calls, however.

You can buy individual preferred stock shares (hundreds of preferred stocks are traded on the New York Stock Exchange), or when the pickings are slim, invest through a mutual fund.

Resource

One fund to consider is Vanguard's Preferred Stock Fund. Ask for a prospectus at (800) 635-1511 or www.vanguard.com.

Real Estate Investment Trusts (REITs)

Imagine owning a stake in America's busiest shopping malls, prime Beverly Hills real estate, or some of the hottest commercial property in the Silicon Valley. You're probably thinking, "Get real." Yet you don't have to be a millionaire to claim bragging rights to an impressive portfolio of real estate. You can invest in a Real Estate Investment Trust (REIT), which is the only practical way for most people to own a stake in property beyond their own homes.

A REIT (rhymes with feet) is a publicly traded company that acquires, owns, and manages income-producing real estate, such as apartment buildings, hotels, warehouses, factory outlets, golf courses, and office towers. More than 300 REITs are operating today.

REITs have traditionally provided investors with a steady stream of income. The historic yield for REITs is about 7 percent. At the same time, REITs have tended to provide better capital appreciation than bonds. Some investors like to jump into REITs when they believe that the real estate market is ready to take off. Largely due to inflation, REITs tend to zig when bonds and stock zag: Stocks and bonds wilt with inflation, but REITs can fare well during interest rate hikes because rental rates also escalate.

Tip   REITs can be used to diversify a portfolio because their returns usually don't track bonds or stocks closely.

During the late 1990s, REITs performed terribly. The hot money was chasing technology stocks, and REITs, which are considered more of a value play, were ignored and performed badly. REITs also took a pounding early in the decade when the commercial real estate market went bust after the 1980s boom, when savings and loan credit fueled overbuilding, leading to decreasing tenant demand and ultimately foreclosures.

In contrast to these troubled times, REITs performed incredibly well in 2000 when the overall market was taking a pounding. In the mid-1990s, REIT also rewarded their supporters with 30 percent to 40 percent returns. During this pre-Internet era, REITs were considered growth stocks. From 1992 to 1997, the REIT benchmark even outmuscled the Standard & Poor's 500.

Caution   One of the aggravating quirks of REITs is that they're cyclical: Overbuilding in boom times can lead to poor performance when the real estate market busts.

Evaluating the different types of REITs

The three types of REITs are equity, mortgage, and hybrid:

✦ **Equity REITs:** Equity REITs are the overwhelming favorite of REIT fans. About 96 percent of REITs fall into this category. These REITs generate most of their income from rental income. Despite the boom and bust cycles of the past, an index of equity REITs shows that the industry has posted negative returns only six times since 1972.

✦ **Mortgage REITs:** Mortgage REITs, which represent just 2 percent of the industry, loan money to real estate developers. The dividend for this type of REIT is typically higher than dividends for equity REITs, but a mortgage REIT allows little chance for your investment to jump in value. For that to happen, interest rates would usually have to slump.

Caution

Table 19-1 demonstrates the miserable performance of mortgage REITs, which get slammed when interest rates increase. These REITs are best avoided.

✦ **Hybrid REITs:** The hybrid REIT, which represents the remaining 2 percent of the market, is a blend of the other two varieties. It invests in property and mortgage loans. It's better to stick with a pure equity REIT play.

Table 19-1		
REIT Historic Returns		
Type of REIT	*Duration*	*Return*
All REITs	1 year	25.89%
All REITs	3 years	−1.50%
All REITs	5 years	9.05%
All REITs	10 years	12.74%
Equity REITs	1 year	26.37%
Equity REITs	3 years	−.19%
Equity REITs	5 years	10.1%
Equity REITs	10 years	13.6%
Mortgage REITs	1 year	15.96%
Mortgage REITs	3 years	−18.16%
Mortgage REITs	5 years	−3%
Mortgage REITs	10 years	5.04%

Source: National Association of Real Estate Investment Trusts. Based on data through Dec. 2000.

Tip

A REIT can be a rich source of income because it must pay out at least 95 percent of its income to investors as dividends. Because dividends are tax hogs, keep REIT investments in tax-protected retirement accounts.

Picking a top REIT

You'll increase your chances of finding a superior REIT by following these tips.

Follow the paper trail.

Do you have a REIT in mind? Before you do anything, obtain the documents that a company must file with the Securities and Exchange Commission. The company can send you these documents for free by mail. A quicker way to get the materials is by downloading them from the Security and Exchange Commission's Web site (www.sec.gov).

Examine the REIT's annual report, which is filed as a 10-K with the SEC, as well as its proxy and quarterly reports, which can also be found at the SEC. As you're reading, ask yourself whether the REIT's management is combat-ready. Has it weathered previous real estate boom-and-bust cycles? Also look at the company's debt level that's listed on its balance sheet in the 10-K. Some professional REIT watchers suggest that debt should not exceed 35 percent of a REIT's total capitalization.

You can also research REITs just as you would other stocks. Mega-financial Web sites, such as Microsoft's MSN MoneyCentral and Yahoo!, can provide lots of information.

Look at diversification.

Some REITs operate in a single region of the country, such as California. If a recession occurs in the Golden State, the REIT will suffer. Many REITs narrowly focus on one sector such as office buildings, hotels, or shopping centers. Remember that you may face more risk with a niche REIT.

Don't let the yield blind you.

Just because a REIT offers a high yield doesn't mean you should bite. The REITs with the most attractive yields are often the riskiest. A factory outlet REIT, for instance, might tantalize with a high yield, but the market may be able to accommodate only a limited number of future outlets. Because the REIT has less growth potential, the yield is higher to attract more investors.

Examine insider ownership and compensation.

Choose a REIT with a high level of insider ownership. That is, the executives have sunk a considerable amount of their own money into the company. The percentage of insider ownership should be at least 10 percent. You can find out this information by checking a company's proxy document.

Also determine whether the pay of the firm's top officers is tied to appreciation of the stock price. (This information is also in a REIT's proxy.) If the top executives have their pay linked to stock performance, they are arguably more motivated to succeed.

Consider investing in REIT mutual funds.

Evaluating REIT candidates, which are traded on the New York, American, and Nasdaq stock exchanges, is not easy. Let mutual fund managers do all the work by investing in one of the better-performing REIT mutual funds rather than picking out an individual REIT yourself.

Begin your research with these funds:

✦ Columbia Real Estate at (800) 547-1707 or www.columbiafunds.com

✦ Security Capital U.S. Real Estate at (888) 732-8748 or www.securitycapital.com

✦ Vanguard REIT Index at (800) 635-1511 or www.vanguard.com

 Resource   To learn more about REITs, contact the National Association of Real Estate Investment Trusts, 1129 20th St., NW, Suite 30, Washington, DC 20036; (800) 3-NAREIT; www.nareit.org.

Summary

✦ Utility stocks can be suitable for both aggressive and conservative investors.

✦ Convertible securities can give conservative investors exposure to high-flying stocks.

✦ Don't expect preferred stocks to skyrocket in value; just appreciate their steady payout.

✦   ✦   ✦

VI

Cashing in Your Chips

Part VI addresses many of the complicated issues that Americans face after retiring or as they approach that milestone. While many publications advise Americans to invest in stocks during the critical savings years, there's little investment advice out there for people who are already retired. You'll learn what the ideal balance of stocks and bonds is during later life and discover smart strategies for retirees to safely tap into their portfolios. This part of the book also contains an estate-planning primer that thoroughly covers the basics. Meanwhile, you'll learn the do's and don'ts of trusts and how to intelligently pick a financial institution and/or individuals to handle any money that you ultimately leave behind in a trust.

Investing and Spending Strategies for Retirees

Just as you wouldn't buy a 10-year-old computer and expect the same results as you'd get from this month's model, you can't rely on outdated advice when considering your retirement income options. This chapter gives you the newest techniques to answer these three critical (and eternal) questions:

- ✦ Will my retirement savings outlast me?
- ✦ How should I invest so this doesn't happen?
- ✦ How much can I realistically spend in retirement?

Traditionally, retirees were supposed to consume their retirement savings the way some little kids eat chocolate cake: lick off all the icing, but leave the cake alone. In other words, they could live off the regular interest checks, but never, ever consume the bonds. The principal was sacred.

Today the ranks of financial advisors who continue praising the merits of income-only portfolios are shrinking. As you'll learn in this chapter, the smart money is now on academic researchers and influential icons in the financial planning world who are encouraging retirees to invest for total return by giving a bond-heavy portfolio a much needed boost with stocks. With Americans living longer and retiring sooner (the vast majority of workers now claim Social Security at 62), growth in the leisure set's portfolios is essential. But the growth needs to be balanced with realistic concerns about risk. You won't hear many financial planners advocating 100 percent stock portfolios for retirees.

The standard measurements used to gauge a portfolio's chances of success often can't answer the practical, fundamental questions asked by most retirees and wannabe retirees, such as: If I have $300,000 and I want to pull out 7 percent a year, can I die with money still in the bank? Yet much of the software that consumers and financial advisors use today, including the freebie calculators found on the Internet, is woefully simplistic. A vastly more sophisticated modeling technique, Monte Carlo simulation software, is described in this chapter.

The Great Guessing Game: Retirement Planning

The weak link in retirement planning has always been human error. You can easily project how long your nest egg will last by crunching numbers on a calculator, but although the math may be correct, the conclusions could be terribly wrong. How is this possible? One simple reason: You are forced to guess a lot. When devising retirement withdrawal strategies, you must make big assumptions about three unpredictable factors:

✦ Your retirement spending needs

✦ The future of inflation

✦ Future market performance

Cross-Reference

To develop a sound retirement withdrawal strategy, you must coordinate your various retirement accounts. In Chapter 21, you learn the right and wrong ways to tap into your IRA, 401(k), pension, and other savings.

Retirement spending predictions

Perhaps the only assumption you can make a reasonably accurate stab at is your retirement spending needs. To some extent, you can base your future spending on your previous patterns. As a general guideline, many planners estimate that retirees will spend 70 to 75 percent of what they did during their preretirement years. Spending is expected to decline as people move into their mid 70s and beyond, but other costs, such as nursing care and drugs, could keep costs from shrinking much. These generalities, however, are just that. Costs may go up or remain the same.

Note

Many people assume that Medicare will pay all the medical bills, but it doesn't cover such things as drugs, nursing homes, dental bills, hearing aids, and glasses.

Plenty of unknowns have to be tossed into the mix. You can't predict if your car is going to need a transmission in two years or whether you'll wind up needing nursing home care. (That cost can at least be mitigated with long-term care insurance, a topic covered in Chapter 30.) But if your projections are way off, you can at least control your discretionary spending. You can cancel your cable television subscription, eat out less, and (in a real financial crisis) move in with the kids.

How much you spend will also ultimately depend upon how long you stick around. Today's average 65-year-old should live for 20 more years. But you sure don't want to put too much stock in that number because your savings could still fall short. Many financial planners are counseling their clients to financially prepare to live until 95 or 100.

Inflation predictions

Inflation, another one of the big unknowns, is completely beyond your control or your best estimates. You just have to fudge this number. During most of the 1990s, inflation averaged just over 3.5 percent, so it would seem safe to plug that figure into your equation. But inflation gets downright ugly during some periods. From 1973 through 1978, for instance, inflation soared by 48 percent. Although Social Security is indexed for inflation, this adjustment wouldn't nearly make up for the impact on a person's lifestyle.

Caution Retirees often overlook what an insidious threat inflation is. With an inflation rate of 5.2 percent, which was the average annual rate between 1974 and 1998, a $2.50 loaf of bread would, in three decades, cost almost $11.50.

Even when inflation is muzzled, it can still dangerously erode the buying power of somebody on a fixed income. Assume that a retiree is living comfortably on $50,000 a year. Even if inflation were a mere 2.4 percent (as it was between 1994 and 1998), the retiree's income would have to double in 30 years to prevent backsliding.

Assuming a modest 4 percent inflation, Table 20-1 demonstrates the amount of principal you will need in the future to maintain purchasing power of $50,000.

Table 20-1 Principal Needed to Maintain Purchasing Power of $50,000	
Number of years	*Amount Needed*
5	$60,833
10	$74,012
15	$90,047
20	$109,556
25	$133,292

Market return predictions

Predicting market performance is also fiendishly difficult. Not knowing what else to do, many retirees determine their yearly withdrawal rates based upon the historic performances of stocks, bonds, and cash. Since the mid-1920s, the stock market has posted a yearly annualized return of 11 percent; bonds have averaged about 6 percent, and cash has averaged 4 percent. In recent times, investors have been treated to even higher gains. During the past decade, the Standard & Poor's yearly return has averaged nearly 17 percent; the broader stock market, which also includes smaller stocks, did about the same. During the same period, government and corporate bonds averaged about a 9 percent return while cash generated 5 percent returns.

Caution   Basing a withdrawal strategy on projected average rates of return can be perilous. The exceptions to the averages create troubles for retirees.

But what if the market drops during your retirement? A retiree forced to regularly draw down savings during such times doesn't have the luxury of sitting on his or her investments for decades like a twentysomething, who can weather the storm.

Example   Imagine retiring in 1969 with the assumption that your stocks would average double-digit increases. During the 1970s, however, stocks returned less than 6 percent a year.

The T. Rowe Price study: Effects of the market

T. Rowe Price, the Baltimore mutual fund company, captured how challenging it is to devise a solid spending strategy with investment returns yo-yoing. In its critically acclaimed research, the fund firm examined what would happen to a $250,000 nest egg that contained 60 percent stocks, 30 percent bonds, and 10 percent cash between 1968 and 1998. During that 30-year period, the portfolio produced an 11.7 percent annualized total return. If a new retiree had withdrawn 8.5 percent from this portfolio during the first year and increased that amount slightly each year to compensate for inflation, the portfolio would have been depleted in the 30th year. That doesn't sound bad, does it? The typical retiree could stay alive into his or her 90s without going broke. However, this sunny scenario is based upon a smooth 11.7 percent yearly return.

Yet the returns during those 30 years were erratic. What really would have happened? The hapless retiree would have been trapped in a financial nightmare. Poor stock performance in the early years, particularly the ferocious bear market of 1973 and 1974, would have crippled the $250,000 portfolio. With the same withdrawal rate, the nest egg would have completely vanished in less than 13 years, not 30. Even if a more conservative 6 percent withdrawal rate was used, the money still would have run out early.

The study clearly illustrates how sheer luck in a retirement's timing can dramatically affect whether someone's nest egg will last. Just look at what happened when the fund company examined how a retiree would have fared if the return patterns had been switched. That is, the bear market years of the 1970s came at the end of the 30-year period, and the high-octane returns of the 1990s kicked off the retirement. The results would have been phenomenally different. Instead of being destitute, the retiree could have joined the ranks of the millionaires. With the average return remaining at 11.7 percent, the model portfolio, at the end of the 30 years, would have been worth $1.2 million. If the withdrawal rate had been limited to 6 percent instead of 8.5 percent, the portfolio would have climbed to $2.6 million.

Caution   Workers suffer if they retire during a bear market because they are forced to pull out more money for living expenses early on. With more of the principal gone at the beginning, less is left to grow when the markets eventually recover.

Monte Carlo Math for Real-World Answers

With so many factors that could go wrong, it's only natural to think that escaping from the workaday world is strictly a crapshoot. But it doesn't have to be. You can feel more confident about your chances for a prosperous retirement if you rely upon some help from a little something called *probability theory,* a sophisticated approach to calculations based on real-world conditions. Applying this theory is complicated, but you don't have to do any of the math yourself. Probability theory is now incorporated in software referred to as a *Monte Carlo simulation* and is being embraced by a growing number of financial advisors, who are using various software programs in their offices.

Cross-Reference   This same mathematical modeling is useful for younger investors who wonder whether they are squirreling away enough to retire on schedule. See Chapter 1 for more information on using Monte Carlo math to develop a savings plan.

Research using Monte Carlo simulations has introduced scientific rigor into the process of spending retirement savings by accounting for thousands of possible financial variables during a retirement period. Such scenarios, for instance, include the possibility that interest rates will be either high or low for certain stretches of someone's retirement or throughout the entire period. A dizzying number of possibilities about investment returns for stocks, bonds, cash are also plugged in the equation. One scenario might have stocks treading water for an entire decade; another could have inflation raging at double-digits for several years. Obviously, some outcomes are more likely than others. The simulation model follows its own bell curve, with the largest group of possibilities clustered near the bulging middle and far fewer at either end. The software runs all these random scenarios thousands of times.

Monte Carlo and Roulettes

Monte Carlo-style calculation, named after the famous European city known for its gambling, is not new. You can trace its history back to the 1940s when scientists involved in the top-secret Manhattan Project used the calculations to predict the possible devastation of the atomic bomb's chain reactions. Many other industries today, including petroleum and banking, employ it in decision-analysis applications.

Some software that uses Monte Carlo simulations can analyze your specific retirement holdings and simulate how they might perform in thousands of scenarios. For instance, you could make projections based on a portfolio of a couple of Janus mutual funds, a Vanguard bond index fund, and a few individual stocks. Other software simply looks at asset classes. Such software, for instance, might project what would happen if you have 70 percent of your retirement money in stocks, 20 percent in bonds, and 10 percent in cash.

Monte Carlo formulations can't provide an iron-clad, guaranteed answer as to whether you have enough money stockpiled, but they come closer than any other approach. What the software typically does provide is an estimate (as a percentage) of your own chances of having enough income to last through your golden years. For instance, a program might conclude that your portfolio of blue chip stocks and bond funds has a 79 percent chance of outlasting you. You must then decide whether you can live with a 21 percent possibility of dying broke. If you don't like the odds, you can postpone retirement, make adjustments to your retirement portfolio, or reduce your standard of living by drawing down the nest egg more slowly.

Tip   A growing number of Internet sites, such as Financial Engines (www.financialengines.com) and Morningstar (www.morningstar.com), provide individuals who are still on the retirement savings track with the tools to conduct Monte Carlo-style analysis themselves.

In the future, Monte Carlo simulation software will probably be as commonplace as paper clips in a financial advisor's office. In the meantime, T. Rowe Price is the first mutual fund firm to develop its own Monte Carlo simulation product, Retirement Income Manager. The centerpiece of this program is software that simulates hundreds of possible market scenarios and retirement income strategies. This powerful software requires an hour on a mainframe computer for each client's case. The cost of the service is $500.

Note Computers can't do everything for you. To benefit from any financial-planning software, you need to know your retirement goals and investing comfort level.

To use the Retirement Income Manager, T. Rowe Price clients must decide how much money they want to spend each month, as well as how many years they'd like their savings to last. In a questionnaire, they rate on a scale of 1 to 10 the importance of leaving an inheritance behind, avoiding market volatility, preserving principal, and many other goals. Based on the answers, the program spits out a model portfolio and two runners up. As part of the advisory service, a Certified Financial Planner reviews the recommendations and counsels the client.

If the customer wants to implement the plan with T. Rowe Price funds, the CFP will make specific fund recommendations. Otherwise, the suggested portfolios don't include fund suggestions. Instead, the proposed portfolios give generic asset allocations from 100 percent stocks to 95 percent bonds and 5 percent stocks. The customer is free to use T. Rowe Price funds or any other ones in building or modifying a portfolio.

Along with the computer-generated investment advice, a T. Rowe Price financial planner discusses with customers how their new action plan meshes with their goals. The firm does not suggest any strategies that pose less than a 70 percent chance of succeeding. For an investor who wants his or her money to last 20 years, but is terrified of becoming destitute, the quoted success rate can be as high as 99 percent with a portfolio designed for maximum security. Someone who has no interest in leaving an inheritance and desires maximum income may be comfortable with a 70 percent possibility of success.

Monte Carlo in Cyberspace

If you want to learn what the experts are saying about Monte Carlo probability, visit a Web site maintained by Lynn Hopewell, whom *The Wall Street Journal* has called the dean of retirement planners, and his partner Glenn Kautt. Although their site (www.montecarlo-simulation.com), which is a repository for a tremendous amount of papers and articles about Monte Carlo techniques, was designed for financial analysts, it provides worthwhile reading for the serious investor as well.

Investing Wisely to Spend More

Regardless of whether you rely upon mathematical calculations in developing a withdrawal strategy, you ultimately need to make this decision: What will your withdrawal rate be?

Frankly, a lot of people, even those sitting on a nest egg of $1 million or more, are stunned by the modest amounts of money that advisors say they can prudently withdraw without jeopardizing their portfolios. Traditional wisdom holds that retirees can earn 10 percent a year on their investments, take out 7 percent annually, and pretty much guarantee that they will die with an impressive chunk of money left behind in a brokerage account. But this traditional wisdom doesn't always wash; just look at the T. Rowe Price statistics given in the previous section. As you'll learn shortly, a super-safe strategy could limit yearly withdrawals to 4 percent of a portfolio's value. But 4 percent of $1 million is only $40,000, and a retiree with a $300,000 nest egg could withdraw only $12,000, which is hardly a princely sum to supplement Social Security and a pension.

Many aggressive investors, who remain fiercely loyal to stocks, no doubt figure that such a modest withdrawal rate doesn't have to apply to them. In their view, a portfolio that's all stocks can grow fast enough to take bigger withdrawal hits. But remaining aggressively committed to stocks can catapult even the brightest investor into trouble.

Caution   Investors are trained to think that if they invest aggressively and remain a disciplined investor over time, they'll do well, but that strategy works only in the accumulation phase, not in the spending phase.

The Trinity study revelations

Stock junkies, as well as die-hard bond fans, may want to do some soul searching after digesting the results of landmark research conducted by three finance professors at Trinity University in San Antonio, Texas. Using data from 1926 to 1995, the researchers examined just what kind of portfolios and payouts would have historically fared the best and worst during that period. This study, as dry as it may sound, was as exciting to the financial-planning community as Mark McGwire's historic home run record was to baseball fans. It has made a significant impact on the world of financial planning.

In what's come to be known simply as the Trinity study, the professors looked at the historical performance for these five model portfolios:

+ 100 percent stocks
+ 75 percent stocks and 25 percent bonds

✦ 50 percent stocks and 50 percent bonds

✦ 25 percent stocks and 75 percent bonds

✦ 100 percent bonds

The researchers determined how these portfolios would hold up during payout periods that lasted anywhere from 15 to 30 years, using annual withdrawal rates ranging from 3 to 12 percent.

Tip   The Trinity study clearly showed that in many payout scenarios a portfolio that mixed bonds and stocks enjoyed the best chance of surviving for 30 years.

Though a stock/bond mix may seem counterintuitive to die-hard stock fans, bonds can play a crucial role in boosting a portfolio's longevity. For example, consider how three different types of portfolios fared during the 71-year period with a 6 percent withdrawal rate. A 100 percent stock portfolio enjoyed a success rate of 90 percent. A stock portfolio that included 25 percent bond exposure fared better with a 95 percent success rate. A portfolio that was split evenly between stocks and bonds enjoyed a 98 percent success rate.

Caution   The worst portfolio to cling to for 30 years was the all-bond one. At a 6 percent withdrawal rate, there was just a 27 percent chance that any money would remain. With a 7 percent withdrawal rate, those dreary odds dropped even further to zero.

As you can see in Tables 20-2 and 20-3, portfolios weighted more heavily in stocks clearly performed better when the researchers focused exclusively on market performance after World War II. Someone who maintained a portfolio that ranged from 50 percent to 100 percent stocks wouldn't have run out of money. In contrast, an all-bond portfolio had even more troubles surviving during this period. If you look at the popular withdrawal rates of 6 percent, 7 percent, and 8 percent, bond portfolios experienced a tougher time surviving.

When glancing at the tables, you may wonder which of the two time frames is more relevant. Philip Cooley, the lead author of the study, believes that the post-war are the more realistic, relevant ones. The Great Depression and World War II affected the capital markets prior to 1945 in ways that are unlikely to be repeated.

Table 20-2
Portfolio Success Rates 1926 to 1995 (Percentage of All Past Payout Periods Supported by the Portfolio)

Withdrawal Rate as a % of Initial Portfolio Value:

Payout Period	3%	4%	5%	6%	7%	8%	9%	10%	11%	12%
100% Stocks										
15 Years	100	100	98	98	93	91	88	77	63	55
20 Years	100	98	96	94	92	84	73	61	47	43
25 Years	100	98	96	91	87	78	70	50	43	35
30 Years	100	98	95	90	85	78	68	54	49	34
75% Stocks/25% Bonds										
15 Years	100	100	100	100	96	95	91	79	63	46
20 Years	100	100	100	96	94	88	71	51	41	33
25 Years	100	100	98	96	91	78	57	46	33	26
30 Years	100	100	98	95	88	73	54	46	37	24
50% Stocks/50% Bonds										
15 Years	100	100	100	100	100	98	91	71	50	36
20 Years	100	100	100	100	96	88	61	41	25	10
25 Years	100	100	100	98	96	70	43	22	7	0
30 Years	100	100	100	98	90	51	37	15	0	0
25% Stocks/75% Bonds										
15 Years	100	100	100	100	100	100	91	50	21	14
20 Years	100	100	100	100	100	71	24	12	4	2
25 Years	100	100	100	100	78	22	9	0	0	0
30 Years	100	100	100	100	32	5	0	0	0	0
100% Bonds										
15 Years	100	100	100	100	100	79	43	38	14	7
20 Years	100	100	100	96	47	35	16	6	0	0
25 Years	100	100	98	52	26	7	2	0	0	0
30 Years	100	100	51	27	0	0	0	0	0	0

Note: Numbers rounded to the nearest whole percentage. The number of overlapping 15-year payout periods from 1946 to 1995, inclusively, is 36; 20-year periods, 31; 25-year periods, 26; 30-year periods, 21. Stocks are represented by Standard and Poor's 500 index, and bonds are represented by long-term, high-grade corporates.

Source: Based on calculations from Philip Cooley, Carl Hubbard, Daniel Walz, based on data from Ibbotson Associates.

Table 20-3
Portfolio Success Rates 1946 to 1995 (Percentage of All Past Payout Periods Supported by the Portfolio)

Withdrawal Rate as a % of Initial Portfolio Value:

Payout Period	3%	4%	5%	6%	7%	8%	9%	10%	11%	12%
100% Stocks										
15 Years	100	100	100	100	100	100	97	86	69	64
20 Years	100	100	100	100	100	97	81	61	45	42
25 Years	100	100	100	100	100	88	77	46	42	38
30 Years	100	100	100	100	100	90	76	52	52	38
75% Stocks/25% Bonds										
15 Years	100	100	100	100	100	100	100	86	69	53
20 Years	100	100	100	100	100	97	77	48	42	32
25 Years	100	100	100	100	100	85	54	42	31	27
30 Years	100	100	100	100	100	81	52	48	38	29
50% Stocks/50% Bonds										
15 Years	100	100	100	100	100	100	94	78	56	42
20 Years	100	100	100	100	100	94	61	39	26	13
25 Years	100	100	100	100	100	69	38	19	4	0
30 Years	100	100	100	100	100	48	33	10	0	0
25% Stocks/75% Bonds										
15 Years	100	100	100	100	100	100	89	53	25	17
20 Years	100	100	100	100	100	68	23	13	6	3
25 Years	100	100	100	100	73	15	8	0	0	0
30 Years	100	100	100	100	19	0	0	0	0	0
100% Bonds										
15 Years	100	100	100	100	100	72	39	33	19	11
20 Years	100	100	100	94	42	29	23	10	0	0
25 Years	100	100	96	54	15	12	4	0	0	0
30 Years	100	100	48	10	0	0	0	0	0	0

Note: Numbers rounded to the nearest whole percentage. The number of overlapping 15-year payout periods from 1946 to 1995, inclusively, is 36; 20-year periods, 31; 25-year periods, 26; 30-year periods, 21. Stocks are represented by Standard and Poor's 500 index, and bonds are represented by long-term, high-grade corporates.

Source: Based on calculations from Philip Cooley, Carl Hubbard, Daniel Walz, based on data from Ibbotson Associates.

Everyone can draw their own conclusions about the research, but you may wonder how the researchers are applying what they learned. Cooley, who is in his 50s, says he expects his portfolio to contain 80 percent stocks and 20 percent bonds in his early retirement years. As he ages, he expects his reliance on stocks to decrease, but he never expects stocks to dip below 50 percent of his holdings. Meanwhile, he plans to withdraw 7 percent of his portfolio a year.

He also suggests that retirees don't need to be wedded to a withdrawal rate that's been 100 percent successful historically. That could require too many financial sacrifices for people, who may have to scale back their standard of living. He suggests that aiming for a 75 percent success rate is a reasonable goal.

Here are some of the Trinity study's significant conclusions:

✦ Early retirees and others who expect to have a very long retirement should plan on more modest withdrawal rates of 3 to 5 percent.

✦ Payout rates exceeding 7 percent of the portfolio's value can be dangerous unless they last for short periods.

✦ The presence of bonds in a portfolio increases the success rate for fairly low withdrawal payouts.

✦ The average retiree ought to have at least 50 percent of his or her portfolio devoted to stocks.

Money at the End of the Line

The Trinity study primarily focused on portfolio endurance. A portfolio was considered a success if any amount of money was left, even if that amount was just a few dollars. The professors also looked at how much money might remain for heirs. Clearly, a heavy dose of stocks increased the chances of an estate windfall. Suppose a retired couple with a $1 million portfolio invested their nest egg in stocks (75 percent) and bonds (25 percent) and took out 7 percent a year. At the end of a 30-year retirement, the average value of those holdings would be worth a whopping $4.2 million. If the stock and bond percentages were flip-flopped, however, the median value would plummet to $122,000.

Bonds provide more certainty. The stock-dominated portfolios faced the risk of running out of money if markets were particularly bad. According to the study, this risk was of little to no concern for investors who limit their stock holdings to no more than 25 percent to 50 percent.

If you're a member of the American Association of Individual Investors, a nonprofit financial education group, you can find the entire study in the group's Internet archives (www.aaii.org). If not, you can obtain the study by signing up for a free trial membership on the AAII's Web site.

The best balancing act: Total return investing

The Trinity research, as well as other studies, suggests that an all-bond portfolio in retirement is courting danger. As you saw in Tables 20-2 and 20-3, a retiree could not be sure that a fixed-income portfolio would last 25 to 30 years unless the annual payout was limited to a modest 3 percent, 4 percent, or possibly 5 percent. But the survival odds improved noticeably if $1 out of every $4 in a predominantly bond portfolio was invested in stocks.

For many retirees, suggesting that bonds make up no more than 50 percent of their holdings is nearly sacrilegious. It's understandable why seniors have clung onto their bonds. With an income portfolio, traditionally only the interest is spent; the principal remains intact. Knowing that the principal isn't being touched can be incredibly reassuring. But what people fail to realize is they need growth to balance the certainty of the bond income. A bond's worst sin is that it fails as an inflation slayer. Whereas stocks are valued for their ability to increase in value (sometimes quite dramatically), you generally can't expect much price appreciation from bonds.

So what's the solution? Many financial advisors are advocating *total return investing*. With this strategy, you devise a more diverse portfolio instead of favoring investments that generate a specific income stream.

Tip
A mixed portfolio, including stocks, bonds, and cash, can provide both growth and stability. Rather than simply pocketing the income, you withdraw a certain percentage from the overall holdings, such as interest income, dividends, and capital gains.

Just what the portfolio looks like depends a lot upon you. Certain types of stocks and bonds are inherently more risky than others. For example, although many folks will live 20, 30, or more years in retirement, most retirees couldn't stomach loading up on technology stocks. Among domestic stocks, the small-cap variety is the most volatile, but over time they have performed better. In the fixed-income world, high-yield or junk bonds are certainly riskier than Treasuries, but they've enjoyed greater, albeit rockier, returns. (See Chapter 17 for a primer on bonds and Chapter 12 for information on the stock world.)

Tip
An important ingredient for total return investing is rebalancing. If you want to maintain a 60/40 mix of stocks and bonds, for instance, you'll want to be mindful of that percentage when you make withdrawals from your account.

A Wise Way to Manage Cash in Retirement

Breaking the nest egg can be traumatic. When workers are drawing regular paychecks, they probably aren't going to agonize about dining out or buying a new VCR. But retirees often cringe at spending because they know their paycheck days are over.

Consequently, planners who advocate that retirees wean themselves from a heavy reliance on bonds know the total return approach can make their clients anxious. It's one thing to feel guilty about spending $60 on dinner, but it's a whole new ball game when the portfolio dips $10,000 in one month. Consequently, the advocates of total return portfolios often suggest that their clients stockpile cash on the side. Some recommend the two-bucket approach. One bucket contains the stock and bond investments; the second holds a cash reserve for one or two years of living expenses. When the financial markets are doing well, withdrawals are drawn out of both buckets. In bad times, only the cash bucket is used. This strategy gives the other investments a chance to recover.

Summary

✦ Consider carefully the assumptions that you make about your retirement years.

✦ Remember that historical stock market averages can be misleading.

✦ Use Monte Carlo calculations when devising a retirement withdrawal strategy.

✦ During retirement, invest for total return rather than constructing an income-only portfolio.

✦   ✦   ✦

Wise Withdrawal Tactics for Retirement Funds

Traumatic. That's probably the first adjective that many people conjure up when they contemplate the inevitable. After saving for decades, reversing the process and spending for possibly decades can be a nerve-wracking prospect. In this chapter, you learn your best defense against the all-too-real possibility of portfolio erosion. Your best bet is to start thinking like a tax accountant. Planning your withdrawals in a way that avoids taxes can significantly boost the buying power of your nest egg. This chapter shares tax-efficient approaches to withdrawing your retirement cache.

You'll also find out how to increase the staying power of America's popular retirement plans. In a stunning development in early 2001, the federal government made it much easier for retirees to keep more of their nest egg in their IRA and other retirement plans, where it can remain immunized from taxes. You'll discover much more about this new development in the next few pages. (To learn more about withdrawal strategies for Social Security, see Chapter 2.)

The Hidden Perils of Retirement Plans

Saving for retirement isn't fun. We can all think of plenty of other ways that we would rather spend our paychecks. After sacrificing mightily for years to fatten our retirement savings accounts, we certainly don't want to watch some of this cash evaporate.

Yet the money can disappear in both obvious and insidious ways, and retirees are not the only ones who need to worry about a cash hemorrhage. Throughout your career, as well as in retirement, you can sabotage your nest egg in many ways. Ultimately, you could lose tens or even hundreds of thousands of dollars to sloppy retirement planning. Incredibly, you may not even realize that you lost so much.

How can this tragedy occur? You can blame part of it on job hopping. Americans are always looking for the better paycheck, the ideal boss, and the roomier cubicle. But when workers empty out their desk, they don't always spend much time contemplating what they should do with their workplace retirement benefits, including a 401(k) and a pension. With a 401(k), for instance, an employee departing for another job must decide whether to take the money out or leave it undisturbed in a tax-insulated cocoon. Pick the wrong choice, and it could ultimately blow up in your face.

Those who are retired or are on the verge of retiring face even more pressure because there are no more years of earnings to make up for mistakes. The decisions at this stage of the game are often irrevocable. Read on for the scoop on identifying and working around the pitfalls.

Tax-Savvy Withdrawal Strategies

Drawing down your life savings can be traumatic enough without making things worse by triggering unnecessary taxes. Carefully deciding which assets to tap can help preserve more of your spending power. If you remain aware of the tax consequences of your spending, your money could last many years longer. When deciding on your withdrawal plans, you might want to use the following guidelines to prioritize your accounts.

Tip   As a general rule, you should leave your tax-sheltered accounts alone as long as possible.

Step No. 1: Empty your taxable (nonretirement) accounts first.

The taxable money should usually go first. Remember that you're already paying the IRS for any earnings that your taxable accounts generate. The cash that you have sitting in a bank account, a mutual fund, or a brokerage account is subject to yearly income taxes and possible capital gain taxes as well. By spending this money first, you eliminate the federal tax liability that can soar as high as 39.6 percent if you're in the highest tax bracket. The tax bite is even bigger if you live in a state with its own income tax.

Step No. 2: Be choosy when you drain your taxable portfolio.

Not all the investments kept in taxable accounts are tax hogs. Consider keeping your more tax-friendly holdings until you absolutely must withdraw funds from them. Municipal bonds fit into this category. The owners of munis, which are issued by state and local governments, avoid paying any federal taxes on the interest income. Some munis even permit you to skip state taxes and, in certain cases, local taxes.

If you don't need the money, allowing stock certificates to gather dust could be shrewd for a couple of reasons. First, individual stocks are incredibly tax-efficient. As long as you don't sell a stock, you don't pay any capital gain tax. Even if you own a stock that has skyrocketed 500 percent since your smart purchase, your capital gain liability through all those wonder years has been a big, fat zero. If you hold on to an individual stock, the only way you'll owe yearly taxes is if it generates dividends. Traditional dividend generators include utility, bank, and tobacco stocks.

Tip   Because stocks are so tax-efficient, you might not want to disturb big stock winners, even if they are sitting in a taxable account.

If you hold on to a stock long enough, the potentially dreadful capital gain liability can vanish. This happens when you own stock upon your death. The *cost basis* (the amount of the original investment) is reset for the new owners to the current value. Only future price hikes are subject to taxation.

Tax Strategizing in Practice

How important is tax planning during retirement? Not long ago, T. Rowe Price, a mutual fund firm, explored that question. In its study, the firm started off with a hypothetical $600,000 portfolio, which was equally split between a traditional IRA and a regular taxable account. The study assumed that the owner was in a combined federal and state income tax bracket of 31.6 percent. In the study, the retiree wanted to withdraw $35,000 annually from the portfolio that grew 9 percent a year while inflation remained at 3 percent.

If the retiree drained the IRA first and only then touched the taxable accounts, the money would run out in 20 years. In contrast, the nest egg would last 25 years if the taxable account was emptied first, before the IRA. The best option, however, was to convert the traditional IRA into a Roth IRA. That move would keep the nest egg going for more than 26 years.

Example   If years ago you bought 2,000 shares of a stock at $2 each, and each share now goes for $150, your profit is $296,000. If you sell now, the long-term capital gain bill is $59,200. But if your heirs receive the stock instead, the cost basis is reset at $300,000.

Finally, if you do sell investments with significant capital gain, try to limit the tax pain. You can do this by offsetting the profits with losses from other investments. You learn more about this in Chapter 16.

Step No. 3: Tap into retirement accounts funded by after-tax contributions.

Need more money? Be just as selective when cracking open your retirement accounts. Your best bet could be drawing cash from accounts whose tax hit won't be so high. One logical place to start is with a nondeductible IRA (see Chapter 10 for definitions of IRA types). This type of IRA is a good bet because a percentage of your withdrawals avoid taxes. Because you can't deduct your contributions to this type of IRA from your income tax return, you won't be expected to pay taxes on the original contributions when you start your withdrawals. (This approach works only if all your IRAs are nondeductible ones.)

Example   Suppose that you funneled a total of $30,000 into a nondeductible IRA over a 15-year period, and the account eventually grew to $200,000. You wouldn't owe taxes on the $30,000, but you'd be liable for the earnings, which in this case are $170,000.

Step No. 4: Access the rest of your retirement accounts.

Retirement accounts that don't contain any after-tax money, such as 401(k)s and deductible IRAs, should be left until the end. That's because every dollar you pull out will be hit with a tax because you didn't pay the tax at the time of deposit into the account.

Step No. 5: Tap into your Roth IRA.

If you've concluded that you won't need all the money sitting in your retirement accounts, don't touch any money that you might have in a Roth IRA. Unlike all other IRAs, the Roth owner never has to withdraw money from the account. Everyone else must begin mandatory IRA withdrawals after age 70½.

In addition, Roth withdrawals for retirees are tax-free if the money has been in the Roth for at least five years. If you do need to tap into your Roth IRA, don't withdraw all the money at once. Instead, take out only what you need — once the money leaves the Roth's tax-free oasis and is deposited into a regular bank or brokerage account, you'll pay taxes on any capital gain or income that the money generates in the future.

401(k)s: Saying Goodbye

You won't always be chained to your desk, and neither will your 401(k). When you retire, both of you will walk out the door. When you do, you'll face several options:

✦ Keep your 401(k) at your old employer.

✦ Deposit all the money in an IRA rollover.

✦ Put everything in an IRA rollover except company stock.

✦ Take the money and run.

Which alternative is best for you depends upon many factors. But making the right choice could save you and your heirs a huge pile of money.

Leave the 401(k) behind.

Before deciding to leave your 401(k) where it is, find out how easily the account can be moved in the future. This might be a satisfactory interim move if you aren't sure what you want to do with your account. Later you ideally should transfer the money into an IRA rollover account, which provides unlimited investment options.

Pluses and minuses exist when leaving cash behind in a 401(k). Here's a drawback: After your death, a spouse is the only beneficiary who can roll the money into a tax-protected IRA. If you leave the 401(k) money to your kids, as a practical matter, they won't be able to stretch out the payments through their lifetime. The reason is that corporations don't want to bother with this hassle. By law, companies can limit payouts to beneficiaries for five years. After that, a 401(k) must be disbanded and the tax benefit is lost. (See Chapter 11 for more on this topic.)

One the other hand, if you discover later that you need to prematurely withdraw money out of your retirement account, the 10 percent early withdrawal penalty can sometimes be avoided if the cash remains in a 401(k) rather than a IRA rollover. That's because anybody who is at least 55 when leaving a job can begin drawing down a 401(k) without getting dinged by the 10 percent penalty. The penalty, however, applies if the worker transferred the 401(k) money into an IRA rollover and then began siphoning it out before the age of 59$\frac{1}{2}$.

If you'd rather not disturb your 401(k), learn how flexible the plan will be after you're gone. Ideally, the access to your 401(k) should be the same as you'd enjoy with an IRA rollover.

Note   Staying put may not be possible if you have $5,000 or less in your 401(k) account. Employers are entitled to close out these modest accounts when workers leave.

Establish an IRA rollover.

If you crave the freedom to invest your 401(k) proceeds any way you like, establishing an IRA rollover is the best option. You can establish an IRA rollover account at just about any financial institution.

When you transfer money into a rollover account, it is classified as a traditional IRA. That means that the money is shielded from taxes until you begin withdrawing the money. At that point, the taxes are based upon your income tax bracket.

Tip   In a rollover account, your money grows much faster than it would if you had cashed out the 401(k), paid the taxes, and put what was left in a taxable account.

If you roll over your 401(k), proceed carefully. In one of its greedier moments, Congress intentionally made the rollover rules complicated in hopes of generating extra cash for the federal Treasury. Make sure that your employer transfers the money directly into your IRA rollover account.

Caution   Do not have the check or stock certificates sent to your home. If you do receive the money directly, 20 percent of your pretax contributions and earnings will be withheld, even if you immediately send your 401(k) proceeds to an IRA custodian.

You will get the money returned if you deposit an identical sum from your own pocket into an IRA or qualified retirement account within 60 days, but you won't receive a refund until after filing your next federal income tax return.

Put everything but the company stock in an IRA rollover.

Although stashing your 401(k) in an IRA rollover is almost always the best move, sometimes it's better not to roll over any company stock. You might want to consider this strategy if you're at least 55, the age at which taxpayers can avoid the 10 percent early withdrawal penalty on 401(k) savings.

If you place the stock in a rollover, no taxes are owed immediately, but when you begin pulling out this money, the cash will be taxed at your ordinary income tax rate. The tax bite can be less onerous if you segregate the stock in a taxable account. If you do this, you'll owe upfront taxes only on the cost basis. The *cost basis* represents what you paid for the company stock during your years in the 401(k) plan. At this point, you won't pay any taxes on the appreciation. Suppose that you paid an average of $30 a share for your company stock over the years, and now it's worth $400 a share. You won't owe taxes on that $370-a-share profit until you unload the stock. When you begin selling it, you'll pay tax on this appreciation, but here's where keeping the stock out of the IRA will pay off: You will owe only long-term capital gain taxes on the windfall, which are no more than 20 percent. And that rate is scheduled to decrease further in the future.

Cash out your 401(k).

Many people love this idea, but they do it at the wrong time. According to one survey, 57 percent of workers cash in their 401(k) chips when they leave their company for another job. They might buy a car, remodel a kitchen, pay tuition, or spend the money in ways that they won't even remember by retirement time. If you follow the herd, you will not have the money when you really need it. And by then, there will be no more salary increases and job promotions to bail you out.

Even more daunting is that the IRS is lying in wait for people who cash out their 401(k)s too early. If you're under the age of 55 when you cash out your 401(k), you'll likely be assessed a 10 percent penalty. And the tax pain might not end there. Cashing in a large 401(k) account could catapult you into a higher tax bracket. State income tax can also nibble away at your windfall. Many people have no idea that the tax pain can be so great.

Example

Say that you're lucky enough to retire at 50 years old with a 401(k) worth $75,000, and you're in the 31 percent tax bracket. Because you are not old enough to avoid the early withdrawal penalty, the IRS will demand 31 percent of that money up front, plus a 10 percent early bird penalty. You also could be liable for state taxes. At a minimum, your tax bill on the $75,000 will be close to $31,000!

Another Lump Sum Option

If you meet the IRS's strict age requirement, there is a way you can cash in a lump-sum distribution and shield it from the full brunt of income taxes. However, you must have been born before 1936 to qualify. The method is called 10-year forward averaging. As you just read, the IRS punishes retirees who cash in the lump sum that they receive through a 401(k) or other workplace retirement plan. But with 10-year forward averaging, the tax bill is lower because it's calculated as if someone had withdrawn the money over an entire decade. (You actually withdraw all the money, and the income taxes are then owed.) This method might be appropriate for someone who will need this money shortly after retirement.

To receive the favorable tax treatment, you must devote the entire balance of your workplace retirement plan to the 10-year averaging strategy. You can't, for instance, stash half of a lump sum in a rollover IRA. If you're interested, consult an accountant, a financial planner, or another expert advisor who is well versed on the strategy.

Cracking the IRA Nest Egg

In general, it makes no difference to the IRS how you tap into your IRA: The agency doesn't care whether you pull out one yearly lump sum or take a steady amount out each month. Nor does it matter if you own more than one IRA, whether you withdraw cash from just one IRA or tap a little bit out of each one. The agency also doesn't care if you siphon out more than it requires you to — that amount which is officially referred to as the *required minimum distribution.* When you decide to begin tapping into an IRA, you use a calculation based on the IRS life expectancy tables to determine the minimum that must be withdrawn each year. And the IRA does care deeply about everyone meeting that minimum, particularly those folks who have turned the magic age of 70½. In fact, the IRS cares so deeply that it changed all the rules in 2001 to make sure that everyone plays fair.

Why the new rules?

Until 2001, the IRA distribution rules were incredibly complicated and confusing. Even attorneys, bank officers, financial planners, and other financial experts weren't always clear what these rules entailed or how to follow them. Consequently, many retirees inadvertently made mistakes that unfortunately couldn't be undone. Those who made poor choices after beginning their distributions sometimes inadvertently cost their heirs great sums of money over their lifetimes.

But just as the countdown to 2001's Super Bowl Sunday had begun, the IRS did something startling. It concluded that the laws governing mandatory IRA withdrawals were too cumbersome. Cynics said that the government did something quite rare: It simplified the rules. The changes were indeed dramatic. One of the biggest results of the wholesale changes was this: The vast majority of American retirees are now allowed to take less money out of their IRAs every year. For seniors who are only grudgingly draining their IRAs, this is great news indeed.

Note The IRS's new distribution rules don't just apply to IRAs. The new regulations also cover mandatory retirement withdrawals from qualified workplace retirement plans such as 401(k)s and 403(b)s. Many times, money from these plans are rolled into an IRA when someone leaves a company or retires.

Why the federal change of heart? The changes were in the IRS's self-interest. Under the old system, individuals weren't always sure if they were withdrawing the right amounts from their IRAs, and the financial institutions safeguarding these accounts weren't always clear, either. With so many convoluted rules, it was easy for institutions and their customers to make mistakes. In all the confusion, it was difficult for Uncle Sam to discern without a great deal of effort whether people were being honest.

With the process streamlined, the IRS now can determine this quite easily. One of the new rules requires financial institutions to report the amount of the required distribution to their customers as well as the IRS. This kind of reporting never existed before. Thanks to the reporting, it will be much easier for the agency to collect the right taxes.

Tip The revised distribution rules were immediately made retroactive to January 1, 2001.

Mandatory withdrawals at age 70^1/$_2$

If you live long enough, someday you will crack open your IRA whether you need to or not. The IRS, which has waited patiently for this day, requires that you begin mandatory withdrawals shortly after reaching the age of 70^1/$_2$ (if you haven't tapped into the account already).

The federal bureaucracy didn't make the mandatory disbursement age an easy one to remember. You must begin siphoning money out of your IRA no later than April 1 of the year following the year in which you turn 70^1/$_2$. For example, if you were born on October 1, 1931, you will reach the age of 70^1/$_2$ in 2002, so you must withdraw your first payment out of an IRA by April 2003.

Tip Roth IRA owners can avoid this mandatory withdrawal rule. If they never touch their IRA, that's their prerogative. One of the other charms of a Roth IRA is that owners can make tax-free withdrawals during retirement.

Of course, taxes are the motivation behind the mandatory withdrawal regimen. When money is pulled out of regular IRAs, the owner owes income taxes on it. The withdrawals are taxed at the individual's income tax rate.

When you've made the mandatory yearly withdrawal, the IRS loses interest in what you do with it. You certainly aren't required to spend the money. In fact, if you don't need it, you can stash your yearly withdrawals in a taxable account. Your best bet could be in a tax-efficient investment, such as tax-free municipal bonds or an index mutual fund.

Timing your IRA payouts

In most cases, you should avoid postponing your first required IRA distribution. If you turn 70^1/$_2$ in 2001, you can delay your first withdrawal until April 1, 2002. But if you do that, you'll have to make two withdrawals in 2002 (your 2001 and 2002 distributions). Often the better option is to take the first distribution by December 31, 2001, to help lower your overall income tax liabilities. However, if you expect an usually large income in 2001 (perhaps from a final workplace bonus) and little income the next year, postponing both payments until 2002 could be a wise move.

Determining your minimum distribution

Until 2001, one of the first chores that people faced as they approached their 70^1/$_2$ birthday was deciding which type of life expectancy to use to determine you're the yearly mandatory IRA withdrawals. The first task was determining whether to base your contributions on your own life span combined with your beneficiary's, called a *joint life expectancy,* or based just on your projected life span, called a *single life expectancy.* Making that decision was difficult because general advice available on this topic was usually couched in a lot of *if*s, *and*s, and *but*s.

But your task wasn't yet finished. You then had to choose an IRA distribution method. Three options existed: recalculation, term-certain, and hybrid. Which one you selected depended on your own unique financial situation and who you wanted to designate as beneficiaries of any money left when you died.

Happily, you no longer need to take these agonizing steps. With one major exception, nearly all Americans can use the same simple life expectancy table. Relying upon the new IRS table in this book (found in Table 21-1), you should be able to figure out how much to withdraw with little effort.

An exception to the rule

One exception to the use of this standard table exists: A retiree with a spouse who is more than 10 years younger and who is the only IRA beneficiary must use the traditional joint life expectancy table, which is published by the IRS. Using this table makes the required minimum IRA payouts even smaller. If this is your situation, you might want to ask a certified public accountant, an estate attorney, a financial planner, or some other experts knowledgeable in the new IRA regulations to help you calculate the withdrawals.

Using the new rule now

Because 2001 is a transition year, a retiree who has already been tapping into an IRA, or somebody who is required to do so in this year, has a choice. These folks can use the old calculations to figure out the distributions (not recommended!) or the new way. There seems little point in choosing the former because everyone will switch to the new method in 2002.

The IRS is allowing the financial institutions that hold IRAs, as well as workplaces that oversee retirement account distributions, to wait until 2002 to begin calculating the withdrawals based on the new regulations. Beginning in 2002, these entities will be required to determine what a customer or former employee's minimum distributions should be.

Note If you don't want to wait until 2002 for your financial institution to provide your updated figures, you'll have to make the new calculations yourself.

The new formula for required distributions

When they reach the magic age for mandatory retirement account withdrawals, most people use the IRS table found in Table 21-1 to calculate the minimum withdrawal. It's a simple formula: Each year, find your life expectancy figure in the chart, and divide the value of your IRA(s) by that number.

Here's an example: Suppose that a retired editor who just observed her 70$^1/_2$ birthday has a total of $100,000 in her combined IRAs at the end of the calendar year.

She is scheduled to take out her first withdrawal by the time she reaches age 71. To find the right amount, she simply divides $100,000 by 25.3. Consequently, her minimum withdrawal is $3,952 ($100,000 divided by 25.3). Suppose that the next year her IRAs grow nicely and, despite last year's withdrawal, are now worth a total of $105,000. The next year's calculation will reflect the IRA's worth on the last day of each calendar year. This time she'll divide by the factor used by 72-year-olds. As a result, her required withdrawal is $4,303 ($105,000 divided by 24.4). As you can see in Table 21-1, the chart continues through to the ripe old age of 115.

	Table 21-1		
	IRS Life Expectancy Chart		
Age	**Life Expectancy (In Years)**	**Age**	**Life Expectancy (In Years)**
70	26.2	93	8.8
71	25.3	94	8.3
72	24.4	95	7.8
73	23.5	96	7.3
74	22.7	97	6.9
75	21.8	98	6.5
76	20.9	99	6.1
77	20.1	100	5.7
78	19.2	101	5.3
79	18.4	102	5
80	17.6	103	4.7
81	16.8	104	4.4
82	16	105	4.1
83	15.3	106	3.8
84	14.5	107	3.6
85	13.8	108	3.3
86	13.1	109	3.1
87	12.4	110	2.8
88	11.8	111	2.6
89	11.1	112	2.4
90	10.5	113	2.2
91	10.5	114	2
92	9.4	115 and older	1.8

Source: Internal Revenue Service

Making those mandatory withdrawals

You can postpone the inevitable for only so long. If you're now faced with mandatory yearly IRA withdrawals, you might be wondering when you should pull out the money. The answer is simple: any time you want, as long as it happens at least once a year. Many people leave their money alone until crunch time at the end of each calendar year. By doing that, you can let an account grow in its tax-deferred cocoon as long as possible. Of course, if you want to empty the IRA faster than is required by law, you're certainly free to do so.

The logistics of draining IRAs can be more challenging. We live in a nation of multiple IRAs. You might have an IRA parked at a mutual fund in Boston, a discount broker in San Francisco, and another one at the savings and loan four blocks away. Does Uncle Sam really expect you to disturb each one every year? Luckily, the tax agency isn't that sadistic. If you have more than one IRA, you can simplify your yearly ritual by tapping into just one. The same holds true for your 403(b) accounts.

Tip　　You might want to withdraw from the IRA that is generating the lowest returns.

Unfortunately, this easy rule doesn't apply to all workplace plans, including 401(k)s and Keoghs. You can't add up all the money incubating in your IRAs and your 401(k), calculate your withdrawal amount, and then take it out of an IRA. You must make withdrawal calculations for your 401(k) separately. If you have more than one 401(k), you'll have to make withdrawals from each of them.

The IRS will be unforgiving if you fail to take out the minimum required amount of money from your IRA by the yearly deadlines. You will have to pay a 50 percent penalty and income taxes on the difference between what you withdrew, if anything, and what you should have taken.

IRA Early Birds

With more people opting for early retirement, interest in cracking open IRAs at younger ages is growing in popularity. What stops some from pulling out IRA money prematurely is the 10 percent early withdrawal penalty. Unless someone is 59^1/$_2$, the penalty is usually unavoidable. One way to jump this hurdle, however, is to annuitize your IRA. These early withdrawals are sometimes called 72(t)s after the appropriate section in the Internal Revenue Code.

You can be any age to annuitize your IRA. When you decide to proceed, you must take a "series of substantially equal periodic payments" from your IRA. The payments must continue for at least five years or until you're 59^1/$_2$ years old. Don't expect the IRS to give you a break if you change your mind. The payments can't be stopped or modified. However, you may annuitize one IRA and leave any others that you have alone. If you're intrigued by this approach, be sure to contact a tax expert.

When you begin draining IRA money through a 72(t), the IRS requires you to keep withdrawing a certain amount of cash for the required time period, even if you return to work, inherit a windfall, or become haunted by second thoughts. A 72(t) can't help you dodge income taxes. No matter what your age is, you'll owe income taxes on whatever you extract from an IRA, other than nondeductible contributions. The only exception, of course, is the Roth IRA, which, if all the conditions are met, permits tax-free withdrawals.

If you've never heard of a 72(t), it's not surprising. If you type "72(t)" into an Internet search engine, you'll discover far more entries for an armored tank that the Soviets previously manufactured in Siberia. But the financial community, always eager to create new business opportunities, is coming up to speed fast on this clever maneuver. Experts capable of droning on about all aspects of 72(t) minutia are now favorite speakers at industry conferences, and news of the 72(t) is trickling down to receptive clients.

Selecting beneficiaries

The new IRS regulations also made dramatic changes to the importance of beneficiaries in someone's distribution calculations. In the past, you needed to designate who your future beneficiaries were by the time you reached that $70^1/_2$ milestone. The identity of those people, as well as their ages, was necessary to calculate the yearly withdrawals. Now, with rare exception, your beneficiary's identity and age don't affect your yearly payouts.

You can choose any lucky person to inherit your IRA — it can be your wife, husband, relatives, friends, or anybody else you care about. A charitable organization, whether it's the American Heart Association, your church, or an organization that protects sea urchins, can also be the recipient.

Tip   Be sure to also name backup beneficiaries. You'll be glad you did if your first choice dies before you do.

You're also allowed to name multiple beneficiaries for the same IRA. If you'd like to mix and match beneficiaries, proceed carefully. Just as you wouldn't want to serve French toast at a Fourth of July barbecue or hot dogs at Thanksgiving, in the world of IRAs, some combinations are unpalatable. For instance, if you want to leave a portion of an IRA to the American Cancer Society, you shouldn't name a person as a co-beneficiary. That's because a charity doesn't have a life expectancy. Pairing a charity with a real, live beneficiary can cause complications. (See Chapter 11 for advice on how to rectify this mistake.)

What if you change your mind about beneficiaries? Thanks to the revised regulations, it's no big deal. You can change beneficiaries as often as you change the oil in your car.

Pension Possibilities

Cashing in on a pension might seem like a no-brainer. After retirement, pension checks begin automatically arriving in the mailbox. What could be easier? Well, like so much in retirement, cashing in a pension is not that simple.

For starters, your company might throw you off balance by giving you two choices: a lifetime supply of checks or a lump sum. When presented with these two possibilities, workers often grab the windfall. The money is just too tantalizing to ignore. But you need to explore your options before deciding which alternative is best for you.

If your company doesn't offer a lump sum option, you might have little to agonize about. If you're married, however, you'll encounter more choices. This section covers what you need to know about all your possible pension options.

Receiving regular pension checks

If you're single when you retire, you will begin receiving what's called a single-life pension or single-life annuity. When you die, the pension dies, too.

Married workers face an extra option. A husband or wife can also choose the same single-life pension. Again, when the retiree dies, the pension vanishes. If you want your pension to continue after your death, you'll want the joint-and-survivor alternative. This pension lasts for two lives: yours and your spouse's. However, when the worker dies, the pension check is typically cut in half for the widow or widower. In other words, if a husband was receiving a $1,000 check each month, his widow may pocket only $500 a month.

You might be wondering why a husband or wife would opt for a single-life pension. That's simple: The monthly pension check is fatter. The payments are more generous because they last for only one life rather than two. It wasn't that long ago that men, the ones most likely to have a pension, routinely deprived their wives of survivor benefits, throwing so many widows into poverty that Congress finally stepped in. Today, a pension for a married worker automatically includes benefits for both a husband and a wife, and it can be changed only if the worker's spouse signs away his or her rights.

Note It's rare that a couple would want to pass up the opportunity for a his-and-her pension. Generally a single-life option is preferable only if the spouse is independently wealthy, is much older, or is gravely ill and not expected to live long.

Beware pension maximization insurance

If you discuss your retirement plans with a stockbroker or an insurance agent, you might be encouraged to take the single-life pension (even when it doesn't appear to make sense) in favor of something called pension maximization insurance. In the vast majority of cases, this life insurance strategy is a bad idea.

Here's the pitch: With pension maximization insurance, you can enjoy the biggest pension benefit possible without jeopardizing your spouse's final years. In theory, you pull this off by purchasing life insurance for yourself. If you die first, your pension disappears, but the surviving spouse won't be condemned to poverty because he or she will receive the life insurance windfall. The life insurance coverage that's necessary to pull this off is based upon the amount of money needed to replace the lost pension checks. This scenario uses the assumption that the insurance premiums will be smaller than the extra cash that you'd pocket with the biggest pension benefit. In many cases, this assumption is incorrect. For one thing, the pensioner might not be healthy enough to buy a policy at a standard or preferred rate.

 Caution A pension maximization insurance policyholder might not be able to continue paying the premiums throughout retirement. Some couples have been forced to cancel their policies, with tragic results: The pension disappears if the breadwinner dies first.

Marriage woes can also jeopardize the finances of a spouse, depending on pension maximization insurance. If the marriage starts to crumble, a policyholder might secretly cancel the insurance or designate a different beneficiary. Or, the policy might not be renewed due to carelessness. Here's yet another danger: If the spouse isn't a co-beneficiary of the pension plan, he or she might be dropped from company health coverage. Finally, if the worker dies and the survivor receives a lump sum from the insurance company, he or she might not know how to properly manage it. It can be tricky turning a large pot of money into a lifetime stream of income.

Taking a pension lump sum

When you retire, should you take a lump sum instead of a pension? A lot of people don't give this issue much thought. They are hypnotized by the dollar signs and want that money now rather than watching it trickle in through monthly checks.

 Tip Some people are better off resisting the lump sum in favor of a regular pension payout.

Reasons to take the lump sum

In some circumstances, taking the money in a lump sum may be a good idea:

✦ **You're an investing whiz, or you hire someone who is.** Some people assume that they can invest a lump sum so intelligently that its value will exceed that of a lifetime of pension checks. Maybe some people can pull off this feat, but many cannot. If you can't manage your windfall, you can always hire a professional. Choosing a top-notch money manager is not always an easy task, though. See Chapters 4 and 5 for more information on selecting a financial advisor.

✦ **Your health is poor.** If you're single and in poor health when you retire, your heirs will lose out if you opt for a series of pension checks. If you die a few months into retirement, your pension benefit disappears. If you chose the lump sum and die early in retirement, you will pass a tidy amount on to your heirs.

Reasons to go with regular checks

Consider these compelling reasons to pick the stream of checks instead.

You're tempted to blow it.

If you take the cash, you should safeguard it in a rollover Individual Retirement Account. By taking this step, you allow the money to continue to grow tax-deferred. The worst thing that you can do is begin to spend the money. Any cash that you don't put into an IRA is taxed at your income tax rate. If your state has an income tax, you'll owe the state as well. What's more, if you haven't reached the age of 59$^1/_2$, you will probably be hit with a 10 percent early withdrawal penalty.

You're entitled to a subsidized pension.

Suppose that at age 55 you are offered an early retirement package that provides you with the same pension that you'd get if you slaved away at your cubicle for another 10 years. This pension is called a *subsidized pension.* The Pension Rights Center suggests that it's not uncommon for an early retiree to lose 35 percent to 40 percent of the pension benefit when taking the lump sum in this circumstance rather than a stream of sweetened pension checks.

Note Concerned that employees might be ignorant of what they could be losing when choosing the lump sum, the U.S. Treasury Department launched an investigation to determine whether corporations are properly notifying their departing employees of the true ramifications of their pension choices.

Why the loss? A company is supposed to equalize a cash buyout and a lifetime pension in calculating a lump sum payment. This equalization, according to the Pension Rights Center, isn't necessary with a subsidized pension benefit. When determining the lump sum, the company wouldn't have to plug those 10 phantom years of service into the equation. So, your lump sum could be based upon your service up to age 55, not to age 65.

If you're married, your spouse could suffer with an early buyout lump sum as well. With the typical pension (which is set up on a joint-and-survivor basis), the monthly benefit is cut in half for your spouse if you die. But with a subsidized pension, your spouse could be entitled to a benefit of 70 percent or so if you die first. However, this pension's extra value won't necessarily be calculated into the lump sum formula.

Cross-Reference You should not rush into a decision about whether to opt for monthly pension checks or a lump sum. If you're about to retire, you should definitely not make this decision alone. Your best bet is to hire an actuary, a CPA, or a Certified Financial Planner who can crunch the numbers for you.

Summary

✦ Withdraw your nest egg tax efficiently.

✦ Don't take a pension lump sum without consulting an expert.

✦ Consider withdrawing 401(k) stock when you leave a company.

✦ Review your IRA distribution choices carefully.

✦   ✦   ✦

The Role of Annuities in Retirement

This chapter covers both the good and bad annuities. Because these products are much more complicated than a mutual fund, knowing how they tick could save you a bundle of money. If you decide an annuity is appropriate for your circumstances, keep reading for the shopping tips.

Beware: Annuity Salespeople Ahead

If you own an annuity, you've probably crossed paths at some point with a stockbroker, an insurance agent, or a financial advisor who lives off commissions. Annuities, which are an insurance product, are complicated, and people usually don't purchase them unless they run up against a hard sell.

Doubtful products peddled

Annuity promoters love to boast about the virtues of using annuities as a smart way to save for retirement. Yet there are often cheaper and easier ways to take advantage of the benefits that annuity salesmen tout. While there are excellent annuities on the market, many annuities are too expensive, too complex, and too hard to get out of. If you ultimately decide that your annuity was a dreadful idea, the penalty for bailing is often so stiff that many disillusioned customers just sit tight.

As if this situation isn't bad enough, some sales practices are so borderline sleazy that the U.S. Securities and Exchange Commission and the National Association of Securities Dealers, which regulates the industry, have expressed great concerns. Meanwhile, trial lawyers have filed class-action suits, alleging deceptive sales practices, against several insurers who peddle variable annuities inside retirement plans.

Worthy products obscured

Despite the controversy swirling around the product, there are two types of annuities that stand out above the crowd. One is the immediate annuity. Ironically, you'll rarely hear insurance agents recommending this solid product. Frankly, some agents don't suggest them because they earn fatter commissions on variable annuities, which are, by far, the industry's hottest product and biggest cash cow.

What's so special about the immediate annuity? As you discovered in Chapter 21, Rube Goldberg couldn't have made the task of turning a nest egg into a dependable stream of retirement income any more complicated. Even the experts bicker about what the right investment approaches are. An immediate annuity can address this challenge by reducing your risk of running short of money. When you buy an immediate annuity, an insurance company, not you, is on the hot seat to invest your money wisely. The insurer, being quite confident that it's up to the task, promises its customers a lifetime of monthly checks. Even if you live past your 100th birthday, those checks will keep on coming. This chapter tells you what to look for in an immediate annuity and how to buy one if it's right for your situation.

Another annuity that's largely ignored but also worth a look is the lowly fixed annuity. As you'll learn, fans of certificates of deposit and Treasuries could find a lot to like about a fixed annuity.

Annuity Types

What separates annuities from other types of investments is insurance. Annuities are created by insurance companies, which can extend certain promises about the security of your investments. For instance, if you are contributing to an annuity and abruptly die, the insurance company will make sure your heirs, at the very minimum, receive your initial investment. They will pay up even if your investment has plunged in value. A similar reassurance is made to retirees who are receiving monthly income from an annuity. The insurance company promises the payments will continue as long as you live and sometimes even longer, even if the money you originally invested in the annuity runs out.

While you're still saving for retirement, you can invest in an annuity in one lump sum or contribute periodically or regularly, just as you would with mutual funds. You can get started with very little cash; the minimums are often similar to mutual funds. Until you begin taking money out, money in annuities grows tax deferred.

Before you can appreciate the strengths and limitations of annuities, you need to understand the various types on the market.

Deferred annuity

The vast majority of annuities sold every year in this country are deferred annuities, a product usually tailored for investors who still have many years before they retire. You can invest either a lump sum or add regularly to a deferred annuity over a lengthy period. The interest generated grows tax-deferred.

Some people who have already maxed out their contributions to an Individual Retirement Account, a 401(k), or other workplace plan gravitate to this type of annuity because of the tax protection. Like a 401(k) or traditional IRA, the tax reprieve evaporates when the cash is eventually withdrawn. At that time, income taxes are due. If you're under the age of 59^1/$_2$ when you tap into your annuity, you'll probably be subject to a 10 percent early withdrawal penalty. Unlike a workplace retirement plan or an IRA, you can shovel as much money as you want into a tax-deferred annuity.

Immediate annuity

With an immediate annuity, you deposit your cash into the investment, and your monthly payments can start immediately. Part of the money you receive each month is tax-free because it represents a return of a portion of your premium. An immediate annuity relieves you of the burden of investing a chunk of your retirement savings on your own. The insurance company assumes this responsibility and promises to send you monthly checks for life. The insurance company makes a bet that you won't live long enough to pull out more than what you originally deposited. Of course, you're hoping that you beat the actuarial odds.

Tip   An immediate annuity can be ideal for someone who is retiring with a 401(k) plan, but is uncertain how to invest it.

An immediate annuity, with its dependable income stream, can be a godsend for retirees without a pension or whose investing skills are shaky. If your only steady monthly check is coming from Social Security, you may want to consider investing some of your assets into an immediate annuity.

Immediate annuities are also appropriate for retirees who need monthly income and otherwise would be drawing cash out of money markets and certificates of deposit. That's because the income from the latter two investments is fully taxable. In contrast, the income in those monthly annuity checks is partially protected from taxes.

Age, gender, and payment options influence how big your monthly check from an immediate annuity will be. Women, for instance, receive smaller checks than men of the same age because they're expected to live longer.

Two more annuity choices

You can choose either a conservative or a more aggressive way to invest your cash within your annuity of choice. Both immediate and deferred annuities come in two investment flavors: fixed and variable.

Fixed annuity

The fixed annuity is marketed to the sort of people who get white knuckles when the stock market is bouncing like a ping pong ball, such as retirees who need a steady income. When you opt for a fixed annuity, you're guaranteed a set rate of return for your investment. The rate of return can never slip below the guaranteed floor set at the time of purchase. Although the rate floor never moves, the actual rate may change as often as every month and these changes do effect how much money builds up in the account. Whether the rate creeps up or down depends upon such factors as the interest rate climate and the performance of a company's typically conservative investment portfolio of government and corporate bonds.

Some people feel safe with the guaranteed rate, but this rate doesn't provide assurance that a fixed annuity will keep up with inflation. Yet a fixed annuity may be suitable for someone who willingly surrenders the potential for higher returns that stocks can provide in exchange for a sure thing.

Tip A fixed annuity can be quite attractive for retirees who are investing a portion of their nest eggs in certificates of deposit or Treasuries.

Fixed annuity rates can be significantly higher than CDs or Treasuries. What's more, the fixed annuity grows tax-deferred. In contrast, an investor must pay yearly income taxes on the interest that a CD generates. Treasury investors must pay federal, but not state, taxes. The tax on a fixed annuity is due only when the money is withdrawn. If you have a CD that's about to mature, you should check out competing fixed annuity rates.

Variable annuity

The variable annuity is a popular choice for persons who are still saving for retirement. This annuity shares a lot in common with a mutual fund, but an annuity offers an insured guarantee against losing even a fraction of your original investment. No regular mutual funds can make such a promise. As the name suggests, the returns on variable annuities fluctuate because there's usually a heavy reliance upon stock funds. Consequently, the value of your investment hinges upon how well the underlying funds are performing. Variable annuities are vastly more popular with Americans than the fixed ones. This situation wasn't the case just a decade ago; when interest rates were higher, the fixed annuity looked more appealing.

Annuity Hanky Panky

If a stockbroker or insurance agent urges you to buy a deferred annuity for your Individual Retirement Account or a workplace retirement plan, run as fast as you can. Chances are this guy is looking out only for himself. Placing an annuity within a retirement account is like using an umbrella inside a house. The double coverage is unnecessary. An IRA or qualified retirement plan allows money to grow without any taxation until the money is withdrawn, as does a deferred annuity. Therefore, putting an annuity into an IRA is pointless. Doing so only forces you to pay higher fees for a feature that an IRA or 401(k) automatically offers for free.

Sadly, this redundancy is incredibly widespread. In one recent year, an estimated 55 percent of variable annuity sales were earmarked for retirement plans. The controversial practice is deservedly under fire. Class-action suits are targeting big annuity players who market annuities for IRAs. Meanwhile, the National Association of Securities Dealers warned its member firms that brokers must divulge to potential customers that the annuity's tax-deferral benefit is unnecessary in retirement accounts.

A variable annuity can be appropriate way to save in a taxable account, but only if you have already contributed the maximum amount to an Individual Retirement Account and your 401(k) or other workplace retirement plan.

Saving for Retirement with Deferred Annuities

As you've learned, you can use annuities in two ways: You can stockpile cash for a retirement nest egg with a deferred annuity or buy an immediate annuity for those guaranteed monthly checks when you're in retirement. This section addresses the advantages and disadvantages of saving for retirement with annuities.

Advantages of deferred annuities

Note that two of the three advantages listed here also made it onto the list of disadvantages, which is why folks need to be cautious before going whole hog with deferred annuities.

Diversification

The overwhelming number of people who rely upon annuities to save for retirement use variable annuities. With a variable annuity, you'll choose which *subaccounts,* which is industry jargon for mutual funds, your money ends up in. An annuity may offer subaccounts that are managed by such well-known fund companies as Janus, Fidelity, T. Rowe Price and Putnam. Within a variable annuity, you should be able to invest in large- and small-cap funds, as well as bond funds and a cash account. Ideally, there are enough fund choices to allow you to properly diversify. If you want to fine-tune your portfolio and shift money out of a bond fund and, say, into a foreign fund, that's fine. You don't have to fret about taxes because you're shuffling money within an annuity.

Note   With a fixed annuity, diversification is not an issue. The insurer selects the investments. You, in turn, are promised a certain rate of return.

Guaranteed death benefit

Deferred variable annuities come wrapped with a death benefit. Actually, you wouldn't be around to claim it, but your heirs would be. The insurer guarantees the value of your annuity even if it dips below your original investment. Suppose someone sunk $40,000 into a variable annuity at the height of a bull market and died two years later when stocks had tanked. The value of the annuity is now $33,000. The heirs aren't penalized for their loved one's ill-timed death, though. The insurance company pays out $40,000.

This same safety net is also available for an investor who deposits money into an annuity sporadically. The total of all the contributions is added to determine the death benefit. In an effort to make annuities more attractive, some insurers offer fancier death benefits that guarantee a minimum return or lock in investment gains after certain periods of time.

Fixed Annuity Detective Work

When you're hunting for a fixed annuity, pay close attention to an insurance company's financial strength. You certainly don't want to risk losing your money if an insurer goes under. Various rating services evaluate whether an individual insurer should be able to meet its obligations. Sticking with the highest-rated companies is important because no FDIC protection exists for insurance customers. Quite a few insurers were taken over by government regulators in the 1990s, so you shouldn't be complacent.

Limit your search to insurers with the highest credit ratings. You should be able to find credit rating information at a good library reference department. Or you can find this information by calling or visiting the Web sites of these credit rating services:

✦ A.M. Best at (908) 439-2200 or www.ambest.com

✦ Standard & Poor's at (212) 438-2400 or www.standardandpoors.com/ratings

✦ Moody's Investors Services at (212) 553-0377 or www.moodys.com

✦ Weiss Ratings at (800) 289-9222 or www.weissratings.com

An insurance company's financial health isn't as critical for variable annuity customers because their money is protected in separate funds—not in an insurance company's general accounts. If an insurer experiences financial difficulties, it shouldn't endanger variable annuity holdings.

The more generous the death benefit is, the higher the annuity fees probably are.

Tax break

Deferred annuities offer a tax break that regular mutual funds can't match. As long as your money stays inside one, it's immune to taxes. The IRS won't expect you to pay taxes on an annuity's capital gains, dividends, or interest until you pull out the money from the annuity. In this way, investing in a deferred annuity is like investing in an Individual Retirement Account or a 401(k). Unlike those popular retirement plans, however, an annuity doesn't have a contribution ceiling. Some financial experts suggest that people should consider deferred annuities an option after they've already made the maximum yearly contributions to an IRA and a 401(k) or other workplace retirement plan.

Disadvantages of deferred annuities

Read this long list of disadvantages carefully before you decide to invest in deferred annuities.

Annuities are expensive.

Deferred variable annuities are so complicated that many people sign the paperwork without even knowing how much they're paying. Some insurance companies count on this confusion, which is why the overall annuity market hasn't worried about making its products price competitive. Many insurers load up these products with bells and whistles that only jack up the prices even further.

Variable products

The annual expenses that variable annuities charge are significantly higher than the average mutual fund. What's more, most annuities penalize you if you decide to cash in your investment early; surrender charges can climb as high as 9 percent. Often the surrender charge declines each year you remain loyal, but the surrender charge, in extreme cases, can linger for 16 years or more thanks to "rolling penalties" that are prolonged if an investor continues making contributions. In other words, each contribution creates its own surrender schedule. In addition to the surrender charge, you are also charged for the life insurance coverage, which is referred to as the mortality and expense risk charge. Insurers also throw in administrative fees.

When it comes to pricing, however, not all annuity providers wear black hats. Some financial institutions offer significantly reduced prices. TIAA-CREF, which has been managing retirement money for college professors and other teachers for decades, has earned the distinction of offering the least expensive annuities in the nation (see Chapter 9).

Annuities and the Roman Empire

Ancient Romans paused long enough during their war-mongering to invent annuities. After depositing money upfront, a customer received a stream of payments that would sometimes last a lifetime. The Romans called these contracts *annua*. Annuities in the Middle Ages had a lottery-style spin. Customers received regular payouts after putting their money in a pool, but as they began dying, those left behind in the pool saw their payments increase. The biggest winner was the final survivor, who pocketed whatever money was left. It didn't take long for annuities to arrive in the New World. Before the Revolutionary War, an annuity program was established for widows of Pennsylvania ministers.

Tip   Consider patronizing these low-cost leaders, who are typically no-load mutual fund firms and discount brokers.

Most individuals fail to buy variable annuities from the cheapest sources because companies such as TIAA-CREF, Vanguard, and T. Rowe Price, don't employ armies of insurance agents or use full-service brokers to drum up sales. These firms sell variable annuities directly to the public, which is a major reason why they can keep prices low. You'll see a list of some of these companies with phone numbers and Web site addresses later in the chapter.

When shopping for a variable annuity, always ask about the following fees. And don't just take an agent's word for it; look them up yourself in the annuity's prospectus:

- ✦ Surrender charge
- ✦ Mortality and expense risk charge
- ✦ Administrative fees
- ✦ Underlying fund or subaccount expenses
- ✦ Fees and charges for special features, such as improved death benefits or a guaranteed minimum income benefit

Fixed products

Fees for fixed annuities aren't as hazardous to consumers because the quoted interest rate that you receive for a fixed annuity already takes fees into account. So if a fixed annuity is currently offering 7 percent, that's the rate you can expect after the fees are deducted. You still need to ask what a fixed deferred annuity's surrender charge is, though. Typically, this charge is lower than what a variable annuity imposes. That's because the surrender charge is tied to the original date of issue versus the variable annuity's rolling penalties.

Advertising can be misleading.

Would you like an annuity that kicks in free money? Who wouldn't? The offer is proving irresistible to many, but the SEC is warning investors to beware. Variable annuities packaged with a bonus credit, which is one of the latest creations from the insurance industry, only appear to offer something for nothing. These annuities promise an investor a bonus credit on each annuity purchase. If you buy a $10,000 annuity, for instance, the insurer will add anywhere from 1 to 5 percent of the purchase price into your account. With a 5 percent bonus, the account's value would instantly increase by $500. Sounds fabulous, right?

But if you spend anytime reading the annuity's prospectus, you'll uncover the mystery of the free greenbacks. The insurer can afford to offer buyers what appears to be a generous bonus by stuffing the annuity with higher fees. Because these stiffer fees erode the annuity's return over time, you would probably be better off with an annuity offering no bonus at all.

Fixed annuities can also stoop to smoke and mirrors. Like carneys at a carnival, insurers try to lure in customers with higher introductory interest rates. Trouble is, that rate could ultimately be replaced with one that's punier than what you would get with a plain vanilla annuity.

Tip Read the fine print carefully to see whether the insurer will make up in fees the bonus you get up front.

The tax break doesn't last forever.

Annuity peddlers love to brag about their product's tax break: Do you hate to pay taxes? Do you want to avoid them as long as possible? Who wouldn't perk up once they understood how an annuity can keep the IRS away? But sadly, customers usually hear only half of the story. The tax break doesn't last. But the reality is worse than that. The eventual tax could be even more than what you'd expect if you put your money into regular mutual funds or individual stocks.

Although taxes are deferred as long as the money remains in the annuity, the tax is stiff once the money is withdrawn because the cash that's pulled out is taxed at your income tax rate. In contrast, if you had invested in traditional mutual funds or stocks in a taxable account, the tax pain wouldn't have been so excruciating. If you hold a mutual fund for more than one year, the maximum long-term capital gains tax is 20 percent. That rate applies even if you are a millionaire in the top tax bracket. The capital gains rate slips to a mere 10 percent if you're in the lowest 15 percent tax bracket.

Example If you're in the highest bracket (39.6 percent), you'll pay close to $40 for every $100 withdrawal from a variable annuity. For somebody in the 28 percent tax bracket, the IRS would collect $28 for every $100 siphoned out of the annuity account.

The death benefit is a psychological crutch.

One of the insurance industry's dirty little secrets is that the annuity death benefit is almost always pointless. Heirs rarely ever need it. By the time a long-term investor dies, an annuity account usually has risen in value. A 2000 study conducted by researchers at York University in Canada and Goldman Sachs suggests that the steep annual price that consumers are paying for the death benefit is completely out of whack with what it's worth. The typical charge is 1.25 percent, which would work out to an annual $312.50 expense for a $25,000 annuity. Using the study's conclusions, a fair death benefit charge for a woman owning a $25,000 annuity should be only $5; a man's charge should be $8.75.

 If you want to see this study, visit one of the researcher's Web site at www.yorku.ca/milevsky.

You have to be extremely patient.

Think about the mutual funds or individual stocks and bonds you now own. Have you held any of them for at least 15 years? If not, you probably won't have the endurance to invest in a deferred variable annuity.

Morningstar's annuity expert estimates that you'd need to remain loyal to a variable annuity for 10 to 15 years before the investment makes sense. Some studies suggest the holding period needs to be even higher. Why are such long holding periods necessary? Blame it on the high fees and the taxes you'll pay when you withdraw the money. Only an extended holding period allows the money to grow tax-deferred long enough to overcome this double whammy. Of course, the buy-and-hold scenario works only if you're happy with your investment.

You need to be patient with a variable annuity for another reason. Generally, if you cash in your annuity before reaching age 59½, you will pay a 10 percent early withdrawal penalty to the federal government.

 Even the most patient investor may no longer find variable annuities compelling. Why? Some wonderfully tax-efficient alternatives, such as index funds, tax-managed mutual funds and exchange-traded funds, exist for stock market investors who have maxed out their retirement contributions and now want to save in their taxable accounts. (See Chapter 15.)

Annuities can spell estate tax disaster.

Remember the tax hit that's lurking for everyone who eventually cashes out his or her annuities? Another one is reserved for heirs. Beneficiaries have to pay capital gains taxes on any jump in the annuity's value. So, if the annuity was originally worth $25,000 and now it's worth $75,000, tax would be owed on the $50,000 gain.

 When someone dies and an annuity is passed to heirs, it could trigger stiffer taxes than other investments.

Annuity Resources

Some of the best sources for annuity information are the following:

✦ **Insure.com:** This consumer-friendly media site covers a wide variety of insurance issues, including primers on annuities. Go to www.insure.com.

✦ **National Association for Variable Annuities:** This trade group maintains a separate Web address for consumers who are interested in learning more about annuities and finding out about specific products. Contact the association by mail at 11710 Plaza America Dr., Suite 100, Reston, VA 20190; by phone at (703) 707-8830; and on the Internet at www.navanet.org or www.retireonyourterms.com.

✦ **U.S. Securities and Exchange Commission:** You can obtain a copy of the SEC's cautionary publication, *Variable Annuities: What You Should Know,* by calling the commission or going to its Web site. You can also call the SEC with annuity complaints. Contact the Office of Investor Education and Assistance, 450 Fifth St., NW, Washington, DC 20549-0213; (202) 942-7040; www.sec.gov.

✦ **National Association of Insurance Commissioners:** This nonprofit organization represents insurance regulators in the 50 states and Washington, D.C. The organization's Web site provides links to the home page of each state's insurance commissioner. You may want to contact your state commission with questions or complaints about annuities. Contact the national association by mail at 2301 McGee, Suite 800, Kansas City, MO 64108-2604; by phone at (816) 842-3600; or on the Internet at www.naic.org.

This tax may seem fair only until you appreciate how other inherited investments are treated. Suppose your dad left you an individual stock or a regular mutual fund that had enjoyed the same appreciation from $25,000 to $75,000. If you sold the investment, you'd owe tax on that $50,000 gain, right? Wrong. These assets enjoy what's called a step-up cost basis. When you inherit a stock or mutual fund, the IRS recalculates the cost basis, which primarily refers to the original cost. The new basis for the investment is $75,000, so if you sold the stock right away, you'd owe no capital gains taxes.

Cashing Out During Retirement: Immediate Annuities

Most people use annuities to save for retirement, but an annuity is much easier to defend once somebody starts consuming instead of saving. Financial salesmen tend to disregard immediate annuities, which represent just a tiny fraction of the bustling annuity market, because the commission schedules are stingier. Because nobody is pushing them, few are buying them.

You can choose between variable or fixed immediate annuities, but fixed immediate annuities far outnumber the variable ones. More variable choices, along with new features, are hitting the market, though.

Advantages of immediate annuities

What makes the immediate annuity worthwhile? Here are several reasons:

Peace of mind

An annuity can soothe the psychological trauma of drawing down your life savings. After decades of squirreling away money, now you're spending. Cashing a monthly annuity check won't necessarily trigger the same anxiety as withdrawing money from a bank account because the immediate annuity is guaranteed to cut you checks each month for the rest of your life.

A steady stream of income

The immediate annuity is ideal for any investor who is unsure how to invest a large sum of money to make it last for the final stretch. By depositing cash into an immediate annuity, you transfer the responsibility of making sure the cash lasts to the insurance company. With a lifetime annuity, the checks continue even if your initial investment has long since been depleted. Obviously, the insurance company hopes you'll die sooner rather than later, but even if your age hits the triple-digit mark, the money will continue rolling in. Some customers roll enough money into an immediate annuity so that the monthly payouts will cover the household bills.

The disadvantage of immediate annuities

Immediate annuities sound tempting to you, but your heirs may hate the idea. Why? Once you annuitize with the traditional immediate product, there's no retreating. If you put $50,000 into an immediate annuity and die in a plane crash a year later, that $50,000 belongs to the insurer, not your loved ones. If you experience second thoughts months after you commit to an immediate annuity, that's tough luck, too.

Although the chances of this happening are remote, it's still a scary possibility. To address this fear, the industry offers easier-to-swallow alternatives to the traditional life-only annuity. Purchasing an annuity with a "life with period certain" option, for instance, means the payments will last for a person's lifetime or a specified number of years, whichever is longer. Suppose you choose an annuity that guarantees payments for at least 10 years. If you die before that time, your beneficiary would receive the checks until the decade ran out. Married couples often use the joint-and-survivor option. When the annuity owner dies, the spouse pockets the payments until his or her death.

This extra protection shrinks the monthly check amounts. In some cases, the reduction is slight, but in others it is dramatic. You can see that for yourself in Table 22-1, which is an example of price quotes on immediate annuities obtained from the Annuity Shopper's Web site.

Table 22-1				
Monthly Check from Immediate Annuities for a 65-Year-Old				
Gender	**Annuity Amount**	**Life Only**	**Life and 10 Year Certain**	**Life and 25 Year Certain**
Woman	$50,000	$384.19	$374.60	$344.59
Man	$50,000	$410.72	$393.73	$348.14
Woman	$100,000	$768.38	$749.21	$689.18
Man	$100,000	$821.43	$787.47	$696.28

Source: www.annuityshopper.com

Annuity Shopping Tips

If you're shopping for an annuity, using these tips will help you track down the best ones.

Immediate annuities

For an immediate annuity, one place to start is Annuity Shopper's Web site (www.annuityshopper.com), which can provide quotes on a variety of immediate annuities. At its Web site, you can type in your age, state, and type of immediate annuity you desire (that is, term-certain, joint-and-survivor, or life-only) and receive fast quotes. Annuity Shopper provides quotes for about two dozen insurers. You can also contact the service by phone at (800) 872-6684. Another excellent source is *Comparative Annuity Reports,* a newsletter that provides information on dozens of immediate annuity options. Subscribers can also obtain brief consultations by phone. Contact Comparative Annuity Reports at (916) 487-7863 or www.annuitycomparativedata.com

Note

Annuity Shopper doesn't provide quotes for some of the low-cost leaders, such as TIAA-CREF, Vanguard, and Fidelity. You will have to contact them on your own; see contact info in the Resource Guide.

Changing Course: Converting Deferred to Immediate

If you already own a deferred annuity, you can essentially convert it into an immediate one and begin to receive payments when you reach retirement. The vast majority of deferred annuity investors pass on this opportunity; their big worry is dying shortly after the payments begin.

Sometimes an insurance company will sweeten the deal if a deferred annuity customer wants to convert to an immediate annuity. Suppose that you have a $200,000 deferred annuity that you want to convert into a regular income stream. Because you don't need to purchase a new annuity to do this, no commission is triggered. Consequently, the insurer may be willing to increase the value of your investment by 2 or 3 percent. It certainly doesn't hurt to ask.

Fixed annuities

For fixed annuity comparisons, you may once again want to turn to the *Comparative Annuity Reports,* which compares and rates the nation's fixed annuities on such factors as current interest rates, base rates and surrender charges.

Another resource is the *Fisher Annuity Index,* which compares current rates and contract features on hundreds of annuities. It includes such information as effective annual yields, surrender penalties, maximum issue age, and minimum premium amounts. The index is available in book form or on a CD-ROM. For more information about the monthly *Fisher Annuity Index,* call (800) 833-1450.

Variable annuities

Variable annuities are the toughest to shop for because many are packaged with so many features. You may want to begin with no-load mutual fund firms and discount brokerage firms. Here are some to get you started:

- ✦ TIAA-CREF at (800) 842-2776 or www.tiaa-cref.com
- ✦ Vanguard at (800) 635-1511 or www.vangaurd.com
- ✦ T. Rowe Price at (800) 638-5660 or www.troweprice.com
- ✦ Fidelity at (800) 343-3548 or www.fidelity.com
- ✦ Schwab at (800) 838-0650 or www.schwab.com

Tip

By contacting T. Rowe Price, you'll be able to order free software that analyzes whether you need a variable annuity.

You can check out a couple of online sites, too:

✦ **AnnuityNet.com:** A calculator on this site helps you assess whether you should consider investing in an annuity. You can also obtain information on some variable annuities. The Web site is `www.annuitynet.com`.

✦ **Annuities Online:** This site provides educational materials on annuities, as well as information about specific ones. Visit it at `www.annuity.com`.

✦ **Morningstar:** Morningstar tracks variable annuities, but its publication, *Morningstar Variable Annuity Performance Report,* is geared toward financial professionals. This report covers more than 11,600 subaccounts and highlights the top performers. The report provides information necessary to compare different annuities. Knowing how an annuity's subaccounts have performed historically is extremely important. You don't want to be saddled with a mediocre basket of funds. Call Morningstar at (800) 735-0700 or visit its Web site at `www.morningstar.com`.

Tip

At $135, Morningstar's annual publication (which includes one update) is pricey. If a salesman or financial planner is trying to sell you a variable annuity, ask him or her for copies of the relevant Morningstar evaluations.

Summary

✦ Avoid expensive variable annuities; read the prospectus carefully to determine the fees, charges, and expenses.

✦ Don't be fooled by tax-benefit claims; your earnings will be taxed at your income tax rate on withdrawal.

✦ Compare certificates of deposit and Treasuries with fixed annuities.

✦ For a lifetime of monthly checks, consider investing in an immediate annuity upon retirement.

✦ Simplify your annuity hunt by using the Internet.

✦ Before buying a fixed annuity, check the insurance company's rating.

✦   ✦   ✦

Estate Planning: Why It's Such a Big Deal

Knowing the basics of estate planning is crucial whether you expect to receive an inheritance or plan to give one away. This chapter and the next provide a condensed course on basic estate planning, including the necessity of coordinating a will with a living trust and naming guardians for underage children. In Chapters 25 and 26, you'll learn more about trusts, as well as how to choose trustees and manage an inheritance. Chapters 27 through 29 discuss approaches to estate planning that could benefit your favorite charities as well as your family.

Note Generalities about estate planning can only go so far. You should consult a legal expert before making any decisions that could impact you and your loved ones for decades.

The Dangers of Doing It Wrong

Everyone in America has a will. Even if you have never paid for or written a will, you have one. The reason is simple. Your state has laws dictating how your bank account, car, furniture, all the junk stacked up in the garage, and your other worldly possession will be divided if you die without an estate plan. Trouble is, you might hate the way the bureaucrats slice the pie.

A lot of people don't seem spooked by the specter of bureaucrats deciding who gets grandfather's gold-plated pocket watch or a lifetime accumulation of General Electric stock. The American Bar Association estimates that 70 percent of Americans die without a will. Delinquents who never bothered to draw one up include such famous people as Abraham Lincoln, Pablo Picasso, and the reclusive Howard Hughes.

Why Americans don't bother with wills

Despite the high stakes, it's understandable why Americans shy away from estate planning. Many find anticipating their own deaths too morbid. The complexity and the cost of the task also intimidate people. Attorneys don't work cheap, but attorney fees aren't as exorbitant as many suspect.

Note   Most Americans should be able to find a qualified attorney to draw up a will, a living trust, and other basic documents for $1,500 to $3,000 or less.

Yet many people don't see the point of writing that check. Some married couples, for instance, assume that when the first spouse dies, everything will end up with the surviving spouse. But in the arcane world of estate law, assumptions can get you in terrific trouble. In many states, a husband or wife isn't automatically entitled to all the money.

If no will exists, state laws take over. Some states, for instance, insist that assets of a childless couple must be split evenly between the surviving spouse and the dead husband or wife's parents. If the parents aren't alive, half the money may be doled out to brothers and sisters. Meanwhile, if a couple has children, a formula can dictate how much the mom or dad must share with the kids. And putting the kids' money in the family kitty can be a no-no. If a state can't find any relatives for the deceased, that person's money typically gets dumped in the state's coffers.

Estate planning isn't something you should postpone just because you aren't yet eligible for an AARP membership. If a couple doesn't choose substitute parents for their kids through a will, a court might do it instead. Or the kids could become caught in a battle among angry relatives, or worse, nobody might step forward.

Caution   Parents with young children who delay estate planning are playing Russian roulette with their children's welfare.

A taxing situation

Despite the mish-mash of state and federal estate laws, most families survive a death without getting dinged by estate taxes. In fact, as little as 2 percent of all estates are hit with these onerous taxes. But thinking that only billionaires and technology moguls must pay these taxes would be a serious mistake. These people can afford the legal firepower to often dodge some of these taxes. What's heart wrenching is to see middle-class families being bludgeoned by estate taxes when such taxes were completely avoidable. This situation often occurs when people follow their hearts instead of the tax code.

The Death of the Death Tax?

Estate taxes have been hanging around as long as the Egyptian pyramids, and the controversy surrounding the tax is just as long-lived. Although the estate tax in this country has existed only since Teddy Roosevelt's presidency, it has been fiddled with countless times.

The tinkering is likely to continue because the estate tax has lately faced tremendous opposition on Capitol Hill and President George W. Bush has vowed to kill it. Politicians in both parties have floated proposals to abolish the tax or scale it back. If changes are made, you'll need to consult an estate attorney or some other professional to see what effect, if any, it will have on your own estate plans. The estate tax's demise has several potential consequences:

✦ Charitable giving could decrease. Wealthy individuals might not feel the need to shovel loads of money into charities to garner those all-important tax breaks. In addition, without the specter of estate taxes, parents and grandparents may not feel compelled to pass on monetary gifts to children before their deaths.

✦ Estate planning would become simpler. By using complicated estate-planning tools, all but the most phenomenally rich individuals can dodge estate taxes. If the tax is eliminated or scaled back, the need for ordinary Americans to have many of these slick and sophisticated arrangements disintegrates, paving the way for more straightforward arrangements.

✦ The motivation to buy life insurance for some estate-planning purposes would disappear, eliminating that expense for those folks with large estates.

For example, one of the worst moves that many Americans can make is leaving behind what estate attorneys derisively call a "sweetheart" will. When the first spouse dies, the other inherits everything from grandma's sterling silver tea set to the cache of Nasdaq stocks. For some married couples, such a will seems the ultimate symbol of their love for each other. Yet a sweetheart will could ultimately force their heirs to pay completely unnecessary federal estate taxes.

Cross-Reference If you have a sweetheart will, see Chapter 24 to determine whether you should rip it up and replace it.

Although everybody focuses on estate taxes, other taxes can be even more problematic for the survivors. In some cases, for instance, income taxes-in combination with estate taxes owed on an inherited Individual Retirement Account can gut up to 80 percent of the assets. And this tax hit can happen whether the IRA is worth $20,000 or $20 million. Something as simple as replacing your parent's name with your own name on the inherited IRA could cost you dearly in taxes and kill your chances of preserving the IRA for your lifetime, as is spelled out in Chapter 11.

Meeting the bare minimum

The more affluent you are, the more complicated your estate planning will be. But at the very least, most people need some combination of these estate-planning building blocks:

✦ Will

✦ Living trust

✦ Durable power of attorney

✦ Health care proxy

✦ Living will

✦ Bypass credit shelter trust

Wills and living trusts are covered in this chapter; the next chapter addresses the last four documents. What's confusing to many people is figuring out just what documents in that list they really need. Nolo.com, the consumer legal publisher, is bombarded with mail, faxes, and e-mail 24 hours a day that ask the same question: Is a will enough?

This question is only natural because the tried-and-true will has been eclipsed by a popular legal phenomenon: the living trust. In recent years, some very vocal financial professionals have insisted that a will isn't enough. Instead, they've championed the living trust as the cornerstone of any worthwhile estate plan. Chiefly, a living trust is portrayed as a weapon against bloated probate court systems that charge inflated prices and take forever. Entire books are devoted to the wonders of living trusts and no doubt, hundreds of thousands of people, if not more, have attended seminars that trumpet the virtues of this document.

Despite all the hoopla, there's no simple answer as to whether you can get by with just a will or whether you also need a living trust. Get a room of legal experts together and you'll hear conflicting answers. Ultimately, every situation is different. You'll have a better idea of what you need if you understand what wills and living trusts, as well as other estate-planning strategies, can and can't accomplish.

Estate Planning: Getting Started

Perhaps the hardest part about estate planning is getting motivated to undertake two equally unappealing enterprises: considering your own death and working with legal documents. But there are some excellent reasons why estate planning should not be ignored.

The $136-Trillion Handoff?

Expecting an inheritance? A lot of people are. In the next 50 years, Americans could inherit enough money to eliminate today's national debt and still have enough left over to buy every single American a $500,000 home.

The inheritance projections have become more startling as the years go by. In the early 1990s, a couple of Cornell University professors grabbed headlines when they predicted that estates would generate a $10-trillion bonanza for younger generations. But the latest research from Boston College researchers suggests that the old estimate was wimpy. During the next five decades, they predict a conservative windfall of $41 trillion. The real amount, they estimate, could soar as high as $136 trillion.

The best reasons to plan ahead

A good estate plan enables you to accomplish the following tasks:

✦ Increase the windfall you leave family and friends if you use estate tax-evasion strategies

✦ Divide your assets as you see fit

✦ Allow your estate to possibly skip probate court

✦ Name surrogate parents for minor children

✦ Arrange in advance to have your estate's assets invested well

✦ Avoid or minimize estate and income taxes

✦ Protect loved ones' inheritances from lawsuits, divorce, and bankruptcy

✦ Establish trusts for any number of beneficiaries

✦ Leave lasting gifts to favorite charities

✦ Provide for a disabled child

✦ Direct how you'd like to be medically treated during your final weeks

✦ Designate someone to act on your behalf if you become incapacitated

✦ Keep your financial affairs confidential after your death

✦ Disinherit undesirable family members

Wills of the Rich and Famous

If you thought estate planning was dull, check out the Web site of Court TV (www.courttv.com). You can read the wills of the rich and famous, including the following people:

Babe Ruth	Richard Nixon
Jacqueline Kennedy Onassis	Jerry Garcia
Diana, Princess of Wales	Marilyn Monroe
Elvis Presley	David Packard
John Lennon	Shoeless Joe Jackson

Perhaps the shortest will you'll find on the Internet was written by former U.S. Chief Justice Warren Burger. The will, which left everything to his two children, was just 176 words long.

Assessing your assets

Do you know how much you're worth? How much is your estate worth? If you died tomorrow, the two figures could be vastly different. Many people don't realize this fact when they dismiss estate planning as crucial only for the rich. Large amounts of term insurance, for instance, can make someone worth considerably more dead than alive. Keep in mind that in 2001, any estate worth more than $675,000 can be hit with federal estate taxes. (Chapter 24 has a schedule of the minimum amounts that will trigger estate taxes, updated through 2006.)

Example   Say a retired schoolteacher's net worth is $175,000 when retirement assets, home equity, and savings accounts are totaled. So far, no need to worry about federal estate taxes. But add in a term life insurance policy worth $750,000. If the policy-holder dies and the death benefit is payable to her estate, the payout would ratchet up the value of the estate to $925,000.

Consequently, you need to know just what assets you have before you begin the estate-planning process. Include these commonly held assets in your calculations:

✦ Individual Retirement Account

✦ 401(k) plan or other workplace retirement accounts

✦ Insurance policies

✦ Home equity

✦ Other real estate

✦ Valuables such as cars, jewelry, and boats

✦ Household furnishings and possessions

✦ Bank, brokerage, and mutual fund accounts

✦ Pensions

✦ Business assets and insurance policies

✦ Annuities

✦ Trust income

✦ Royalties, patents, and copyrights

Once you've compiled an inventory of your assets, keep the list with your other estate-planning documents.

Writing a Will

Although the debate rages on about the merits of living trusts, this much is clear: Every adult needs a will.

Caution   Even someone who favors using a living trust to pass along a fortune needs a backup will.

A *will* is the document that directs where you want your property to go after your death. In a will, you can leave your property to people, charities, schools, churches, or any organizations you please. In addition to major assets such as a house or a brokerage account, your will can dictate who gets your sentimental possessions. For instance, you might give your personal journals to a daughter, your World War II medals to a son, and a rocking chair to a favorite niece.

You also use a will to appoint an *executor* who'll be responsible for carrying out your final wishes. The executor, who can be a spouse, friend, relative, attorney, accountant, or some other third party, handles the inevitable paperwork that's triggered by a death. The executor locates your will upon your death, files a final tax return, writes checks to creditors, and pays the funeral expenses. After all the bills are paid and all the assets are tracked down, the executor passes along what's left to the heirs.

The probate court's role

Overseeing this whole process is probate court. One of the probate judge's most important tasks is determining that your will is authentic. The probate process also officially gives the executor the authority to represent the estate. Unless the will specifically waives the requirement, often the judge requires that this person post a bond just in case he or she disappears with the money. (If you don't feel a bond is necessary for your hand-picked executor, say so in your will.) The probate court is expected make sure that the executor carries out all of his or her responsibilities.

Whether probate court is something to be feared depends upon which state you live in and perhaps the particular probate district within the state. In states such as California, New York, and Florida, probate court may turn out to be an expensive and time-consuming ordeal. In such states as Pennsylvania and Georgia, it's more likely to be a far simpler process. Many states have streamlined their probate systems to simplify the process for small- and medium-sized estates.

Choosing an executor

Many people believe that naming an oldest child or a trusted friend as an executor is a great honor. Think again. An executor's job often boils down to menial paper shuffling that requires a phenomenal commitment of time. Think long and hard before you select somebody to do the grunt work. Because of the responsibility involved, ask the person's permission before making the designation official in your will.

When drawing up a will, you can name more than one executor. You could choose two relatives, or you could pair a family member with an attorney or accountant. If a family member serves solo, he or she can always decide to hire outside help. The estate would pay the tab.

When you choose an executor, keep in mind his or her age. All too often, by the time a will is read, the executor is already dead. When this happens, the court selects an executor unless you have made adequate provisions for successors. To avoid this situation, list one or two backups, called *successor executors,* in your will. You should also be aware that a handful of states, such as Illinois, Florida, and Ohio, either forbid or place restrictions on out-of-state executors.

Many family members serve as executors without compensation, but because of the enormity of the task, you may want to arrange, through your will, to compensate a relative. In many states, executors are entitled to "reasonable fees." A court determines what reasonable means. In other states, such as California, Maryland, and Hawaii, a statutory fee schedule dictates how much an executor must be paid.

Executors: In for the Long Haul

If you agreed to be an executor, know that the responsibility could last about two years for a sizable estate. The Internal Revenue Service has that long to review estate income tax returns. Creditors can also appear out of nowhere long after you've doled out the inheritance. If you haven't followed proper notification procedures, you could be personally liable. Perhaps the only job that's more thankless is to serve as a trustee (see Chapter 25). That chore can sometimes last for decades.

Advantages of a will

A will is indispensable for many reasons. The major ones are explained in this section.

A will substitutes for a comprehensive estate plan.

Not everyone has the desire or the need to pay for a full-blown estate plan that may include one or more trusts. Someone with assets that are below the federal estate tax radar could decide an inexpensive will is all he or she needs.

A will can also be ideal for a young and healthy person who should be alive for decades. Someone who fits this category may decide that it's not worth the extra hassle to also obtain a living trust, which can cost more money and require considerably more paperwork. A simple will can also suffice for many parents of modest means, allowing them to name a guardian for their young children.

A will directs who will raise minor children.

A will allows you to name substitute parents for your minor children in case of your premature death. You can do this only through a will. You can't use a living trust to name a guardian, which is just one reason why a living trust should be linked with a will. If you want, you can name one guardian to raise the children and another to manage the children's money.

Although there's no guarantee that your wishes will be followed, chances are excellent that a court will honor them. A judge usually balks only when the would-be surrogate parent is a drug abuser, has a criminal history, is mentally disturbed, or has other characteristics that would make him or her a horrible parent.

Caution   If you make unofficial arrangements with a friend or relative to take care of your kids, but you never write it down in a will, relatives and ex-relatives have an open invitation to bicker about who gets the children.

Many people turn to their parents to be guardians if the parents are young enough. The children's aunts and uncles are also a popular choice. If there's a big enough age gap, a grown child can be tapped to take care of a younger brother or sister.

Ideally, a couple should name the same guardian in each of their wills. Yet parents, especially divorced ones, don't always agree on such an emotionally charged issue. Dueling guardianship provisions usually aren't a problem because a surviving parent is the natural guardian of the child. If both parents die simultaneously, then the court decides.

Tip   If the person who'd be the best mom or dad might not be the ideal candidate to oversee your son or daughter's finances, you can name a separate trustee to handle the money you bequeath to your kids.

Can I Write My Own Will?

Not everybody needs a lawyer to compose a will. People who don't face potential federal estate taxes or require complicated trusts may be able to get by on their own. It depends upon how extensive the estate is.

However, if any of following statements applies to you, you'll want to use an attorney:

✦ You want to establish trusts.

✦ You are a business owner with succession issues.

✦ You need to arrange for the long-term care of a disabled child.

✦ You have an estate that could be subject to estate taxes.

✦ You fear challenges to your will.

✦ You want to disinherit or leave very little to your spouse.

For self-starters, easy-to-understand resources exist. Nolo.com., the highly acclaimed legal consumer publisher, offers a variety of books and software that guide people through the estate-planning process. WillMaker, a software package, and *Nolo's Will Book* were developed for those who want to write their own wills. You can also find a great deal of free information about estate planning on the publisher's Web site at www.nolo.com.

If you compose your own will, type out your instructions and have it witnessed by two people who aren't named in the document. (Some states may still require three witnesses.) You don't have to have it notarized. Keep your will in a safe place with your other important papers, such as in a clearly labeled folder in your file cabinet.

You also can use your will to create a trust for the money you leave behind for your children and designate the trustee. The trustee invests the trust money, decides what to spend, and files an annual trust income tax return. If you don't designate that the child's guardian or a separate trustee will handle the money, the court takes on the burden. The guardian will then have to ask the court's permission to get expenditures approved. You certainly don't want that to happen.

Tip   Name backup guardians and trustees in case your first choices can't accept the responsibility when the time comes.

A will distributes assets through a catchall provision.

In a will, you can name a beneficiary who inherits all of your miscellaneous personal property. This property can include personal belongings such as cars, furniture, clothing, televisions, and household goods.

A will can put a deadline on creditor claims.

Imagine this nightmare: your father's estate was settled two years ago. The debts were paid, and the heirs split what was left. Now a long-lost creditor from one of dad's old business ventures has appeared and is demanding to be paid a princely sum of money to settle an old debt. One of the nice things about passing an inheritance through a will is that the probate court generally puts a time limit on creditors' demands.

When a will is probated, creditors usually have just a few months to come forward and demand payment. If the proper procedures are followed, an estate won't be liable if a creditor surfaces much later. You typically can't enjoy this shorter time period with a living trust.

Drawbacks to a will

There are some clouds to the silver linings of wills. This section details the major ones.

Probate court can be an expensive hassle.

If you've written a will, your heirs will ultimately spend time prowling the halls of probate court. In some states, probate court deserves its bad rap of being expensive and lengthy. Often probate takes several months to a year or more to complete. While the family waits, if the executor is not sensitive, the assets can be frozen, which may create hardships. Relatives might find themselves asking the executor to release some of the money in advance and if the executor refuses, there may be an appeal to the probate judge.

In some cases, court and attorney fees can eat up 5 percent or more of the deceased's estate. Probate fees in certain states can seem exorbitant. For example, if a $500,000 house ends up in probate in California, attorney and court fees may be based on that amount. If the owner had only $100,000 in equity in the house, that's too bad. By statute, that $500,000 house could generate $22,300 in legal and executor fees. A judge could permit even higher fees if special problems are encountered.

Many states permit smaller amounts of property to pass to heirs without any probate process or through a simplified version that might tie up loose ends in a matter of weeks instead of months or years. As you'll learn later in this section, some types of property, such as Individual Retirement Accounts and 401(k)s, won't be ensnared by probate. Instead, the money goes directly to the beneficiaries.

Wills are public documents.

Outsiders don't know how much money you have in the bank, but that kind of privacy can disappear upon death. Strangers may stroll into a courthouse and scrutinize anybody's probate records. They can easily learn who the heirs are, what they inherited, where they live, and many other details. Thanks to this open-door policy, for instance, it's public knowledge that more than half of Marilyn Monroe's $800,000 estate was gobbled up by estate taxes.

A Guardian Checklist

Nobody is going to raise your children as well as you can. But you need to ask yourself who would be the next best choice. Never name anybody as a guardian without having a heartfelt discussion with this person first.

Ask yourself these questions about a potential guardian:

+ Is your first choice willing to take on the responsibility?

+ Would your youngsters have to move?

+ Is the individual too old to serve?

+ Does the person have children roughly the same age?

+ What is the relationship between your children and the would-be guardian?

+ Can the candidate raise your children and handle the money you leave behind for them?

+ Do you approve of the person's lifestyle and values?

+ Will there need to be special arrangements provided for in the will, for example, a provision to allow the named guardians to add an addition on to their house?

Many times parents are inclined to pick a couple to be guardians, but it may be better to designate just one person. That way, there won't be any confusion about who is responsible for your children if the surrogate parents get divorced.

No matter who you pick, you should leave a letter, which you can file with your will, that discusses how you'd like your children to be raised, including your thoughts about religious upbringing, values, education, and other issues.

Of course, your mom or dad's will isn't going to attract the kind of attention that John F. Kennedy Jr.'s last will and testament generated. But families understandably want to keep their financial matters from prying eyes, including those of salespeople who try to contact the survivors to pitch their financial services. These vultures like to focus on vulnerable widows who may be scared and confused about what to do next.

Caution Scam artists, as well as legitimate businesses, routinely comb through probate records in search of prospective customers.

Wills don't control all property.

Most people probably assume they can and should use a will to bequeath everything they own to loved ones. That's not true. For example, homes and other real estate can be passed directly to a co-owner through what's called "joint tenancy" or "tenancy by entirety." When one partner dies, the other automatically gets the other half of the property. No will is necessary for the transfer.

Over the years, the assumption that the will controls all assets has caused tremendous heartache. Some assets, particularly financial products, transfer directly to the beneficiaries named on the account paperwork. For these types of accounts, you designate whom you want to inherit this money when you fill out the initial paperwork:

✦ Individual Retirement Accounts

✦ 401(k), 403(b), and other workplace retirement accounts

✦ Annuities

✦ Life insurance proceeds payable to third parties

✦ Pensions

Note

The person you name as the beneficiary of such an account is entitled to the money upon your death, regardless of what your will says.

Bank accounts can also passed along through a beneficiary designation. If your bank account has been established as a "pay-on-death" account, the beneficiary you name on the bank form will be the one that counts. Even if your will leaves the $50,000 in your savings account to your daughter, Uncle Joe gets the cash if he's the one on the beneficiary form. Many states are now also allowing stocks and bonds outside of retirement accounts to be passed along with a transfer-on-death form.

Don't Be Weak-Willed

If you write your own will, you'll want to make it bulletproof. The chances of the will being contested or thrown out will decrease if you avoid these types:

✦ **Fill-in-the-blank wills:** You can find boilerplate will forms in stationery stores, but relying upon them is unwise. These forms may not come with instructions and can be oversimplified.

✦ **Handwritten wills:** A judge once accepted a will scrawled with lipstick on a cocktail napkin. Nonetheless, typing the will on white paper is the preferred method. Most states do not consider *holographic* (handwritten) wills legitimate. At the very least, all the handwriting on the will must match the penmanship of the signature.

✦ **Video wills:** States haven't caught up with newer technology. At this point, no state allows a multimedia will.

✦ **Oral wills:** Most states refuse to honor verbal wills. You might get some leeway with a spoken will if you're dying on a battlefield, but otherwise, write it down. Only a minimal amount of property would be allowed to be effectively disposed of in this way.

The paperwork's potential for trouble

People who believe that a will is the final arbiter on who gets what after a death can run into trouble: Suppose a widower leaves an IRA to his friend in his will. She gets the money when he dies, right? Not so fast. His will certainly is clear on that point, but the will is irrelevant. What counts is a document that he signed years ago and obviously forgot about.

When he established the IRA, he filled out a beneficiary form. Since he was a widower back then, he named his brother and sister as beneficiaries. Trouble is, he forgot to change this designation after he became involved with his friend several years later. Because the beneficiary form takes precedence, the friend won't be entitled to the IRA windfall. Oversights like this also explain why an ex-husband or ex-wife can gleefully walk away with a former spouse's fortune.

Tip If you want to disinherit someone, don't forget to remove that person's name from the beneficiary slot on all your accounts' paperwork.

Because of this potential land mine, double-checking whom you've designated as beneficiaries on assets that aren't probated is critical. Contact your human resources department if you aren't sure whom you've designated as beneficiaries of your workplace retirement plans. If you have an IRA or IRA rollover at a brokerage firm, mutual fund company, or another financial institution, it should have your beneficiary forms on file.

The upside to the system

The big advantage to passing along assets through beneficiary forms is that money left this way doesn't have to go through probate court. Loved ones can receive the money much more quickly and without the legal expense. Yet there's a hidden danger to titling all your assets to avoid probate. As you'll learn later in the next chapter, passing a sizable chunk of money to a surviving spouse in this way can trigger unnecessary estate taxes upon the death of the second spouse.

Skipping Probate with Mutual Funds

Being able to quickly pass mutual funds to heirs through direct designations is a fairly new concept. Even though IRA owners have always enjoyed this convenience in the past, a patchwork of state probate laws had thwarted this option for the shareholders of taxable mutual funds. Now just about every state allows mutual fund shareholders to fill out paperwork that will directly transfer the assets to heirs after the shareholder dies.

All the major fund companies provide the "transfer on death" paperwork. You can obtain information by calling your fund company's toll-free number. You should name one or more beneficiaries, as well as backups.

If you inherit a mutual fund account this way, notify the fund company after the death. Typically, the firm will ask you to provide a death certificate before it releases the money. If you prefer to keep the money in the same fund, the firm will provide you with a new account form.

Shaking Off the Dust

Once you've written a will, don't forget about it. About every three years, you should review your will and any other estate-planning documents and decide whether modifications are necessary. Do the same thing if a major change occurs in your life, such as marriage, divorce, the birth of a child, a death, or an inheritance. It's also imperative to pull out these documents anytime Congress passes new laws that affect estate taxes.

Wills can be contested.

Wills are public documents, which means anyone can take a peek at them once probate court assumes control after a death. This openness can encourage angry survivors to challenge its content. Contesting a will is easy; you can even do it without an attorney. Sometimes heirs would rather settle with a malcontent than risk an ugly court battle that could eat up an inheritance or see the money end up in the protestor's bank account.

A will can't help if you become incapacitated.

A will kicks in only after your death. But what if you can no longer bathe and feed yourself, much less keep track of your finances? A will can't help during this kind of crisis. Your executor is legally powerless to help.

Enter the court system. If you haven't made prior arrangements for a surrogate and a relative or other interested person takes the matter to court, a judge will decide whether you're legally incompetent. Attorneys and physicians can be summoned to weigh in on the issue. The court proceedings may degenerate into a legal brawl if more than one relative or friend is vying to be your guardian. All this can get expensive, messy, and, for you, humiliating. Ultimately, what's best for you might get lost in the court paperwork.

Tip To avoid all this heartache, make sure you fill out a durable power of attorney form in addition to your will. Chapter 24 teaches you how to fill out this form and what the form entails.

Creating a Living Trust

A living trust is a document that allows an estate to pass its assets directly to the deceased's heirs instead of going through probate court. If you put everything you own in the name of the trust, there's nothing for probate court to oversee when you die. The avoidance of probate is the living trust's biggest selling point. If there's no living trust, an estate has to go through court if there are any probate assets. For many Americans, the living trust has replaced the will as the centerpiece of their estate plan. Particularly for those in ill health or in their 50s and 60s or older, a living trust can be invaluable.

A living trust does require doing some extra work that you don't have to do with a will: Once you create a trust on paper, you have to flesh it out by putting in the trust's name all the stuff you don't want going through probate (the house, the car, the brokerage accounts, the baseball cards, and whatever else you have). Every time you buy something new, you'll need to put it in the trust's name.

If you want all that stuff back in your name, don't worry: A living trust is a revocable trust, which means you can change the terms any time you'd like or simply get rid of it. In contrast, many other types of trusts are irrevocable, which means they can't be nullified. (As a general rule, revocable trusts are created to avoid probate; irrevocable trusts are created to minimize taxes.) You're in control of what goes in and out of the living trust. Many people name themselves as trustee; a spouse is often tapped as a co-trustee. Even if you designate someone else to be trustee, such as a relative, a friend, or a financial institution, you can always replace your trustee because while you're alive you're still in control of the trust, which is why it's called a living trust.

Tip If you plan to hire an attorney to prepare a will, adding a living trust to the tab may cost only a few hundred dollars more.

Advantages of a Living Trust

Living trusts have become popular for many reasons. This section highlights the main ones:

You avoid probate court.

Probate court inspires the same dread as an IRS audit. As mentioned earlier, an odyssey through probate court can be lengthy, costly, and traumatic. It's often best to avoid this experience when possible. The assets within a living trust can often be dispensed to heirs in a matter of weeks. In contrast, probate can drag on for months or even years.

By dodging probate, the costs of settling the estate may be considerably less. Expenses will also be held down if the trustee doesn't require the assistance of an attorney or other outside professional help or decides to forego a personal fee. Meanwhile, because the assets in a living trust don't go through probate court, you and your family's privacy will be preserved.

Note A living trust can be invaluable if you own property in different states. Placing distant properties in a trust allows your family to skip probate hassles in other states.

A living trust avoids court supervision if you become incapacitated.

A living trust can be a godsend if you can no longer take care of yourself. That's because it allows you, in advance, to name whom you'd like to step in if you can't handle your financial and legal affairs. He or she can write checks, sell assets, apply for disability benefits, and do much more. The person who agrees to take on this responsibility is called the *successor trustee.*

The beauty of this arrangement is that you can decide in advance how it will be determined when you can no longer care for yourself. You can direct, for instance, that certain physicians must agree that you can't manage your own affairs. This transition occurs without any court hearing or attorney involvement. But you can insert checks and balances into the trust document to make sure the successor trustee doesn't become overzealous.

Tip Choose your successor trustee with the same care and consideration you give to choosing a will's executor.

A successor trustee for a living trust will also serve after you die. At this point, the job description is similar to that of a will's executor. The trustee will settle all your outstanding debts, distribute the assets as you directed, and file the final tax returns. After all these tasks are completed, the trust normally disappears.

Living trusts are difficult to challenge.

Living trusts are harder to contest than a will. With a will, someone can protest your final wishes without even hiring an attorney. The open nature of the probate process also makes it easier for disgruntled heirs to challenge a will. Trust administration is a much more private and therefore protected process.

Challenging a living trust's provisions is tough because assets can typically be divided up much more quickly. By the time somebody protests, the checks may have already been mailed out. At this point, the challenger would face the daunting prospect of separately suing the beneficiaries and the trustee.

The secrecy of a living trust could also cut down on potential challenges. Family members, for instance, may never discover that a special friend or a charity was given a generous bequest. For the same reason, a living trust can also be handy if you plan to give unequal inheritances to your children.

Limitations to a living trust

Although a living trust can be a wonderful estate-planning device, it can't do everything. This section explains a living trust's limitations.

You still need a will.

You can't get by with just a living trust; you still need a will. When a will is drawn up in conjunction with a living trust, the will typically is called a *pour over will.* Any assets that weren't included in the trust, whether it's Grammy's cameo ring, the threadbare furniture in the basement, or some forgotten stock certificates, are distributed through a will.

Beware of Living Trust Hype

Want a living trust? Plenty of unqualified people are anxious to sell you one. Look at newspapers in many communities, and you can find ads for free living trust seminars. Those who buy a trust at a seminar, however, may discover that they didn't obtain one at all. Instead, what they purchased were fill-in-the-blank forms with little or no instructions.

Trust promoters who portray their living trusts as wonder documents scare the elderly into thinking that consequences of not getting one will be cataclysmic. In one such case pursued by the Federal Trade Commission, two companies claimed that local attorneys drew up documents tailored to their state laws, but in fact thousands of these trusts were mass-produced by one lawyer for clients throughout the United States. The two companies overcharged clients ($2,000 to $3,000 per trust) for a generic form and then didn't bother to help their victims transfer their assets into the trusts.

Also beware of peddlers who sell trusts through organizations with names that resemble the AARP. The AARP does not sell or endorse any living trust packages. State attorneys general have sued outfits with names such as the American Senior Citizen Alliance and the American Association for Retired Citizens.

Seminar sponsors may also try to wheedle audience members into buying life insurance as well. Insurance, a speaker may insist, is necessary to defray punitive estate taxes. Don't be swayed by scare tactics. A living trust by itself can't reduce estate taxes, and the vast majority of people won't need extra insurance. If you arrange your estate properly, there probably won't be any estate tax obligation waiting at the end of the line.

If you attend a seminar, check the credentials of the speakers. If you need an estate attorney, it's best to find one through more traditional channels. (See Chapter 6 for tips on locating an estate attorney.)

Even if you believe that you've tucked all your assets into the living trust, you might have overlooked something. Or perhaps you bought a car or received your own inheritance after drawing up your living trust. If you don't have a will, your state directs who gets the orphaned property when you die. Each state uses a formula to determine how any assets will be divided among relatives.

Tip

With a backup will, you can direct who will inherit assets that weren't specifically left to an individual or charity through the living trust.

Transferring your assets to the trust can be a pain.

Creating a trust is a two-step process: First, you establish the trust on paper, and then you put your assets in the trust's name. People frequently postpone or forget to follow through on this critical second step, but a living trust won't work if it's empty!

How do you get your valuables into the trust? It's not complicated, but it requires a flurry of phone calls and paper shuffling. You need to retitle the names on your brokerage accounts, stocks, bonds, house, mutual funds, and other valuables so that the owner of all these assets officially becomes the trust. The attorney who draws up your estate plans can provide the standard retitling forms that you need to send to your financial institutions. Some attorneys will do this work for you for an extra fee.

Note Transferring your assets to a living trust while you're alive has absolutely no effect on your income tax obligations.

Obviously, not everything needs a new name on its title. A wedding ring, artwork, tools, computers, and other possessions don't have titles to begin with. To include these kinds of belongings in a trust, you simply itemize them on a trust schedule.

Tip Once you've established a trust, remember to designate your trust as the owner each time you open a new bank account or buy property.

Occasionally, people with living trusts encounter problems later, for example, if they seek to refinance their homes because the original mortgage might prohibit the property from being placed in a trust. Homeowners may have to retitle the house back into their names before the refinancing can sail through.

Living trusts cost more than a simple will.

Usually, you'll spend more to draw up a living trust than you would to draw up a simple will. How much more depends upon what lawyers charge in your area. If you're establishing a living trust to avoid the cost of probate, check the going rates for probate court and executors in your state first. Otherwise, you may spend more money setting up a living trust than you would having your estate probated.

A living trust doesn't control all property.

Just like a will, a living trust isn't always the final authority on how a fortune, whether big or small, will be divided among heirs. As you read earlier, some assets are bequeathed in other ways. A house held in joint tenancy or joint entirety gets passed on directly to the remaining property owner. Retirement accounts and IRAs are also transferred directly to the beneficiaries listed on the account's paperwork. Although some people believe a living trust can neatly provide for all heirs in one document, it just ain't so.

A living trust doesn't automatically adjust to a divorce.

If you get divorced, your living trust won't automatically remove your ex-spouse as a beneficiary. You have to amend the trust to do this. In contrast, wills have the handy feature of instantly removing a former husband or wife without any additional paperwork.

Living trusts can't reduce estate taxes.

Many people believe a living trust is a miracle document that can make estate taxes disappear, but that's a myth. Various irrevocable trusts can reduce or eliminate taxes, but a living trust can't.

You can take advantages of strategies to whittle away or reduce estate taxes regardless of whether your estate plan includes a living trust. As you'll learn in Chapter 25, a will or a living trust can be coupled with a bypass trust and a marital trust so that you can often eliminate all federal estate taxes.

Do you need a living trust?

Many people obtain a living trust as they near retirement or their health declines. That's when the chances of needing the benefits of a living trust increase. Whether you should obtain one is a highly personal decision. If the following characteristics describe you, you may not need a living trust.

You're young.

If you're in your 30s, 40s, or younger, you may conclude that a living trust is an unnecessary hassle. Remember, the living trust's most alluring selling point is avoiding probate. But for people this age, chances are that probate court isn't going to be a problem for many years. If you sign up for a living trust now, you could conceivably face decades of retitling property. As you approach retirement age, you should reevaluate your decision.

You're just getting by.

If you have little money, you're not going to worry about losing a modest amount of your heirs' inheritance through the probate process.

You have a sizable amount of debt.

If you have a lot of debt, your heirs might be happier if your estate does grind through probate. Why? When an estate is probated, creditors are on the clock. If creditors don't make a claim in a timely manner (typically 90 days after a death), they are out of luck. A living trust provides no definitive cut-off period for creditors' claims. Somebody with complicated business arrangements might also fare better in probate.

Your only concern is appointing a guardian for your children.

Remember, you can't designate a guardian for your kids through a living trust. You can do this only through a will.

There's no reliable person to serve as successor trustee.

Because a living trust eliminates the need for court supervision after your death, you must appoint someone who is extremely trustworthy. Chances are that no one will be looking over this person's shoulder. If there's no one you feel comfortable with to take on this responsibility, you should probably skip using a living trust.

Summary

✦ Don't delay writing a will.

✦ Understand a will's limitations and make arrangements to work around them.

✦ Leave your children in good hands; use a will to name guardians.

✦ Beware of living trust seminars that overpromise and overprice.

✦ Decide whether you need a living trust.

✦ Don't forget to transfer assets into a living trust once it is created.

✦   ✦   ✦

More Estate-Planning Basics

This chapter describes estate-planning moves that benefit you while you're alive and your family and heirs after you're gone. Estate planning, after all, involves more than dictating who gets your money and your lifetime accumulation of stuff. If you believe a will can handle it all, think again. Many times it won't. A will is just a bare-bones document.

Merely contemplating what else needs to be done is enough to discourage even the most responsible among us. Keep in mind that estate planning is in some respects life planning. The preparations you make in advance, which shouldn't take much time, could become invaluable when you are most vulnerable. You can dictate in advance, for instance, when it's acceptable for someone to legally step in and help you with your finances should you become physically or mentally incapacitated. You can also provide explicit guidance to whomever you select to look after you in a medical crisis. These decisions and instructions are hardly the most glamorous aspect of estate planning, but they are crucial nonetheless. Perhaps more immediately rewarding is writing an ethical will, a document that gives you the chance to put on paper those things you value more than money.

Understanding how estate taxes work can also prove to be immediately rewarding, giving you the chance to determine quickly whether your estate will be liable and whether you need to take evasive action. This chapter explains the estate tax exemption and rate schedule and provides some key figures you need to add in when figuring out whether your estate will fly below the tax radar.

Durable Power of Attorney

What happens if you become senile or slip into a coma after a car accident or somehow lose your ability to take care of yourself? If you have a living trust, your financial interests can be protected because in the trust document you named a successor trustee who can legally fill in for you by doing such things as write your checks and filing a disability claim. To allow the trustee the maximum amount of flexibility, your assets should be in the living trust, since that's what the trustee has authority to manage. Because you don't need any court involvement, the transition for you and your legal protector can be seamless. (See Chapter 23's treatment of wills for more information.)

If you don't have a living trust, you should fill out a durable power of attorney form to enjoy the same kind of protections. With one of these documents, you choose whom you'd like to act on your behalf if you no longer can take care of yourself. In awkward legalspeak, this person is referred to as an *attorney-in-fact*. The term *durable* is used because the responsibility remains intact when someone is incapacitated. Giving someone this authority in advance does not mean the designated person can start running your life at any time. This person can act only during a time of crisis. So long as you can handle your own affairs, your trusted backup should have absolutely no power. To protect yourself, you should make this clear in the document and hold onto it.

Tip   Keep the power of attorney document with your will and other estate-planning paperwork.

What kinds of things can your attorney-in-fact handle for you? This person could

   ✦ Pay your everyday expenses (using your own assets, of course).

   ✦ Arrange for and collect benefits from Social Security, Medicare, or other such federal bodies.

   ✦ Conduct transactions with your bank and other financial institutions.

   ✦ Buy and sell such assets as your home, insurance policies, stocks, bonds, and mutual funds.

   ✦ File your income taxes and pay your property taxes.

   ✦ Locate and hire qualified help to represent you in court.

   ✦ Oversee your retirement accounts.

This much authority, even if it's never needed, is an awesome responsibility, so you should select someone who is completely trustworthy. Married couples typically pick each other for the task. You will probably want to name someone who lives nearby for practical reasons. Make sure you select an alternate in case something happens to your first choice. Also discuss with your lawyer what wording should be used. You can give either sweeping or limited authority to whomever you chose.

Two shoes to fill

You have two guardian spots to fill: someone specifically appointed to handle your financial affairs and someone to make medical decisions on your behalf. You give the latter person authority in a document that's called a *health care proxy* or *a durable power of attorney for health care* (that document is covered in the next section).

One person can take on both jobs, but make sure that he or she is well qualified. If your sister is a physician or a nurse, for instance, giving her the durable power of attorney for health care could make sense. You want to pick someone who won't be flustered by medical terminology and who is gutsy enough to stand up to physicians or family members who disagree with your wishes. On the other hand, a family member with investment experience could serve as the financial caretaker.

The dangers of delaying

Drawing up these papers might not seem urgent when you're young and healthy and the fall television season is monopolizing your free time. But you jeopardize your own welfare by postponing this task. If you never select a representative and you become incapacitated, the court will appoint a guardian.

Sometimes, the court appoints a complete stranger as guardian, also called a *conservator*. People appointed by a court may do an outstanding job, but most of use would prefer to make our own decisions. This person, who could be an attorney looking to generate extra income, might make decisions that you hate. He or she has the power to decide such things as where you live, whether your home or family business should be sold, what cash can be spent, and how your money is invested. The court imposes strenuous reporting requirements on the conservator, regardless of whether a family member or an outsider is serving in the role. Meanwhile, the courts often prefer that your assets be invested quite conservatively, which might require the sale of some of your holdings.

This legal intrusiveness can happen even if you're blessed with loving family. Just consider what happened to a financial planner in the South who had been handling his mother's modest finances for 15 years. When Alzheimer's disease finally forced the mother into a nursing facility, the children agreed her house needed to be sold. But because the mother had never signed a durable power of attorney document, her family wasn't legally permitted to sell it. After notifying all his siblings, the son petitioned the court to become his mother's conservator so that he could sell her house. It would have been a routine matter, but one of the daughters inexplicably protested the appointment.

Confronted with a family feud, the judge postponed his decision and scheduled a hearing for several months later. In the interim, the court appointed a temporary guardian: an attorney fresh out of law school. From that point on, it was the young lawyer and not the family who signed checks and was legally responsible for the mother's medical care. After several thousand dollars in legal costs, a judge ultimately appointed the son as guardian.

Pave the Way for Your D. P. of A.

Have your parents asked you to legally step in if they can no longer manage their financial affairs? You might be named on mom or dad's durable power of attorney form, but that doesn't mean you'll be taken seriously later on. Even if you have the signed document in your hand, banks and other financial institutions might be reluctant to hand over the reins to someone else's account. Their big fear is being sued by the person who's losing the control, particularly if the bank suspects that the surrogate might use the funds for him- or herself instead.

If you are tapped as someone's legal stand-in, suggest that that person follow these suggestions to strengthen your ability to do good on their behalf:

✦ Update the paperwork every couple of years. Institutions get very nervous when they are asked to honor a stale document.

✦ Find out whether the financial institutions the person works with have their own durable power of attorney forms, as some banks and brokerages do. Prepare two durable powers of attorney with identical information, using your own form and the forms provided by your bank or brokerage.

Health Care Proxies and Living Wills

Americans inadvertently set up relatives for untold anguish because they never write down, much less discuss, what medical treatment they favor or want to avoid near the end of their lives. As you contemplate your own mortality, you need to give the person who you want to entrust with your life as much advance guidance as possible.

Luckily, providing this guidance doesn't have to be difficult. When you fill out a durable power of attorney for health care or health care proxy, you can detail your wishes. Another popular way to spell out your medical care preferences is with a living will, which you might also see referred to as a "directive to physicians," "advance directive," or a "declaration regarding health care." In a health care proxy, you tell your designated intermediary how you want your medical care to be handled. With a living will, you state your desires in a document addressed directly to medical personnel.

Note   In theory, a physician who refuses to honor the wishes that you've outlined in a living will must transfer your care to another doctor.

These documents can ease the dying process and make someone's final days or months more comfortable. How? You can direct what kind of (or whether) medical treatment is desired when death is near. These directives can also encourage families to discuss end-of-life issues long before they have to.

At this point, you might be asking yourself, "How many of these forms do I need? Will one suffice?" Once again, no one answer fits all situations. What forms you need mostly depends upon what your particular state requires. You can find this out by contacting an attorney.

Note Although all states recognize living wills, some don't permit you to use it to name a person to supervise your medical care. In this case, you'd have to designate a health care proxy separately.

Finding the right forms

Unfortunately, attorneys and state bureaucrats teamed up to write many of the health directives that are in use today. These documents can be ridiculously difficult to comprehend and use. Even so, make sure that you use a form that your state accepts.

Tip If you use more than one form, make sure they provide the same information. You don't want to state in your living will that you'd prefer not being kept alive with a feeding tube, but then reverse yourself on another form.

You can typically find these state-authorized forms at the following locations:

✦ Senior citizen agencies

✦ Nursing homes

✦ Hospitals

✦ Local senior centers

✦ Physicians' offices

✦ Nonprofit organizations benefiting the elderly

User-friendly living wills

Many people are intimidated by the sterile, boilerplate living will documents that states often favor. But now there's a better alternative: a living will called Five Wishes, which is distributed by a nonprofit group called Aging with Dignity. Named for its five parts, Five Wishes was developed by a former attorney for Mother Theresa and has received the American Bar Association's seal of approval. In its first two years, the organization distributed 1 million copies of this document.

Like standard living wills, Five Wishes permits someone to direct what kind of medical treatment is desired or unwanted when death is imminent and name a medical proxy. But Five Wishes is refreshingly easy to read and also addresses a person's spiritual and emotional wishes. For example, you can stipulate in the document whether you'd like someone to hold your hand when you're not responsive to voice or touch. You could express the desire for family and friends to pray at the bedside or favorite music to be played or poetry to be read as death approaches.

Winging it Without an Attorney

Do you need an attorney to fill out a living will, a durable power of attorney for health care, or similar documents? Chances are, you don't. One place you can find a fill-in-the-blanks form is from Nolo.com, the publisher of many handy do-it-yourself legal forms and software.

In order for these health care forms to be valid, however, most states require that you use two witnesses for your signature. A few states require that the documents be notarized. You will need to check with an attorney about the requirements specific to your state.

Aging with Dignity worked with the ABA to make the document legally acceptable in as many states as possible. It's valid in 33 states and the District of Columbia, but it's not recognized in 17 states, including California, Ohio, and Wisconsin, because certain statutory language, which is not in the document, is required. But thousands of people in these states have filled out the Five Wishes living will and used it in conjunction with their state-approved forms.

 Resource You can preview or order copies of Five Wishes at the group's Web site: www.agingwithdignity.org. If ordering by mail, include $5 per copy: P.O. Box 1661, Tallahassee, FL 32302-1661.

Partnership for Caring, a nonprofit group that focuses on end-of-life issues, is another one-stop source for health directives. The organization keeps updated advance forms for all 50 states and Washington, D.C.

 Resource Call (800) 989-WILL to order forms from Partnership for Caring or download the appropriate state form from the Web site at www.choices.org. The mailing address is 1035 30th St. NW, Washington, DC 20007.

Limitations of health care directives

Is this your worst nightmare? You helplessly spend the last few days or weeks of life hooked up to machines. You eat through a feeding tube, breathe with a ventilator, and can barely move with the tangle of wires attached to your body. None of this medical intervention can cure you; it's simply delaying what might have been a peaceful death.

Health care directives such as living wills are supposed to prevent such medical indignities from happening. But as many have discovered, these documents don't always do the trick. A living will takes effect when someone is unconscious or terminally ill. Unfortunately, families find themselves bickering among themselves or with physicians about the definition of terminally ill. What's more, many doctors resist when families insist they don't want their loved ones kept marginally alive through superhuman efforts, fearing lawsuits if they obey a living will's instructions.

Tip
To make a health care directive harder to ignore, fill in all the blanks on all the forms and be very specific in what you want. You may be tempted to skip those sections in the forms that make you uncomfortable, but doing so only gives your doctor leeway later to make those decisions for you.

In addition to your written directives, sit down and share your feelings about your medical care with family and your physicians long before death is at hand. Keep in mind, too, that a living will doesn't do any good if no one else knows about it. It's estimated that one out of every four or five American adults have signed a living will, but all too many of these documents are stuffed into a drawer and forgotten.

Tip
Make sure you give copies of any health directives to your doctors and close relatives or friends.

Ethical Wills

Legally preparing for your own death isn't easy. But the emotions that swirl around this process are never reflected in the dry, sterile, estate-planning documents. You have an opportunity to make your legacy more meaningful by writing your own ethical will. The ethical will, which has been enjoying a robust revival, is not a legal document; it's a love letter to your family. Unlike a traditional will that dictates who gets the fine china and granddad's gold pocket watch, an ethical will bequeaths personal and spiritual values, life's lessons, hopes for the future, and forgiveness.

Note
Ethical wills are not new; they've just been rediscovered. Hebrew scripture first described them in Biblical times. Ethical wills from the Medieval and Renaissance periods still survive.

Today, parents often write these wills and share them with family long before they die. Here are just a few of the reasons why you might want to consider writing an ethical will:

✦ The process can reveal a lot about you.

✦ It can heal family wounds by asking for forgiveness and forgiving those who have hurt you.

✦ It can be easier to die having shared what's important to you with your loved ones.

✦ It can reduce the difficulty of writing a legal will, a living trust, and other estate-planning documents.

✦ It can be a spiritual experience.

✦ It can help you deal with your own mortality and provide closure.

You can be a dreadful writer and still create a lovely ethical will. No one's going to care about dangling participles or typos. Also, don't treat the creation of an ethical will like a timed test. You don't have to write this letter all at once. The process can evolve over many weeks. When you are composing your thoughts, consider these questions:

✦ What do you cherish about your children and grandchildren?

✦ What are your hopes for those you leave behind?

✦ What important lessons have you learned in life from your family members or others?

✦ What were the milestones in your life?

✦ What has given you the great pleasure in your life?

✦ What are your biggest regrets?

✦ What are your spiritual beliefs?

 For inspiration, get a copy of *The Ethical Will Resource Kit* by Barry K. Baines, M.D. or visit www.ethicalwill.com, a clearinghouse for articles on and helpful suggestions for ethical wills.

Bypass Shelter Trusts

Perhaps you're feeling smug at this point. You have an updated will tucked in a filing cabinet. You've compiled an inventory of all your assets. You've signed legal papers designating who will handle your financial and medical affairs if you lay dying in a hospital bed. Maybe you've also been motivated to transfer all your assets into a living trust. Now you can rest because your estate is in great shape, right? Not so fast.

None of the strategies covered so far will protect your hard-earned fortune from the IRS. Married couples need to consider two more moves before they finish their basic estate plan. (Chapters 25 and 26 explore more elaborate options involving trusts regardless of whether you're married or single.) Even couples who assume their net worth isn't large enough to fret about federal estate taxes need to at least explore the feasibility of pursuing these two options:

✦ Creating a bypass shelter trust

✦ Retitling assets to balance his-and-her estates

Many married couples fail to take these steps because they seem like a cruel joke to play on a marriage. What's mine is yours, and what's yours is mine. How could someone possibly suggest that a husband bump his wife's name off the deed of the family home? Or that the wife eliminate her husband's name from a stock portfolio? Although this kind of advice might seem bizarre, it can make perfectly sound financial sense.

Tasting the sour side of a sweetheart will

These two valuable strategies are also overlooked because married couples generally know that when the first one dies, the widow or widower receives all the joint property without paying a single cent in estate taxes. This free ride, which is legally referred to as the "unlimited marital deduction," can be enjoyed by any married couple, as long as they are both U.S. citizens. Even billionaire Bill Gates and his wife could claim this tax privilege. Understanding this, many people can't appreciate the dangers of keeping a *sweetheart will,* which leaves all the earthly possessions to the surviving spouse. The danger is that you can postpone taxes with a sweetheart will, but you can't necessarily avoid them. Without proper planning, the ultimate tax bill could be a lot worse than it ever had to be after the death of the second spouse.

Granted, the federal government isn't interested in collecting estate taxes from everybody. Death is inevitable, but federal estate taxes are not. As you can see in Table 24-1, if your estate doesn't surpass a certain value, no estate taxes are owed because the Internal Revenue Code provides each person with a credit against the estate tax. The credit shelters an amount referred to as the exemption equivalent. This value is $675,000 in 2001, and it will continue to climb until 2006. When someone dies in 2006, no estate tax will be owed if the assets left behind don't exceed $1 million.

Table 24-1 Individual Federal Estate Tax Exemption	
Year	**Amount of Exemption**
2001	$675,000
2002	$675,000
2003	$700,000
2004	$850,000
2005	$950,000
2006	$1,000,000

The amount of tax owed depends upon the amount by which your estate exceeds the exemption amount. The federal estate taxes can be brutal, with percentages ranging from 37 to 55 percent. If your net worth doesn't surpass these amounts, you won't have to worry about estate taxes, and you can ignore the strategies that follow. But you want to be sure you're working with the right figures.

Example

Say a couple's assets total $400,000. If one of them owns a term life insurance policy worth $500,000, the estate catapults into the estate-tax zone upon that spouse's death.

If the net worth of you and your spouse does not exceed these amounts and you don't expect your estate to ever do so, you can ignore the strategies that follow. Otherwise, you'll want to ask an attorney about bypass shelter trusts. Bypass shelter trusts allow each spouse to pass a huge amount of money to heirs tax-free. The first spouse to die can't posthumously claim that sizable exemption unless it's tucked into a bypass trust.

Spelling out the numbers

Suppose a husband dies in 2002, leaving behind an estate worth $1.3 million. His $675,000 exemption is put into a bypass trust that was established before his death. Because the money is earmarked for a trust that is set up in a way that will keep it out of the second spouse's estate at her death, no estate tax will ever be owed on it. What's more, if the $675,000 skyrockets in value over the years, no estate tax will be due on that appreciation either. Technically, the widow can't claim this money outright because it's in a trust. But as a practical matter, the trust can be liberally drawn so that the wife enjoys access to it. She typically collects the income from the trust and can dip into the principal for a variety of reasons. The most popular trust language gives the survivor as much income and principal needed with a huge latitude to use the trust for "health, maintenance, education, and support."

Of course, not all the survivor's money is tied up in the bypass trust. Only the amount necessary to claim the husband's exemption goes into the bypass trust. The widow is free to invest or spend the rest anyway she wants. In this example, she's entitled to $625,000 with no strings attached. When she dies, she'll claim her own credit as well. Because both husband and wife claimed their credits, no estate taxes will be owed on any of the money. The heirs will pocket it free and clear.

What would have happened if the husband's tax exemption hadn't been created by putting those funds in a trust? His $675,000 chunk of the estate, not to mention any appreciation, would ultimately have been subject to estate taxes when his wife died. Suppose his widow died in 2003, when she could claim an estate tax exemption of $700,000.

$1,300,000	(total estate on hand)
−$700,000	(amount of wife's estate tax exemption)
$600,000	(estate now vulnerable to taxes)

Here's the bottom line: Because the husband claimed an estate tax credit through a bypass trust, the estate owed no tax when the widow died two years later. Had that trust not been established, that vulnerable $600,000 would generate $222,000 in estate taxes due in a 37 percent estate tax bracket.

Bypassing the biggest trust mistake

Unfortunately, establishing his-and-her bypass trusts won't automatically allow you to dodge estate tax bills. These trusts won't work unless they can be funded at death. If you and your spouse have everything you own tied up in both your names, nothing will be available to be distributed to the bypass trust on the death of the first spouse. Couples in their 50s and older should examine how all their assets are titled.

Let's go back to the original example of the husband who channeled his estate tax credit into a bypass trust. Suppose all the couple's property had been held jointly. When the man dies, $675,000 is slated to go into that trust. But the couple's attorney discovers a nasty surprise: Nothing in the couple's tidy fortune was strictly in his name. The house, the stocks, the individual bonds, certificates of deposit, and everything that's eligible to put in the trust has both names on it. So upon the husband's death, everything automatically goes to the wife instead of the trust. If there's nothing left to stash in the bypass trust, the late husband's credit can't be used.

Caution

If you and your spouse follow the popular practice of jointly owning property, stocks, bonds, and everything else, there are no individually titled assets to transfer into the bypass trust, meaning that the trust loses its power to protect.

What can you do to prevent this kind of nightmare? If you're married, consider dividing up your property as evenly as possible with your partner. That means splitting up such things as your house, vacation home, cars, a boat, antiques, and investment portfolios.

Creating a new deed for your home and retitling investment portfolios and other holdings can be a pain, but at least this shuffling of titles won't trigger any tax bill. (Ask an attorney about possible exceptions if one spouse is not an American citizen.) The biggest hurdle in balancing an estate is probably an emotional one: It can be excruciating to divide a lifetime of possessions. Remind yourself that the motivation for doing this busy work is to shield your estate from Uncle Sam, which is a most worthwhile goal.

Summary

✦ Pick someone you trust to handle, if necessary, your medical and financial affairs.

✦ You don't need an attorney to write a living will.

✦ Consider leaving behind an ethical will.

✦ Consider a bypass trust to avoid estate taxes.

✦   ✦   ✦

A Primer on Trusts

In the decades after President Theodore Roosevelt authorized the estate tax, a vast army of attorneys, insurance agents, financial planners, and bank officers became a formidable and relentless force in finding creative ways to stiff the government. The favorite tool in their arsenal has always been the trust. In this chapter, you learn what trusts are capable of doing and which ones might best serve your needs. You also learn what steps are crucial in designing a model trust.

Although this chapter is by no means an exhaustive treatment of trusts, it gives you the highlights. Admittedly, trusts can be complicated and leaden documents that induce insomnia. But you should never consent to a trust that's being promoted by your attorney without doing at least some outside research on your own.

The living trust, which is covered extensively in Chapter 23, is America's most popular trust, but plenty of other trusts are available. This chapter outlines the general characteristics of all trusts and describes these specialized trusts:

- ✦ Living trusts
- ✦ Bypass shelter trusts
- ✦ Marital trusts
- ✦ Trusts for children
- ✦ Trusts for disabled children
- ✦ Spendthrift trusts
- ✦ Qualified personal residence trusts

Why Use a Trust?

The Rockefellers have trusts. Bill Gates, no doubt, has some, too. But if you think trusts are merely for the extremely wealthy, guess again. Millions of trusts exist in this country for both the affluent and those far from it. In the next few decades, trillions of dollars could pass from one generation to the next through trusts. The Internal Revenue Service has already noticed a heavy increase in the use of trusts.

Note   Chances are excellent that you'll either inherit money through a trust or create one of your own.

The motivations for creating a trust are boundless. Some parents and grandparents establish trusts out of a heartfelt desire to do what's best for the people they love the most. The motivation behind other trusts is strictly dollars and cents. There are equally compelling reasons why people may want to avoid bulking up on trusts. In worst-case scenarios, trusts can tear apart families and backfire horribly.

Caution   When used properly, trusts may offer considerable rewards, but their effectiveness can be jeopardized by flawed documents padded with unreasonable or inflexible stipulations. Before you agree to the use of trusts, be sure to intensively review the advisability of using them with your advisor.

You want to understand all the ramifications of a trust before your attorney hands you a pen for a signature. Trust documents are becoming increasingly intricate, and their powerful hold over heirs is tending to last for longer periods of time. Because trusts often exist for many decades, a great deal of thought must go into their creation. You may not be around to witness a trust's shortcomings, but your loved ones will have to live with the consequences of miscalculations you made for 20, 30, 40, or more years.

Yet you may never hear an estate attorney, who seems so keen on trusts, mention any hidden dangers. Why the disconnect? The more trusts stuffed into your estate plan, the stiffer the final legal bill will be. What you may not be told is that many times there are simple and cheap alternatives to a variety of trusts. These alternatives are noted in the chapter within the specific trust descriptions.

Defining a Trust

After deciding which potential heirs make your final cut, you can proceed down one of two paths. The first option is the direct bequest. This option means you pass along your hard-earned money and property to family, friends, charities, churches, or others outright. Once your heirs receive that cash, investment portfolio, or vacation home in the Rocky Mountains, they can do whatever they desire with these gifts.

Estate Taxes and Trusts

If the federal estate tax is killed or dramatically scaled back, the popularity of trusts, as an estate tax savings tool, will diminish. Without an estate tax, some of the cat-and-mouse games that older taxpayers, in particular, play with the IRS could be unnecessary. But even if the estate tax no longer exists, some trusts will still be necessary to deal with non-tax concerns, such as caring for disabled children and preventing adult children from squandering inheritances.

The second option is to bequeath all or some of your worldly possessions through trusts. Trusts, which come with an extra legal layer, aren't as simple as direct bequests. With a trust, you attach strings to your generosity. A trust established for a grown child, for instance, might stipulate that the money is parceled out over the course of a decade or two. Some trusts are intentionally designed to endure for two generations or more. The first heirs in line, who are often the adult children, receive the income generated by a trust's investments. There is often discretion given to the trustee to also distribute principal as required. They are sometimes referred to as *income beneficiaries.* The grandkids, or whoever are the backup heirs, receive what's left of the estate after their parents are dead. These heirs are called *remaindermen,* which makes sense because they get what remains.

A trust's language contains the distribution rules, which dictate how much money the beneficiaries will receive over the years or under what circumstances. Some trusts are written broadly so the beneficiaries have greater access to the assets; others can be infuriatingly restrictive.

Caution   A trust's provisions often can't anticipate all the questions that will arise about the use of the funds once the trust's creator is long gone.

Suppose money is set aside in an educational trust for a child to obtain a college degree. What if the high school graduate decides he wants to be a palm reader and take classes at a fly-by-night school? Or consider all the potential interpretations of this very common trust provision: the money is to be used for a person's "health, education, maintenance, and support." Is a beneficiary entitled to buy a Saab, or would a car that's $20,000 cheaper be more appropriate for the heir's "maintenance and support"? Experienced trustees, considering many factors, can make what they consider an appropriate decision. The beneficiary may disagree.

The person who makes these tough, and often thankless, decisions is the trustee. The trustee could be an outside financial institution, a family member, a friend, or some kind of combination of these choices. They hold title to the trust property and money held in the trust. In the next chapter, you'll learn much more about trustees and why selecting excellent candidates is crucial.

A Trust Glossary

Whether you are creating or inheriting a trust, you should know the terminology:

✦ **executor:** Person or institution named in a will to carry out its instructions. A woman selected for this job is called an *executrix*.

✦ **fiduciary:** A person who holds a position of trust. Trustees and executors are called fiduciaries because the law requires that they responsibly carry out a will and or trust's dictates. A bank or trust company that serves this role is called a corporate fiduciary.

✦ **grantor:** The person who creates a trust; also can be called a settlor or trust creator.

✦ **irrevocable trust:** A trust that can't be canceled or changed by its grantor after it's established.

✦ **remaindermen:** The people who receive what's left of a trust when it terminates.

✦ **revocable trust:** A trust that can be changed or dismantled while the grantor is still alive (such as a living trust).

✦ **successor trustee:** Person or institution who takes over as trustee when the original trustee(s) has died or become incapacitated.

✦ **testamentary trust:** A trust created by a will.

✦ **trust corpus:** Name for property that's put into a trust.

✦ **trustee:** Holds legal title to the trust assets for the benefit of the beneficiaries.

The types of trusts out there run the gamut from living trusts, which are used by millions of ordinary Americans, to instruments tailored for the kind of people who have to stop and think about how many houses they own. Living trusts are a popular tool for people who want their heirs to avoid the expenses and hassles of probate court. Any living trust can be revocable. That means it can be changed at any time. If you decide a week, a month, or years later that you don't want the trust, or you want to modify it in anyway, it's okay.

Note Because a revocable trust can be edited or torn up at any time, it provides no tax advantages.

Some trusts, including those set up to gain tax advantages, are irrevocable, which means you can't tinker with their terms later. That's the case with many charitable trusts. Once you've designated a nonprofit organization as the beneficiary of a charitable remainder trust, for instance, it's too bad if you desperately need the money later on or are plagued with second thoughts about your generosity. Sometimes a trust becomes irrevocable only after the creator dies. That is often the case with a living trust as well as a bypass trust, which allows a husband or wife to ultimately pass a huge amount of tax-free money to heirs. However, even irrevocable trusts can sometimes be modified through a court order or thanks to changes in law.

 Note With an irrevocable trust, you lose control over the assets, but you may be rewarded with certain perks, such as tax breaks and protection from creditors.

The Benefits of a Trust

Why would anyone need a trust? A well-crafted trust may be able to provide several benefits:

✦ **A trust can reduce estate taxes.** Many trusts can be used to sidestep estate taxes. The bypass trust, which is also referred to as a shelter trust, is the most common one used for this purpose.

 Note Many people think that a living trust can be used to avoid estate taxes, but that's a huge misconception. See the descriptions of various trusts later in this chapter to identify the tax shelter-ready trusts.

✦ **A trust can protect against creditors, court judgments, and ex-spouses.** Inheritances are meant for loved ones. But without the protection of a trust, heirs may end up sharing money with people they detest, such as an ex-spouse or a legal adversary. Suppose you leave your fortune to your daughter, who marries a ne'er-do-well. Maybe he's an alcoholic, a wife abuser, an adulterer, or in some other way just plain bad news. Even if your daughter divorces the bum, he could still be entitled to a share of her inheritance depending on the state in which your daughter lives. If the money is left to her in a trust, however, this money grab might be impossible.

✦ **A trust can stretch out the money for more than a generation.** Some benefactors love the idea of making their money outlast their children. Consequently, trusts can be tailored to ultimately benefit two generations. With a trust, for instance, you could leave money for your children and grandchildren. The kids would receive whatever income the trust spins off during their lifetime, and eventually the grandchildren would pocket whatever is left at the end.

✦ **A trust can provide for heirs who aren't capable of managing the money themselves.** Trusts may be a logical way to leave money to beneficiaries who you fear aren't capable of handling a windfall outright. You may worry that they will waste the money on jewelry, vacations, cars, gambling, drugs, or frivolous purchases. A trust can guarantee that an inheritance won't be blown during one terrible night at a Las Vegas blackjack table by functioning as a spigot that releases the funds gradually over a person's lifetime or at specific ages.

Example   Rather than getting all the cash at a tender age, a 20-year-old daughter might not get her final yearly check until she's 40, an age at which she's presumably mature enough to handle the money.

✦ **A trust can benefit your favorite causes.** Although you can donate directly to a charity or church, there are benefits to tucking the money, stock, or other assets into a trust. With a sophisticated trust, you and the charity can both benefit financially. After a donation into a charitable trust, for instance, you could receive a stream of income for the rest of your life. (See Chapter 29 for information on charitable trusts.)

✦ **A trust ensures privacy.** When you leave your possessions through a will, anyone can trot down to the courthouse and find out who has what. This doesn't happen when assets are tucked away in a revocable living trust. Often the creators of the trust are more worried about protecting their privacy from their own families than nosy outsiders. They may not want anyone to know they are bequeathing money to a live-in companion, a mistress, or a child born out of wedlock. A trust also enables someone to make anonymous gifts to people or institutions.

The Recipe for a Great Trust

Different trusts have different requirements to fulfill and procedures to follow, but overall the tips in this section will help you no matter what kind of trust you want to create.

Determine whether you need a trust.

Certain trusts can be a necessity, such as a bypass trust and those established for minor children and disabled heirs. But the sort of trusts that are established solely to allow mom and dad to direct the kids' lives from the grave can cause tremendous turmoil in a family. If your children are mature grownups, you should seriously consider leaving them money directly.

Some attorneys, who make a living drawing up trust papers, vigorously argue that trusts can protect even model children from life's unforeseen hazards, such as divorce, business failures, or lawsuits. But although trusts may be able to insulate heirs from a potential financial setback, ask yourself if it's worth the potential downside of having an unresponsive stranger in some bank trust department controlling your kids' cash forever. In most cases, the answer will probably be no.

Caution   Think hard before establishing trusts for responsible adult children. The overwhelming number of grown children should be able to inherit outright.

One of the biggest mistakes people can make is not having a very clear sense of whether they need to deal with trusts at all. Deep reflection is advisable if you want to use a trust; very often, you can handle your estate-planning issues in a far simpler manner. For example, as you'll learn in this chapter's description of marital trusts, trusts for second or third marriages are a popular way to give both a spouse and children a piece of an estate, but outright gifts to the kids and the stepparent would be far easier to deal with.

Decide how many trusts are necessary.

Leaving all your money in one trust might be easy, but it can booby-trap your family's future harmony. Most brothers and sisters have a hard time agreeing on something as mundane as what to watch on TV. Add money into the equation and the emotions can become incendiary.

Another advantage to breaking your estate into different trusts instead of consolidating it into one large one is that it diminishes the incentive of a bank or other corporate trustee to fiercely hold onto its power if beneficiaries are unhappy with the institution. If your dad left behind a $2 million estate in one big, juicy trust, a bank isn't going to be anxious to let the heirs escort the trust to another financial institution. In contrast, a bank might not protest with a much smaller trust that generates fewer fees.

In other instances, one trust might be best. Perhaps you want to put a few acres of land into the trust for the benefit of several grandchildren. The land might be more valuable if it's not broken up into smaller pieces. You may want to arrange to have the property sold and the proceeds parceled out at a specific time, such as the youngest grandchild's 21st birthday.

Don't hamstring a trust with rigid language.

Trusts that provide incentives for heirs to receive extra cash are becoming more popular. One of these trusts might dole out more money if the beneficiary gets a college degree, stays off drugs, or becomes a stay-at-home mom. Directing your heirs' lives from the grave can be destructive, though. But even parents who aren't that controlling can booby-trap their trusts. Some dictate how a trust's investments should be made or forbid the sale of the family home. Even the language in the best-intentioned trusts can backfire.

Allow for a flexible investment policy.

Trusts have traditionally been designed to generate steady income for beneficiaries. But with stock dividends at historic lows, today's trust portfolios are often loaded with bonds to produce decent income. These sluggish portfolios often won't leave lots of appreciation for the grandkids once the trust expires. But a new alternative called the total return unitrust can invest heavily in the stock market because payouts aren't dependent upon dividends and interest. A certain percentage of the portfolio, often 4 percent, is skimmed off the top each year. This dramatic change in investment strategy can make a huge difference. (See Chapter 20 for an explanation of the total return concept.)

Test-drive your trustee.

As you'll find out in the next chapter, most people never meet face-to-face with their designated trustee. They might name a bank trust department as trustee upon the recommendation of their attorney. But the person who is being entrusted to make many difficult and intimate decisions on your beneficiaries' behalf should be tested ahead of time. Some people wisely start with a fairly modest trust and see how the trustee fairs. Observe how the trustee invests the money and handles your inquiries and those of your family. If the trustee is aloof, irresponsible, or incompetent, you want to find out before it's too late. Because it can be very difficult for angry beneficiaries to fire an incompetent or greedy trustee, you should test out a trustee before a family is stuck with one permanently.

Tip   Insert a trustee-removal clause to allow your beneficiaries the leverage to boot a bad trustee. Today all trusts drawn by competent attorneys will likely address the trustee removal question.

Regularly update your trusts.

Trusts are not like fine wine; they don't get better as they age. The older they are, the more likely they are to need revising. The problem is that only revocable trusts can be modified easily. You may be able to amend an irrevocable trust, however, especially if the circumstances have changed and all parties are in agreement.

Caution   Avoid making changes that jeopardize a trust's favorable tax treatment.

Allow your trust a change of address.

You may not want your trust forever locked into the state where you now live. If you happen to move to another state, you may want the trust to move with you. By providing for this, you can avoid the expense and hassle of having a new trust prepared. Avoiding taxes can be another reason to give your trust the ability to change addresses.

Hire a top-notch estate-planning attorney.

Plenty of attorneys write wills and trusts, but you should think twice before hiring someone who also handles divorces or relishes suing Starbucks when a client burns her tongue slurping coffee. Trusts are not for amateurs. Your dream candidate is a specialist who isn't distracted by other kinds of law. He or she should focus exclusively on estate and trust matters and be experienced in setting up the kind of trust you desire.

Resource These two Web sites can provide the contact numbers for the bar in your state: Findlaw.com at `www.findlaw.com` and the California State Bar at `www.calbar.org`.

The best way to begin your search is by contacting the American College of Trust & Estate Counsel at 3415 S. Sepulveda Blvd., Suite 330, Los Angeles, CA 90034; (310) 398-1888; `www.actec.org`. You may also want to contact your state bar to obtain the names of estate-planning attorneys who have received extra credentialing. In some states, lawyers can earn an additional designation that indicates that they are highly skilled estate and trust attorneys. To achieve this distinction, an attorney typically must be a veteran in the estate and trust field, pass occasional tests, and attend continuing education courses annually.

Cross-Reference Chapter 6 contains more information on selecting an estate-planning attorney.

Bad Trusts

Beware of trusts that promise as many rewards as an infomercial. These trusts may, for tax purposes, be found to be bogus. The Internal Revenue Service has investigated hundreds of thousands of trusts suspected of snubbing the tax code.

Purveyors of shady trusts often advise customers to try to claim tax write-offs that are not legitimate. For instance, individuals will be told that they should try to write off personal living expenses on a tax return after putting their homes in trusts. Although homes can be placed in legitimate trusts (you'll learn later in this chapter about the qualified personal residence trust), other suggested schemes simply flaunt the law. In hyping abusive trust schemes, for instance, a promoter may insist that you can treat your home as if it was a rental property. Only landlords, however, can deduct expenses incurred in maintaining their property. Other frauds include claiming tax deductions after establishing illegal charitable trusts. No charity benefits from these phony trusts. A person, for instance, might write a check for college tuition out of the trust's assets and then claim it as a tax-deductible donation to the college.

Who is behind these sham trusts? Con artists and shady financial advisors are big boosters. They may try to lure customers by offering free investment, tax, or estate-planning seminars. They sometimes charge exorbitant amounts of money to customers, who may only receive preprinted legal forms.

On occasion, the IRS issues alerts on some of the fraudulent organizations that keep popping up. While the IRS is prosecuting these promoters, the taxpayers with these trusts, who may be innocent victims, are paying a heavy price, too. Those who become audit targets can end up owing back taxes, as well as penalties and interest.

A Guide to Major Trusts

Trusts are limited only by someone's imagination. One of the strengths of trusts is that they can be tailored to anyone's specifications. This section describes a few of the more common (as well as some of the more specialized) trusts that you may run across.

Living trusts

Nothing is simple in the arcane world of estate planning. Just try getting a consensus from experts about whether you need a living trust. Some insist that it's absolutely essential for everyone; others suggest it's unnecessary for most people until they hit their 50s or 60s. It's probably safe to say that most elderly people should consider having a living trust.

What is a living trust, exactly? It's a trust that remains under the control of its creator until his or her death and is therefore classified as revocable. Many people appoint themselves as trustee; a spouse is typically named as a co-trustee. Even if you designate someone else to be trustee, such as a relative, a friend, or a financial institution, you're still in control because you can always replace your trustee. The main reason living trusts are so popular, though, is because they enable heirs to avoid getting trapped in probate court. If all assets are placed in the trust, the probate court has nothing to oversee.

Note   Most estates covered by a living trust will probably be subject to at least a limited probate court review because it may be impractical for most people to place everything they own in the trust. If the living trust is to be used exclusively to avoid probate, it would be wise to check on how onerous probate is in your jurisdiction. It may turn out that probate is not as big a problem as it's made out to be.

A living trust can also establish a valuable financial lifeline during medical emergencies or if the grantor becomes physically or mentally incapacitated. With this trust, you name a surrogate (your trustee) you'd like to help out if you can't manage your own financial and legal affairs. You also can dictate the terms under which someone would take over. This same person can settle your affairs upon your death.

Another advantage is that living trusts are generally harder to contest than a will. With a will, someone can protest your final wishes without even hiring an attorney. The open nature of the probate process also makes it easier for disgruntled heirs to challenge a will.

Cross-Reference   See Chapter 23 for detailed coverage of living trusts and wills.

Bypass shelter trusts

If you're married and your estate has any chance of being smacked by federal estate taxes, you'll want a bypass shelter trust. A bypass shelter trust allows a husband and wife to each enjoy what's rightfully theirs: a limited free ride on estate tax obligations.

If you're smart enough to claim it, the federal government offers each person an estate tax credit. In 2001, an estate valued at no more than $675,000 would escape estate taxes entirely. When a single person dies, his or her estate automatically claims this nice credit, which is scheduled to reach $1 million by 2006.

The process is trickier for married couples. Suppose a man died in 2001, leaving behind his wife and a $1 million estate. All this money ends up with the widow, and no tax is owed. Sounds great, right? But the tax-free transfer is a temporary one; the IRS is laying in wait. By the time the wife dies, the nest egg has grown to $2 million, and her estate posthumously claims her exemption. If she died in 2004, her exemption would be $850,000. It's only now that her kids discover that mom and dad weren't so smart after all. Sure enough, mom's automatic exemption drops her taxable estate to $1,150,000. But, oops, dad never claimed his credit. (It's not an automatic credit when the first partner dies.) Remember, in the year he died, the exemption was $675,000. So instead of the heirs owing tax on just $475,000 ($2 million minus both partner's exemptions), the estate tax, which ranges from 37 percent to 55 percent, is based upon the $1.15 million value.

This extra tax blow was unnecessary. It could have been averted if the husband's $675,000 exemption had been sheltered in a bypass trust upon his death. Not only would no federal estate tax have been owed on this money when the last partner died, but the assets also could have grown considerably over the years with no future worry about estate taxes.

With the money in a bypass trust, a widow or widower won't enjoy the same access to the money as he or she did before. The trust's terms dictate the survivor's rights to this money. Typically, a widow or widower collects income from the trust and the trustee, who can be the surviving spouse, has the right to dip into the principal for a wide range of reasons. Boilerplate trust language commonly gives a survivor the ability to use the money for "health, maintenance, education, and support."

Marital trusts

A variety of marital trusts exist to fit different situations. One type is favored for people who have been married more than once. Another variety is used when one spouse is not an American citizen. Still another kind is considered appropriate for an average couple who has been happily married for decades.

Spouses must talk openly with each other, as well as with their estate attorney, before establishing a marital trust. Before proceeding, each partner needs to know what the ground rules would be.

General power of appointment trust

Often it's a husband who is anxious to establish a marital trust for his wife. The genesis for this desire can be traced back to the country's earlier history when women were legally powerless and were thought to have little or no aptitude for money. Although that situation no longer exists, perceptions about a widow's abilities to deal with finances haven't necessarily changed all that much. Some husbands fear that their widows will be exploited by con artists whose suave demeanors will disarm them and ultimately cause them to empty their accounts. Even when this isn't a concern, some men worry that their wives aren't capable of adroitly handling the family's fortune if it's passed to them directly.

The general power of appointment trust is meant to address these fears. Depending upon how the document is written, the trust can provide a widow (or widower) with a great deal of flexibility in using the money as he or she sees fit. These trusts are quite restrictive because they must be drawn to meet the exact requirements of the Internal Revenue Code. The trust may allow an outside trustee to wield total power over how the money is invested. What's more, the trustee could determine when a widow (or widower) is entitled to money. Some marital trusts are fashioned to provide the widow or widower only with the income generated by the trust's principal. In cases like these, he or she may not be able to tap directly into the principal. If she doesn't ask some pointed questions beforehand, a woman may not appreciate what she's giving up by consenting to this type of marital trust until it's too late.

Tip Even if a surviving wife or husband knows little about investing, a trust isn't the only solution. Excellent financial advisors can be hired in advance to oversee the assets.

Qualified Terminable Interest Property Trust (QTIP)

The average American marriage doesn't survive its seven-year anniversary. As long as the divorce rate remains high, there's no danger of the Qualified Terminable Interest Property Trust (QTIP) becoming obsolete. This kind of trust is often used as a way to call a truce between children and their stepmother or stepfather because it is designed to protect the interests of the children and a stepparent after the biological parent is dead. With a QTIP in place, both sides may be less interested in unleashing legal attack dogs.

Tempers can easily flare up if such a precaution is not taken. For instance, a father may die with his loyalties equally divided between his second wife and the children from his first marriage. If he leaves everything to his wife, his children might explode in anger. They could privately seethe as they watch their stepmother spend what they consider to be rightfully theirs. Without a QTIP, the father's money might not go to the kids after the stepmother's death. Instead, it could end up with her biological children, a charity, or maybe a new husband. On the other hand, if the kids get all of the money from the start, the widow may struggle to maintain her lifestyle.

With a QTIP, the surviving spouse is entitled to all the income generated by the trust but has no right to the trust's principal. The spouse who creates the QTIP designates how the money will be dispersed once the widow or widower dies. Once those wishes are stated in the trust, they cannot be ignored.

Is a QTIP always necessary? Not at all. Some people might prefer a less complicated solution. Instead of tying up the money indefinitely in a trust, the father in this scenario could have split the money any way he desired between his wife and his kids and perhaps informed everyone involved prior to his death that he expects his wishes to be honored without argument.

Tip By bequeathing the money outright to loved ones, parents can avoid the expense and hassles of a trust.

Qualified Domestic Trust (QDT)

If your spouse is not a United States citizen, the Qualified Domestic Trust (QDT) could be invaluable. A spouse from Canada, Mexico, or any other country can't take advantage of a traditional marital trusts that can shield a tremendous amount of money from estate taxes at the first death. Why the prohibition? The government worries that a foreigner who inherits money on U.S. soil will grab the money and leave the country, thereby avoiding U.S. taxes at death.

As an alternative, a couple can set up a QDT for the foreign spouse. An unlimited amount of money can be siphoned into this trust, but there is a catch. The widow or widower is entitled only to the income the trust generates. If the surviving spouse dips into the trust's principal, he or she will be hit with estate taxes. Therefore, you should avoid relying solely upon a QDT.

Tip To decrease reliance on the QDT, a couple could start transferring money into the foreign spouse's name in preparation. Up to $100,000 a year can be moved between spouses within any calendar year without triggering estate or gift taxes.

Trusts for children

Because leaving money to a child outright may not be wise, there's no need to agonize about the merits of this kind of trust. If you intend to bequeath money or other assets to a minor child, you should definitely consider establishing a trust to avoid the expense and hassle of probate.

If you leave a big chunk of money directly to a child, almost invariably a probate court will appoint a legal guardian to watch over a child's windfall. At this point, micromanaging commences. The court will demand an accounting for all the money spent on the child. In some cases, a judge will veto a guardian's proposed expenditures, and the limitations don't end there. Some states impose incredibly restrictive guidelines on how a child's money is invested. What's more, certain states won't allow a child's remaining parent to manage the inheritance. Meanwhile, the guardian may be required to post a bond, which must be paid with the child's assets.

The guardian oversees a child's financial affairs until the child is legally considered an adult. In almost all states, a youth reaches that milestone at age 18. But a teenager who may be hanging out at fraternity parties probably won't be mature enough to handle a windfall.

Advantages of a child's trust

When money is left to a child through a trust, these headaches disappear. The trust serves as a spigot that releases the funds gradually until the child ideally is competent to handle money. The document also names a trustee so there's no need to worry about the judicial system meddling in your family's financial affairs.

As with other trusts, you enjoy a great deal of flexibility in the creation of a child's trust. When the child is a minor, the trustee makes all the financial decisions, and the money is spent according to guidelines set in the trust documents. Typically, the trust assets can be tapped if the cash is used for a child's health, education, maintenance, and support. At some point, the heir's involvement in such spending decisions is often healthy. Some heirs begin receiving all the trust income, with no strings attached, shortly after college graduation for a trial run at handling the money. After that, he or she may be on a time schedule that ultimately ends with the release of all the money. Before the trust is completely emptied, some parents stipulate that the now-adult child serve as a co-trustee.

Custodial accounts

Trusts can also be used to give money to children long before a person's death. Many people don't realize that trusts are an option and instead gravitate to the far more widely known and easier to establish custodial or kiddie accounts. And where small amounts of money are involved, this may make the most sense. Depending upon what state you live in, two kinds of custodial accounts are available: the Uniform Gifts to Minors Act (UGMA) and the Uniform Transfer to Minors Act (UTMA). With one of these accounts, the money belongs to the child, but an adult is also listed on the paperwork. The adult controls the account until the child reaches the age of majority, which in most states is 18, but in a few it's 21. Each state dictates at which age the child reaches majority so he can grab the money. For the parents, these are one-way accounts: once the money is given to the child via deposit into the account, the parent cannot withdraw it for personal use.

Many parents use custodial accounts to stash cash away for a child's college years. These accounts are easy to open at brokerage firms, mutual fund firms, and banks. Parents are attracted to these accounts because of a built-in tax advantage. With a custodial account, the first $700 in earnings are tax-free every year. Suppose you sold your child's mutual fund shares and moved the money to a different fund. If you made a profit, you'd owe capital gains tax, but you wouldn't be dinged for that first $700 in profit. After a child reaches the age of 14, all investment gains and earnings are taxed at the kid's rate instead of the parent's, and the kid's rate is presumably the lower of the two.

Caution   With custodial accounts, children receive all the money at an early age. Having this amount of money in his or her name can hurt a child's chances for financial aid for college.

Trusts for children with disabilities

If you have a child who is severely handicapped, your estate plans will be more complicated. You may want to create a special needs trust that won't jeopardize any government assistance that the child is receiving. Once a special-needs child passes into adulthood, his or her right to Medicaid and Social Security is based upon the assets he or she personally holds. To be eligible, someone essentially has to be destitute. With a trust, you can ensure that the child doesn't control this pot of money in any way so that the government benefits aren't threatened.

Another advantage of a trust is that it allows you to ensure that the money will be professionally managed. Make sure your estate attorney has experience drawing up a special-needs trust because faulty language could imperil your child's future. The following trusts are commonly used to provide for people with disabilities:

✦ Medicaid trust

✦ Pooled trust

✦ Special-needs trust

✦ Discretionary trust

Caution   Don't even think about hiring a general practice lawyer to create a trust for your special-needs child. With eligibility rules constantly in flux, finding an attorney who stays current in this area of the law is critical.

If you're contemplating what to do, parents of other disabled children can be an invaluable resource. So can local nonprofit organizations that focus on your child's particular handicap, such as United Cerebral Palsy, the National Alliance for the Mentally Ill, and The Arc. You can learn how these parents have prepared their own estate plans. Your contacts should also generate names of financial planners, estate attorneys, and others who are familiar with the needs of people with disabilities.

When you establish one of these trusts, choosing an appropriate trustee is important. Some nonprofit advocacy groups such as The Arc, an advocacy group for the mentally retarded, are now offering trustee services. They hire outside investment firms to manage the money. Short of serving as trustee, some advocacy groups will step in as trust watchdogs.

 Resource   Contact The Arc at 1010 Wayne Ave., Suite 650 Silver Spring, MD 20910; (301) 565-3842; www.thearc.org.

Spendthrift trust

The name of the spendthrift trust suggests that it's tailor-made for a family's black sheep, such as a son who is addicted to betting on horses or a daughter whose appetite for credit cards is unparalleled. Although this trust was initially designed for the poster children of irresponsibility, its use has expanded to cover people you'd never dream would need such protection, such as physicians, business owners, and other professionals. The reason for this increased use is that the spendthrift trust enables a beneficiary to shelter money from creditors who are eager to confiscate it.

Tip   The spendthrift trust's protection from creditors has prompted parents of responsible children to create these trusts. Why? The trust could protect the funds from future lawsuits, divorce settlements, or business debts.

There is one catch to this Teflon-coated trust: The money is safe only as long as it remains in the trust. When a beneficiary pulls out the money, the cash is fair game to creditors. There is one way to address this dilemma: The trustee can directly pay someone's bills. If a check isn't made out directly to the beneficiary, there is nothing for creditors to fight over. Depending upon the trust's language, the trustee may be able to withhold payments to the beneficiary if a creditor is in an excellent position to grab them.

Of course, some people have ethical problems with a spendthrift trust. Is it morally right to shield someone who made business mistakes or lives recklessly from the financial consequences of his or her actions? Should someone who loses a lawsuit, for instance, be able to duck paying the plaintiff by hiding behind a trust? Others may conclude that protecting mature adults from financial mishaps that may or may not happen is an unfortunate overreaction.

Note   If your heir is a grown, responsible person, think twice before taking the drastic action of creating a spendthrift trust.

Taking Care of Fido

Ever worry about what would happen to your pet if you died first? You may be petrified that your frightened dog or cat would be carted off the animal pound. A trust could prevent this tragedy. Through a trust, you can leave a friend or any other person a sum of money to be used for the pet's veterinarian services, food, toys, and other expenses. In the trust, you can be as specific as you want about how you want your pet to be treated. Before you go to this trouble, however, make sure your two-legged trustee is willing to accept this responsibility.

Qualified personal residence trust

For many people, their house is their most valuable possession, and they want to leave their home to family, but they don't want to saddle them with an estate tax bill. A house no longer has to be a mansion or a beachfront bungalow to catapult someone's net worth into the estate tax danger zone. What's the solution? Some people ultimately conclude that federal estate taxes can be reduced with a qualified personal residence trust.

Caution

If there's no chance of estate taxes, don't give this complicated trust a second thought. It also won't be a wise move if you can't trust your own kids or whomever will be the trust's recipients.

Here's how the trust works: You place your home or vacation getaway into a trust that exists for a prearranged period of time, such as 10 or 15 years. During that period, you continue living in your house. When the trust expires, the house belongs to your kids or whomever you named as beneficiary. If you live in the house after that point, you must pay rent to the beneficiary, or the IRS will become suspicious of the arrangement. In the worst-case scenario, you could be booted out of your family home when the trust terminates and you no longer legally own the home.

Why on earth would you set yourself up to lose your home? Some older Americans, fearing that letting go of cash could expose them to financial hardship, prefer to reduce their estate taxes by giving away a house rather than cash, stocks, or bonds. Some folks are just attracted by the tax break: By giving away your house this way, you can secure a significant tax break on the gift. How so? Because the house won't belong to your beneficiary for many years, the gift tax on the house will be dramatically discounted, and you don't have to pay it upfront. Instead, the amount of gift tax assessed is applied against the estate tax exemption amount to which every person is entitled (as covered in Chapter 24). The shorter the length of the trust is, the better the discount. In contrast, if you waited until your death to transfer the house to an heir, the full value of the residence would be used when tallying an estate's total worth rather than the discounted value determined by the trust's length.

Caution   If you die before the trust does, the whole intricate arrangement was a futile exercise. The full value of the home's current market value is included in the estate.

On the other hand, if you outlive the terms of the trust, you'll have to pay rent to your kids to avoid estate and income tax problems. Depending upon family dynamics, this situation may have its own complications.

Summary

✦ Know the strengths and limitations of a trust before signing one.

✦ Resist controlling your loved ones from the grave with explicit trust stipulations.

✦ Make a trust's language as flexible as possible.

✦ Use a highly qualified estate attorney to draw up trusts.

✦ Beware of trust peddlers.

✦   ✦   ✦

Hiring and Firing Trustees

Now that trusts have become more popular with the middle
class as well as the wealthy, recognizing the trustee's role in a
trust's success is more important than ever. This chapter provides solid
advice on choosing trustees and on getting rid of bad trustees. The
financial community has been scrambling to provide trust services, so
more trustee choices abound now than at any time in the nation's
history. This chapter spells out all the options and aims to simplify your
selection process.

Even the greatest trustees, however, can't overcome a basic flaw in
millions of trusts. This chapter reveals dramatic changes in how
Americans' trust funds can now be invested. Antiquated investment
rules that required trusts to bulk up on bonds or, horror of horrors, a
state-approved list of investments, have been repudiated. Dozens of
states have passed legislation that is pushing trust investing into the
21st century. At the same time, an increasing number of attorneys are
devising investment strategies for their clients' heirs, which should
curtail some of the cross-generational warfare that frequently erupts
over inherited money.

The Trustee's Crucial Role

The widow of a wealthy businessman has tried her darndest
for years to embarrass a prominent national bank. Sometimes
she slips a sandwich board on over her clothes before pacing
in front of bank locations in Manhattan and Palm Beach. When
the sandwich board lost some of its shock value, this otherwise distinguished concert pianist borrowed a huge inflatable
pink rat and made some unflattering comparisons between
the bank and the rodent.

Why on earth has this woman picketed the bank more than 100 times? As she patiently explains to any passers-by who'll listen, she believes that she's been victimized by the bank's trust department. She's disgusted by the way the bank, which was handpicked by her late husband to oversee the estate's assets, has invested her family's dwindling trust funds.

Matchmaker, make me a match

Sure, this case is extreme. Although roughly $1 trillion in trust money is parked at banks today, most of us will never witness a beneficiary picketing a trust department. But that doesn't mean that all is well in the sleepy land of trusts. Across the country, beneficiaries who lack the socialite's sense of the dramatic are trapped in unhappy relationships with banks and other financial institutions. When a marriage experiences irreconcilable differences, divorce is an option. But trusts often don't have such an option. Trusts are typically designed to last for many decades, and all too frequently only the trust's creator, who instigated the union in the first place, can okay a split. This person, however, has usually long since died.

Financial institutions aren't the only ones catching flak. Banks manage approximately 1 million trusts, but millions more are overseen by family members, friends, attorneys, certified public accountants, and others. Although banks are criticized for allegedly committing a wide variety of transgressions, family trustees are usually responsible for the most heinous abuses. Financial institutions must adhere to strict regulations on overseeing trust money, but the rules are much more lax when an eldest son or an old family friend is running the show. There are no federal bank examiners peering over their shoulders. Further, railing against a faceless bank bureaucracy is easier than criticizing your big brother. But when a parent, a sibling, or dad's old golfing buddy must make tough decisions that could ultimately determine whether, say, you drive an Eddie Bauer Expedition or a Hyundai, conflicts can become quite personal and destructive.

It could be you

In all fairness, trustees, no matter who they are, are easy targets. Just because a beneficiary is complaining doesn't mean that the grievance is justified. In fact, it can be so difficult to figure out when complaints are justified that sometimes a judge must ultimately decide. For a son or daughter who resents having money tied up in trusts instead of receiving an outright bequest, dumping their anger on a trustee is only natural. Of course, you might believe that only the sort of people profiled in *Vanity Fair* enjoy the luxury of fuming about a trust fund. But that is a huge misconception. The number of trusts has increased dramatically in recent years, and middle-class Americans have enthusiastically embraced their use.

Note   Irrevocable trusts, ones whose language and conditions are essentially dried in cement, draw the most fire from discontented heirs. Revocable trusts, which can be amended or dissolved, often become irrevocable when the trust's creator dies.

Unfortunately, the Americans who are drawing up all these trusts often spend little time contemplating who should oversee them. The trust paperwork looks awfully impressive bound in leather, but the true test is whether it still holds up when the pages are yellowed with age. Undoubtedly, a key factor in ensuring a trust's success is the selection of the trustees.

Types of Trustees

You're sitting in your attorney's office discussing your estate plan when you're asked this question: Whom do you want for a trustee? You shrug your shoulders. You go with your natural inclination, which is to rely upon your lawyer's advice. He suggests a local bank or trust company, and you agree. Maybe he makes his recommendation because his choice is the best in town. Or perhaps he does so because the bank rewards him for his referrals. If this is your selection process, chances are you'll never meet the outside trustee, much less ever shake a trust officer's hand. You may even forget whom you named. After your funeral, your heirs are the ones who make that first phone call.

This scenario presents the wrong way to choose a trustee. Remember, choosing a trustees is probably one of the most important decisions you'll ever make. Your choice could dramatically impact the financial and emotional well-being of your loved ones for decades.

By one estimate, the average trust in America lasts for about 45 years, which is a long time for beneficiaries to live with a lemon. Unfortunately, bad trustees are like nasty colds; they're tough to shake. The reason is simple: The trust world isn't democratic. Once you're dead, your heirs can be trapped with a mediocre trustee thanks to language inadvertently contained in your trust documents.

As you contemplate whom to name as a trustee for your estate, consider the pros and cons of the three types of trustees:

Family or friends: Advantages

For many people, the inclination to choose a trusted friend or blood relative as trustee is overwhelming because of the personal connection. Some will also see it as the cheapest way to go.

The personal touch

Most people name a relative or friend as a trustee, and this choice is certainly understandable. After all, you need to have absolute confidence in whomever you choose to oversee the trust once you're gone. Chances are no one will be regularly scrutinizing the person charged with handling the assets. You're in the best position to know whether a wife, daughter, grandchild, or close friend is honest and conscientious enough for the job.

Keeping the job within the family can also make for a friendlier experience for the heirs. Beneficiaries with concerns or questions won't run the risk of being shunted to a bank's toll-free assistance number; they can just call Uncle John.

Less cost

Relying upon family trustees can sometimes be the most economical alternative. The trust can avoid fees that a bank or other financial institution serving as a professional trustee charges.

Although choosing a family member who has a working knowledge of investments is often best, the job description doesn't require the instincts of a Warren Buffett. That's because the trustee need not double as the money manager. The trustee can choose to parcel out the financial tasks to a certified financial planner, an investment firm, or someplace else. Outside professionals can also be hired, as needed, for tax and legal advice. Of course, the cost of paying these outside professionals may offset cost savings resulting from having a relative be the trustee.

Family or friends: Disadvantages

If you think Thanksgiving dinner with relatives is no picnic, try throwing money into the mix. Are you cringing yet?

Family resentment

Because of family dynamics, picking appropriate trustees within a circle of relatives and friends can be tricky. Perhaps your daughter would be the most obvious choice. She's a corporate executive who enjoys a great deal of success managing her own portfolio. If her siblings, however, resent her accomplishments and would bristle at her direction, she might not be the best candidate. You also don't want to choose someone who is experiencing drug, alcohol, gambling or financial troubles.

Tip   Look beyond the obvious reasons that would eliminate someone from consideration. For instance, you might want to pass on someone who tends to procrastinate or shy away from tough decisions.

Many parents think their oldest child or eldest son will consider it an honor to serve as trustee, but a family member won't be the best solution every time. You could inadvertently focus all the hard feelings and disagreements with the estate on that one person. One woman, for instance, turned to an independent trust company to manage her mother's trust after her angry brothers repeatedly berated her for spending too much money on their ailing mother's care. The siblings were in line to pocket whatever was left after their mother died. The conflict degenerated to such a point that she didn't dare meet with her brothers in person because she feared they'd strike her. Of course, that's the woman's story. The brothers may tell an entirely different tale.

Don't Hide Your Intentions

Parents should generally tell their children up front whom they want to name as trustee and why. The resulting family discussions might prompt mom and dad to change their minds. At the very least, children will understand the game rules and won't be shocked after their parents' deaths. They will also be able to support or complain about a choice while their parents are still alive to hear it.

Example

In one publicized case, a family trustee allegedly took several years to sell his late brother's medical practice. The delay cost the family millions because the patients had all found other physicians.

Complaints less likely

When relatives or friends are running a trust, some family members are less inclined to protest when the trustee is floundering. Typically, in court family trustees aren't held to as high a standard as corporate trustees.

Corporate trustees: Advantages

If you rule out family or friends as trustees, you may want to use a financial institution instead.

Continuity and professional management

Banks, trust companies, mutual fund companies, brokerage firms, and other financial institutions all fit into the category of corporate trustees. One big advantage that this type of trustee enjoys over a relative or friend is that a trust can't outlive a corporate trustee. An institution provides continuity. In contrast, a relative could eventually become too infirm to continue in the role or could die before the trust expires.

A corporate trust can also inject a measure of professionalism into the management of a trust. Complicated trusts that contain sizable amounts of money or specialized assets such as commercial real estate or oil and gas interests could benefit from professional management.

Note

A corporate trustee is much more likely to keep abreast of trust law changes in your state.

No emotional attachment

A financial institution can dispassionately administer a trust. A family trustee might buckle under pressure from a sister or a cousin to release money when it's not in the interest of most beneficiaries. A corporate trustee should be immune to emotional blackmail.

Corporate trustees: Disadvantages

Consider as well the flipside of involving a corporate trustee in your heirs' lives.

Impersonal service

In this age of mega bank mergers, a trust that was initially established at a small, local bank might now be overseen by a national bank conglomeration that's 3,000 miles away. When banks or brokerage firms merge, the acquirer steps in as the trustee. To save money, the institutions that gobble up their competitors sometimes eliminate on-site trust officers and replace them with toll-free assistance instead. So much for personal service.

Financial institutions are increasingly focused solely on managing trust assets profitably. Although some independent trust companies and upper-crust banks, such as Northern Trust and U.S. Trust, are highly regarded for their personalized service, many institutions wouldn't be interested, for instance, in taking the time to find nursing care for a widower.

High fees

Beneficiaries love to gripe about bank trust fees. Sometimes these complaints are justified and other times they aren't. A bank's fee schedule could pose a particular hardship for smaller trusts because there can be a minimum annual fee imposed regardless of the assets involved. The minimum fee for some banks is in the $5,000 to $10,000 range.

Caution   Never underestimate a bank's ability to concoct new fees. Fight back if a bank starts charging your trust account gratuitously.

One bank, for instance, tacked a $600 fee onto its trust accounts for what it called "regulatory compliance compensation." No matter that the expenses incurred for following federal regulations were included in the bank's overhead. Beneficiaries won a class-action suit against the bank for charging this fee and received refunds.

Other professional trustees: Advantages

Financial institutions and family aren't the only trustee choices. Attorneys, investment advisors, and accountants offer another alternative.

An Ally for Beneficiaries

Feeling trapped in beneficiary hell? You aren't alone. Thousands of beneficiaries have sought help from Heirs Inc., a nonprofit group that promotes trust and estate reform. The organization can help assist members in creating beneficiary-friendly trusts, as well as provide advice to unhappy beneficiaries. It also maintains a referral network of estate attorneys, as well as litigators.

Heirs Inc. has published a hefty book for its members that discusses ways to design model trusts, fire trustees, and boost trust performance. Through hundreds of footnotes, the book also provides many other resources. Contact Heirs Inc. at P.O. Box 292, Villanova, PA 19085; (610) 527-6260; www.heirs.net.

A financial planner, an accountant, or a lawyer can be quite adept at running a trust. An accountant or financial planner, in particular, should be able to handily oversee a trust's investment portfolio. These professionals may have a broad understanding of a client's financial picture and could provide what amounts to holistic advice. On the other hand, a lawyer may excel at drawing up estate documents, but he might know far less about investing trust money.

These professionals are also likely to be covered by liability insurance. If any problems should arise, such as stolen money or recklessly invested assets, beneficiaries could seek compensation and, hopefully, have someone to collect from if they win a judgement.

Other professional trustees: Disadvantages

Choosing a professional advisor as a trustee can get tricky.

Conflicts of interest

The very nature of an investment advisor's job description could trigger conflicts of interest. A financial planner, for instance, may be tempted to trade stocks, mutual funds, and other investments simply to generate commissions for himself.

An attorney could face even thornier conflicts. Suppose the attorney drew up the original trust and is now serving as trustee. If the relationship disintegrates into a legal battle, your former ally could unleash legal firepower against you for very little expense. In pressing your cause, you might experience difficulty finding an attorney who doesn't mind butting heads with a colleague. Finding an attorney who will sue a corporate fiduciary may be even harder.

Note

Some states maintain ethic laws that prohibit an attorney from volunteering to be a trustee. It should give you pause if an attorney has lobbied for the job.

Lack of personal service

These professionals might pose the same potential problem as a bank trust officer: lack of time for and empathy with the beneficiaries. They won't necessarily have the personal skills required to deal with, say, a confused widow. If an attorney or an accountant maintains a hectic practice, he or she may not be able to devote enough time to the trust.

Co-trustees: The best of both worlds

Some benefactors ultimately decide to link a professional trustee with a family trustee. The corporate trustee usually makes the investment decisions. The family member serves as a sounding board for the beneficiaries and acts as a watchdog for the professional trustee. In some cases, the roles are divided differently. For instance, if a family business is included in a trust, a family member may be in charge of the business while the other trustee manages the rest of the assets. If you want to pair a family trustee with a corporate one, consider giving the family member the right to replace the corporate co-trustee with another institution as needed.

Caution   A family member co-trustee can also be a trust beneficiary, but the IRS frowns on appointing only beneficiaries as trustees.

For example, a widower might want to leave all his money in trust to his son and daughter and name them as the sole trustees. The arrangement, however, could prompt the IRS to investigate. Why? Trusts often generate tax breaks because heirs don't have direct control of the money and so can't freely use the money any way they want. If the kids are trustees, though, there's nothing to stop them from doing just that. Consequently, the trust's tax advantages could be jeopardized.

Another alternative is naming two relatives or friends. Note, however, that although this arrangement can provide checks and balances, it could inadvertently stymie intelligent investment decisions. This problem could occur if the trustees hopelessly deadlock on decisions. For instance, a daughter who is a co-trustee doesn't want to sell any of the stocks in her dad's portfolio because she considered him a brilliant investor. She believes that unloading his stocks, even if some are teetering on the edge of bankruptcy, would be a betrayal. Her dad's best friend, the other trustee, may want to jettison the investments. So although there is no prohibition against designating more than one trustee, having more people involved in the decision-making results in a greater possibility of squabbling and losing money due to wasted investment opportunities.

A third possibility is giving your family the option of using a trust protector if trustees disagree. You can name this third party or leave it up to your heirs to choose someone if the need arises. The trust protector could be given the power to remove a troublesome trustee. This person may also be expected to mediate disputes. The authority of a trust protector will depend upon what powers are given to him or her when estate-planning documents are drawn up.

Don't Forget an Escape Hatch

You can save your heirs future grief by designing a trust with an eject button. Make sure you include language that indicates that if a majority of the beneficiaries vote to oust the original trustee, that trustee is gone. When beneficiaries have the power to vote out a trustee, they can better protect their own pot of money.

You may also want to specifically address a common problem encountered by beneficiaries: bank mergers. Consider stipulating in the trust documents that beneficiaries have the right to find another corporate trustee if that trustee is gobbled up by another financial institution.

Traditionally, firing a trustee has been nearly impossible. Most old trusts don't allow the surviving loved ones to switch trustees. Why the prohibition? Some trust creators feared that the beneficiaries would switch corporate trustee institutions just so they could squeeze more money out of the trusts. If beneficiaries didn't like how one bank was doling out the cash, another one might be more generous. After all, trust payouts are typically structured around the rather loose provision that the money is to be used for a person's "health, education, maintenance, and support." A different trustee might have a looser interpretation of that open-ended language.

Even the option of legal retaliation hasn't been much comfort to beneficiaries because a besieged trustee can use the trust funds to fight off a legal challenge. Just the thought of the trustee spending thousands of dollars in attorney fees can stifle any thoughts of rebellion. So make it easy on your heirs by providing a legal escape hatch in the trust.

Selecting a Corporate Trustee

Naming a family member or friend to act as trustee can be a quick and intuitive process: You know whom you trust and whom you expect to be around for a while. In contrast, with many financial institutions and advisors scrambling to get into the trust business, your choices of professional trustees are increasing every year. Mutual fund companies, full-service and discount brokerage firms, independent trust companies, insurance companies, and financial planners are now competing with bank trust departments. All of them want to cash in on the historic transfer of wealth that everybody has been anticipating. There is no one best place to turn for a corporate trustee. You'll need to evaluate your own needs and choices before deciding.

This section provides a closer look at your alternatives:

Bank trust departments

If you have money tied up with an outside trustee, chances are it's sitting in the bowels of a bank. Banks have traditionally been the most popular place to stash trust assets, which is understandable: The institutions are financially sound, and they've managed trusts for many generations.

If you have an excellent relationship with your bank, you may wish to buttonhole the institution to serve as a trustee in the future. Before deciding, you will want to learn more about the bank's trust operations. Now that banks are defending their territory against a slew of interlopers, in some cases they are sabotaging their own best efforts. Trust departments were never the banking industry's cash cow; banks always made their big money elsewhere. So when the industry began reeling from merger mania, it was often the trust departments that were battered by cost-cutting measures. A customer who might have once shared a leisurely cup of coffee with a trust officer may now be dialing a toll-free number to reach someone. A trust officer who might have handled 100 to 150 accounts in the past may now be swamped with many, many more. At the same time, many banks have become disinterested in the small fry. If a trust has assets under $500,000 or even $1 million, the chance for personalized service is slim. Some institutions do not even accept smaller trusts.

Tip   Not all banks are downsizing client service. Some of the premier trust institutions, such as Northern Trust and U.S. Trust (which have locations scattered around the country), continue to provide a high level of personal service well beyond asset management.

Independent trust companies

As banks continue to swallow each other up, countless trust officers have lost their jobs. Some of the more enterprising bank refugees have created their own trust companies.

Tip   In contrast to the typical bank, these boutique trust companies are more likely to be involved in meeting a family's personal needs.

For example, a staffer at a trust company may spend time hunting for an adult daycare center for an elderly client or explain to a widow, who knew nothing about her husband's finances, how to balance a checkbook. Trust officers also find themselves counseling widows and widowers about the financial implications of remarrying late in life. (Often elderly clients crave companionship, but they hesitate to remarry for fear of robbing their children of a portion of their inheritances.)

These trust officers also may focus their attention on a family's younger generations. One trust company, for instance, spent time researching whether an adult child's wish to obtain a degree in astrology fit in with her deceased parents' instructions that only legitimate education expenses be funded. After researching the issue, the trust officer concluded that a major in astrology passed the test. These boutique firms also serve more decadent needs. For instance, trust officers at boutique firms will do the legwork for a client who wants to buy a luxury car. After receiving an e-mail from a client on safari in Africa who had lost his luggage, a trust officer tracked down identical luggage and shipped it express mail to Kenya.

The fee schedules for these smaller trust companies are usually similar to what banks charge, but the minimum investment required can be smaller. You don't have to live in the same state as the trust company to become a customer. Here's a list of a few of these independent shops for you to consider:

✦ Kanaly Trust in Houston, Texas at (800) 882-8723

✦ Idaho Trust in Coeur d'Alene, Idaho at (888) 664-6448

✦ Trust Company of Illinois in Glen Ellyn, Illinois at (630) 545-2200

✦ Reliance Trust Co. in Atlanta, Georgia at (404) 266-0663

✦ Cypress Trust Co. in Palm Beach, Florida at (800) 439-8745

✦ Legacy Trust Co. in Overland Park, Kansas at (913) 338-4530

✦ Caldwell Trust Co. in Venice, Florida at (800) 338-9476

For a more complete list, contact the Association of Independent Trust Companies, which is a trade organization, at 710 E. Ogden Ave., Suite 600, Naperville, IL 60563; (630) 579-3230; www.aitco.net.

Financial planners

Former bank officers are not the only ones who are jumping into the trust business. Certified Financial Planners are beginning to create their own trust companies. Often they make this move after growing tired of being stymied by their efforts at intergenerational planning; when a husband or wife dies, a planner all too often loses the account because it's shipped off to a bank trust department. Experienced financial planners can be a worthwhile resource for your trust needs.

Some of the trust pioneers in this field belong to the National Association of Personal Financial Advisors at 355 W. Dundee Rd., Suite 200, Buffalo Grove, IL 60089; (888) FEE-ONLY; www.napfa.org.

Brokerage firms' trust services

Brokerage and mutual fund firms, including Merrill Lynch, Fidelity, Salomon Smith Barney, Vanguard, and TIAA-CREF, are now busily marketing their own trust services. Charles Schwab created quite a stir in the financial industry by gobbling up U.S. Trust. The move toward trust services makes perfect financial sense. Brokerage firms are tired of losing their most affluent clients' money to trust companies that cater to the wealthy. It's also part of a move to provide one-stop financial services covering everything from college planning to trust management.

See Chapter 5 for the whole story on financial planners.

Giving a Trustee a Test Run

Trust services are no different than anything else you buy. Some are wonderfully efficient and helpful, but others just across town could be dreadful. You wouldn't know that, however, if you didn't shop around. Few people would dream of buying a car without a test drive. Yet with stakes much higher, few people test their trustees.

What you don't want to do is leave your heirs with an untested trustee. At the very least, you'll want to evaluate a corporate trustee before it's too late. How do you do that? Don't wait until a death to have your trusts funded. You may want to invest some of the assets you have in a living trust with an institution that you're curious about. (Chapter 23 tells you all about establishing living trusts.) You can then evaluate the service you receive while it's still possible to change institutions.

If your trust is funded at a full-service brokerage firm, be wary if you're lobbied to invest heavily in the firm's own brand of mutual funds.

A brokerage's proprietary funds usually charge high expenses and can be poor performers. And the troubles don't end there. Suppose you later decide to move the money to an independent trust company. The proprietary funds, which aren't transferable, would have to be cashed out, and capital gains taxes would be owed. This cost could prove to be such a financial hardship that you feel compelled to stay put.

Family offices

A family office is, by far, the most exclusive option for a trustee. Family offices were created by the kind of millionaires who get university schools of business and major downtown streets named after them. Families of oil tycoons and other industrial magnates originally created these offices just to serve their own extended families. But in recent years, they've opened up the doors to mere millionaires. To gain admission, you typically need at least $2 to $3 million.

Some of the notable one family offices include the following:

✦ Bessemer Trust in New York City

✦ Pitcairn Trust in Jenkintown, Pennsylvania

✦ Laird Norton Trust in Seattle, Washington

✦ Whittier Trust in South Pasadena, California

✦ Glenmede Trust in Philadelphia

Resource

To find out more about family offices, contact this clearinghouse: Family Office Exchange, 137 N. Oak Park Ave., Suite 310, Oak Park, IL 60301; (708) 848-2030; www.familyoffice.com.

Corporate trustee cost considerations

As you narrow a search for a corporate trustee, don't forget about the costs. Remember, the only time you'll enjoy leverage on price is before sealing the deal. Always inquire about price breaks. If a trust company or bank wants your business badly enough, it can tear up its standard fee agreement. After you're gone and the heirs are locked into the arrangement, negotiating more attractive fees will be tough. Unhappiness over fees is one of the biggest complaints you'll hear from heirs.

Tip   To combat fee inflation, request that all fees be paid according to a fixed fee schedule. You might not get this concession, but it's worth a try.

Fees vary dramatically. Corporate trustees typically charge anywhere from 1 to 1.5 percent of assets for portfolios that are $1 million or less. Trusts that exceed $1 million may get price breaks on these annual fees. Find out about any other costs the trust will incur. Some institutions, for instance, charge a sizable redemption fee when the trust is cashed out. Try to establish an agreement that forbids this fee, which is sometimes used to discourage beneficiaries from jumping to another institution.

When you are interviewing corporate trustee candidates, add the following to your list of questions:

- ✦ Who will be my personal trust officer?
- ✦ What is the background of the trust officer?
- ✦ What is the turnover rate of your trust department staff?
- ✦ What is your minimum for trust assets?
- ✦ What services can I expect based on my trust's net worth?
- ✦ When I have questions, will I be directed to an 800 number or can I speak with someone local or in person?
- ✦ Will you accept an unconditional trustee removal clause?
- ✦ What fees do you charge and how often are they raised?
- ✦ Will you provide references?

Considerations for Potential Trustees

If your parents, another relative, or a friend asks you to be a trustee, you may be flattered. A more realistic reaction might be unadulterated fear. Be prepared for a thankless job. By controlling the money, you're setting yourself up to be the bad guy. You might be better off suggesting that you be one of a group of trustees.

This section addresses some of the challenges you may face as a trustee.

Awesome responsibility

As the trust's fiduciary, the buck stops with you. Your responsibility is to make the trust run smoothly. The duties include touching base regularly with the beneficiaries, overseeing investment strategies, filing income tax returns, keeping careful records, and maintaining the trust's purse strings. If real estate is left in the trust, you'll be responsible for such grunt work as making sure locks are changed and that the home is properly insured. You can hire professionals to do these jobs, but ultimately the responsibility is yours. You may decide to be compensated for some of your work, but this compensation may cause resentment among family members.

Emotional drain

Standard gear for a trustee is a flack jacket. Beneficiaries, perhaps your own brothers or sisters, may resent what you're doing for all the wrong reasons, or if you're not handling the job well, for all the right reasons. They could be furious that mom and dad didn't bequeath the money directly to them. But with the parents gone, you're the only convenient target.

You may also be called upon to make difficult decisions. Should an heir receive trust money to fund an abortion or perhaps buy a bigger house in a top school district? A trustee must also balance the competing interests of relatives who favor trust investments that produce a lot of income versus those who lobby for growth stocks. The decisions can become even more tortuous if the trust assets include a closely held family business.

Potential legal action

If beneficiaries want to accuse you of incompetence, negligence, or unscrupulousness, they can sue. Perhaps you left a big chunk of money uninvested. That's a no-no. On the other hand, maybe your only crime is failing to coddle impossible beneficiaries.

If a family business is in a trust, there can be even more potential legal headaches. Courts may react harshly if you allow a closely held family business to be the dominant trust asset and over time that business fails. A family business is by nature an extremely risky venture, and it may face even harder times with the family's patriarch dead. Operating a business through a trust can cause no end of grief. If you're sued, you can often defend yourself with the trust's money. If you lose the lawsuit, the plaintiffs may go after your personal assets.

If you decide to plunge ahead, use these methods to help protect yourself:

✦ Review the trust documents so you thoroughly understand your future responsibilities.

✦ Recommend any changes to the trust document that could clarify your responsibilities as well as liabilities.

✦ Discuss your duties with any co-trustees so that everyone is clear about their roles.

✦ Never mix your personal assets with the trust's assets. And do not purchase assets from or sell your personal assets to the trust. These rules apply to your friends and family as well.

✦ Document all your actions as a trustee and keep meticulous records.

✦ If you are on the verge of making a significant investment decision, try to obtain the written consent of beneficiaries before following through.

✦ Hire a top-notch lawyer or accountant to prepare the trust's tax returns.

✦ Keep in frequent touch with the beneficiaries.

Trust Investment Issues

No one needs to tell you that the financial world is changing, but does someone need to tell your trustee? Back in the mid-1990s, not a single soul traded stocks online, but today many millions do. Stock trading continues well past the market's official closing at 4 p.m. Eastern time. The tremendous curiosity about all things money has spawned the creation of television channels devoted exclusively to stock tips, hunches, and breathlessly delivered financial news.

The string of revolutionary changes has affected most investors in both positive and negative ways. But trust investment strategies have remained stubbornly mired in the Stone Age. Antiquated laws have dictated how trust investments have been managed for generations. Maybe these laws worked in simpler times, but today they are hurting the investment returns of countless trusts.

Prudent investing decisions

One such law, commonly referred to as the *prudent man rule,* requires a trustee to evaluate potential investments to determine whether they are a prudent (meaning conservative) choice. In effect, this law limits a conscientious trustee to investments that are super safe, such as U.S. government bonds, some blue chip stocks, and certificates of deposit.

The prudent man rule was designed to protect beneficiaries from trustees who managed trust money recklessly. This intention sounds good, but the rule is inherently flawed. Could a small-cap technology stock meet the prudent test? Almost certainly not. What about junk bonds or a foreign stock fund? No way. Initial public offerings? Get real. Yet in recent years, Nobel laureates and other economic power hitters have repeatedly insisted that the most successful portfolios need to be balanced with a wide variety of investments. And that variety includes the investments sitting at the far end of the risk spectrum. Ironically, these experts long ago concluded that adding small-cap stocks, junk bonds, and other firecrackers could actually dampen a portfolio's risk while at the same time boosting overall returns.

Caution

When you are making an investment decision, it's foolish to focus on a solitary investment and decide whether it's appropriate (as the prudent man rule dictates trustees do) rather than considering the entire portfolio.

Although it's taken an achingly long time for the world of trusts to embrace this mindset, a breakthrough occurred in the mid 1990s when the National Conference of Commissioners on Uniform State Laws recommended the scuttling of the prudent man rule. (The goal of the nonprofit conference, which has been around since 1892, is to encourage the uniformity of state laws. The 300-plus commissioners, who are primarily attorneys, judges, and law professors, draft uniform acts and then encourage state legislatures to adopt them.) The Uniform Prudent Investor Act spawned the prudent investor rule. Under this rule, a trustee must look at the entire portfolio and determine what the best mix of investments should be. The rule permits more diverse and dynamic portfolios by sanctioning the use of a panoply of investments. The new marching orders, over time, should boost the typical trust's total returns. The rule also concluded that trustees should oversee a portfolio with an eye toward keeping taxes and costs low. This guideline may sound like common sense, but it's a big deal in the trust world.

Those states that establish trust law within their own boundaries are under no obligation to adopt the prudent investor rule. So far, however, 35 states (listed in Table 26-1) have approved the rule, and more are expected to do so.

Table 26-1
States That Have Approved the Prudent Investor Rule

Alaska	Maine	Ohio
Arizona	Maryland	Oklahoma
Arkansas	Massachusetts	Oregon
California	Michigan	Pennsylvania
Colorado	Minnesota	Rhode Island
Connecticut	Missouri	Utah
District of Columbia	Nebraska	Vermont
Hawaii	New Hampshire	Virginia
Idaho	New Jersey	Washington
Indiana	New Mexico	West Virginia
Iowa	North Carolina	Wyoming
Kansas	North Dakota	

Source: National Conference of Commissioners on Uniform State Laws

Examining a trust's investments

Just because your state has adopted the prudent investor rule doesn't mean that you should relax. The definition of what qualifies as prudent varies widely. You must determine whether trust money is being managed intelligently and the returns and the level of risk are acceptable. You should also pay close attention to how well your trustee is keeping taxes and costs to a minimum.

Note   The prudent investor rule should prod more trustees into using index funds, which are both cheap and tax-friendly.

In many cases, index funds are far superior to a bank's proprietary mutual funds. However, some banks that are in the corporate trustee role invest trust assets in their own mutual funds even though these funds, as a group, can be mediocre performers. Rarely will you see a personal finance magazine rave about a bank mutual fund. One reason why they plod along in obscurity is that the fees are often high, which cuts into performance. What's more, the funds can be tax-sloppy, which is particularly bad news for taxpayers in the highest brackets.

If the trust is worth $500,000 to $1 million, beneficiaries may not need to use a bank's in-house funds. Before signing up a bank as trustee, find out what the investment policies are and whether common trust funds are available. Common trust funds, which are pooled assets managed in-house, aren't shackled by the high retail costs of the regular mutual funds, but they operate in the same way: A manager of a common trust fund selects equity investments just as a mutual fund manager would. These common funds were created as a way to address the logistical nightmare of overseeing an overwhelming number of small trust accounts, each with their own stock and bond holdings. The attraction is that beneficiaries can expect more attention focused on their investments in a common trust fund than in an individually managed portfolio that's considered small potatoes.

Tip   If you want to go with a bank trustee, avoid the bank's mutual funds as trust investments; the bank's common trust funds make a better choice.

If you choose an independent trust company, a money management firm, or some other corporate trustee to invest the assets, you'll want to check its performance records. You should know whether the manager invests in individual stocks or from a favored roster of mutual funds. Either way, you should check the long-term track record of each investment. You should also inquire about any bias the manager has toward investing styles. Some managers may favor value over growth investments; others might be big boosters of index funds.

Tip   Always compare performance figures of potential money managers with well-established benchmarks such as the Standard & Poor's 500 and the Russell 2000.

A Trust That Pleases Everybody

The prudent investor rule can't possibly lay to rest all the investment issues that have haunted trustees and beneficiaries alike. Throughout the nation's history, the traditional trust has managed to infuriate just about anyone who is in line to receive money. And beneficiaries are still angry today. For example, immediate beneficiaries often complain that a trust's investments aren't spinning off enough income. The next in line, who are often the grandchildren of the trust's creator, couldn't care less about the income. They want to see the trust's portfolio packed with growth stocks.

The once intractable tensions between competing relatives no longer have to trigger generational warfare. Today, a potential solution exists: It's called a total return unitrust. This trust is designed to appease beneficiaries with very different objectives. But to appreciate how this trust can ease tensions, you need to understand how trusts have historically worked.

The bad old days

For more than 200 years, Americans have embraced what is called the income-only trust. The premise of this trust is simple: A family's patriarch (or matriarch) leaves his money in a trust to two generations, usually his children and grandchildren. But the children get first crack at it. Throughout their lives, the children siphon off whatever income is generated by the trust's investments. Except for certain circumstances, they are not allowed to touch the trust's principal. Of course, these beneficiaries prefer to tap into rich veins of dividend and interest income from utility and tobacco stocks, bonds, and certificates of deposit. They aren't focused on how fast the portfolio grows but on how much income it produces. With stock market dividends at historic lows, however, investing for income has become a thankless job.

Note   Today's trust portfolios must be stuffed with stodgy bonds to produce decent income. To get just a 5 percent annual payout from a trust, some trustees find they must sink as much as much as 95 percent of the assets into bonds.

A portfolio that by today's standards has a decent amount of stocks (65 percent) to bonds (35 percent) provides a pathetic income stream. A $1 million portfolio invested with that mix of stocks and bonds would produce a mere $25,000 or so after the trustee's expenses were deducted. That kind of annual payout is shocking to beneficiaries, who think a $1 million portfolio should stretch a lot farther than that.

This investment strategy doesn't fill the grandkids with much joy because they sometimes must wait decades before receiving anything. Only after their parents die are they entitled to whatever trust money is left. At this point, the trust legally terminates. If you were in a grandchild's shoes, would you prefer a trust that had clung to U.S. Treasury bonds or one that was fueled by stock in such growth companies as Intel, Oracle, Home Depot, and Wal-Mart? A trust stuffed with growth stocks for many years could conceivably far exceed the value of the original trust that granddad left behind. But if a trust is bloated with low-performing bonds, there may be little to divvy up when the last generation finally gets its turn. At the very least, the portfolio's real value shrinks with inflation. Trustees try to weigh the concerns of both types of inheritors, but typically there's been more of a bias toward pleasing the first relatives to feed at the trust trough.

Unitrust to the rescue

Enter the concept of the *total return unitrust,* proposed by trust and estate law specialist Robert Wolf. With this approach to trust investing, trustees aim for growth by investing heavily in the stock market and using the principles of total return investing, in which the success of a portfolio is not judged strictly on the amount of income it kicks out, but on how much it appreciates over time. Bulking up on bonds is unnecessary because payouts aren't dependent upon dividends. Instead, a certain percentage of the portfolio, 4 percent is often recommended, is skimmed off the top each year.

With this type of trust, current beneficiaries aren't clamoring for income because they receive a stable percent of the trust's principal unrelated to the income earned by the trust. These principal withdrawals shouldn't jeopardize the trust because it should be growing at a fast enough clip to more than make up for the difference. The relatives who are first in line would receive a percentage of trust's assets each year. If the trust creator wants to be more conservative, he can use 2 percent or 3 percent for the percentage. By aiming for the best returns, both generations of beneficiaries can finally back the same horse.

Although the unitrust has been acclaimed in legal circles, some critics warn that dipping into principal could backfire during an extended bear market. In response, the unitrust's creator examined what would happen to a $100,000 trust funded in 1960 using both methods. A trust invested evenly between intermediate Treasury bonds and the Standard & Poor's 500 would have been worth $346,171 in 1998. In comparison, the total return trust, which was invested in stocks (80 percent) and bonds (20 percent), would be worth $832,482. And that's with annual 4 percent payouts. A portfolio invested entirely in stocks would have mushroomed to $1.57 million.

Hope for beneficiaries of traditionally invested trusts

When you're drawing up trust documents, the best strategy is to make provisions for a unitrust from the start. But that advice doesn't help those stuck with the traditional trust language. Beneficiaries shouldn't automatically despair. Instead, talk with the trustees. They may conclude that there is nothing in the trust that prevents this switch in investing styles. Your chances of succeeding could be better if the trust doesn't specifically state that payouts must be exclusively limited to income. You should also be encouraged if the original trust permits principal to be touched for certain worthy purposes such as education, medical bills, maintenance, and support. A few states, such as New York and Pennsylvania, are exploring legislation that would make trust conversions to unitrusts much easier.

Meanwhile, there's hope on one other front. The National Conference of Commissioners on Uniform State Laws has once again weighed in. The conference recently approved the Uniform Principal and Income Act, which should also make it easier for existing trusts to switch from traditional all-income strategies to the total return unitrust approach by giving trustees more flexibility. Table 26-2 lists the states that have adopted the act.

Table 26-2	
States That Have Adopted the Uniform Principal and Income Act	
Alabama	Kansas
Arkansas	North Dakota
California	Oklahoma
Colorado	Tennessee
Connecticut	Virginia
Hawaii	West Virginia
Iowa	

Source: National Conference of Commissioners on Uniform State Laws

Resource Many other states are considering adopting the Uniform Principal and Income Act. For the latest list of states, visit the National Conference of Commissioners on Uniform State Laws' Web site at www.nccusl.org.

Busting a Trust

Maybe mom or dad picked a terrible trustee. The corporate trustee is charging unreasonable fees, and the kids have been placed on terminal hold when calling with questions or complaints. Or perhaps the family trustee is pouring the trust money into shaky land deals or other lousy investments.

Tip Before you try to get rid of a trustee do some soul searching. Are you sure your trustee is mediocre or worse? Or are your expectations inflated? Some beneficiaries who switch trustees remain unhappy with their new choices.

If you want to give your trustee the boot, here's how to proceed:

✦ **Examine the trust's documents.** You might find language that permits you to switch trustees after all. Don't assume the trust doesn't permit it.

✦ **List the trustee's shortcomings.** In writing, thoroughly document what you perceive to be the corporate trustee's failings. If investment performance is shameful, compare the portfolio's returns with widely recognized benchmarks, such as the Standard & Poor's 500 and the Russell 5000. You'll also want analyze a trust's tax efficiency. To do this, you need more than the K-1 tax form that's sent to beneficiaries each year. You have the right to obtain a copy of the trust's tax return. The return includes such information as trustee fees and trading activity. If you have the numbers to back up your complaints, you stand a better chance of making yourself heard.

Tip

Once you have the list of problems in hand, find out who at the trustee institution handles trust disputes. At banks, that person will probably be the ombudsman.

✦ **Get help.** You may want to use an attorney, an accountant, or a financial planner to help evaluate a trust's subpar performance, as well as gather damning evidence.

Resource

Managing Family Trusts, Taking Control of Inherited Wealth by Rob Rikoon and Larry Waschka (John Wiley & Sons), a book written for professional advisors, gives detailed instructions on how to evaluate a trust and ultimately boot the trustee.

✦ **Threaten to sue.** You'll get a corporate trustee's attention if you threaten litigation. The trustee may be hesitant to receive bad publicity. After you sue, you lose leverage.

Caution

Remember that a corporate trustee can legally tap into a trust's assets for to pay its own legal fees when defending itself against the beneficiaries.

✦ **Disclaim interest in a trust.** This is a drastic move, so you need to consult an attorney and proceed carefully, if at all. Suppose you're the sole income beneficiary with two kids. If you wave your right to future trust checks, the trust would dissolve. The money would be distributed to your kids, and the trustee would walk into the sunset. Under this scenario, you'd be dependent upon your children to give money back to you. (That would probably be the scary part.)

More Help on the Horizon

The National Conference of Commissioners on Uniform State Laws has approved a model trust code that should make it a bit easier to remove a trustee. Under the new Uniform Trust Code, which was approved in August 2000, beneficiaries can petition a court to remove a trustee as long as they all agree and there was a "changed circumstance" affects the trust. (Yes, this wording is awfully vague.) Some beneficiary advocates suggest that a bank merger or even a sustained change in the economic climate would meet that standard. The code would apply to all trusts, even old ones that make no mention of trustee removals. But you can't take advantage of the code's provision unless your state adopts it. To find out if your state has, contact the National Conference of Commissioners on Uniform State Laws at 211 E. Ontario St., Suite 1300, Chicago, Ill. 60611; (312) 915-0195; www.nccusl.org.

Summary

✦ Grill your trustee candidates and give them a test run.

✦ Don't keep your trustee choices a secret.

✦ Include an escape hatch in your trust.

✦ Pay close attention to trustee fees.

✦ Consider choosing a total return unitrust to benefit all beneficiaries.

✦ Know how to boot a trustee.

✦   ✦   ✦

Being Generous for All the Right Reasons

In Part VII, you will discover the wisest ways to share your wealth with loved ones, as well as with organizations and causes dear to your heart. You will learn that giving to worthy causes can involve more than just writing a check and pocketing a tax deduction. Some charitable giving plans give back to you, and one plan allows you to essentially run your own mini-foundation. After reading this section, you can decide whether any of the charitable strategies covered have a place in your estate plan.

Managing the Family Dynamics of Inheritance

Inheritance issues relate to retirement because people planning the financial aspects of their retirement should consider not only how they will spend their money during retirement but also how they will gift the assets left over. This chapter provides practical tips for those folks as well as for people who can use inheritances they receive to benefit their own retirement nest egg.

The Big Inheritance Issues

Along with mom's spaghetti recipe, yellowed *National Geographics,* and dusty knickknacks, trillions of dollars will be handed down from one generation to the other in the next few years.

Those sitting on all this money face a huge responsibility. They have to decide when to hand it off to their loved ones. Traditionally, mom and dad tightly hold onto their money until they die. But for those parents who don't need every penny, there are admirable and pragmatic reasons to contemplate playing Santa Claus earlier. But that decision is probably one of the easier calls to make.

Older Americans must also grapple with tough questions like these: Can we rely upon the kids to make good financial decisions, or should we tie up their inheritance in trusts? Are we being fair if we give each child the same inheritance? (Second and third marriages make this issue even more complicated.) Should a child who is a neurosurgeon receive the same inheritance as her sister who is a waitress? Families can ultimately be emotionally ripped apart by such issues.

In turn, future heirs need to examine their own expectations and understand what responsibilities they face. Baby boomers and younger Americans who are saving haphazardly for retirement or not at all because they anticipate an inheritance are living most dangerously. Researchers at Cornell University suggest that the average boomer will inherit a $90,000 estate, but other studies estimate that the figure could be as low as $23,000. Only an infinitesimal fraction of Americans can expect big bonanzas. A third of the inherited loot is expected to end up with just 1 percent of all baby boomers. No matter who gets what, the logistics of this high-stakes game of financial musical chairs are mind-boggling.

Note

Most inheritances will be modest. The nation's retirees, who are healthier than in the past, are leading longer and more active lives, so there will be less in their bank and investment accounts to pass on when they die.

Advice for Benefactors

These tips will help to keep the peace between benefactors and their heirs.

Don't keep your intentions a secret.

Money is America's last taboo. Television talk show guests chat about sex, therapy, and other incredibly intimate details of their lives, but you'll never see anyone pull out financial statements and spread them across a coffee table. This reluctance to talk about money is certainly practical in a television studio, but it can create havoc within a family.

More than three-quarters of senior citizens who participated in an AARP survey failed to discuss their estate with their would-be heirs. Remaining quiet is understandable, and some financial experts still insist that it's the best strategy. But if you're tempted to keep your inheritance plans secret, think long and hard about the consequences.

Even if you remain mum, you're likely to send unintended messages after your death to your heirs. No family is perfect. Scratch beneath the surface and you'll often find hurt feelings, jealousies, and resentment. Inherited money won't heal those wounds, but it might inflame them. Suppose a couple dearly loves their three grown children, but only the son works in the family business. The couple wants to divide assets evenly, but is it fair to ignore the son's hard work and indirect contribution to the pot of money left behind? If the estate is divided equally upon the parents' deaths, the son may focus his anger on his siblings and forever strain those relationships.

Without communication, children are likely to misinterpret the intentions of a dead parent or grandparent. Suppose a husband and wife leave their grown children money in trusts. The kids are incensed that they didn't receive the money outright and feel that mom and dad treated them like babies. If the parents had sat down and explained their reasoning, the children might have felt okay about the parents' decision. Or after a family meeting, the parents might have felt compelled to rewrite their estate plan to better fit their children's wishes.

Tip   As a practical matter, heirs are less likely to challenge an estate plan after your death if you share it with them ahead of time.

Even the wealthy need to be candid.

Rich parents often think that the advice to be candid doesn't apply to them. They believe if they reveal too much about family wealth, the children will drop out of school, fail to pursue a career, and become lifelong slackers. However, this mums-the-word embargo often backfires. When the kids eventually get the money, they may feel isolated, guilty, and haunted with no real purpose. They might indeed blow the money because they've never been trained how to deal with sudden wealth.

Many wealth consultants suggest that wealthy parents (or any parent) begin talking with children about money as soon as the kids express an interest, just as they might discuss sex with a child.

As the kids grow up and their questions grow increasingly sophisticated, the parents reveal more about the subject. A seven-year-old, for instance, isn't going to ask about trust funds, but she might be curious about why her house is nicer than her friend's house. Later on she may ask where the money came from, how large the fortune is, and when she could expect some of it herself.

Note   You should convey to your children that asking questions about money at home is okay. Make it clear that home is the safest place to talk about money and to share feelings, no matter how conflicted or irrational they may seem.

Ideally, parents should serve as good role models. They should talk openly about the role of money in their lives and their own feelings about it. What they shouldn't do is pretend they aren't rich. However, they can tell the truth and remain low key. In response to children's questions, a parent might acknowledge that the family is more fortunate than most, but that good fortune means the family can help others, which is an exciting responsibility. It's wise to acquaint children with charitable works at an early age so they become a natural part of the children's lives later on.

A wealthy family should convey to children the pitfalls and advantages of wealth. One instructive way is to point to examples of families who are handling their money in both good and reckless ways. As they grow older, kids can participate in discussions about the ethical responsibilities that wealth brings.

Speaking from the Grave

An increasing number of parents and grandparents are passing along inheritances with strings attached by tying up their money in family incentive trusts.

As with other trusts, the money isn't awarded to a son or daughter all at once. But although many trusts parcel out money when children reach certain ages, an incentive trust requires the heirs to earn the money. To do this, the heirs must meet their dead parents' expectations.

Parents, for example, might release more cash for a child who earns a college or post-graduate degree, starts a business, or decides to be a stay-at-home parent. To discourage loafing, the trust might provide financial matches for a child's salary. Some trusts have even established their own family Nobel Prize awards. Every few years, a panel of judges convenes to decide which family member has made the most meaningful contribution to society. The winner pockets a sizable chunk of money.

Meanwhile, some trusts stipulate that children are docked money if they fail to establish a prenuptial agreement, flunk a periodic drug test, become alcoholic, or join a cult. A man whose brother was killed in a car accident stipulated that his kids would get an extra $10,000 for each year with a clean driving record. Another person released more money if a child spent a few months on a kibbutz.

Creators of incentive trusts, which were introduced in the 1990s, originally assumed that only the extremely rich would bite. After all, many wealthy people are petrified that their kids will be spoiled rotten by too much money. But a lot of the people embracing these trusts only recently became wealthy. Often this wealth is due to stock options and the rewards of a lengthy bull market. Because these parents made it on their own, they are biased against giving their kids a free ride.

Dictating from the grave brings its own perils. Children may understandably resent their parents' interference. For example, a couple might provide a financial incentive for a daughter to stay home with a child. But if the daughter quits a job she loves to earn the trust payments, the resentment may haunt her for a lifetime. Meanwhile, incentives tied to a person's professional career can also trigger anger. The sister who became a Wall Street analyst might receive far more money from a trust than the brother who became a teacher. That sort of value judgment about a grown child's vocational choices is bound to inspire anger.

Families who appreciate these perils are trying to make the trust documents more flexible. Trusts that used to be 20 pages long may now run 45 pages. After fashioning one of these documents, some parents are afraid to share the news with their children. Do this and run the risk of alienating your children when reconciliation is no longer possible.

Are these trusts a good idea? In almost every case, they aren't. Most experts agree that it just isn't healthy for your family to feel that you are controlling them from the grave.

Stagger an inheritance.

There's no reason to dump money on a child or grandchild all at once. Your estate documents can dictate that a loved one receives money at certain stages in his or her life. When to open the money spigot is an individual decision. Many parents dictate that their child begins receiving the money at the age of 25, an age when they feel their children are beginning to be financially responsible. After that, distributions are staggered until the age of 35 or 40. Staggering the inheritance keeps large amounts of money from being spent frivolously in a short period of time.

Although you might be inclined to delay the inheritance as long as possible, you should resist this temptation. Withholding the money until heirs are in their 40s and 50s won't do them nearly as much good. By then they will be well into their careers and, with any luck, will be accumulating a sizable nest egg. Holding the money back may also convey the message that you don't trust your kids.

Put it in writing.

Heirs don't hesitate to fight over the oddest things. A war medal, an old brooch, a box of faded letters, a grandfather clock, trophies, and other keepsakes can all stir passionate debates. A bitter family fight over a glockenspiel that a father played in Shriner parades once even made it into *The New York Times*.

Fights among siblings or other relatives don't have to be inevitable. Parents or grandparents can turn the division of their sentimental possessions into a family project. Ask the children what they want and write it down. An easy way to do this is as a supplement to a will. That way, an attorney won't have to get involved every time you add something to the list.

If parents die without leaving written record of who gets what, hold a family meeting to divide up the keepsakes. Get creative with distribution methods:

- ✦ Heirs can take turns putting an adhesive note on the items they want. (Draw names out of a hat to see who goes first.)

- ✦ Allow trading. If your sister selected Mom's pearl necklace and you cherish it, consider relinquishing two of your turns in exchange for the jewelry.

- ✦ Establish that any gift given to a parent by a child automatically reverts to the original giver.

- ✦ If more than one person wants the parents' wedding pictures, have the photographs scanned; once framed, a laser copy on photo-quality paper is just as lovely as the original.

- ✦ Divide and conquer: If everyone is clamoring for the sterling silver, divide the silverware into place settings. Parcel out the charms on your mother's favorite bracelet.

Consider gifting while you're still around.

Giving financial gifts to loved ones while you're still alive is worth considering for two reasons. First, it's an excellent way to avoid estate taxes. The money you give away tax-free now reduces the size of your estate. The goal for many generous parents is to die with an estate that doesn't trigger any estate taxes.

Even if the estate tax is killed or eventually phased out, there's another excellent reason to play Santa Claus: You can give grown children their inheritances at an age that they can best use it. You can watch your children or nieces and nephews enjoy the money and derive satisfaction from that. Of course, the downside is that you might be watching the money being handled badly. Keep in mind that hardly anyone will spend money the way you would.

Ground rules for gifting to individuals

You can bestow annual $10,000 gifts on whomever you'd like without worrying about any tax consequences. Federal gift taxes, which are identical to the estate tax schedule, kick in only when you give someone more than $10,000. (The $10,000 amount is indexed to inflation, so it won't remain frozen at that level.) If you're married and can afford to be even more generous, you and your spouse can give a total of $20,000 per person a year. How is this possible? A husband and a wife can each give $10,000 to the same person without triggering taxes.

Cross-Reference   Chapter 24 contains the estate tax schedule.

There is no limit to how many $10,000 checks (or smaller ones) you can distribute. If you want to give each of your five grandchildren checks along with your favorite cousin, a dear friend, and anybody else in one year, it's okay.

Note   The IRS doesn't care if you give away a fortune as long as each individual pockets no more than $10,000 a year from you.

What happens if you write a check that exceeds $10,000? The amount over $10,000 is essentially subtracted from your estate tax exemption. As you might recall from Chapter 24, the exemption in 2001 is $675,000. Suppose you give your daughter a $25,000 check in 2001. Of that amount, $15,000 would be applied to the exemption, so now your estate would avoid estate taxes if its net worth doesn't surpass $660,000 ($675,000 minus $15,000). As long as your lifetime gifts — not counting the yearly $10,000 gifts — don't exceed the exemption threshold (which increases to $1 million in 2006), you won't need to write a check to pay federal gift tax.

Are there circumstances when a generous soul will face gift taxes, as opposed to having his or her estate tax exemption whittled down? Yes. It would happen if someone gives a huge gift to an individual that, in one fell swoop, exceeds the estate tax exemption. The payment of gift tax could also be triggered by enough gifts over the years to exceed the limit. You, not the recipients, pay the gift taxes.

Cash isn't the only gift that qualifies for the $10,000 tax exemption. Try these avenues of generosity:

✦ Forgive a personal loan.

✦ Sign over a mortgage to another person.

✦ Transfer the title to a car, boat, or other property.

✦ Gift stocks, bonds, and stock options.

✦ Make an interest-free loan (the waived interest is the gift).

Breaking through the $10K ceiling

The IRS waives the $10,000 gift-tax ceiling if the money is used to pay medical bills or school tuition. But the rules are quite precise on how the money must spent. For instance, the gift waiver only applies to tuition and not room and board, supplies and other college expenses. What's more, if someone reimburses a child for college tuition, the gift is not tax-exempt. The grandparent, for example, must send the check directly to the school. A new option for grandparents is to contribute the money into a state-sponsored tuition savings program, which is often referred to as a 529 plan. The rules also apply to medical expenses. A wealthy uncle, for instance, would have to send a check directly to the medical provider instead of the patient.

Gifting large sums and stock

If you'd like to give away considerable sums of money, think strategically. An ideal gift is property that you expect to appreciate substantially in the future. Suppose that you recently bought a $30,000 block of a blue chip stock that you anticipate will grow nicely in the years to come. By giving it to, say, a son, you remove it from your estate. By transferring the stock to your son, your estate won't get dinged years later if the stock helps to hoist your estate out of the tax-free zone. For estate purposes, the stock's value is locked in at today's prices and not what it's worth when the benefactor dies. If the son was going to get the stock anyway, it could make sense to give it to him now rather than later.

Tip   Don't assume, however, that all stocks make great gifts. You should hold onto stocks that have already skyrocketed in value.

Suppose you bought Dell Computer stock in 1990 and watched it skyrocket by an average of 97 percent annually during the next 10 years. You probably shouldn't give this stock to your son. Let him inherit this terrific stock pick instead. Why? Because if you hand him the shares now, his capital gains tax when he sells will be based on your original purchase price (the stock's cost basis).

If the stock isn't passed on until after your death, the IRS won't use the original value of the stock to determine capital gains taxes when your son sells the stock. Instead, the stock value will be based on the stock's market price at the time of your death; this figure is known as the *stepped-up basis*. Thanks to the method used to value stocks in estates, your son can avoid paying any capital gains tax on that eye-popping appreciation.

If Your Parents Won't Talk

Have your parents discussed their estate plan with you? Chances are they haven't. This section suggests ways to get them talking to you about estate issues without appearing greedy.

Get your own estate in order.

Mom and Dad aren't the only ones who need an estate plan. Most people require at least a no-frills version no matter what their age. All parents of minor children, for instance, should have a will to designate who would care for the kids if both parents die. Estate planning should really be considered lifetime planning to preserve and protect what you own, regardless of age. Waiting until retirement to begin estate planning can result in serious financial mishaps that can't be reversed.

Knowing this, you can legitimately ask your parents for estate-planning advice. Ask them what estate-planning documents they found necessary. (If they've done nothing, you'll at least know.) Query them about their choice of an estate-planning attorney. With any luck, your questions can lead to a meaningful discussion.

Use a death to start a conversation.

Look for an opening to begin a dialogue. The death of a family friend or a celebrity could provide an excuse to begin talks that evolve over time.

If your parents balk, ask them at least for the basics.

Okay, your parents feel uncomfortable talking about inheritances. Even if money is taboo, you should at least pin them down on four critical estate-planning necessities, listed in this section. Assure your parents that dollar figures needn't enter the conversation. Explain that sharing this information can protect them when they are in most need of help. The following questions are the four key points you need to discuss with them.

Who has power of attorney?

The durable power of attorney document names the person who can make financial and legal decisions for your mother and father when they no longer can do it themselves. It's possible that your mom might one day suffer from Alzheimer's or your dad might be paralyzed by a stroke. If they didn't designate anyone in advance, they need to know that a court will do so if it becomes necessary. The judge may select a person who doesn't even know your family.

Do they have a will?

A will dictates where someone's property goes after death. In a will, you can leave your property to people, charities, schools, churches, or any organizations you please. In addition to major assets like a house or a brokerage account, your will can dictate who receives your sentimental possessions. Dying without a will can create havoc for your family.

 See Chapter 23 for details on creating a will and making it official.

Who is the health care proxy?

Imagine that your dad's a widower and he suffers a massive heart attack. Who'll be his advocate at the hospital? A document called a health care proxy gives a loved one the authority to make medical decisions when a person is not physically or mentally able to do so himself. If your parents fail to fill out this form, which can often be obtained at hospitals and nursing homes, they risk having a court-appointed attorney take control of medical decisions away from the family.

 Learn more about health care proxies, as well as living wills, in Chapter 24.

Where is the list of assets?

You should know where your parents keep their assets. After someone's death, survivors are often forced to rifle through desks, filing cabinets, bookcases, and under mattresses in the hopes of finding investment records, a safety deposit key, and insurance policies. To prevent this search, a list of assets should be kept in an easy-to-find place.

Families are unfortunately not always successful in discovering all the assets. Sometimes missing heirlooms can trigger distrust. In one family dispute, missing jewelry raised suspicions. Only later was it discovered underneath floorboards.

Ask parents what they need.

Grown children need to know if parents will have the resources to take care of themselves. A retirement portfolio, for instance, can be wiped out if a parent spends years languishing in a nursing home. If parents are unable or unwilling to pay for long-term care insurance, children might want to pitch in and buy it for them. (See Chapter 30 to determine whether they need the insurance.)

An aging widow or widower, on the other hand, may be having trouble keeping track of their finances or, due to deteriorating eyesight or health, may need assistance writing checks, filling out a tax return, and filing financial papers. Studies indicate that roughly one out of every four persons over the age of 85 needs assistance with routine money matters. A parent may welcome the help, but he or she may be too proud to ask for it. You might offer to help mom or dad get their finances in order by organizing bank and brokerage statements, reviewing insurance policies, and possibly merging accounts.

Consider asking a therapist for advice.

If you aren't sure how to approach your parents, consider seeking the advice of a family therapist. Sometimes an outsider who is an expert on family dynamics can address deep-seated issues that keep family members from confiding in each other.

Advice for Heirs

In many ways, inheriting money isn't any different than receiving a big pile of cash after quitting a job, cashing in stock options, or winning a legal settlement. But there's one huge difference: An inheritance can be booby-trapped by a lifetime of emotional baggage. Whether we like it or not, people use money as a way to quantify love. This section is an heir's survival guide:

Spend a small portion.

For some people, the temptation will be great to spend all or most of an inheritance on a car, a house, or other pricey items. Unless you're independently wealthy, you should resist this temptation. Spending a modest amount of an inheritance may help you resist the urge to spend it all. Some heirs may want to spend a little money to buy something that would serve as a reminder of the father, mother, or other benefactor who left behind the gift; for example, heirs might make a contribution to a charitable organization to honor the deceased's interests.

Strengthen your own financial position.

Most people know what they need to do to get their finances in order, but they might not have the money to do it. An inheritance provides you with the opportunity to straighten out your finances. Here's what you should initially do with the money:

- ✦ Wipe out credit card debt.

- ✦ Establish an adequate emergency fund.

- ✦ Review your insurance needs, including life, disability, and long-term care, and make sure you have adequate coverage.

- ✦ Begin making the maximum contribution to a 401(k), 403(b), Keogh, or other tax-deferred retirement account.

✦ Contribute $2,000 annually to an Individual Retirement Account.

✦ Start a college fund for your children.

After all that is accomplished, congratulate yourself. Now you can move on with the fun stuff, which is deciding how to invest leftover money.

Invest tax efficiently.

The good news is that you probably won't owe income taxes on the money you inherit. Also, the estate paid any estate taxes before distributing the assets to beneficiaries. But that tax protection doesn't last forever.

The earnings your inheritance generates once you take possession of it will be subject to taxes. An exception is money you inherit through an Individual Retirement Account. (See Chapter 11 for more on inherited IRAs.) Inherited IRAs can be extremely prickly. If you inherit an IRA, don't touch it until you seek professional help. For some rules of the road, visit the Web site of Ed Slott, a CPA and nationally known IRA expert, at www.irahelp.com.

To shield your inheritance from the IRS, consider these tax-efficient investments:

✦ Index mutual funds

✦ Tax-efficient mutual funds

✦ Exchanged-traded funds

✦ Municipal bonds

✦ Individual stocks

Whatever you do, don't let sentiment sway your investment decisions. Some people vow not to touch a parent or grandparent's stock portfolio because it would be dishonorable. Others believe that their benefactor was such a wise investor that it would be foolish to tamper with success. But investments that were appropriate for a 70- or 80-year-old person probably won't be desirable for someone much younger.

Take your time.

Don't rush into spending or investing the money. Develop a solid game plan before proceeding. Until that time, you may want to put any cash into a money market, which should offer a better interest rate than a savings account.

If your inheritance is sizable, you may wish to invest through dollar-cost averaging. By using this approach, you don't have to decide all at once what to do with the money. With dollar-cost averaging, you allocate money into a specific investment monthly or quarterly. Doing this provides you with breathing room. It can also bolster your courage to invest regardless of whether the financial markets are soaring or being battered.

Consider counseling.

Ever hear of the sudden wealth syndrome? If you inherit a sizable portfolio, you might experience it. It's not confined to heirs; persons winning a lottery or legal settlement or those who make a killing on stock options can also experience the same feelings. In just the Silicon Valley alone, by one fairly recent estimate, about 64 new millionaires were being created each day.

Sudden wealth syndrome sounds like a nice malady to catch, and that's the problem. There aren't many people who are going to sympathize with somebody who just inherited enough money to pay off the mortgage. Heirs can feel alienated from their friends and don't dare talk about their emotional demons. A windfall might also seriously strain a marriage. The person who inherited money might feel superior; the other spouse might be battling a sense of inadequacy. If the beneficiary makes all the decisions surrounding this new money, the tension may only be exasperated. Heirs might also worry that people are friendly just because of the newfound wealth.

One way to deal with new wealth and a bewildering flood of emotions is to seek counseling. Certain family therapists specialize in the problems of the wealthy. Another excellent resource is the growing list of organizations that are geared toward those who inherit money or who have earned a great deal on their own (see the sidebar). In addition to providing advice and networking, many of these groups are big proponents of mixing wealth with philanthropy.

Getting involved in a good cause can help someone dispel any feelings of shame and at the same time find a sense of purpose. Once someone becomes involved with philanthropy, guilt can dissipate. There's been an explosion of ways that affluent people can get involved with good causes.

Resources for Sudden or Inherited Wealth

These organizations can help you adjust to your newfound wealth:

✦ Money, Meaning & Choices Institute at P.O. Box 803, Kentfield, CA 94914; (415) 267-6017; www.mmcinstitute.com

✦ The Inheritance Project at P.O. Box 503, Ivy, VA 22945; (804) 961-0876; www.inheritance-project.com

Also, check out the book *Seven Stages of Money Maturity* by George Kinder (Dell Books). John Levy, a wealth consultant, has written a variety of publications on inherited wealth. You can write him at 842 Autumn Lane, Mill Valley, CA 94941 or call (415) 383-3951.

Understand how trusts work.

You may receive your inheritance outright, but many heirs don't. Your money could be parceled out through a trust. The trust terms dictate when you receive the money.

Sometimes an heir is named as a co-trustee, but sometimes not. A trustee could be a relative, attorney, accountant, bank, brokerage firm, or trust company. A trustee manages a trust's assets and complies with any trust instructions. Some disgruntled heirs have become active in fighting what they believe are antiquated trust arrangements. An organization called Heirs Inc. represents the interest of aggrieved inheritors. See Chapters 25 and 26 for full details on handling trust issues.

Caution   You won't know what your rights are unless you thoroughly understand the terms of a trust. Do your homework to find out how it works and what it means for you.

Watch out for sharks.

Once you inherit, be aware of financial sharks. If your inheritance passes through the probate court system, legitimate financial advisors, as well as shady characters, can pluck your name out of public records. Vulnerable widows can be targets of these con artists. Never hire a financial advisor who calls you out of the blue.

There are excellent organizations that can easily provide you with a list of qualified financial experts in your area. The National Association of Personal Financial Advisors (800-FEE-ONLY) and the Financial Planning Association (800-282-PLAN) are great resources.

Cross-Reference   See Chapter 5 for solid information on picking a financial advisor.

Summary

✦ Consider tax-free gifting to family while you're still alive.

✦ Discuss your estate plans with your heirs ahead of time, so no one's feelings get hurt.

✦ Talk to your parents about their estate plan and other legal arrangements.

✦ After you inherit money, put your own finances in order first.

✦   ✦   ✦

Getting Involved with Charitable Organizations

✦ ✦ ✦ ✦

In This Chapter

Riding the new wave in charitable giving

Assessing a charity's worth

Being a mini-Rockefeller on a macaroni budget

Considering family foundations (for the mega wealthy)

✦ ✦ ✦ ✦

*I*n this chapter, you learn how to find charities that most deserve your money, time, or both. For individuals, including retirees, who want a hands-on-role with their favorite philanthropic endeavors, finding out whether a charity can accommodate the desired level of involvement is also critical.

This chapter also gives you the basics on two of the more satisfying ways to give: donor-advised funds, which have become tremendously popular, and family foundations.

New Trends in Charitable Giving

Never in the history of America has there been so many people contemplating the disposal of so much money.

Cross-Reference Curious about the nitty-gritty of establishing charitable funds that provide tax benefits? See Chapter 29 for information on strategies such as charitable remainder trusts, charitable gift annuities, and pooled-income funds.

Yet an increasing number of Americans are unwilling to wait until the funeral to be eulogized as a truly generous person. Many want to make a difference while they still have a pulse. This desire to do good in both traditional and innovative new ways has ushered in what some are now calling a new age of philanthropy.

In this era, the United Way is no longer the knee-jerk choice of magnanimous souls. Checkbook philanthropy will never go out of style, but a growing number of do-gooders are demanding hands-on experiences. Many entrepreneurs with newfound wealth as well as others wish to see their donations of time and money generate impressive results. New age philanthropists hope their cash and business smarts will produce the kind of competitiveness and accountability that some charities may lack.

Tip The reward for charitable good works isn't limited to a warm, fuzzy feeling. Donations can help reduce taxes in ways that have probably never occurred to you (you'll learn more about this later in this chapter).

Finding the Right Charities

Which charity deserves your money? Choosing the right one to support isn't much different than finding the best stocks to invest in. Both assignments require research, and both quests can seem daunting at the outset. After all, about 1.4 million tax-exempt organizations exist in the United States. What follows are steps you can take to winnow down the field.

Do your homework.

Before contributing to a charity, read as much as you can about it. A charity should provide you with literature, including its annual report, which should include its mission statement, board of directors, and financial statement. Also ask for the group's annual information return, IRS Form 990. If the charity is reluctant to provide you with a copy, strongly consider scratching it off your candidate list. Keep in mind that churches and many small charities are not required to file this government form. The returns of many charities are available through Guide Star (www.guidestar.org).

In addition to your research, find out what the pros think. The following organizations can provide a seasoned perspective. Make sure you familiarize yourself with each watchdog group's standards for assessing a charity's finances and operations.

✦ **National Charities Information Bureau:** You can purchase an in-depth report on a specific charity from the NCIB for $9.95. To see a sample report, visit the bureau's Web site at www.give.org. You can also receive an introductory copy of the group's *Wise Giving Guide,* a quarterly publication that includes a complete summary of its evaluations of national charities. You can contact this organization by mail at 19 Union Square West, New York, New York 10003, and by phone at (212) 929-6300.

✦ **American Institute of Philanthropy:** The American Institute of Philanthropy is another watchdog organization that rates hundreds of charities. The institute suggests that charities spend 60 percent or more of their contributions on program services. However, new or less popular groups might spend more on administration than on charitable programs. You can contact this organization at 4905 Del Ray Ave., Suite 300 W., Bethesda, MD 20814; (301) 913-5200; www.charitywatch.org.

What's in a Name?

Do you know the difference between the Make-A-Wish Foundation and the Grant-A-Wish Network? It can be difficult to distinguish the nation's best-known charities from those with familiar-sounding names. Make-A-Wish isn't the only organization fighting the confusion. The American Cancer Society, the American Heart Association, the Arthritis Foundation, and the National Multiple Sclerosis Society are some of the long-established charities that have been confused with obscure organizations that have similar names. Before donating, make sure you know your money is going to the right charity. Check out a charity with the rating resources given in this chapter before you contribute your time or money.

✦ **Philanthropic Advisory Service of the Council of Better Business Bureaus:** The Better Business Bureau's Philanthropic Advisory Service collects information on hundreds of nonprofit organizations. It also sets its own standards for charitable operations. You can obtain reports on individual charities, as well as contact the BBB with complaints about nonprofits, at 4200 Wilson Blvd., Suite 800, Arlington, VA 22203-1838; (703) 276-0100; www.bbb.org.

✦ **Evangelical Council for Financial Accountability:** This council is made up of evangelical Christian charities that meet certain standards for fundraising, accountability, money management, and other criteria. The council reviews organizations annually for compliance. Contact the council at P.O. Box 17456, Washington, DC 20041-0456; (800) 323-9473; www.ecfa.org.

Consider volunteering.

You'll not only receive an emotional reward from volunteering, but you'll also better appreciate whether a charity deserves your time and money. Contact your local United Way, an arts association, or another umbrella organization that knows about the work of many agencies. If you have a charity already in mind, contact it directly.

Tip To find opportunities, see if your community has a volunteer center, a voluntary action center, or a volunteer bureau, which should act as a clearinghouse for volunteering opportunities.

The Internet also serves as a matchmaker. Do you want to know what volunteer needs are going unmet in your community? No problem. Many charitable Web sites can pinpoint opportunities after you type in your zip code. To start your search, explore these four Web sites:

✦ **SERVEnet.org** at www.servenet.org allows people to perform customized searches for volunteer opportunities based on location, skills, and interest.

✦ **Helping.org** at www.helping.org, backed by the AOL Foundation, is a one-stop source for finding volunteer and giving opportunities.

✦ **Idealist.com** at www.idealist.org, a project of Action Without Borders, provides a search engine and other resources for locating thousands of volunteer opportunities here and abroad.

✦ **VolunteerMatch** at www.volunteermatch.com allows individuals to research thousands of one-time and ongoing volunteer opportunities by zip code, category, and date.

Research your options.

If you don't have a particular charity in mind or want to see what's out there, take a good look around: There are wonderful charities doing great things, but you may not even know about a meritorious one just down the street. To learn more about nonprofits and charitable trends, try these excellent resources on and off the Web:

✦ *The Chronicle of Philanthropy* is the world of philanthropy's trade publication. Contact it at 1255 23rd St. NW, Washington, DC 20037; (800) 728-2819; www.philanthropy.com.

✦ **GuideStar** is a nonprofit clearinghouse that maintains information on more than 660,000 charities. You can contact it at 427 Scotland St., Williamsburg, VA 23185; (757) 229-4631; www.guidestar.org.

✦ **Independent Sector,** the national organization of nonprofit groups, publishes reference guides. You can contact it at 1200 18th St., NW, Suite 200, Washington, DC 20036; (202) 467-6100; www.indepsec.org.

✦ **The Internet Nonprofit Center** provides a charity locator, essays and analysis of nonprofit trends, and FAQs at its Web site at www.nonprofits.org.

✦ *NonProfit Times* is a publication geared towards persons working in the nonprofit world, but it contains articles of interest to philanthropists; www.nptimes.com.

✦ **More than Money,** a nonprofit group, publishes a catalogue called *Taking Charge of Our Money, Our Values, and Our Lives,* and it lists hundreds of resources on charity, philanthropy, and money. You can contact this organization at 2244 Alder St., Eugene, OR 97405; (800) 255-4903; www.morethanmoney.org.

Setting Up a Donor-Advised Fund

Has your desire to help good causes outgrown buying Girl Scout cookies or writing a yearly check to your alma mater? After spending years of writing modest checks to all sorts of worthy causes, many people have grown dissatisfied with this scattershot approach to philanthropy. What they want to do is organize their giving to make it more effective.

If you feel that way, too, perhaps you should consider funding your own mini foundation. It doesn't cost nearly as much as you might assume. In some cases, you can begin for as little as $5,000 or $10,000 through a community foundation or through independent charities established by such financial institutions as Fidelity, T. Rowe Price, and Vanguard.

To get started, you need to establish a donor-advised fund. Donor-advised funds, which share a great deal in common with family foundations that millionaires favor, are revolutionizing the world of philanthropy. People who would never consider themselves rich can now act and feel like big-time philanthropists. For those with much deeper pockets, at least $1 million or $2 million, a family foundation is an alternative. You'll find more information on these near the end of the chapter.

Tip   In comparison to traditional foundations, donor-advised funds are cheaper to launch and sustain, and the legal and accounting hassles are nearly nonexistent.

How a donor-advised fund works

To establish a donor-advised fund, you set aside a pool of money and pick either a community foundation or a financial institution to act as an intermediary between you and worthy charities. The foundations use professional money managers to invest the pool of donor money. To pay for these services, an annual fee, often 1 percent, is extracted from the fund. Filling out the paperwork to set up a donor-advised fund shouldn't take more than a few minutes.

As the donor, you'll make decisions about which favorite cause you'd like to money to be directed to. You don't have to be locked into a cause forever, though. All in all, a donor-advised fund has many advantages, which are described in the following sections.

Note   You can change the recipients, but once you've contributed to a donor-advised fund, your money can't be returned. The gift is irrevocable.

Freedom to choose charitable causes

A benefactor's interests can be quite specific. A donor with the Maine Community Foundation, for instance, earmarked money for clam restoration. Through the Cleveland Foundation, an equestrian established a therapeutic riding program for people with disabilities. Someone in St. Louis bought a greenhouse for an inner city school.

The money in a donor-advised fund can be distributed to any legitimate charity. To win the IRS's seal of approval, the charity must be classified as a 501(c) 3 organization. Schools, churches, hospitals, museums, environmental causes, performing arts, youth sports groups, and traditional charities such as the American Cancer Society and American Lung Association have all been grateful recipients of donor-advised money. Why not just send the money directly, instead of working with community foundations or other go-betweens? You can get the inside information from a community foundation on what compelling needs are out there, how a charity works, and how your money will be used.

Tax breaks for cash donations

Just like any other charitable gift, the money earmarked for a donor-advised fund is tax-deductible. You receive an immediate tax break for the cash you funnel into a fund.

 Example   Suppose you place $10,000 in a donor-advised fund and you're in the 31 percent federal tax bracket. Your tax deduction would be $3,100.

Cash contributions can be used to write off up to 50 percent of someone's adjusted gross income for any one year. If the gift is in securities, such as stocks, mutual funds, and bonds, the ceiling drops to 30 percent of the giver's adjusted gross income. Any portion of a charitable deduction that's not claimed due to the ceiling may be carried forward and used as a deduction for up to five years.

No capital gains tax for stock donations

Donor-advised funds can be an ideal way to donate appreciated securities. You not only claim the tax write-off, but you also dodge a potentially painful capital gains tax bill. Suppose you bought 1,000 shares of General Electric stock when it was trading at $8 and years later it's priced at $55. Your stake has skyrocketed from $8,000 to $55,000. If you donate the stock to a donor-advised fund, your tax deduction is based upon $55,000, even though your original investment was worth much less. If you're in the 31 percent tax bracket, that write-off is worth $17,050. By donating appreciated stock, you'll skip paying capital gains on the $47,000 profit. (You can take advantage of the same deduction if you directly donate stock to a charity.)

If the generous GE investor sold the stock first, realizing the $47,000 profit, and then placed the proceeds in a donor-advised fund, the stock sale would trigger the long-term capital gains tax. For most people, the long-term capital gains tax is 20 percent. Thus the transaction would generate a $ 9,400 long-term capital gains tax bill. If the philanthropist makes a gift of securities directly to a charity, including a donor-advised fund, there's no capital gains tax involved and the charity's benefit is exactly the same.

A lasting gift

Just like huge foundations established by wealthy families such as the Lillys and Rockefellers, a donor-advised fund doesn't have to die with its benefactor. What delights many benefactors about these funds is that their gifts keep on giving. After the original benefactor's death, family or friends may, in some cases, continue to recommend that money go to worthy causes through a donor-advised fund.

Even a fund that's launched with, say, $10,000 or $20,000 can continue indefinitely because donors are strongly urged to allocate only a small portion of their fund annually to good causes. Traditionally, small amounts, such as 5 percent, are directed to good causes each year through donor-advised funds so that these pools of money can continue growing for future giving. Donors are also encouraged to add to their initial contribution throughout their lifetimes.

Community foundation donor-advised funds

The traditional way to establish a donor-advised fund is through one of the nation's 500 or so community foundations. A community foundation is an independent charitable organization that oversees a permanent collection of endowed funds for the long-term benefit of a defined geographic area. Community foundations are located in major cities, but even some places as small as Findlay, Ohio, operate them. In more sparsely populated states, such as Maine, New Hampshire, Vermont, Idaho, and Montana, one foundation serves the entire state. Interest in community foundations has exploded in this country. Half of the existing community foundations were created during the past decade.

A volunteer board runs each foundation. At the St. Louis Community Foundation, for instance, board members recently included a retired CEO, an executive at a prominent public relations agency, and the publisher of a black newspaper. (At the end of this chapter is a listing of some of the community foundations operating in all 50 states and the District of Columbia.)

Advantages of a community foundation donor-advised fund

Establishing a donor-advised fund at a community foundation has two main advantages.

Training wheels for budding philanthropists

Many people who gravitate to community foundations feel that their previous gift giving didn't make a difference. They want to learn more about the charities they support, such as how they work and what they need. For these motivated philanthropists, community foundations serve as mentors. A community foundation lets donors know where the deserving charities are in their area. A person might wish to help troubled teenagers, but she might not have any specific charity in mind. The foundation can pinpoint what worthwhile charities need, whether it's more books for a literacy program or wool blankets for a homeless shelter. They take donors on tours of various charities and suggest volunteer opportunities.

Note
: The foundation staff also handles paperwork and monitors how gifts are spent once they are in the charity's hands.

Low minimum hurdle

Although the investment necessary to get started in a donor-advised fund varies, it can be fairly low. Initial donations of $5,000 to $10,000 are common. In contrast, mutual fund companies and brokerage firms often require an initial commitment of at least $10,000 and sometimes $25,000. Yet some community foundations do insist upon a healthier upfront commitment. The Community Foundation of Silicon Valley, which is flush with tech stocks, requires an initial minimum contribution of $25,000. The Cleveland Foundation, which has been a popular cause for the city's wealthy for many decades, makes its new patrons pony up $50,000.

Typically, community foundations don't set minimums on additional contributions, which can be a real plus for the philanthropically minded. For example, a couple who sets up a donor-advised fund can request that friends send contributions to the fund instead of giving gifts at birthdays, holidays, or anniversaries.

Disadvantages of a community foundation donor-advised fund

Community foundation donor-advised funds have a couple of disadvantages as well.

Foundation oversight

Some people might chafe at a community foundation's oversight responsibility for a donor-advised fund. As the name of the fund implies, a donor only "advises" the foundation where it should direct the cash. Once the money is put into a donor-advised fund, it no longer belongs to the charitable giver. The foundations, which are overseen by a volunteer board of directors, have historically maintained veto power over any contribution. For instance, donors ordinarily can't use money in their funds to pay for tickets to celebrity golf tournaments or fundraising dinners, nor can they direct donations to a specific person.

Note   In the vast majority of cases, the donor's wishes are swiftly honored.

Community foundations also have their own rules in place concerning how much of their donors' money must be allocated to charity each year. Again, the recommended amount is often 5 percent of a fund's assets, but these rules vary from foundation to foundation.

Geographic limits

Suppose you were born in Denver, but now you live in San Diego. The San Diego Foundation would be the most convenient one to establish a donor-advised fund, but you might prefer supporting worthwhile causes in the Rocky Mountain state. While most community foundations would try to help you make the occasional out-of-state donation, they are primarily designed to serve their local area.

Donor-Advised Funds: Wall-Street Style

If you decide to open a donor-advised fund through a financial institution, here are some of the bigger players:

Name of Fund	Minimum Donation	Phone Number
Fidelity Charitable Gift Fund	$10,000	(800) 952-4438
Vanguard Charitable Endowment Program	$25,000	(888) 383-4483
Schwab Fund for Charitable Giving	$10,000	(800) 746-6216
T. Rowe Price Program for Charitable Giving	$10,000	(800) 564-1597

Financial institution donor-advised funds

It probably wouldn't surprise you that the Salvation Army and the YMCA were recently ranked as the No. 1 and No. 2 biggest charities in America. But you might be flabbergasted by the identity of No. 5: the Fidelity Charitable Gift Fund. Fidelity's donor-advised program has attracted billions of dollars since it was launched in 1992. Following Fidelity's lead, other financial institutions have entered the donor-advised arena. More are expected to follow.

The same rules generally apply to these donor-advised or charitable gift funds that apply to donor-advised funds at community foundations. The tax write-offs are the same. Fidelity and the other institutions invest donor contributions in mutual funds that grow tax-free. When you want to make a contribution to a good cause, the institution dispatches the money to your charity.

Are the nation's community foundations thrilled that the Fidelitys of the world are horning into their territory? Hardly. Their supporters worry about the entry of Wall Street into the charity business. They accuse the financial heavyweights of getting involved in good works simply as a way to generate profits. But contrarians insist that the financial world's involvement with charities has provided this method of giving with much higher visibility. As more dollars flow into both philanthropic alternatives, more charities ultimately profit.

Advantages of financial institution donor-advised fund

A financial institution donor-advised fund has two main advantages:

✦ **There are no geographic boundaries.** You can live in Minneapolis and contribute money to children's programming at the Denver Natural History

Museum. Because the donor-advised funds operated by mutual funds and brokerage firms are national in scope, you can instruct the institution to donate money anywhere in the country.

✦ **You can decide what organization to give to later.** After donating the money, you can immediately claim a tax deduction. As with community foundations, you don't have to rush into deciding what good cause will be the ultimate recipient. The money will continue to grow while you're making your decision.

Disadvantages of financial institution donor-advised fund

The financial institution donor-advised fund also has its disadvantages:

✦ **You're on your own.** A brokerage firm may excel at investing the pool of money in a charitable fund, but the money managers are not philanthropists. If you want to know whether a particular battered women's shelter in Chicago will use a donation wisely, don't expect Fidelity or Vanguard to have an opinion. Financial institutions are not equipped to help you uncover worthwhile causes or explore the many charitable options in your city or state. You're strictly on your own. This is by far the biggest disadvantage of these funds.

✦ **Fees can be high.** Some mutual fund firms are doing a better job at keeping costs low than others. Recently, Vanguard offered the lowest prices. The higher the fees are, the less money will wind up with charities.

✦ **Initial investment requirements can be stiff.** Although some community foundations will warmly greet donors who have as little as $5,000 to contribute, mutual fund firms require more. (See the sidebar earlier in this chapter.) The Vanguard Group imposes the steepest hurdle with its initial $25,000 investment. Some institutions require subsequent investments be at least $1,000; Vanguard will only accept additional contributions of at least $5,000.

Establishing a Family Foundation

In 1998, more than 800 people crowded into a swank Los Angeles hotel to listen to the heirs of David and Lucile Packard of Hewlett-Packard fame and Hollywood director Rob Reiner share experiences about their own family foundations. Ten years earlier, the annual affair hosted by the Council on Foundations barely attracted a few dozen would-be benefactors.

A family foundations is a kind of private foundation, a charity that's essentially controlled by one company or one small group of people. Private foundations are subject to much stricter rules than are public charities, such as donor-advised funds. The advantage of a private foundation is the total control that donors and other board members can retain over how their money is spent.

With the stock market operating in a gravity-free zone during much of the 1990s, it's no surprise that the number of family foundations has been rapidly increasing. In the 1990s, more wealthy families decided to create their own charitable legacies than in any other decade in history. Although precise numbers don't exist, it's estimated that more than 30,000 family foundations across the country are quietly performing good deeds.

Essentially, family members (though others can be invited to sit on their boards) create these foundations to direct money to charitable activities that the relatives feel passionately about. These foundations can be modest affairs run by somebody's bank trust officer. On the other end of the spectrum are the Goliath organizations such as the one funded by Eli Lilly & Co.'s namesake, which was launched back in 1937. Until Microsoft founder Bill Gates and his wife's foundation overtook it, the Lilly Endowment was the largest family foundation in the country.

Most family foundations aren't nearly so grand as the ones that generate media attention. It's estimated that three-quarters of family foundations have less than $1 million in assets. They often start out as "kitchen table philanthropy," which is the way Lucile Packard described her and her husband's early charitable pursuits back in the mid-1960s. Sitting in her kitchen, she wrote checks to what grew into an incredibly long list of worthy causes. Now the David and Lucile Packard Foundation gives away hundreds of millions of dollars a year.

Although interest in family foundations is high, not everyone with a heart of gold should launch a family foundation. Consider the following pros and cons.

Donor-Advised Funds and Family Foundations: Getting Started

Want to learn more about donor-advised funds at community foundations or family foundations? Here's where to begin:

✦ **Council on Foundations:** The nation's largest association of foundations provides many guides on the practical aspects of philanthropy. You can contact this organization at 1828 L St. NW #300, Washington, DC 20036; (202) 466-6512; www.cof.org.

✦ **National Center for Family Philanthropy:** This nonprofit organization helps families create their own foundations. Contact it at 1220 Nineteenth St. NW, Suite 804, Washington, DC 20036; (202) 293-3424; www.ncfp.org.

✦ **The Foundation Center:** You can find the center's various publications on charitable giving and organizations at its five regional libraries in New York, Washington, D.C., Atlanta, Cleveland, and San Francisco. You can also obtain the center's materials at 210 public and university libraries in all 50 states. You can contact this organization at 79 Fifth Ave., New York, NY 10003; (212) 620-4230; www.fdncenter.org.

On-the-Job Training

The Rockefeller Foundation is willing to train seriously committed people with deep pockets to be philanthropists. The foundation conducts year-long philanthropy workshops. The price is $10,000, and space is limited. Only 12 people are accepted into the program each year. For information, contact the Rockefeller Foundation at 420 Fifth Ave., New York, NY 10018-2702; (212) 869-8500; www.rockfound.org. The Council on Foundations offers much cheaper conferences. You can reach the Council at 1828 L St., NW, Washington, DC 20036; (202) 466-6512.

Advantages of a family foundation

Here are the advantages of establishing a family foundation:

A family foundation can create a lasting legacy.

For anyone toying with the idea of making one big splash, writing a huge check to fund a wing of a hospital, for instance, might seem more exciting than establishing a foundation. But the goodwill someone generates with a single check could evaporate before the building needs tuck-pointing, and down the road another philanthropist might give even more money and replace the name on the building. A family foundation, however, creates a lasting legacy.

A family foundation is a way to share values with your children.

The genesis of many family foundations springs from heartfelt reasons. Wealthy parents often want to bestow upon their children, who may grow up thinking a BMW on their 16th birthday is an entitlement, a sense of obligation to those who will spend their entire lives riding the bus.

Foundations can also bind families together in ways that aren't possible at birthdays, weddings, and holidays. A family foundation allows parents, children, and perhaps other relatives to get together when they're not just eating. A family foundation is a way to bring people together to talk about society's ills and how the family's good fortune can make a difference. It's also a way of transmitting one generation's values to the next.

The money can last for more than a lifetime.

The gift-giving can continue for more than just a generation. Although some philanthropists plan to disburse all the money in a single lifetime, others hope the foundation will continue to exist for generations.

Disadvantages of a family foundation

Here are the key drawbacks of creating a family foundation:

A huge investment requirement

Many experts insist that a donor needs at least $1 to $2 million in seed money, and some suggest that $5 million is the bare-bones minimum to make a foundation financially feasible.

Red tape and legal fees

As a private foundation, not only must a family foundation comply with a stricter set of rules than apply to public charities, such as donor-advised funds, but the initial set-up costs more as well.

Establishing a boilerplate foundation can initially cost $5,000 or so; more complicated varieties, such as one that intends to make grants outside the United States, could generate a much higher legal start-up fee. Ongoing costs include income tax return preparation, investment management, and legal fees. And somebody must decide where to award the donations.

Whether someone can realistically operate a more modest foundation may depend on how much work that person can shoulder. The work shouldn't be underestimated. If you expect to write checks to your alma mater, the local opera, and a few other pet causes, you could very well handle the job yourself. But the task will be trickier if you want to fund, for instance, the most innovative programs in early childhood development. Before seeking proposals, you need to establish guidelines for submission and be prepared to evaluate a deluge of hopeful applications.

Tip   If you're daunted by the prospects of running the show alone, but can't justify hiring a staff, alternatives are available. Some foundations share staff, and for a fee, certain public foundations will handle the administrative details.

Mandated giving schedule

Federal law requires that approximately 5 percent of a family foundation's net investment assets must be annually distributed for charitable purposes. This requirement isn't imposed on those who contribute through donor-advised funds although distributions from these funds often equal or exceed this amount.

A lesser tax break

Attractive tax and estate-planning advantages do exist for family foundations, but the tax breaks aren't nearly as good as the ones you'd receive if you simply wrote a fat check or donated a block of stock to the National Kidney Foundation or any other public charity. When you contribute cash to a public charity, you may deduct an amount up to 50 percent of your adjusted gross income. But you can deduct no more than 30 percent of your adjusted gross income for any money you place into your foundation. In either scenario, if a donation exceeds the limits, you may carry over the excess for the next five tax years. The tax rules for giving appreciated property, such as stock or land, are different, but public charities still offer the best break: a 30 percent deduction versus a 20 percent deduction.

Example

If you donate $1 million worth of stock to the Salvation Army, you can receive a deduction that's worth up to $300,000. But that deduction shrinks to a maximum value of $200,000 if the stock is earmarked for a family foundation.

For a family foundation, the tax payoff for donating most types of appreciated assets, such as land and artwork, is downright dismal. You can claim only the cost basis for these kinds of donations. In contrast, you can capture the full fair market value of your Andy Warhol painting if you give it to a regular charity.

Note

Anyone holding ancient shares of General Electric or Microsoft, however, can take heart. Family foundations can deduct the full market value of publicly traded stocks rather than the original cost.

Questions to ask before establishing a family foundation

Although a family may get warm and fuzzy anticipating all the great philanthropic causes they can embrace, laying a firm groundwork is important. Initially, deciding whether all future direct descendants will be welcomed on the board or whether there will be qualifications might not seem important, but anticipating future conflicts is crucial.

With hundreds of permutations possible in a family foundation, families will be much happier if they think about these issues in advance.

Here are some questions to ask yourself and any other family members who want to get involved in a family foundation:

✦ How much of your wealth do you want to leave to charity and to your family?

✦ What expectations do you have for your family philanthropy?

✦ What are your charitable goals?

✦ How involved would you want to be in the management and investment of the foundation's money and operations?

✦ Do you expect to hire others?

✦ What causes or institutions would you like to help?

✦ Should the foundation last for one lifetime or perpetuity?

✦ What role should family members play in the foundation both now and in the future?

✦ Should spouses be welcomed on the board?

✦ What happens if the children get divorced?

✦ What role, if any, should stepchildren play?

✦ Can future generations change the fields of interest you wish to support?

Ideally, family members who want to be involved in the foundation should reach some sort of consensus about the foundation's aims and parameters. This list of questions can generate a detailed discussion that brings to the surface conflicting goals or ideals that should be worked out well ahead of sending the letterhead design off to the printers.

Finding a Community Foundation Near You

Approximately 500 community foundations exist, from the wealthy New York Community Trust to foundations in tiny towns. What follows is a partial list of community foundations in each state.

To find the community foundation nearest you, contact the Council on Foundations at (202) 466-6512 or use the community foundation locator at the council's Web site at www.cof.org.

Alabama
Community Foundation of
Greater Birmingham
2027 First Ave. North,
Suite 410
Birmingham, AL 35203
(205) 328-8641

Alaska
The Alaska Community
Foundation
701 W. 8th Ave.
P.O. Box 100360
Anchorage, AK 99510
(907) 265-6044

Arizona
Arizona Community
Foundation
2122 E. Highland, Suite 400
Phoenix, AZ 85016
(602) 381-1400

Arkansas
Arkansas Community
Foundation
700 S. Rock St.
Little Rock, AR 72202
(501) 372-1116

California
California Community
Foundation
445 S. Figueroa St.,
Suite 3400
Los Angeles, CA 90071
(213) 413-4130

Community Foundation
Silicon Valley
60 S. Market St., Suite 1000
San Jose, CA 95113
(408) 278-2200

Peninsula Community
Foundation
1700 S. El Camino Real,
Suite 300
San Mateo, CA 94402
(650) 358-9369

The San Diego Foundation
1420 Kettner Blvd.,
Suite 500
San Diego, CA 92101
(619) 235-2300

The San Francisco
Foundation
225 Bush St., Suite 500
San Francisco, CA 94104
(415) 733-8500

Colorado
The Denver Foundation
950 S. Cherry St., Suite 200
Denver, CO 80246
(303) 300-1790

Connecticut
Community Foundation
for Greater New Haven
70 Audubon St.
New Haven, CT 06510
(203) 777-2386

Hartford Foundation for
Public Giving
85 Gillett St.
Hartford, CT 06105
(860) 548-1888

Delaware
Delaware Community
Foundation
P.O. Box 1636
Wilmington, DE 19899
(302) 571-8004

District of Columbia
Community Foundation
for the National Capital
Region
1112 16th St. NW, Suite 340
Washington, DC 20036
(202) 955-5890

Florida
Dade Community
Foundation
200 S. Biscayne Blvd.,
Suite 505
Miami, FL 33131
(305) 371-2711

Community Foundation of
Central Florida
P.O. Box 2071
Orlando, FL 32802
(407) 872-3050

Community Foundation of
Tampa Bay
4950 W. Kennedy Blvd.,
Suite 250
Tampa, FL 33609
(813) 282-1975

Georgia
Community Foundation
for Greater Atlanta, Inc.
The Hurt Building,
Suite 449
Atlanta, GA 30303
(404) 688-5525

Hawaii
Hawai'i Community
Foundation
900 Fort Street Mall,
Suite 1300
Honolulu, HI 96813
(808) 537-6333

Idaho
Idaho Community
Foundation
210 W. State St.
Boise, ID 83702
(208) 342-3535

Illinois
Chicago Community Trust
222 N. LaSalle St.,
Suite 1400
Chicago, IL 60601
(312) 372-3356

Indiana
Indianapolis Foundation
615 N. Alabama St., Suite 119
Indianapolis, IN 46204
(317) 634-2423

Iowa
Greater Des Moines
Foundation
P.O. Box 7271
Des Moines, IA 50309
(515) 883-2626

Kansas
Wichita Community
Foundation
151 N. Main, Suite 140
Wichita, KS 67202
(316) 264-4880

Kentucky
Community Foundation of
Louisville
Waterfront Plaza,
Suite 1110
325 W. Main St.
Louisville, KY 40202
(502) 585-4649

Louisiana
Baton Rouge Area
Foundation
406 N. Fourth St.
Baton Rouge, LA 70802
(225) 387-6126

Maine
Maine Community
Foundation
245 Main St.
Ellsworth, ME 04605
(207) 667-9735

Maryland
Baltimore Community
Foundation
2 E. Read St., 9th floor
Baltimore, MD 21202
(410) 332-4171

Massachusetts
The Boston Foundation
One Boston Place,
24th floor
Boston, MA 02108
(617) 723-7415

Michigan
Community Foundation
for Southeastern Michigan
333 W. Fort St., Suite 2010
Detroit, MI 48226
(313) 961-6675

Minnesota
Minneapolis Foundation
A200 Foshay Tower
821 Marquette Ave. S.
Minneapolis, MN 55402
(612) 339-7343

Mississippi
Foundation for the
Mid South
308 E. Pearl St., 2nd floor
Jackson, MS 39201
(601) 355-8167

Missouri
Greater Kansas City
Community Foundation
1055 Broadway, Suite 130
Kansas City, MO 64105
(816) 842-0944

St. Louis Community
Foundation
319 N. Fourth St., Suite 501
St. Louis, MO 63102
(314) 588-8200

Montana
Montana Community
Foundation
101 N. Last Chance Gulch,
Suite 211
Helena, MT 59601
(406) 443-8313

Nebraska
Nebraska Community
Foundation
317 S. 12th St., Suite 200
Lincoln, NE 68508
(402) 323-7330

Nevada
Nevada Community
Foundation
1850 E. Sahara Ave.,
Suite 207
Las Vegas, NV 89104
(702) 892-2326

New Hampshire
New Hampshire
Charitable Foundation
37 Pleasant St.
Concord, NH 03301
(603) 225-6641

New Jersey
Community Foundation of
New Jersey
P.O. Box 317
Morristown, NJ 07963
(973) 267-5533

New Mexico
New Mexico Community
Foundation
1227 Paseo de Peralta
Santa Fe, NM 87501
(505) 820-6860

New York
New York Community
Trust
2 Park Ave., 24th floor
New York, NY 10016
(212) 686-0010

North Carolina
Foundation for the
Carolinas
1043 E. Morehead St.,
Suite 100
Charlotte, NC 28204
(704) 376-9541

North Carolina
Community Foundation
P.O. Box 2828
Raleigh, NC 27602-2828
(919) 828-4387

North Dakota
North Dakota Community
Foundation
1025 N. 3rd St.
P.O. Box 387
Bismarck, ND 58502
(701) 222-8349

Ohio
Greater Cincinnati
Foundation
200 W. 4th St.
Cincinnati, OH 45202
(513) 241-2880

Cleveland Foundation
1422 Euclid Ave.,
Suite 1400
Cleveland, OH 44115
(216) 861-3810

Oklahoma
Oklahoma City
Community Foundation
P.O. Box 1146
Oklahoma City, OK 73101
(405) 235-5603

Oregon
Oregon Community
Foundation
US Bancorp Tower
111 SW Fifth Ave.,
Suite 3600
Portland, OR 97204
(503) 227-6846

Pennsylvania
Philadelphia Foundation
1234 Market St., Suite 1800
Philadelphia, PA 19107
(215) 563-6417

Pittsburgh Foundation
One PPG Place, 30th floor
Pittsburgh, PA 15222
(412) 391-5122

Rhode Island
Rhode Island Community
Foundation
One Union Station
Providence, RI 02903
(401) 274-4564

South Carolina
Community Foundation
Serving Coastal South
Carolina
90 Mary St.
Charleston, SC 29403
(843) 723-3635

South Dakota
South Dakota Community
Foundation
207 E. Capital-Box 296
Pierre, SD 57501
(605) 224-1025

Tennessee
Community Foundation of
Greater Memphis
1900 Union Ave.
Memphis, TN 38104
(901) 728-4600

Texas
Greater Houston
Community Foundation
4550 Post Oak Place,
Suite 317
Houston, TX 77027
(713) 960-1990

Communities Foundation
of Texas
4605 Live Oak St.
Dallas, TX 75204
(214) 826-5231

Utah
Salt Lake Foundation
9 Exchange Place, Suite 959
Salt Lake City, UT 84111
(801) 883-0941

Vermont
Vermont Community
Foundation
Three Court St.
P.O. Box 30
Middlebury, VT 05753
(802) 388-3355

Virginia
Arlington Community
Foundation
2250 Clerendon Blvd,
Suite J
Arlington, VA 22201
(703) 243-4785

Washington
The Seattle Foundation
425 Pike St., Suite 510
Seattle, WA 98101
(206) 622-2294

West Virginia
Community Foundation
for the Ohio Valley
P.O. Box 1233
Wheeling, WV 26003
(304) 242-3144

Wisconsin
Milwaukee Foundation
1020 N. Broadway,
Suite 112
Milwaukee, WI 53202
(414) 272-5805

Wyoming
Wyoming Community
Foundation
221 Ivinson Ave., Suite 202
Laramie, WY 82070
(307) 721-8300

Summary

✦ Investigate a charity before contributing to it.

✦ Use the Internet to learn more about charitable giving trends and get the low-down on specific charities.

✦ Consider giving through a donor-advised fund if you want more involvement with charitable giving.

✦ Know the differences between donor-advised funds set up through community foundations and those set up through financial institutions.

✦ Only millionaires should contemplate establishing a family foundation, and they should consider the lack of tax breaks involved.

Charitable Gifts That Give Back to You

Most people assume that charitable giving is a one-way street. You write a check to a wonderful cause and congratulate yourself after dropping it in the mail. But this chapter reveals a secret: The good feeling you experience doesn't have to be your only payoff. Some charitable donations can provide a lifetime of income for donors and perhaps their family members, which is a benefit above and beyond the automatic tax deduction.

This sort of symbiotic relationship is doable for those who are contemplating gifts of at least $5,000 or higher to one of the nation's charities, colleges and universities, hospitals, and other nonprofit organizations. The charity benefits from the donation; the donors and sometimes even their heirs benefit from the sound estate-planning arrangements that are outlined in this chapter.

Here are the four methods of giving that you will learn more about:

+ Charitable remainder trusts

+ Charitable lead trusts

+ Pooled-income funds

+ Gift annuities

If you've never heard of these strategies, it's no surprise. Establishing trusts, in particular, can be complicated and require outside help. People who might benefit from these arrangements typically hear about them through attorneys, accountants, and financial planners. Planned giving officers at many well-established charities are another source of information, as are the nonprofit organizations' Web sites.

The number of financial advisors who are combining estate-planning strategies with charitable giving has jumped dramatically. You have to proceed with care, however, if your charitable plans extend beyond simply writing a check to the Salvation Army. As creative philanthropic giving has become hot, the lines between charity and greed have blurred. Some controversial and possibly illegal strategies now being hyped sometimes barely benefit charities at all.

Whom should you trust? Often charities have planned giving officers on the staff who can assist potential donors. You may also want to consult an attorney, a Certified Financial Planner, or a certified public accountant who specializes in nonprofit organizations. It's a good sign if the professional you're considering belongs to a local planned giving council. Currently, there are more than 110 such councils in the United States.

Resource To find a planned giving council in your area, contact the National Committee on Planned Giving at 233 McCrea St., Suite 400, Indianapolis, IN 46225; (317) 269-6274; www.ncpg.org.

Charitable Remainder Trusts

A charitable remainder trust is basically an estate-planning device that allows a person to donate assets to a charity and in return receive tax breaks, as well as a lifetime stream of income. When the donor dies, the assets become the property of the charity. Charitable remainder trusts (CRTs) were once the preserve of America's most affluent families, but today they are also a practical option for the upper middle class.

Who are the prime candidates for a charitable remainder trust? Typically they are older Americans who own stock, property, or land that has appreciated tremendously. The holdings might be quite valuable, but the investment is not providing the owners with what they now crave: income. Ideally, they'd like to bail out of the stock or vacant piece of land and move the money into an investment that produces income or generates more income than they now receive. Possible income producers could be bonds, real estate investment trusts, a balanced mutual fund (holds stocks and bonds), utility stocks, or any number of other alternatives.

Of course, nothing is stopping someone from unloading, say, Intel stock and putting the proceeds into any income-generating investment on his or her own. How does the charity fit in? For starters, the charity can help the Intel shareholder dodge what may be a heart-stopping capital gains tax bill. Consider what would happen to a shareholder with $250,000 worth of stock who sells it on his or her own. If the stock originally cost $40,000, the appreciation of $210,000 would be subject to capital gains tax.

Note The top long-term capital gains tax rate is presently 20 percent, which applies to investments that are held for more than one year. The top rate for securities held for five years beginning in 2001 will drop to 18 percent.

The tax bill decreases the amount left over for an income-producing investment, which is a problem because income-oriented portfolios typically generate returns somewhere in the ballpark of only 6 percent. Here's how the numbers play out in this scenario:

Stock's present value:	$250,000
Stock's original cost:	$40,000
Taxable portion:	$210,000
Capital gains tax rate:	20 percent
Tax owed:	$42,000 ($210,000 multiplied by 20 percent)
After-tax profit:	$208,000
Expected earnings rate:	6 percent
Yearly income:	$12,480 ($208,000 multiplied by 6 percent)

As you can see, the IRS hit is considerable, and this scenario doesn't even take into consideration state income taxes. Obviously, the tax bill shrinks the amount of income an investor can expect after investing the equity proceeds.

In contrast, the investor wouldn't absorb any tax hit if he or she established a charitable remainder trust. The trustee of this trust could sell the stock without incurring capital gains taxes. (The trustee could be the charity, a financial institution or, in some cases, the donor.) Consequently, more money would be available to sink into income-producing investments. The following list clearly shows the difference:

Stock's original cost:	$40,000
Stock's present value:	$250,000
Capital gains taxes owed:	$0
Proceeds from sale:	$250,000
Expected earnings rate:	6 percent
Yearly income:	$15,000 ($250,000 multiplied by 6 percent)

The taxes are avoided because the assets are held in trust for the charity. Usually, the trustee sells the stock and since the beneficiary of the trust is a nonprofit, the sale doesn't generate any immediate capital gains taxes. The former shareholder no longer owns the assets that sit in the trust; instead, they belong to the charity. But the charity can't legally touch the money until the donor dies. Until that occurs, the philanthropist enjoys a steady stream of income from the trust.

The donor even gets to determine each year's payout from the trust within certain guidelines. There are two approaches to determining the payout, depending on which of the two kinds of CRTs a donor establishes. The two flavors are the Charitable Remainder Annuity Trust (CRAT) and the Charitable Remainder Unitrust (CRUT).

Charitable Remainder Annuity Trust (CRAT)

With a CRAT, you receive a fixed dollar amount each year. When the trust is created, you specify the payout as a percentage of the fair market value of the assets placed in it. The payout must be 5 percent or more of the fair market value of the assets on the day the trust is funded. The higher the payout is, the lower the charitable deduction will be. The payout, by the way, can't be unreasonable and must follow IRS guidelines. The chief advantage to a CRAT is that your income is predictable, but it doesn't provide inflation protection. You also won't reap the benefit of a runaway portfolio that skyrockets in value because your payout remains frozen. If the portfolio in a bad year doesn't produce enough income, the principal can be invaded.

Tip This type of trust can be attractive for retirees in their 70s or older because the high payouts are guaranteed as long as any assets remain in the trust.

Charitable Remainder Unitrust (CRUT)

The CRUT is the more popular option because the income grows as the assets do. When establishing a unitrust, you select a yearly payout rate that represents a percentage of trust assets. You must follow IRS rules when choosing it. The minimum rate is 5 percent. When the portfolio does well, you will do well. But even during lousy years on Wall Street, some trusts allow you to dip into the principal to make up for an income shortfall. Unlike the CRAT, a unitrust permits subsequent contributions to it.

Advantages to a CRT

The charitable remainder trust provides other advantages as well. Here are the major ones:

A CRT guarantees a tax deduction.

Someone establishing a charitable remainder trust also pockets an upfront income tax deduction on the contribution for a portion of its fair market value. Just what that tax deduction will be varies depending upon such factors as the value of the gift, the life expectancy of the income beneficiary, the frequency of payments, and the formula chosen to determine the income stream. The tax break is more generous the older you are because actuarial charts assume that 80-year-olds won't live long enough to pocket as much trust income as those in their 60s or 70s.

 Caution   The more income you expect from the trust, the lower your tax write-off will be. There are federal limits on how much income you can squeeze out of the trust.

The deduction is also dependent upon how many people will share the income. A married couple will typically want each other to receive income throughout their lifetimes. So if the husband dies, the trust will remain intact until the wife passes away. A trust that provides for multiple beneficiaries, whether this group includes a spouse, children, grandchildren, or nonfamily members, will produce a smaller upfront tax write-off.

A CRT reduces the taxable estate.

Upon the last beneficiary's death, what's left in the trust won't be taxed in the estate because it belongs to the charity. A charitable remainder trust is a proven way to reduce someone's taxable estate.

CRTs require less cash to establish.

Charitable remainder trusts are an option for more people today because they can be established with less money than in the past. Some financial advisors suggest that you can create one for as little as $50,000; others suggest that these trusts should be funded with at least $100,000, or even $200,000.

Another reason CRTs are more practical and accessible today is that they've been standardized. Now an increasing number of financial advisors, attorneys, and tax experts know how to draw up the documents by using standard software and boilerplate legal forms. A decade ago, all the documents had to be generated from scratch by specialists.

Disadvantages of a CRT

Your desire to generate comfortable retirement income while benefiting a charity has to be balanced with the discomfort you or your heirs may feel with a CRT. Consider the following disadvantages.

Heirs can be left in the cold.

Understandably, heirs might not be thrilled with a charitable remainder trust. After all, when the trust expires, the charity claims all the money. So much for the kids' inheritance.

To keep would-be heirs smiling, consider using the money saved from the tax breaks to buy second-to-die life insurance with a death benefit that equals the value of the assets given to the trust. When the last parent dies, the insurer pays off the beneficiaries.

If you decide to buy life insurance, be sure to put the policy in an irrevocable insurance trust. Another alternative is to gift the money for the premiums to your children and they can write the insurance premium checks. Before buying insurance, consult with an expert in this specialized field. Ask a charity's planned giving officer, if it has one, for suggestions about insurance. You may also want to consult a fee-only insurance analyst. (See Chapter 6 for advice on locating such an expert.)

There are annual costs.

In addition to setup costs, which on a $1 million trust could run from $4,000 to $15,000, there are annual administrative costs, and a separate trust tax return must be filed each year. Generally, the costs are 1 percent to 1.5 percent of the fair market value of the trust assets.

You may lose control of the money.

Donors can sometimes control the assets inside their trusts by naming themselves trustees. Trustees manage the money and are responsible for the distributions. If a donor acts as the trustee, his or her powers must be limited in certain ways. Many larger charitable organizations balk at individuals naming themselves trustees. They wish to serve as trustee. If you relinquish management of the trust to the charity, investigate how successful it's been in managing money. Ask your attorney or certified public accountant to help with this chore.

Tip   A better alternative is naming yourself as a co-trustee with the charity or with a bank or trust company that understands all the trust requirements.

Charitable Remainder Trusts for the Nonmillionaires

Charitable remainder trusts can sometimes present a solution to those who don't fit the traditional definition of affluent. Consider the real case of a couple who took advantage of one of these trusts after watching their assets dwindle rapidly. The husband, a former doctor who had been struck by a debilitating disease during his prime earning years, had been living in a nursing home for many years. The monthly tab was $3,000 a month. With the money disappearing, his wife was forced to consider selling one of the couple's last major assets: a rental home. She hesitated because the capital gains tax would be sizable, and the proceeds could ultimately get sucked into Medicaid's coffers if and when she could no longer foot those nursing home bills.

At the advice of her certified financial planner, the wife established a charitable remainder trust and put the deed to the property into it. The trustee found a buyer and sold the $225,000 house. She avoided the capital gains bite because the eventual recipient of the money is a hospital foundation. Until their deaths, however, the couple will receive quarterly income checks from the trust, which exceed the rent they used to collect. The couple also claimed a substantial income tax deduction. The wife was thrilled that she could help herself and a charity at the same time.

Charitable Lead Trust

The charitable lead trust isn't nearly as popular as a charitable remainder trust because its usefulness is limited to a far smaller universe. It can, however, be a valuable estate-planning tool for the very wealthy. Jackie Kennedy Onassis, for instance, left her estate to a charitable lead trust. Her trust, which provides for a variety of charities, will exist for 24 years. After the trust expires, the remaining estate reverts to her family. This strategy will reportedly save her family tens of millions of dollars in estate taxes.

There are big differences between charitable remainder trusts and charitable lead trusts. With CRTs, the charity's payoff begins when the last income beneficiary dies. Up until then, the beneficiaries collect the interest generated by the trust's assets. With a charitable lead trust, the charity begins receiving that income as soon as the trust is established. The charity returns the principal to the donor or, more typically, to the donor's heirs after a set number of years or when the trust's creator(s) die. Often money or property is tied up in a charitable lead trust for 15 to 20 years. The charitable lead trust can be initiated before or at a benefactor's death.

Advantages of a charitable lead trust

If you are wealthy enough to need a charitable lead trust, here's how one can benefit you.

The inheritance grows tax-free.

There's a huge payoff for patiently tying up loads of money. When assets are placed in the trust, the value of the gift is essentially frozen for gift and estate tax purposes. The donor reports the gift on a gift tax return when the lead trust is established and pays any gift tax due at that time. If the assets escalate in value, they pass along tax-free at their higher value to the heirs. Any growth is not subject to estate taxes. A charitable lead trust is commonly used as a way to give ownership to a closely held company to one's heirs at a minimal tax cost.

The charity benefits right away.

Instead of waiting many years for the money, a charity can put the trust income it receives to work immediately. Organizations such as the American Cancer Society and the Parkinson's Disease Foundation, which are working on cures for dreaded diseases, greatly appreciate the upfront money.

Tip Charitable lead trusts are sometimes used in combination with charitable remainder trusts — which can be a sound technique to generate a large tax deduction in the year of the gift.

Disadvantages of a charitable lead trust

Here are a couple of drawbacks to the charitable lead trust:

Charitable lead trusts are a niche strategy.

A charitable lead trust isn't appropriate for the vast majority of Americans. Because this trust requires lending a charity assets or property for a lengthy period, sometimes up to 20 years. The donors generally need to be quite wealthy to find this arrangement appealing.

Heirs have to wait a long time for an inheritance.

Charitable lead trusts could hurt relatives who were counting on an inheritance right after a family member's death. For relatives who anticipated an inheritance, a 20-year wait can seem like eternity.

Pooled-Income Funds

The pooled-income fund is a poor man's alternative to the charitable remainder trust. You can typically participate in a charity's already established pooled-income fund with a contribution of as little as $5,000 to $10,000. Many national charities, universities, churches, large religious organizations, and art institutions offer pooled-income funds. As the name suggests, these funds pool and invest all the donors' contributions and then generate income for these donors.

Like a charitable remainder trust, a pooled-income fund will gladly accept your gift of stock and other assets, sometimes even real estate. In return, the fund will provide you with a lifetime stream of income. You'll also enjoy the upfront federal and state tax deduction. Your tax break is calculated similarly to the way a charitable remainder trust contribution is determined. In addition, you avoid paying any capital gains tax.

After your contribution, you'll receive a certain number of units or shares in the charitable fund. The regular income you can expect depends upon your number of shares. This arrangement is how a regular mutual fund works. When you send a mutual fund a check, the number of shares you obtain depends upon how much you invest and what the current value of the shares is.

As with a charitable remainder trust, you can designate more than one person to receive the quarterly income checks from the pooled-income fund over their lifetimes. Often, the money lasts over the lifetimes of a husband and wife. Upon the death of the last income beneficiary, all the shares revert to the charity.

Note Because there's no central clearinghouse for the thousands of pooled-income funds in existence, the best way to learn about their availability is to call individual charities that interest you.

Advantages of a pooled-income fund

Here's why a pooled-income fund may be appropriate for some charitable souls:

Pooled-income funds provide hassle-free investing.

You don't have to fret about how the money in a pooled-income fund is invested. The charity handles that responsibility by hiring professional money managers. This can be a relief for those who are not financially savvy.

A pooled-income fund may be cheaper.

The pooled-income fund is a practical alternative for relatively smaller donations of $5,000 or more because expenses don't automatically eat into your contribution. The charity, whether it's your alma mater, the Red Cross, or some other institution, will generally assume all the costs of running the fund and setting up your account.

Some charities, however, expect you to pay for the ongoing costs of the pooled-income fund out of your share of the fund's income. Consequently, you should know the rules before committing. If you want to donate to a fund that passes costs on to you, find out what the expenses are and how you will pay.

Tip   It's better to choose a charity that takes expenses out of its pooled-income fund's principal rather than the earnings. Charging expenses to the earnings could noticeably reduce the amount of your quarterly income checks.

Pooled-income funds welcome gradual donations.

You don't have to make just one lump-sum donation to a pooled-income fund. Although a minimum contribution (often it's $5,000) is necessary to get started, later donations can be much smaller, such as $1,000. Some people add to the fund while they're still earning a living, realizing that they may grow dependent upon the income as they age.

Disadvantages of a pooled-income fund

Here are the potential drawbacks to a pooled-income fund:

Pooled-income funds suffer during low inflation.

When inflation isn't a threat, pooled-income funds aren't nearly as popular. To understand why, you have to appreciate how pooled-income funds usually are invested. Many funds are heavily invested in bonds. Typically, the net interest generated from the bonds is passed along to the donors. When bonds are generating measly interest rates, which has been the case for many years, the return for these funds are mediocre. To cope with this problem, some charities now offer two fund choices, which encompass either a conservative or more aggressive approach that includes stocks.

But even a fund that's stuffed with stocks isn't a panacea for donors who dream of juicier returns. That's because traditionally only the dividends have been skimmed off stocks and passed on to the fund's investors. Unfortunately, stocks aren't robust dividend sources anymore. Many of today's most successful stocks don't even fool with dividends. To make these funds more alluring, a minority of charities are now allowing up to 50 percent of the capital gains generated by a fund each year to be distributed to the donors.

> **Tip**
>
> If you want to invest in a fund stuffed with stocks, find out in advance whether you'll be stuck with just dividends or if you can claim a stake of the fund's stock market successes.

Pooled-income funds have no investment flexibility.

If a pooled-income fund sounds good, you'll have to accept the ground rules. Your money is mingled with everybody else's in the pool. You can't instruct the charity to invest your donation in U.S. Treasury bonds, your favorite utility stock, or anything else for that matter. The charity's money managers make the financial decisions.

> **Note**
>
> Because you have no control over how the assets are invested, it pays to know a fund's historic rate of return. The size of your checks will partially depend upon how successfully the outside financial institution handles the charity's assets.

You can easily find out what a fund's performance record is by contacting the charity's planned giving office. Just ask for the fund's prospectus, which every charity is required to provide to a potential donor. A section of the prospectus must lay out in plain English how the fund works. The prospectus also mentions what investment firm, mutual fund company, or bank is handling the portfolio and how long it's served in this capacity. In addition, the document should include a 10-year history of the fund's performance.

Performance statistics can be especially crucial when you're considering which charity's fund to go with. Maybe you're torn between pooled-income funds offered by the American Association of University Women and by Greenpeace. The deciding factor could be which one has done a better job of investing the money.

Pooled-income funds provide fewer tax options.

Compared with a charitable remainder trust, a pooled-income fund isn't as tax efficient. The quarterly checks are taxed as ordinary income, which means the tax will be based on an individual's federal tax bracket. (Capital gains taxes could be triggered if the fund also passes along a portion of the fund's capital gains in those checks.) Suppose that your yearly payout totals $4,000. If you're in the 31 percent tax bracket, you'd owe $1,240. The bill for somebody in the highest 39.6 percent bracket would be $1,584.

Unfortunately, pooled-income funds are prohibited by law from investing in tax-exempt securities such as municipal bonds, which would lighten the tax burden. A pooled-income fund also can't accept assets that earn tax-free income.

The Charitable Gift Annuity: A Low-Hassle Alternative

When interest rates are low, the charitable gift annuity is by far a more popular alternative than the pooled-income fund. Thousands of charities offer the gift annuity option, which is essentially the exchange of a donation for a stream of fixed payments continuing for one or two lives. The income tax deduction depends on such factors as the donor's age, the payout, and interest rates.

These funds can be ideal for charitably inclined people who would like to make more modest donations than are practical with a CRT, and still receive fixed payments for life. You can invest in a gift annuity for as little as $2,500 or $5,000.

Advantages of gift annuities

Here are the top reasons to go with a gift annuity:

The gift annuity provides a stream of checks.

With a gift annuity, your charitable donation is exchanged for guaranteed, fixed payments for life. If desired, the payments can be spread out over two lifetimes. The size of the payment depends upon your age and the amount of the contribution. The older you are, the higher the annuity rate. After your donation, you can expect regular, fixed payments. Part of the payment is taxable as income and part is a tax-free return of principal. The steady checks can be appealing for retirees who are sitting on assets that spin off little income.

The National Kidney Association provides this example: A couple contributes $40,000 in stock to the charity. The stock had been paying a 3 percent dividend, which meant a $1,200 check per year for the couple. The annual payments from the charity's gift annuity, however, are significantly higher at $2,880. In the year of the gift, the couple avoided paying full capital gains taxes on the stock sale by the charity, and their income tax deduction came to $14,607.

The gift annuity is more tax-efficient.

Compared to a pooled-income fund, the gift annuity is more tax-friendly in one big respect: A portion of each check that a donor receives is tax-free. That's not the case with a pooled-income fund. The tax-free portion is the fair market value minus the charitable deduction. Consider the tax obligation of the couple who donated to the National Kidney Foundation. When the $2,880 yearly annuity payment is dissected, $1,564 is taxed at the couple's income tax bracket, $987 is taxed as capital gains, and $329 is tax-free. Because of the tax-break, the annuity's total return is even higher than the quoted interest rate would suggest.

It's easy to comparison shop for a gift annuity.

Approximately 80 percent of the nation's charities follow the gift annuity rate chart recommended annually by the American Council on Gift Annuities. Some charities prefer to be even more generous. Some Jewish and Catholic groups, in particular, offer higher annuity rates. Years ago, these religious groups felt compelled to begin paying better rates to remain competitive after a couple of non profits raised the stakes. In contrast, some nonprofits geared toward women, such as women's colleges, are known to pay lower annuity rates. A rationale is that women donors live longer so their rates should be lower. Keep in mind that the higher the payout, the less is ultimately left for charity and the smaller is the charitable deduction that the donor can claim.

 Resource   Contact the American Council on Gift Annuities at 233 McCrea St., Suite 400, Indianapolis, IN 46225; (317) 269-6271; www.ncpg.org/acga.html.

Table 29-1 lists gift annuity rates recommended by the council for gift annuities in which only one person will receive the payments. The gift annuity rate for two people is slightly lower than the single rate of the youngest in the pair. The council decides each spring whether the rates need changing. You can find the latest rates by visiting the Web site of the American Council on Gift Annuities.

Table 29-1
Gift Annuity Rates for Single Recipients

Age	Annuity Rate	Age	Annuity Rate
40	5.5%	60	6.6%
45	5.7%	61	6.7%
50	5.8%	62	6.8%
55	6.1%	63	6.9%
56	6.2%	64	6.9%
57	6.3%	65	7%
58	6.4%	66	7.1%

Age	Annuity Rate	Age	Annuity Rate
67	7.2%	80	9.2%
68	7.3%	81	9.4%
69	7.4%	82	9.6%
70	7.5%	83	9.9%
71	7.6%	84	10.2%
72	7.7%	85	10.5%
73	7.8%	86	10.8%
74	8%	87	11.1%
75	8.2%	88	11.4%
76	8.3%	89	11.7%
77	8.5%	90+	12%
78	8.7%		

* Rates are effective until at least July 2001. They may be adjusted as often as once a year.

Gift annuity payments are attractive for retirees who are 70 or older.

If you look at Table 29-1, you'll see that annuity interest rates are much higher for the oldest senior citizens. It would be hard to find an investment offering such a big guaranteed return. Consequently, gift annuities among Americans who are at least in their 70s are a more popular choice than pooled-income funds.

You can defer payments until retirement.

Perhaps you're in your peak earning years and don't need the payments right now, but you'd like to have more income starting in 10 to 15 years. You can establish a gift annuity and stipulate that the payments begin at the age you expect to retire. Some parents of young children also invest in gift annuities and defer payments until their children enter college when they need the money for college expenses. In this scenario, larger annual payments could be made over four or five years rather than have the smaller payments stretch across a lifetime.

Disadvantages of gift annuities

Here are the potential drawbacks of a gift annuity:

Payouts are smaller.

The charitable gift annuity payments are intentionally smaller than what you'd get from the regular annuities offered by life insurance companies. The gift annuity rates are lower because charities don't want to be perceived as competing with private insurance companies for business. What's more, a charity would love to have a significant contribution left at the end of the annuity. Finally, if gift annuity rates were the same as commercial annuity rates, there would be no charitable deduction, which must be at least 10 percent of the amount given to make the arrangement legal. Most deductions are between 30 percent and 70 percent of the amount given.

Gift annuities aren't feasible for all age groups.

Pooled-income funds could be a better choice for people in their 50s and 60s. That's because the rates for a gift annuity at those ages usually aren't as competitive. Because of the higher rates of return for more elderly donors, this investment pays off better for the 70 and older set.

Would-be heirs receive nothing.

When the donor(s) dies, all the money in the gift annuity belongs to the charity.

Summary

- ✦ In the world of charity, you can give and receive cash.
- ✦ A charitable remainder trust can be an ideal way to sell appreciated securities.
- ✦ Only millionaires should consider a charitable lead trust.
- ✦ Investigate a pooled-income fund's past performance before agreeing to donate to it.
- ✦ Charitable gift annuities are popular with the oldest Americans.

✦   ✦   ✦

Insuring Your Financial Health

In Part VIII, you'll learn the best ways to protect your income, your career, and ultimately your retirement nest egg. While saving for retirement, many people don't give much thought to protecting their investments from unexpected crises or unplanned developments, such as a workplace disability or a stay in a nursing home. This section will teach you how to evaluate your need for life, disability, and long-term care insurance. You will also discover the questions you need to ask when searching for an ideal policy.

The Impact of Insurance on Your Retirement Plans

Whether you are retired or far from that milestone, in this chapter, you'll learn how to determine what insurance you may need and how to evaluate your options. This chapter explains how to simplify the hunt for life, long-term care and disability insurance, and exposes some of the industry's dirty little secrets as well. Without proper insurance, the best-laid retirement savings plans can be sadly blown apart.

The Great American Hard Sell

Have you ever been trapped in your own living room by an insurance agent who shows no signs of getting off the couch? With the agent testing the outer limits of your hospitality, you may be willing to do anything to get him to pack up his literature and leave. To reclaim your couch, perhaps you'll even do something drastic like buying a policy.

If you've experienced something similar, you already appreciate what people in the industry readily admit: insurance policies are *sold,* not *bought.* Few people wake up in the morning and vow to themselves that this is the day they begin their search for a cash value life insurance policy. Even fewer souls start the day with a search for a disability or long-term care insurance policy. So unless a next-door neighbor, your brother-in-law, or a friend of a friend cajoles you into buying a policy, it might not ever happen.

The decision to obtain insurance coverage should obviously not depend upon whether your sister marries an insurance agent. But people get pushed into purchasing coverage all the time without evaluating what they truly need. Although it's not the most exciting prospect, most folks do need to spend some time considering their insurance needs and shopping for necessary policies in a methodical way instead of buying something just to get someone off your couch. Read on for the lowdown on the insurance products most critical to your financial health.

Life Insurance

Buying life insurance is about as thrilling as replacing worn tires on your car, yet it is just as necessary. Because it is a thankless task, many people don't devote enough energy into properly evaluating what they need. This lack of planning can lead to all sorts of problems years later when the consequences of a hasty or haphazard decision may haunt you or your loved ones. After all, when you buy life insurance, you are really buying protection for the necessary income your livelihood produces. To obtain the right coverage, you need to take the steps outlined in this section.

Tip   You can shop online for many types of policies and thus reduce the amount of hard-sell tactics or cheap suits you'll have to endure.

Deciding what type you need

Countless insurance policies exist today, which is a huge reason why people loathe insurance shopping. Yet all these options can be broken down into two broad categories: term life insurance and cash value life insurance, which you'll also see referred to as permanent insurance. Term life insurance is by far the simplest and cheapest way to go and is the superior choice for the vast majority of people.

Term insurance

The purpose of this no-frills insurance is to replace your income for any dependents left behind. You buy this coverage in chunks of time, such as 10-, 15-, or 20-year terms. Many people time their term insurance to expire when their youngest child graduates from college. If you outlive the term of your insurance, you receive nothing. The insurer keeps all your premiums. Research done by Pennsylvania State University in the early 1990s discovered that only 1 percent of the 20,000 term policies in the study resulted in a death claim.

People usually buy this type of coverage when their death would cause tremendous financial hardship for a family. Parents whose children are still living in the home are heavy users of this insurance. A childless couple would also find the insurance especially valuable if only one person worked outside the home. This type of insurance is rarely appropriate for retirees because the premiums at older ages are exorbitant. But, of course, most older people won't need life insurance anyway: If you have left the workforce, you have no paychecks to insure.

Cash value insurance

Policyholders of cash value insurance are interested in more than just a death benefit. They may wish coverage on a permanent basis with a level premium. This insurance also provides a customer an opportunity to accumulate a "cash value" inside the policy. A policy's cash value is a lot like a savings account. After the steep commissions are paid, your premiums are invested, which allows the value of your policy to grow. This money may eventually be withdrawn or borrowed against, or the entire amount can be left to heirs. The cash value should not be confused with the policy's face amount. The *face amount* is the money paid at death or at the policy's *maturity* (the point at which the accumulated cash value equals the face amount of the policy), minus any outstanding loads and or previously withdrawn funds. When the policy reaches maturity, the face amount can be paid out to the policyholder, if he or she is still alive. Today's policies mature typically when the owner is between 95 and 120 years old. The three major types of cash value insurance are whole life, universal life, and variable life.

Whole life insurance

Whole life insurance, which is also called ordinary or straight life insurance, used to be the most common variety of cash value life insurance. The premium amount generally is fixed for the life of the policy. Typically these policies command the highest premiums of all the permanent insurance choices.

A traditional policy's cash value often grows at a fixed rate though there are some interest-sensitive policies as well. The insurer, who is solely responsible for the investing strategies, usually guarantees a minimum amount for the cash value and the death benefit.

Universal life insurance

Universal life insurance is the most flexible of the cash value alternatives. These policies were developed in the 1970s as a way for stodgy insurers to better compete with the financial services industry. As with whole life, the insurer makes the investment decisions. With one of these policies, you can choose how much you want to sink into the policy every year. The insurer suggests a target premium, which is the amount necessary to keep the policy in force until you hit age 100. In some years, you may be able to skip the premium entirely.

You're free to decide how big the death benefit will be. Of course, your decision involves trade-offs. If you want an increasing death benefit, your policy's cash value will be lower. If you want a level death benefit (a fixed amount), the cash value will increase. These policies guarantee a minimum death benefit and cash value.

Variable life insurance

Variable life insurance is the conservative insurance industry's attempt to be more competitive and to transfer more investment risk to shareholders. The underlying mix of investments that are contained in the policy are generally selected after a customer fills out a questionnaire that asks questions about the individual's investment risk tolerance. The possible asset allocations can range from a more risk-averse portfolio that's devoted primarily to bonds to a far more aggressive one that contains a heavy concentration in stocks. This kind of policy is more appropriate for individuals, who don't mind some volatility in their underlying investments.

Ironically, while the investments can be riskier, these types of policies are safer in one respect. Since the money in these policies are invested in separate accounts, they should be protected for the policyholders if an insurer declares bankruptcy. This protection isn't automatic with the other two types of cash value insurance because the investments are contained within an insurer's general account funds, which are fair game for creditors. Policyholders would have to stand in line with other creditors to get their money from a bankrupt insurer if they have universal or whole life coverage.

Comparing term insurance with cash value insurance

In the overwhelming number of cases, term insurance is the best choice. For most people, there's little point in looking elsewhere. People who choose cash value insurance run the risk of buying an expensive policy that they don't need. What's tricky about these policies is that you may not even know whether you've been ripped off. The pros and cons of each type of life insurance are outlined in this section.

Tip   Although insurance agents talk up the investment features of cash value insurance, most people would be better off investing the premium difference between a term and cash value policy into solid, low-cost mutual funds.

Term insurance advantages

Note that term insurance has some solid strong points.

Term insurance is cheap.

Because term insurance has no investment component, the cost can be significantly lower. Initially, term premiums are cheaper than those of permanent insurance. The low cost allows someone to buy higher levels of coverage at a younger age when the need for protection is often the greatest.

Term insurance provides flexibility.

With term insurance, you choose your own coverage period, such as 10, 15, or 20 years and whether you wish to lock in prices. You can obtain annual renewable term insurance, which may result in the premium increasing yearly. The price of this coverage can be cheaper during the first few years than the other alternative, which is level premium term. With this type, the premium is guaranteed not to budge for a set period of time, such as 10 years. After that, you may face annual increases. The longer the premium must remain unchanged, the higher the premium will be. If you obtain level premium term insurance, you'll want to know what happens when the level period expires. Some insurers may then begin increasing your cost every year; others will allow you to lock in prices for another fixed period.

Term Insurance Quote Sources

If you're buying term insurance, you can do most of the legwork yourself. Quote services provide prices on a wide variety of policies. Because each quote service deals with its own pool of insurers, you should contact more than one for rates.

Don't assume, however, that you are entitled to the most attractive rates you hear. The cheapest rates are reserved for the healthiest among us. If you don't meet the criteria in the following list, you'll probably pay more. Here are typical requirements you must meet to obtain the best prices:

✦ Stringent height/weight requirements

✦ Low cholesterol

✦ Don't smoke

✦ No deaths from cancer or heart disease in parents or siblings before age 60

✦ No drunk-driving convictions

✦ No serious illnesses

✦ Blood pressure below 140/90 without medication

✦ Don't fly in private planes

✦ No more than three moving traffic violations in the past three years

Some customers mistakenly assume that the rates will be lower because an agent isn't involved. That's usually not true. The quote service pockets the commission just as an agent would. The chief advantage to going this route is obtaining lots of quotes quickly. After that, it's up to you to evaluate the financial stability of the insurers. (See sidebar on evaluating insurers later in this chapter.) The disadvantage is you don't have an agent to represent you.

The following are a few of the firms providing quotes:

✦ QuickQuote at (800) 867-2404 or www.quickquote.com

✦ Quotesmith.com at (800) 431-1147 or www.quotesmith.com

✦ InstantQuote.com at (888) 223-2220 or www.instantquote.com

✦ AccuQuote at (800) 442-9899 or www.accuquote.com

✦ Quicken Insurance at (800) 695-0011 or www.insuremarket.com

✦ SelectQuote at (800) 343-1985 or www.selectquote.com

Term insurance disadvantage

Term insurance can be too costly for older Americans and most companies don't even offer it to people once they reach their 70s. Here's one example of just how unbelievable the price can be. Suppose an 85-year-old wanted a $1 million policy that would last 10 years. The annual premium would recently have been $127,000. Obviously, most seniors won't need life insurance anyway. Their children will be grown, the mortgage will be paid, and with any luck, they will have an adequate retirement nest egg.

Cash value insurance advantages

Be sure to balance the pros against the cons when considering your cash value life insurance options.

A practical alternative to paying estate taxes

Older, affluent Americans who find term insurance too costly often use cash value insurance. Often these customers want insurance to pay for potential estate taxes after their deaths.

> **Note**   Estate taxes won't be a concern for most folks because only about 2 percent of Americans end up paying them.

A tax advantage

Money grows tax-free inside a cash value life insurance policy. You can also withdraw money without triggering taxes as long as the withdrawal amount doesn't exceed the amount that you've contributed to the policy. The death benefit when the policyholder dies is also free of income tax.

What many people don't appreciate, however, is that the insurance payout, if it's big enough, can trigger estate taxes that could swallow up to half of the death benefit proceeds. This potential nightmare can happen if the policy is owned by the insured person. To avoid the tax liability, the policy must be owned by another person or entity. Another solution is to establish an irrevocable life insurance trust. This kind of trust enables the policyholder to keep the insurance out of his or her estate and free of estate taxes. With one of these trusts, you neither own nor control the insurance policy. A trustee, whom you name, oversees the trust for the benefit of your eventual heirs. The trustee could be one of the policyholder's future heirs.

> **Cross-Reference**   See Chapters 25 and 26 for more information on trusts.

A loan provision

A cash value life insurance policy builds up a cash value that can be borrowed against. The term "loan" is a misnomer because the money doesn't have to be repaid. If the money is not returned with interest, however, beneficiaries will receive a smaller death benefit. You can also borrow money from the policy to pay the policy's premium. Some older policyholders on a fixed-income resort to this method to keep the policy in force for the benefit of their heirs.

 Caution Although agents love to tout this lending feature, it can backfire terribly. If too much cash is withdrawn over time, the policy can collapse. In this case, coverage evaporates, and the policy's owner can face a substantial tax bill on the earnings.

Policy loans are quite complex so you should have an expert evaluate your policy before you take out a loan against it. You may want to read the article "The Pitfalls of Policy Loans," which appeared in A.M. Best's November 2000 issue of *Best Review;* the article is posted on the author's Web site, www.asisyourlife.com.

Cash value life insurance disadvantages

You need to take these disadvantages into account when considering the purchase of a cash value life insurance policy.

Cash value life insurance is costly.

A cash value life insurance policy can be a terrible idea, especially for someone who needs coverage only for 10 years or less. The Consumer Federation of America, which clearly favors term insurance for most people, estimates that people who don't hold onto their policies for at least 20 years could lose money. Steep costs keep policies in the red for a long time.

Note An agent's commission can eat up more than 100 percent of the first year's life insurance premium.

Lower cost alternatives do exist. Some insurance companies do not use agents, so the built-in costs of these policies should not be as steep. You can obtain policies directly from the insurers or though fee-only financial planners and fee-for-service life insurance advisors, who do not accept commissions. These policies are referred to as low-load insurance. Here are some low-load insurers:

✦ Ameritas Life Insurance at (800) 552-3553

✦ ING Southland Life at (888) 968-5433

✦ USAA Life Insurance at (800) 531-8000

✦ Paragon Life Insurance at (800) 685-0124

✦ Great-West Life Assurance at (800) 537-2033

Cash value insurance is too complicated.

If someone sells you a cash value policy, you probably wouldn't know if you were buffaloed. You can blame some of this confusion on the insurance policy's illustration. An illustration represents a set of actuarial projections that are supposed to predict how your policy will fare over your lifetime. The operative word here is "predict." An insurance company must project such things as the policy's investment returns, mortality charges, and inflation. Obviously, no one knows how a company's portfolio will fare.

Aggravating an already bad situation is this sad reality: While some agents are very ethical, others won't tell you if the projections are baloney.

Caution   The system is rigged against consumers because insurance agents operate with a built-in conflict of interest. If you don't buy a policy from them, they earn nothing. So some agents may forget to mention a policy's weaknesses or to hype questionable benefits. Just as bad, a well-meaning agent might not understand all of a policy's nuances.

Getting fair, practical advice

Is there anyone you can turn to for unbiased insurance help? Yes. The Consumer Federation of America provides an excellent and inexpensive resource. Through the federation, James H. Hunt, a nationally known insurance actuary and former state insurance commissioner, can analyze an existing policy or those that you're considering purchasing. Hunt can determine whether a cash value policy makes sense and provide an opinion on different insurance candidates. In addition, he can help you decide whether an existing policy should be swapped for another one. You can contact James H. Hunt at the Consumer Federation of America, 8 Tahanto St., Concord, NH 03301-3835; (603) 224-2805; www.consumerfed.org. The cost of the analysis is $45 for the first policy and $35 for an additional one that's submitted at the same time.

Caution   Insurance agents are notorious for encouraging people to bail out of one policy to sign up for another. This kind of switch generates fat commissions for agents, but it is usually a dreadful idea for customers.

Another possibility is contacting a fee-only insurance advisor or fee-only financial planner who does not sell insurance or take commissions. (See Chapters 5 and 6.) Never buy cash value insurance from an agent without consulting an outside expert who won't profit one way or another from a sale.

Determining how much life insurance you need

How much life insurance do you need? There are a couple of quick methods to estimate it. One is to obtain a policy that represents five to six times a person's salary. Another way is to determine the amount of money necessary to generate an income stream that would adequately support the surviving family. For instance, a $1 million insurance payment invested to return 7 percent a year would annually generate $70,000.

Evaluating the Insurers

Insurance protects you from the financial impact of catastrophes. But what happens if the insurer faces its own demise? Insurance companies do fold, and when that happens policy-holders can suffer tremendous losses. To avoid that nightmare, you need to know what the experts think about an insurance company's financial stability.

Finding independent assessments of any insurer is easy. Rating services provide a letter grade to each one. Each service uses its own criteria and each rating will mean something a bit different. Don't bother with any insurer with a "B" rating or below. Stick with those who have earned an "A" rating. The "A" ratings vary from service to service. For instance, Standard & Poor's highest mark is AAA; Moody's top ranking is Aaa.

Here are the major rating services:

✦ A.M. Best at (908) 439-2200 or www.ambest.com

✦ Fitch, IBCA, Duff & Phelps at (800) 853-4824 or www.fitchratings.com

✦ Standard & Poor's at (212) 438-2400 or www.standardandpoors.com/ratings

✦ Moody's Investors Services at (212) 553-0377 or www.moodys.com

✦ Weiss Ratings at (800) 289-9222 or www.weissratings.com

For the most part, you can obtain an insurer's report card free of charge by calling or visiting a rating service's Web site. You can also ask an agent for the ratings, but as a precaution, you should double-check the information with that of an unbiased source. If you get the rating from an agent, make sure it's less than a year old.

Of course, these quick methods aren't foolproof. For your own peace of mind, estimate what the family's needs would be after a death—including long-term expenses. Expenses might include the funeral, a mortgage, the usual household costs, medical bills, and future college tuition or student loans. When considering potential expenses, many people forget to factor in inflation and taxes. Explore what resources the family would have to cover these costs, such as a 401(k) plan or an Individual Retirement Account that might be left behind.

Tip   Don't forget to purchase life insurance for a stay-at-home parent who takes care of young children. In case of that parent's death, childcare could become a huge expense.

Single people aren't usually life insurance buyers, but there will be cases when it's a practical move. If you've bought a house with a live-in partner, your share of the mortgage could be paid off with life insurance. Purchasing life insurance may also be a wise move if your parents are financially dependent upon you or you want to leave money to a friend, relative, or charity.

Long-Term Care Insurance

Imagine a bomb blowing up your nest egg. That sort of graphic imagery frightens millions of us when we start to think about the health problems that often accompany aging. If you, a parent, or grandparent ends up requiring expensive home health care or must be admitted into a nursing home, the money that's been set aside for retirement could quickly vanish.

An increasing number of older Americans are trying to avoid this nightmare by purchasing long-term care insurance. Interest in this complicated product has skyrocketed, as have the misconceptions. Long-term care insurance is supposed to protect policyholders from financial implosions by picking up at least some of the tab for all this expensive care, which theoretically leaves more money available for the frail policyholder, a spouse, and possibly heirs.

Is long-term care insurance necessary? At first glance, it might seem absolutely indispensable. Spine-tingling statistics abound. The federal government, for instance, has estimated that a 65-year-old faces at least a 40 percent chance of requiring nursing home, assisted living, or home care expenses at some point. The numbers and the price tag are expected to continue to balloon.

What does long-term care insurance cover?

Long-term care insurance can pay for assistance you may require if you are suffering from a chronic disability or illness that leaves you unable to take care of yourself. Many people buy such policies because they want to avoid living their final years in a nursing home. The insurance may allow those folks who need help with eating, dressing, or bathing to remain in their homes and hire some help. Long-term care policies may also cover the costs of an adult day care center, home care agencies, senior centers, and retirement communities. These services are expensive, and they typically fall through the health insurance safety net.

Caution Neither private health insurance nor Medicare pays for nursing home care except in very limited circumstances for a brief time period.

Do you need long-term care insurance?

Despite the grim statistics, not everybody needs long-term care insurance. If you have few assets, don't give this type of coverage a second thought. Why? The government will eventually pay for your care. Americans are expected to foot a nursing home tab until they are on the verge of running out of money. Once someone's bank account contains just $2,000 to $3,000, he or she is eligible for state-run Medicaid, which medically insures the poor of any age. A person on Medicaid may keep a car, burial plot, furniture, and a home if the spouse or dependent or disabled child lives at the house.

A Helping Hand

Because you may ultimately sink tens of thousands of dollars into a policy, picking the most appropriate one is critical. With so much is at stake, you may want to consult an elder law attorney or a financial planner who has a great deal of experience in this field.

Another resource (and this one is free) is the State Health Insurance Assistance Program (SHIP). SHIP is a government-sponsored counseling program that helps older Americans with health insurance-related questions. You can find the program nearest you by calling the Eldercare Locator at (800) 677-1116.

The state of Maine's Web site posts cyberlinks to many states' counseling services. Visit www.state.me.us/dhs/beas/hiap/statelinks.htm.

A couple who barely manages to pay all their bills shouldn't consider this insurance either. It makes no sense to buy a long-term care insurance policy if you can't commit to payments for many years. If you can afford the premium while you're still working, think about whether you could still shoulder the cost when you're 70 and primarily dependent upon Social Security and a pension. If you can't make an open-ended commitment to this coverage, you could discover 10 or 15 years later that you've been tossing checks into a money pit.

Caution   The whole investment in long-term care insurance will be wasted if you ultimately cancel the policy because it's no longer affordable.

On the flip side, wealthy people probably don't need this coverage either. Millionaires should be able to pay for long-term care costs out of their own investments. The Consumers Union, publisher of *Consumer Reports,* suggests that long-term care insurance isn't necessary for those who can afford to invest $160,000 to cover four years of nursing home care while still leaving enough money for a spouse or dependent child. Why four years? Ninety percent of elderly nursing home patients remain in their nursing home less than four years.

So the folks who find this protection most desirable are the middle class and upper middle class because they stand to lose the most assets if they encounter catastrophic bills, and may not be able to accumulate the large amount of cash necessary to foot long-term care expenses.

While insurance agents love to promote long-term care insurance for any age, realistically it's better purchased by those who are older. There is no magic age when purchasing a policy makes sense; however, according to industry statistics, the average age of individuals buying these policies is 66. Younger people typically have more pressing needs for their money, such as paying for their children's college costs. For younger folks, probably the more important priority is insuring their livelihoods with disability insurance.

Ironically, people who know they'll almost certainly need the insurance, such as those diagnosed with Parkinson's disease, heart disease, or some other persistent medical condition such as Alzheimer's, are generally unable to get policies. As far as the insurance industry is concerned, these folks are untouchables.

How do you buy the best long-term care insurance policy?

If you're interested in buying long-term care insurance, choosing an appropriate policy is extremely important. The task is much trickier than picking the best term life insurance. Unlike Medigap insurance policies, long-term care policies aren't standardized. (Medigap policies, which are issued by private insurers, extend coverage to expenses that Medicare doesn't pay.) Policies on the market vary tremendously; therefore, understanding the fine print is critical. This section explains what you need to know about selecting a long-term care policy.

Be leery of the cheapest policies.

When shopping for a long-term care policy, your instincts as a savvy consumer won't always serve you well. Choosing the cheapest policy, for instance, may ultimately prove to be a disastrous move. Some of the most aggressive writers of long-term care insurance have traditionally attracted interest by undercutting the competition with lower prices. Also, they may insure less healthy people, such as diabetics or recovered stroke victims, that other insurers would automatically reject.

Premiums are based on actuarial studies that indicate how policies must be priced to pay for eventual claims. Pricing these policies is tricky because long-term care insurance is still a relatively new product, which means there is little history to base premiums upon.

Caution   If prices turn out to be too low, the insurer is not the one that suffers. Policy loopholes that allow premium increases enable insurers to pass high costs on to customers.

Rock-bottom prices recently created turmoil for customers of two of the biggest long-term care insurers. Although the companies promised their premiums wouldn't increase as the customers aged, hundreds of thousands of customers were hit with significant price hikes. The costs became so exorbitant that some policyholders had no choice but to drop their coverage.

The price hikes were legal because the insurers used a popular loophole. Most states prohibit an insurer from raising the customers' rates as they grow older. However, an insurer typically can increase premiums to all customers who own the same type of policy if it demonstrates that it is paying out more in claims that it initially projected. For this reason, some hapless policyholders watched in disbelief as their premiums climbed 100 percent.

Don't believe the sales literature.

If you experience trouble with your long-term care insurance, realize that the only promises that matter are the ones contained in the contract, which you should thoroughly read. An agent, who will pocket a commission that can range from 30 to 65 percent of the first year's premium, may promise the world. At the risk of losing a commission, the agent could also be unwilling to disclose a policy's weaknesses. Typically, you have 30 days after signing a contract to change your mind. But before you make your final decision, it's better to ask an agent for a "specimen policy," a blank policy that you can read at your convenience.

 Caution

Never make a purchasing decision based upon an insurance agent's slick sales presentation or the promotional literature—only the contract counts.

Be leery if an agent tries to scare you into buying a policy by sharing horror stories of seniors losing their home because of a chronic illness. Also resist pressure from agents who insist that you must make a decision immediately because prices are going up any day now.

Do the math.

One of the most infuriating aspects of long-term care insurance is that it's economical at ages when there's almost no chance of needing it. You could spend decades paying yearly premiums for coverage that you thankfully don't use. The premiums for the elderly, who are the most likely to use the coverage, are astronomical.

Insurance agents urge people to sign up for long-term care insurance when they are younger and the premiums are much cheaper. Younger customers believe that they've locked in lower premiums forever, but that isn't necessarily the case. Premiums can and often do escalate. As a result, many people who have been contributing faithfully to a long-term care policy for years reach the point where their premiums are unaffordable.

If you are considering purchasing a policy and you are in your 40s or 50s, consider whether you could protect yourself better by establishing a rainy-day medical fund. Suppose a 40-year-old invested the typical annual premium indicated in Table 30-1, $595, into a brokerage account. Assume that the account earns 11 percent, which is what stocks have historically earned. In 30 years, the investment would be worth $118,417. In 20 years, a 50-year-old annually stashing away $888 would have $57,012. Will that much cash pay for four years of long-term care? The answer really depends upon the rates for care in your area and the extent of care that you'll need—which is another frustrating aspect of deciding whether to purchase long-term care insurance. No one can look into the future and discover how much care or coverage will be necessary. At least when you invest the money yourself, you'll have something at the end, if you end up not needing the care.

Don't purchase more than you need.

You can cut the costs of long-term care insurance in some sensible ways. For example, you may typically purchase a policy that provides coverage anywhere from one year to a lifetime. The longer the coverage is, the bigger the premium. When you are deciding how long your coverage should be, keep in mind that the average stay at a nursing home is 19 months and nearly 90 percent of elderly nursing home patients remain less than four years.

 Tip   Given the statistics about the length of nursing home stays, a policy providing four years of coverage is probably a safe compromise.

You can also economize by picking a longer elimination period. An *elimination period* is essentially the policy's deductible; it dictates when the benefits begin.

Example   With a 30-day elimination period, for instance, a person entering a nursing home would have to pick up the tab for the first month.

Consider inflation protection.

Insurance with inflation protection is pricier, but without it, your policy's purchasing power may fizzle. Suppose nursing homes in your area are now charging $3,300 a month. You pick a policy that today would pay most of this tab. You might, at this point, congratulate yourself. Depending upon your age, however, the more relevant cost figures could still be 10 or 20 years away. Assuming an inflation rate of 5 percent, that same nursing home bed will cost $5,375 in a decade and $8,756 in 20 years. So much for the peace-of-mind protection you purchased.

How quickly can nursing home prices increase? You can make some rough projections on your own by using the Rule of 72. This handy math formula determines how long it takes for a price to double. Simply divide the rate of growth you anticipate into 72 to find out how many years it'll take a price to double. To get some idea of how much nursing home costs are rising in your area, contact the State Health Insurance Assistance Program (SHIP) in your state (see the sidebar "A Helping Hand" earlier in this section).

 Example   Suppose a $100-a-day nursing home increases its prices by 6 percent a year. Divide 72 by 6 to find out that the price will double in 12 years. If the price of nursing home care jumps 8 percent a year, prices would double in 9 years.

Those interested in inflation protection have two choices — compounded-inflation protection and simple-interest increases. With the latter, interest is calculated strictly on the original amount of money invested. In contrast, compound interest is calculated upon the original investment plus the accumulated interest so it provides more protection. The compounded-inflation feature, which is pricier, is more realistic for younger policyholders, who aren't likely to need the coverage for quite a few years and thus can benefit from the interest building up for a longer period. In contrast, someone in his or her 70s may prefer to stick with the simple-interest protection. The decision will be a harder one for persons between the ages of 65 to 70; closely examine prices when deciding.

Agents often belittle inflation coverage because they fear it will scare away customers. That's because the cost of inflation protection, as you can see in Table 30-1, increases premiums quite a bit.

The premiums in Table 30-1 are for a hypothetical four-year policy with a 20-day elimination period. The coverage pays for $100-a-day nursing home care, $80 a-day assisted-living facility care, or at least $50-a-day home care. Rates for care vary by area, so it's tough to say whether these coverage amounts are sufficient.

Table 30-1		
Average Annual Premiums for Long-Term Care Insurance, 1997		
Age	*Premium*	*Premium with 5% compounded inflation protection*
40	$274	$595
50	$385	$888
65	$1,007	$1,850
79	$4,100	$5,800

Source: Health Insurance Association of America

Look closely at the policy's features.

Even little differences among policies can be important. For instance, the ideal policy requires just one deductible so that if you need services off and on over the years, you won't have to pay a deductible each time you require care. (Realistically, however, by the time your poor health necessitates the coverage, chances are you'll be relying upon it for the rest of your life.) Also, you're better off with a policy that goes into effect even if you haven't been hospitalized; not having to meet the hospitalization criteria allows you greater flexibility in getting the care that you need when you need it.

Know the hallmarks of a blue-ribbon long-term care policy.

The AARP recommends choosing a policy with these features:

✦ Offers 5 percent compounded inflation protection.

✦ Doesn't require a hospital visit to trigger benefits.

✦ Allows policyholders to downgrade coverage if they can't afford the premium.

✦ Guarantees the policy's renewability as long as the premiums are paid.

✦ Uses one deductible for the life of the policy.

✦ Covers preexisting conditions without a waiting period if they are disclosed when you apply.

Long-Term Care Hot Spots

More than half of the long-term care policies that have been sold since the late 1980s (when the insurance was introduced) have been sold in these nine states:

California	Iowa	Pennsylvania
Florida	Missouri	Texas
Illinois	Ohio	Washington

As you shop for a policy, here are questions to ask insurers:

✦ Which of these services are covered?

- Nursing home care

- Home health care

- Assisted living facility

- Adult day care

- Respite care

- Other

✦ How much does the policy pay per day for these services?

✦ What's the waiting period (also known as the elimination period) before coverage begins for each of these services?

✦ Are Alzheimer's disease and other organic mental disorders covered?

✦ What does the policy cost with and without inflation protection?

✦ Is the policy's renewability guaranteed?

Where can you find out more about long-term care insurance?

As with any insurance purchase, the more you know, the better off you are. Consult these resources:

✦ **The National Association of Insurance Commissioners,** which represents state insurance regulators, publishes a variety of insurance booklets, including *A Shopper's Guide to Long-Term Care Insurance* and *Life Insurance Buyer's Guide.* Contact this organization at 2301 McGee, Suite 800, Kansas City, MO 64108; (816) 842-3600; www.naic.org.

✦ **United Seniors Health Cooperative** publishes a 100-page book entitled, *Long-Term Care Planning: A Dollar & Sense Guide,* which can be ordered by contacting the organization at 409 Third St., Suite 200, Washington, DC 20024; (202) 479-6973; `www.unitedseniorshealth.com`.

✦ **The American Health Care Association,** which is a federation of long-term care providers, has posted a detailed explanation of long-term care insurance issues on its Web site, `www.ahca.org`. You can also contact this organization at 1201 L St. NW, Washington, DC 20005; (202) 842-4444.

✦ **The Consumer Law Page,** operated by a California law firm, has posted on its site an exhaustively detailed long-term care buyer's publication entitled *Avoiding Fraud When Buying Long-Term Care Insurance, A Guide for Consumers and Their Families.* This lengthy guide should spur readers into researching their options carefully. You can visit this Web site at `www.consumerlawpage.com`.

Disability Insurance

You insure your car, your house, your health, and your life. What about your career? Most people ignore that one, but insuring your career can be extremely important. Imagine the fate of a pianist diagnosed with progressively worsening osteoarthritis or a carpenter who has muscular dystrophy. How about a reporter or software programmer who is crippled by Carpal Tunnel Syndrome after years of typing on a keyboard? Could you survive financially if an injury or disease kept you away from your job for long stretches of time or perhaps forever? And, of course, if you can no longer work in your profession, your retirement savings goals can be obliterated.

Should you consider a disability policy?

The chances of becoming disabled are greater than you might assume. The Health Industry Association of America says that 30 percent of Americans between the ages of 35 and 60 will become disabled for at least 90 days. Although interest in disability insurance has picked up recently as the baby boomers feel less invincible, most Americans still aren't buying. Those who do purchase policies are primarily white-collar workers.

Some people pass on the coverage because they think they're already protected through a workplace policy, workman's compensation, or Social Security. However, most corporate coverage lasts only for a brief period, from a few days to no more than six months. A few states, such as New York, New Jersey, Rhode Island, and Hawaii, require six months of coverage; California insists upon one year. Worker's compensation covers only disabilities that occurred on the job or were caused by it.

> **Tip**
>
> In all likelihood, you'll want to supplement your workplace coverage with your own personal policy, which can be expensive. Prices should be cheaper if you go through a professional or trade association.

Social Security is not a sure thing either. It imposes extremely tough standards in winnowing out those who qualify for disability payments. Those eligible must be unable to perform any job. Suppose you were a teacher before suffering partial brain damage in a car accident. If the only job you can now handle is sweeping the floor at a fast food restaurant, that's your tough luck. Social Security won't help. Recently, the average monthly disability payment from the government was just $733.

Like all insurance, you can mix and match disability coverage in many ways. Some features cost more than others. The trick is finding an affordable policy that can realistically provide for your needs. This section highlights the points you need to consider.

What is the definition of disability?

Insurers' definitions of disability differ dramatically. Before sinking money into a policy, know how the insurer defines disability. The more liberal the definition is, the higher the premium will be. The three common ones are own occupation, any occupation, and income replacement occupation.

Own occupation

If you want Cadillac coverage, own occupation coverage is it. However, the cost for own occupation coverage, is steep. With this definition, you're considered disabled if you can't perform your own occupation. An orthopedic surgeon who lost fingers in a car accident would collect payments because he could no longer perform operations. With this kind of coverage, it wouldn't matter if the surgeon could still make the same amount of money teaching at a medical school or becoming an administrator.

Back in the mid-1990s, insurers were hit by an increase in own-occupation claims (many from physicians) and boosted the price of these policies. In some regions, own-occupation coverage isn't even offered anymore. But the policies, where available, remain popular with executives and other high-paid professionals.

Many of these policies provide own-occupation coverage for two to five years and then revert to a less onerous standard for the insurer. After the period has expired, the disability checks would be based on the loss of income.

> **Example**
>
> A policy that initially provided a $5,000 monthly benefit would decrease payments to $3,000 if the policyholder began working at a job that represented 40 percent of his or her old salary.

Disability Untouchables

Have you ever been in therapy? Been diagnosed with Carpal Tunnel Syndrome? Are you a police officer, an oil-field worker, a pilot, a miner, or somebody else with a hazardous job? If so, you could have a much tougher time getting disability coverage, if it's possible at all. Chances are your premiums will also be more expensive than somebody who doesn't pose as great of risk of needing the insurance. It can also be extremely difficult for self-employed people who work at home to obtain coverage. Insurers feel that they have no way to verify whether these people are capable of working.

Blue-collar workers, such as baggage handlers, carpenters, and others whose job description requires heavy labor, could also experience a great deal of trouble finding reasonably affordable insurance. Women, unless they can obtain a unisex policy, also tend to pay more because historically women have made more claims.

Any occupation

The any occupation definition is the toughest definition to meet and consequently provides the least protection. Before you're qualified for benefits, you'd have to be unemployable. The requirements can be just as stiff as those imposed by Social Security. Not surprisingly, policies relying upon this definition are the cheapest.

Income replacement occupation

The income replacement occupation definition is the most cost-efficient pick. Your income is covered rather than your specific job title. Suppose a disability forced an attorney to work as a paralegal where he would have less responsibilities and stress. The insurance company would make up part of the difference between what the lawyer was formerly making and what his salary is today.

What should you consider when buying a policy?

To make the best choice, consider not only the level of occupation covered by a disability insurance policy but the following factors as well.

Size of benefit

There is a limit to how big monthly disability checks can be. Obviously, an insurer won't let you buy coverage that provides more cash than you currently make because then you would have no incentive to return to the rat race. Policies typically replace 60 to 70 percent of someone's monthly income. Higher income workers are often not allowed to replace even this much of their compensation. Although the replacement may not seem adequate, keep in mind that your disability checks won't be taxed as long as you pay for the policy. If your former employer paid for the coverage, you'll owe taxes.

Renewing Your Policy

Obtain a policy that guarantees your right to renew each year. With a "guaranteed renewable" policy, an insurer can't refuse to sign you up for another year, nor can it change the policy's terms except premium costs. Even then, your premiums can't rise unless they do for everybody in your same classification.

Even better, sign up for a "noncancellable" policy. With these policies, which are becoming harder to find, the premium remains the same, and the insurer can't drop your coverage.

Length of coverage

The longer you want disability payments to continue, the pricier the policy will be. A policy that lasts one to two years will be far cheaper than one remaining in force until age 65 or your death. The vast majority of disabilities don't last more than a year, but you can't count on it.

For almost everyone, obtaining lifetime benefits is prohibitively expensive. You'll save money by having the benefits stop at age 65, when you could claim Social Security and possibly a pension. Of course, you don't have to stay locked into paying premiums for decades. If you retire early, you'll cancel your policy, and if you build up considerable assets, you may not need it either. If you can't afford to pay for coverage that lasts until age 65, try to obtain the longest coverage that you can.

At the same time, you'll need to determine when the benefit should kick in. This amount of time is called the elimination period. The shortest waiting period is 30 days, but you'll pay more for this short lead time. If you agree to a 90-day elimination period or even a longer one, the policy won't cost as much.

Summary

✦ Find an outside, unbiased source to evaluate any cash value insurance policy.

✦ Be highly skeptical if an agent urges you to switch life insurance policies; agents earn commissions each time you switch.

✦ Evaluate whether you need long-term care insurance.

✦ Don't look for the cheapest long-term care policy; search for the best policy with a highly rated company.

✦ Consider obtaining disability insurance to safeguard your earning potential.

✦   ✦   ✦

Resource Guide

401(k) Plans

401Kafe
www.401kafe.com

Annuities

Annuity.com
www.annuity.com

AnnuityNet.com
(877) 569-3789
www.annuitynet.com

Comparative Annuity Reports
(916) 487-7863
www.annuitycomparativedata.com

Fisher Annuity Index
(800) 833-1450

Morningstar Variable Annuity Performance Report
(800) 735-0700
www.morningstar.com

National Association for Variable Annuities
11710 Plaza America Dr., Suite 100
Reston, VA 20190
(703) 707-8830
www.navanet.org
www.retireonyourterms.com

TIAA-CREF
(800) 842-2776
www.tiaa-cref.org

U.S. Securities and Exchange Commission
Office of Investor Education and Assistance
450 Fifth St. NW
Washington, DC 20549-0213
(202) 942-7040
www.sec.gov

WebAnnuities.com
(800) 872-6684
www.annuityshopper.com

Bonds

Bond Market Association
www.investinginbonds.com

Bondsonline
www.bondsonline.com

Bureau of the Public Debt: Savings Bonds
(304) 480-6112
(800) 4US-BOND (Automated)
www.savingsbonds.gov

TreasuryDirect
U.S. Treasury Department
(800) 722-2678
www.publicdebt.treas.gov

Certificates of Deposit

Bankrate.com
www.bankrate.com

BanxQuote
www.banxquote.com

iMoneyNet.com
imoneynet.com

MaxRate.com
(877) 462-9435
www.maxrate.com

Divorce

DivorceNet
www.divorcenet.com

Institute of Certified Divorce Planners
(800) 875-1760
www.institutecdp.com

Elder Care

AARP
601 E St., NW
Washington, DC 20049
(800) 424-3410
www.aarp.org

American Bar Association: Commission on Legal Problems of the Elderly
www.abanet.org/elderly

American Bar Association: Section of Real Property, Probate & Trust Law
www.abanet.org/rppt/home.html

CaregiverZone
www.caregiverzone.com

CareGuide
www.careguide.com

CareScout
www.carescout.com

Eldercare Locator
(800) 677-1116

ElderWeb
www.elderweb.com

National Academy of Elder Law Attorneys
1604 N. Country Club Rd.
Tucson, AZ 85716
(520) 881-4005
www.naela.com.

National Alliance for Caregiving
4720 Montgomery Lane, Suite 642
Bethesda, MD 20814
www.caregiving.org

National Family Caregivers Association
10400 Connecticut Ave., Suite 500
Kensington, MD 20895
(800) 896-3650
www.nfcacares.org

National Senior Citizens Law Center
East Coast office
1101 14th St., NW, Suite 400
Washington, DC 20005
(202) 289-6976

United Seniors Health Cooperative
409 Third St. SW, 2nd floor
Washington, DC 20024
(202) 479-6973
www.ushc-online.org

West Coast office
3435 Wilshire Blvd., Suite 2860
Los Angeles, CA 90010
(213) 639-0930
www.nsclc.org

Estate Planning

Aging with Dignity
P.O. Box 1661
Tallahassee, FL 32302-1661
(850) 681-2010
www.agingwithdignity.org

**American College of Trust &
Estate Counsel**
3415 S. Sepulveda Blvd., Suite 330
Los Angeles, CA 90034
(310) 398-1888
www.actec.org

Heirs, Inc.
P.O. Box 292
Villanova, PA 19085
(610) 527-6260
www.heirs.net

**National Conference of Commissioners
on Uniform State Law**
211 E. Ontario St., Suite 1300
Chicago, IL 60611
(312) 915-0195
www.nccusl.org

Nolo.com
www.nolo.com

Partnership for Caring
1035 30th St. NW
Washington, DC 20007
(202) 338-9790
www.choices.org

Exchange-Traded Funds

American Stock Exchange
(800) THE-AMEX
www.amex.com

Barclays Global Investors
(800) 474-2737
www.ishares.com

Nasdaq
www.nasdaq.com

U.S. House of Representatives
(202) 224-3121
www.house.gov

U.S. Senate: Federal Legislation
(202) 224-3121
www.senate.gov

Financial Planners

**American Institute of Certified Public
Accountants**
Personal Financial Planning Division
Harborside Financial Center
201 Plaza Three
Jersey City, NJ 07311-3881
(888) 999-9256
www.aicpa.org.

Financial Planning Association
(800) 282-7526
www.fpanet.org

**National Association of Personal
Financial Advisors**
355 W. Dundee Rd., Suite 200
Buffalo Grove, IL 60089
(888) FEE-ONLY
www.napfa.org

Government and Industry Regulators

Certified Financial Planner Board of Standards
1700 Broadway, Suite 2100
Denver, CO 80290-2101
(888) CFP-MARK
www.cfp-board.org

National Association of Securities Dealers (NASD)
125 Broad St., 36th floor
New York, NY 10004
(212) 858-4400
(800) 289-9999
www.nasdr.com (a resource for investors and the securities industry)
www.nasdadr.com (a forum for securities dispute resolution)

NASD District Offices:
District 1
525 Market St., Suite 300
San Francisco, CA 94105
(415) 882-1234

District 2
300 S. Grand Ave., Suite 1600
Los Angeles, CA 90071
(213) 627-2122

District 3
Republic Plaza Building
370 17th St., Suite 2900
Denver, CO 80202
(303) 446-3100

Two Union Square
601 Union Street, Suite 1616
Seattle, WA 98101
(206) 624-0790

District 4
12 Wyandotte Plaza
120 W. 12th St., Suite 900
Kansas City, MO 64105
(816) 421-5700

District 5
1100 Poydras St., Suite 850
New Orleans, LA 70163
(504) 522-6527

District 6
12801 North Central Expressway,
Suite 1050
Dallas, TX 75243
(972) 701-8554

District 7
3490 Piedmont Rd., NE
One Securities Center, Suite 500
Atlanta, GA 30305
(404) 239-6100

District 8
10 S. LaSalle St., Suite 1110
Chicago, IL 60603
(312) 899-4440

Renaissance on Playhouse Square
1350 Euclid Ave., Suite 650
Cleveland, OH 44115
(216) 694-4545

District 9
581 Main St., 7th floor
Woodbridge, NJ 07095
(732) 596-2000

1835 Market St.
11 Penn Center, Suite 1900
Philadelphia, PA 19103
(215) 665-1180

District 10
33 Whitehall St.
New York, NY 10004
(212) 858-4000

District 11
260 Franklin St., 16th floor
Boston, MA 02110
(617) 261-0800

North American Securities Administrators Association
10 G St. NE, Suite 710
Washington, DC 20002
(202) 737-0900
www.nasaa.org

Securities and Exchange Commission
450 Fifth St. NW
Washington, DC 20549-0213
(202) 942-7040
(800) 732-0330
www.sec.gov

Money, Meaning & Choices Institute
Pamphlet: *Inheritances and Sudden Wealth*
P.O. Box 803
Kentfield, CA 94914
(415) 267-6017
www.mmcinstitute.com

Index Funds

Indexfunds.com
www.indexfunds.com

Vanguard Group
(800) 871-3879
www.vanguard.com

Individual Retirement Accounts

Ed Slott's *IRA Advisor*
(800) 663-1340
www.irahelp.com

The Inheritance Project
P.O. Box 503
Ivy, VA 22945
(804) 961-0876
www.inheritance-project.com

IRAjunction
www.irajunction.com

George Kinder
Seven Stages of Money Maturity: Understanding the Spirit and Value of Money in Your Life, Dell Books, 2000.

John L. Levy, wealth consultant
Assorted publications on inherited wealth
842 Autumn Lane
Mill Valley, CA 94941
(415) 383-3951

Insurance

Consumer Federation of America
1424 16th St., NW, Suite 604
Washington, DC 20036
(202) 387-6121
www.consumerfed.org

Insure.com
www.insure.com

National Association of Insurance Commissioners
2301 McGee, Suite 800
Kansas City, MO 64108-2604
(816) 842-3600
www.naic.org

Society of Financial Service Professionals
270 S. Bryn Mawr Ave.
Bryn Mawr, PA 19010-2195
(610) 526-2500
(800) 392-6900 (for orders and registration for products and events only)
www.financialpro.org

Insurance Ratings Services

A.M. Best
(908) 439-2200
www.ambest.com

Fitch (formerly Duff & Phelps)
One State Street Plaza
New York, NY 10004
(212) 908-0500
(312) 368-3100
(800) 753-4824
www.dcrco.com

Moody's Investors Services
99 Church Street
New York, NY 10007
(212) 553-1658
www.moodys.com

Standard & Poor's
(212) 438-2000
www.standardandpoors.com/ratings

Weiss Ratings
(800) 289-9222 (sales)
(800) 291-8545 (customer service)
(800) 627-3300 (corporate offices)
www.weissratings.com

Investment Clubs

Bivio.com
www.bivio.com

Motley Fool
www.fool.com

National Association of Investors Corp.
P.O. Box 220
Royal Oak, MI 48068
(877) 275-6242
www.better-investing.org

Investor Education

American Association of Individual Investors
626 N. Michigan Ave.
Chicago, IL 60611
(312) 280-0170
(800) 428-2244
www.aaii.org

Investorama
www.investorama.com

National Association of Investors Corp.
P.O. Box 220
Royal Oak, MI 48068
(877) 275-6242
www.better-investing.org

Medicare

Medicare
(800) MEDICARE
www.medicare.gov

Medicare Rights Center
(800) 333-4114
www.medicarerights.org

Mutual Funds

Morningstar
(800) 735-0700.
www.morningstar.com

Mutual Fund Education Alliance
www.mfea.com

Online Retirement Advice

DirectAdvice
www.directadvice.com

Financial Engines
www.financialengines.com

Monte Carlo for Financial Planners
Montecarlo-simulation.org

Morningstar's ClearFuture
www.morningstar.com

mPower
(415) 875-2000
www.mpower.com

Quicken 401k Advisor
www.quicken.com

Pensions

American Academy of Actuaries
1100 17th St. NW, 7th floor
Washington, DC 20036
(202) 223-8196
www.actuary.org

American Society of Pension Actuaries
4245 N. Fairfax Dr., Suite 750
Arlington, VA 22203
(703) 516-9300
www.aspa.org

Pension and Welfare Benefits Association
U.S. Department of Labor
200 Constitution Ave., NW
Washington, DC 20210
(202) 693-4650 (main office)
(202) 219-8771 (public disclosure room)
(800) 998-7542 (hot line)
www.dol.gov/dol/pwba

Pension Benefit Guaranty Corp.
1200 K St. NW
Washington, DC 20005-4026
(202) 326-4000
(800) 400-7242
www.pbgc.gov

Pension Rights Center
1140 19th St. NW, Suite 602
Washington, DC 20036
(202) 296-3776
www.pensionrights.org

Administration on Aging's Pension Counseling Projects:

Alabama
Legal Counsel for the Elderly
University of Alabama
School of Law
P.O. Box 870392
Tuscaloosa, AL 35487
(205) 348-4960

Arizona
Pension Rights Project
Pima Council on Aging
5055 E. Broadway, Suite C104
Tucson, AZ 85711
(520) 790-7262

California
Pension Rights Project
1610 Bush St.
San Francisco, CA 94109
(415) 474-5171
(800) 474-1116

Illinois
Pension Information Effort
Chicago Department on Aging
(Serving greater Chicago area)
1767 E. 79th St.
Chicago, IL 60649
(312) 747-0189

Massachusetts
New England Pension Assistance Project
Pension Action Center
Gerontology Institute
University of Massachusetts
100 Morrissey Blvd.
Boston, MA 02125
(617) 287-7300
www.pensionaction.org

National Pension Lawyers Network
Gerontology Institute
University of Massachusetts
100 Morrissey Blvd.
Boston, MA 02125
(617) 287-7332

Michigan
Legal Hotline for Michigan Seniors
115 W. Allegan St., Suite 720
Lansing, MI 48933
(517) 372-5959

Minnesota
Pension Rights Project
Minnesota Senior Federation
1885 University Ave. West
St. Paul, MN 55104
(651) 645-0261
www.mnseniors.org

Missouri
Pension Benefits Project
Older Women's League
Pension Benefits Project
2165 Hampton Ave.
St. Louis, MO 63139
(314) 725-1516

New York
New York Pension Hotline
Legal Services for the Elderly
130 W. 42nd St., Floor 17
New York, NY 10036
(212) 997-7714 (New York City residents)
(212) 391-0120

Virginia
Virginia Pension Rights Project
(Serving eastern half of state)
Crater District Area Agency on Aging
23 Seyler Dr.
Petersburg, VA 23805
(804) 732-7020

Mountain Empire Older Citizens
(Serving western half of state)
P.O. Box 888
Big Stone Gap, VA 24219
(540) 523-4202

Philanthropy

American Council on Gift Annuities
233 McCrea St., Suite 400
Indianapolis, IN 46225
(317) 269-6274
www.ncpg.org/acga.html

American Institute of Philanthropy
4905 Del Ray Ave., Suite 300 W.
Bethesda, MD 20814
(301) 913-5200
www.charitywatch.org

The Chronicle of Philanthropy
1255 23rd St. NW
Washington, DC 20037
(800) 728-2819
www.philanthropy.com

Council on Foundations
1828 L St. NW
Washington, DC 20036
(202) 466-6512
www.cof.org

Evangelical Council for Financial Accountability
P.O. Box 17456
Washington, DC 20041
(800) 323-9473
www.ecfa.org

The Foundation Center
79 Fifth Ave.
New York, N.Y. 10003
(212) 620-4230
www.fdncenter.org
Also maintains five regional libraries in New York, Washington, D.C., Atlanta, Cleveland, and San Francisco.

GuideStar
427 Scotland St.
Williamsburg, VA 23185
(757) 229-4631
www.guidestar.org

Independent Sector
1200 18th St. NW, Suite 200
Washington, DC 20036
(202) 467-6161
www.independentsector.org

Internet Nonprofit Center
www.nonprofits.org

More than Money
2244 Alder St.
Eugene, OR 97405
(541) 343-2420
(800) 255-4903
www.morethanmoney.org

National Center for Family Philanthropy
1220 Nineteenth St. NW, Suite 804
Washington, DC 20036
(202) 293-3424
www.ncfp.org

National Charities Information Bureau
19 Union Square West
New York, New York 10003
(212) 929-6300
www.give.org

Philanthropic Advisory Service of the Council of Better Business Bureaus
4200 Wilson Blvd., Suite 800
Arlington, VA 22203
(703) 276-0100
www.bbb.org

Real Estate Investment Trusts

National Association of Real Estate Investment Trusts
1875 Eye St. NW
Washington, DC 20006
(202) 739-9400
(800) 3-NAREIT
www.nareit.org

Social Security

Social Security Administration
(800) 772-1213
www.ssa.gov

Women and Social Security Project
National Council of Women's Organizations
www.women4socialsecurity.org

Stock Indexes

Indexfunds.com
www.indexfunds.com

Nasdaq 100 and composite
www.nasdaq.com

Russell 2000
www.russell.com

Standard & Poor's 500
www.spglobal.com

Wilshire 5000
www.wilshire.com

Stock Research

CBS MarketWatch
headwww.cbsmarketwatch.com

Edgar
U.S. Securities and Exchange Commission
www.sec.gov

Morningstar
www.morningstar.com

Motley Fool
www.fool.com

MSN MoneyCentral
www.moneycentral.com

Silicon Investor
www.siliconinvestor.com

TheStreet.com
www.thestreet.com

Value Line Investment Survey
(800) 634-3583
www.valueline.com

Yahoo! Finance
http://finance.yahoo.com

Taxes

Internal Revenue Service
(800) 829-3676 (publications)
(800) 829-1040 (tax questions)
www.irs.gov

Internal Revenue Service Office of the Director of Practice
(202) 694-1891

National Association of Enrolled Agents
200 Orchard Ridge Dr., Suite 302
Gaithersburg, MD 20878
(301) 212-9608
(800) 424-4339 (hot line)
www.naea.org

Trust Services

Association of Independent Trust Companies
710 E. Ogden Ave., Suite 600
Naperville, IL 60563
(630) 579-3290
www.aitco.net

Family Office Exchange
137 N. Oak Park Ave., Suite 310
Oak Park, IL 60301
(708) 848-2030
www.familyoffice.com

Index